Fair Trade
and Harmonization

The American Society of International Law
2223 Massachusetts Avenue, N.W.   Washington, DC   20008-2864
(202) 939-6000   Fax (202) 797-7133

Fair Trade and Harmonization

Prerequisites for Free Trade?

Volume 2
Legal Analysis

Edited by
Jagdish Bhagwati
Robert E. Hudec

The MIT Press
Cambridge, Massachusetts
London, England

This book was set in Palatino by Asco Trade Typesetting Ltd., Hong Kong and was printed and bound in the United States of America.

Library of Congress Cataloging-in-Publication Data

Fair trade and harmonization : prerequisites for free trade? / edited
 by Jagdish Bhagwati, Robert E. Hudec.
  v. ⟨1,   ⟩; cm.
  Includes bibliographical references and index.
  Contents: v. 1. Economic analysis. v. 2. Legal analysis.
  ISBN 0-262-02401-2 (v. 1)
  ISBN 0-262-02402-0 (v. 2)
   1. International trade. 2. Competition, Unfair. 3. International economic relations.
 4. Foreign trade regulation. 5. Environmental policy. 6. Free trade. 7. Competition,
 Unfair—Japan.
I. Bhagwati, Jagdish, 1934—   . II. Hudec, Robert E.
HF1379.F34   1996
382—dc20   95-46605

Contents

Fair Trade
and Harmonization

Introduction to the Legal Studies

Robert E. Hudec

This volume of legal studies is one of two volumes produced by a Ford Foundation sponsored research project investigating a growing conflict that is taking shape between international trade policy and certain domestic social policies of national governments. As governments find their economies becoming more and more intertwined in a world of expanding international commerce, they are finding that their domestic social policies are having a greater and greater impact on each other. To the extent that domestic policies differ from one country to another, that heightened impact has become a source of conflict.

This book focuses on three areas in which differences in national domestic policies seem to be causing the most significant problems in international trade relations—environmental policy, labor policy, and competition (or antitrust) policy. In each of these areas, some governments have adopted fairly rigorous regulation of private behavior, while others impose only weak or nonexistent regulation. The policy differences that exist in these three areas have become a major point of friction in the trade relations between developed and developing countries, although they also create certain problems between developed countries as well.

Differences between domestic social policies can create two kinds of friction in a world of integrated economic relations. At one level, differences between domestic policies may appear to distort the international economic exchange that goes on between nations, leading one side to perceive that it is being unfairly disadvantaged. At another level, some countries may feel that their own domestic policies are being frustrated by the divergent domestic policies of other countries, and these countries may wish to condition further economic exchanges on correction of these policy shortcomings.

The three areas of domestic policy examined in this study—environment, labor, and competition—have been especially prominent in generating such policy conflicts. The conflict in each policy area tends to center around complaints by countries with high standards against the countries with low standards. In "environmental" affairs—a term which in this context usually includes health and safety regulations and concerns about mistreatment of animals—high-standards countries complain about the adverse effects of low standards upon the environment, claiming that the failure to regulate certain harmful practices constitutes an injury to themselves. They also complain about the economic effects of low environmental standards, asserting that the absence of suitable environmental requirements confers an unfair cost advantage upon producers in low-standards countries, thereby causing economic injury to their own producers and workers. In addition to complaining about the economic injuries themselves, the high-standards countries contend that these adverse economic effects also have a political impact by increasing opposition to environmental regulation within their own countries. In the other direction, countries with particularly rigorous environmental standards are sometimes accused of employing excessive environmental regulations for the purpose of restraining trade.

Similar complaints are made about low standards in the area of national labor policy. Countries with high labor standards object to the adverse effects of weak labor policies on the workers in those countries, a complaint that rests more on human rights concerns than on any sense of injury to themselves. And, as in the case of weak environmental policies, the high-standards countries also complain about the unfair cost advantage enjoyed by producers in countries with low labor standards, an advantage that both injures producers and workers in the high-standards country and thereby also increases political opposition to high labor standards in that country.

In the area of competition or antitrust policy, the high-standards countries complain that weak competition policies in other countries impede their exports to those countries, because producers in the low-standards country are permitted to create private restraints on trade that exclude their exports. The high-standards countries also complain that the protected home markets created by private trade restraints in low-standards countries allow firms in those low-standards countries to "dump" exports into the markets of high-standards countries.

In each of these three policy areas, the primary solution advocated by complaining governments is to raise standards in the low-standards country. This goal has been pursued along a wide diplomatic front. Improvements in environmental standards and practices are regularly negotiated in

free-standing international conferences, conferences that have already produced a large body of international environmental agreements. Ameliora-
tion of labor policies is likewise pursued through independent international
negotiations, chiefly through the conventions negotiated under the International Labor Organization (ILO). Regional agreements such as the European Union or the North American Free Trade Area (NAFTA) have also
pursued improvements in environmental and labor standards on a regional
level. To date, international harmonization of competition policies has not
proceeded quite as far. The European Union has produced a single Com-
munity-wide competition law, but most other international efforts have
been bilateral and have limited their focus to matters of administration and
enforcement.

Notwithstanding these continuing efforts toward international harmonization, the present situation continues to be one of substantial divergence
of domestic policy in the areas indicated. Governments concerned about
the adverse effects of divergent domestic policies have begun to consider
proposals calling for more direct action to eliminate these unwanted effects. The policy tools being considered are primarily economic measures,
mainly trade measures. It has been proposed that governments employ
trade restrictions for several purposes: (1) to enforce international agreements already achieved, (2) to induce recalcitrant governments to enter
such agreements, and (3), in the absence of international harmonization, to
neutralize the adverse economic and political effects of divergent domestic
policies.

The proposals for the use of trade restrictions in these circumstances
often raises the possibility of conflict with the rules of the General Agreement on Tariffs and Trade (GATT). Officials responsible for international
trade policy matters have seriously questioned both the correctness and
the GATT-legality of this call for trade measures. In response, those proposing the use of trade measures argue that GATT must learn to accommodate itself to these other important social policy interests, either by
changing its rules or by interpreting them to permit the sort of trade
measures being advocated. The result has been an increasingly noisy policy debate between "trade" advocates on the one side and advocates for
the competing domestic policies on the other side. The debates have come
to be known by the shorthand terms "trade-and-environment," "trade-and-
labor," and "trade-and-competition" policies. Because the GATT rules and
institutions are already firmly established, these debates usually center on
the issue of what GATT should do to accommodate these potentially
conflicting interests.

This volume of legal studies is designed to examine the "trade-and-" debates in conjunction with the economic studies in Volume I. The core issue in these debates is the conflict between the economic policy values of the present GATT/WTO trade regime and the important values underlying environmental, labor, and competition policies. This conflict is a subject particularly amenable to the tools of legal analysis. The legal scholar's craft begins with the identification and definition of the values underlying social conflict, and its principal focus is on sorting and weighing the normative and institutional means for resolving such conflict. The studies in this volume seek to apply these tools to the problem at issue.

The studies divide into three parts. First, the initial study in this volume describes the GATT's general legal response to the use of trade measures in this setting. Second, a group of six studies examines the intersection of trade policy with each of the three domestic policy areas that have been chosen for investigation—environmental policy, labor policy, and competition policy. Third and finally, two studies analyze the "fairness" norms that are invoked whenever it is claimed that policy divergence creates "unfair" conditions of trade.

The several studies have been designed to cover the main issues in the current debate. However, because the studies are a collection of free-standing works by individual scholars with expertise in each particular area, they offer neither the completeness nor the uniformity of viewpoint that might be found in a comprehensive book by a single author. Nor do they completely avoid duplication. The logic of such a study is that the cumulative expertise of the individual scholars and the variety of perspectives they represent add more in depth than is lost by lack of single comprehensive view.

I.1   The GATT Legal Framework

Frieder Roessler's chapter on the general GATT legal response to these problems opens the volume. Roessler begins by presenting an analysis of the three key legal concepts that GATT law uses to draw a line between "trade policy measures" and "domestic policy measures": (a) the border adjustment rules, (b) the national treatment rule, and (c) the unconditional most-favored-nation (MFN) rule. Roessler's analysis argues that these three GATT legal concepts leave member countries with full autonomy to pursue domestic policies within their jurisdiction. GATT rules step in only when internal taxes or regulations have the purpose or effect of protecting domestic industries from import competition. GATT also steps in under the MFN rule when domestic policy measures seek to interfere with the policy autonomy of other member countries.

Roessler then analyzes proposals to change these GATT rules to authorize trade restrictions that will facilitate the adoption of high-standards policies. With regard to trade restrictions designed to offset the increased costs of higher standards within the *importing* country, he points out that GATT rules actually do allow governments to grant subsidies or increase tariffs to protect domestic industries in these situations, provided that governments compensate trading partners for the trade agreement rights they are abrogating or impairing. The main effect of proposals to remove GATT legal obstacles to such trade protection, he observes, is to avoid the duty to compensate trade partners. As for the argument that such trade protection may be necessary to forge domestic political coalitions in support of high-standards policies, Roessler argues that no international legal order would be possible if members enjoyed such a political-necessity exception. He points out that GATT has neither the mandate nor the capacity to measure or compare the political importance of domestic policy goals.

With regard to trade restrictions designed to influence the policies of other governments, Roessler canvasses the limitations upon GATT's ability to promote positive harmonization in other policy areas. He concludes that GATT's prior experience confirms that there are serious institutional barriers to its serving such a harmonization function.

In the end, Roessler articulates a legal design that seeks to achieve a reconciliation of trade policies and other domestic policies by a sharp delineation of respective competences. Given that GATT has neither the mandate nor the capacity to make judgments about the worthiness of various social policy goals, he argues that the GATT can best serve its role by, first, maintaining clear and fixed legal rights about market-access commitments and, second, by offering flexible procedures under which governments can negotiate for the modification of those legal commitments when they wish to accommodate other more important social policies. Roessler acknowledges that clarity often makes policy making more difficult by reducing a government's ability to reconcile competing interests at the expense of other, under-represented interests.

I.2   Specific Policy Conflicts

The volume then turns to a series of six studies dealing with the three specific areas of environmental policy, labor policy, and competition policy.

In each case, the studies seek to present the specific factual background to the controversy in each area, and then to analyze the competing positions.

I.2.1   Environment

In the first of the two chapters on the trade-and-environment debate, Daniel Farber and Robert Hudec consider GATT legal restrains on domestic environmental regulations that have a trade-restrictive effect—the sort of claim that a country with lower domestic policy standards might make against countries with arguably excessive standards. Farber and Hudec begin by noting that any system of free trade between individual sovereign entities requires some arbiter to police the domestic policy actions of individual member governments, in order to make sure that they are not using domestic policy measures to achieve disguised restrictions on trade. The GATT's role in this regard, they argue, is in essence no different than the role played by the Supreme Court of the United States under the "dormant commerce clause" of the U.S. Constitution or the role played by the European Court of Justice under Articles 30 and 36 of the Treaty of Rome. They note that each of these surveillance mechanisms has been quite controversial, evoking serious objections to judicial intrusion into what are regarded as legislative perogatives. In order to evaluate the criticisms of GATT in this regard, the authors set out to compare the GATT's jurisprudence in this area with the commerce clause decisions of the U.S. Supreme Court.

The authors point out that, while neither the Supreme Court nor the GATT has had much difficulty with domestic policy measures that explicitly discriminate against foreign commerce, both institutions have had difficulty with facially neutral regulatory measures that have a discriminatory purpose or effect. They suggest that decisions with regard to facially neutral measures appear to involve intertwined judgments about both the actual motives behind the measure and the adequacy of the social policy justifications for it. Noting the political objections to second-guessing legislative actions on such grounds, the study details the ways that both commerce clause doctrines and GATT doctrines are shaped to incorporate such controversial judgments indirectly.

Farber and Hudec conclude that there is no simple solution to the conflicting demands placed on the judicial institutions called upon to make these decisions. They take encouragement from the fact that the institutions performing this function in Europe, the United States, and GATT have so far been skillful enough to maintain acceptance and authority. They suggest that with skillful judges the GATT should be able to continue performing this adjudicatory function, taking advantage of the underlying recognition of its necessity.

The second trade-and-environment chapter by Robert Hudec considers GATT legal restraints on trade restrictions directed against the environmental policies of other governments. Hudec begins with a review of the large number of both actual and proposed government actions in this category. He divides the subject into two parts: (1) trade measures explicitly authorized by international environmental agreements and (2) all other, unilateral, trade measures directed against foreign environmental policies.

In the first category, Hudec recommends amending GATT Article XX to permit the recognition of trade measures called for by certain international environmental agreements, following the legal structure already established for commodity agreements in Article XX(h). That structure would make it easier for governments to introduce trade policy perspectives into the negotiation of such environmental agreements without asking GATT itself to render formal judgments about the environmental policies adopted in those agreements.

With regard to unilateral restrictions, Hudec acknowledges that unilateral trade measures may on occasion be necessary to deal with at least the most serious environmental harms. He then examines the various legal structures under which GATT might try to impose meaningful controls on such unilateral measures. His main conclusion is that GATT would not be able to administer any legal rule requiring judgments about environmental policy. The realistic options, then, are three: (1) to adopt a procedure that would control only for protectionist purposes, (2) to follow a suggestion of the second *Tuna/Dolphin* panel by also allowing for measures that discriminate by country, and (3) to follow the first *Tuna/Dolphin* panel by declaring all externally directed trade measures GATT-illegal. The final option, leaving it to political processes to validate measures that are in fact required by threat of serious and irreversible environmental harms, resembles the legal design suggested by Roessler.

I.2.2 Labor

In the first of two studies on the trade-and-labor debate, Virginia Leary begins by tracing in rich detail the history of efforts to achieve international harmonization of certain labor rules since the mid-nineteenth century.

She points out that international harmonization has been seen from the beginning not only as a desirable end in itself, but also as a necessary condition to adoption of higher labor standards in any one country. Leary's study reviews the organization and the accomplishments of the International Labor Organization, the as-yet unsuccessful efforts of the United States to introduce a labor clause in GATT, and the as-yet unique approach taken in the recent NAFTA side-agreement on labor policy. The story is brought up to date with a discussion of current and proposed U.S. legislation imposing trade sanctions to enforce internationally recognized workers rights, and with an account of the continuing ILO discussions of a possible "social clause" to be implemented cooperatively between ILO and GATT. The discussion of U.S. legislation includes a description of some of the weaknesses of the unilateral U.S. approach. The latter subject includes the ILO's analysis of the ways a social clause might be incorporated into a multilateral process based on Articles XX or XXIII of the GATT.

Leary concludes that it is desirable to defuse the current tension relating to linking workers' rights with trade, since the conflict is detrimental both to the expansion of world trade and to the protection of workers' rights. She points out that considerable common ground can be discerned between both advocates and opponents of a social clause. Opponents of linkage generally concede that "some things are beyond the pale," and both advocates and opponents frequently state that a country should be free, for example, to bar imports made from forced labor and that comparative advantage should not be based on egregious violations of workers' rights. Leary urges that this common ground be stressed in future negotiations.

Those who advocate linking workers' rights to trade should, for their part, recognize the legitimate worries that a social clause might serve as an excuse for protectionism, Leary argues. States should be encouraged to forego unilateral approaches to trade measures relating to workers' rights in exchange for a multilateral approach. Leary suggests that it should be possible for the ILO and GATT to agree on the principle that comparative advantage in trade should not be based on the violation of the most fundamental workers' rights: freedom of association, prohibition of forced labor, and prohibition of the egregious use of child labor and discrimination in employment. She recommends that governments agree to include such a principle in the GATT. Leary maintains that a social clause should not include other more technical labor standards relating to wage differentials and occupational safety and health, for example. She recommends that primary emphasis should be placed on moral suasion through the use of

ILO procedures, with GATT-authorized trade measures serving only as a last resort for particularly serious violations, determined through ILO procedures.

The second chapter on the trade-and-labor debate is Brian Langille's essay addressed to the question whether labor policy should be one of the subjects included in trade agreement negotiations. Langille takes issue with what he considers the prevailing orthodoxy among trade economists and trade policy officials—the view that trade should *not* be linked to labor policy issues.

Langille's essay presents the contrary view from two perspectives. First, addressing the conventional case for free trade, he argues that the assumptions of conventional theory are contradicted by the fact that government policies inevitably affect conditions of competition, in the same way that tariffs and subsidies do. He contends that these political influences on trade flows cannot be wished away, and that the only rational way to deal with them is to negotiate them explicitly. Second, Langille steps outside the assumptions of conventional economic theory to support the same conclusion on other grounds. He argues that North American labor law represents a policy based upon a set of values different than those contained in the assumptions of conventional free trade theory. In his view, labor laws that mandate collective bargaining and specific conditions of employment represent a rejection of market-determined outcomes in favor of a politically determined set of outcomes based on concepts of justice and individual autonomy.

Langille argues that the political settlement represented by North American labor law is currently threatened by an imbalance of political power in favor of capital, due to capital's mobility in the present world economy—a mobility that neither labor nor the state possesses. He envisions the possibility of a "race to the bottom" as states compete for mobile capital resources by relaxing their domestic labor policies. Langille rejects unilateral trade sanctions as a solution to this threat. He states that using trade negotiations to establish an international baseline of basic labor rights is the most promising way for a society to preserve a balanced labor settlement.

I.2.3   Competition Policy

In the first of two chapters devoted to harmonizing divergent competition laws, Daniel Gifford and Mitsuo Matsushita address the connection between trade disputes and differences in domestic competition laws. The concern is that private arrangements among business firms (through cartels or otherwise) not be allowed to impede the participation of foreign producers in domestic markets. Generally, nations look to the competition laws of their trading partners to ensure that their trade agreement rights of access are not nullified or impaired by private cartels. Yet differences in the competition laws of the trading nations and in their enforcement policies can give rise to misunderstanding.

A significant number of trade disputes—especially between the United States and Japan—have involved allegations that private cartels or other privately engendered market restraints impede market access of foreign suppliers. In these disputes, the United States government has complained that the Japanese Antimonopoly Law has not been effectively enforced. Although the U.S. and Japanese governments have grappled with these matters for many years, they have had mixed results in resolving their disputes.

Gifford and Matsushita believe that the difficulties in resolving these disputes lay largely in a failure of communication. The underlying issues are sufficiently complex that a structured dialogue is necessary to produce successful negotiations. The extent to which private business arrangements that have market-restraining effects are tolerated within any jurisdiction involves complex matters of policy, which are not always readily understood by outside observers. Moreover, they note, nations differ in the extent to which governments intervene to correct market failures or otherwise to skew the market for policy reasons. Especially difficult problems arise from the varying approaches which the major trading jurisdictions have taken to matters of industrial policy.

In an effort to structure this dialogue in ways that will identify the underlying policy issues, Gifford and Matsushita suggest that all of the major trading jurisdictions accept efficiency as an important normative goal and therefore that efficiency play a key role in this dialogue. They also propose that when one jurisdiction determines that its competition law will not be enforced against a privately engendered trade restraint, a burden of justification or at least of explanation be borne by the nonenforcing jurisdiction. That burden would be fully carried if the nonenforcement is justified under an efficiency rationale. Even if it cannot be justified under an efficiency rationale, the exercise of explaining the policy reasons for allowing an inefficient restraint would be salutary for all parties. International understanding would be improved and the jurisdiction tolerating the inefficient restraint would reconsider its own policy in the process. A constraint on the dialogue would be drawn from the GATT:

In no case could a nation's competition law legitimately permit private business firms to impose a trade restraint that their government was barred from imposing under the GATT.

Gifford and Matsushita then apply their approach to a number of current trade issues. They also observe that approaching trade issues from an efficiency orientation provides a new perspective for domestic reform. The most obvious candidate for reform, they find, is the U.S. antidumping law. That law fails the efficiency test by a wide margin and is difficult to justify in its present form. The authors suggest that there are a variety of other domestic laws which restrain trade and cannot be justified under an efficiency rationale.

In the second of the two chapters on the intersection of competition policy and trade policy, Brian Hindley explores the possibilities of policy convergence by examining the possibility of adding an agreement on competition policy to the current GATT/WTO trade rules. Hindley argues that a substantial part of the legitimate aims of a WTO agreement on competition policy can be achieved by relatively simple actions to facilitate the application of GATT Article XXIII:1(b) to cases in which GATT access concessions are nullified or impaired by:

1. anticompetitive practices or outcomes that derive from governmental laws or acts, and

2. private anticompetitive practices which are open to attack under the law of the jurisdiction in which they occur, but have not been attacked under that law.

Hindley discusses the necessary content of more complicated agreements, and suggests that they would be difficult to negotiate. He raises the question of whether, if an agreement to facilitate the application of Article XXIII can be negotiated, the *incremental* gains from a more complicated agreement will be worth the costs of negotiating it. He concludes that there are good grounds for skepticism on that score.

I.3   Fairness Norms

The final two studies in the volume examine two sets of "fairness" norms that are frequently invoked in complaints about the trade effects of divergent domestic policies. One study deals with complaints that comparatively weak regulatory policies in other countries give the exports of those countries an unfair advantage when they enter another country's market—a set of complaints that are usually labeled "social dumping" or "regulatory subsidies" and that are propelled by the normative premises of the antidumping and countervailing duty laws. The second study deals with unfairness claims made against foreign laws, practices, and institutions that impede one's own exports to foreign markets, the kind of unfair trade complaints commonly presented under Section 301 of the U.S. Trade Act of 1974. Both studies deliberately suspend judgment about the *bona fides* of such fairness complaints, take them at face value, and try to illuminate the normative values on which they rely for their persuasive appeal.

Ronald Cass and Richard Boltuck begin their analysis of the fairness concepts underlying U.S. antidumping and countervailing duty laws by first questioning the general metaphor of the "level playing field," asking whether it is possible, given all the differences in competitive conditions from one country to another, to specify the baseline of equitable competition that the metaphor presumes. In considering fairness explanations for antidumping laws, the authors identify concerns that price cutting has been based upon certain advantages of superior access to capital and/or protected home markets. After noting that complaining countries themselves do not hesitate to ameliorate such conditions for their own producers, they can find no basis on which to define what might be the "equitable" degree of firm size, capital access, or market protection. With regard to foreign subsidies subjected to countervailing duty law, they undertake a detailed consideration of the grounds on which subsidies might be distinguished from other government-assistance policies that can also harm foreign producers. (On this point, Brian Langille's study draws a considerably different conclusion from the existence of the same ambiguities.)

Cass and Boltuck then apply their analysis to the specific claims of unfairness directed against low environmental and labor standards, pointing again to the same basic difficulties of defining normative baselines in government regulatory activity. A concluding section considers possible second-best justifications for antidumping and countervailing duty laws.

The second chapter on fairness concepts is Kenneth Abbott's study of the normative underpinnings of the "unfairness" concerns underlying Section 301 in U.S. trade legislation. Section 301 unfairness claims are directed almost exclusively at barriers in foreign markets, in contrast to the unfairness claims made against imports involving dumping or subsidies. Abbott catalogues seven major normative claims that are made against foreign barriers, which he calls "norms of fairness." They range from violation of legal commitments to disappointing trade results that fall short of mercantilist objectives. Abbott ranks the norms in the order of their recognized legitimacy, and then dissects each of them according to criteria of coherence, internal consistency, and workability. Special attention is given to separating and evaluating the many faces of "reciprocity," which emerges as a protean concept capable of being molded to fit the complaints of any and every unhappy trader.

Abbott also identifies three key "norms of responsibility" that add to or subtract from the normative force of particular unfairness claims—(1) the extent to which private behavior can be attributed to governments, (2) the extent to which states can appropriately be held responsible for the trade effects of various domestic policies, and (3) the culpability of the government's motives.

Abbott's study concludes with a comparison between Section 301 unfairness claims against foreign trade barriers and the unfairness claims leveled against low standards in the environmental, labor, or competition policies of other governments. These two sets of claims often overlap, especially in the areas of labor and antitrust, though harmonization claims range more broadly than Section 301, with its more limited focus on barriers to exports. Abbott concludes that the harmonization type of unfairness claims typically rest on norms of fairness that enjoy relatively low levels of legitimacy, compared to many of the claims advanced under Section 301.

I.4 Analytic Themes

Clearly, the studies in this volume were not designed to supply an overall policy prescription for dealing with the problem of divergent national social policies. Each author approaches the issues with a somewhat different policy perspective, and none have tried to reconcile their own prescriptions with those of the other authors. Nevertheless, several interesting themes can be traced through the different studies.

1. All of the studies concede the validity of the values and the concerns on both sides of the "trade-and-" debates. All see the problem as one of designing ways to accommodate the respective interests. Accommodation does not mean total acceptance of all claims on both sides. To the contrary, both sets of claims have to be pared down by subjecting them to honest, possibly even hostile, criticism.

One way of looking at that process of critical screening is to consider the analysis in terms of a cost-benefit analysis. Each of the studies in this volume can be understood as an effort to contribute some element of clarification to the reader's understanding of the costs and the benefits involved in the policy area being discussed. Although each author looks carefully at both sides of the picture, each author's particular contribution inevitably reflects that authors' professional perspectives. Those authors who work primarily in trade policy will tend to raise the most questions about the costs of trade measures (the costs of trade measures are usually undervalued), and will tend to call attention to excesses in the value claims on behalf of competing domestic policies. Those who work primarily in the other areas of environmental, labor, or competition policy are naturally drawn to other observations; although they have not dwelt at length on the social importance of those policy goals (at least by comparison to other studies of this kind), they have missed few chances to point out the anomalies and inconsistencies in prevailing trade policy doctrine and theory. A major premise of the study is that both sides of the equation could use a great deal more clarification of this kind.

2.   Many of the studies stress the difficulties that trade institutions will have in evaluating particular domestic policy goals, and vice versa. Many call attention in particular to the GATT/WTO's lack of competence to render judgments about the substantive content of policies such as environmental policy, labor policy, and, to some degree, competition policy as well. These limitations on institutional competence necessarily affect the structure of whatever solutions one wishes to consider.

For Roessler, the solution is to leave GATT pretty much as it is, but to confine GATT law to trade policy matters. Roessler acknowledges that trade rules may impede other social policies on occasion, but he proposes to deal with such situations by political processes to override the rules, rather than trying to build some general accommodation into the rules themselves.

On environmental policy, Hudec's proposals for dealing with trade measures directed against foreign environmental policies follow a line similar to Roessler's. The chapter by Farber and Hudec acknowledges that GATT tribunals confront the same competence problem when investigating whether social policy measures are being used for trade purposes. Conceding that GATT tribunals will have to defer on genuinely close questions, they contend that a significant proportion of such cases will involve relatively clear cases that can be decided authoritatively.

Leary's chapter on labor policy argues that GATT should take a more positive role in considering the linkage of international labor rights with trade, but her study attempts to define institutional arrangements by which substantive issues of labor policy will be dealt with primarily in the ILO rather than GATT. Langille's chapter does not focus on these institutional issues, but in calling attention to the North American setting he reminds us of the NAFTA "side agreements" that have created a place for separate labor and environmental bureaucracies.

With regard to GATT's possible involvement in competition policy, the two studies in this volume offer somewhat differing judgments. Hindley's chapter does assume that GATT can play some role in dealing with government-supported private restraints or private restraints in violation of local competition law, but he raises serious doubts about GATT's ability to negotiate—or renegotiate—the substance of national competition law. Gifford and Matsushita propose a dialogue in which both trade and competition policies would be examined and justified according to the concern for efficiency—the core policy norm that arguably unites competition policy and, in its better moments, trade policy. Although they do not weigh the practical problems raised by two rather independent (and possessive) bureaucracies and by the darker side of trade policy reflected in the antidumping laws, Gifford and Matsushita do make a convincing case that competition policy may be the one area in which the GATT's intellectual foundations could support an in-house effort to reconcile divergent national policies.

While one might reserve judgment about competition policy, the other studies do give some reason to question the wisdom of trying to integrate trade policy with environmental or labor policy in one international institution. Just as the existence of the ILO clearly changes the center of gravity in the "trade-and-labor" debate, so would a parallel international institution for environmental policy. Such an institution deserves serious consideration.

3.   Regardless of the particular solutions recommended, the studies generally agree that unilateral trade measures are not a desirable solution in any of the policy areas examined. The basis for this conclusion was not necessarily the same in each case. By necessary implication, the preference for multilateral solutions involves some underlying assumptions about the acceptability of the likely outcomes that a multilateral process is likely to produce. In general, it suggests an expectation that the important core values are likely to be achieved, and that objectives that cannot be achieved multilaterally may not be important enough to justify the cost of unilateral action. Such expectations, in turn, will depend both on the amount of negotiating success anticipated and on the line drawn between critical and

noncritical objectives. In each of the areas discussed—environment, labor, and competition policy—the studies have identified some goals as to which they raise doubts about value of harmonization. The two "fairness" studies also call attention to the weaknesses in the prevailing trade policy concepts of fairness that frequently motivate these unilateral actions.

In some cases, a preference for multilateral solutions may also rest on a belief that some or many unilateral trade measures are not actually necessary to achieving their declared goal—that they are just a way of shifting the cost of a policy to weaker interests. In other cases, the equation may also reflect serious doubts about the efficacy of unilateral measures—questions about the durability of solutions achieved by unilateral coercion, and the costs of using such measures in terms of other diplomatic relations.

In the end, the case against unilateralism is one dimension of the larger cost-benefit issue presented by this entire area. The multilateralism–unilateralism axis is one of the lines on which these studies try to contribute greater clarity.

4.   Quite apart from the various forms of accommodation suggested in particular studies, the final two studies dealing with the fairness question make what may be the most important point on how to approach these questions. Complaints about divergent domestic policies usually come to rest on an assertion that the economic or social policy results of that divergence are "wrong" in some sense—wrong enough to justify the application of diplomatic pressure and perhaps coercive economic force as well. The degree and character of these normative starting points are an absolutely critical element in the effort to reconcile the contending policy objectives.

The Cass-Boltuck and Abbott studies take a much needed, hard look at the leading "fairness" norms that are generated by some of the commercial interests that participate in the trade policy side of the debate. Whatever the merits of a commitment to fairness in general domestic social policy, these studies do make it clear that the norms by which current political institutions tend to judge international trade issues leave a great deal to be desired in terms of coherence, consistency, and objectivity. This is not surprising. All nations have a tendency to distort the norms of fairness they apply to other countries. They assume that what they do at home is normal, and natural, and pleasing to God, while at the same time feeling perfectly free to criticize superficially different practices of others that are in no rational way distinguishable from their own.

The double standards and the self-serving distinctions revealed in these studies of "fairness" norms are not unique to the trade sector. They are common ingredients in most kinds of moral outrage that spurs government action. Whenever they are present, they produce a level of self-righteousness that exacerbates conflict, and that also blurs the real issues in a way that serves as a screen for many less worthy motivations. The first step in the process of paring down conflicting value claims to their essentials should be a very critical look at all of the fairness norms and other kinds of moral imperatives underlying this conflict. The first step to sensible accommodation is self-awareness.

GATT Legal Framework

1   Diverging Domestic Policies and Multilateral Trade Integration

Frieder Roessler

1.1   Introduction

Two types of policies affecting trade can be distinguished: first, policies that discriminate between domestic and foreign products or between products sold abroad and those sold domestically and, second, policies that merely discriminate between different categories of products without taking into account their origin or destination. The former will be referred to in this paper as "trade policies," the latter as "domestic policies." The rules of the General Agreement on Tariffs and Trade (GATT) primarily aim at the reduction of barriers between markets, not at the harmonization of competitive conditions in markets. They therefore impose in principle only constraints on trade policies, but leave the contracting parties free to conduct their domestic policies.

As the liberalization of world trade progressed through multilateral negotiations under the auspices of the GATT, the pressure to negotiate rules on domestic policies in the GATT rounds of trade negotiations has increased. The first efforts to regulate in detail domestic policies affecting trade were made in the 1973–79 Tokyo Round: an Agreement on Technical Barriers to Trade supplementary to the GATT was negotiated, which governs the preparation, adoption, and application of technical regulations. The results of the 1986–93 Uruguay Round of Multilateral Trade Negotiations have been incorporated into the Agreement Establishing the World Trade Organization (WTO) to which—in addition to the GATT—15 agreements have been annexed.[1] These include a slightly modified version of the Agreement on Technical Barriers to Trade, an Agreement on Trade-Related Aspects of Intellectual Property Rights, an Agreement on the Application of Sanitary and Phytosanitary Measures with detailed rules on domestic policy measures affecting human, plant, and animal life or health, an Agreement on Agriculture under which commitments on domestic support measures in favor of agricultural producers have been assumed, and a General Agreement on Trade in Services that contains provisions on domestic regulations, including quantitative market access limitations applied equally to domestic and foreign services and service suppliers.

This trend is likely to continue. As the Uruguay Round came to a close at the Ministerial Meeting in April 1994 in Marrakesh, new demands for bringing domestic policy matters into the multilateral trade order were made. During the course of this meeting, delegations stressed the importance of examining the relationship between the trading system and the following domestic policy matters:

- environmental policies
- internationally recognized labor standards
- competition policy
- company law
- investment
- immigration policies
- monetary matters, including debt
- development, political stability, and alleviation of poverty.[2]

This chapter analyzes the relationship between trade policies and domestic policies under the GATT and the WTO Agreement. It is organized as follows. It first examines the distinction between trade and domestic policies under the provisions of the GATT governing the application of domestic taxes and regulations to imported products and products sold for export (border adjustment rules), the treatment of imported products in internal taxation and regulation (national treatment provisions), and the treatment of products from countries with different domestic policies (principle of unconditional most-favored-nation treatment). The main purpose of this analysis is to determine the borderline drawn between trade and domestic policies under GATT jurisprudence. The paper then analyzes the objectives behind the current proposals to link trade and domestic policies under the multilateral trade order and the extent to which these objectives have been realized under the various agreements annexed to the WTO Agreement. The main purpose of this examination is to determine the legal, procedural, and institutional scope for such issue linkages. A summary concludes the chapter.

1.2   The Distinction between Trade and Domestic Policies under the General Agreement

1.2.1   Border Adjustment Rules

Under the provisions of the GATT on national treatment, export subsidies, and restrictions on the sale for export, each contracting party may in principle apply to imported products the taxes and regulations it applies to domestic products and may exempt from its domestic taxes and regulations the products that are exported.[3] The resort to these provisions is optional: The contracting parties have the right but not the obligation to impose the burdens borne by domestic products also on imported products. Equally, the contracting parties may, but need not, apply to products sold abroad the measures applied to products sold domestically.[4] A product exported from A to B could therefore be subject to four different forms of treatment:

1. It could be exempted from domestic taxes or regulations by A upon exportation, and then taxed or regulated by B upon importation (*destination principle*).

2. It could be taxed or regulated by A and exempted from taxes or regulations by B (*origin principle*).

3. It could be taxed or regulated both by A and B (*double taxation or regulation*).

4. It could be taxed or regulated by neither A nor B (*tax or regulatory exemption*).

Table 1.1 summarizes the four possible forms of tax treatment to which a product exported from one country to another may be subjected under the border adjustment rules of the General Agreement.

Table 1.1

		Importing Country	
		Taxes	Does not tax
Exporting Country	Does not tax	Tax at *destination*	Tax *exemption*
	Taxes	*Double* taxation	Tax at *origin*

The GATT's system of border adjustment preserves all the contracting parties' policy options regarding the treatment of products entering international trade. This can perhaps best be illustrated with the example of two countries that apply a special environmental tax to chemical products that cause pollution either at the time of production or at the time of consumption, or both. Take first a product that causes pollution at the time of consumption. In this case the exporting country may wish to refrain from applying the tax to exported products because the pollution does not take place within its territory; the importing country, however, may wish to apply its environmental tax so as to discourage the consumption of the product. The two countries would then follow the destination principle. If a product causes pollution only at the time of production, the country of production might wish to tax both domestic and foreign sales, while the importing country would have no reason to apply an environmental tax to that product. In this case the origin principle would prevail. If the product causes pollution both at the time of production and of consumption, both countries may wish to apply the environmental tax and hence subject it to double taxation. Conversely, if neither the production nor the consumption of the product causes pollution, neither the exporting nor the importing country would have any reason to apply the tax. The product would then benefit from tax exemption.

1.2.2   The National Treatment Principle

The central provision in the General Agreement regulating the application of domestic policies to imported products is Article III, which requires contracting parties to accord national treatment to imported products. Article III:4 reads in part:

The products of the territory of any contracting party imported into the territory of any other contracting party shall be accorded treatment no less favourable than that accorded to like products of national origin in respect of all laws, regulations and requirements affecting their internal sale, offering for sale, purchase, transportation, distribution or use.

This provision applies to all internal measures except those of a fiscal nature. These are regulated in Article III:2, the first sentence of which states that imported products

shall not be subject, directly or indirectly, to internal taxes or other internal charges of any kind in excess of those applied, directly or indirectly, to like domestic products.

The second sentence of Article III:2 broadens this rule by declaring that

no contracting party shall otherwise apply internal taxes or other internal charges to imported or domestic products in a manner contrary to the principles set forth in paragraph 1.

Paragraph 1 of Article III states, *inter alia*, that

The contracting parties recognize that internal taxes and other internal charges, and laws, regulations and requirements affecting the internal sale, offering for sale, purchase, transportation, distribution or use of products ... should not be applied to imported products so as to afford protection.

While the principle underlying these provisions is clear, its application in specific situations gives rise to a series of interpretative issues. The resolution of two of these issues has significant consequences for the range of domestic policy options open to contracting parties. The first is the definition of the term "no-less-favorable treatment." If the treatment of imported and domestic products under a domestic tax or regulation is determined by comparing the actual economic impact of the measure, contracting parties would be prevented from adopting regulations that tend to affect the actual sales of imported products to a larger extent than the sales of domestic products, for instance a tax on automobiles with high gasoline consumption in a country in which such automobiles are mainly imported. If one compares instead the competitive opportunities afforded to imported and domestic products, contracting parties would merely have to ensure that the conditions under which imported products may be sold are no less favorable than those under which domestic products may be sold.

The second interpretative issue significantly determining the range of domestic policy options under the national treatment provision arises from the term "like products." "Like" means both "identical" and "similar." If two products are distinguished that are identical except for their origin, the application of the term "like product" presents no problems. For instance, a regulation prohibiting the sale of foreign but not of domestic beer would clearly be inconsistent with Article III. However, if a contracting party's tax or regulation does not distinguish two products exclusively on the basis of their origin but on the basis of other factors, for instance on the basis of their price, a determination that the two products are, notwithstanding these factors, "like products" implies a determination that they may not be distinguished on the basis of these factors, and consequently also represents a determination of the range of domestic policy options available to the contracting party. The following example illustrates this

Table 1.2

Domestic Whiskey	Domestic Gin
Imported Gin	Imported Whiskey

point: Suppose there are two categories of products—whiskey and gin—of two different origins—domestic and imported. An internal tax could in this case distinguish between pairs of the following four products in Table 1.2.

If whiskey and gin are considered to be like products, imported whiskey would have to be treated no less favorably than domestic gin and imported gin no less favorably than domestic whiskey. As a consequence, the tax on whiskey and on gin would have to be the same. To determine that two products are "like products" is thus to limit the scope of tax policy options open to WTO Members.

The following paragraphs examine in detail the GATT's jurisprudence on these two interpretative issues.

Article III does not require formally equal but only no-less-favorable treatment and thus clearly permits contracting parties to treat domestic and imported products differently; the only obligation imposed upon them is to ensure that any difference in treatment is not less favorable for imported products. The drafters chose the no-less-favorable standard for good reason. First of all, formally equal treatment can in certain circumstances lead to severe discrimination. To ensure an effective equality of treatment, contracting parties must therefore have an obligation to accord formally different treatment to domestic and imported products in such circumstances. Moreover, it is in practice frequently not possible to accord formally equal treatment to domestic and imported products. For instance, one method of taxing domestic products is to tax the turnover of domestic enterprises. In this case contracting parties cannot apply to imported products a tax that is formally identical to that applied to domestic products. For these reasons the text of Article III does not require formal equality, nor would it make sense to interpret it to impose this obligation.

If the treatment of domestic and imported products may be formally different—and in certain circumstances even has to be different—then the question arises about which differences constitute a treatment of imported products that is no less favorable. Two standards have been considered in GATT practice: The treatment is less favorable if it has an *economic impact* that is less favorable. And: The treatment is less favorable if it accords *competitive opportunities* that are less favorable.

The economic impact criterion has been consistently rejected by the GATT Contracting Parties, the first time in 1949 in a working party report on a dispute related to Brazilian internal taxes, which notes that

[t]he delegate of Brazil submitted the argument that if an internal tax, even though discriminatory, does not operate in a protective manner the provisions of Article III would not be applicable. He drew attention to the first paragraph of Article III, which prescribes that such taxes should not be applied "so as to afford protection to domestic production".... The delegate for Brazil ... suggested that where there were no imports of a given commodity or where imports were small in volume, the provisions of Article III did not apply.... [The majority of the working party] argued that the absence of imports from contracting parties during any period of time that might be selected for examination would not necessarily be an indication that they had no interest in exports of the product affected by the tax, since their potentialities as exporters, given national treatment, should be taken into account. These members of the working party therefore took the view that the provisions of the first sentence of Article III, paragraph 2, were equally applicable whether imports from other contracting parties were substantial, small or non-existent.[5]

In 1987 the Contracting Parties adopted a panel report which set out in detail the rationale for the rejection of the economic impact criterion:

An acceptance of the argument that measures which have only an insignificant effect on the volume of exports do not nullify or impair benefits accruing under Article III:2, first sentence, implies that the basic rationale of this provision—the benefit it generates for the contracting parties—is to protect expectations on export volumes. That, however, is not the case. Article III:2, first sentence, obliges contracting parties to establish certain competitive conditions for imported products in relation to domestic products. Unlike some other provisions in the General Agreement, it does not refer to trade effects. The majority of the members of the Working Party on the "Brazilian Internal Taxes" therefore correctly concluded that the provisions of Article III:2, first sentence, "were equally applicable, whether imports from other contracting parties were substantial, small or non-existent" (BISD Vol. II/185). The Working Party also concluded that "a contracting party was bound by the provisions of Article III whether or not the contracting party in question had undertaken tariff commitments in respect of the goods concerned" (BISD Vol. II/182), in other words, the benefits under Article III accrue independent of whether there is a negotiated expectation of market access or not. Moreover, it is conceivable that a tax consistent with the national treatment principle (for instance, a high but non-discriminatory excise tax) has a more severe impact on the exports of other contracting parties than a tax that violates that principle (for instance a very low but discriminatory tax). The case before the Panel illustrates this point: the United States could bring the tax on petroleum in conformity with Article III:2, first sentence, by raising the tax on domestic products, by lowering the tax on imported products or by fixing a new common tax rate for both imported and domestic products. Each of these solutions would have different trade results, and it is therefore logically not possible to determine the difference in trade impact ... resulting from the non-observance of that provision. For these reasons, Article III:2, first sentence, cannot be interpreted to protect expectations on export volumes; it protects expectations on the competitive relationship between imported and domestic products. A change in the competitive relationship contrary to that provision must consequently be regarded ipso facto as a nullification or impairment of benefits accruing under the General Agreement. A demonstration that a measure inconsistent with Article III:2, first sentence, has no or insignificant effects would therefore in the view of the Panel not be a sufficient demonstration that the benefits accruing under that provision had not been nullified or impaired even if such a rebuttal were in principle permitted.[6]

The most precise definition of the treatment required by Article III can be found in the report of the Panel on "United States—Section 337 of the Tariff Act of 1930":

... The words 'treatment no less favourable' in paragraph 4 call for effective equality of opportunities for imported products in respect of the application of laws, regulations and requirements affecting the internal sale, offering for sale, purchase, transportation, distribution or use of products. This clearly sets a minimum permissible standard as a basis. On the one hand, contracting parties may apply to imported products different formal legal requirements if doing so would accord imported products more favourable treatment. On the other hand, it also has to be recognised that there may be cases where application of formally identical legal provisions would in practice accord less favourable treatment to imported products and a contracting party might thus have to apply different legal provisions to imported products to ensure that the treatment accorded them is in fact no less favourable. For these reasons, the mere fact that imported products are subject under Section 337 to legal provisions that are different from those applying to products of national origin is in itself not conclusive in establishing inconsistency with Article III:4. In such cases, it has to be assessed whether or not such differences in the legal provisions applicable do or do not accord to imported products less favourable treatment. Given that the underlying objective is to guarantee equality of treatment, it is incumbent on the contracting party applying differential treatment to show that, in spite of such differences, the no less favourable treatment standard of Article III is met.[7]

Criteria that have been suggested for determining whether two products are "like products" within the meaning of the national treatment provisions include: the product's end-uses in a given market; the product's properties, nature, and quality; consumer tastes and habits; and the classification of the product in tariff nomenclatures.[8] The proponents of these criteria appear to base themselves on the assumption that the process of determining the likeness of two products is a process of comparing the characteristics of two physical objects, one imported and the other domestic.

In fact, the starting point of the analysis cannot be the concrete objects to which an internal tax or regulation is applied but only the abstract categories of products distinguished by the contracting party. For instance, in the context of an analysis under Article III it is meaningless to say that the imported cup in my left hand is like the cup of domestic origin in my right hand because their properties, nature, quality, and end-uses are the same and that, consequently, the cup in my left hand must be accorded no less favorable treatment than the one in my right hand. It may be true that the two objects might be the same when considered as cups but the fact that they are cups may not at all be relevant under the domestic legislation at issue. One of the cups might under that legislation fall under the category of "nonrecyclable beverage container" (subject to an environmental tax), "material producing poisonous gases when incinerated" (subject to a sales prohibition), or "household utensil" (subject to a reduced value-added tax). To compare the two objects as cups when they are not distinguished by the contracting party as cups is arbitrary. In order to examine whether the contracting party's measure meets the no-less-favorable standard, one has to compare the categories of products that are distinguished by it, not two individual products that happen to fall within the categories created.

Whether two products that are not identical are nevertheless considered to be like products depends on the perspective from which they are viewed: A fox and an eagle are like animals to a hare but not to a furrier. Article III:1 prescribes the perspective from which products are to be compared by declaring that domestic taxes and regulations should not be applied "so as to afford protection to domestic production." The term "so as to" suggests that both the intent and the effect of the regulation or tax are relevant. In determining whether two products are alike, the central issue thus is whether the product categories under which they fall have been distinguished with the intent and effect of affording protection. The 1992 Panel Report on "United States—Measures Affecting Alcoholic and Malt Beverages," in its examination of a Mississippi wine tax according a more favorable treatment to wine produced from a particular type of grape which grows only in the southeastern United States and the Mediterranean region, noted that

The purpose of Article III is ... not to prevent contracting parties from using their fiscal and regulatory powers for purposes other than to afford protection to domestic production. Specifically, the purpose of Article III is not to prevent contracting parties from differentiating between different product categories for policy purposes unrelated to the protection of domestic production. The Panel considered that the limited purpose of Article III has to be taken into account in interpreting the term "like products" in this Article. Consequently, in determining whether two products subject to different treatment are like products, it is necessary to consider whether such product differentiation is being made "so as to afford protection....."[9]

The Panel, noting *inter alia* that "the United States did not claim any public policy purpose for this Mississippi tax provision other than to subsidize small local producers," concluded that the distinction made was one between "like products."[10]

An objection against the above analysis might be that the purpose and effect of a distinction should not be taken into account in the determination of the likeness of products under Article III but in the context of Article XX, which establishes broad exceptions from the obligations under the General Agreement for measures required in the pursuit of policy objectives other than that of affording protection. For instance, it might be argued that meat with hormones is "like" meat without hormones within the meaning of Article III because of the similar physical characteristics of the two products and that the question of whether meat with hormones may be accorded less favorable treatment than that accorded to meat without hormones should be examined in the context of Article XX(b), which permits measures necessary to protect human health.

This approach is, however, problematical. Article XX lists only ten policy goals as justifying measures deviating from the other provisions of the General Agreement, but there are far more legitimate policy goals that can only be attained by distinguishing between different product categories. For instance, policies designed to harmonize technical standards, to avoid the accumulation of waste, or to tax the consumption of luxury goods are not among the policies covered by the exemptions in Article XX. If one were to rely in the context of Article III only on the characteristics or uses of the products and examine the purpose of the product distinctions only in the context of Article XX, one would arrive at the conclusion that distinctions between physically similar products or products serving similar end-uses could only be made for the ten purposes listed in Article XX, a result that was probably not intended by the drafters of the General Agreement and that would hardly be acceptable to the contracting parties.

This thought has been expressed by the Panel on "United States— Measures Affecting Alcoholic and Malt Beverages," which examined the justification of distinguishing between beers of different alcohol content, as follows:

The Panel recognized that the treatment of imported and domestic products as like products under Article III may have significant implications for the scope of obligations under the General Agreement and for the regulatory autonomy of contracting parties with respect to their international tax laws and regulations: once products are designated as like products, a regulatory product differentiation, e.g. for standardization or environmental purposes, becomes inconsistent with Article III even if the regulation is not "applied ... so as to afford protection...." In the view of the Panel, therefore, it is imperative that the like product determination in the context of Article III be made in such a way that it not unnecessarily infringe upon the regulatory authority and domestic policy options of contracting parties.[11]

1.2.3   The Principle of Unconditional Most-Favored-Nation Treatment

Contracting parties to the GATT not only enjoy domestic policy autonomy but must also respect the exercise of that autonomy by other contracting parties. This is reflected in the provisions of Article I of the GATT, according to which most-favored-nation treatment must be accorded unconditionally. The main practical purpose of the principle is to ensure that the right of access to a market not be made conditional on reciprocal market access concessions of the trading partner, but its fundamental function is to ensure that each contracting party accord access to its markets independently of *any* of the policies of the trading partner, including domestic policies.

The argument that the provisions of the General Agreement should be interpreted to permit actions against contracting parties with different domestic policies was made for the first time in the history of the GATT by the United States in the proceedings of the panel established at the request of Mexico in 1991 to examine the United States restrictions on imports of tuna from contracting parties which permit fishing methods endangering dolphins.[12] At the request of Mexico, who wished to settle the matter bilaterally, the Council has not yet considered the adoption of the report. Its basic conclusions have been confirmed by another panel established at the request of the EC to examine the same measures.[13] The report of this panel has also not yet been adopted. While the report of the panel established at the request of Mexico has been derestricted, the report on the complaint by the EC is still restricted and is therefore not cited in this paper.

In the proceedings of the panel which examined the Mexican complaint, the United States argued that its tuna import embargo was part of an internal measure subject to Article III that was applied equally to imported and domestic products and consequently consistent with this provision. It stated that

> where the United States had requirements in place regarding the production method for a particular product, such as in the current proceeding on tuna, the United States could then exclude imports of that product that did not meet the United States requirements, provided that such regulations were not applied so as to afford protection . . . .[14]

The Panel rejected this contention. It found that Article III

> calls for a comparison of the treatment of imported tuna *as a product* with that of domestic tuna *as a product*. Regulations governing the taking of dolphins incidental to the taking of tuna could not possibly affect tuna as a product. Article III:4 therefore obliges the United States to accord treatment to Mexican tuna no less favourable than that accorded to United States tuna, whether or not the incidental taking of dolphins by Mexican vessels corresponds to that of United States vessels.[15]

Article III does not distinguish between domestic legislation that one would wish to see in all countries, such as legislation protecting dolphins, and legislation in areas where different countries justifiably adopt different solutions. An acceptance of the United States interpretation of Article III would therefore have had implications far beyond the issue area before the panel. It would have meant that imports could be restricted or taxed because of any difference in policy even if the policies pursued by the exporting country do not have an impact on the product, and the sale of the product would therefore not prevent the importing country from effectively implementing its policies within its jurisdiction. The General Agreement would then have provided legal security only for the trade between pairs of countries with identical domestic policies. In short, the principle of unconditional most-favored-nation treatment set out in Article I of the GATT would have been eliminated in respect of internal measures through a new interpretation of the term "product" in Article III.

The United States further considered the embargo on tuna from Mexico to be justified by Article XX(b), which exempts from the obligations under the GATT "measures ... necessary to protect human, animal, or plant life or health." It stated that the "embargo was necessary to protect the life and health of dolphins. No alternative measure was available or had been proposed that could reasonably be expected to achieve the objective of protecting the lives or health of dolphins."[16] The Panel concluded that

Article XX(b) allows each contracting party to set its human, animal or plant life or health standards. The conditions set out in Article XX(b) which limit resort to this exception, namely that the measure taken must be "necessary" and not "constitute a means of arbitrary or unjustifiable discrimination or a disguised restriction on international trade," refer to the trade measure requiring justification under Article XX(b), not however to the life or health standard chosen by the contracting party.... The Panel considered that if the broad interpretation of Article XX(b) suggested by the United States were accepted, each contracting party could unilaterally determine the life or health protection policies from which other contracting parties could not deviate without jeopardizing their rights under the General Agreement. The General Agreement would then no longer constitute a multilateral framework for trade among all contracting parties but would provide legal security only in respect of trade between a limited number of contracting parties with identical internal regulations.[17]

The Panel emphasized that this interpretation of Article XX did not prevent the Contracting Parties from acting jointly to address international environmental problems which can only be resolved through measures in conflict with the present rules of the GATT. In that respect it stated:

It seemed evident to the Panel that, if the Contracting Parties were to permit import restrictions in response to differences in environmental policies under the General Agreement, they would need to impose limits on the range of policy differences justifying such responses and to develop criteria so as to prevent abuse. If the Contracting Parties were to decide to permit trade measures of this type in particular circumstances it would therefore be preferable for them to do so not by interpreting Article XX, but by amending or supplementing the provisions of the General Agreement or waiving obligations thereunder. Such an approach would enable the Contracting Parties to impose such limits and develop such criteria.[18]

The Panel's finding can be seen as an example of judicial restraint. Rather than proposing an interpretation responding to a wide-ranging political problem on which the text of the General Agreement gives no guidance, it proposed that a negotiated solution be found.

A number of authors have argued that Article XX should be interpreted to permit trade sanctions against countries which do not participate in multilateral agreements protecting the global commons, such as the Montreal Protocol.[19] While many of the arguments of these authors are convincing *de lege ferenda*, they must be rejected as arguments for the interpretation of Article XX. This provision does not distinguish between unilateral and multilaterally agreed action. Any interpretation of a treaty must respect the expression of the will of its parties. To assume, as these authors do, that the Contracting Parties have already expressed in Article XX their consent to the imposition of trade sanctions against them in the framework of a multilateral agreement which they have not accepted is to leave the realm of interpretation and enter into that of lawmaking.

If Article XX were interpreted to permit contracting parties to apply trade sanctions against countries pursuing different domestic policies, in particular in the field of the environment, that are different from their own, GATT panels would have to settle conflicts of values and interests that are, in the absence of any guidance for their resolution neither in the legal instruments accepted by the contracting parties nor in any common practice, hardly justiciable. As the panel on the tuna dispute pointed out, Article XX does not establish any constraints on the type of domestic policies that contracting parties may pursue. Article XX(b) in particular does not require a demonstration from the contracting party invoking it that its health policies are "necessary." What must be demonstrated to be necessary is merely the trade measure requiring justification under that provision.[20] Since the General Agreement essentially prohibits only measures discriminating between products as to their origin or destination, the contracting party invoking Article XX(b) normally only has to demonstrate that its health policies require a measure that favors domestic products over imports or imports from one contracting party over imports from another. A typical example would be a prohibition of imports of cattle from countries where hoof-and-mouth disease is widespread. The question of whether an import restriction is necessary to protect human or animal health within the jurisdiction of the importing country is a technical issue, the resolution of which does not require the settlement of conflicts between the values and interests of different contracting parties. These conflicts have been clearly settled in Article XX(b), which declares each contracting party's health interests to prevail over the trade interests of the other contracting parties.

It has also been suggested that the term "necessary" be used to distinguish between the policies that may be imposed on other contracting parties consistently with Article XX(b) from those that cannot be applied extra-jurisdictionally. If the term "necessary" were interpreted to refer not to the inconsistency requiring justification but to the health policy itself, then GATT panels would have to pass judgment on the justification of the contracting party's health policy itself rather than the trade measure implementing it, and this in spite of the absence of any guidance on this issue in Article XX(b). One can safely assume that the drafters of the General Agreement, had they considered that only "necessary" health policies could be implemented through trade restrictions, would have given some guidance on the criteria to be used in assessing the necessity of the contracting parties' health policies. The significant differences between the health policies of the contracting parties, the conflicts of values that have to be resolved when a health policy is adopted, the enormous difficulty of agreeing among the now 128 contracting parties on common criteria for judging health policies, and the inappropriateness of undertaking such a task in a body not composed of representatives of health ministries should convince anyone of the wisdom of the panels when they interpreted the term "necessary" to refer to the GATT inconsistency rather than the health policy.

If Article XX(b) were interpreted to permit contracting parties to impose trade restrictions not only for the purpose of implementing their own health policies within their jurisdiction but also for the purpose of imposing sanctions on countries with different health policies, the interpretation of the term "necessary" would raise not merely technical issues relating to the effective implementation of health policies. An import restriction designed to change the health policies of other countries would be "necessary" if the import restriction was the only measure reasonably available to induce the other countries to change their policies. To answer this question GATT panels would have to proceed to an examination of the alternative measures available to the contracting party invoking Article XX(b). Would an interruption of diplomatic relations have been sufficient? Would a refusal of landing rights for the national airline have induced a policy change? Or the removal from the list of beneficiaries of GSP tariff preferences? These examples show that an extra-jurisdictional interpretation of Article XX would force panels to assess the foreign policy options of Contracting Parties and the effectiveness of applying alternative means of exerting pressure available to them. In the tuna case the representative of the United States proposed an interpretation of Article XX(b) that would have implied the need to examine the foreign policy means available to the United States to force Mexico to change its domestic policies. ("The embargo was necessary to protect the life and health of dolphins. No alternative measure was available ... that could reasonably be expected to achieve the objective of protecting ... dolphins."[21]) However, it seems unlikely that in practice the United States and other contracting parties to the GATT would be ready to accept an interpretation of Article XX according to which the scope of their trading rights and obligations would vary with foreign policy means available to them to coerce other countries into a change of their domestic policies.

1.3 Links between Trade and Domestic Policies under the WTO Agreement

1.3.1 The Purposes of Linking Trade and Domestic Policies

Proposals such as: the WTO should become "green," the WTO should "take up" labor rights, trade and competition policies should be "integrated," and human rights and trade should be "negotiated together" are in essence proposals to permit trade restrictions designed to facilitate or promote a change in domestic policies in these areas. The motivations behind these proposals can be categorized as follows.

The market-opening commitments under the GATT and the WTO are sometimes seen as obstacles to the adoption of domestic public interest laws that raise the cost of production and are therefore opposed by import-competing industries, such as laws requiring the installation of costly anti-pollution equipment by industries facing competition from products produced in countries that do not impose similar requirements. Trade restrictions are proposed as an instrument **to offset differences between domestic policies**. Ralph Nader, in a recent statement before the U.S. Senate Finance Committee on the results of the Uruguay Round, said:

> U.S. corporations long ago learned how to pit states against each other in 'a race to the bottom'—to provide the most permissive corporate charters, lower wages, pollution standards, and taxes. Often it is the federal government's role to require states to meet higher federal standards.... There is no overarching 'lift up' jurisdiction on the world stage.... The Uruguay Round is crafted to enable corporations to play this game at the global level, to pit country against country in a race to see who can set the lowest wage levels, the lowest environmental standards, the lowest consumer safety standards. Notice this downward bias—nations do not violate the GATT rules by pursuing too weak consumer, labour ... and environmental standards.... Any ... demand that corporations pay their fair share of taxes, provide a decent standard of living to their employees or limit their pollution of the air, water and land will be met with the refrain, 'You can't burden us like that. If you do, we won't be able to compete. We'll have to close down and move to a country that offers us a more hospitable business climate.'[22]

The market access opportunities created by the rules of the GATT and the WTO are sometimes viewed as instruments to induce other countries to adopt regulations that raise the cost of production of their industries to that of the importing country's industries. The purpose of the trade restriction is in this case to help **eliminate differences in domestic policies**. Steve Charnovitz writes in a paper on Environmental Harmonization and Trade Policy:

How can an agreement on minimum standards be achieved among a hundred countries with different values and resources? One approach is to devise a clever mix of carrots and sticks from a diverse enough issue garden to allow a cross-fertilization of concerns. The goal is not only to obtain an agreement, but also to maintain its stability. The carrots are the basic tool. Because countries face different economic trade-offs ... an assistance mechanism can be developed to enable gainers to compensate losers and rich nations to 'bribe' poor ones. This assistance could be in the form of financial aid or technology transfer ..., or it could be trade concessions.[23]

The rules of the GATT and the WTO are also seen as obstacles to domestic regulations reflecting tradeoffs between public interests and the interests of import-competing industries, in other words as obstacles to **domestic bargaining across issue areas**. Ralph Nader, in his statement before the U.S. Senate Finance Committee on the Uruguay Round results, criticized that WTO Agreement for creating obstacles to the achievement of domestic policy goals that are attainable only through measures restricting trade and gave the raw log export bans in two U.S. states as an example. He said:

Raw log export bans are one of the most trade restrictive means to attain the goal of conserving our nation's forests. Yet, after years of debate, raw log bans were the only politically feasible approach because they accommodated the interest of providing alternative lumber processing jobs to those who would no longer be cutting down forests. Laws with such mixed economic and social purposes, of which there are many, would likely fall before challenge under the World Trade Organization's rules.[24]

The denial of market access may also serve to generate political support by the exporting industry of the exporting country for a measure considered desirable by the importing country. The link between trade and domestic policies is then made for the purposes of **international political bargaining across issue areas**. Steve Charnovitz adds to his considerations of how international environmental agreements can be negotiated:

But carrots alone may not be sufficient. Uncooperative countries might attempt to extract more assistance or concessions than the global community is willing to provide.... In such cases, sticks like trade sanctions may be needed to force free-riding countries to enter multilateral agreements.[25]

There are thus in essence four motivations behind the proposals to link trade and domestic policies, as summarized in Table 1.3 (on p. 38).

The following paragraphs analyze to what extent links between trade and domestic policies serving the above purposes have been incorporated into the various trade agreements annexed to the WTO Agreement and

Table 1.3

Reason	Example
Offsetting differences between domestic policies	Import duties on products from countries with low environmental standards
Eliminating differences between domestic policies	Ban on imports of tuna harvested with dolphin-endangering fishing methods
Domestic bargaining across issue areas	Restrictions on raw logs to preserve national forests and help saw mills
International bargaining across issue areas	Exchange of commitments on environmental policies and market access

the legal, procedural, and institutional scope for such links under that Agreement.

1.3.2   Offsetting Differences between Domestic Policies

There is no provision in the WTO Agreement that permits trade restrictions specifically designed to offset differences in domestic policies. WTO Members may impose countervailing duties on products that benefit from a subsidy, and this right can be seen as a right to limit the access to the domestic market conditional upon the exporting country's policies.[26] However, a countervailing duty may be imposed even if the importing contracting party also accords a subsidy. Two contracting parties granting the same fiscal advantages to their steel industries could both impose countervailing duties on the steel products exported to each other. In fact, countervailing duties are frequently applied in such situations. Moreover, the right to levy a countervailing duty is triggered not merely by the existence of the subsidy; there must also be a determination that the subsidy causes material injury to the domestic industry. The countervailing duty provisions of the WTO are therefore not provisions permitting measures designed to offset policy divergences; they are provisions permitting the protection of import-competing industries contingent upon the protection of an exporting industry in another country.

This observation can also be made in respect of another provision in the GATT that permits import controls contingent upon the domestic policies of another contracting, namely Article XX(e), which exempts measures related to the products of prison labor from the obligations under the GATT. It is true that the domestic policies of another contracting party trigger in this case the right to impose import controls, but that right may be exercised independently of the prison labor regulations of the contracting party imposing the import control. A contracting party could consequently permit the sale of products produced in domestic prisons while restricting the sale of those made in foreign prisons. Article XX(e) is therefore essentially a provision that accords the right to protect the domestic industry by restricting imports of products not produced under normal competitive conditions.

WTO Members have the right to give tariff preferences to the developing countries in accordance with the Generalized System of Preferences (GSP).[27] The GSP preferences are accorded on an autonomous basis and may therefore be withdrawn in whole or in part at any time. This has led some contracting parties to grant preferences conditional upon the pursuit of policies by the exporting country unrelated to trade. For example, in order to obtain tariff preferences under the United States GSP scheme, a developing country must, *inter alia*, not

• expropriate or otherwise seize control of property owned by a United States citizen, including patents, trademarks, and copyrights

• repudiate an agreement with a United States citizen

• impose taxes or other exactions with respect to property of a United States citizen, the effect of which is to expropriate that property

• refuse to cooperate with the United States to prevent narcotic drugs from entering the United States unlawfully

• aid or abet any individual or group which has committed an act of international terrorism

• deny its workers internationally recognized rights, including acceptable minimum wages

• refrain from enforcing arbitral awards

• be a member of the Organization of Petroleum Exporting Countries.[28]

Chile, having been denied GSP benefits by the United States because of its labor policies, requested consultations under the GATT with the United States on that denial, claiming that the U.S. action was inconsistent with the principle that GSP benefits must be accorded to all developing countries on a nondiscriminatory basis.[29] Chile did not pursue the matter under the GATT dispute settlement procedures and there is therefore no GATT panel ruling on Chile's claim. While it is debatable whether GSP benefits may be granted on domestic policy conditions, it is undeniable that there is no obligation to grant GSP benefits at all. Any inconsistency resulting from the conditional denial of GSP benefits can therefore always be corrected by denying GSP benefits altogether. As a practical matter, there is therefore little a GSP recipient can do to prevent a donor country from linking the grant of GSP benefits to the pursuit of specified domestic policies.

The statement by Nader quoted above suggests that a government could not, consistently with its obligations under the WTO Agreement, protect from import competition those domestic industries that have to bear the economic burden of regulations not applied by other countries. The following example demonstrates that this is not correct.

Suppose the WTO Member Patria considers adopting a law which would prohibit the production of eggs with caged hens. This law is opposed by Patria's farmers, who claim that the price of eggs would have to be raised by 20 percent to compensate for the higher cost of producing eggs with free-range hens. As a consequence domestic eggs would no longer be able to compete with imported eggs. The proposed prohibition would therefore merely transfer the production of eggs with caged hens from Patria to other countries. How could Patria, consistent with its obligations as a Member of the WTO, protect both hens and farmers?

The first option of Patria would be to permit that a "free-range hens" label be affixed to the package in which eggs are sold and to protect this label against fraudulent use. In this case each individual consumer would have the right to determine whether he or she wishes to incur the cost of maintaining free-range hens. Such labeling regulations are permitted under the GATT. The tuna panel, in its findings on the U.S. legislation protecting the "dolphin-safe" label, confirmed this.[30]

The second option would be to accord farmers a subsidy that would offset the rise in production costs. In this case the taxpayer would pay for the cost of prohibiting hens in cages. Production subsidies are in principle permitted under the WTO Agreement. If the subsidy impairs a tariff concession, injures a domestic industry of another WTO Member, or otherwise causes serious prejudice to another WTO Member, the Member according the subsidy may have to renegotiate the impaired tariff concession, bear the consequences of countervailing duties, or remove the adverse effects of the subsidy, for instance through an export tax. It is, however, not obliged to withdraw the subsidy.[31] These constraints apply only to subsidies that are specific to an enterprise or industry or group of enterprises or industries, not to more generally available subsidies.[32]

The third option of Patria would be to introduce a 20 percent import tariff. The WTO Agreement permits the imposition of trade barriers in the form of import and export tariffs provided the tariff does not exceed the maximum tariff rate bound as a result of negotiations under the GATT.[33] Tariff bindings may be withdrawn after negotiations with the WTO Members with whom the tariff binding was originally negotiated or who have a principal supplying interest.[34] If Patria has bound its import tariff for eggs in its schedule of concession, this measure could only be introduced after a renegotiation of the concession. It is thus possible to impose trade barriers in the form of tariffs to protect an industry from foreign competition, but as a rule only after any negotiated market access right adversely affected by the tariff increase has been renegotiated.

The WTO Agreement consequently permits WTO Members to take a domestic regulatory measure raising the cost of production in combination with subsidies or tariffs that maintain the competitive position of the domestic producers that have to bear these costs. Hens and farmers can be protected at the same time. However, to the extent that the assistance accorded adversely affects the interests of other Members, in particular their negotiated market access rights, procedures designed to remove the adverse effects of the subsidy and to re-establish the negotiated balance of concessions must be observed. Proposals to create under the WTO Agreement the right to offset the economic consequences of regulatory differences between WTO Members are therefore in fact proposals to eliminate the rights that WTO Members have when a Member exercises the already existing right to assist a domestic industry threatened by such differences.

It is the combination of rigid market access rules with flexible safeguards and impairment procedures that permitted multilateral trade liberalization to proceed without any domestic policy harmonization. It is this subtle compromise that has permitted two opposing principles, domestic policy autonomy and trade cooperation, to coexist. Any proposal to introduce into the WTO Agreement new rules permitting WTO Members to offset differences between their domestic policies, or obliging WTO Members to reduce such differences, is therefore likely to be viewed in the light of the political balance underlying this compromise: The more safeguards and impairment procedures are available to WTO Members, the less need will be felt for domestic policy harmonization; the more WTO Members harmonize their domestic policies affecting trade, the fewer safeguards and impairment procedures will be considered to be justified. The so-called "peace clause" of the Agreement on Agriculture annexed to the WTO Agreement is a reflection of this phenomenon. For a period of nine years, it exempts domestic support measures conforming to the Agreement from the imposition of countervailing duties and from the procedures governing the impairment of tariff concessions.[35]

1.3.3 Eliminating Differences between Domestic Policies

There is only one agreement annexed to the WTO Agreement that establishes positive standards for the conduct of domestic policies, the Agreement on Trade-Related Aspects of Intellectual Property Rights, which
establishes minimum standards concerning the availability, scope, and use
of intellectual property rights. This Agreement can be enforced through
the integrated WTO dispute settlement procedures which, in case the
results of the procedures are not implemented, permit "cross-retaliation",
that is, the suspension of obligations in one area in response to a failure to
observe obligations in another.[36] All other agreements on domestic policy
matters annexed to the WTO Agreement establish negative standards.
The Agreements on Technical Barriers to Trade and on the Application of
Sanitary and Phytosanitary Measures, for example, do not oblige any
WTO Member to adopt domestic regulations to protect the health or
safety of its citizens. They oblige WTO Members to observe certain rules
if they choose to adopt any technical regulation or sanitary measure. The
essential purpose of these rules is thus not to promote domestic policy
goals but merely to ensure that market access rights are not undermined
through technical regulations and sanitary measures that are in fact disguised restrictions on trade. The harmonization of domestic policies under
the WTO Agreement is thus of limited scope: Apart from the area of intellectual property rights, the rules on domestic policies are essentially rules
on trade policies in the guise of domestic policies, rules that are ancillary to
the market access commitments exchanged under the WTO Agreement.

  Any proposal to harmonize domestic policies through the GATT or the
WTO raises the question of whether the optimal area for the harmonization of the policies at issue coincides with the area covered by the multilateral trading system. To propose that international policy harmonization
be achieved through the WTO is to propose policy harmonization on a
worldwide scale. It cannot be assumed that an international harmonization
of internal regulations increases efficiency, and—to the extent that it
does—that multilateral harmonization is superior to harmonization within
regional groupings because differences in regulations between nations or
regions may reflect differences in values, tastes, and circumstances. Its
worldwide scope makes the WTO an attractive forum for worldwide harmonization efforts, such as those that led to the Agreement on Trade-
Related Aspects of Intellectual Property Rights, but the range of policies
for which worldwide harmonization is desirable and attainable is likely to
be very small.

An international harmonization of domestic policies generally implies a national harmonization of policies within federal states. Within the framework of the GATT and the WTO, governments have so far been reluctant to accept international obligations that have to be performed at subfederal levels of government. Most of the agreements annexed to the WTO Agreement and the WTO dispute settlement procedures contain special provisions for measures taken by regional and local governments and authorities in federal states.[37] The wording of these clauses varies but their practical consequences are largely the same, namely:

• The obligations under the WTO Agreement apply in principle to all governmental measures irrespective of the level of the government.

• The duty to perform these obligations in respect of measures taken by regional and local governments and authorities is mitigated: The WTO Member concerned merely has the duty to take such reasonable measures as may be available to it to ensure observance.

• If the WTO Member does not secure observance, it owes compensation to the adversely affected WTO Members or must bear the consequences of a suspension of obligations by them.

The federal clause in Article XXIV:12 of the GATT has had little practical relevance because most of the trade policy matters covered by the GATT are within the competence of the central government even in very decentralized states, such as Canada. In the few cases in which this clause was invoked the failure to observe the General Agreement probably did not result from the constitutional delegation of powers to the subfederal government but from a failure of the federal government to assert the powers assigned to it under the constitution. However, numerous matters covered by the WTO Agreement—such as technical regulations, sanitary and phytosanitary measures, quantitative restrictions on the supply of services, etc.—fall within the jurisdiction of subfederal governments. The federal clauses in the WTO Agreement are therefore likely to be of great practical relevance.

The federal clauses of the WTO Agreement create a legal imbalance between a unitary state and a federal state by relaxing the latter's duty to perform its obligations. They partly correct this imbalance by according to the WTO Members adversely affected by a failure to perform obligations the right to compensation or retaliation. This approach is an appropriate and practicable one when the essential purpose of the domestic policy obligations is to ensure/that market access concessions are not impaired through domestic policy measures, for instance to ensure that tariff concessions for agricultural products are not rendered valueless because of arbitrary phytosanitary measures. But to resolve the federal problem through compensatory or retaliatory adjustments of market access rights is inappropriate and impracticable if the domestic policy obligations are not ancillary to the exchange of market access concessions. For instance, if child labor is to be prohibited for its own sake, not as a source of competitive advantage, it would be inappropriate to differentiate in the duty to prohibit child labor between unitary and federal states and to correct the resulting imbalance through market access adjustments. It would also be impracticable because the consequence of a failure to observe the prohibition of child labor could not be measured in terms of market access.

1.3.4   Domestic Political Bargaining across Issue Areas

Policy goals can usually be attained through a variety of policy instruments. The theory of optimal intervention ranks these instruments in accordance with the efficiency with which they attain the policy goal. The optimal instrument is the one that attains the policy goal with the least amount of undesired side-effects, usually the one that attacks the identified problem directly at its source.[38] Suppose the policy goal is to protect domestic forests. Banning the *export* of raw logs—but not sales in the domestic market—and banning only the sale of *raw* logs—but not processed lumber—furthers the goal of conserving forests only to a very limited extent, if at all. A trade-neutral measure, one perfectly consistent with the GATT, that is a tax or restriction on the sale of all trees whatever their destination and degree of processing, would be the optimal instrument to achieve that goal. If the government responds to the demand for protection of the national forests by prohibiting the export of raw logs it illustrates a point made by the Director-General of the GATT in a recent speech: "The erection of new trade barriers under the banner of environmental protection is likely to be bad environment policy as well as bad trade policy."[39]

Conflicts between domestic taxes or regulations and the GATT or the WTO Agreement tend to arise from measures supported by coalitions of interests pursuing public policy goals and producer interests seeking competitive advantages. In many instances it may politically not be feasible to realize the public policy goal without forging such a coalition. For instance, the parties to the Montreal Protocol agreed to phase out the use of ozone-depleting chemicals by reducing the production and import of such chemicals. The decline in the domestic supply of these chemicals combined with import controls generates rents for the domestic producers during the phaseout period and the scheme therefore won their support. The phase-out of the chemicals could have been achieved through internal measures consistent with the national treatment principle, for instance a system of sales licenses. However, such a system would have imposed only burdens on the producers of the chemicals and would probably not have won their support.[40] The import controls were thus not needed to protect the ozone layer, but to protect the producers of ozone-depleting gases and to gain their political support.

Public interest groups often fight their battles in a domestic constitutional framework for decision making that is hostile to their cause. They face governments that act under procedures which induce them to shift the burdens of public interest legislation to ill-informed domestic citizens, future generations, and foreigners. The need to compensate trading partners under WTO law when a domestic political compromise on a domestic policy issue can only be attained through trade restrictions that shift regulatory burdens from domestic producers to ill-informed domestic consumers and non-voters abroad partially correct these constitutional deficiencies.[41] It is that constitutional function of the WTO law which exposes public interest groups to a dilemma: On the one hand, the need to compensate the trading partners adversely affected by the trade measure tends to favor these groups' goals by inducing governments to impose trade-neutral measures that achieve the public policy objective more fully and efficiently; on the other hand, the provisions of the WTO Agreement render the adoption of public interest legislation more difficult by creating obstacles to the formation of political alliances with producer groups seeking competitive advantages in the guise of public interest regulations. The WTO Agreement thus encourages the very measures the public interest groups wish to attain, but also makes the politically feasible, partial step in the direction of these measures more difficult. The debate on the relationship between trade and the environment would no doubt benefit from open recognition of this dilemma.

It is difficult to conceive how an international trade order could function with a general rule that permits discriminatory trade measures which are not required *to implement* a domestic policy but needed merely to generate the political support needed *to adopt* a domestic policy. Such a rule would not be based on any justiciable principle; in fact, its very purpose would be to permit policy making not based on any principle. A sovereignty-conscious government would not wish to submit itself to an international obligation that would make its domestic political constraints subject to multilateral scrutiny. A trade order would not provide legal security if the market access rights under it varied with the haphazardness of domestic political bargaining. The only adjustments of the WTO rules that one can therefore reasonably expect are adjustments in the form of limited *ad hoc* endorsements of specific results of past domestic political struggles with inefficient outcomes, such as a waiver for a widely accepted international environmental agreement with trade provisions required for political reasons.

1.3.5   International Bargaining across Issue Areas

The use of trade sanctions as sticks in international negotiations would generally be inconsistent with the WTO Agreement because of the unconditional nature of its most-favored-nation clauses. Such sanctions could only be introduced if the obligations under that Agreement were changed or if it were replaced by a new agreement with different obligations. The procedural obstacles to a change or replacement of the WTO Agreement are significant. Under the WTO Agreement, a waiver from obligations may only be granted with the consent of three fourths of the WTO Members and only for a limited period of time. New policy obligations cannot be created by majority decision under the WTO Agreement. Amendments that change the rights and obligations of the WTO Members take effect upon their acceptance by two thirds of the Members but only for the Members that have accepted them.[42] This means that all new policy obligations have to be agreed among the WTO Members and that the benefits accorded as a result of such negotiations would in principle have to be extended to all WTO Members whether or not they have accepted these obligations. This limits the possibilities to use, within the legal framework of the WTO, the threat of a withdrawal of market access rights as an incentive to induce other Members to accept new commitments on their domestic policies or, more generally, to link trade and domestic policy issues for international bargaining purposes.

In the Uruguay Round the obstacles to issue linkages created by the GATT's unconditional most-favored-nation clause have been overcome through the concept of the "single undertaking." The Uruguay Round covered 15 negotiating areas. The commitments assumed under the General Agreement and in each of these areas have been incorporated into a single legal instrument—the Agreement Establishing the World Trade Organization—which must be accepted in its totality.[43] The integrated dispute settlement system under which failures to observe commitments in one area could result in retaliatory action in another is to hold the negotiated package of commitments together. Trade and domestic policy issues thus have been successfully linked in the Uruguay Round because the negotiators decided to create a new legal system that will eventually replace that of the GATT rather than attempting to amend the GATT or supplement it with new agreements. It was this approach that permitted bargaining across issue areas that have so far led separate lives in separate institutions, such as trade and intellectual property rights. Also in the future, major changes in the domestic policy obligations of the WTO Members could be achieved only with great difficulty through a process of changing the rules of the multilateral trade order or of supplementing it with additional agreements. Probably its replacement by a new agreement would be necessary. However, that can realistically be envisaged only in the context of a major new negotiating round with a scope comparable to that of the Uruguay Round.

The possibility of periodically replacing the multilateral trading system with a new system creates the possibility of total bargaining, of linking any issue with any other. However, while there may be no legal obstacle to total bargaining there are certainly numerous procedural and institutional constraints. The main purpose of international bargaining in the GATT and the WTO is to create regimes, systems of rules, and procedures making governmental actions more predictable. Each of these regimes cannot function if it is constantly exposed to the need to adjust to breakdowns in other regimes. How can, for instance, an international regime governing intellectual property rights or trade in financial services function if the balance of rights and obligations established in these regimes can at any time be disturbed by failures to observe obligations in the field of trade in textiles or agricultural products? The negotiators in the Uruguay Round have recognized this by agreeing that retaliation across sectors should be permitted only in exceptional circumstances.[44] This is the first indication that the issues linked in the negotiations will not necessarily be linked in the implementation of their results.

Attempts to link trade policies with policy matters not directly related to trade have frequently been made in the past in the GATT. For instance, the GATT adopted resolutions on investment for economic development, disposal of surplus products, liquidation of strategic stocks, and freedom of contract in transport insurance. The GATT also considered proposals to insert articles into the General Agreement on double taxation, freedom of establishment, tied loans and monopolistic practices in transport and shipping, and a proposal for the creation of an "aid club."[45] An analysis of how some of the proposals that were accepted subsequently fared illustrates the difficulties of maintaining a linkage made in negotiations in the implementation phase.

Article XII permits import restrictions to safeguard the external financial position. The first sentence of paragraph 5 of this provision states:

If there is a persistent and widespread application of import restrictions under this Article, indicating the existence of a general disequilibrium which is restricting international trade, the Contracting Parties shall initiate discussions to consider whether other measures might be taken, either by those contracting parties the balances of payments of which are under pressure or by those the balances of payments of which are tending to be exceptionally favourable, or by any appropriate intergovernmental organization, to remove the underlying causes of the disequilibrium.

Discussions under this provision were proposed in 1949 in connection with an agreement of the Commonwealth countries to endeavor to reduce dollar-area imports by 25 percent from their 1948 level. Discussions were, however, referred to the International Monetary Fund.[46] In the 1955 Review Session two proposals were made to deal with a persistent surplus of a major trading nation causing a general scarcity of its currency. These proposals were rejected because Article XII:5 was considered sufficient to deal with such a problem.[47] The provision has been dormant since then.

Under Article VII of its Articles of Agreement, the International Monetary Fund can declare the currency of a persistent surplus country scarce if the demand for that currency seriously threatens the Fund's ability to supply it. Such a declaration operates as an authorization to impose temporarily limitations on the freedom of exchange operations in the scarce currency, which in turn provides under Article XV:9 of the General Agreement a legal basis for imposing restrictions on the trade with the surplus country. The Fund has never declared a currency scarce. In a monetary system based on currencies fully convertible into each other, a persistent surplus does not necessarily lead to a rise in demand for the Fund's holdings of the surplus country's currency, and it is therefore doubtful whether the situation that can trigger the scarcity declaration could arise in the current circumstances.[48] Article VII of the Fund Agreement and the corresponding provision in the General Agreement are therefore likely to remain dead letters.

The 1973 Ministerial Declaration launching the Tokyo Round of Multilateral Trade Negotiations included the following phrases: "The policy of liberalizing world trade cannot be carried out successfully in the absence of parallel efforts to set up a monetary system which shields the world economy from the shocks and imbalances which have previously occurred.... The Ministers recognize that they should bear these considerations in mind ... throughout the negotiations."[49] These sentences were included at the suggestion of France, which favored at that time a return to a fixed exchange rate system and argued that it would not make sense to negotiate a reduction in tariffs when exchange rate changes could from one day to the next eliminate the competitive advantages resulting from such a reduction. The issue linkage was not carried through. The Tokyo Round and the negotiations on monetary reform proceeded independently. The amendments of the Articles of Agreement of the International Monetary Fund legalized flexible exchange rates, contrary to the wishes of France. Nevertheless, throughout the Tokyo Round the decision to bear in mind the link between trade liberalization and monetary reform was ignored.

In 1958, the GATT Contracting Parties appointed a group of experts on restrictive business practices "recognizing that the activities of international cartels and trusts may hamper the expansion of world trade ... and thereby frustrate the benefits of tariff reductions and of the removal of quantitative restrictions...." In its 1960 report the group agreed "that the Contracting Parties should now be regarded as an appropriate and competent body to initiate action in this field ... and should encourage direct consultations between contracting parties with a view to the elimination of the harmful effects of particular restrictive practices." In the light of these recommendations, arrangements for consultations were agreed.[50] However, during the past 34 years, these arrangements have never been used.

William Wallace writes that linkages across operationally unrelated issue areas are usually not maintained beyond the negotiation phase: "Whenever detailed ... implementation becomes important, particularisation reasserts itself and grand designs break down."[51] The experience of the GATT confirms this observation. It suggests that the WTO would be most successful in dealing with those domestic policy issues which are not only politically but also operationally linked to its principal tasks and which the political forces channeled through the WTO are interested in pursuing on a day-to-day basis.

1.4   Summary

The analysis of the GATT's border adjustment rules, national treatment provisions, and most-favored-nation clause showed that domestic policy autonomy and international trade coexist under the current multilateral trade order. The border adjustment rules of the GATT permit, but do not oblige, each country to apply its domestic policies to goods entering international trade. Thus, domestic taxes and regulations applied to domestic products may, but need not, be applied to imported products; and domestic taxes and regulations applied to products sold in the domestic market may, but need not, be applied to products sold abroad. These border adjustment rules maximize each country's domestic policy options.

There is no conflict between the national treatment provisions in Article III of the GATT and the pursuit of policies other than those designed to afford protection to domestic producers. In interpreting the term "like product" in Article III, the GATT panels have respected the right of Contracting Parties to distinguish products for any reason other than that of affording protection. One panel made this clear by stating that "the purpose of Article III is not to prevent Contracting Parties to differentiate between product categories for purposes unrelated to the protection of domestic production." In interpreting the term "necessary" in the public policy exceptions in Article XX(b) of the GATT, the panels have respected the right of Contracting Parties to implement their domestic policies through restrictive trade measures if no alternative measures are reasonably available. One panel stated emphatically that this exception "clearly allowed Contracting Parties to give priority to human health over trade liberalization." The panels have thus consistently avoided interpretations that would have required Contracting Parties to weigh the objectives of the GATT against the objectives of their domestic taxes or regulations.

Contracting Parties to the GATT not only enjoy domestic policy autonomy but must also respect the exercise of that autonomy by other Contracting Parties. This is reflected in the provisions of Article I of the GATT according to which most-favored-nation treatment must be accorded unconditionally. The main practical purpose of the principle is to ensure that the right of access to a market not be made conditional on reciprocal market access concessions of the trading partner, but its fundamental function is to ensure that each contracting party accord access to its markets independently of *any* of the policies of the trading partner, whether trade policies or domestic policies. The panels on the tuna disputes between the United States, on the one hand, and Mexico and the EC, on the other, have confirmed that the GATT's general exceptions in Article XX permit Contracting Parties to apply import restrictions to implement their law within their jurisdiction but do not allow them to impose discriminatory trade restrictions to force other Contracting Parties to change their domestic policies within their jurisdiction.

The links between domestic and trade policies under the WTO Agreement have been analyzed in this chapter in the light of the principal purposes for which linkages between domestic and trade policies have been made or proposed. These purposes are:

- to offset differences between domestic policies
- to eliminate differences between domestic policies
- to permit domestic bargaining across issue areas
- to permit international bargaining across issue areas.

There is no provision in the WTO Agreement that specifically permits import restrictions designed to offset the economic consequences of a difference in domestic policies. If the costs of production of an import-competing industry rise as a result of a domestic regulation different from that applied by other countries and the government wishes nevertheless to maintain the level of production it could, consistently with the WTO Agreement, grant a subsidy or impose an import tariff. If the subsidy impairs a tariff concession, causes material injury to the domestic industry of another Member, or results in serious prejudice to the interests of another Member, the Member granting the subsidy may have to face compensatory actions by other Members, in particular countervailing duties, but is under no legal obligation to remove the subsidy. If the tariff exceeds that provided for in its schedule of concessions the government would have to renegotiate the concession. To claim that the WTO Agreement should permit WTO Members to impose import restrictions designed to offset the economic consequences of differences in domestic policies is therefore to claim that governments should be able to take such offsetting measures without having to bear compensatory measures by their trading partners and without having to renegotiate the affected market access concessions negotiated with them, concessions for which their trading partners have made reciprocal market access concessions.

It is the combination of rigid market access rules with flexible safeguards, impairment, and renegotiation procedures that has permitted multilateral trade liberalization to proceed so far without any domestic policy harmonization. It is this scheme that has made it possible for two opposing principles, domestic policy autonomy and trade cooperation, to coexist. Any proposal to permit WTO Members to offset differences in production costs due to differences in domestic regulations or any proposal to oblige them to avoid such differences through international harmonization will therefore be viewed as a proposal changing the political balance underlying this subtle compromise.

Multilateral negotiations on market access and negotiations on domestic policies have so far been successfully linked for the purpose of eliminating differences between domestic policies only in the area of intellectual property rights. The Agreement on Trade-Related Aspects of Intellectual Property Rights annexed to the WTO Agreement and enforceable through the WTO dispute settlement procedures establishes positive obligations to set minimum standards concerning the availability, scope, and use of intellectual property rights. The other domestic policy provisions of the WTO Agreement are of a negative nature. The basic purpose of these rules is not to prescribe the attainment of specific domestic policy goals but to ensure that the policies the WTO Members have chosen to adopt do not constitute disguised restrictions on trade. The scope of positive harmonization under the WTO Agreement is limited because it is intended to be of worldwide application and the domestic policies for which universal harmonization is both desirable and attainable, as in the case of intellectual property rights, are limited. Harmonization across nations implies harmonization within nations and consequently shifts in regulatory powers within federal states. The many clauses in the WTO Agreement that mitigate the obligation of WTO Members to perform the WTO Agreement in respect of measures by local governments and authorities indicate how reluctant governments are to accept domestic policy obligations that imply such shifts. This, too, limits the scope for positive harmonization through the WTO.

There is no provision in the WTO Agreement giving special status to trade measures designed to forge domestic political coalitions between public interest groups pursuing a domestic policy goal and import-competing industries seeking protection from foreign competition, that is, trade restrictions resulting from domestic political bargaining across issue areas such as a raw log export restriction designed to protect forests and wood-processing industries. Unlike trade-neutral domestic measures consistent with the WTO Agreement, the trade restrictions resulting from such coalitions generally constitute inefficient measures that attain the domestic policy goal only partly. This exposes public interest groups to a dilemma: The WTO Agreement encourages the very measures they wish to attain but subjects partial steps towards such measures to legal constraints. It is difficult to conceive of an international trade order with a rule permitting trade restrictions that are not technically necessary to *implement* a domestic policy but politically required to *adopt* a domestic policy. Such a rule would not be based on any justiciable principle; its very purpose would be to permit unprincipled policy making. And it would expose WTO Members to a multilateral scrutiny of their domestic political constraint—a prospect most of them would no doubt shun.

The unconditional nature of the WTO Agreement's most-favored-nation clauses limits the possibilities of WTO Members to use the threat of a discriminatory withdrawal of market access rights as an incentive to induce other Members to accept new commitments on their domestic policies or, more generally, to link trade policies and domestic policy issues for international bargaining purposes. Under the WTO Agreement a change in rights and obligations cannot be imposed through majority decisions on Members unwilling to accept them. A threat of a discriminatory withdrawal of market access rights for the purpose of obtaining domestic policy commitments could therefore be made only in the context of a broad negotiation aiming—just as the Uruguay Round did—at the replacement of the existing multilateral trade order by a new order. While this creates the possibility of total bargaining, of linking any trade issue with any domestic policy issue, there are numerous procedural and institutional obstacles to such links. The experience of the GATT suggests that it is easy to link disparate policy issues in Ministerial declarations, difficult in negotiations and impracticable in the subsequent administration of the results of the negotiations. The domestic policy issues that could be taken up by the WTO with the greatest chance of success are therefore those that are directly and operationally linked to the tasks already assigned to it and that the political forces channeled through the WTO can be expected to pursue on a day-to-day basis.

NOTES

Frieder Roessler is the Director, Legal Affairs Division, GATT Secretariat and Professeur associé, Université Jean Moulin, Lyon. The opinions expressed are the personal views of the author.

1. Final Act Embodying the Results of the Uruguay Round of Multilateral Trade Negotiations, Apr. 15, 1994 (done at Marrakesh).

2. GATT Doc. MTN.TNC/45(MIN) at 12.

3. *See* GATT art. VI:4 and the notes to arts. III and XVI.

4. *See* GATT Working Party on Border Tax Adjustments Report in GATT Basic Instruments and Selected Documents [hereinafter BISD] 18th Supp. 97, ¶ 11 (1972).

5. Report of the Working Party. *Brazilian Internal Taxes*, 2 BISD 181, ¶ 16 (1952).

6. *United States—Taxes on Petroleum and Certain Imported Substances*, BISD 34th Supp. 136, ¶ 5.1.9 (1988).

7. Report of the Panel. *United States—Section 337 of the Tariff Act of 1930*, BISD 36th Supp. 345, ¶ 5.11 (1990). A definition of national treatment inspired by that developed in this panel report was included in the General Agreement on Trade in Services (GATS) annexed to the WTO Agreement. Article XVII of the GATS entitled "National Treatment" reads:

1. In the sectors inscribed in its Schedule, and subject to any conditions and qualifications set out therein, each Member shall accord to services and service suppliers of any other Member, in respect of all measures affecting the supply of services, treatment no less favourable than that it accords to its own like services and service suppliers.

2. A Member may meet the requirement of paragraph 1 by according to services and service suppliers of any other Members either formally identical treatment or formally different treatment to that it accords to its own like services and service suppliers.

3. Formally identical or formally different treatment shall be considered to be less favourable if it modifies the conditions of competition in favour of services or service suppliers of the Member compared to like services or service suppliers of another Member.

A note to this provision states:

Specific commitments assumed under this Article shall not be construed to require any Member to compensate for any inherent competitive disadvantages which result from the foreign character of the relevant services or service supplier.

8. *See* Report of the Working Party. *Border Tax Adjustments*, BISD 18th Supp. 97, ¶ 18 (1972).

9. Report of the Panel. *United States—Measures Affecting Alcoholic and Malt Beverages*, BISD 39th Supp. 206, ¶ 5.26 (1993).

10. *Id.*

11. *Id.* at ¶ 5.72.

12. *United States—Restrictions on Imports of Tuna*, BISD 39th Supp. 155, ¶ 3.19 [hereinafter *U.S.—Tuna*].

13. GATT Doc. DS/29/R. The panel's conclusions are discussed in Philippe Sands, *GATT 1994 and Sustainable Development: Lessons from the International Legal Order*, GATT BULL. TRADE & ENV'T, July 28, 1994, at 27–30 (paper presented at GATT Symposium on Trade, Environment, and Sustainable Development).

14. *U.S.—Tuna*, note 12 above, ¶ 3.19.

15. *Id.* at ¶ 5.15.

16. *Id.* at ¶ 3.33.

17. *Id.* at ¶ 5.27.

18. *Id.* at ¶ 6.2.

19. *See, e.g.*, Sands, note 13 above.

20. Report of the Panel. *Cf. Thailand—Restrictions on Importation of and Internal Taxes on Cigarettes*, BISD 37th Supp. 200 ¶¶ 72–81 (1991).

21. Full quote is in text accompanying note 16 above.

22. Statement of Ralph Nader before the Senate Finance Committee on the Uruguay Round Agreements of the General Agreement on Tariffs and Trade, March 16, 1994 (mimeo.).

23. Steve Charnovitz, *Environmental Harmonization and Trade Policy*, in TRADE AND THE ENVIRONMENT: LAW, ECONOMICS, AND POLICY 282 (D. Zaelke, P. Orbuch & R. F. Housman, eds., 1993).

24. *Id.*

25. *Id.*

26. GATT art. VI.

27. Decision of the Contracting Parties to GATT of 28 November 1979 on *Differential and More Favourable Treatment, Reciprocity and Fuller Participation of Developing Countries*, BISD 26th Supp. 203 (1980).

28. Trade Act of 1974, Pub. L. No. 93-618, subch. V, 88 Stat. 1978 (1975).

29. GATT Doc. L/6298 (Jan. 22, 1988).

30. *U.S.—Tuna*, note 12 above, at ¶¶ 5.41–5.44.

31. *Cf.* Agreement on Subsidies and Countervailing Measures, arts. 5, 6, 7.

32. *Id.* art. 2.

33. GATT art. II:1(a).

34. GATT art. XXVIII.

35. Agreement on Agriculture, art. 13, in 1994 Uruguay Round Final Act, note 1 above.

36. Understanding on Rules and Procedures Governing the Settlement of Disputes, art. 22, in 1994 Uruguay Round Final Act, note 1 above.

37. *See, e.g.*, GATT art. XXIV:12; Understanding on the Interpretation of Article XXIV of the General Agreement on Tariffs and Trade 1994, ¶¶ 13–14; Agreement on Technical Barriers to Trade, arts. 7, 14.4; Agreement on the Application of Sanitary and Phytosanitary Measures, art. 13; Understanding on the Rules and Procedures Governing the Settlement of Disputes, art. 22:9, all of which are in 1994 Uruguay Round Final Act, note 1 above.

38. For an analysis of the rules of the GATT in the light of the theory of optimal intervention, *see* Frieder Roessler, *The Constitutional Function of the Multilateral Trade Order*, in 8 NATIONAL CONSTITUTIONS AND INTERNATIONAL ECONOMIC LAW 53–62 (M. Hilf & E.-U. Petersmann, eds., 1993).

39. *The New Multilateral Trading System: What Is at Stake?*, GATT Doc. GATT/1619 (address by Peter D. Sutherland to the Swedish-American Chamber of Commerce, New York, Mar. 3, 1994).

40. *Cf.* Alice Enders & Amelia Porges, *Conventional Success and Successful Conventions: The Montreal Protocol*, in THE GREENING OF WORLD TRADE ISSUES (K. Anderson & R. Blackhurst, eds., 1992).

41. On this function of GATT law, see more generally the contributions to the volume cited in note 38 above, and Frieder Roessler, *The Constitutional Function of International Economic Law*, 41 AUSSENWIRTSCHAFT, Heft II/III, 467–74 (1986).

42. Agreement Establishing the World Trade Organization, arts. IX, X, in 1994 Uruguay Round Final Act, note 1 above.

43. *Id.* art. XIV.

44. Understanding on Rules and Procedures Governing the Settlement of Disputes, art. 22:3, in 1994 Uruguay Round Final Act, note 1 above.

45. *See* the references in Frieder Roessler, *The Competence of GATT,* 21:3 J. WORLD TRADE L. 78 (1987).

46. GATT Doc. GATT/CP.3/SR.42, at 19–21.

47. GATT Doc. L/332/Rev.1; Report of the Working Party. *Quantitative Restrictions,* BISD 3rd Supp. 170, ¶¶ 14–23 (1955).

48. *See* Frieder Roessler, *Pressures to Adjust Balance of Payments Disequilibria. An Analysis of the Powers of the International Monetary Fund,* 30 INT'L ORG. 433 (1976).

49. *Declaration of Ministers, Approved at Tokyo on 14 September 1973,* BISD 20th Supp. 19, ¶ 7 (1974).

50. *Restrictive Business Practices, Arrangements for Consultations,* BISD 9th Supp. 28, 170 (1961).

51. William Wallace, *Issue Linkage Among Atlantic Governments,* 52 INT'L AFFAIRS 163 (1976).

II · Environmental Standards

2 GATT Legal Restraints on Domestic Environmental Regulations

Daniel A. Farber
Robert E. Hudec

2.1 Introduction

The so-called conflict between trade and environment arises from the simple fact that nations have different environmental policies. At one end of the spectrum are the "high-level" countries, who have rigorous laws rigorously enforced. At the other end of the spectrum are the "low-level" countries that make lesser demands—countries with equally rigorous laws that are not so rigorously enforced, or with less rigorous laws, or with no laws at all.

Differences in national environmental policy can produce two kinds of trade disputes. Both are triggered by actions by high-level countries. The first type of conflict involves regulations that seek to protect environmental quality within the territory of the high-level country, such as a local auto emission or fuel efficiency standard. The high-level country unquestionably has jurisdiction to impose such regulations, but conflict can arise if a regulation has a particularly burdensome effect on imports. Other countries may claim that the burdensome qualities of the high-level regulation are unnecessary to the claimed environmental purpose of the regulation, and thus constitute a barrier to market access that is prohibited by GATT.

The second type of conflict involves efforts by the high-level country to employ trade restrictions to pressure other governments or their nationals to improve the level of environmental quality elsewhere in the world. A recent example is the U.S. embargo on tuna imports from countries that allowed their fishing fleets to employ dolphin-unsafe harvesting methods. The conflicts in such cases involve an attack upon the high-level country's legal authority to regulate foreign conduct in this way. The target countries complain that trade restrictions conditioned on behavior outside the territory of the regulating country are another kind of barrier to market access that GATT obligations prohibit.

The legal restraints imposed by GATT law in these areas are by no means illusory. Both types of environmental regulatory action, domestic and outward looking, have sometimes been found in violation of GATT law. Moreover, the recently concluded Uruguay Round trade negotiations have added several new GATT rules that are intended to reinforce certain parts of this legal discipline. The two changes raising the most concern among environmentalists are the new code on the Application of Sanitary and Phytosanitary Measures[1] and the new and expanded rule on trade-restricting technical specifications in the GATT's Standards Code.[2] Both make explicit that differentially burdensome regulations that deviate from internationally accepted standards may be subject to legal challenge.

The central thrust of the current "trade and environment" debate is an attack by environmental groups on the GATT legal restraints that curtail these two kinds of regulatory activities by high-level countries. Our focus in this paper will be on the first area, i.e., regulations protecting the domestic environment of the high-level country. The primary complaint is that the GATT rules governing domestic environmental regulations are simply too strict. The GATT rules themselves, it is claimed, place too great a burden on the accused government to prove the necessity of the particular regulation. The GATT's administration of the rules, it is argued, also tips the scales against environmental interests, due to GATT's inability or unwillingness to understand the importance of the environmental interests at stake. Environmental groups want to change GATT rules to give the regulating government the benefit of the doubt. They also seek a more balanced adjudicatory forum—more open to the public, more balanced in the selection of judges, and more receptive to environmental interests in general.

Perhaps the most thoughtful of the recent environmentalist critics is Daniel Esty. In his recent book, *Greening the GATT*,[3] Esty acknowledges the danger that environmental regulations may be captured by protectionists who will use them as a "guise for erecting barriers to imports."[4] He criticizes more extreme environmentalists for overlooking the lessons of history about "the temptation to slip into protectionism, the dynamics of trade retaliation, and the need to promote international cooperation...."[5] On the other hand, he fears that GATT's current rules set "an almost impossibly high hurdle for environmental policies."[6] After surveying current GATT issues and analogous problems involving the U.S. commerce clause, he proposes a modification in GATT law to reduce the scrutiny given environmental regulations. Under his proposed approach, an environmental regulation would withstand attack if its trade effects are "not *clearly* disproportionate" to its environmental benefits, taking into account "equally effective policy alternatives that are reasonably available."[7]

Because *Greening the GATT* is one of the most cogent statements of the environmentalist position, we will devote substantial attention to Esty's arguments. We agree with him about the need to strike a balance between environmental and trade concerns, but we draw different lessons from current GATT and U.S. decisions. With respect to facially discriminatory measures, we would follow current GATT law in requiring a strong showing of necessity. We believe that current GATT law is at least as favorable to discriminatory environmental regulations are U.S. judicial decisions, which Esty cites approvingly.[8] With respect to non-discriminatory measures, we believe that current GATT law is a good deal more flexible than Esty recognizes, and much closer to U.S. judicial decisions.

2.2 Tensions between Environmental Regulation and Free Trade

Applying GATT to environmental regulations involves some complex legal issues. These issues are best evaluated with a clear awareness of environmentalist concerns and with an understanding of how other legal systems handle analogous problems. We will begin by surveying environmentalist criticisms of the GATT (only some of which are endorsed by Esty). We will then follow Esty's lead in looking to U.S. case law for guidance, before turning to a legal analysis of GATT.

2.2.1 Environmentalist Concerns about GATT

The claims currently being made against GATT range from scholarly discussions, such as Esty's, to the hysterical. The latter are typified by the text of the well-known *Sabotage* advertisement that appeared in several national newspapers in April and December of 1992, a full-page ad taken out by Sierra Club, Public Citizen, Greenpeace, Friends of the Earth, Clean Water Action, and a number of other smaller environmental groups.[9] The ad warns that a "secretive foreign bureaucracy" will be given "vast new powers to threaten American laws that protect your food, your health, your wilderness and wildlife, your job, and democracy itself." GATT is called a threat to "thousands of laws in countries around the world that give priority to clean food and clean water," preserve natural resources, and restrict pesticides. Among the specific examples are "European laws to stop the sale of beef shot up with carcinogenic hormones like DES," "Japanese laws that keep out dangerous food colorings known to cause cancer," and Thailand's anti-smoking campaign.

Setting aside its debatable factual assertions,[10] the *Sabotage* advertisement does point to many of the recurrent themes in this area. GATT has a number of rules which permit tribunals to invalidate measures as undue restrictions on trade. In particular, the new agreement on Sanitary and Phytosanitary Measures and the new Standards Code evaluate health and product safety standards under legal standards such as "disguised restriction on international trade" or "unnecessary obstacles to international trade."[11] These new agreements also encourage governments to use accepted international standards in their regulations because uniform international standards are likely to cause the least trade disruption.[12] In a country like the United States, which has many regulations that are more demanding than international standards, this emphasis on international standards leads to fears of pressures to "harmonization down." Failure to prove a scientific basis for such higher-level regulations could result in rulings of GATT illegality when such regulations impose differential burdens on foreign sellers.[13] The end result might thus be a weakening of the strict regulations that environmentalists have fought long and hard to achieve. For this reason, it is not surprising that even thoughtful critics like Esty are quite concerned about GATT's potential impact.

Environmental groups often cite GATT complaints brought by the United States against high-level regulations of other governments as examples of the downward pressure that will occur. Two cases mentioned in the *Sabotage* advertisement are most often cited. The *Hormones* complaint against the EC involves a claim that the hormone ban serves no valid purpose, because there is no scientific evidence that the hormone-produced meat contains any harmful substance. Critics who object to this complaint argue that its implicit standard of judgment—demonstrated harmful effects—is too high; they content that such trade policy rules will override much risk-preventing regulation that should be allowed.[14]

Another favorite target is the U.S. complaint against Thailand's cigarette embargo. Thailand claimed that the embargo was part of an anti-smoking campaign. The GATT panel rejected this defense, pointing out that Thailand's claimed objectives could have been achieved by measures that did not discriminate between imports and domestic producers. Critics, usually with a somewhat distorted view of holding,[15] object to the panel's second guessing the Thai government's view of what was needed to reduce smoking. Trade policy officials would concede that, factual errors aside, policing of disguised trade restrictions does require a tribunal to look behind claimed motives for restrictive regulation.

A potentially more telling example is the U.S. complaint brought under the Canada–U.S. Free Trade Agreement against a Canadian landing requirement for salmon and herring caught in Canada's West Coast waters.[16] Although the landing requirement was facially neutral in its application to domestic and foreign fish buyers, it had a clearly differential impact on foreign buyers. That effect was ruled an export restriction *prima facie* in violation of GATT. The panel then rejected the environmental justification for the measure because of the minimal environmental gain produced by the 100 percent landing requirement, as compared to the gain offered by less restrictive alternatives. This gain, in the panel's view, would not have been deemed large enough to have justified the economic burden imposed by the measure, if Canadian fish buyers had been the ones to bear it.

Another U.S. complaint, which seems not to have drawn the attention it should, was President Bush's complaint, during his ill-fated visit to Tokyo in December 1992, about the excess rigor of Japan's auto emission standards. Had it been brought to GATT, it would have been a perfect example of how environmental regulations more rigorous than the international norm can be attacked. Ironically, U.S. automobile regulations themselves have been attacked in GATT for targeting foreign imports. In addition to certain expressly discriminatory features, the U.S. fuel efficiency tax also weighed more heavily on European producers of luxury cars because domestic producers are able to calculate fuel efficiency based on the average gas consumption of their entire fleets,[17] a complaint that Esty found meritorious.[18]

The ultimate position taken by the critics of GATT rules in this area tends to vary. The more extreme critics call for a broad zone of sovereign immunity, allowing no international restrictions at all in the important areas of health, safety, and environmental regulation. One version simply argues that the economic cost of tolerating disguised trade barriers in this area is less than the environmental cost of depressing national standards. At a loftier level, the argument wraps itself in the flag of "democracy," claiming that democratic choices made by national and local legislatures deserve preference over rules and decisions of international bodies. This is the subliminal message of the *Sabotage* advertisement's references to a "secretive foreign [not international, mind you, but 'foreign'] bureaucracy," and its listing of "democracy itself" among the victims of that sinister foreign instrument.[19] Ultimately, the fear seems to be directed against international institutions as opposed to trusted (or at least familiar) national governments.

Other critics, such as Esty, do recognize the need for some international supervision of trade restrictions disguised as environmental or health-and-safety measures.[20] They focus on making the rules and procedures more environment-friendly than they perceive GATT to be. The complaint on procedures is set forward in the *Sabotage* ad itself:

Under GATT, when one country sues another, a panel of three trade officials is formed to hear the case.... The hearings are secret. No environmental, consumer, health, labor, or citizens organizations have a right to testify. No press, no public. The manner of deliberations is still unknown.[21]

Although we believe that these questions of process are extremely important, they fall outside the scope of this paper. On the substantive side, critics like Esty call for shifting the burden of proof, so that complainants would have to prove the absence of regulatory necessity, rather than requiring the regulating country to prove that its measures are necessary.[22] A further substantive change might be to explicitly endorse some version of the precautionary principle.

These critics have been effective in forcing a re-examination of how GATT regulates, or might regulate, claims of disguised trade restriction. Pushing aside the more extreme claims on each side—the deregulatory fervor of some GATT defenders and the "sovereign immunity" position of the more isolationist environmental groups—there is a fairly broad range of agreement on the need to strike a balance. Like thoughtful environmentalists such as Esty, we agree on the need to find a set of rules and procedures that can accommodate the desires for, on the one hand, effective policing of disguised trade restrictions, and, on the other hand, adequate protection of the environment.

2.2.2 U.S. Experience with the Dormant Commerce Clause

Like Esty, we believe that U.S. judicial decisions provide a useful starting point in analyzing the analogous GATT issues. American courts now have almost two centuries of experience in dealing with internal trade barriers. Under what has been called the "dormant commerce clause" doctrine, the Supreme Court has viewed the Constitution as placing implicit limits on state regulations that impact trade. The U.S. experience suggests both some of the intellectual quandaries involved in this exercise and some possible doctrinal resolutions.[23]

Esty views current U.S. doctrine as establishing a two-prong test. Laws that appear to apply even-handedly are subject only to what Esty calls a "light" balancing test (which is sometimes extremely light.) Laws that discriminate on their face against interstate commerce are subject to strict scrutiny, as are laws that are superficially neutral but plainly discriminatory in effect.[24] Although this is not a bad summary of U.S. law, it suffers from oversimplification.[25] This oversimplification not only misses some significant features of U.S. doctrine, but also somewhat obscures the way in which U.S. courts are struggling to juggle conflicting values.

Current doctrine distinguishes three categories of cases. The first category consist of facially discriminatory measures. Here, it may be an understatement to speak of "strict scrutiny" as Esty does, for the Court has suggested that such discrimination is virtually prohibited.[26] A second category involves facially neutral statutes with a "discriminatory effect," and here the state has the burden to justify the regulation in terms of its benefits and the unavailability of nondiscriminatory alternatives.[27] The third category of cases involve regulations that place "incidental" or "indirect" burdens on commerce, and here the Court applies a balancing test.[28]

Although this three-part scheme has the appearance of tidiness, in practice it involves difficult line drawing. Indeed, a recent Supreme Court decision rather casually lumps the first two categories together as involving "clearly discriminatory" statutes.[29] Similarly, the line between the second two categories has proved permeable, as the Supreme Court has also observed.[30]

Though the task of assigning cases to categories has proved unexpectedly difficult, the consequences of that assignment are striking. In practice, the strict scrutiny applied to discriminatory statutes has usually proved fatal. Indeed, particularly as to statutes that discriminate on their face against interstate commerce, the courts have sometimes referred to an almost categorical rule of invalidity.[31] To uphold the statute, the state must show that the discrimination is "demonstrably justified by a valid factor unrelated to economic protectionism."[32] Only a few statutes have survived this test.[33] In contrast to strict scrutiny, the balancing test in practice has seemingly become lax in the most recent cases. Indeed, there is some argument that it requires only that the state present *some* evidence of a regulatory benefit, particularly when public health or safety is at stake.[34] Courts have been reluctant to "second-guess the empirical judgments of lawmakers concerning the utility of legislation."[35] Because of the sharp differences between the results of these two types of scrutiny, the crucial question in most cases is which type applies. Unfortunately, as we found in an extensive survey of recent U.S. decisions,[36] courts have not addressed this question in a particularly cogent fashion. Often, they simply pronounce that a statute is or is not "discriminatory"; having attached this label, they then apply the requisite level of scrutiny. Thus, though he is wrong about the doctrinal details, Esty is right that the crucial issue is the degree of judicial scrutiny provided different statutes.

When reading the actual cases, as opposed to overviews like Esty's, one is immediately struck by the difficulty the Court seems to have in applying its purportedly straightforward tests. For example, *Kassel v. Consolidated Freightways Corp.*[37] is often viewed as a classic example of the milder balancing test. The case involved an Iowa regulation banning a certain type of semi-truck; because neighboring states allowed such trucks, the regulation added significantly to transportation costs.[38] This apparently straightforward problem, however, produced a fractured Court. The plurality opinion applied a balancing test and found essentially no evidence of any safety benefit to offset the regulatory burden. Two concurring Justices rejected even this limited use of the balancing test, but found evidence of discriminatory intent, while the dissenters insisted that the statute was a valid safety regulation.[39]

A more recent decision demonstrates that the Court's difficulties have not abated. *C & A Carbone v. Town of Clarkstown*[40] involved what is called a garbage flow-control ordinance, which required that all garbage within the town be sent to a government-financed disposal facility. The Court divided 5-4 on whether this ordinance should be considered discriminatory against out-of-state disposal sites, or whether it should be governed by the more lenient balancing test. To add to the confusion, one of the four advocating application of the balancing test thought the ordinance failed that test, while the other three disagreed.

As we see it, the U.S. courts are struggling with a dilemma. Open-ended balancing is widely perceived to give far too much power to federal judges at the expense of legislatures. Drawing back from the implications of balancing, judges are tempted to limit themselves to policing for discriminatory intent. But intent is often difficult to prove, so the temptation is to substitute an objective proxy. For instance, if the judge is confident that a statute will produce no regulatory benefits, he or she may reasonably conclude that the motive must have been protectionist. Yet a "no-benefits" test would be too weak, since a statute may produce minor benefits but be overwhelmingly protectionist. The impulse then is to strengthen the test, leading back toward balancing. None of these solutions seems wholly satisfactory. The resulting difficulties are papered over with conclusory references to "discrimination."

Because of the difficulty of finding an adequate doctrinal formulation, judges find it hard to articulate the bases for their decisions except where there is clear, explicit discrimination. Based on our own studies of the cases, we believe that both the choice and application of the doctrinal test is strongly influenced by the judge's initial evaluation of the government regulation. If the regulation bears the earmarks of protectionist motive, the burden of proof is likely to be effectively placed on the government to justify the regulation. In other cases, a challenge to a regulation will face a skeptical audience.

There are two important conclusions to be drawn from the U.S. experience. The first is that a commitment to free trade almost inevitably requires scrutiny of local regulations for signs of protectionism. Thus, it is not surprising that GATT has embarked on a similar venture, nor can GATT reasonably be expected to abandon the field. The second lesson is that, particularly absent any explicit discrimination against foreign commerce, this judicial task may not be at all easy to accomplish. It requires a delicate balance between concern for free trade and deference to legislative prerogatives.

2.3   GATT Rules Governing Challenges to High-Level Regulations

Unlike the constraints imposed on state government under the dormant commerce clause, the similar GATT restraints imposed on member governments rest on an explicit mandate. GATT is a formal international agreement containing explicit prohibitions of certain kinds of protectionist trade barriers. GATT begins with "tariff bindings" setting a maximum rate for tariffs on an item-by-item basis.[41] Then, to protect against other measures that would subvert the commercial opportunity created by tariff bindings, the GATT agreement adds a rather detailed code of rules prohibiting most other forms of trade barriers.[42]

GATT's prohibitions are qualified by GATT Article XX, which authorizes exceptions whenever trade barriers are found to be required by other widely accepted government regulatory objectives such as health, safety, or law enforcement.[43] Application of Article XX requires GATT tribunals to analyze the extent to which claimed regulatory objectives are served by a particular trade-restricting measure.

Recent interpretations and additions to GATT law tend to merge the issues of protective effect and justifying purpose. An example is the 1994 Standards Code prohibition of measures that create "unnecessary obstacles to international trade."[44]

The application of GATT rules ultimately raises the same type of issues confronted by U.S. courts. Although Esty recognizes the distinction in U.S. law between facially discriminatory and facially neutral regulations,[45] his recommendations for reforming GATT tend to blur the significance of this distinction in GATT law. We find the importance placed on this distinction in U.S. decisions to be paralleled in GATT decisions, and will organize our discussion of GATT accordingly.

2.3.1   Cases Involving Explicit Discrimination

GATT law imposes the greatest restraints on measures that explicitly discriminate between domestic and foreign goods. This category includes border measures such as quotas and other restrictions that limit the volume of foreign goods allowed to enter the national market, and also "internal" taxes or regulations that explicitly provide more onerous treatment of foreign goods. The U.S. case law often suggests that such explicitly discriminatory measures are all but *per se* prohibited under the Commerce Clause, but in practice does recognize some narrow exceptions.[46] Under GATT, such discriminatory measures are *prima facie* outlawed by the rules of the agreement,[47] but GATT Article XX permits even explicitly discriminatory measures when such discrimination is necessary to legitimate regulatory objectives.

GATT's *Section 337* case offers a good example of GATT's approach to this category of cases.[48] Section 337 is a U.S. patent-enforcement law that applies only to imports. Under GATT, an internal regulatory measure that makes an explicit differentiation between foreign and domestic goods calls for a two-step analysis. The first question is whether the different treatment is "less favorable" to the foreign products—in other words, whether the measure is a *prima facie* violation of GATT Article III:4. Measures providing explicitly different treatment of foreign goods are scrutinized quite severely under this test. In the *Section 337* case, the GATT panel held that any difference that *could* result in less favorable treatment in some cases was enough of a disadvantage to establish a violation.[49] For example, the shorter time limits of the Section 337 procedure were held to be less favorable treatment even though not all foreign defendants were disadvantaged by them, and even though some defendants might find this disadvantage outweighed by other advantages. The fact of differential treatment is thus treated as a badge of potential discrimination, placing a measure into a suspect category in which any harmful commercial effect will trigger a finding of *prima facie* violation.

Second, once a measure is found to be in violation of Article III, the defendant government may seek to establish a justification for the measure under Article XX. The Article XX defense is difficult to establish, for once a *prima facie* violation is established, GATT imposes a demanding framework of analysis in which the burden is on the enacting government to demonstrate each element of the claimed excuse.[50] In the *Section 337* case, the United States sought to establish an Article XX defense, claiming that different procedures were required for imports because of the special difficulties of enforcing patent rights against foreign parties. The GATT rejected most of the Article XX defense, finding that the United States had failed to demonstrate that unavailability of effective, nondiscriminatory alternatives.[51] But GATT did rule that one part of the special enforcement procedure was justified, holding that the difficulty of enforcing injunctions against foreign producers justified the use of special *in rem* remedies.[52]

The main difference between the treatment of explicitly discriminatory measures under GATT and U.S. doctrine is the GATT's tendency to give somewhat greater attention to possible justifications for such measures. The explicit terms of GATT Article XX encourage defendant governments to raise justification claims, and require GATT legal decisions to address the issue of justification explicitly. As a result, the legal analysis of claims of justification tends to be more fully elaborated in GATT. The demanding requirements of Article XX, however, limit its successful use.

Facial discrimination is the most attractive basis for GATT intervention, and correspondingly difficult for environmentalists to defend. Perhaps for this reason, environmentalists such as Esty have seemingly found it difficult to formulate a clear position regarding such regulations. On the one hand, Esty recognizes the argument for strict scrutiny of discriminatory regulations. On the other hand, his "not clearly disproportional" test, which is much weaker, seems to be designed to apply even to measures that explicitly differentiate between foreign and domestic goods.[53] In the end, discrimination seems to serve only as one of several factors in his analysis.

We would give discrimination a more pivotal role. U.S. experience under the dormant commerce clause suggests that facially discriminatory regulations pose special risks of protectionism and should be viewed with suspicion. The current GATT analysis is, if anything, a bit less demanding than its U.S. counterpart. At another point in his analysis, Esty does appear to concede a special place for discriminatory measures when pointing out that very few domestic environmental regulations have ever run afoul of the GATT test:

> The GATT does provide broad leeway for countries to pursue *domestic* environmental regulation. As long as the nondiscrimination strictures of GATT Articles I and III are met, governments can impose pollution taxes, enact deposit-refund requirements, set ceilings on emissions, and even bar the production or sale of certain goods. Indeed, in the 45 years of GATT's existence, nations have promulgated tens of thousands of environmental regulations affecting domestic production and the consumption of products, whether domestic or imported. Only a handful of these environmental rules have been found to be discriminatory and judged to be inconsistent with GATT.[54]

Given the risk of protectionist motive posed by discriminatory regulations, we believe that facially discriminatory regulations should continue to be subject to the current rigors of Article III/Article XX analysis.

2.3.2   Cases Involving Facially Neutral Measures with Disparate Effects

Like U.S. doctrine, the GATT law also deals with facially neutral measures that may have a trade-restricting effect. For example, a different tax or regulatory burden may be placed on products with certain characteristics; it "just happens" that all or most foreign products fall into the disadvantaged category. An example might be emission controls that impose less burdensome requirements for large-bore engines used in domestic automobiles than for small-bore engines normally used in foreign autos.[55]

Facially neutral regulations invariably fall in the category of so-called "internal" measures—tax or other regulatory measures that are imposed on imported goods (together with domestic goods) after the imported goods have cleared customs and entered domestic commerce. Article III requires that internal taxes and internal regulations treat foreign goods "no less favorably" than the "like" domestic goods. This is the so-called "national treatment" rule. Any measure found in violation of Article III would be a *prima facie* violation, and thus in the same category of explicitly discriminatory measures. Any regulatory justification for such a measure would have to establish strict conformity with the requirements of Article XX.

Where the treatment of imports is both explicitly different and more burdensome, the Article III violation is clear, and issues of excuse come under Article XX with the burden of justification being on the enacting government. Esty seems to assume that the same burden of justification would exist for all regulations burdening trade. When the more burdensome treatment is the result of a facially neutral regulation, however, the meaning of Article III remains unclear. This interpretative difficulty requires an extended explanation. We will begin by exploring this problem in the context of facially neutral product definitions that in fact disadvantage foreign products.

Product Definitions
Facially neutral product definitions are taxes or regulatory measures that prescribe different treatment according to distinctions between two or more types of product—for example, a law permitting grocery stores to sell beer in bottles but not beer in cans. If we look to U.S. law on this type of facially neutral measure, we find that the validity of such measures seems to turn on the balance between the measure's trade-distorting effects and its purported regulatory purpose. Where the trade-restricting effects are substantial while the regulatory benefits are nil or minuscule, we expect to find courts ruling against the measure—either on the ground that its regulatory benefits are outweighed by its burden on commerce or on the ground that its lack of any credible regulatory purpose is evidence of a protectionist purpose. The U.S. courts tend to issue *a priori* characterizations of a measure as "discriminatory" or merely "incidentally" burdensome. We believe that these *a priori* characterizations are the means by which courts adjust their degree of scrutiny according to their initial common sense perceptions of the likely purpose of the measure.

This preliminary sorting operation seems quite useful in view of the great diversity of regulatory measures that fall into this category. At one extreme are the devious product standards aimed solely at disadvantaging foreign goods; at the other are a very large number of quite ordinary regulatory measures that happen to impose some greater degree of burden on foreign producers. If the mere existence of greater burdens on foreign producers were to call for strict scrutiny of the measure, governments would be required to mount a major defense for almost every regulatory action they take. We agree with critics such as Esty in finding this possibility unacceptable.

On the surface, Article III seems to offer less flexibility than U.S. doctrine in dealing with this wide variety of facially neutral measures. Article III appears to separate the question of legal violation from the issue of regulatory justification. The issue of violation is framed solely as a matter of whether the treatment of foreign goods is "less favorable"—in other words, commercially disadvantageous. If the commercial disadvantage is ruled "less favorable treatment," then the measure is a *prima facie* GATT violation, and the regulatory justification, if any, will be considered only under Article XX. Hence, GATT may find it difficult to control disguised protectionist measures at one end of the spectrum without having to find all other regulation with adverse trade effects to be in violation (and thus subject to the strict tests of Article XX).[56]

Thus, GATT's treatment of facially neutral regulations seems vulnerable at first blush to the charge of excessive rigidity raised by Esty and others. If the existence of a disparate impact did not constitute discrimination under Article III, any good lawyer could disguise protectionism in the form of superficially neutral regulations. On the other hand, if disparate impact always constitutes discrimination, many regulations would violate Article III, and any defenses would be subject to the demanding standards of Article XX. Esty's critique assumes that disparate impact will be equated with discrimination, and, given that assumption, his argument has considerable force. But GATT tribunals have found ways to avoid inflexible application of Article III, so that in many situations facially neutral regulations need never face the standards of Article XX.

A recent GATT decision articulates an interpretation of Article III that permits GATT to scrutinize such measures according to the credibility of their claimed regulatory purpose. The case involved a Mississippi tax on wines which placed a lower rate on wines made from the *vitus rotundifolia* grape used by most Mississippi vintners; wines made from all other types of grape were taxed at a higher rate.[57] Under Article III, equal treatment is required for all "like" products. The issue was whether wine from the *rotundifolia* grape was a "like product" to wine made from other grapes. The GATT tribunal concluded that the "likeness" issue turns on the purpose of the Article III "like product" standard, which is to distinguish between protectionism and good-faith regulation. The tribunal concluded that the "likeness" of the two types of wine must depend on whether any nontrade regulatory purpose was served by distinguishing between them.[58]

The actual decision on this point was aided by a U.S. concession that the product distinction did not serve any independent tax or regulatory purpose apart from subsidizing small local producers.[59] The various types of wine in question thus were all like products. Under Article III, therefore, all the imported wine products were entitled to be treated as well as any domestic product in that category. The heavier tax against the non-Mississippi types of wine was thus a violation of Article III.[60]

Formalistically, a finding of an Article III violation would set the stage for an Article XX defense. In this setting, however, Article XX is superfluous. The regulatory justification for the product distinction had already been considered and rejected when deciding the "like product" issue as a part of the question of violation under Article III. Indeed, the test stated by the GATT decision would always require simultaneous consideration of regulatory justification as a part of the decision under Article III. Hence, the narrowness of the Article XX defenses that so concerns Esty is irrelevant.

Because of the U.S. concession, the Mississippi wine decision was not required to say anything about the burden of proof on the issue of whether the product distinction served any regulatory purpose. Burden of proof may be crucial in environmental cases, where substantial factual uncertainty may well exist about the benefits of a regulation. There being no finding of *prima facie* violation at this stage of the analysis, the Article XX rationale for placing the burden of justification on the defendant would not apply. At this early stage, the only fact before the decision maker was the bare fact that the tax measure in question was trade restricting—that is, it resulted in a commercial disadvantage for almost all non-Mississippi wine, foreign or domestic. Should that trade-restricting effect be enough, by itself, to render the measure suspect, with the burden on the defendant to justify it? Or should a tribunal still apply the usual rule that the initial burden is on the complainant to establish at least a *prima facie* violation?

As discussed previously, we believe that U.S. courts adjust the burden of proof based on their intuitive perception of protectionism (or its absence). On this basis, they label a statute as "discriminatory" or not, and then shift the burden of proof accordingly.

GATT tribunals may find it more difficult to manipulate the burden of proof in this kind of case—or at least to do so openly. Under Article III, the burden is on the complaining party to establish a violation, and one component of the violation is establishing that two "like" products have been treated differently. Thus, the formal burden will be on the complaining party. Yet intuition suggests that, in practice, a decision-making tribunal will probably be influenced in its approach by an initial common sense characterization of the measure. There will be some cases, like the Mississippi wine tax, where the impact on trade seems clear and where the criteria seem bogus, and these initial appearances will result in a strong initial presumption of protectionist purpose. On the other hand, there will be some cases where the smell of ulterior motive is absent—cases, perhaps, where disadvantages are not distributed so unevenly to foreign goods or where the measure's criteria may have a plausible regulatory ring to them. Tribunals will probably follow these initial presumptions in determining the "likeness" of the products affected by the regulation.

The GATT legal proceeding that dealt with the Mississippi wine case also contained another claim requiring application of the "like product" test. The other claim involved marketing regulations by several U.S. state governments distinguishing between sales of 3.2 percent beer and sales of beer with higher alcohol content.[61] Most of the beer imports from the complaining country were beer above 3.2 percent.[62] "Beer is beer," said the claimant, arguing that all kinds of beer should be treated as "like products" and treated the same.[63] Not so, said the GATT decision. The panel concluded that the history of the distinction in alcohol content showed a bona fide concern for health, and also for revenue maximization, and not any trade purpose; consequently, the two types of beer should *not* be classified as like products.[64] One suspects that U.S. courts would have reached the same result, calling the trade-restricting effects of these beer-marketing regulations an "incidental burden on commerce." It was not a hard case under either approach.

A further discussion of the "like product" issue is found in the recent *CAFE* decision.[65] The *CAFE* decision may not be a particularly reliable forecast of GATT doctrine in this area, because the decision was rendered under extreme pressure due to the much noted danger that a finding of violation against the United States might impede Congressional ratification of the WTO Charter and the Uruguay Round agreements. The *CAFE* decision does take a very confined view of GATT's powers to review facially neutral regulatory measures, and the decision contains signs of strained logic in reaching that result. Nonetheless, the theory of the *CAFE* decision will certainly occupy a central position in further developments of GATT doctrine in this area. The panel decision in the *CAFE* case endorsed the approach taken in the Mississippi case under which likeness turns on whether the regulatory distinction was made "so as to afford protection to domestic production."[66] The panel defined the phrase "so as to afford protection" as follows:

The Panel noted that the term "so as to" suggested both aim and effect. Thus the phrase "so as to afford protection" called for an analysis of elements including the aim of the measure and the resulting effects. A measure could be said to have the *aim* of affording protection if an analysis of the circumstances in which it was adopted, in particular an analysis of the instruments available to the contracting party to achieve the declared domestic policy goal, demonstrated that a change in competitive opportunities in favour of domestic products was a desired outcome and not merely an incidental consequence of the pursuit of a legitimate policy goal. A measure could be said to have the *effect* of affording protection to domestic production if it accorded greater competitive opportunities to domestic products than to imported products.[67]

Applying this test, the panel determined that cars costing more than $30,000 were "unlike" cars costing less for purposes of a luxury tax, and that cars with high gasoline consumption were "unlike" more efficient cars for purposes of a "gas-guzzler" tax designed to reduce gasoline consumption.

The panel's discussion of the luxury tax was more extensive than its discussion of the gas-guzzler tax. In determining the aim of the luxury tax, the panel seemingly gave little weight to legislative history that suggested protectionist motives. Instead, the panel emphasized that the apparent aim of the legislation was to raise revenue by means of a luxury tax, a widely used tax measure in many countries, and that the $30,000 level did identify the upper end of the automobile market.[68] As to the effect prong of the test, the panel found considerable uncertainty about composition of the market near the threshold, due to the unclear relationship between list and actual sales prices. It emphasized that a high selling price did not appear to be "inherent" to EC or other foreign automobiles, and that EC, U.S., and Japanese manufacturers could and did manufacture cars on both sides of the threshold. In addition, the panel found the gradually incremental structure of the tax was reasonable, and that the threshold did not appear "arbitrary or contrived in the context of the policies pursued."[69]

The analysis of the gas-guzzler tax followed similar lines. Notably, in considering the aim of the tax, the panel did not consider it relevant that a fuel tax might have been a much more effective method of pursuing conservation.[70] Again finding that the nature and level of the distinction made at the threshold "were consistent with the overall purpose of the measure and did not appear to create categories of inherently foreign or domestic origin," the panel also concluded that the tax's effect was not to afford protection. Hence, foreign automobiles below the 22.5 mpg threshold were "unlike" domestic automobiles above the threshold.

Given the evidence of protectionism in the legislative history, as well as the fairly dramatic disparate impact claimed by the EC, it would not have been difficult to find that the taxes in question were protectionist. The *CAFE* decision appears to say that, even in the presence of such indicia of protectionism, nations will have considerable discretion to adopt otherwise plausible regulatory measures. So long as the measure seems rationally related to its purported purpose, the only major restriction under

CAFE seems to be provided by the need to avoid singling out "inherently foreign" traits of goods. The panel's definition of "inherently foreign" is one of the narrowest elements of the decision. It seems to distinguish between characteristics of the foreign goods that are merely due to market specialization and characteristics that are "inherent" in the sense of being a necessary and unavoidable part of the foreign industry's position. The decision suggests that a government will not be charged with a protective purpose, or effect, if the government's regulations target the existing market characteristics of a foreign producer.[71]

Disparate Effects

We turn now to another type of facially neutral measure that can have trade-restricting effects—the regulation or product standard which, though imposing exactly the same requirements for all products, bears more heavily on foreign producers than on domestic producers. A simple example would be a container reuse requirement, which would obviously be more burdensome for foreign producers.

In the long run, the trick to making Article III a sufficiently flexible and sensitive legal standard lies in finding some way to interpret the "less favorable treatment" standard to limit its application to more egregious measures involving little or no genuine regulatory purpose. As we saw, this has been done for product classifications via the "like product" test of Article III. To some extent, this approach may work for a broader range of facially neutral regulation. For example, if a country allows certain goods to be sold with a warning label but not without, one might fruitfully consider whether the labeled and unlabeled versions are "like" products.[72]

This approach may seem somewhat artificial, however, particularly when the difference between permitted and forbidden products is invisible to the consumer. It also seems strained when the basis for regulation is not a physical attribute of the product itself. Consider the example of a German packaging law requiring reuse of shipping containers; this law creates a special burden for Kenyan flower growers.[73] It is unclear whether the analysis of the validity of this regulation is advanced by asking whether flowers shipped in containers that will later be subject to reuse are "like products" with flowers shipped in containers that aren't later reused. The question here is either too easy (the flowers themselves are identical), or too metaphysical (the likeness of the flowers depends on the exigencies of waste regulation). The panel in the *CAFE* decision held that regulatory distinctions cannot be justified under Article III "based on factors not directly relating to the product as such," such as the average fuel efficiency of the manufacturer's fleet.[74] Query whether a packaging, recycling, or labeling requirement relates to the "product as such." In cases like these, where the "like product" approach is problematic, GATT needs an alternative method of introducing flexibility and thereby avoiding the criticisms raised by Esty and others.

A possible answer may have been created, in the National Treatment provision of new Uruguay Round Services Agreement.[75] The new provision restates the national treatment concept in more detail than GATT Article III. It begins by employing the old less-favorable-treatment standard. It then resolves the important question of whether facially neutral measures are covered, saying yes, that the prohibition applies to both "formally identical and formally different" measures whenever they "modify conditions of competition" in favor of domestic suppliers.[76] But the new text then goes on to add that the prohibition does not apply to "inherent competitive disadvantages which result from the foreign character of the relevant services or service suppliers."[77] When will a competitive disadvantage be considered "inherent [to] ... the foreign character" of the foreign supplier? The answer, presumably, is when all of the causal weight regarding the commercial disadvantage is placed on "inherent disadvantage" rather than on the regulatory feature in question. And when will that be? When, it is submitted, the regulation has the kind of routine normalcy (dare we say, credibility?) that makes it look like innocently ordinary domestic regulation with no protectionist purpose. The word "inherent" is synonymous with "inevitable" here, the reality that regulators, even if operating with the purist of motives, cannot always avoid disadvantaging the foreign supplier. In short, by introducing the all-purpose concept of causation, the draftsmen of the Uruguay Round Services Agreement may in fact have found another way of introducing the issue of valid regulatory purpose into the legal definition of "less favorable treatment."

This National Treatment provision of the new Services Agreement can be viewed as an updated restatement of the national treatment concept adopted by all GATT governments. The exclusion of "inherent competitive disadvantages" from the category of actionable violations could thus also be incorporated into Article III itself, as a gloss on the meaning of its own "less-favorable-treatment" language. In either context, incidentally, the concept of "inherent competitive disadvantages" would likely function as a less-than-fully-explained category, not unlike the concept of "incidental burden" in U.S. cases.

The *CAFE* decision also focuses on "inherent" attributes of foreign producers but in quite a different way. The Services Agreement excuses competitive burdens that are inherent in the regulatory process in the sense that they cannot be avoided by regulation in any other form. An example might be the risk of multiple regulation inherent in any business that operates in more than one jurisdiction. The *CAFE* decision, on the other hand, looks to whether a regulation has been shaped to seize upon some inherent (unavoidable) characteristic of the foreign producer, thereby imposing a competitive disadvantage that could easily have been avoided by using a different form of the same regulation. In the former case, the inherent characteristic is causal, while in the latter case it is the regulation that is the active cause of commercial disadvantage. Or so one could say. In any given situation, the question will be whether the regulatory burden linked to the inherent characteristic was natural and inevitable (the Standards Code approach) or whether instead it is unnatural and invidious (*CAFE*).

Leaving the puzzle of Article III, we turn to two sets of supplemental GATT rules that also deal with the issue of facially neutral measures. Both sets of rules involve products standards. One is the new GATT Standards Code, initially promulgated in 1979, that applies to any and all product standards.[78] The other is the new Uruguay Round Agreement on Sanitary and Phytosanitary Restrictions (SPS Agreement), pertaining to product standards relating to human, animal, and plant health and safety.[79] The Standards Code will be treated as *lex specialis*, superseding Article III to the extent that they overlap, and the SPS Agreement, being even more specific, will be treated as superseding both Article III and the Standards Code to the extent that it overlaps.

Both the Standards Code and the SPS Agreement escape the dilemma created by the seemingly bifurcated approach of Articles III and XX. Both contain rules that permit tribunals to weigh a measure's trade-restricting effects and its regulatory justification at the same time. Article 2.2 of the Standards Code provides as follows:

Members shall ensure that technical regulations are not prepared, adopted or applied with a view to or with the effect of creating unnecessary obstacles to international trade. For this purpose, technical regulations shall not be more trade-restrictive than necessary to fulfil a legitimate objective, taking account of the risks non-fulfillment would create. Such legitimate objectives are, *inter alia*, national security requirements; the prevention of deceptive practices; protection of human health or safety, animal or plant life or health, or the environment. In assessing such risks, relevant elements of consideration are, *inter alia*, available scientific and technical information, related processing technology or intended end use of products.

The text clearly calls for an analysis and evaluation of the regulatory purpose of the measure.

The SPS Agreement contains a rather lengthy and convoluted set of legal standards, but the basic provisions are similar to those of the Standards Code. Paragraphs 6 and 7 of the Agreement provide:

6. Members shall ensure that any sanitary or phytosanitary measure is applied only to the extent necessary to protect human, animal or plant life or health, is based on scientific principles and is not maintained without sufficient scientific evidence, except [as later provided].[80]
7. ... Sanitary and phytosanitary measures shall not be applied in a manner which would constitute a disguised restriction on international trade.

The concept of "disguised restriction" has been interpreted to refer to cases where a claimed regulatory purpose is found to be of so little importance, or so little served, that it can be called a disguise.[81] Note that here the regulatory justification is considered as part of the initial analysis of violation, rather than being relegated to the role of an affirmative defense.

The GATT's policy toward administering these standards remains to be defined. If the recent *CAFE* decision is indicative (which it may not be), GATT regulation will be extremely restrained. The part of the panel decision dealing with the *CAFE* fuel efficiency standards themselves is quite striking in this regard. The *CAFE* standards allow manufacturers to average fuel efficiencies over their entire fleets. The averaging method favors U.S. manufactures, who sell a broad range of cars in the U.S., over European firms that often sell only luxury cars here. The discrimination is compounded by the fact that light trucks, sold in large numbers by U.S. firms, are excluded from the average. Esty himself suggested that CAFE should be struck down because its "modest" benefits are "likely to be deemed clearly disproportionate to the significant trade impacts on European automakers, estimated at as much as $100 million per year."[82] As Esty pointed out, *CAFE* is not simply a case of arguably overzealous environmentalism:

The US Congress could have selected other less trade-distorting mechanisms for improving fuel efficiency—for instance, a higher gasoline tax or a "sipper-guzzler" fee system on all cars, subsidizing the purchase of cars that get good mileage and penalizing owners whose cars do not. But Congress *intentionally* selected the CAFE mechanism to protect the US auto industry jobs and the automobile market share of the Big Three US automakers.[83]

Taking a more deferential view than Esty himself, the GATT panel chose to overlook these indications of protectionism. Although it found the

CAFE standards to violate Article III on an unrelated ground, the panel volunteered an explanation of the ultimate ruling it would have made otherwise, explaining that it would have found the fleet-averaging measure justified by Article XX(g).[84] The panel concluded that overall goal of the averaging scheme was to improve fuel efficiency, and that an exemption for foreign cars would have undermined this goal.[85] If anything, the *CAFE* decision seems to indicate that GATT may err on the side of excessive deference when considering facially neutral environmental regulations.

Although GATT law is concededly still in the process of development, it is much less rigid than believed by some critics. GATT is by no means committed to stringent scrutiny of every regulation that affects trade flows. In the end, GATT is merely the sum of its Member nations, and they are unlikely to countenance incursions on their legitimate regulatory powers. Instead, GATT has sought to distinguish between protectionism and bona fide regulation. We offer some thoughts below about future efforts to implement this distinction.

2.4   Motive and Inadequate Regulatory Benefit as Signs of Protectionism

This may be an appropriate point at which to assess the relationship between our analysis and that of Esty (our designated thoughtful environmentalist). To begin with, we agree with environmentalists that trade rules should not be allowed to interfere with needed environmental regulations. We believe that these environmentalists overestimate, however, the extent of the threat from GATT. GATT treats facially discriminatory regulations somewhat less harshly than do the U.S. courts. Despite the superficial rigidity of Article XX as a mechanism for considering environmental justifications, GATT has also begun to evolve more flexible and nuanced legal doctrines regarding facially neutral regulations. While this flexibility provides a means of addressing the problem effectively, its very flexibility leaves in question just how the necessary judicial analysis is to be performed. Unlike Esty, we are skeptical that a simple doctrinal formula can resolve the difficult and complex problem posed by the tension between trade and environmental objectives.

The problem we have been discussing involves two main elements: (1) a trade-restricting measure (whether explicitly discriminatory or facially neutral) and (2) some kind of justification for the measure in terms of recognized, nontrade regulatory purpose. The central substantive issue is the way that these two elements are to be evaluated and balanced by the decision maker. One particularly delicate problem is the role that legislative motivation should play in this analysis. On the one hand, a tribunal can do a cost-benefit analysis, asking whether the trade-restricting effect of the measure is justified by its regulatory benefit. On the other hand, a tribunal can examine the question of whether the measure has a protectionist purpose or motive. The same evidence about regulatory impact often tends to support a guilty verdict under either standard.

In GATT, as in U.S. cases, critics challenge the capacity of tribunals to make accurate judgments about the effects of regulatory measures and the political legitimacy of their making such judgments in the first place. The main difficulty is found when tribunals try to make judgments about the regulatory *benefits* of such measures.[86] GATT tribunals have few credentials to assess the success or social value of regulatory measures nor any recognized political mandate to do so. The competence of federal courts in this area is also suspect, though perhaps to a lesser extent. The difficulty varies, however, according to the particular facts and issues presented.

GATT tribunals have received a fair degree of acceptance for one type of decision holding that a regulatory measure produces no benefit at all. These decisions conclude that the same regulatory benefit can be achieved by an alternative measure that is less trade restricting or not trade restricting at all. Esty and others have suggested that this search for less restrictive alternatives presents a severe challenge to environmental regulations.[87] In theory, this approach can be abused, given that it is always possible to imagine *some* less restrictive alternative to any given regulation. In practice, however, GATT tribunals have exercised good judgment and common sense in this exercise.

In the *Section 337* case, for example, the panel was able to secure acceptance of its judgment that the special, expedited U.S. procedure for foreign patent violations did no more to protect patent owners against irremediable injury than could be accomplished by various trade-neutral preliminary remedies.[88] Likewise, in the much discussed *Thai Cigarette* case, the panel was able to find that a complete ban on imports of U.S. cigarettes accomplished no more than would trade-neutral restrictions on all cigarette sales.[89] Although comparison of alternatives will often be constrained by the difficulty of the technical or scientific judgments involved,[90] these cases show that this type of comparison can be a very powerful legal tool. Particularly in cases involving discriminatory measures, U.S. courts have also found it easy to point out equally effective but nondiscriminatory alternatives.[91]

In a fair number of other cases, the facts have been clear enough to allow a credible finding of no regulatory benefit. In the first *Salmon and Herring* decision, tried before a regular GATT panel, the panel was able to reject Canada's assertion that an export restriction had a conservation purpose, simply because Canada imposed no limits on export or consumption once the fish had been processed.[92] Likewise, a GATT panel readily rejected a claim that an import ban on tuna was in aid of conservation measures by noting that the United States had no conservation limits on its own fishermen.[93] This case illustrates the fact that many claims of regulatory purpose are quite transparently bogus, having been dreamed up in the lawyers' offices only after the measure was challenged. A fairly large number of justifications fall into this category.[94]

It will be substantially more difficult for tribunals to find that apparently neutral health, safety, or environmental regulations produce no regulatory benefit at all. Although the new GATT SPS Agreement does contain a requirement that such measures must have a scientific basis,[95] the Agreement does permit risk-avoidance measures when the scientific evidence is unclear,[96] and governments will insist on having a fair degree of leeway in defining and weighing risks of the unknown.[97] We suspect that tribunals will be likely to make such judgments only when a regulation seems so otherwise arbitrary that protectionism appears to be the only reasonable explanation.

The most difficult case for GATT tribunals will be the one in which the regulation in question does produce some possible regulatory benefit, but that benefit seems clearly too small to justify the cost in terms of trade restriction.[98] This is the type of case in which the term "balancing" can correctly be applied. It is the type of case in which the greatest objection may be raised against judicial intrusion into the political process. A ruling that a regulatory benefit is too small to justify the cost of trade restriction will usually be challenged as a usurpation of the government's political functions. Arguably, such a decision was made by the panel convened under the Canada–U.S. Free Trade Agreement in the second *Salmon and Herring* case, when the panel ruled that the regulatory gain of a 100 percent landing requirement would not have been large enough, compared to less trade-restrictive alternatives, to justify the commercial burden if that commercial burden had been placed on Canadian fish buyers.[99] The decision has already been criticized on these grounds.[100] It remains to be seen whether a tribunal constituted under the GATT itself would construe its mandate to authorize such candidly expressed judgments.

Esty's proposed "grossly disproportionate" test seems to contemplate some scope for GATT judgments about the balance of costs and benefits for a regulation. We would not reject the possibility of such an analysis, but are less sanguine than Esty for two reasons. First, experience with similar problems in U.S. administrative law suggests that Esty may be too optimistic about the prospects for applying his test. There is considerable dispute about whether U.S. courts have intruded too deeply into the regulatory process under the guise of the similar "arbitrary and capricious" test.[101] Second, we would expect governments, as well as the environmental community, to object strongly to findings that they have overvalued the goals of risk avoidance or environmental preservation.

When some small (but arguably inadequate) regulatory gain is present, a GATT decision that sounds like a cost-benefit analysis may draw the heaviest criticism, for it will sound like second-guessing the value judgments of a national government. A decision which uses the same evidence to support a finding of protectionist purpose may to some extent avoid that objection, albeit at the expense of eliciting another objection against impugning the motives of a client government. As we saw earlier, U.S. judges seem to be driven to consider the bona fides of a regulation *en route* to using their three-prong test. Interestingly, the second *Salmon and Herring* decision was articulated partly in terms of purpose, albeit not enough to escape criticism for second-guessing.

Despite the obvious hazards of decisions based on purpose or motive, GATT does have one frequently employed legal standard that seems to legitimize some consideration of the governmental purpose behind a measure. The preamble to GATT Article XX calls for rejection of regulatory justifications that are found to be a "disguised restriction on international trade." Although the word "disguise" can be viewed as an objective criterion merely connoting the inadequacy of a regulatory justification in cost-benefit terms, its more literal meaning suggests a conclusion about purpose—about a real purpose hiding behind a disguising purpose.[102] The prohibition against "disguised restrictions" seems to have gained even greater currency recently, having been employed again in several new Uruguay Round agreements.[103] It is not surprising to find governments expressing legal standards in terms of the real purpose behind regulatory measures, because that is what they are in fact thinking about when they see protectionist measures. They do so even though they would certainly not welcome tribunals examining their own behavior on that ground. The presence of these mixed attitudes present a delicate challenge for GATT tribunals.

The general problem we have addressed in this study has resisted the best efforts of the Supreme Court (for over 150 years), GATT tribunals, international negotiators, and a host of talented legal scholars. The reason, we believe, is that in some ultimate sense the problem is unsolvable. Taken to their logical conclusion, either free trade or local autonomy could virtually eliminate the other, and negotiating a workable border between the two depends as much on history, politics, and local terrain as on any overarching vision. No matter how a legal test is articulated, it cannot satisfactorily resolve the tensions between local autonomy and free trade in all conceivable cases. In the end, the law must have a certain irreducible messiness in dealing with such fundamental tensions.

Messiness is not, however, the same as chaos. Both the Supreme Court and GATT do have fairly adequate ways of dealing with facially discriminatory measures. Both place a heavy burden on the regulating government to justify the measure (though the GATT experience suggests that the articulated U.S. standard may be too high). Both run into trouble with facially neutral measures, which run the spectrum from devious bad faith on the one hand and innocent run-of-the-mill regulation on the other. Even here, however, there are a considerable number of easy cases. The difficult cases are those in the middle of the spectrum—where a clear but limited benefit exists, or the benefit is hard to predict (perhaps because of scientific uncertainty), or assessing the benefit requires a difficult and possibly culturally based value judgment. GATT tribunals are just now beginning to confront these harder cases.

Particularly in these difficult cases, common sense tells us that most tribunals are likely to be strongly affected by their perceptions about the probable motive of the government that enacted the measure. The conclusion that protectionism was in fact the government's purpose is the most powerful possible condemnation. In reality, it will be the thought running through almost everybody's mind, whether the conclusion is reached because the purported benefits seem so minuscule or because of actual evidence of historical motive. Concerns about government motive may not be fully articulated in the final opinion. Even the U.S. courts have sometimes treated the subject of legislative motive gingerly. GATT tribunals have a weaker institutional position and even more reason to be wary, as the CAFE decision may evidence. Overt or not, however, consideration of motive seems inevitable, and a more explicit treatment of the issue by tribunals would probably be helpful.

Despite the conceptual difficulties posed by regulatory trade barriers, both U.S. and international tribunals seem to have largely struggled their way to defensible results. The modern regulatory state shows little sign of withering away. Hence, tension between free trade and local regulatory policies is inevitable. As a practical matter, however, it is possible to find workable (if sometimes messy) accommodations. Because of the difficulty of constructing a clean doctrinal solution, the quality of the process and that of the decision makers are and will remain critical. In our view, the next stage of the debate should focus less on the question of substantive standards and more on these critical issues of legal process.

NOTES

Daniel A. Farber is the Acting Associate Vice President for Academic Affairs, Associate Dean of Faculty, and the Henry J. Fletcher Professor of Law, University of Minnesota.

Robert E. Hudec is the Melvin C. Steen Professor of Law, University of Minnesota.

1. Agreement on the Application of Sanitary and Phytosanitary Measures [hereinafter 1994 GATT SPS Agreement], in Final Act Embodying the Results of the Uruguay Round of Multilateral Trade Negotiations, [hereinafter 1994 Uruguay Round Final Act], at 69–83. Apr. 15, 1994 (done at Marrakesh).

2. Agreement on Technical Barriers to Trade [hereinafter 1994 Standards Code], in 1994 Uruguay Round Final Act, note 1 above, at 117–37.

3. Daniel C. Esty, Greening the GATT: Trade, Environment, and the Future (1994).

4. *Id.* at 45.

5. *Id.* at 58.

6. *Id.* at 48.

7. *Id.* at 222 [emphasis in original].

8. *Id.* at 113–14, 234. It is unclear to us how Esty reconciles his expressed agreement with these cases and his "not clearly disproportionate" standard.

9. *See* N.Y. Times (Midwest ed.), Apr. 20, 1992, at A9; N.Y. Times (Midwest ed.), Dec. 14, 1992, at A12. The principal sponsors were also the plaintiffs in the recent successful lawsuit calling for the Clinton Administration to submit an environmental impact statement for NAFTA. *Public Citizen v. Office of the United States Trade Representative*, 5 F.2d 549 (D.C. Cir. 1994), *cert. denied* 114 S.Ct. 685 (1994).

10. For example, the EC hormone restriction currently being challenged in GATT does not deal with DES, a proven carcinogen long ago prohibited, but with synthetic copies of natural hormones that Codex Alimentarius has so far found to have no harmful effects at all. *See* Adrian R. Halpern, *The U.S.-E.C. Hormone Beef Controversy and the Standards Code: Implications for the Application of Health Regulations to Agricultural Trade*, 14 North Carolina Int'l L. & Com. Rev. 135 (1989); Note, *The EC Hormone Ban Dispute and the Application of the Dispute Settlement Provisions of the Standards Code*, 10 Michigan J. Int'l L. 872 (1989). Likewise, Thailand's so-called "anti-smoking campaign" consisted of prohibiting the importation of foreign cigarettes while the domestic producers of cigarettes, a state enterprise,

were increasing production. *See Thailand—Restrictions on Importation of and Internal Taxes on Cigarettes,* GATT BASIC INSTRUMENTS AND SELECTED DOCUMENTS [hereinafter BISD] 37th Supp. 200 (1991) (hereinafter *Thailand—Cigarettes*) (GATT panel decision upholding U.S. complaint).

11. The term "disguised restriction on international trade," which comes from GATT Article XX, is found in paragraphs 7 and 20 of the 1994 GATT SPS Agreement, note 1 above. The term "unnecessary obstacles to international trade" is contained in Article 2.2 of the 1994 GATT Standards Code, note 2 above.

12. 1994 GATT SPS Agreement, note 1 above, ¶¶ 9–10.

13. The 1994 GATT SPS Agreement permits standards higher than international standards, but only on condition that (1) there is a scientific justification or (2) that parties follow a prescribed risk-assessment procedure. *Id.* ¶ 11.

14. The case for regulating risks of potentially irreversible harm that are inadequately understood or documented is sometimes referred to as the "precautionary principle." Principle 15 of the 1992 Rio Declaration, for example, states: "Where there are threats of serious or irreversible damage, lack of full scientific certainty shall not be used as a reason for postponing cost-effective measures to prevent environmental degradation." *See generally* Naomi Roht-Arriaza, *Precaution, Participation, and the "Greening" of International Trade Law,* 7 J. ENVIR'L L. & LITIG. 57 (1992).

15. *See* note 10 above. More recently, Thailand has allowed U.S. imports but has instituted a ban on cigarette advertising. *See Complaint Against Thai Cigarette Barriers Trade Issue, Not Health Matter, Exporters Say,* 6 Int'l Trade Rep. (BNA) 1181 (1989).

16. 12 Int'l Trade Rep. Decisions (BNA) 1026 (1991). The parties accepted the report in November 1989.

17. The GATT decision is discussed in the text at notes 65–71 below.

18. ESTY, note 3 above, at 45.

19. For further analysis of this issue, see Robert E. Hudec, *Circumventing Democracy: The Political Morality of Trade Negotiations,* 25 NEW YORK UNIV. J. INT'L L. & POL. 311–22 (1993).

20. Critics seldom challenge, for example, two other GATT decisions in which panels rejected transparently untenable claims of environmental purposes. *United States—Prohibition on Imports of Tuna and Tuna Products from Canada,* BISD 29th Supp. 91 (1983) [hereinafter *U.S.—Tuna & Tuna Products*]; *Canada—Restrictions on Export of Unprocessed Herring and Salmon,* BISD 35th Supp. 98 (1989) [hereinafter *Canada—Salmon & Herring I*] (the first GATT phase of the FTA salmon-and-herring dispute described above).

21. N.Y. TIMES, note 9 above. For more measured criticisms in the same direction, see Stephen J. Porter, *The Tuna-Dolphin Controversy: Can the GATT Become Environment Friendly?,* 5 GEORGETOWN INT'L ENVIR'L L. REV. 91–116 (1992) (discussing means for bringing greater expertise to bear on environmental issues).

22. *See, e.g.,* Peter Lallas, Daniel Esty & David van Hoogstraten, *Environmental Protection and International Trade: Toward Mutually Supportive Rules and Policies,* 16 HARVARD ENVIR'L L. REV. 271–342, at 337 (1992).

23. For a more comprehensive analysis of U.S. law and its relationship to GATT, see Daniel A. Farber & Robert E. Hudec, *Free Trade and the Regulatory State: A GATT's-Eye View of the Dormant Commerce Clause,* 47 VANDERBILT L. REV. 1401 (1994).

24. ESTY, note 3 above, at 113–14.

25. A fuller summary of current doctrine can be found in JOHN E. NOWAK & RONALD D. ROTUNDA, CONSTITUTIONAL LAW 275–89 (4th ed. 1991).

26. The leading case is *City of Philadelphia v. New Jersey*, 437 U.S. 617 (1978).

27. *See Hunt v. Washington State Apple Advertising Commission*, 432 U.S. 333 (1977).

28. *See Pike v. Bruce Church, Inc.*, 397 U.S. 137 (1970). Professor Stewart reads *Pike* as establishing a test of "net proportionality." Richard B. Stewart, *International Trade and Environment: Lessons from the Federal Experience*, 49 WASHINGTON & LEE L. REV. 1329, 1336 (1992).

29. *Fort Gratiot Sanitary Landfill v. Michigan Dept. of Natural Resources*, 112 S.Ct. 2019, 2024 (1992).

30. "[T]here is no clear line separating the category of state regulation that is virtually *per se* invalid under the commerce clause, and the category subject to *Pike v. Bruce Church* balancing approach." *Brown Forman Distillers Corp. v. New York State Liquor Authority*, 476 U.S. 573, 577 (1986).

31. *See City of Philadelphia v. New Jersey*, 437 U.S. 617, 624 (1978); *Old Bridge Chemicals v. New Jersey Dept. of Envir'l Protection*, 965 F.2d 1287, 1293 (3d Cir. 1992).

32. *Fort Gratiot Sanitary Landfill v. Michigan Dept. of Natural Resources*, 112 S.Ct. 2019, 2023–24 (1992) (citing *New Energy Co. of Indiana v. Limbach*, 486 U.S. 269, 274 (1988)).

33. *See, e.g., Maine v. Taylor*, 477 U.S. 131 (1986), discussed in note 97 below.

34. *See Electrolyte Corp. v. Barry*, 737 F.2d 100, 113 (D.C. Cir. 1984); *National Kerosene Heater Ass'n v. Massachusetts*, 653 F. Supp. 1079, 1092 (D. Mass. 1986). *See also J. Filibreto Sanitation, Inc. v. New Jersey*, 857 F.2d 913, 922 (3d Cir. 1988); *Norfolk Southern Corp. v. Lamberts Point Barge Co.*, 822 F.2d 388, 401 (3d Cir. 1987).

35. *Kassel v. Consolidated Freightways Corp.* 450 U.S. 662, 679 (Brennan, J., concurring in the judgment), discussed in Part III below.

36. *See* Farber & Hudec, note 23 above.

37. 450 U.S. 662 (1981).

38. *Id.* at 674.

39. *Id.* at 668, 679–87, 686, 704–05.

40. 114 S.Ct. 1677 (1994).

41. Tariff bindings are established by periodic negotiation, and then recorded in individual country schedules that are given binding effect by GATT Article II.

42. The main provisions are the prohibition of nontariff restrictions under GATT Article XI:1 and the prohibition of discriminatory internal taxes and regulations under the so-called "national treatment" rule of GATT Article III. The text of Article XI:1, which is subject to numerous exceptions, provides quite simply and broadly,

1. No prohibitions or restrictions other than duties, taxes or other charges, whether made effective through quotas, import or export licenses or other measures, shall be instituted or maintained by any contracting party on the importation of any product of the territory of

any other contracting party or on the exportation or sale for export of any product destined for the territory of any other contracting party.

The two key provisions of the National Treatment rule of GATT Article III are paragraphs 2 and 4:

2. The products of the territory of any contracting party imported into the territory of any other contracting party shall not be subject, directly or indirectly, to internal taxes or other internal charges of any kind in excess of those applied, directly or indirectly, to like domestic products. Moreover, no contracting party shall otherwise apply internal taxes or other internal charges in a manner contrary to the principles set forth in paragraph 1 [i.e., internal measures should not "afford protection to domestic production."].

. . . .

4. The products of the territory of any contracting party imported into the territory of any other contracting party shall be accorded treatment no less favourable than that accorded to like products of national origin in respect of all laws, regulations and requirements affecting their internal sale, offering for sale, purchase, transportation, distribution or use. . . .

43. Article XX reads as follows:

Subject to the requirement that such measures are not applied in a manner which would constitute a means of arbitrary or unjustifiable discrimination between countries where the same conditions prevail, or a disguised restriction on international trade, nothing in this Agreement shall be construed to prevent the adoption or enforcement by any contracting party of measures:

(a) necessary to protect public morals;

(b) necessary to protect human, animal or plant life or health;

(c) relating to the importation or exportation of gold or silver;

(d) necessary to secure compliance with laws or regulations which are not inconsistent with the provisions of this Agreement, including those relating to customs enforcement, the enforcement of monopolies operated under paragraph 4 of Article II and Article XVII, the protection of patents, trade marks and copyrights, and the prevention of deceptive practices;

(e) relating to the products of prison labour;

(f) imposed for the protection of national treasures of artistic, historic or archaeological value;

(g) relating to the conservation of exhaustible natural resources if such measures are made effective in conjunction with restrictions on domestic production or consumption;

(h) [commodity agreements]

(i) [price-controlled products]

(j) [short supply situations].

44. 1994 Standards Code, note 2 above, art. 2.2.

45. *See* text accompanying note 24 above.

46. *See* notes 31–33 above.

47. *See* notes 25, 42 above.

48. *United States—Section 337 of the Tariff Act of 1930*, BISD 36th Supp. 345 (1990) [hereinafter *U.S.—Section 337*].

49. *Id.* ¶¶ 5.13–5.20.

50. Important GATT panel decisions construing Article XX include, in chronological order: *U.S—Tuna & Tuna Products*, note 20 above; *Canada—Salmon & Herring I*, note 20 above; *U.S.—Section 337*, note 48 above; *European Community—Regulation on Imports of Parts and Components*, BISD 37th Supp. 132 (1991); *United States—Restrictions on Imports of Tuna*, BISD 39th Supp. 155 (1993) (the celebrated, initial "Tuna/Dolphin" decision). On the general importance of such burden-of-proof standards to GATT decision making in general, *see* ROBERT E. HUDEC, ENFORCING INTERNATIONAL TRADE LAW: THE EVOLUTION OF THE MODERN GATT LEGAL SYSTEM 267–68 (1993).

51. *U.S.—Section 337*, note 48 above, ¶¶ 5.28–5.35.

52. *Id.* ¶¶ 5.32, 5.33.

53. The confusion may stem from Esty's effort to provide a unified test for two quite different categories of cases: those involving the application of domestic regulations to foreign goods and those involving border measures intended to affect foreign environmental conditions. The problem is that all of the regulations in the second category distinguish between goods on the basis of geographic origin, and are therefore discriminatory, but Esty wants to uphold a considerable amount of national power in this domain. The result seems to be a lack of clarity regarding the role of discrimination in the analysis.

54. ESTY, note 3 above, at 102 (emphasis in original).

55. Another example, more European in flavor, might be an alcoholic beverage tax distinguishing between fruit-based distilled alcohol and grain-based distilled alcohol, in a country where most domestic production of alcoholic beverages falls into the former category while most imports fall into the latter.

56. The "less-favorable-treatment" standard in Article III:4 was interpreted to cover facially neutral measures in two earlier decisions, neither very authoritative. The GATT's *Section 337* decision contained a single sentence of dictum that a facially neutral measure may constitute less favorable treatment of imported goods if it creates a commercial disadvantage for imports. *U.S.—Section 337*, note 48 above, ¶ 5.11. The second was a decision of a panel constituted under the Canada–U.S. Free Trade Agreement, which applied GATT obligations incorporated in that Agreement. *In the Matter of Canada's Landing Requirements for Salmon and Herring*, 12 Int'l Trade Rep. Decisions (BNA) 1026 (1991) [hereinafter *Canada–Salmon & Herring II*]. The case involved facially neutral landing-cum-inspection requirement (an internal regulation) that imposed a substantial burden on would-be export sales of fish as compared with domestic sales. Applying the GATT Article XI:1 analogue to Article III:4 that covers internal measures affecting export transactions, the panel held that, even though the inspection requirement was facially neutral, the greater commercial burden on the export sales made it a "restriction" (i.e., "less favorable treatment") falling within the GATT prohibition. *Id.* ¶¶ 6.08, 6.09, 6.12, 6.13. The panel's ruling was expressed somewhat narrowly; instead of the broad proposition that any significant commercial disadvantage would constitute a "restriction" within the meaning of Article XI:1, the panel appeared to rest its conclusion on the fact that the primary effect of the landing requirement was to alter the way exports were made:

6.09 . . . The panel concluded that where the primary effect of a measure is in fact the regulation of export transactions, the measure may be considered a restriction within the meaning of Article XI:1 if it has the effect of imposing a materially greater commercial burden on exports than on domestic sales.

For the answer to this question given in the Uruguay Round Services agreement, see text accompanying note 67 below.

57. *United States—Measures Affecting Alcoholic and Malt Beverages*, BISD 39th Supp. 206 (1993) [hereinafter *U.S.—Malt Beverages*] (GATT panel report analyzing numerous claims of violation against U.S. federal and state laws affecting alcoholic beverages, including beer). The *vitus rotundifolia* grape was a variety suitable for warmer climates, including the Mediterranean basin.

58. *Id.* ¶ 5.25. The foundations for this ruling were laid by a relatively unnoticed GATT legal ruling in 1987 involving an Article III complaint against Japanese taxes on (of all things) alcoholic beverages. *Japan—Customs Duties, Taxes and Labelling Practices on Imported Wines and Alcoholic Beverages*, BISD 34th Supp. 83 (1988). In a long and complex opinion, the panel, *inter alia*, established the separateness of the Article III "like-product" test (*see id.* ¶ 5.6), rejected discrimination based on an arbitrary product characteristic (*see id.* ¶ 5.9(d)), and held that the tax treatment of certain unlike but directly competitive or substitutable products constituted a protection of domestic production in contravention of the second sentence of Article III:2 (*see id.* ¶¶ 5.7, 5.11).

59. *U.S.—Malt Beverages*, note 57 above, ¶ 5.26.

60. *Id.* The fact that the invalidated measure was a state rather than federal law has given rise to exaggerated concerns about the effect of GATT on state autonomy. *See GATT Threatens to Preempt States' Rights to Make Policy, Annual Meeting of NCSL Told*, 9 Int'l Trade Rep. (BNA) 1344 (1992).

61. *U.S.—Malt Beverages*, note 57 above, ¶ 2.32, Table 4.

62. *Id.* ¶¶ 3.127, 3.129.

63. *Id.* ¶ 3.120.

64. *Id.* ¶¶ 5.74, 5.75.

65. *United States—Taxes on Automobiles*, GATT Doc. DS31/R (Sept. 29, 1994) [hereinafter *U.S.—Taxes on Automobiles*].

66. *Id.* ¶ 5.9.

67. *Id.* 5.10.

68. *Id.* ¶ 5.12. The panel noted that the proportion of foreign and domestic cars selling below and above this threshold was unclear, particularly since non-EC imports might be affected differently.

69. *Id.* ¶ 5.14.

70. *Id.* ¶ 5.24.

71. The panel did not regard the fact that some producers concentrate on exporting luxury autos to the U.S. market as "inherent," since many had "the design, production, and marketing capabilities to sell automobiles below the $30,000 threshold." *Id.* ¶ 5.14. Similarly non-inherent were (1) the sale of high fuel consumption autos (*Id.* ¶ 5.25) and the choice not to export light trucks (*Id.* ¶ 5.34).
    While the panel did not give any examples of a characteristic it would consider "inherent," a possible example, in an export context, might be the need to transport exports to another destination—the characteristic that made the landing requirement in the second *Salmon and Herring* case necessarily burdensome. *Canada—Salmon & Herring II*, note 56 above.

72. This argument is developed in Frieder Roessler, *Diverging Domestic Policies and Multilateral Trade Integration*, Chapter 1 in this volume.

73. ESTY, note 3 above, at 102.

74. *U.S.—Taxes on Automobiles*, note 65 above, ¶ 5.54.

75. General Agreement on Trade in Services (GATS), art. XVII, *in* 1994 Uruguay Round Final Act, note 1 above, at 283–317.

76. *Id.* art. XVII:3.

77. *Id.* art. XVII:1, n.11.

78. The current 1994 version of the Standards Code includes both standards defined in terms of the characteristics of the product as well as standards defined in terms of production processes insofar as they affect the quality of the products themselves. 1994 Standards Code, note 2 above.

79. 1994 GATT SPS Agreement, note 1 above.

80. Paragraph 11 of the 1994 GATT SPS Agreement provides for acceptance of measures that conform to internationally accepted standards, but higher standards may be adopted if a country determines that the relevant international standard is "not sufficient to achieve its appropriate level of protection." *Id.* ¶ 11, n.2. The "appropriate level of protection" is to be determined under paragraphs 14–23, which require a country to consider the relevant scientific evidence before choosing an acceptable level of risk. Annex A to the SPS defines the appropriate level to be the "level of protection deemed appropriate by the Member establishing a sanitary or phytosanitary measure to protect human, animal or plant life or health within its territory. " The use of the phrase "deemed appropriate" seems to suggest a high level of discretion. The main constraint on this determination seems to be paragraph 20, which requires each country to "avoid arbitrary or unjustifiable distinctions in the levels [of risk] it considers to be appropriate in different situations, if such distinctions result in discrimination or a disguised restriction on international trade." For further discussion, see Steve Charnovitz, *The World Trade Organization and Environmental Supervision*, INT'L ENVIR'L REP., Jan. 26, 1994, at 89. For discussion of the parallel provisions of NAFTA, *see* Daniel Magraw, *NAFTA's Repercussions: Is Green Trade Possible?*, 36:2 ENVIRONMENT 14, 18–20 (Mar. 1994); John Kim & James Cargas, *The Environmental Side Agreement to the North American Free Trade Agreement: Background and Analysis*, 23 ENVIR'L L. REP. 10720, 10723–35 (1993).

81. This interpretation was adopted by a dispute settlement panel convened under the U.S.–Canada Free Trade Agreement. *Canada—Salmon & Herring II*, note 56 above, ¶ 7.11 & n.20. To be sure, this interpretation is at odds with the view taken in two GATT panel decisions that "disguised" means not publicly announced. *See United States—Imports of Certain Automotive Spring Assemblies*, BISD 30th Supp. 107, ¶ 56 (1983); *U.S.—Tuna & Tuna Products*, note 20 above, ¶ 4.8 (1983). The latter interpretation makes no sense. It seems clear that the governments who agreed to the recent incorporation of the "disguised restriction" formula into several new Uruguay Round agreements were doing so in agreement with the former meaning.

82. ESTY, note 3 above, at 128.

83. *Id.* at 45 (emphasis added).

84. Note that Article XX(g), unlike XX(b), does not state the standard in terms of necessity, but requires only a relation to conservation. Query whether the purpose of CAFE was to conserve U.S. oil reserves or to limit imports (thereby "conserving" OPEC oil reserves). Would the latter purpose be permissible?

85. *U.S.—Taxes on Automobiles*, note 65 above, ¶ 5.65.

86. Judgments about the *harms* caused by such measures—the existence and degree of competitive disadvantage—have not proved too troublesome. In GATT law, the issue of commercial disadvantage is not whether some specific commercial loss can be proved (usually impossible due to the number of separate factors influencing any business outcome). Rather, the issue is whether the measure has changed "the conditions of competition," in the words of the Services Agreement. Assessment of the competitive impact is essentially a matter of rather simple business economics, applied to undisputed facts. GATT decisions have not encountered much criticism on this score. So far as we are aware, the identification of burdens on interstate commerce has also been relatively non-controversial in U.S. cases.

87. *See, e.g.,* Esty, note 3 above, at 45.

88. *See* notes 48–51 above and accompanying text.

89. *See Thailand—Cigarettes*, note 10 above. For another decision employing the same type of analysis, *see Japan—Customs Duties, Taxes and Labelling Practices on Imported Wines and Alcoholic Beverages*, BISD 34th Supp. 83, ¶ 5.13 (1988) (GATT panel ruling that achievement of a social policy of taxing alcoholic beverages according to ability to pay did not require using GATT-illegal discriminatory taxes).

90. *See, e.g.,* the criticism of the second *Salmon and Herring* decision, notes 99–100 below and accompanying text.

91. *Dean Milk Co. v. City of Madison*, 340 U.S. 349 (1951) is the leading case. *See also Hunt v. Washington State Apple Advertising Commission*, 432 U.S. 333, 354 (discussing nondiscriminatory alternatives to state labeling requirement).

92. *Canada—Herring & Salmon I*, note 20 above, ¶ 4.7. Local processing requirements have been similarly disfavored under the DCC. *See C & A Carbone v. Town of Clarkstown*, 114 U.S. 1677, 1682–83 (citing cases).

93. *U.S.—Tuna & Tuna Products*, note 20 above, ¶¶ 4.10–4.13.

94. Although such bogus claims of justification may seem unworthy of responsible governmental behavior, it must be remembered that the officials representing a government owe a responsibility to defend its actions. The way in which such defenses are actually made and handled deserves careful examination.

In most cases, government lawyers will maintain such defenses for only a decent length of time, and will not protest too strongly when they lose. Government attorneys are usually sensitive to the fact that they represent the government as a whole, and not the special-interest group that managed to obtain the protectionist measure. This is certainly true in GATT litigation, where the tenor of legal practice is a far cry from the "scorched-earth" methods for which large U.S. law firms are so well known—an important point to remember, incidentally, when considering proposals to allow private legal representation in GATT proceedings. Arguably, the level of government legal practice in U.S. litigation is quite similar to the practice in GATT, in both respects. The decision-making capacity of U.S. courts is no doubt enhanced by these tendencies.

95. 1994 GATT SPS Agreement, note 1 above, ¶ 6.

96. *Id.* ¶ 22.

97. The U.S. Supreme Court sometimes has apparently given leeway to states, even for discriminatory measures. In *Maine v. Taylor*, 477 U.S. 131 (1986), the Court upheld a Maine statute banning the importation of bait fish. The Court gave great deference to the testimony of three experts who claimed that Maine's fisheries might be placed at risk because of parasites present only in out-of-state bait fish. Despite a contrary opinion from another expert, the Court concluded that Maine was justified in regulating even without definite scientific proof:

Maine has a legitimate interest in guarding against imperfectly understood environmental risks, despite the possibility that they may ultimately prove to be negligible.... [It need not] sit idly by and wait until potentially irreversible environmental damage has occurred or until the scientific community agrees on what disease organisms are or are not dangerous before it acts to avoid such consequences.

Id. at 148.

98. Perhaps in recognition of the difficulty of this kind of environmental risk assessment, the GATT SPS Agreement tries to furnish regulators with another handle on the process of risk assessment. It provides that Members "shall avoid arbitrary or unjustifiable distinctions in the levels [of protection against risks] it considers appropriate in different situations, if such distinctions result in discrimination or a disguised restriction on international trade." *Id.* ¶ 20. The drafters apparently believed that GATT tribunals would be able to compare levels of risk avoidance from one case to another, and thus would be able to use the government's own standards as a basis for finding that some levels of risk avoidance were excessive.

99. *Canada—Salmon & Herring II*, note 56 above, ¶¶ 7.09, 7.10, 7.35–7.38. The ultimate issue being decided by the panel could be described as one of motive, in formal rather than historical terms. An earlier GATT decision had interpreted GATT Article XX(g) as covering measures "primarily aimed at" conservation. *Canada—Salmon & Herring I*, note 20 above, ¶ 4.6. The panel in this case applied the "primarily aimed at" test as follows:

7.10 [T]he Panel concluded that in determining whether the Canadian landing requirement would have been adopted for conservation reasons alone, the central issue was whether the conservation benefits of the landing requirement would have been large enough to justify imposing the commercial inconvenience in question. To comply with the trade neutrality required by Article XX(g), the issue must be posed in terms of whether Canada would have adopted the landing requirement if that measure had required an equivalent number of Canadian buyers to land and unload elsewhere than at their intended destination.

100. *See* David A. Wirth, *The Role of Science in the Uruguay Round and NAFTA Trade Disciplines*, 27 CORNELL INT'L L. J.817 (1994) (taking the view that the panel improperly substituted its own conclusions as to the statistical necessity of a 100 percent sample for the conclusions of Canadian government scientists).

101. *See* Daniel A. Farber, *Environmental Regulation as a Learning Experience*, 27 LOYOLA (L.A.) L. REV. 791, 805–06 (1994). Interestingly, Esty seems to contemplate the use of precisely this test by international tribunals. *See* ESTY, note 3 above, at 129.

102. This nuance was relied on in *Canada—Salmon & Herring II*, note 56 above, ¶ 7.11 ("The preamble of GATT Article XX, which expressly prohibits 'disguised' restrictions on

international trade, is an acknowledgement by the Parties that they will submit the purposes of trade-restricting conservation measures to third-party scrutiny."). For another view of this provision, see the two GATT panel rulings cited in note 81 above.

103. The term has been adopted as a legal standard in: (1) Article 3 of the TRIPS Agreement, cited as Agreement on Trade-Related Aspects of Intellectual Property Rights, Including Trade in Counterfeit Goods, in 1994 GATT Final Act, note 1 above, at 319–51; (2) Article XIV of the 1994 Services Agreement, note 67 above; and (3) paragraphs 7 and 20 of the 1994 GATT SPS Agreement, note 1 above.

3 GATT Legal Restraints on the Use of Trade Measures against Foreign Environmental Practices

Robert E. Hudec

3.1 Introduction

The current policy debate that goes by the name "trade and environment" involves a conflict between international trade policy, chiefly as expressed in GATT, and environmental policies. As used in this debate, the term "environmental policies" is usually understood to encompass not only strict environmental concerns—concerns about degradation of the planet's physical environment—but also concerns about human health and safety, consumer protection and, significantly, the killing or mistreatment of animals.

The current trade-and-environment debate involves at least three distinct areas of potential conflict between trade and environmental policies. The first area of conflict involves domestic environmental regulations—regulations that countries impose to protect their own territory. International trade conflicts can arise whenever domestic environmental regulations discriminate against imports or when they have a distinctively burdensome commercial impact on imports. If the burdensome qualities of those environmental regulations cannot be justified by some credible regulatory purpose, they can be attacked as trade barriers in violation of GATT obligations.

The second type of conflict involves efforts by countries with more rigorous environmental policies to "level the playing field" by imposing some kind of supplemental trade restriction, such as an antidumping or a countervailing duty, against goods from countries with less rigorous policies. Such level-playing-field measures are quite naturally resisted by the countries whose exports would be prejudiced by them.

The third area of conflict involves trade restrictions imposed against another country or countries, or against certain exporters, to induce them to correct behavior that is causing environmental harm somewhere else in the world. A recent example of a trade restriction used for this purpose is the U.S. embargo on tuna imports from countries allowing their tuna fleets to employ fishing methods that cause the death of large numbers of dolphins. The core objection to such trade restrictions is the assertion that the government in question is seeking to regulate external matters beyond the appropriate reach of national power.

These first two areas of potential conflict are dealt with by other chapters in this volume.[1] This chapter deals with the third area of conflict.

For ease of reference, this study will refer to the central type of trade restriction involved in this third kind of conflict as "externally-directed trade restrictions." Not all the trade measures in this category have the same degree of external orientation. Generally, externally-directed trade restrictions will have two main characteristics: (1) The trade measure seeks to regulate behavior that occurs outside the territory of the regulating country. (2) The goal of the trade measure is to prevent environmental harms occurring predominantly outside the country.[2]

The external character of the environmental harms in question will often be a matter of degree and, to some extent, values.[3] Certain global harms such as depletion of the ozone layer do in fact threaten some physical impact upon the territory of regulating countries. Also, governments tend to consider themselves directly affected by any environmental harm that causes them concern—harms ranging from extinction of a species anywhere in the world to mistreatment of certain farm animals. In the eyes of other governments, however, except to the extent that some tangible physical harm to a country's territory is imminent, these other more intangible kinds of actual or potential local impact are seldom accepted as a sufficient justification for coercive behavior against others. Even though governments are generally willing to confer about such problems and even to enter agreements about them, they tend to regard them as predominantly external and thus draw the line at coercion. To cover the full range of these objections, the term "externally-directed trade measures" will include all trade measures aimed at environmental harms perceived to occur predominantly outside the territory of the state imposing the restriction.[4]

The purpose of this study is to analyze the policy question of whether governments should be allowed to impose externally-directed trade restrictions for environmental purposes, and, if so, under what circumstances and under what limitations.

The question is usually framed as a question of GATT law, because most governments have undertaken reasonably well-defined GATT obligations limiting their rights to employ trade restrictions. The question of externally-directed trade measures has already been submitted to GATT, and the results of the first GATT legal proceedings on this issue have provided a strong indication of legal opposition. But a contrary position has been stated forcefully by a large number of claims—claims by governments, by environmental interest groups, and by commentators—arguing that GATT law should give governments clear legal authority to use externally-directed trade restrictions for environmental purposes. This paper does not attempt to provide an analysis of what the current GATT law *is*. Rather, it endeavors to analyze what the GATT's ultimate legal response *should be*.

This section begins with a survey of the various assertions and proposals calling for GATT law to authorize the use of trade measures against foreign environmental practices. The survey concentrates on claims made by formal government action. It begins by listing both international agreements and national trade laws authorizing the use of externally-directed trade restrictions. It then goes on to examine other proposed laws that would carry these claims even further. Although the survey does not exhaust all the numerous other proposals made by environmental advocates and academics, the government claims it does represent the core demands that immediately confront the GATT in this area.

The next section provides some introductory observations about the political and legal setting in which the debate over externally-directed trade measures is taking place.

The final sections take up the merits of the question, each dealing separately with one of the two main legal categories of externally-directed trade measures. Section 3.4 considers the problem of what to do about trade measures authorized by international environmental agreements. Section 3.5 then offers an analysis of the possible ways that GATT could deal with so-called "unilateral" trade restrictions—externally-directed trade restrictions imposed by individual governments acting without any multilateral approval.

3.2 A Survey of the Claims for GATT Legal Authorization

At the present time, a number of international agreements and national laws require or authorize the imposition of trade restrictions for the purpose of deterring environmentally harmful behavior. In addition, a steady stream of new legislative proposals of the same kind continue to be introduced. Each of the existing legal provisions and each of the new proposals is itself a claim upon GATT law—a demand that GATT's rules make room for the type of externally-directed trade measure authorized by these various legal instruments.

3.2.1　Agreements and Laws Authorizing Trade Restrictions

International Agreements

The leading international agreements requiring or authorizing trade measures are quite familiar. The Convention on International Trade in Endangered Species of Wild Fauna and Flora, known as CITES, has as its central mechanism the prohibition of imports and exports of endangered species and products made therefrom. The prohibitions apply to all trade, including trade with nonparties.[5]

The Montreal Protocol on Substances That Deplete the Ozone Layer imposes a system of consumption and production limitations on the use of ozone-depleting substances, primarily chlorofluorocarbons (CFCs).[6] The Protocol prohibits trade with nonparties in various products—trade in the ozone-depleting CFCs themselves, trade in products containing CFCs, and possibly trade in products made with the use of CFCs but not containing CFCs.[7] The prohibition against trade with nonparties does not apply to nonparties who have observed the Protocol's consumption and production limitations.[8]

The Basel Convention on the Control of Trans-Boundary Movement of Hazardous Wastes and Their Disposal requires signatories to limit both exports and imports of hazardous wastes in cases where safe disposal is not assured.[9] The Convention prohibits all trade in hazardous wastes with nonparties, unless bilateral agreements meeting the conditions of the Convention have been concluded.[10]

In addition to international environmental agreements with mandatory trade provisions, others merely contain an explicit authorization for the use of trade measures to carry out the purposes of the agreement. The Wellington Convention of 1989 for the Prohibition of Fishing with Long Driftnets authorizes measures, "consistent with international law," to prohibit landing or importation of fish and fish products taken with driftnets.[11]

A 1993 study by the GATT Secretariat identifies 19 international environmental agreements that contain trade provisions, out of a total of 140 international environmental agreements identified.[12] A 1991 study by the U.S. International Trade Commission identifies five other U.S. bilateral environmental agreements in that category.[13]

In addition to the explicit trade provisions found in these 19 multilateral agreements, these and other environmental agreements often contain other provisions under which the parties may take further decisions to implement the agreement; such decisions may include the recommendation or authorization of trade measures. For example, Charnovitz reports that the CITES Standing Committee has, on several occasions, issued resolutions inviting members to take measures, including trade measures, against members (and nonmembers) in response to certain behavior deemed inconsistent with the purposes of the agreement.[14] Similarly, although the International Convention for the Regulation of Whaling (ICRW) contains no explicit trade provisions as such, the International Whaling Commission (IWC) has issued a number of resolutions calling upon members to bar trade with nonmembers in whale products and whaling equipment.[15] Given the presumption that the signatories of such agreements are competent to interpret them, such actions can, if no party objects, be viewed as authorized by the decision-making provisions of the agreements in question.[16] Since similar actions could be taken under the governance provisions of almost any international environmental agreement, it is impossible to gauge the exact extent of the existing authority for such *ad hoc* authorized trade actions without knowing the actual experience and practice under all these agreements.

To the extent these international environmental agreements require or authorize trade restrictions among signatories, they can be viewed as a waiver, between the parties, of any conflicting GATT obligations that might otherwise prohibit such measures.[17] But to the extent that they authorize otherwise GATT-illegal trade restrictions against GATT members who are not parties to the agreement, they are potentially in conflict with the GATT rights of such nonparties. To that extent, these agreements represent a claim for recognition of an exception to GATT obligations for such environmental measures.

United States Laws and Regulations

A number of existing U.S. laws provide for trade restrictions seeking to induce foreign countries and/or their nationals to comply with higher environmental standards. Some of the laws are designed to enforce the obligations or agreed principles of international environmental agreements, but most such laws go beyond what the international agreements themselves require. The laws are often overlapping, frequently duplicative, and together often furnish a menu of diverse trade options to deal with a particular environmental problem.

The area with the greatest concentration of laws imposing such trade restrictions appears to be wildlife conservation, a subject that has come to include moral objections to needless killing or cruelty to animals. Wildlife protection laws are not a recent occurrence in the United States. Although not enacted in conjunction with an international convention, the Lacey Act,[18] which prohibits the importation or exportation of fish or wildlife taken in violation of U.S. or foreign conservation laws, dates back to 1900. Since the early 1970s, however, there has been a near explosion of such laws.[19]

The cluster of legislation that has grown up around the CITES agreement is representative. CITES does not prescribe specific measures that parties must use to enforce the Convention. Instead Article VIII requires parties to take "appropriate measures to enforce the present Convention and to prohibit the trade in specimens" in violation of the Convention. The Endangered Species Act of 1973 (ESA), which implements CITES in the United States, prohibits the import into, or export out of, the United States of endangered species.[20] In addition, ESA prohibits the taking of endangered species within the United States, on the territorial seas of the United States, or upon the high seas.[21] Although ESA import controls could be used to bar imports of wildlife from noncomplying countries,[22] the act does not authorize restrictions against other kinds of trade— restrictions that might be used as a sanction to induce other countries to observe CITES obligations in their trade with countries other than the United States.

In order to enhance the enforcement of CITES, in 1978 the U.S. Congress extended the scope of another statute, the Pelly Amendment. In its original form, the Pelly Amendment authorized trade restrictions on fish products against countries whose nationals were harvesting fish in a manner that "diminishes the effectiveness" of international fisheries agreements.[23] The 1978 amendment extended the Pelly Amendment to behavior impeding the objectives of wildlife conservation agreements, authorizing trade restrictions on "wildlife products" to sanction misbehavior in this area.[24] The trade restrictions authority of the Pelly Amendment is limited to restrictions that are in compliance with GATT.[25]

The United States has in the past "certified" a number of countries under the Pelly Amendment.[26] President Clinton recently imposed the first trade restrictions ever ordered under the Pelly Amendment when he ordered restrictions against Taiwan for its continued trade in rhinoceros horns and tiger parts.[27] Although the Pelly Amendment currently authorizes the President to ban the importation of "any products,"[28] President

Clinton limited the import ban to $22 million worth of trade in wildlife products.[29]

Another recent move to invoke the Pelly Amendment occurred in 1993 when Norway announced its intention to kill a quota of 296 minke whales in disregard of a moratorium on commercial whaling declared by the International Whaling Commission (IWC) under the provisions of the International Convention for the Regulation of Whaling (ICRW).[30] The U.S. Commerce Department certified Norway under the Pelly Amendment, finding that Norway's actions were diminishing the effectiveness of an international fishery conservation program.[31] Norway contested the finding, pointing out that the IWC's own scientists had concluded that minke whales were no longer threatened, and arguing that the moratorium was an "animal-rights" measure rather than a conservation measure, a purpose nowhere provided for in the Convention.[32] Although the certification authorized President Clinton to impose trade sanctions against Norway, the President delayed such action until the United States could "[exhaust] all good faith efforts to persuade Norway to follow agreed conservation measures."[33] However, the President did direct that a potential list of sanctions be prepared against Norway to protest their decision to resume commercial whaling.[34]

In May 1994, the IWC extended its moratorium on commercial whaling until 1995, and Norway again announced that it would disregard the moratorium by taking 301 minke whales. Although the Commerce Department had not issued another certification by the end of 1994, in June 1994 the Clinton Administration undertook an independent scientific study to determine whether Norway's killing of 301 minke whales could occur without endangering the species' survival.[35]

A number of recent additions to the Pelly Amendment have provided explicitly for the application of its trade sanctions to specific environmental problems. For example, one recent statute applies to whaling in violation of the International Convention for the Regulation of Whaling,[36] and a recently introduced bill would, *inter alia*, extend the Pelly Amendment's trade restrictions to countries whose citizens are "engaging in trade in products made from rhinoceros or tigers."[37] Laws such as these appear to add nothing to the authority that already exists under the general terms of the Pelly Amendment. It would appear that there is political gain in making highly visible attacks on the environmental problem of the moment.

In 1992 the High Seas Driftnet Fisheries Enforcement Act[38] extended the Pelly Amendment to require the President to ban the importation of fish, fish products, and sport fishing equipment from countries that violate the U.N. driftnet moratorium imposed by the Wellington Convention.[39] Furthermore, it goes on to authorize the President to embargo any product from the offending nation if that country is still driftnetting six months after a ban has been imposed on imports of its fish or if the offending nation retaliates against the first round of trade restrictions.[40]

The Marine Mammal Protection Act of 1972 (MMPA),[41] source of the celebrated "Tuna/Dolphin" GATT complaint brought by Mexico against the United States,[42] contains a variety of restrictions against trade in products harvested in ways harmful to marine mammals, including a prohibition against imports of marine mammals themselves taken in violation of the exporting country's laws.[43] On the subject of dolphin-safe tuna harvesting, the Act has been amended twice since the first GATT decision. The first was a 1992 amendment authorizing the Secretary of State to enter into international agreements establishing a global moratorium of at least five years on the harvesting of tuna through the use of purse-seine nets deployed on or to encircle dolphins or other marine mammals.[44] If a country that signs such an agreement later breaches the agreement, the Secretary of the Treasury must first ban the importation of all Yellowfin Tuna and Yellowfin Tuna products from that country.[45] If, after 60 days, the offending country has not complied, the Secretary must ban the import of additional fish and fish products having an aggregate customs value equal to at least 40 percent of the total value of all fish and fish products imported from that country during a one-year period.[46] As of November 1994, no such international agreements had been concluded. The second amendment to the MMPA was an amendment, effective in June 1994, prohibiting the sale in the United States of any tuna not caught in a "dolphin-safe" manner, whether caught by domestic or foreign vessels.[47]

Similar in kind to the Marine Mammal Protection Act is the Sea Turtle Conservation Act.[48] After requiring the initiation of negotiations with the governments of the relevant fishing countries, the Act goes on to prohibit importation of shrimp or shrimp products harvested with commercial fishing technology which adversely affects sea turtles.[49] In 1993, the U.S. State Department banned imports of shrimp from French Guiana, Honduras, Suriname, and Trinidad and Tobago under this statute.[50] The ban was subsequently lifted from Honduras and Trinidad and Tobago after those countries adopted measures to comply with U.S. standards.[51]

The United States has also protected sea turtles through the Pelly Amendment. The United States certified Japan under that law because Japan was importing Hawksbill Sea Turtle Shells and Olive Ridley Turtle Skins. Both species were listed on CITES Appendix I. The U.S. Commerce and Interior Departments found that Japan's actions were diminishing the effectiveness of CITES. The United States threatened to ban imports of pearls and other animal products, including $300 million of fish; from Japan. Even though Japan was not violating CITES (it had insisted upon a reservation on the relevant turtle species when it joined the Convention in 1981), it nonetheless agreed to ban imports of the turtle products by the end of 1992 and so no sanctions were imposed.[52]

The foregoing list of U.S. wildlife preservation laws with trade provisions is by no means exhaustive.[53] It does, however, represent a reasonably accurate cross section of the menu of trade options that the U.S. Congress has authorized for the president in dealing with this most sensitive area of international environmental problems. The number of trade measures actually imposed, of course, are a great deal fewer. Almost all of these laws merely authorize the president to impose trade measures, but the president has discretion whether to use the powers in any particular case.[54]

In this connection, a recent pronouncement by the Clinton Administration was an important guide to how these powers will be used over the next few years. The Administration listed four circumstances in which it will consider the use of unilateral trade measures to deter a country from harming the environment:

(1) when trade measures are required by an international environmental agreement to which the [United States] is a party, assuming non-discriminatory treatment of non-parties;

(2) when the environmental effect of an activity is partially within [U.S.] jurisdiction, and there is reasonable scientific basis for concern;

(3) when a plant or animal species—wherever located—is endangered or threatened, or where a particular practice will likely cause a species to become endangered or threatened, assuming there is a reasonable scientific basis for concern; and

(4) where the effectiveness of a scientifically-based international environmental or conservation standard is being diminished, provided the standard is specific enough that the judgment as to whether it has been "diminished" can be made objectively.[55]

The wildlife laws surveyed here, as applied according to these principles, constitute the main area of potential conflict with present GATT law.[56] As such, they are a catalogue of the main claims upon GATT law currently being made by U.S. environmental policy. Of all the claims being made by governments all over the world, these are the most demanding.

Other National Laws and Regulations
This study does not purport to present an equally comprehensive review of laws in other countries authorizing externally-directed trade restrictions for environmental purposes. Even a more limited survey reveals four things:

(1) Notwithstanding their declared aversion to such restrictions, other countries do occasionally use such restrictions.

(2) At least once in a while, the United States ends up on the receiving end—as is currently the case under the European Union's (EU) "leghold trap" regulation.

(3) So far, the volume of authorizing legislation in other countries appears to be significantly less than in the United States.[57]

(4) As in the United States, most of the externally-directed trade measures imposed by other countries involve wildlife preservation and animal rights.

A few countries have acted alongside the United States in some of the environmental problems mentioned previously. For example, during the recent whaling controversy, Britain[58] and Australia[59] have condemned Norway's decision to resume commercial whaling, but have not as of this writing initiated trade sanctions. On driftnetting, New Zealand has also acted by prohibiting the landing of any fish or marine life taken using a driftnet.[60] Although the European Commission has proposed a ban on driftnet use by EU member states by 1997, this proposal has not yet been adopted.[61] On dolphin-unsafe fishing practices, in 1992 the EU approved a regulation prohibiting member states from using purse-seine nets on marine mammals.[62] However, they decided not to adopt an embargo on the import of dolphin-unsafe tuna into EU member states.[63]

The European Union has taken two widely reported measures in the area of wildlife protection. The first was a 1983 ban on the importation of seal pup fur, designed to restrict commercial harvesting in Canada and Norway. A GATT lawsuit was filed by Canada but never pursued, as Canada eventually decided to adopt roughly the same protective measures sought by the EU.[64]

The second was a regulation banning the importation of pelts and manufactured goods of certain wild animal species originating in countries that permit the use of leghold traps, to take effect January 1, 1996.[65] The import ban is limited to pelts and manufactured goods of 13 different species that are predominantly caught in leghold traps.[66] The United

States, which allows the use of such leghold traps, has expressed concern to the EU regarding the regulation's likely negative effects on U.S. fur exports to Europe. The U.S. position is that an international body, such as the International Organization for Standardization (ISO), should determine the criteria for humane trapping methods—not the EU.[67] Canada has initiated GATT consultations.[68]

A policy similar to the EU leghold trap policy was argued by the European Commission in a 1990 case challenging a 1936 Netherlands law that banned the importation of numerous European wild birds.[69] The case involved a lawsuit brought by an importer of red grouse from the United Kingdom.[70] The EC Commission argued on behalf of the Netherlands, stating that the "transfrontier nature of bird protection" allows a member state to "take measures to protect bird life not only on its own territory, but even outside of it."[71] The European Court of Justice did not rule directly on the point, finding that the case did not raise the issue because the red grouse is neither "migratory nor endangered."[72]

The EU has also enacted a directive, scheduled to become effective in 1998, that will prohibit the use of animal testing for cosmetics research. An accompanying provision will ban the marketing of cosmetics, domestic or foreign, containing ingredients that have been tested on animals.[73]

Frogs have become a subject of concern. Germany, after proposing unsuccessfully that several frog species be added to CITES,[74] has acted unilaterally to protect frogs from overharvesting by banning frog imports from Indonesia.[75]

Most recently, the British Ministry of Agriculture, Fisheries, and Food canceled a large contract to import ostrich meat from South Africa because of that country's "barbaric" practice of plucking feathers from the birds while they are still alive.[76] The British government felt that this practice violated the U.K.'s Charter on Animal Welfare.

Recently, several European countries have enacted internal laws protecting domestic animals from cruel treatment. The European Union has passed a directive setting minimum space standards for cages used to house laying hens.[77] Sweden and Switzerland have gone one step further and banned the use of cages to house laying hens within their borders.[78] In addition, in 1988 Sweden adopted an extensive animal protection ordinance that widely regulates animal treatment.[79] Although these measures contain no trade provisions at the moment, both competitive pressures and expanded horizons could well lead to trade measures.

3.2.2   Recent U.S. Proposals to Authorize Trade Restrictions

A survey of recent legislative proposals in this area reveals a number of proposals seeking to enforce international conservation agreements already in existence. For example, Senator Moynihan proposed a General Agreement on Tariffs and Trade for the Environment Act that would use international environmental agreements as standards for imposing trade sanctions.[80] The bill's main purpose was to authorize a study of the effects of international environmental agreements on international trade. It would also, however, have amended Section 301 of the Trade Act of 1974 to declare any action by a foreign nation that "diminishes the effectiveness of any international agreement on the environment or on the conservation of animals or plants" to be "unjustifiable" for trade purposes.[81] The U.S. Trade Representative could then have imposed Section 301 duties or restrictions or taken additional action on imports from nations whose conduct was so classified.

A similar proposal by Senator Baucus included a provision completely banning imports of products whose production violated internationally recognized environmental norms.[82] Senator Baucus's proposal involved creating a GATT environmental code modeled after the subsidies code.

Proposals related to specific problems have continued to emerge. A 1989 proposal would have required the president to revoke most-favored-nation status for any country that did not have, or did not enforce, appropriate protection of elephants.[83] A similar bill in 1990 would have required certification of China under the Pelly Amendment, and eventually prohibited the importation of fish and wildlife products from China, if China did not withdraw its reservation regarding listing the African elephant as an endangered species under CITES.[84]

A bill introduced in 1993 would have required the president to impose economic sanctions against countries that engage in whaling not authorized and approved by the International Whaling Commission.[85] Likewise, a resolution was introduced in 1993 to support the efforts of the International Commission for the Conservation of Atlantic Tunas by allowing for Pelly Amendment certification of countries that violate the Commission's recommendations.[86] Finally, in June of 1994, a bill was introduced requiring inclusion of provisions relating to workers' rights and environmental standards in any trade agreement entered into under any future trade-negotiating authority.[87]

3.3   Some General Observations about Proposals to Authorize Externally-Directed Trade Measures

3.3.1   The Battle for the Rhetorical High Ground

Environmentalist proposals for GATT legal reform often begin with an attempt to capture the rhetorical high ground by characterizing GATT as an institution representing values inferior to those of the environmental movement. A typical way of introducing the GATT is to describe it as an "obscure" international institution that has intruded rather unexpectedly into environmental matters. The word "obscure" suggests several nodules of inferiority:

• The GATT's obscurity suggests that its accomplishments since 1947 are not important enough to have commanded the attention of a reasonably well-informed observer.

• Similarly, GATT's obscurity means that its work involves arcane and narrowly technical issues lacking the moral urgency of things like environmentalism.

• Finally, GATT's obscurity means that the 50 years of government policy decisions that stand behind the GATT legal code must have occurred somewhere in the hidden recesses of government, out of view of the democratic electorate and its intellectual leaders, and thus must lack the political legitimacy of true democratic approval.

The same point about the superiority of environmental values is usually advanced with the repeated assertion that GATT has no expertise in environmental affairs. The suggestion is that any GATT opposition to environmental trade measures must be based upon a failure to understand environmental problems. Concerns based on GATT values, it is implied, would certainly give way once the environmental concerns are properly understood.

A number of international law scholars have contributed another dimension to this normative hierarchy by pronouncing the large number of international agreements and declarations espousing environmental values to be a form of "emerging international law." GATT's own long legal history is implicitly treated as a lower form of legal ordering, one that must give way before this newly emerging international law.

The present study will probably be somewhat irritating to those who accept the rhetorical stance just described. The study rejects the notion that any and all harms called "environmental" are always and everywhere more important than the GATT policy goals they would displace. To the contrary, this study is based on the view that the ultimate policy goals of the GATT are of roughly equal importance—important enough to deserve serious consideration, and accommodation, in any case where they are actually in conflict with environmental goals. To be sure, there will be cases where GATT policy goals must give way before more important policies, as the GATT itself does in the exceptions made for other policy needs in Articles XX and XXI. But that conclusion, like any other accommodation, always requires careful examination of the competing policies at issue in each case.

The GATT serves two major policy goals that can claim major importance. One is economic, and the other is political. Each deserves equal attention.

The GATT's economic goal is to promote, through liberal international trade policies, the greater effectiveness of national economies. Effective economic performance makes a contribution to the well being of all economic participants, but it is especially important for the alleviation of human poverty. The GATT regime has made a major contribution to alleviating poverty in the postwar era. The GATT trading system provided the base for the recovery from the wartime devastation of Europe and Japan. Later on, it provided the foundation for the spectacular growth of many third-world economies. Most recently, the GATT trading system has served as the engine for yet another burst of vigorous, export-led economic growth in still other countries, many of them still very poor. Poverty remains a critical problem affecting the quality of human life on this planet. Those who would minimize the importance of the GATT's economic work are either ignoring that poverty or else are taking for granted the economic processes that have done so much to reduce it.

There has been nothing surreptitious about the political mandate for the GATT's economic work. In the United States, the trade agreements program has been endorsed by no less than 17 acts of Congress between 1934 and 1994, with each of the last five authorizing acts (in 1962, 1974, 1979, 1988, and 1994) having been a major item on the nation's legislative agenda.[88] As for the rest of the world, perhaps the most striking evidence of well-considered political commitment has been the collective decision of some 120 countries to negotiate a massive expansion of GATT in the 1986–94 Uruguay Round negotiations. Unlike many of the resolutions and declarations adopted in international environmental matters, the 120 or so signatures on the Uruguay Round Final Act involve a firm legal

commitment to immediate and substantial economic and social change—
the clearest evidence of serious purpose.

The GATT's political mission was established by a generation of postwar leaders acutely conscious of the threat to international peace posed by
the power diplomacy of the 1930s. GATT was part of a larger plan to
establish a better system of international relations, one based on rules
voluntarily agreed upon. To be sure, the larger plan has not been fully
achieved, and GATT itself has fallen short in many ways. But on the
whole GATT has succeeded in constructing a remarkably well-developed
legal order in the area of international economic affairs. The heart of that
legal order is the proposition that economic coercion must be limited by
law—by rules voluntarily accepted and objectively applied. Explaining the
political objectives of the ITO Charter from which GATT was taken, the
chief United States delegate said:

We have introduced a new principle in international economic relations. We have
asked the nations of the world to confer upon an international organization the
right to limit their power to retaliate. We have sought to tame retaliation, to
discipline it, to keep it within bounds. By subjecting it to the restraints of international control, we have endeavored to check its spread and growth, to convert
it from a weapon of economic warfare to an instrument of international order.[89]

This particular political objective has been at the center of GATT operations since 1947. Today, it is supported by an international consensus as
broad and as firm as is any of the propositions in the so-called "emerging
international law of the environment."

The competition between the goals of the GATT and those of the
environmental movement can take various forms. The conflict of greatest
interest to this study is the one that occurs when environmentalists propose that governments employ trade restrictions to deter environmentally
harmful behavior. Environmentalists argue that the value of the environmental goals in question justify overriding GATT rules against trade
restrictions. So far, the GATT has been unwilling to concede the displace-
ment of its own rules without carefully weighing the justification, the
alternatives, and the costs.

The GATT's skepticism is rooted in long experience. Environmentalists
are not the first group to come to GATT seeking to appropriate the use of
trade-restricting measures for beneficial purposes. A similar argument was
advanced by the leading schools of development economics of the 1950s
and 1960s, promising breakthroughs in economic development if trade
were just properly managed. Another movement, with many similarities to

the current environmentalist movement, was the campaign for a New International Economic Order (NIEO) in the 1970s, in which trade intervention was advocated in the name of the remedying the unjust disparity of wealth and power in the world. Then as now, international law scholars declared that the principles of the NIEO were an "emerging international law," and urged the GATT to alter its precepts to reflect this new body of higher legal principles.

Although it bent before these pressures for a number of years, the GATT's ultimate reaction was to resist any meaningful commitment to the interventionist principles being advocated, on the ground that they were simply bad economics and bad legal policy. The GATT's judgment was eventually vindicated. Most developing-country governments have learned over time that interventionist trade policies do not produce the desired economic results, and during the 1980s one government after another abandoned them. The remedial trade measures called for by the NIEO suffered a similar fate. In retrospect, the NIEO's claim to be "emerging international law" stands as an embarrassing monument to well-intentioned legal theorizing built on bad economics and naive politics.

For the most part, the current environmentalist proposals do not rest on the same wrong-headed economics that animated these earlier appeals for interventionist trade policy. But a comparison to these earlier proposals does suggest many similarities in the lack of attention to the economic and legal-political costs of the trade measures being advocated. Consequently, the GATT has good reason to be skeptical of the cost-benefit justifications being offered for these environmentalist proposals, and so has every reason to insist on making an independent judgment as to the trade measures being proposed.

3.3.2   Identifying the Players

The conventions of writing about trade policy lead one to refer to "the GATT" as though it were a separate and independent actor with its own values. In reality, of course, the GATT is the creation of its Member governments, and the values it expresses are the values given it by the Member governments.

Governments, in turn, consist of many overlapping bureaucracies, each tending to its own area of responsibility. The policies expressed in GATT are actually those of the bureaucracy responsible for international trade affairs—in most governments the trade ministry. While the government as a whole will generally have endorsed the main elements of GATT policy, other government bureaucracies within that government will have their own policy agendas and they will not always take care to follow the directions of GATT policy. Thus it can happen that a government will simultaneously affirm certain GATT trade policy norms with one hand (its trade bureaucracy), while with the other hand (another bureaucracy) act in conflict with those norms. Such conflict is actually a fairly normal state of affairs.

The international setting created by GATT can actually cause the divergent strands of policy to widen somewhat, for the international setting tends to draw greater attention to the benefits of international cooperation and thus to elicit even more demanding policies than were agreed to back home. Thus the international product often becomes somewhat more ambitious than the sum of its more modest parts. Being more ambitious, GATT norms may diverge even further from the agendas of other bureaucracies.

The larger debate between GATT and the environmentalists, therefore, is very often a case of conflict *within* governments. The policies of a government's trade bureaucracies are being challenged by its environmental bureaucracies and by the environmental interest groups collected around them. Although the GATT will be the focus of the debate, the actual resolution (to the extent that there is one) will have to be worked out within the Member governments, between the contending bureaucracies and interest groups. The GATT will ultimately do what its Member governments tell it to do.

It is impossible to discuss the trade-and-environment debate without giving careful attention to the collection of GATT policy norms that represent one side of the debate. It is a convenient convention to refer to those norms as "GATT policy" or "the GATT view" or even just "GATT." It would be tedious to keep reminding the reader of the realities that lie behind those terms. Only an occasional reminder is planned.

3.3.3   The Concept of Environmental Harm

The basis for almost every externally-directed environmental trade measure is the assertion that practices of another country or its citizens are causing some kind of harm to the environmental interests of the complaining countries. Terms such as "transborder" or "transboundary" are often employed to describe the idea that an activity has adverse effects on other countries, but the range of impacts covered by these terms is quite broad.

The range varies from events with a physical impact on other countries to events that take place entirely within the borders of the target country.

The cases that most clearly entitle an affected state to act are those in which some harmful physical substance is transmitted across borders into the complaining country and causes traceable damage. The example usually cited is the so-called *Trail Smelter* case involving transborder emission of toxic sulfur dioxide fumes from a lead and zinc smelter.[90] These are the easy cases. Once the scientific facts are established, the "wrong" in such cases is almost universally acknowledged. Legal liability can be established, and remedies of retorsion and retaliation, including proportional trade retaliation, are taken for granted—so much so that cases involving this sort of direct impact do not occupy very much space in the current trade-and-environment debate.[91]

Most proposals advocating the use of externally-directed trade measures are targeted upon environmental practices whose outward effects are less direct, less immediate, or less damaging. As a consequence, they often present some degree of controversy over whether intervention is justified.

Scaled in terms of the directness of the physical impact on others, the list of possible adverse environmental effects is usually presented something as follows:

(1) At the upper end, we find practices that have an effect on the overall environment of the planet, such as degradation of the ozone layer or global warming, whose eventual impact will affect most other territories.

(2) Next we find practices that cause damage to certain global resources in which other countries claim a common interest, such as (a) the oceans and other territories known as "global commons" or (b) the so-called "biosphere" consisting of the basic stock of plant and animal life on the planet.

(3) Then there are some toxic substances, such as hazardous wastes, whose effects are so dangerous that all countries feel threatened by uncontrolled disposal wherever it occurs.

(4) Finally, we find actions involving cruelty to animals or wanton destruction of animal life—actions that, although not presenting any immediate threat of extinction of species, are considered morally offensive.

There can be wide differences in perceptions about the seriousness of the harm to human welfare, as well as perceptions about the immediacy of the harm and the reversibility of the harm. The seriousness of any environmental harm can be augmented by one's sense of the accumulation of many small cuts. One's perception of the immediacy of a threatened harm can be influenced by the urgency one feels about the need to start doing things differently. One's sense of whether particular harms are irreparable depends in part on the assumption one makes about the reliability of political commitments to corrective action once problems are identified. And differences can run deeper. It is sometimes difficult, for example, to identify the line between these judgments about the seriousness of harm and ethical objections to tampering with Nature.

The almost infinite variability of environmental harms does not mean that there cannot be clear cases in which a broad consensus in favor of action can be found. The vast number of existing multilateral and bilateral environmental agreements testifies to wide areas of shared concern. But the clear cases are seldom the ones that cause the greatest trouble. The cases where trade restrictions or other forms of coercion are most likely to be employed are precisely those in which there is some basis for disputing the directness, seriousness, immediacy, and irreparability of the environmental harm in question.

Given the normative (some would say political) quality of the notion of environmental harm in these disputed cases, one must be prepared for at least two conclusions. (1) It will not be possible to write a legal definition of environmental harm that can be applied with complete objectivity. Indeed, it will probably not even be possible to obtain agreement on any very meaningful definition. (2) No government or international institution will be able to claim complete objectivity in its own judgments on the existence and seriousness of environmental harm. Such decisions will be viewed as political, and their authority will depend more on the political legitimacy of the institution making the decision than on any objective criterion.

3.3.4 Policies toward Trade Restrictions

Except among trade policy officials, trade restrictions appear to be a much favored instrument of governments in international relations. Whenever simple diplomacy fails and some kind of force is believed necessary, trade restrictions seem to offer just the right blend of coercion and civility.[92] To date, trade restrictions have been just about the only type of coercive measure even considered in discussions of international environmental policy—in international environmental agreements, in national laws, in proposed national laws, in interest group advocacy, and in academic writing.

The relative popularity of trade sanctions is often based in part on an undervaluation of their true cost. The average politician, and far too many

advocates and writers, reveal a solid grounding in mercantilist misperceptions about international trade. They treat trade restrictions as something
that only hurts the targeted country. If trade restrictions have any domestic effects at all, they assume, the effects are mildly helpful in saving jobs
for local workers. It is interesting that no one ever proposes sanctions
where the harm to one's own citizens is clearly perceived: restrictions on
tourism, for example.

Trade Restrictions in GATT
One of the most common misperceptions about trade restrictions is the
belief that the strength of the GATT legal system rests on the GATT's
power to authorize trade sanctions. In truth, trade restrictions are not used
nearly as frequently in international trade affairs as they are in other more
political areas. Indeed, they have been scarcely used at all in GATT legal
affairs. According to the author's own statistical study of GATT adjudication from its inception in 1948 until the early 1990s, trade retaliation was
authorized in only one of the 123 successful legal proceedings conducted
during that period.[93] The force of GATT law has rested, first, in its ability
to make objective legal rulings and, second, in the tendency of such rulings
to elicit community pressure for compliance. Ultimately, GATT law works
because governments want it to work, not because they are bullied into
compliance by trade sanctions.[94]

Trade retaliation on the fringes of the GATT legal system has played
only a slightly more prominent role in GATT affairs. The GATT agreement does allow governments to make "compensatory withdrawals" to
maintain the balance of reciprocity whenever other governments take
advantage of exceptions allowing extraordinary trade restrictions for various reasons. A scattering of such compensatory withdrawals has occurred
in GATT history, in cases where the affected government wished to show
its displeasure with the invocation of the exception in question.[95] Most of
the instances are not even remembered.[96]

Trade retaliation completely outside the GATT legal system has played
a more significant role in GATT policy, in just the past decade. The
primary practice in question has been unilateral trade retaliation by
the United States, both actual and threatened. Beginning in about 1985,
the United States began to use such retaliation as an instrument to wage a
rather aggressive campaign against what it considered unfair or unreasonable practices restricting United States business interests.[97] These actions
are widely credited with having helped to induce developing-country
governments to agree, in the Uruguay Round trade negotiations, to ex-

pand GATT to cover subjects as trade in services, intellectual property rights, and foreign investment.

While the unilateral United States trade restrictions of the late 1980s are often viewed as a model instrument for environmental policy, GATT itself was never inclined to treat these trade measures as a model for anything. GATT law has always been quite clear in limiting the use of trade sanctions to cases in which there has been a violation of GATT norms, and not until such a legal violation has been objectively determined by third-party adjudication.[98] GATT viewed the wave of unilateral United States restrictions as a major departure from this norm. Despite the arguably valuable contribution made by the U.S. restrictions to the Uruguay Round, the GATT response to the U.S. trade measures was to reject them unequivocally, by establishing a new and stronger dispute settlement procedure that would explicitly oblige the United States to follow GATT procedures and third-party rulings in the future.[99]

GATT imposes one other kind of limitation on trade retaliation that is sometimes overlooked by proposals to employ trade restrictions against environmental harms. It has to do with limitations on the quantum of retaliation. The official purpose of all retaliatory measures is to maintain the balance of reciprocity that has been upset. All GATT retaliation is limited to a "compensatory" amount—that is, an amount equivalent to the value of the trade obligation being nullified or impaired by the other party. The compensatory limit applies to retaliation for legal violations, for nullification and impairment, and as compensation for an authorized withdrawal of obligations. The amounts to be compared are measured by the money value of trade covered by the obligations withdrawn.[100]

The main significance of the compensatory limit is that it rejects a more aggressive approach toward sanctions—specifically, the approach under which a legal sanction must be large enough to produce the desired change of behavior. In mercantilist terms, the "pain" of GATT's compensatory sanctions is only as large as the "gain" from the avoidance of obligations that triggers it. Balance of reciprocity, not deterrence, is the standard.

Trade Restrictions for Environmental Purposes
Trade measures imposed in response to claimed environmental harms, whether in concert or unilaterally, are usually designed to deter or prevent the behavior that is causing, or contributing to, the harm.[101] Trade restrictions can serve that deterrent purpose in a variety of ways.

Trade restrictions may act directly on the economic motivation of the individual actors causing the harm. Restrictions may, for example, eliminate

the international market for the product whose production is causing the
environmental harm. One example would be the CITES restrictions on
trade in products of endangered species, such as the prohibition on trade in
ivory as a way of deterring the killing of elephants for profit. Or trade
restrictions may seek to disable a production process that is causing harm.
An example would be the Montreal Protocol's ban on trade in materials,
capital goods, and technology needed for the production of CFC gasses.

Trade restrictions may also seek to prevent the environmental harm by
inducing a change in the environmental policy of the government whose
citizens are causing the problem. Any kind of trade restriction that imposes
an economic loss on the target country can serve this purpose. In many
cases, trade restrictions on the product associated with the harm-causing
practice will have a sufficiently painful effect to induce such a change in
policy by itself. Thus, the U.S. restrictions on imports of tuna have seemingly been effective in changing Mexico's policies toward dolphin-safe
fishing practices.

But there will be other cases in which the retaliating country's imports
of the harm-causing product will not be large enough to make a good
hostage, not even a symbolic one. For example, most countries that oppose whaling do not import whale meat in the first place. When the
harm-causing product is not traded, governments seeking to deter the
environmental harm will consider using trade restrictions on a broader
range of products.[102] Some of the U.S. laws authorizing broader sanctions
along these lines are the driftnet legislation authorizing restrictions on
sports-fishing equipment,[103] or the dolphin-protection legislation authorizing an embargo on all fish products.[104]

If environmental trade restrictions were limited to restrictions on trade
in those products whose production is causing the environmental harm,
that would be a quantitative limit of sorts, albeit a rather haphazard one
depending on the volume of trade in such products. On the other hand,
once environmental trade restrictions cross the threshold into deterrent
sanctions on any and all trade, the built-in limit vanishes.[105] As will
become clear below, this question of quantum limits on trade sanctions is
likely to be an issue of major importance.

3.3.5   The GATT Legal Status of Externally-Directed Restrictions

Under customary international law, a state is free to deny market access to
any other state for any reason or for no reason at all. Likewise, a state is
free to impose trade restrictions discriminatorily. The legal problem with

externally-directed trade restrictions for environmental purposes rests on the contractual obligations of the GATT.

At present, the GATT has not made a clear and authoritative ruling on the legal status of trade restrictions imposed by one GATT member upon the trade of another GATT member in response to that country's inadequate environmental practices. This issue has been addressed most directly in two recent GATT panel reports dealing with U.S. restrictions on tuna imports from countries that did not meet U.S. standards on dolphin-safe fishing practices.[106] Both reports, which are commonly referred to as *Tuna/Dolphin I* and *Tuna/Dolphin II*, found the United States restrictions in violation of GATT. Neither panel report had been officially adopted by the end of 1994.[107] But both panel reports have received the general support of 39 of the 40 GATT member countries that have so far taken a position on the matter—all, that is, except for the United States.[108]

The first part of both *Tuna/Dolphin* rulings dealt with the question of whether the U.S. trade restrictions could be justified under national treatment rule of GATT Article III. Article III states a very liberal standard toward internal regulations—regulations that apply to goods after they enter the country. As a practical matter, Article III allows a government to adopt whatever internal regulations it wishes, and to apply them to foreign products as well as domestic products so long as the regulations treat foreign products no less favorably than like domestic products.[109] The United States regulation involved in the *Tuna/Dolphin* cases was a regulation directed to preventing the killing of dolphins on the high seas. The United States had argued that its regulation treated domestic and foreign producers equally; it prohibited all producers, U.S. and foreign, from using dolphin-unsafe fishing methods. The United States argued that its dolphin-saving regulation should be judged under the equal-treatment test of Article III, and thus was authorized by GATT.

The GATT decisions in the two *Tuna/Dolphin* cases found that the permissive equal-treatment rule of Article III applies only to regulations governing the impact that imported products themselves will have inside the country, as opposed to harms elsewhere in the world that might be caused by the production process for those products. The ruling on this issue is sometimes referred to as the "product-process" distinction. The panel explained that, if governments could regulate imports according to the production process by which they were made, the rules of GATT Article III would allow governments to require imports to conform to any type of social regulation currently imposed on the production process of domestic producers. It would allow governments to condition market access on compliance with domestic laws governing working conditions, such as minimum wage laws, or any of the myriad obligations carried by domestic employers.

Having limited Article III's authorization of equivalent regulations to regulations based on the domestic impact of imported products, the panel reports concluded that externally-directed regulations like the *Tuna/ Dolphin* embargoes had to be treated as an extra burden on imports. In that case, the restriction took the form of an embargo imposed at the border, and so the restriction was found to be a violation of the GATT Article XI:1 prohibition against nontariff border restrictions.[110]

Each of the two *Tuna/Dolphin* rulings then considered the United States argument that its dolphin-protection regulations were justified under Article XX. Article XX is the exception that authorizes governments to employ otherwise GATT-illegal measures when such measures are necessary to deal with certain enumerated social policy problems. The panels considered the exception in XX(b) for measures "necessary to protect human, animal or plant life or health," and the exception in XX(g) for measures pertaining to conservation of exhaustible resources. Although both decisions rejected this argument, each took a somewhat different approach to interpreting the relevant Article XX provisions.

The *Tuna/Dolphin I* panel decision interpreted the Article XX exceptions to apply only to measures relating to health or conservation "within the jurisdiction" of the country imposing the restriction. Although most commentators noted that the word "jurisdiction" was not the same as "territory," most assumed that jurisdiction was essentially limited to direct harms occurring within the regulating state's territory.[111] Under this widely held interpretation, all trade restrictions directed against environmental harms outside the national territory would have failed to qualify for an exception under Article XX, and would thus have remained GATT-illegal.

The panel decision in *Tuna/Dolphin II* stated in the course of its analysis that Article XX does allow governments to pursue environmental concerns outside national territory. It suggested that trade measures to protect the life of dolphins in the world's oceans might thus be permitted. But, said the second panel, the Article XX exceptions apply only to trade measures that do in fact have a direct conservation or protective effect. Article XX, it said, does not authorize trade measures that will have conservation or protective effects only by coercing other governments to adopt the desired conservation or protective policy.[112] The U.S. restrictions in question were held to be of this coercive design.[113]

The implications in *Tuna/Dolphin II* about the kind of restrictions that Article XX *permits* were dicta. The ruling in the case was that the U.S. law was in violation of GATT because of its coercive design. The panel was not called upon to define exactly what characteristics would be required for a permitted trade restriction. Nonetheless, the decision seems to be suggesting that restrictions would be permitted if aimed directly at harm-causing behavior by individuals regardless of their nationality. The decision thus appears to approve restrictions like the CITES embargo on all trade in ivory products, aimed at the economic motivations of individual elephant hunters, even though it applies to harms outside national territory. Or, in the tuna/dolphin matter, the decision would seem to allow a trade restriction requiring that all imports of tuna, whatever their nationality, be accompanied by a certificate that the tuna was harvested by dolphin-safe fishing methods.[114]

As noted above, the strict interpretation of the *Tuna/Dolphin I* panel report was supported by every GATT country that took a position on the matter except for the United States. On the other hand, the decision has been subjected to considerable criticism. Much of this criticism argues for a broad validation of externally-directed trade restrictions, even broader than would be allowed by the implications of *Tuna/Dolphin II*.[115] The rest of the critics take a number of intermediate positions.[116]

The only thing certain so far is that the debate has not come to rest with the panel decision in *Tuna/Dolphin II*. In the meanwhile, GATT governments have firmly established Trade and Environment as a major topic of debate and negotiation for the new WTO.[117] The mandate for these negotiations includes the direction to "make appropriate recommendations on whether any modifications of the provisions of the multilateral trading system [i.e., GATT] are required...."[118]

At this point in the debate, another closely reasoned analysis of the legal sources is unlikely to have much impact upon the mountain of legal commentary already in place. Besides, governments are likely to resolve most of these issues before the legal commentators do. The most useful contribution to the debate at this point will be to concentrate less on what the GATT law *is* at the moment than on what it *should be*. In order to present the issues from that perspective, the following analysis will simply assume that GATT law permits nothing until GATT agrees to permit it. Hence the study will continue to speak of the environmentalist demands for GATT authorization of externally-directed trade restrictions as proposals for an addition to GATT law.

3.3.6   The Two Main Proposals for GATT Legal Authorization

There are two main proposals to permit the use of environmental trade restrictions for externally-directed purposes.

First, there seems to be relatively broad agreement that GATT should permit trade restrictions authorized by international environmental agreements like CITES, the Montreal Protocol, and/or the Basel Convention. The issues in this first area are less *whether* such an exception should be recognized, but more when, how, to what extent, and on what conditions.

Second, the large body of actual or threatened unilateral actions described in Part I above can be viewed as a group of related proposals for changes in GATT law. These claims present the question of when, if ever, individual governments should be allowed to impose externally-directed trade restrictions unilaterally for environmental purposes.

The remainder of this study will be devoted to a detailed examination of each of these two major proposals for change in GATT law.

3.4   Trade Measures Authorized by International Environmental Agreements

3.4.1   The Basic Issues

One of the main legal reforms now being discussed in GATT's trade-and-environment debate is a proposal to remove GATT legal barriers against trade restrictions required or authorized by certain international environmental agreements. The type of international environmental agreements GATT governments have in mind are the three major environmental agreements that currently authorize such trade restrictions—the CITES convention, the Montreal Protocol, and the Basel Convention.[119] Since each of these three agreements has been ratified by all or most of the GATT's most powerful countries, the conditions for GATT legal accommodation of these particular agreements are quite favorable. The key issue that remains to be decided is exactly what kinds of legal accommodation should be made: What kind of international environmental agreements should be included? What kind of trade restrictions, for what kind of purposes? What specific form of legal accommodation is required or appropriate? And what, if any, conditions should the GATT impose?

The GATT has only a limited, one-directional power to make the sort of legal decisions required. The GATT Contracting Parties have no power to rule upon the relative legal status of GATT and other international agreements. They can only rule upon what their own agreement means, and, if necessary, can amend the GATT agreement to make it say what they want it to say. If the Contracting Parties decide that GATT law should give way before another agreement (or in any other circumstance), they can certainly define GATT law in a way that will achieve that result. But if they decide that GATT law should not give way to the commands of some other agreement, their decision is merely a refusal to step aside; it is not an authoritative ruling that GATT obligations are superior to those of the other agreement. Only a tribunal with competence to adjudicate the overall international legal relationship of the parties would have the authority to make such a ruling.

Notwithstanding the GATT's lack of power to make an authoritative application of the international legal principles governing the relationship between agreements, GATT governments will almost certainly endeavor to follow those principles in attempting to reconcile GATT obligations with those of other international agreements. In general, these principles would suggest that GATT should step aside whenever a GATT member government has signed an international environmental agreement authorizing other signatories to impose trade restrictions against it. The general concept is that GATT members who sign such an agreement can quite properly be deemed to have waived their GATT legal rights against such trade restrictions.[120]

In most cases the waiver concept would be recognized under the rule of international treaty interpretation known as *lex posterior:* When two agreements signed by the same parties are in conflict, the agreement later in time is presumed to be controlling.[121] Most if not all of the international environmental agreements in question postdate the original 1947 GATT agreement, and most also postdate the accession of most major GATT members.[122]

In addition, the waiver concept can also be based on the fact that the environmental agreements are clearly more specific than GATT in terms of their subject matter. Under the principle of *lex specialis* it is normally presumed that the more specific of two agreements is meant to control, even when the more general agreement happens to be later in time.[123]

Prior to 1994, these two principles would both have dictated treating most if not all international environmental agreements as a waiver of GATT rights by signatory governments. That being the long-established relationship, it is extremely unlikely that governments would have wished to alter that relationship for governments acceding to GATT in the last few years, or that governments would have intended the 1994 recreation of GATT into the WTO to change the established relationship. Even if an international tribunal might not be required so to rule, GATT does have the power to so interpret its own obligations in this way, and will very likely do so.

If GATT chooses to treat signature of the trade provisions of an international environmental agreement as a waiver, two major legal issues will remain. First, GATT will have to find some way of dealing with uncertainty about what trade restrictions such agreements do in fact require or authorize. As noted earlier, the institutions that administer such agreements sometimes call for trade measures in cases where the authority for taking such measures is less than clear.[124] Problems may arise when a signatory government disputes the agreement's authorization of such measures. For example, one could well imagine such a dispute occurring if the International Whaling Council were to call for trade sanctions against Norway for its refusal to abide by a total moratorium on commercial whaling.[125]

The second major issue that GATT will have to resolve is the very difficult question of what to do about GATT members who have *not* signed such international environmental agreements. No waiver of GATT rights may be attributed to countries that do not sign the agreement. Absent some other justifying principle, GATT-illegal trade restrictions imposed against non-signatories would continue to be GATT-illegal. Each of the three centerpiece agreements—CITES, Montreal, and Basel— require trade restrictions against nonsignatories.[126] The proposal to legitimate the trade provisions of these three key agreements is in major part a proposal to permit the signatories of those agreements to impose trade restrictions against GATT members who are nonsignatories.

The discussion which follows will concentrate on the second of these questions—what to do about the GATT rights of GATT member countries who have not signed international environmental agreements. This is the more important of the two questions. Even though the number of affected nonsignatories is often not very large, the "free-rider" problem looms large in every new negotiation. In addition, the way that the GATT chooses to resolve the issue of nonsignatories will establish its basic approach toward international environmental agreements, and this approach will provide the setting for how GATT deals with the question of what those agreements mean.

3.4.2   Weighing GATT Legal Rights against Environmental Agreements

The problem of reconciling the GATT legal rights of nonsignatories with the policies being advanced by international environmental agreements is a problem that cannot be resolved by conventional legal analysis. To be sure, if the principles of certain environmental agreements were to achieve the status of *jus cogens*, that conclusion would answer the question in favor of overriding GATT. But no such status can be claimed for international environmental agreements as a class.

Absent a higher legal authority, the GATT itself is the only competent authority that can define the status of the GATT legal rights of its member governments. The GATT agreement gave rise to those legal rights, and it provides no other means to accomplish their interpretation, their amendment or, if need be, their waiver or abrogation. The international environmental agreements cannot act for GATT; they do not have the same parties, nor are they constituted under the authority of the GATT agreement.

In some cases, the GATT agreement itself has made its legal rights subservient to the actions of another international organization. GATT Article XXI(c) provides that GATT legal rights are subservient to United Nations obligations in the area of international peace and security.[127] Similarly, GATT Article XV:2 requires GATT to abide by the findings of the International Monetary Fund on whether the financial condition of a GATT member country satisfies the criteria for using balance-of-payments trade restrictions. These provisions amount to a complete cession of regulatory jurisdiction over the subject matter in question. The GATT does not claim the right to review the basis of United Nations or IMF actions in this area.

Some proposals seem to be asking that GATT resolve the problem of non-signatories by exercising a similar deference to international environmental agreements. That relationship might be established one day if there were an international environmental organization with the same standing as the United Nations or the IMF. But the United Nations and the IMF are finite institutions that possess established constitutions defining their decision-making procedures and representing at least a minimum degree of international consensus as to what powers they should and should not exercise. It is impossible to cede legislative jurisdiction in advance, in blanket fashion, to something as amorphous as the environmental movement, or to any class of agreements yet to be negotiated. As is amply demonstrated by the 1992 Earth Summit, the governments of the world are still quite far from a working consensus on environmental policy, much less on an allocation of power to achieve that policy. Nor, indeed, is it possible to define with any precision the class of agreements that should qualify as "international environmental agreements." As a group, the existing agreements are quite varied, and they themselves are often vague and extremely tentative as to the specific policy measures they ordain.

As a practical matter, it is likely that GATT will be required to defer to broadly based agreements like CITES and the Montreal Protocol, where the more than 120 signatories include all, or almost all, GATT countries of any significance. It is also likely that GATT will in fact need to defer to other important agreements. But these practical realities are highly contingent. Until the world is ready to define a master institution for international environmental affairs, the only practicable and sensible course would be to recognize that GATT possesses at least some kind of joint competence over the trade measures called for by such international environmental agreements.

The boundaries of influence between the GATT bureaucracy and the environmental bureaucracy are likely to be rather subtle. As just noted, it is likely that, despite the GATT's primary legal competence, GATT governments will not be willing to reverse, or even modify, broad-based international environmental agreements once they have already been ratified. This has been the GATT's own experience with customs unions and free trade-area agreements—agreements that are completely within its area of competence. But while GATT has not been able to alter the content of those agreements once negotiated, it is clear that the GATT rules on customs unions and free trade areas (Article XXIV) have had a considerable effect on the negotiation of those agreements.[128] The same type of influence is probably the most that GATT can hope for with regard to international environmental agreements.

That is, if governments acting through GATT were to formulate rules expressing their own policy views with regard to the use of trade restrictions in international environmental agreements, it is likely that these GATT rules would influence the negotiating process for such agreements. The GATT rules would become an item on the agenda of internal decision-making processes for each government in the negotiations, giving the respective bureaucracies an opportunity to resolve their differences within each government, rather than lobbing hand grenades at the each other's international work product.

What the GATT requires, therefore, is a structure that permits it to articulate its own policy toward these environmental trade measures without ignoring the practical reality that it is unlikely to be able to reverse or even modify the trade provisions of a broadly-based international environmental agreement once ratified. One good structure for doing so would be a legal rule that would have two "lines."

(1) On one line, governments acting through GATT would set out rules stating what they regard as the appropriate accommodation between the GATT contractual rights of nonsignatories and the needs of environmental protection. GATT would review agreements for conformity with these rules. The review would have little or no prospect of a negative decision. Indeed, the procedure might provide for accepting the express findings of the negotiating conference on compliance. But the parties to the agreement would be expected to present a case for compliance and respond to criticism.

(2) On the second line, the rules should contain an alternative procedure under which GATT could grant *ad hoc* approval to whatever international environmental agreements the signatory governments decide to submit.

The second-line procedure would always be available for agreements that did not conform to the first-line rules set down by GATT. Even if every environmental agreement were dealt with under the *ad hoc* procedure, the first-line rules would still be able to serve their main purpose of influencing internal government debate and international negotiations—just so long as governments know that at least some kind of GATT review will be required before GATT acceptance.

A model for this two-line type of rule can be found in GATT Article XX(h). Article XX(h) creates an exception for GATT-illegal trade measures imposed pursuant to obligations in international commodity agreements, overriding the GATT rights of nonsignatories as well as signatories. The first part of Article XX(h) sets out its own first-line criteria as to the substance, structure, and negotiating procedure that commodity agreements must meet in order to qualify for a XX(h) exception.[129] The second part goes on to provide that the exception may also apply to any commodity agreement submitted to the GATT Contracting Parties and not disapproved by them.[130]

The remainder of Part III of this paper is devoted to an analysis of how the Article XX(h) model might be adapted to deal with the trade provisions of international environmental agreements. The main body of the analysis addresses the substantive and procedural criteria that GATT might announce as the preferred basis for excepting such trade provisions from GATT obligations—criteria that this paper refers to as "first-line" criteria. Then a brief concluding section considers the structure of an alternative "second-line" procedure—a procedure under which GATT would consider *ad hoc* exceptions for whatever other international environmental agreements that parties might choose to submit.

3.4.3   Defining the First-Line Criteria

Basic GATT Policy toward Regulatory Conditions
Before considering the specific criteria that GATT might wish to impose, it will be helpful to step back and look at GATT's basic policy toward regulatory conditions imposed by the importing country.

The GATT agreement rests on exchanges of commitments by governments promising access to each other's markets. For the exchange to be meaningful, the access commitments must have a certain degree of reliability; there is no point in trading for access rights that can be taken away at will. The ability to condition market access on compliance with regulatory norms is obviously a limitation on the right of access to a market. Each regulatory norm becomes a hurdle that has to be surmounted in order to gain access to that market. To make access rights meaningful, GATT must strike a balance between access and regulatory policy.

The teaching of the *Tuna/Dolphin* cases is that regulatory conditions may be divided into two kinds. The most common conditions are those regulating the impact of the imported product within the territory of the importing country. In this category are all the regulatory conditions relating to the impact of imports on domestic health and safety, consumer protection, and the like. The second kind of regulatory conditions are those that concern behavior of foreign producers that impacts outside the importing country. This second category contains all those regulatory conditions that we are calling "externally directed."

For regulations concerning the impact of imported goods within the importing country, the GATT already gives national governments very wide latitude. GATT Article III gives the importing government the right to impose as many regulatory requirements as it wants to, so long as those requirements bear equally on foreign and domestic products, or at least have a bona fide regulatory purpose. The powers are broad, because all governments insist on freedom to regulate their internal affairs. Although these conditions obviously have a limiting effect on trade, they have always been there, and international trade flows have always shaped themselves to accommodate them.

When governments of importing countries seek to condition market access on the exporter's conduct affecting other parts of the world, they claim a relatively new, and obviously greater, power to limit market access. On the surface, there is some appeal to the idea that the production process of foreign manufacturers should follow the same rules as local producers. Upon reflection, however, it can be seen that unlimited power to impose such conditions could easily erect a regulatory barrier to all market access. If, for example, foreign producers could not enter the market unless their home factories complied with the importing country's social legislation, that condition would effectively cancel out most comparative advantage, not to mention subjecting the home factory to a welter of potentially inconsistent requirements from every different export market. In sum, the exporter's right to access would be worth little or nothing.

The GATT obviously has an interest, therefore, in having some regulatory control (or at least regulatory influence) over the scope of externally-directed regulatory conditions on market access. The nature of the limitation that GATT will want to impose is fairly obvious. The case for allowing externally-directed environmental trade restrictions is that governments need to be able to employ such measures in order to protect the planet against environmental degradation, as well as against other "environmental" harms. The GATT's interest is to confine the use of externally-directed trade restrictions to cases in which such an environmental need does in fact exist. Moreover, its interest is to limit such action to cases in which the threatened harm is important enough to justify interfering with the GATT system of market-access commitments.

Most environmentalist proposals implicitly concede that the power to impose externally-directed restrictions must be limited somehow. When they recommend authorizing governments to use trade restrictions against foreign environmental practices, they almost always put these proposals forward as a special-case exception—a power justified by the special importance of environmental needs. Although environmentalists resist the idea that any environmental measure can ever be GATT-illegal, most proposals are in fact put forward under either the letter or the spirit of GATT Article XX—the provision that allows governments to employ measures that are otherwise GATT-illegal when such measures are necessary to achieve certain high-priority social policies. The main target of criticism in the two *Tuna/Dolphin* decisions has not been their conclusion that externally-directed regulations are *prima facie* GATT-illegal (both rulings are quite firm on that point), but the additional conclusion in each ruling that the measures in question could not be justified under a special Article XX-type exception for environmental policies.

GATT Article XX is a relevant precedent for dealing with this issue, although its legal structure is not exactly a perfect model. As a precedent, Article XX does express a policy of allowing measures harmful to market access when there is a sufficient social policy justification. As a model, however, the terms of Article XX itself do not produce the same degree of restraint when applied to externally-directed measures as they do when applied to domestic policy measures such as local health or safety requirements. The weakness of Article XX in this regard requires some explanation.

When applied to domestic policy measures, the terms of Article XX tend to produce a rather tight and narrow exception. Article XX does not require that the social policy reason for the exception be particularly important, just so long as it fits within the named categories such as "health" or "conservation." The strictness of Article XX lies in the requirement that the trade-restricting measure be "necessary" to achieving the particular societal policy in question.[131] "Necessity" can be rather hard to prove in a domestic regulatory setting, where the government has total regulatory control over all participants within its territory. With that much government control over the situation, there are usually many other trade-neutral means of accomplishing domestic regulatory goals. It is the exceptional case in which a GATT-illegal trade measure is really needed.

The "necessity" test of Article XX would not impose the same kind of restraint when applied to externally-directed regulatory measures. Unlike the domestic setting where trade-neutral alternatives abound, the only policy instruments that governments can use to influence externally-directed behavior are two: diplomatic negotiation and coercion. Once negotiation has been tried and failed, trade restrictions will be necessary every time.

And once "necessity" is reduced to a minor limitation, the rest of Article XX imposes little other restraint. The gravity of the problem does not matter under Article XX. For example, once it is decided that preventing the death of dolphins is a policy involving protection of the environment, it matters not whether the survival of the species is threatened or how many dolphins are at risk. The only additional requirement that Article XX adds is that the policy goal be genuine, rather than a "disguised restriction" on trade. Whenever many governments join to conclude a multilateral environmental agreement, this is never a problem.

If GATT wishes to erect a limitation on externally-directed regulatory conditions that has some degree of rigor, it must go beyond the terms of Article XX. It must prescribe that an exception for externally-directed trade measures will be allowed only when the measure is "necessary" to avert a "serious environmental harm."

Defining "Serious Environmental Harm"
The concept of "environmental harm" is very flexible at the margin. The concept involves two related ideas: (1) the conclusion that the subject matter of the harm is "environmental" and (2) the conclusion that the effects of the harm are legitimately the concern of other countries, an idea usually represented by terms such as "transborder" or "global." If one examines the list of existing and proposed "environmental" trade measures described in Part I of this paper, it can readily be seen that powerful governments, particularly the United States and the European Union, have been extending the concept of transborder environmental harm to include some quite contentious concerns—particularly claims regarding treatment of animals such as dolphins, whales, baby seals, marine mammals in general, and animals caught in leghold traps. Proposed international agreements in these areas are likely to involve a substantial degree of dissent.

The same flexibility can be found in the term "serious." In his recent book *Greening the GATT*, Daniel Esty presents a simplified matrix showing just a few of the possible gradations in the seriousness of environmental harms: major harm versus "narrower" harm; rapid harm versus less rapid harm versus least rapid harm; certain harm versus less certain harm versus least certain harm; irreversible harm versus reversible harm.[132] Esty goes on to suggest that avoiding less serious degrees of harm may not be worth the damage caused by certain kinds of trade restrictions. Drawing these lines is also likely to be a matter of considerable disagreement.

Consequently, any criterion requiring that externally-directed trade measures be justified by serious environmental harms is likely to generate an extraordinary amount of disagreement over its meaning. As important as such a limitation may be to GATT policy, the GATT itself will not have the institutional capacity—either the political mandate or the technical expertise—to negotiate a more precise definition of its meaning. An effort to negotiate that meaning in advance would plunge GATT into a diplomatic and political morass. And the GATT would have even less capacity to make an adjudicatory judgment after the fact. In sum, if a sufficiently large and representative number of governments are concerned enough about a certain "harm" to conclude an international agreement authorizing trade restrictions to remove the harm, there is probably nothing GATT can do to challenge that appraisal—whether it involves the ozone layer or the habitat of egg-laying chickens.

The only way the concept of serious environmental harm can be made effective as a limitation on externally-directed trade measures is during the negotiation of the international environmental agreement itself—when those charged with negotiating that agreement must decide how much trade action is justified. The GATT's objective in preparing such criteria, therefore, should be primarily to influence those negotiations. To do so, it will want to make the issue an item on the agenda of the negotiations, in a way that permits the trade bureaucracies of national governments to raise objections on that ground. For that purpose, a general requirement of "serious environmental harm"—without further definition—is as good as a more precise definition.

Although it would not be essential, the GATT could add one additional requirement to intensify its influence on the negotiations. The GATT criteria could require that the international agreement expressly state its intention to displace GATT legal obligations owed to nonsignatories. This requirement would dramatize the issue of overriding the legal rights of others, both in domestic debate and in the negotiations themselves. It will be a clear ticket of admission for the trade bureaucracy to enter the debate at this point if not before.

In order for the GATT criteria to have any meaningful influence, the GATT will need to have a review proceeding to give negotiators some incentive to pay attention to GATT criteria. It has already been suggested that GATT can effect such a review by employing a two-line legal provision, a provision that states GATT's policy criteria in the first line while at the same time offering an alternative *ad hoc* approval procedure in the second line. Neither procedure would render an adjudicatory decision, but both would call for explicit discussion of the extent to which the criteria had been satisfied, the first directly and the second by way of justifying departures.

The "Necessity" of Trade Restrictions

The second key element in the environmental justification of externally-directed trade measures will be the conclusion that trade measures are "necessary" to averting the environmental harm in question. As with the definition of harm itself, the GATT is unlikely to be able to adjudicate the necessity of trade measures in actual international agreements. The one case that would present a clear issue—trade sanctions against a nonsignatory whose conduct conforms to the agreement—is unlikely ever to arise. Otherwise, if GATT is presented with a broadly representative agreement in which signatories have decided that they wish to use trade measures against noncomplying countries, GATT would be hard pressed to make an independent appraisal of necessity contradicting that finding. Nonetheless, the GATT can help to place the issue of necessity before the negotiators and their home governments. A GATT rule stating the proposition—that trade restrictions should be used only to the extent necessary to accomplish the objectives of the agreement—would have this effect.

One of the most common "necessity" problems likely to arise under international environmental agreements involves the use of trade restrictions to deter "free-riding." Free-riding usually means one of two things: (1) the nonsignatories are reaping the environmental benefits of the agreement without paying the same price in terms of honoring obligations or (2), even worse, they are earning greater profits by selling the prohibited product or service at an elevated price. Free-riding does not *necessarily* interfere with achieving the environmental objectives of the agreement. For example, the divergent conduct of nonsignatories may not be significant enough to add a meaningful degree of harm. In such cases, it can be argued that, strictly speaking, the trade restrictions are unnecessary.

Free-riding can make it difficult, however, for other signatories to justify accepting the agreement's obligations in the domestic political setting back home. Should this sort of *political* necessity be recognized as a justification for trade sanctions against free-riders? In the normal Article XX situation, GATT cannot afford to recognize political necessity as a justification for an otherwise "unnecessary" protectionist regulation. The reason is clear: Every protectionist regulation ever written could be justified by arguing that the support of the protected industry was necessary in order to achieve some other good regulatory purpose.

Arguably, however, a political necessity claim based on the need to satisfy the principle of equal sharing of burdens is a different case. The underlying political demand is not as disreputable, nor is meeting it as likely to subvert the goals of the GATT system.

The frequent imprecision of the trade provisions in international environmental agreements poses another kind of "necessity" problem. Many agreements "authorize" but do not "require." Many are unclear about exactly what measures are supposed to be taken, and by whom.[133] A typical scenario might well have some member countries employing one trade measure, some employing other measures, and others employing none at all. GATT rules could make a contribution if they could merely force negotiators to think more clearly about what remedies are needed and to clarify their answers.

Trade Restrictions: The Degree of Coercion Allowed
Assume it is established that the problem in question is a serious environmental harm. Assume further that negotiations have been unsuccessful and that the signatory governments believe some kind of coercive trade measure is needed to deter the harm-causing behavior. The next question is to decide what kind of trade measures to authorize.

Once again, the political reality of a broad-based international agreement may ultimately force the GATT to accept the answers provided in the particular agreements themselves, no matter how imprecise. But these are issues that are as much within the GATT's competence as they are within the competence of environmental institutions. GATT can legitimately express its views on the substance of these matters, and a limiting rule of this issue would arguably not exceed its political mandate.

The setting of an international environmental agreement removes some of the inherent limitations that apply to trade restrictions authorized under Article XX for domestic policy purposes. In the domestic regulatory setting, where a government is trying to protect its own territory from some threat to health, life, morals, environment, or whatever, the only kind of trade measure that is ever "necessary" is the limitation or exclusion of the harm-causing product from entering that territory. Governments have no need to use punitive sanctions on other products, and they are never even proposed.

The normal objective of an international environmental agreement, however, is the regulation of environmentally harmful conduct that takes place outside the territory of signatory countries. The parties to the agreement must be able to influence the conduct of a nonsignatory country or its citizens. Stopping trade in the harm-causing product may exert enough coercion to deter the unwanted conduct, but it may not. In those cases where it does not, the logic of having an international agreement in the first place would appear to support using more coercive trade sanctions, specifically, punitive sanctions on other products traded by the offending country or its citizens.

That logic is carried out in some of the United States laws that authorize unilateral trade restrictions in support of environmental goals. Some of the more prominent U.S. laws provide authority for trade restrictions against a much wider range of products in order to create a more effective deterrent.[134]

Interestingly, however, the international community has shown a rather consistent tendency to limit trade measures to the harmful products themselves. The trade restrictions authorized by the three international agreements everyone has in mind—CITES, Montreal, and Basel—have generally been limited to restricting trade in the products associated with the environmental harm. The Basel convention restricts trade in hazardous wastes between members and nonmembers, but these restrictions do little to deter other kinds of improper disposal arrangements between nonmembers. Under Montreal, restrictions are limited to CFC products, products and technology used to make CFCs, and possibly products made with the use of CFCs. Thus far, these restrictions appear adequate to achieve the goals of diminishing CFC production and consumption, but this would not stop domestic production in any large nonsignatory. And although the CITES Standing Committee has sometimes called for broader trade measures,[135] the CITES agreement itself calls only for restrictions on trade in the products of endangered species.

The same limited approach toward trade coercion has been well represented in the GATT's working party on trade and the environment. In 1992, the European Community deposited a paper arguing that, where trade restrictions are authorized by international environmental agreements, the power to impose trade restrictions against nonsignatories should be limited to products that are environmentally damaging themselves or products whose production is environmentally damaging.[136] The EC explained that an exception allowing trade restrictions on unrelated products "would be practically limitless."

To some commentators, this reticence to use the full power of trade restrictions seems puzzling. These commentators argue that the emergence of environmental problems on a global scale makes it obvious that governments must use strong measures to correct them. Environmentalists frequently describe the reluctance to use wider trade sanctions against noncomplying states as an attachment to outdated notions of sovereignty—outdated because it ignores the need to organize global solutions to today's global environmental problems.

The opposing point of view refuses to dismiss considerations of sovereignty this easily. For good or ill, it argues, the world is still made up of nation-states, and solutions have to work through them. International legal relations, it contends, cannot be conducted according to the norms of domestic legal institutions. In domestic law, when something is wrong, the government is usually expected to pass a law (use state coercion) to make it right. Nation states may sometimes have to bow before coercion at the hands of one or more powerful states, but there is no civic consensus accepting the authority of such coercion. The differences between domestic and international settings may be less evident to American commentators (because it is the familiar and trusted United States government that does most of the coercing in either case). Things do not look the same from the perspective of other countries.

Other governments, particularly smaller governments, do not have confidence in the objectivity or fairness of the sort of international coercion that is likely to be practiced under international environmental agreements. The kind of agreement-based coercion we are discussing rarely if ever takes the form of action by the entire community of signatory governments. Instead, the agreements merely "authorize" trade measures, and it is taken for granted that the large countries will be the ones who do most or all of the coercing. And smaller countries simply do not trust the larger countries to use those coercive powers impartially or without a bias in favor of their own self-interest.[137] And, of course, the large country never uses such powers against itself.

Another element in the opposition to very strong coercion is the belief that most of the goals of international environmental agreements can be accomplished without it. It is not true that agreements lacking enforcement provisions are by definition ineffective. Governments comply voluntarily with the vast majority of all international undertakings, and that is the operative assumption on which most states behave.[138] The great majority of international agreements do not involve coercive enforcement at all. It is no surprise that only 19 of the approximately 140 environmental agreements surveyed by the GATT Secretariat bothered to authorize trade restrictions.[139]

The governments favoring the more restricted approach to trade coercion are not, of course, arguing that trade restrictions should be avoided entirely. These governments generally support a GATT exception for trade restrictions authorized by international environmental agreements. They do see a case for some expression of community displeasure. They would acknowledge, as they must, that occasional trade sanctions do succeed in stimulating reconsideration of policies.[140] But they would insist that trade sanctions are effective primarily as a symbol of community condemnation, and that their symbolic function can be served well enough by more limited forms of restriction.

The two contending positions here can be summed up in terms of two different legal theories that might be used to explain the authorization of trade restrictions against countries that have not signed these environmental agreements. The narrower view might be called the trade agreement view. It rationalizes the power to restrict environmentally harmful trade in terms of the implicit understandings of the parties to a trade agreement. It argues that a country entering a trade agreement with another country must be aware of certain implicit exceptions when it receives the market access commitments. The Article XX exceptions for threats to life, health, morals, and so forth merely make explicit what should have been implicit: "In granting you access to my market, I am obviously not promising to accept goods that will harm me." The exception for trade restrictions authorized by an international agreement is just an extension of the notion of "harm me." It says, "In addition, I will obviously not be ready to accept any trade that undercuts agreements dealing with serious environmental problems." It is a small extension, limited to trade that is actually causing harm. It fits the Article XX tradition.

The broader view looks upon the power to employ trade restrictions more as an exercise in legislative power. It might be called the community self-defense view. It starts with the proposition that the international community is being threatened by a global environmental harm, and asserts that the community is entitled to defend itself against that harm by whatever means are necessary to prevent it. This is not a trade agreement interpretation. It is an assertion of a collective power to legislate, wholly separate of the GATT or any other agreement.

As pointed out above,[141] the GATT's own traditions of using trade retaliation have followed a quite narrow and limited course. GATT has seldom authorized retaliation at all. The GATT law controlling retaliation limits it to a compensatory rather than punitive amount, and authorizes retaliation only on the basis of objective, third-party determinations. Perhaps it is only natural, therefore, that the GATT's deliberations up to this point have had some difficulty in embracing the broader claim of international legislative power underlying the proposals for broader sanctions. If GATT follows the teachings of its own experience in this matter, its first-line criteria will express a preference for the more limited form of trade sanctions.[142]

Arbitrary Discrimination and Disguised Restrictions

If the GATT exception for international environmental agreements were framed as an addition to Article XX—a new Article XX(k)—the exception would inherit the two other legal requirements stated in the preamble to Article XX. First, the preamble prohibits trade measures that treat countries differently unless the discrimination is justified by a relevant difference. In the normal Article XX case involving protection of the domestic market, this requirement is meant to allow selective application of trade restrictions against only those countries that pose a threat to the domestic market—for example, countries where a particular animal disease is known to exist. But a restriction barring trade from only some of the countries where a particular disease prevails, while allowing trade from the other countries equally affected by the disease, would be prohibited.

Since trade restrictions authorized by international environmental agreements typically discriminate against nonsignatories, such discrimination would have to be justified by some relevant criterion. The question of whether membership is a relevant condition is essentially the same as the "necessity" issue discussed in a previous section, and one could expect the same results. Thus, if the trade restriction were based on nothing more than the status of nonsignatory—for example, if the nonsignatory's conduct was in full compliance with the agreement—the restriction would fail both the necessity requirement and the prohibition against arbitrary discrimination. An anti-free-rider restriction, on the other hand, would present the same close issue under both tests.

The second requirement in the preamble to Article XX is an injunction against trade restrictions that are a "disguised restriction on international trade." The term is a stylized way of saying that the good social purpose claimed in the justification must in fact be the purpose of the trade measure, rather than just a "disguise" for a protectionist purpose. While this sort of disguise is frequently practiced by national governments on behalf of domestic industries, it is unlikely to be a problem when the regulation is being promulgated by 50 or 100 governments in an international agreement. Whatever else may be wrong with trade restrictions authorized by international environmental agreements, their purpose is usually what governments say it is.

First-Line Criteria on the Structure of an Agreement

We turn now to the structural requirements that the GATT might impose on an international environmental agreement as a condition for granting a GATT legal exception for trade measures authorized by such an agreement. GATT Article XX(h), which deals with international commodity agreements, provides a precedent for this type of structural requirement. GATT governments have already begun to discuss the possibility of applying these Article XX(h) requirements, *mutatis mutandis*, to international environmental agreements.

To explore the kind of structural criteria that might be applied, we must begin with a detour explaining the substance of Article XX(h).

The Rules of Article XX(h) Article XX(h) states an exception from GATT obligations. The exception applies to trade restrictions required by certain international commodity agreements. Some commodity agreements, known as "commodity control agreements," seek to stabilize (and usually to elevate) the price of a primary commodity in world markets by imposing restraints on production and/or marketing. Typical trade measures required by commodity control agreements are export quotas limiting the amounts producers will sell or import quotas limiting the amount major markets will take.[143] The trade restrictions required by a commodity control agreement would normally be in violation of GATT. In order for the desired market effects to occur, these trade controls must also be applied to the trade of nonsignatories. The Article XX(h) exception is, in effect, an exception authorizing the signatory governments to override the GATT rights of those nonsignatories.

As noted earlier, the Article XX(h) exception contains a two-line formula. The first line provides for automatic acceptance of agreements that meet certain specified criteria. The second line provides that individual agreements may be accepted if they are submitted to the GATT and not disapproved. The first-line criteria established by Article XX(h) are those found in the ITO Charter exception for commodity control agreements.[144]

The ITO criteria begin with a substantive requirement. In brief, commodity control agreements may be negotiated only when there is a burdensome surplus of the commodity which cannot be cleared by market forces without excessive hardship or unemployment.[145] This requirement can be satisfied, however, by a finding made by the negotiating conference itself. In other words, while the ITO Charter defines the type of problem that must exist, it allows the signatory governments to certify that such a problem exists. Much the same arrangement can be anticipated for the type of environmental exception being discussed; GATT would limit the exception to agreements addressing a serious environmental problem, and then GATT's review procedure would accept a finding by signatories that the agreement does.

The ITO Charter exception then establishes a structural requirement to protect the interests of potential nonsignatories. For any commodity, the world can be divided into producing countries (sellers) and consuming countries (buyers). Although the numbers of sellers and buyers are seldom equal, the Charter exception for commodity control agreements requires that the number of votes must be divided 50-50 between sellers and buyers regardless of their actual numbers.[146] For nonsignatories, this 50-50 provision would tend to assure that the provisions of any such agreement would be minimally agreeable to both buyers and sellers, and thus to any nonsignatory on either side.

Seller-buyer compromise is feasible in commodity agreements because the economic effects of a commodity agreement are not a zero-sum game. The agreement is a form of cartel that substitutes level prices for the volatility of the free market. The surrender of GATT rights involved in a commodity control agreement is less a surrender than a forced trade.[147]

The ITO Charter exception also deals with the planning and negotiating stages of the negotiating process, assuming that they would be under ITO supervision. One of the key protections required is the requirement that the planning process and the negotiating conference be open to all parties who consider themselves interested.[148] The ITO exception then goes on to require that, once the commodity agreement is concluded, membership should be open to all ITO Members, initially on equal terms and thereafter on terms approved by the ITO.[149]

Finally, the ITO Charter exception imposes still more requirements pertaining to the particular treatment of nonsignatories. It requires that signatory countries give "equitable treatment" to nonsignatory ITO Member countries, and treat the nonsignatories who are ITO Member countries no less favorably than other nonsignatories are treated.[150] The Charter permits the signatory countries to consider, in determining the level of treatment owed nonparticipants, "policies adopted by nonparticipants in relation to obligations assumed and advantages conferred under the agreement."[151] The implication was that nonmembers whose conduct conforms to the requirements of the agreement should be treated as well as members, and if not, not.

The ITO Charter exception did not require that commodity agreements be signed by some minimum number of signatories or be otherwise representative of the ITO membership. Commodity agreements simply did not have the same need for the legitimacy conferred by a broad membership. In contrast to the typical environmental agreement which legislates that certain practices are wrongs, commodity agreements involve a voluntary accommodation of buyer and seller interests. The important thing is to enlist most buyers and sellers, and this tends to occur automatically, because (except for the occasional OPEC agreement) commodity agreements cannot work at all unless they have the participation of most of the major market participants.

The Structural Requirements of a New Article XX(h) for International Environmental Agreements   A GATT exception for trade restrictions authorized by international environmental agreements will not lend itself to the same nice, self-balancing sort of procedural controls that can be applied to commodity agreements. Countries affected by environmental agreements are not divided into neat classes of producers and consumers who, with 50-50 voting power, can be expected to strike a balance between their interests.

The fact that an international environmental agreement has been concluded does not give us enough information to render a very reliable judgment about its impact on the interests of the various signatories and nonsignatories. Among the signatories, it is fair to assume that the sponsoring governments do believe the environmental benefits are worth the cost to them. One probably has to make the same assumption, *faute de mieux*, about the cost-benefit balance for other signatories, but at the same time one cannot place too much normative weight on that assumption. Poorer countries sometimes do attach different values to the costs and benefits of such agreements, and threats of unilateral trade sanctions sometimes do figure in their decision to sign such agreements. To be sure, it is equally difficult to identify the true interests of nonsignatories, whose motives may range from an honest difference in cost-benefit calculations to a cynical attempt at free-riding.

Since there are no procedural arrangements that will ensure that the terms of any particular international environmental agreement are fair to everyone, it is necessary to establish the legitimacy of coercion under such agreements by a more complex series of requirements. It is still important, of course, to adopt requirements that maximize the chances that divergent interests will be accommodated. But more attention must also be given to the number and representativeness of signatories, in order to establish what might be called the "legislative" legitimacy of the conference process that produces the agreement.

Size and Representativeness   The problem of defining the necessary number of signatories, and their character, is likely to place developed and developing countries in unaccustomed positions. Developed countries normally go to great pains to argue that the super-majority of developing countries in the United Nations cannot be accorded law-making powers. The situation with regard to most environmental agreements is that all the developed countries will have signed, and will be arguing that fewer rather than more developing-country signatures are needed. Developing countries are likely to borrow a page from the developed country songbook in arguing that nonacceptance by a significant minority of developing countries is disabling.

Although it is unlikely that a GATT exception would establish any firm numerical threshold, some outside guideposts can be noted. The new WTO agreement provides that a three-fourths vote of the entire membership is needed for the membership to adopt a legal interpretation of any WTO agreement.[152] A three-fourths vote is also required to impose an amendment on the entire WTO membership.[153] In short, three-fourths is the vote needed to make WTO legal actions binding on all members. And, finally, a three-fourths vote is required for a temporary waiver of obligation.[154]

Article 18 of the United Nations Charter sets two-thirds as an appropriate General Assembly vote for important questions, and UN practice tends to treat two-thirds as the sort of majority that will give United Nations endorsement to a negotiating conference or its product.

The numbers game becomes more complex when the geographical or subject-matter scope of the agreement reduces the number of potentially interested governments. The requirement of a "broadly representative" membership then poses the question: "Representative of what?" The potential variations are infinite. The only practical solution is a provision stating that representativeness must be judged on a case-by-case basis.

Some observers have suggested an additional membership requirement based on interest in the regulated activity. One such proposal specifies that the agreement should be ratified by "a substantial proportion of the activity giving rise to the agreement...."[155] Although it seems anomalous to require the consent of those who are causing the environmental problem and whose behavior the agreement is trying to alter, participation by a substantial percentage of such countries would certainly enhance the legislative legitimacy of the agreement achieved.

In the end, the GATT is likely to adopt a general criterion, like "broadly representative of the international community," with an indicative list of factors pertaining to representativeness—participation in the regulated activity, injury from the harm, geography, level of economic development, and absolute numbers. Such a general criterion may not really be necessary to induce negotiators to seek the broadest possible membership, for they will normally do that anyway. A formal requirement of representativeness could have some impact, however, in whatever GATT review procedure is undertaken. A determined opposition by a significant minority will probably lead to some accommodation of their interests. A representativeness requirement would strengthen the hand of such a minority.

Fairness   In addition to the representativeness of the agreement process, an equally important element in establishing the legitimacy of decisions reached at an international conference is the fairness of the negotiating procedure toward all interested participants. Nonsignatories must at least have an adequate opportunity to press their point of view that corrective action is not required or appropriate. To be sure, the GATT is unlikely to play the same supervisory role that the ITO envisioned for itself in the negotiation of commodity agreements. Fairness conditions in a GATT exception would serve more as advance guidance than enforceable requirements.

The ITO Charter exception for commodity control agreements appears to be a good model for this purpose. Like the ITO provision, a GATT exception for international environmental agreements should require that all countries have access to the negotiating process.[156] Like the ITO Charter, the GATT rules should make a special effort to ensure that all countries have an opportunity to participate in the "study group" or other initiating committee that determines the need for an agreement and the agenda of its negotiations.

In addition to fair participation, legitimacy also requires fair treatment compared to members and other nonmembers. Again, the ITO Charter provisions state a useful set of minimal rights. Membership in the agreement must be open on terms no less favorable than those applicable to existing members.[157] The ITO's general requirement of "equitable treatment as between participating countries and nonparticipating countries" suggests the useful principle that equal conduct deserves equal treatment, member or not.

3.4.4   The Second-Line Approval Procedure: *Ad Hoc* Review

GATT Article XX(h) offers what looks like a very easy second-line route to approval of commodity control agreements. After creating an exception for agreements that conform to its first-line criteria, it also contains a second-line procedure that grants an exception to any other commodity agreement that is submitted to the GATT Contracting Parties and not disapproved by them.[158] Given the GATT practice of deciding as many issues as possible by consensus, a practice formally adopted in the WTO Agreement,[159] it would be extremely difficult to obtain a formal decision of disapproval. Thus it would appear that any agreement so submitted is virtually guaranteed of approval. GATT has had no actual experience with this procedure, however, because no commodity agreement has ever been submitted for approval. Most likely, the agreements were not contentious, and governments did not expect the review procedure to change anything.

If there were serious disagreement about an international environmental agreement, the *ad hoc* review procedure would probably have some regulatory impact. Most governments would be extremely reluctant to ram through approval of such an agreement. Except, possibly, for cases involving an imminent threat of major irreversible damage to the environment, the instincts of most GATT participants would be to negotiate an accommodation of the interests of the dissenters. The environmental agreements in which major dissent occurs are most likely to be those involving borderline problems in the first place.

If one wished to tighten up the GATT's control of this second-line approval procedure, two changes might be suggested. The first, repeating a suggestion made earlier, would be to add a requirement that, if any environmental agreement is to override GATT rights of nonsignatories, it must contain an express provision stating its intention to override such GATT legal rights. In effect, this requirement would say that the price of approval would be deliberation within each signatory government of the decision to override GATT obligations.

The second possible change to the Article XX(h) procedure would be to reverse the burden of action, and to require that GATT actually make a decision approving the agreement. With a large majority of members in favor of the agreement, it should not be that difficult to obtain a decision of approval. While the consensus practice might allow individual dissenters to block agreement for a while, this is the type of situation in which GATT would be likely to vote. GATT has always voted on waivers, and since this *ad hoc* approval procedure would be analogous to a permanent waiver, voting would not be that unusual. To be sure, one must bear in mind the point made above: In cases of very intense dissent, the first instinct of GATT participants will be to negotiate an accommodation. That is what should happen first, and it usually will.

On balance, however, a rule requiring approval would probably cause more controversy than it is worth. GATT can get most of the reviewing pressure it needs from a procedure that requires submission and discussion. To avoid an impasse on this issue, those who understand the way GATT really works would be wise to recede before the wishes of those who don't.

3.5   Unilateral Trade Restrictions against Foreign Environmental Practices

The term "unilateral trade restriction" has a somewhat flexible meaning. The central element is a trade restriction imposed by one government for the purpose of preventing or discouraging some foreign practice deemed to be wrong. The term "unilateral" means that the government has acted without any kind of multilateral approval. Usually, but not invariably, the term is used to indicate the conclusion that the trade restriction is GATT-illegal.[160]

In the trade and environment debate, the term "unilateral trade restriction" usually refers to a trade restriction (1) imposed by one government against a foreign environmental practice, (2) without formal authorization in any GATT legal proceeding, and (3) without any express legal authorization in any international environmental agreement. Critics of such measures argue that they are GATT-illegal. Environmental advocates argue that they either are, or should be, GATT-legal.

3.5.1   The Standard Scenario

As described by environmental advocates, the case for unilateral measures usually presents a standard scenario. It goes like this:

A leading government discovers that commercial practices somewhere in the world are causing what it considers to be serious harm to the environment. To its credit, the government first restrains its own nationals from engaging in the harmful behavior. It then becomes aware that nationals of other governments are continuing to engage in the harmful behavior, and that the effects of their conduct are causing harms of serious magnitude. The leading government makes representations to the governments of the harm-causing nationals. Those governments agree to discuss the matter, and consultations or possibly a conference are convened. The leading government displays commendable patience in trying to achieve a solution by negotiation, the degree of patience being calibrated to the seriousness and immediacy of the environmental harm in question.

Nonetheless, the other governments, or at least a significant number of them, decline to restrain the harmful behavior of their nationals. At some point, the leading government concludes that the problem can wait no longer. So it threatens to apply coercion in the form of trade restrictions against the trade of the recalcitrant governments or directly against trade in the products causing the harm.

The threat usually produces more intensive discussions. New deadlines are set, and deadlines are usually extended if solutions appear to be near. A significant percentage of problems is resolved before the threat is actually carried out.

In some cases, however, lack of progress and the impending harm will cause the leading government to conclude that it is necessary to carry out the threat. Initially, the trade restrictions are held to a moderate level, something proportional to the environmental harm in question. All the while, of course, the leading government continues to negotiate, hoping to obtain the voluntary cooperation of the recalcitrant governments so that the restrictions can be withdrawn.

Trade sanctions sometimes do create the extra incentive needed to bring about a solution. But not always. If not, the leading government will face a choice between impasse and escalation. The leading government will probably have legal authority to escalate (one or two U.S. laws actually seem to require escalation).[161] There will be fairly strong pressure not to escalate, however, for fear of triggering a total rupture in commercial relations. An indefinite state of impasse is another possible outcome, in which case at least the point will have been made and the leading government will at least not be participating in the harmful commerce.[162]

To date, the scenario has not occurred with great frequency. Only a very small number of unilateral trade restrictions have actually been imposed against foreign environmental practices. If one adds in the cases in which unilateral restrictions were seriously threatened, the number becomes somewhat larger, but remains fairly small.

On the whole, trade sanctions or the threat of sanctions appear to have succeeded quite often in producing some changes in government or private behavior, whole or partial.[163] Other threats have been less successful[164] In the long run, the outcome seems to depend on how much support the proposed environmental standard can command in the public at large, in all the countries involved. Given the relationship between strong public support and victory, it is always difficult to measure the actual effectiveness of trade sanctions themselves, for one can never know what would have happened to widely supported claims without such coercive measures. Nonetheless, it is clear that actual or threatened trade sanctions have produced movement in several cases where none seemed to be forthcoming at the time.

One of the key features of the standard scenario is the identity of the "leading government." The term "leading government" was meant to indicate that, as a practical matter, only a few GATT members have both the power and the inclination to make significant use of unilateral trade restrictions for environmental purposes. The only two frequent participants are the United States and the European Union. Indeed, only the United States seems to have a consistent interest in employing such measures. The European Union has taken a few celebrated unilateral measures on environmental matters, but in GATT it has taken a strong position against the GATT-legality of unilateral trade restrictions.[165] The singular interest of the United States in using this form of trade coercion is evidenced both by the number of instances in which it has employed such measures, as well as by the amount of U.S. legislation threatening, authorizing, and sometimes mandating the use of such coercion—a volume of legislation that no other government comes close to matching.[166]

As a consequence, when one considers the pros and cons of unilateral trade restrictions, one must always bear in mind that one is considering the pros and cons of deputizing the United States, and maybe the European Union, to act as an enforcer of environmental standards. While many U.S. commentators seem to have no problems with this idea, a less sanguine view is taken in other quarters.

3.5.2   The Size of the Problem

The importance of the legal debate over unilateral trade restrictions depends to a large degree on the number of times such measures are likely to be employed in the future. So far the volume has been fairly small. But it is only recently that environmental concerns have been able to command major political attention, and many of the laws providing for trade sanctions are relatively new. While the evidence does not all point in one direction, the possibility of a substantial increase in the number of unilateral environmental measures appears to be quite strong.

To be sure, the near unanimous opposition of GATT countries to unilateral trade measures should be a force for restraint. Moreover, unilateral trade restrictions against particular countries are a hostile act, and even the superpowers are reluctant to poison political relations unless they feel there is no choice. Government officials often reinforce the idea of restraint, uttering calming statements that action is likely to be taken in only a few cases.[167]

On the other hand, the U.S. Congress has authorized quite a wide range of restrictions, and keeps adding more authorizing laws every year. The statement of Executive Branch policy described earlier in this study promises to consider taking action whenever scientifically based international environmental standards are being "diminished" or whenever plant or animal species are "threatened."[168]

The politics of the situation lean in favor of expanded use. Once a government has decided to prevent its own nationals from performing certain practices thought to be environmentally harmful, there will be little political counterweight to environmentalist demands to extend such prohibitions to foreign producers. The scales will be tipped even further when there is a local tuna or shrimp fleet that stands to benefit by such measures. The likely scenario is not so much pure protectionism as it is protectionism coming to the aid of genuine but possibly far-reaching environmentalist demands.

The moral and emotional intensity that accompanies many "environmental" claims is a further element that tends to magnify the political power of those concerned. It is interesting to note that a quite high percentage of the coercive measures taken or threatened by the United States and the European Union so far have involved essentially moral objections to killing or mistreatment of animals—baby seals, dolphins, whales, leghold traps. Although these types of "environmental harm" are often quite some distance from the conventional justification for unilateral trade measures (the threat of serious, immediate, and irreversible harm to the global ecosystem), they now appear to have stronger political appeal than more conventional environmental concerns about harm to the ecosystem.

3.5.3   The Debate on the Merits

The arguments against the use of unilateral trade restrictions for environmental purposes are well known. Trade restrictions that can be imposed at the will of any one government obviously pose a threat to the value and reliability of GATT market-access commitments. Moreover, unlike trade restrictions authorized by international agreements, unilateral measures do not have even the pretense of international authority or international control. The government in question acts as prosecutor, judge, and executioner. Such measures are the antithesis of international legal order, in the same sense that vigilante justice is always treated as a form of lawlessness.

These undesirable qualities have been condemned repeatedly. As noted earlier, 39 of the 40 GATT governments that took a position on the unilateral restrictions in the two *Tuna/Dolphin* cases spoke in opposition to such measures. All of the governments represented at the 1992 Earth Summit signed a declaration that contained the following passage:

Unilateral actions to deal with environmental challenges outside the jurisdiction of the importing country should be avoided. Environmental measures addressing transboundary or global environmental problems should, as far as possible, be based on an international consensus.[169]

Most proponents of unilateral trade measures for environmental purposes readily acknowledge that multilateral solutions are better. They point out, however, that multilateral solutions are not always available. They assert that situations will arise in which serious environmental harm is about to occur, there is no more time to wait for agreed international action, and only coercive action by individual countries can stop the harm. At some level of seriousness, the argument runs, environmental harms are obviously more important than the costs of stopping them—the costs in terms of legal control and damage to the trading system.

Given a sufficient degree of seriousness, of irreparability, and of immediacy, most observers would probably agree on the justification for unilateral trade action. The real debate here is not whether, but when and how often.

Judging by the actions taken by the United States and the European Union to date, the standards of serious environmental harm followed by these governments are fairly broad—particularly in the area of animal protection. Critics would probably agree that genuine threats to species preservation are indeed serious harms, but they would argue that many of the actions taken by these governments involved no immediate threat to the species in question. For most critics, the cases in which unilateral action is actually justified are extremely rare. Indeed, as just noted, most GATT governments are prepared to start from the premise that unilateral trade restrictions are GATT-illegal.

The spectrum of pro and con opinions can be described by presenting a series of increasingly rigorous legal positions that might be taken toward unilateral trade measures for environmental purposes.

The National Security Precedent
The most liberal standard that might be adopted is simply no legal control at all. There is one GATT precedent for this type of legal status. Trade restrictions for certain kinds of "national security" purposes are authorized by Article XXI(b). The scope of Article XXI(b) has been expanded by GATT common law to virtually any trade restriction justified by the words "national security."[170] Moreover, GATT has arrived at a common-law understanding that bars any GATT review of the justification for such measures.[171] The explanation is that no government can accept GATT

supervision on what is or is not a threat to its security. In their more expansive moments, some environmentalists assert that environmental policy has—or should have—a similarly "untouchable" status.

The odd thing about the *carte blanche* authority granted on national security matters is that GATT and its system of reciprocal market-access commitments have managed to survive for almost 50 years in the face of this gaping hole in GATT legal protection. With only a few exceptions, the power to restrict imports has been used only in cases of a complete breakdown of political relations.[172] The United States employed import restrictions when political relations collapsed with Czechoslovakia, then with Cuba, and then with Nicaragua. The European Community, Canada, and Australia barred trade with Argentina during the Falkland Islands War. The Arab League boycott of Israel was another instance of a meltdown in political relations, as was Ghana's boycott against goods from Portugal. Finally, in 1991, before U.N. sanctions were created, the European Community withdrew trade concessions from the former Yugoslav Republic.

The two exceptions to the political-breakdown scenario were a long-standing U.S. restriction on oil and oil products in the decades before OPEC, and a short-lived Swedish restriction on shoes. It has been said that the GATT's only defense against protectionist abuse of Article XXI has been the power of collective laughter against obviously bogus claims. Laughter seems to have worked quite well, except for the U.S. oil restrictions.

It might be argued that GATT could also tolerate a *carte blanche* exception for unilateral environmental trade measures. If it were true, as governments often say, that unilateral restrictions would be imposed only rarely, that might be a viable answer.

As pointed out earlier, however, both the declared attitude of governments toward environmental trade sanctions and the political setting in which these issues are decided make expanded use of such sanctions more likely than not, especially if international restraints are removed. Moreover, there is no reason for GATT to take this risk. However powerful environmental claims may sometimes appear, there is simply no comparison to the power of national security issues. To the extent that national security is actually involved, no major country has ever had the political ability to subject its national security to third-party governance. And to the extent the problem is simply a deterioration in political relations, GATT governments have likewise been steadfast in the view that no international legal relationship between national governments can be maintained without a minimal base of civilized political relations. These are fundamental limitations upon international legal relations. Except, possibly, for the case of immediate and tangible physical harms from transborder pollution, environmental claims simply do not reach to this level.

The Preamble to GATT Article XX
Some commentators have suggested that the only limitations that should be imposed on the use of unilateral environmental measures are the two that are stated in the preamble to Article XX.[173] These are: (1) The injunction against measures which are a "disguised restriction on international trade," which prohibits measures that have a protectionist rather than a regulatory purpose. (2) The prohibition against arbitrary discrimination between countries in which the same conditions obtain.

The first criterion would screen out the case where the environmental problem is a trumped-up excuse. To that extent, it would take care of those critics who fear that unilateral environmental measures can be used for entirely economic purposes. But trade restrictions directed against foreign environmental practices are seldom lacking in genuine environmental concern. The proponents are usually genuinely interested in stopping whatever foreign practice is under attack, and they have usually demonstrated the genuineness of their concern by imposing the same restrictions against domestic producers. For example, the current U.S. policy to protect dolphins and other marine mammals rests on quite genuine concerns about the treatment of such animals, applied to U.S. citizens before any others. The main problem here is not pure protectionism, but an excess of zeal over what are essentially moral claims, an excess that is merely helped along by economic interests in search of protection against competition.

That, of course, is the point of a test limited to the "no-protectionism" standard. It is intended to grant governments broad legal authority to impose unilateral trade restrictions in support of whatever environmental policies they impose upon their own producers. It would provide a GATT blessing for virtually all the current U.S. legislation calling for unilateral trade restrictions in this area.

The second criterion in the Article XX preamble would address a genuine problem, because governments acting unilaterally are quite capable of applying environmental measures in a discriminatory manner that punishes enemies more harshly than friends.[174] This criterion would be rather difficult to apply, however, for it would be difficult to stimulate complaints. The complainant would have to be a country suffering trade restrictions because of its environmental behavior, seeking to prove that some other country was behaving no better. Discrimination of this kind is just one of the prices one would have to pay for allowing unilateral restrictions.

A "Serious-Harm" Exception

A commonly suggested solution is that, in addition to the Article XX prohibition against discrimination and "disguised restrictions on international trade," GATT would also require that unilateral trade measures be necessary to avert an environmental harm found to be "serious, immediate and irreparable."

A legal requirement of seriousness might well have some use in stimulating more vigorous domestic debate on these issues, but it would give GATT itself almost no foothold from which to criticize actions once taken. The issue of "seriousness" is essentially a normative question. Characterizing harms as "immediate" or "irreparable" also involve mixed value judgments. If such issues were adjudicated in GATT, the question will be whether the values of those who have acted are the same as those of the rest of the GATT community. As noted several times earlier, the GATT's mandate does not really run to making political value judgments about the seriousness or importance of environmental goals.

Once GATT is compelled to accept the characterization of a given environmental harm as "serious," it likewise has to accept the goal of stopping that harm as a legitimate objective. This being sò, the issue of "necessity" becomes a question of the means chosen to stop the harm. Since the harm by definition involves conduct outside the territory of the government taking the trade measures, the "necessity" issue once again boils down to just two alternative ways of influencing that foreign conduct—negotiation and trade coercion. In all cases that follow the standard scenario, some attempt at negotiation will have been made, and failed. It will be extremely difficult for a GATT tribunal to impose a conclusion that more negotiations will produce a solution, especially upon a government that has already concluded to the contrary.[175]

Could more effective legal discipline be achieved with a more detailed standard? Once again, the problem is that these are value judgments in an area in which GATT itself has little or no competence. It is difficult to imagine a GATT debate over whether, for example, particular animal protection claims are or are not matters of "serious" environmental harm. It is even more difficult to imagine GATT applying them in the face of a superpower decision to the contrary.

In sum, if GATT were to express something like a "serious, immediate and irreparable" standard, the standard might have some influence on internal government debate, but GATT would find it impossible to apply such a standard. If requiring some kind of seriousness threshold is a GATT objective, some other way of doing so will have to be found.

The Standard Suggested in Tuna/Dolphin II

The *Tuna/Dolphin II* decision offered an interpretation of GATT Article XX that would have permitted a fairly broad exception for unilateral environmental measures. In that decision, it will be recalled, the panel left open the possibility that Article XX(b) and/or Article XX(g) could be read to authorize the imposition of unilateral trade restrictions for the purpose of protecting against threats to life and health, or threats to conservation, that occurred elsewhere in the world. The dictum suggested, but did not say, that governments might be allowed to impose trade restrictions to protect the life of dolphins anywhere in the world, provided the trade restrictions applied directly to the trade of persons causing the harm to dolphins—for example, by restricting imports of fish caught by dolphin-unsafe methods. What the GATT prohibited, the ruling seemed to be saying, was trade restrictions applied to the trade of particular countries in order to coerce them into adopting a U.S.–type dolphin-protection policy.

The interpretation of Article XX suggested in *Tuna/Dolphin II* would end up authorizing a rather broad category of unilateral restrictions. In simple terms, it would allow an importing country to impose on foreign producers, anywhere in the world, any environmental requirement it is willing to impose against its own producers. The only limitations on that environmental policy would be: (1) It would have to fall within the subject matter categories of Article XX(b) or (g) (protecting life, health, or conservation) and (2) It would also have to comply with the preamble to Article XX—that is, it would have to be a genuine regulatory goal (a requirement easily met by applying the regulation to one's own producers) and could not discriminate arbitrarily. Any domestic animal-protection policy applicable to things like dolphins, whales, farm animals, or whatever would qualify. Article XX has never had any "seriousness" requirement.[176]

The Article XX "necessity" requirement would not do much to limit the exercise of this power. As pointed out several times before, negotiation and trade restrictions are the only two viable policy instruments that governments have at their disposal to accomplish the externally-directed policy, and almost every case will have some history of failed attempts to negotiate an answer.

The most significant limitation in the formula suggested in *Tuna/Dolphin II* (and it must be stressed that it is only a rather vague dictum) is the prohibition of direct coercion against other governments. Implicit in this prohibition is the requirement that the unilateral trade restriction must be limited to trade in the product actually associated with the environmental harm—fish caught by dolphin-killing methods, products whose manufacture or use causes depletion of the ozone layer, and so forth. A rule prohibiting coercion of other governments necessarily prohibits the use of trade sanctions imposed on "other" products for punitive effect. It would prohibit measures like the recent U.S. statute calling for an embargo on 40 percent of a country's entire fish exports to the United States for using dolphin-unsafe fishing methods.[177] The anti-coercion limitation is reminiscent of the EC's proposal limiting the kind of trade restrictions that would be allowed under the trade provisions of international environmental agreements.[178] Indeed, the panel ruling in *Tuna/Dolphin II* could well have been inspired by it.

The prohibition against direct coercion of governments has one advantage that a "seriousness" standard does not have. It is administrable. GATT does have the competence to draw the necessary distinction between trade measures that coerce environmentally-offending citizens and those that coerce governments. Judgments about the nature and effects of trade measures would involve no second-guessing of environmental policy judgments. So, however broad this standard may be in other respects, the limitation against direct coercion of governments will be enforceable.

Undoubtedly, the prohibition in *Tuna/Dolphin II* against direct coercion of governments would encounter objections in those cases where restrictions on the harm-causing products are ineffective to remove the practice complained of. But this is not necessarily fatal to its acceptability. GATT governments have been known to accept certain rules while silently (or not so silently) reserving the right to transgress them in an emergency.[179] Given a present situation in which many environmental-sanctions laws are in probable violation of GATT, this relatively smaller amount of legal friction would not necessarily bar acceptance.

Legal Prohibition as the Baseline: Tuna/Dolphin I
The alterative that promises the greatest legal control over unilateral trade restrictions is a rather complex piece of legal architecture that begins by reaffirming the legal prohibition of the *Tuna/Dolphin I* decision—the decision that outlaws all unilateral trade measures directed at environmental conduct outside the territory of the government imposing the restriction.

Reaffirming the *Tuna/Dolphin I* ruling would have the effect of channeling unilateral trade measures into a legal universe where measures must prove their justification by clearing one or more of three hurdles. (1) It must surmount its own government's aversion to violating GATT legal obligations—essentially by making a case that the threatened environmental problem is important enough to warrant civil disobedience. (2) It must succeed in obtaining a waiver under the new GATT/WTO waiver process in order to obtain short-term legal permission to use the measure. (3) In order to obtain long-term legal authority to employ such a measure, it must successfully negotiate an international environmental agreement establishing the desired environmental standard and authorizing trade remedies to enforce it.

Framing the issue, for purposes of the internal policy decision, in terms of "civil disobedience" is the most effective way to require a truly serious justification for unilateral trade action. In the normal case, justification will require a strong demonstration of genuinely serious, immediate, and irreversible environmental harm, and a persuasive case that coercion is needed to stop it. "Civil disobedience" would be an apt characterization of the relatively lawless character of unilateral trade measures.

Requesting a waiver through the new GATT/WTO waiver procedure would be an occasion for the trade-restricting government to lay out its justification for multilateral inspection—normally, an explanation of the terrible environmental consequences if nothing is done to stop the environmental practice in question. The waiver would not commit the GATT to permanent approval of the measures. It would be a temporary measure to deter harm pending negotiation of an international agreement.[180] The decision whether to grant the waiver, which requires a three-fourths vote, would not be a legal one. Governments are asked for a political judgment on the question of whether excuse is warranted. The political debate would probably still focus on issues of seriousness and necessity, but the judgment would be discretionary, and the burden of persuasion would be on the party seeking the waiver. Given the size and power of the United States and the European Union, the two most likely claimants, the process would not be as one sided as the three-fourths requirement might suggest.

An agreement to open negotiations looking toward a long-term solution could enter the picture as a condition to a waiver, but most governments imposing unilateral measures begin by affirming their willingness to search for a negotiated solution (on their terms, of course). Any government that claims a principled justification for taking the law into one's own hands will invariably do so anyway.

The first objection to adopting this legal approach to unilateral trade measures would be that it is simply politically impossible. Viewed from within the United States, it certainly seems that way; the U.S. Congress has made a rather large investment in legislation that authorizes or requires unilateral environmental measures. While it is never prudent to minimize the problem of changing U.S. behavior, and especially when

Washington is convinced of its righteousness, the fact remains that the United States is isolated on this issue. Every other GATT member country that has announced a position on the ruling in *Tuna/Dolphin I* has supported the panel's conclusion that the unilateral environmental measures in that case were GATT-illegal.[181] If this nearly unanimous legal position proves to be a durable consensus, and if its proponents pursue their views with conviction, a change in the U.S. position would not be completely out of the question. The decision could take the form of a decision by the Executive Branch acceding to a legal ruling, noting that as a practical matter the door would always be open, for a price, to use the congressionally mandated powers in cases of genuinely serious environmental harms.[182]

Another similar objection is the possibility that governments would not be able to live up to these rules even if they did adopt them. It would not be necessary, of course, that every unilateral environmental measure that a government decides upon be approved by GATT. A government can legitimately decide that the rest of the world is wrong, that it is justified in standing firm on the need for trade action, and that it will just have to pay the price (retaliation) of its convictions. That much flexibility is built into all GATT law. But the legal system would crack if, repeatedly, one action after another ended in such impasse. The reason for worrying about this policy is that, on the record to date, governments have shown a tendency to use coercion over highly emotional but environmentally marginal causes.

It is probably too early to tell whether the political attitudes behind present environmental laws and measures will continue to be as forceful as they seem to be today, or whether longer exposure to the process of international debate will produce political counterweights that will restrain them to some extent. Consequently, it would be premature to reject the possibility of a legal approach based on the rigorous rule of *Tuna/Dolphin I*. Given the alternatives, it is fair to conclude that that rule offers the shortest and most sustainable legal approach to really effective legal discipline over unilateral trade restriction. It would be worth taking a little more time to test its ultimate viability.

3.5.4   Employing Unilateral Trade Restrictions to Enforce Environmental Agreements

As noted earlier in this study, the GATT's own trade-and-environment study is giving separate consideration to international agreements that contain trade provisions—provisions expressly authorizing the use of trade restrictions to achieve the goals of the agreement.[183] The tacit premise of the GATT study has been that GATT law should probably be adjusted to accommodate trade restrictions taken under the authority of such trade provisions, provided the agreement meets certain conditions of representativeness and fairness. The analysis in section 3.4 of this chapter supported the general case for GATT acceptance of such trade measures.

The category of authorized trade measures may well extend to some instances in which, although the international agreement itself contains no explicit trade provision, it does contain governance provisions, and the governing body of the agreement issues a decision calling for trade measures. This will be a troublesome grey area.

But several U.S. laws provide for trade restrictions in support of international agreements that have neither trade provisions or other forms of multilateral approval. The chief example is the Pelly Amendment, which authorizes restrictions against conduct which "diminishes the effectiveness" of fisheries and wildlife agreements.[184] The same formula is employed in the recent statement by the Clinton Administration about its policy toward the use of environmental trade measures.[185] Environmental advocates frequently argue for granting a special class of GATT legal authorization for trade measures of this kind.[186]

In essence, the issue being raised here is whether GATT law should extend the same (or similar) systematic legal recognition to trade restrictions taken in support of *any* international environmental agreement, even though the agreement contains no express authorization of such trade measures. Should GATT authorize this special class of unilateral measure, whatever the legal status of other unilateral measures?

It is possible that such a power may exist as a matter of general international law. Unless the international environmental agreement in question is wholly hortatory, it will represent legal commitments between all the signatories. If one signatory breaches the obligations of the agreement, and if the agreement contains no authoritative legal decision-making process, in theory each member government has the right to take unilateral remedies against that breach. These remedies may include the withholding of legal obligations, in proportion to the breach. In theory, this could conceivably involve withholding application of separate trade agreement obligations.

Governments would probably consider trade retaliation if the breach of legal obligation were a serious international tort such as occurred in the *Trail Smelter* case. But as a general remedy for nonperformance in the very large number of international environmental agreements without trade provisions, such a theory would be highly problematic.

It is most unlikely that governments entering such agreements expect and understand that they are handing every other signatory government the power to judge their conduct and impose trade restrictions in return. They would naturally expect any aggrieved party to be released from reciprocal obligations under the same agreement, but the use of other more coercive sanctions would not be taken for granted. The absence of a trade provision is significant in this regard. Governments do not just forget to talk about such things. Even if a significant number of signatories had wanted trade sanctions in the agreement, the fact that they eventually settled for an agreement without trade sanctions is as much a consciously agreed decision as if it had been decided unanimously in the first instance.

In actual international practice, the decision to decline the use of coercive sanctions is quite common. However "outmoded" traditional concepts of national sovereignty may be, it is still fact that governments dealing with each other in international agreements prefer to proceed on a cooperative basis, respecting each government's autonomy, and trusting in each government's respect for legal obligations and for community consensus. Not only are noncoercive agreements widely used, but there is actually a widespread belief in the efficacy of such agreements.[187]

To be sure, the noncoercive approach to these problems involves a considerably longer time frame than the time parameters set by environmental groups. It is worth remembering, however, that haste can make matters worse rather than better. If Step One—an agreement in principle— will automatically lead to GATT-legal trade sanctions against noncomplying countries, it is quite likely that fewer governments are going to be willing to take Step One in the first place.

In weighing the respect that should be given to a negotiating decision not to authorize sanctions, it is well to remember that one factor that weighs heavily in government positions on this issue is the knowledge that the practical effect of a trade sanctions provision will be to grant a license to the United States (and maybe the European Union) to operate as the policeman who will enforce the agreement. Neither leading government is likely to use such policing powers with complete impartiality.[188] Countries considering granting such a hunting license to the United States or European Union understand that it is not easy to control these biases. It is not hard to see why governments would decline the offer of such an enforcement instrument.

Consequently, the mere fact that an international agreement establishes certain environmental norms or obligations should not be viewed as constituting legal authorization of trade sanctions. To call such unilateral trade measures a tool of "legal enforcement" is a serious misnomer. To the contrary, it would be imposing sanctions where none were intended.

3.5.5   A Concluding Thought about the Debate

Proposals calling for GATT to legitimate the use of externally-directed trade restrictions usually rest upon a perception that the world needs to change its environmental behavior—more rapidly and more radically than most governments are willing to contemplate. The call for trade sanctions is a demand to apply greater coercive power in support of the demand for change.

There is fairly broad agreement about the use of coercive power when it is authorized by international environmental agreements. The GATT's main function with regard to trade sanctions of this kind is to make certain that the costs of such measures to the GATT trading system are understood and carefully considered in the negotiating process leading up to international environmental agreements.

There is also a fair measure of agreement about the need for at least some unilateral trade sanctions to promote change. Most observers would concede that there will be situations in which multilateral negotiation will be unable to halt an immediate threat of serious and irreparable environmental harm, and that unilateral use of coercive power in that situation can be better than doing nothing.

A great difference of opinion exists, however, over the size of the need for unilateral coercive measures, and the overall approach to be taken to them. The environmentalist side seems to begin with a belief that there is a need for very broad change in environmental behavior, and that the changes that can be wrought by agreed multilateral instruments fall quite a bit short of what is needed. In their view, it falls to individual governments to make up the shortfall. Since change is needed on a large number of fronts, individual governments must have fairly broad freedom to create pressures for such change. Viewed from this perspective, unilateral trade measures are seen as a positive contribution to international welfare, to be applauded rather than punished. Proponents of such measures acknowledge that they may work a radical change in the existing international system, but they answer that environmental problems cannot be solved in time by the existing system.

The opposing point of view, largely from the trade policy side, perceives a smaller list of environmental problems that should be classified as urgent, and is more skeptical of the feasibility of conducting international relations through such coercive measures. The opposing view regards the environmentalists' belief in the viability of such coercive measures as a somewhat naive extension of the assumptions of domestic legal policy— the assumptions that state power can supply a coercive solution to every major problem. Instead, the opposing view regards the need to use coercive power upon other governments as an ugly and very costly necessity— something to be used only when necessary to avoid a truly serious harm.

The difference is illustrated by the GATT's experience in dealing with a similar situation in the 1980s. In the early 1980s, it became clear to the United States that the political commitment to trade liberalization was being undermined by the inadequacy of international legal protection for certain kinds of economic transactions. Efforts to negotiate an improved GATT were initially rebuffed. Then, as the political situation continued to deteriorate, the United States concluded that unilateral measures had to be used to bring other governments to the table. In retrospect, the U.S. perception of the problem has been widely credited, and the unilateral U.S. trade measures in response have generally been recognized as having made a positive contribution to a negotiated solution.

Despite the acknowledged utility of the U.S. trade measures, the GATT never made any move to legalize such action. To the contrary, the Uruguay Round agreements created a stronger dispute settlement system designed to make it harder to get away with such unilateralism in the future. The U.S. action may have been condoned privately as a necessary response to an ugly situation, but GATT never even considered making such action into a sacrament. Most GATT participants appear to feel the same way about unilateral environmental measures.

In the end, a certain part of the distance between the two positions is probably irreducible, because it rests on a difference in values towards things such as animal suffering. Another part may be due to stubbornly different degrees of risk aversion, manifested in differing degrees of commitment to the precautionary principle. Each side tends to believe, however, that the other is to some degree rooted in error, one insufficiently informed about environmental problems, and the other too naive about international relations. If one or both are right, there will be reason to hope that further discourse will narrow the distance.

NOTES

Robert E. Hudec is the Melvin C. Steen Professor of Law, University of Minnesota.

1. On domestic environmental regulations, see the article by Daniel A. Farber and Robert E. Hudec, at Chapter 2 in this volume. On level-playing-field issues, see the article by Ronald A. Cass and Richard D. Boltuck, at Chapter 8 in this volume.

2. Some regulations addressed to external behavior are nonetheless considered domestic regulation, because they are directed to preventing purely internal harms. The most common example is the requirement that imported meat products have been processed in an approved slaughterhouse—a regulation directed to protection of domestic consumers.

3. To date, the most thorough analysis of these and other differences in degree is found in Steve Charnovitz, *A Taxonomy of Environmental Trade Measures*, 6 GEORGETOWN INT'L ENVIR'L L. REV. 1–46 (1993).

4. One reliable indicator of the general concern that attends trade measures with a conspicuous degree of external focus is the effort expended by environmental advocates to claim a tangible *domestic* impact for whatever foreign environmental harms they wish to regulate. Thus, we find that the term "spillover" has been stretched out of shape to make such claims. The term was originally used to describe pollution that physically moves from the offending country into the territory of the complaining country. Now it has grown to include the concept of "psychological spillover," a way of claiming that moral distress over death and mistreatment of animals in other parts of the world causes the same kind of "internal" harm as physical harm to one's own territory, and thus is equally deserving of redress. A similar claim of "internal" harm underlies the term "political spillover," recently coined to describe the anti-environmentalist objections that local producers tend to make when they are forced to compete with producers in other countries with lower environmental standards.

5. Convention on International Trade in Endangered Species of Wild Fauna and Flora, *opened for signature* Mar. 3, 1973, 993 U.N.T.S. 243, 27 U.S.T. 1087, T.I.A.S. No. 8249 [hereinafter CITES]. CITES seeks to regulate trade in wildlife through the use of a three-tier classification schedule which accords varying levels of protection to species based on the species' threat of extinction. Appendix I provides the greatest amount of protection. It lists species currently threatened by extinction, prohibits all commercial trade in such species, and allows no noncommercial trade without the prior grant of a permit by both the importing and exporting states certifying "exceptional" circumstances. *Id.* arts. II(1), III(3)c. Less strict import/export rules apply to Appendix II species which, while not currently threatened by extinction, "may become so unless trade in specimens of such species is subject to strict regulation." *Id.* art. II(2)(a). Appendix III provides parties with an opportunity to list species within their own jurisdiction which they feel need to be regulated in order to avoid exploitation. *Id.* art. II(3). Trade under Appendixes II and III requires only a permit from the exporting country certifying that exports will not be detrimental to the survival of the species, and with such permits can include commercial trade. *See generally* DAVID S. FAVRE, INTERNATIONAL TRADE IN ENDANGERED SPECIES: A GUIDE TO CITES (1989).

CITES does not require the parties to use specific measures to enforce the convention. Rather, it requires that:

The Parties shall take appropriate measures to enforce the provisions of the present Convention and to prohibit the trade in specimens in violation thereof: [including] a) to penalize trade in, or possession of, such specimens, or both....

CITES, art. VIII(1). It is up to the parties to determine what these "appropriate measures" will be.

6. Montreal Protocol on Substances That Deplete the Ozone Layer, *opened for signature* Sept. 16, 1987, S. Treaty Doc. No. 10, 100th Cong., 1st Sess. (1987), reprinted in 26 INT'L LEG. MAT. 1550 (1987), *amended and adjusted* S. Treaty Doc. No. 4, 102d Cong., 1st Sess. (1991), reprinted in 30 INT'L LEG. MAT. 537 (1991) (entered into force Jan. 1, 1989).

7. *Id.* art. 4.4.

8. *Id.* art. 4.8.

9. Basel Convention on the Control of Transboundary Movements of Hazardous Wastes and Their Disposal, *opened for signature* Mar. 22, 1989, reprinted in 28 INT'L LEG. MAT. 649 (1989). More specifically, the Basel Convention recognizes a party's right to prohibit the import of hazardous wastes, so long as it notifies the other parties. *Id.* art. 4.1(a). In addition, the Convention preamble acknowledges that a state has a sovereign right to "ban the entry or disposal of foreign hazardous wastes in its territory."

10. Article 4.5 prohibits parties from exporting hazardous wastes to, or importing hazardous wastes from, a nonparty, but article 11.1 permits such trade pursuant to bilateral agreements conforming to the management principles of the Convention.

11. Convention for the Prohibition of Fishing with Long Driftnets in the South Pacific, Nov. 24, 1989, entered into force May 17, 1991 [Wellington Convention], reprinted in 29 INT'L LEG. MAT. 1449 (1990). Article 3, paragraph 2 states:

Each party may also take measures consistent with international law to:

a) prohibit the landing of driftnet catches within its territory;

. . . .

c) prohibit the importation of any fish or fish product, whether processed or not, which was caught using a driftnet.

12. GATT Doc. TRE/W/1/Rev.1 (Oct. 14, 1993).

13. U.S. INT'L TRADE COMM'N, INTERNATIONAL AGREEMENTS TO PROTECT THE ENVIRONMENT AND WILDLIFE, Publ. No. 2351 (1991), at 5-1 to 5-2. The Commission survey identified 170 international environmental agreements, multilateral and bilateral, of significance to the United States.

14. Steve Charnovitz, *Environmental Trade Sanctions and the GATT: An Analysis of the Pelly Amendment on Foreign Environmental Practices*, 9 AMERICAN UNIV. J. INT'L L. & POL'Y 751, 769–71 (1994). Charnovitz expresses some doubt as to the treaty's authority for such actions. One possibility is the provision in CITES Article VIII (1) calling upon parties to "take appropriate measures to enforce the provisions of the present Convention." For other examples of similar CITES actions, see Charnovitz, *Taxonomy*, note 3 above, at 26–27.

15. *See* Charnovitz, *Taxonomy*, note 3 above, at 19.

16. To measure the exact legal dimensions of such collective decisions, one would have to consider, on the one side, the rights of dissenting governments and, on the other, the extent to which such decisions can be regarded as equivalent to amendments of the agreement. Neither the agreements in question nor their administration are noted for clarity on these issues—a form of uncertainty that should be familiar to analysts of GATT legal structure.

17. For a discussion of the principles of *lex posterior* and *lex specialis* under which such a waiver would probably be found, see text accompanying notes 121–123 below.

18. 16 U.S.C. § 3372.

19. For a good overview of most of the key provisions, see Ted L. McDorman, *The GATT Consistency of U.S. Fish Import Embargoes to Stop Driftnet Fishing and Save Whales, Dolphins and Turtles*, 24 GEORGE WASH. J. INT'L L. & ECON. 477–525 (1991).

20. Endangered Species Act of 1973, Pub. L. No. 93-205, 87 Stat. 884 (codified as amended at 16 U.S.C. §§ 1531–1543 (1988)). *See in particular* 16 U.S.C. § 1538(1)(A).

21. 16 U.S.C. § 1538(1).

22. Such authority was used to bar wildlife imports from Singapore when Singapore, then a nonmember, was found not to be complying with CITES documentation requirements. 51 Fed. Reg. 34, 159 (1986).

23. Pelly Amendment to the Fishermen's Protective Act of 1967, Pub. L. No. 92-219, 85 Stat. 786 (1971) (codified at 22 U.S.C. § 1978(a)(1) (1988)).

24. Act of Sept. 18, 1978, Pub. L. No. 95-376, 92 Stat. 714 (codified at 22 U.S.C. § 1978(a)(4) (1988)). The activity that triggers the wildlife provisions is "engaging in trade or taking which diminishes the effectiveness of any international program for endangered or threatened species."

25. 22 U.S.C. § 1978(a)(4) (Supp. 1994). Recent GATT panel decisions, as yet unadopted, have interpreted GATT obligations to prohibit many of the trade restrictions authorized by the Pelly Amendment. *See* text accompanying notes 106–113 below. So far, however, the Executive Branch has seemed to be little affected by the GATT consistency clause when threatening action under the Act. The one trade measure actually imposed so far was imposed against Taiwan, not yet a GATT member.

26. Certification is a formal finding that a government's conduct qualifies for trade restrictions under the Pelly Amendment. For a comprehensive review of Pelly Amendment certifications, see Charnovitz, *Environmental Trade Sanctions*, note 14 above.

27. *President Clinton Announces Sanctions on Taiwan for Rhino, Tiger Parts Trade*, 11 Int'l Trade Rep. (BNA) 576 (1994). The sanctions took effect August 19, 1994.

28. The trade restrictions authority in the Pelly Amendment was expanded to all products by the High Seas Driftnet Fisheries Enforcement Act, Pub. L. No. 102-582, 106 Stat. 4900, 4904 (1992) (codified at 22 U.S.C. § 1978(a)(4) (Supp. 1994)).

29. 59 Fed. Reg. 22,043 (Apr. 28, 1994). The import ban covered the following major categories of wildlife and wildlife parts and products from Taiwan:

(1) reptile leather shoes, handbags, etc.;

(2) jewelry made from coral, mussel shells, and bone;

(3) edible frogs' legs;

(4) live goldfish and tropical fish for the aquarium trade;

(5) bird feathers, down, and specimens.

30. International Convention for the Regulation of Whaling, *opened for signature* Dec. 2, 1946, 161 U.N.T.S. 72. For an account of the many other threats of trade action that had been employed to induce membership in the ICRW and cooperation with IWC resolutions, see McDorman, note 19 above.

31. *Commerce Notifies President That Norway's Resumption of Whaling Is Basis for Embargo*, 10 Int'l Trade Rep. (BNA) 1358 (1993).

32. *See* Clay Erik Hawes, *Norwegian Whaling and the Pelly Amendment: A Misguided Attempt at Conservation*, 3 MINNESOTA J. GLOBAL TRADE 97 (1994).

33. *President Clinton Delays Whaling Sanctions on Norway*, 10 Int'l Trade Rep. (BNA) 1678 (1993).

34. *Id.*

35. *U.S. Wants to Study Norway's Whaling Plan*, THE RECORD, June 9, 1994, *available in* LEXIS, News Library, Allnws File. *See generally* Mari Skare, *Whaling: A Sustainable Use of Natural Resources or a Violation of Animal Rights?*, 36 ENVIRONMENT, Sept. 1994, at 12.

36. 16 U.S.C. § 1821(e)(2)(A)(i).

37. Rhinoceros and Tiger Conservation Act of 1994, H.R. 3987, S. 1925, 103d Cong., 2d Sess. (1994). The bill was later withdrawn following application of sanctions to Taiwan under the general authority of the Pelly Amendment.

38. High Seas Driftnet Fisheries Enforcement Act, Pub. L. No. 102-582, § 101(b), 106 Stat. 4900, 4902, 16 U.S.C. § 1826a(b) (Supp. 1992). Introduction of this legislation in 1991 was widely credited with persuading Japan to agree to a moratorium on large-scale driftnetting. *See* Carol Emert, *U.S. Lawmakers Claim Credit for Japan's Ban on Driftnetting*, States News Service, Nov. 26, 1991, *available in* LEXIS, News Library, Allnws File.

39. Wellington Convention, note 11 above. As pointed out in note 11 above, the Wellington Convention authorizes members to impose trade sanctions, but does not mandate them.

40. *See Japan Fishery Group Warns of Retaliation if U.S. Action on Driftnets 'Unjustified'*, 8 Int'l Trade Rep. (BNA) 1464 (1991). The Act also requires the Secretary of Commerce to deny driftnetting vessels from countries engaged in large-scale driftnetting activity access to any U.S. port for refueling and resupplying. *See* David J. Ross, Note, Making GATT Dolphin-Safe: Trade and the Environment, 2 DUKE J. COMP. & INT'L L. 345 (1992).

41. Pub. L. No. 92-522, 86 Stat. 1027 (codified as amended at 16 U.S.C. §§ 1361–1407).

42. *See* United States—Restrictions on Imports of Tuna, GATT Basic Instruments and Selected Documents [hereinafter BISD] 39th Supp. 155 (1993) (Report of the Panel) [hereinafter *Tuna/Dolphin I*]. For an account of the evolution of the MMPA provisions involved in the case, including the many previous tuna embargoes, see McDorman, note 19 above, at 490–95.

43. 16 U.S.C. § 1372(c)(1)(B).

44. International Dolphin Conservation Act of 1992, Pub. L. No. 102-523, 106 Stat. 3425 (codified at 16 U.S.C. §§ 1411–1417 (Supp. 1992).

45. 16 U.S.C. § 1415(b)(1).

46. 16 U.S.C. § 1415(b)(2).

47. 16 U.S.C. § 1417. The law defines "dolphin safe" to exclude any tuna caught by either driftnets or by purse seine nets encircling dolphins or other marine mammals.

48. Pub. L. No. 101-162, 103 Stat, 988, 1037 (1989) (codified at 16 U.S.C. § 1537). This legislation arose after U.S. domestic shrimp fishermen complained that a 1987 U.S. regula-

tion (50 C.F.R. § 227.72(e)(ii)(2) (1992)) requiring turtle excluder devices gave foreign producers a competitive advantage.

49. The statute exempts countries who maintain regulatory programs similar to the United States program, and who have incidental taking rates comparable to those of the U.S. fleet.

50. 58 Fed. Reg. 28,428 (1993). *See* Charnovitz, *Taxonomy*, note 3 above, at 30–31.

51. 58 Fed. Reg. 30,082 & 40,685 (1993).

52. *See* David E. Sanger, *Japan, Backing Down, Plans Bar on Rare Turtle Import*, N.Y. TIMES, June 20, 1991, at D6.

53. Mention might be made of the following laws with similar characteristics:

The Antarctic Marine Living Resources Convention Act, 16 U.S.C.A. § 2435 (West Supp. 1992), which prohibits import or export of any living resource harvested in violation of the Convention;

The African Elephant Conservation Act (16 U.S.C. § 4221), which restricts the importation of African elephant ivory;

The Wild Bird Conservation Act of 1992 (16 U.S.C. § 4901), which bans the importation of birds taken from the wild in tropical countries.

54. A notable exception, of course, is the trade sanctions provision of the Marine Mammal Protection Act, which required the Secretary of Commerce to impose sanctions; the requirement was enforced by a judicial order obtained by a private environmental interest group. *See Earth Island Inst. v. Mosbacher*, 929 F. 2d 1449 (9th Cir. 1991).

55. Testimony before the Subcomm. on Foreign Commerce and Tourism of the Senate Comm. on Commerce, Science and Transportation, 103d Cong., 2d Sess. (1994) (statement of the Honorable Timothy E. Wirth, Counselor, Department of State).

56. One other area of U.S. national law with a strong concentration of trade measures directed at improving foreign practice is the area of toxic substances. These are the somewhat more benign laws, however. They refuse to allow export of dangerous substances, or drugs, that may pose a health problem to the recipient country. Examples are the Toxic Substances Control Act, 15 U.S.C. § 2611; the Federal Insecticide, Fungicide and Rodenticide Act (FIFRA), 7 U.S.C. § 136; the Drug Export Act of 1986, 21 U.S.C. § 382(b)(4); the Export Administration Act, 50 U.S.C. app. § 2402(13). *See generally* Peter Lallas, Daniel Esty, & David van Hoogstraten, *Environmental Protection and International Trade: Toward Mutually Supportive Rules and Policies*, 16 HARVARD ENVIR'L L. REV. 271–341, at 298–301 (1992).

Trade restrictions dealing with hazardous wastes fall into the same category. *See, e.g.*, 42 U.S.C. § 6938 (1938).

57. Part of the difference is due, no doubt, to the fact that authorizing legislation is an important medium for transmitting policy initiatives from the U.S. Congress to the Executive Branch, whereas in parliamentary governments the legislators do not need to use such formal messages to communicate with the executive.

58. Charles Clover, *Fury Over Norway's Whaling Defiance*, DAILY TELEGRAPH, June 8, 1994, *available in* LEXIS, News Library, Allnws File.

59. *Australia Protests at Norwegian Whaling Decision*, Reuters, June 14, 1994, *available in* LEXIS, News Library, Allnws File.

60. Driftnet Prohibition Act 1991 § 8, reprinted in 31 INT'L LEG. MAT. 218 (1992).

61. Fish Council: EU Ministers' Letter Condemns Canadian Fishing Ban, EUROPEAN REPORT, June 14, 1994, *available in* LEXIS, News Library, Allnws file.

62. Council Regulation 92/3034, 1992 O.J. (L 307). The Regulation states: "It shall be prohibited to undertake encirclements with purse seines on schools or groups of marine mammals when aiming to catch tuna or other species of fish."

63. *EC Acts on Pledge to Save Dolphins*, PR Newswire, Oct. 19, 1992, *available in* LEXIS, News Library, Allnws File.

64. *See* GATT Doc. L/5940 (Dec. 19, 1985), described in ROBERT E. HUDEC, ENFORCING INTERNATIONAL TRADE LAW: THE EVOLUTION OF THE MODERN GATT LEGAL SYSTEM (1993) at 529.

65. Council Regulation 91/3254, 1991 O.J. (L 308). The regulation also bars internal EU use of leghold traps. Countries that do not prohibit leghold traps can avoid the import ban if it is found that their "trapping methods meet internationally agreed humane trapping standards."

66. These 13 species are: beaver, otter, coyote, wolf, lynx, bobcat, sable, raccoon, muskrat, fisher, badger, marten, and ermine. *Id.* Annex I. The ban is imposed country by country; once a country is listed, there do not appear to be any exceptions for pelts of the above 13 animals caught by approved traps or raised on a fur ranch.

67. U.S. TRADE REPRESENTATIVE, 1994 NATIONAL TRADE ESTIMATE REPORT ON FOREIGN TRADE BARRIERS 79 (1994). For a comparable U.S. statute, see the Meat Inspection Act, 21 U.S.C. § 620(a), requiring that all meat imports comply with the standards of the Humane Slaughter Act, 7 U.S.C. §§ 1901–1906.

68. *See* GATT Doc. DS51/1 (Apr. 6, 1994).

69. Vogelwet, Dec. 31, 1936, art. 7 (bans the import of all wild birds not listed in the Jachtwet (Law on Hunting)).

70. Criminal Proceedings Against Gourmetterie Van den Burg, Case C-169/89, para. I-2143 (1990) [hereinafter Van den Burg]. The complaint challenged the law as a violation of the EC Council Directive on the Conservation of Wild Birds, 79/409, 1979 O.J. (L 103) 1.

71. Van den Burg, note 70 above, at 2149.

72. *Id.* at 2153.

73. Council Directive 93/35, 1993 O.J. (L 151).

74. Tara Patel, *French May Eat Indonesia Out of Frogs; Exports May Lead to Frog Extinction*, NEW SCIENTIST, Apr. 10, 1993, *available in* LEXIS, News Library, Allnws File.

75. Ernst-Ulrich Petersmann, *Settlement of International Environmental Disputes in GATT and the EC: Comparative Legal Aspects, in* TOWARDS MORE EFFECTIVE SUPERVISION BY INTERNATIONAL ORGANIZATIONS 165, 172 (Niels Blokker & Sam Muller, eds., 1994).
India banned the export of frogs from its borders in 1987 when it realized the frogs' decline in India had caused an unacceptable increase in the insect population. Patel, note 74 above.

76. Inigo Gilmore, *Ostrich Trade Faces Losses After British Meat Ban*, THE TIMES, July 4, 1994, at 15.

77. Council Directive 88/166, 1988 O.J. 74.

78. Swiss Act on Animal Welfare and Regulations (1981); Swedish Animal Protection Ordinance, SFS 1988:539. According to officials at the Swedish Embassy in Washington, DC who were interviewed, Sweden also plans to ban the importation of chicken meat from chickens raised in cages, but not the importation of eggs produced by chickens raised in cages.

79. Animal Protection Ordinance, S.F.S. 1988:539. Some of the provisions include: cattle are entitled to be put out to graze; sows are not to be tethered and must be provided with sufficient room to move; cows and pigs must have access to straw and litter in stalls and boxes; slaughtering of animals must be as humane as possible; and certain animals are not to be exhibited at circuses.

80. S. 59, 102d Cong., 1st Sess. (1991). *See* 4 GEORGETOWN INT'L ENVIR'L L. REV. 421, 428 (1992). The bill was not enacted or reintroduced.

81. S. 59, 102d Cong., 1st Sess. § 5 (1991).

82. 137 Cong. Rec. at S13,169. *See also* Ross, note 40 above, at 361. Senator Baucus cites driftnet fishing as an example of a practice that violates international norms.

83. H.R. 2519, 101st Cong., 1st Sess. (1989).

84. H.R. 4563, 101st Cong., 2d Sess. (1990).

85. H.R. 1955, 103d Cong., 1st Sess. (1993).

86. H. Con. Res. 169, 103d Cong., 1st Sess. (1993).

87. H.R. 4710, 103d Cong., 2d Sess. (1994).

88. The Trade Agreements Act of 1934, 48 Stat. 943, launched the U.S. trade agreements program that eventually led to GATT. The '34 Act remained in force more or less continuously from 1934 to 1961, as a result of successive legislative extensions in 1937, 1940, 1943, 1945, 1948, 1949, 1951, 1953, 1954, 1955, and 1958. The extension enactments are collected in John H. Jackson, *The General Agreement on Tariffs and Trade in United States Domestic Law*, 66 MICHIGAN L. REV. 249, 332, app. D (1967). The same negotiating authority was then enacted in the three major negotiating-authority laws since 1962. Trade Expansion Act of 1962, 76 Stat. 872; Trade Act of 1974, 88 Stat. 1978 (1975); Omnibus Trade and Competitiveness Act of 1988, 102 Stat. 1121. The two strongest Congressional endorsements of GATT have been the Trade Agreements Act of 1979 ratifying the results of the Tokyo Round, 93 Stat. 144, and the 1994 Uruguay Round Agreements Act ratifying the results of the Uruguay Round and the creation of the World Trade Organization, 108 Stat. 4809.

89. U.N. Doc. E/PC/T/A/PV/6 at 5 (meeting of June 2, 1947).

90. *The United States v. Canada* (the Trail Smelter arbitration), *in* 3 UNITED NATIONS REPORTS OF INTERNATIONAL ARBITRAL AWARDS at 1938 (1941).

91. This is not to say that governments do not dispute the facts in such cases, drag their feet about correcting such situations, or sometimes demand compensation for ceasing the offending activity.

92. For a comprehensive review of the use of trade sanctions for political matters, see 1 & 2 GARY C. HUFBAUER, JEFFREY J. SCHOTT, & KIMBERLY A. ELLIOTT, ECONOMIC SANCTIONS RECONSIDERED (2nd ed. 1990).

93. There were 139 valid legal complaints during this period; the 123 successes represented an 89% success rate. Robert E. Hudec, ENFORCING INTERNATIONAL TRADE LAW: THE EVOLUTION OF THE MODERN GATT LEGAL SYSTEM 285, table 11.6 (1993). The one instance of retaliation occurred in a 1952 legal proceeding by Netherlands against the United States. *Id.* at 425–26.

94. The legal reforms of the recent Uruguay Round negotiations conveyed a somewhat different message, because, largely at the insistence of the United States, one key target of the legal reform was the upgrading of the GATT's retaliation machinery, making it work rapidly and automatically. It is clear that politicians in Washington believed this was a key to a successful legal system. The most likely outcome, however, is that GATT law will continue to rely on the things that have made it successful in the past, so that it will continue to rely on community pressure as the primary—indeed, almost exclusive—form of enforcement.

95. This category of quasi-sanction is discussed in Robert E. Hudec, *Retaliation Against "Unreasonable" Foreign Trade Practices: The New Section 301 and GATT Nullification and Impairment*, 59 MINNESOTA L. REV. 461, 507–10 (1975).

96. The exception was the 1963 U.S. retaliation against the European Community known as the "Chicken War." *See* Andreas F. Lowenfeld, *"Doing Unto Others..."—The Chicken War Ten Years After*, 4 J. MARITIME L. & COM. 599 (1973).

97. *See* Hudec, ENFORCING INTERNATIONAL TRADE LAW, note 93 above, at 203–06, 222–34.

98. To be sure, GATT law does allow unilateral compensatory action under Articles XIX:3 and XXVIII:3, as well as unilateral antidumping or countervailing duty action under Article VI. Article XXI national security actions might also be mentioned. None of these actions, however, involves sanctions for violation of GATT norms.

99. Understanding on Rules and Procedures Governing the Settlement of Disputes, *in* Final Act Embodying the Results of the Uruguay Round of Multilateral Trade Negotiations, April 15, 1994 (done at Marrakesh) [hereinafter 1994 Uruguay Round Final Act]. Article 23 of the Understanding is the explicit anti-unilateralism provision.

100. Since the essential reciprocity of any trade agreement is established by an exchange of market opportunities in different products, steel for ribbons, it is only natural that trade measures to restore reciprocity should employ the same freedom of product selection. Thus, there are no limits on the choice of product on which retaliation may be imposed.

101. Conceptually, it is possible that a trade restriction will be motivated solely by a desire to protect one's own citizens from the moral discomfort of lending commercial support for the harm-causing activity. Trade restrictions for this limited purpose are discussed in the literature, but their actual occurrence is likely to be extremely rare. Measures which are intended to satisfy a political need to express concern by "doing something" (even if not effective) fall into the deterrence category. Indeed, the purpose of most deterrent trade retaliation is as much, if not more, symbolic as economic.

102. The GATT's own practice of authorizing trade restrictions in response to wrongful trade barriers has no such tendency to link the response to the offending practice. In GATT theory, all wrongful trade restrictions are fungible, each being measured in a common currency of lost trade opportunities. GATT's authorization of trade barriers is meant to serve as an offset for the lost trade opportunities, and for this purpose a retaliatory restriction on one product serves as well as a restriction on any other.

103. *See* text accompanying notes 38–40 above.

104. *See* text accompanying note 46 above.

105. To risk explaining the obvious, it should be pointed out that GATT's practice of permitting retaliation on any product does not present a problem of quantum controls because GATT already has quantum controls in its "compensatory," dollar-for-dollar limitation. The reason that any product retaliation in the environmental context presents problems is that there is no dollar-for-dollar limitation, nor any way to measure one.

106. *Tuna/Dolphin I*, note 42 above; *United States—Restrictions on Imports of Tuna (Tuna II)*, GATT Doc. DS29/R (June 16, 1994) (known as *Tuna/Dolphin II*). For a description of the decisions, see Joel P. Trachtman, *International Decision: GATT Dispute Settlement Panel*, 86 AMERICAN J. INT'L L. 142 (1992); Steve Charnovitz, *Dolphins and Tuna: An Analysis of the Second GATT Panel Report*, 24 ENVIRONMENTAL L. REP. (BNA) 10567−87 (1994).

107. The complainant in *Tuna/Dolphin I*, Mexico, did not press for immediate adoption of the report, being dissuaded from doing so because of the pending ratification of the NAFTA agreement by the U.S. Congress. At this writing, with NAFTA safely ratified, Mexico has begun to press its suit once more. The ruling in *Tuna/Dolphin II* is too recent to have been processed for adoption at this writing.

108. The following 39 countries wrote, spoke, or were spoken for in the GATT debate over *Tuna/Dolphin I*: Argentina, *Australia, Bolivia, Brazil, *Canada, Chile, Columbia, Costa Rica, Cuba, *EEC, Hong Kong, India, *Indonesia, Jamaica, *Japan, *Korea, Mexico, Netherlands, New Zealand, *Norway, Pakistan, Peru, *Philippines, El Salvador, *Senegal, Sweden (on behalf of all Nordic countries), Switzerland, Tanzania, *Thailand (on behalf of all ASEAN countries), Uruguay, *Venezuela. All but one (New Zealand) supported the conclusion of GATT-illegality, and New Zealand subsequently supported that position in a brief filed in *Tuna/Dolphin II*. See *Tuna/Dolphin I*, note 42 above; GATT Docs. C/M/254, -255, -257, -258 (GATT Council meetings of Feb. 18, Mar. 18, June 19, and July 14, 1992). Countries that filed a brief in support of Mexico's legal claim in *Tuna/Dolphin I* are preceded by an asterisk (*).

In the second *Tuna/Dolphin* ruling, the following governments filed briefs in support of the claims of GATT-illegality filed by the EC and the Netherlands: Australia, Canada, Costa Rica, Japan, New Zealand, Thailand, and Venezuela. In discussions of the case in the GATT Council for the rest of the year, essentially the same list of governments spoke in favor of the second panel report.

To old GATT hands, the degree of support shown for these two panel rulings amounts to virtual unanimity, because the rest of the 110-odd GATT member countries either do not attend Council meetings or almost never speak anyway.

109. For a fuller treatment of the rules of Article III pertaining to domestic regulation see the companion study to this one, by Daniel A. Farber and Robert E. Hudec, at Chapter 3 of this volume.

110. In the subsequent *CAFE Standards* case, a GATT panel held that an externally-directed measure that took the form of an internal regulation had to be considered an extra burden on imports in violation of the "no-less-favorable" treatment standard of Article III:4. United States—Taxes on Automobiles, GATT Doc. DS31/R at ¶¶ 5.52−5.55 (Sept. 29, 1994).

111. The term "jurisdiction" was also understood to include the power to regulate the behavior of one's nationals anywhere in the world.

112. The panel's conclusion that coercive measures could not meet the requirements of Article XX was based on an interpretation of the requirements in Article XX(b) that the

trade restriction be "necessary" for the life-saving purpose, and in XX(g) that the restriction be "primarily aimed at" the conservation purpose. The panel suggested that coercion of an intermediary country was an accomplishment too remote from accomplishing the required purpose.

113. The tuna restrictions against Mexico were based on the dolphin mortality record of the Mexican fleets and applied to all yellowfin tuna imports from Mexico caught in purse seine nets. Although the measure was not too far from the current law that simply bans the sale of dolphin-unsafe tuna regardless of country, the MMPA provisions in question also conditioned entry to the U.S. market on several other requirements concerning the regulatory regime of the Mexican government itself. The second *Tuna/Dolphin* decision also involved the secondary boycott aspect of the U.S. restrictions—application of the restrictions to imports from other countries which imported Mexican tuna; this was an *a fortiori* case of coercive purpose.

114. If GATT were to adopt this interpretation, it would seem to validate the 1994 amendment to the Marine Mammals Protection Act forbidding the import of all dolphin-unsafe tuna regardless of country of origin. *See* text accompanying note 47 above.

115. *See, e.g.*, Steve Charnovitz, *Exploring the Environmental Exceptions in GATT Article XX*, 25:5 J. WORLD TRADE 37–55 (1991).

116. Several have argued, for example, in favor of allowing trade restrictions in support of international environmental agreements. *See, e.g.*, Ernst-Ulrich Petersmann, *International Trade Law and International Environmental Law*, 27:1 J. WORLD TRADE 43–81 (1993); Betsy Baker, *Protection, not Protectionism: Multilateral Environmental Agreements and the GATT*, 26 VANDERBILT J. TRANSNAT'L L. 437–68 (1993).

117. A GATT committee on Environmental Measures and International Trade, created in the 1970s but long dormant, was reawakened in November 1991, and conducted extensive meetings up to the end of the Uruguay Round. At the Marrakesh Ministerial meeting that adopted the Uruguay Round Final Act, ministers agreed to establish a Trade and Environment Committee of the WTO, and to create a subcommittee of the WTO Preparatory Committee to carry on its work in the interim. *See* Ministers Decision on Trade and Environment of 14 April 1994, *in* GATT Doc. MTN.TNC/MIN(94)/1/Rev.1 (Apr. 11, 1994).

118. *Id.* at 5.

119. *See* GATT Doc L/7402 (Feb. 2, 1994) (Report of the Chairman of the Group on Environmental Measures and International Trade). The reform proposal currently being studied does not include the relationship between trade restrictions and other types of international environmental agreements that *do not* contain a provision authorizing trade restrictions. Proposals to allow governments to impose trade restrictions for the purpose of enforcing this latter type of international environmental agreement raise a different problem, and will be dealt with in the Part IV (Sec. 4.17) of this study, on unilateral trade restrictions.

120. For purposes of the waiver, it is not necessary that the agreement actually *require* signatories to impose trade measures; it is enough that the agreement *authorizes* them to do so.

121. *See* Vienna Convention of the Law of Treaties, arts. 30(3) & 30(4). *See also* Restatement of the Law of Foreign Relations § 323 (1986). For a specific discussion of this point relating to GATT and environmental agreements, see Baker, note 116 above, at 446–47.

Although the Vienna Convention is not in terms applicable to GATT, which predates it, most governments consider the Convention declaratory of customary international law, and GATT panels themselves have cited the Vienna Convention as authority.

122. The effective date of the GATT agreement for the original 23 members is January 1948. For those who acceded afterwards, the effective date is the actual date of their accession. By 1980, 85 of the GATT's current 120-plus members had acceded.

123. *See generally,* SIR IAN SINCLAIR, THE VIENNA CONVENTION ON THE LAW OF TREATIES 93–98 (2d ed. 1984); 1 OPPENHEIM'S INTERNATIONAL LAW 1280 (9th ed. 1993).

124. *See* text accompanying notes 14–16 above.

125. *See* text accompanying notes 30–35 above.

126. The member governments of the International Convention for the Regulation of Whaling (ICRW) have also imposed trade restrictions against nonmembers.

127. "Nothing in this agreement shall be construed ... (c) to prevent any contracting party from taking any action in pursuance of its obligations under the United Nations Charter for the maintenance of international peace and security."

128. The effect can be seen in the largely GATT-consistent content of regional agreements between developed countries. The GATT consistency of regional agreements between developing countries was an early casualty of the rising tolerance for discrimination favoring developing-country trade.

129. Actually, the statement of first-line criteria in Article XX(h) is rather artfully concealed. The text of XX(h) says nothing at all about criteria. An Ad Note, however, informs the reader that "The exception provided for in this subparagraph extends to any commodity agreement which conforms to the principles approved by the Economic and Social Council in its resolution of 30 (IV) of 28 March 1947." That ECOSOC resolution, in turn, recommends that members of the United Nations follow the principles set out in Chapter VI of the ITO Charter—the Charter's section on commodity agreements. The relevant rules and principles of Chapter VI are discussed in detail in the text accompanying notes 143–151 below.

130. Although many commodity agreements have been negotiated since 1947, none has ever been submitted to GATT under this procedure.

131. Strictly speaking, the words "necessary" or "essential" are used only in subsections (a), (b), (d), and (j) of Article XX, relating to morals, health, law enforcement, and short-supply situations. A similar nexus is required, however, in the subsection (g) requirement that the purpose of the measure be for conservation.

132. DANIEL C. ESTY, GREENING THE GATT: TRADE, ENVIRONMENT AND THE FUTURE 283, app. E (Inst. Int'l Econ., 1994).

133. On the ambiguity of what enforcement activity the CITES agreement authorizes, see note 14 above.

134. *See, e.g.,* text accompanying notes 38–40 and 44–46 above.

135. *See* text accompanying note 14 above.

136. GATT Doc. TRE/W/5 (1992).

137. An example of large-country power being wielded for altruistic purposes that is known to many governments is the United States' administration of its law regarding

denial of GSP benefits for countries whose labor policies fail to honor internationally recognized workers' rights. Of the 108 worker rights petitions filed from January 1987 to May of 1994, ten resulted in either termination or suspension of GSP privileges. The three countries that had their rights terminated (Liberia, Nicaragua, and Romania) and most of the seven that received suspensions (Burma, CAR, Chile, Mauritania, Paraguay, Sudan, and Syria) were countries with whom the United States had poor political relations. Commentators have concluded that friendly states with equally substantial worker rights problems were not sanctioned. *See* Harlan Mandel, Note, *In Pursuit of the Missing Link: International Worker Rights and International Trade?*, 27 COLUMBIA J. TRANSNAT'L L. 443, 463−72 (1989); Juli Stensland, *Internationalizing the North American Agreement on Labor Cooperation*, 4 MINNESOTA J. GLOBAL TRADE 141 (1995).

A common type of political bias—excusing large countries while punishing small ones— was widely perceived in the decision of the Clinton Administration to employ trade sanctions against Taiwan, but not against China, for continuing trade in rhinoceros horns and tiger parts. Although the explanation was that China had been making progress, Taiwanese officials and other observers attributed the difference in treatment to China's power and political influence—not to mention China's sensitivity over any Clinton-sponsored trade sanctions for moral purposes. *See, e.g.,* James Sheehan, *Most Favored Fauna Treatment,* WASHINGTON TIMES, May 31, 1994, at A12.

A well known example involving the use of coercive measures in the field of ordinary trade policy was the first, and so far only, application of the "Super 301" provision, a law that requires the U.S. Executive Branch to attack the most prominent trade barriers affecting U.S. exports. Omnibus Trade and Competitiveness Act of 1988, § 1302, 102 Stat. 1107 (codified at 19 U.S.C. § 2420 (1988)). The Bush Administration chose to attack Japan (fair enough), but then bypassed the European Community and all other candidates to strike at Brazil and India alone, the two most outspoken opponents of the U.S. agenda for the Uruguay Round trade negotiations. *See* Section 301 proceedings 301−73 to 301−78, June 16, 1989.

138. There is an extensive international relations literature on the extent of compliance without enforcement. The literature is reviewed in LAWRENCE E. SUSSKIND, ENVIRONMENTAL DIPLOMACY 107−13 (1994). In particular, see Abram Chayes & Antonia H. Chayes, *Compliance Without Enforcement: State Behavior Under Regulatory Treaties*, 7 NEGOTIATION J. 311, 311−12 (1991):

International lawyers and others familiar with the operations of international treaties take for granted that most states comply with most of their treaty obligations most of the time....

. . . .

. . . [I]nducing compliance with treaties is not a matter of "enforcement" but a process of negotiation.

139. The aversion to coercion can also be found in the administration of the international environmental agreements that do authorize trade restrictions. For an account of the non-confrontational approach toward enforcement of the Montreal Protocol taken by government representatives in a 1989 UNEP seminar, see SUSSKIND, note 138 above, at 100−02.

140. *See* authorities cited in note 163 below.

141. *See* text accompanying notes 93−100 above.

142. It bears noting that the rule suggested by the second *Tuna/Dolphin* ruling also follows the limit suggested here.

143. Other forms of commodity agreement may seek to stabilize prices by direct market intervention, using pooled funds to purchase and sell when prices move below or above the desired price ranges. Such market practices by themselves would involve no GATT violation.

144. *See* note 129 above.

145. HAVANA CHARTER FOR AN INTERNATIONAL TRADE ORGANIZATION, art. 62, Dep't of State Pub. No. 3117, Commercial Policy Series 113 (1948) [hereinafter ITO CHARTER].

146. ITO CHARTER art. 63(b).

147. For sellers, the trade involves exchanging (1) the right to sell as much as one can in an open market for (2) a right to sell a limited quantity at a higher price. For buyers (in theory, anyway), the trade involves exchanging (1) the right to buy at whatever price prevails in a somewhat volatile free market for (2) a right to buy at a more stable (albeit higher) price. To be honest, it should be noted that in many commodity agreements involving products made primarily by third-world producers (such as coffee, cocoa, and sugar), the ability to find common ground often depends on there being a resource-transfer motive by the developed-country governments, who, as buyers, sometimes agree more easily to higher-than-market prices.

148. ITO CHARTER arts. 58–59.

149. ITO CHARTER art. 60.

150. ITO CHARTER art. 60(c).

151. *Id.*

152. Agreement Establishing the World Trade Organization [hereinafter WTO Agreement] art. IX:2, *in* 1994 Uruguay Round Final Act, note 99 above.

153. WTO Agreement art. X:3. The three-fourths vote enables the WTO to require those who do not accept the amendment to leave the organization. An amendment *per se* can be adopted by a two-thirds vote, but amendments so adopted are binding only on those who sign them.

154. WTO Agreement art. IX (3–4).

155. *See, e.g.,* Statement of the United States Council for International Business on International Environmental Agreements and the Use of Trade Measures to Achieve Their Objectives, Dec. 15, 1993 (Council press release) at 4–5:

Such provisions shall require participation by countries which account for a substantial proportion of the activity giving rise to the agreement.... There should be an appropriate balance between producers and parties affected by the activity reflecting the fact that such agreements are designed to deal with "global commons" issues.

156. ITO CHARTER, note 145 above, arts. 58–59.

157. *Id.* art. 60:1(a). Initial membership was to be open to anyone on the same terms, but subsequent membership was made subject to the terms of the agreement, presumably to allow for adjustments due to the difference in time.

158. The full text of GATT Article XX(h) creates an exception for "any measure undertaken in pursuance of obligations under any intergovernmental commodity agreement which conforms to criteria submitted to the Contracting Parties and not disapproved by

them and which is itself so submitted and not disapproved." It is the Ad Note to Article XX(h) that extends the exception to agreements that conform to the principles stated in Chapter VI of the ITO Charter. *See* note 129 above.

159. WTO Agreement, note 152 above, art. IX:1.

160. The term "unilateral" is seldom employed to describe trade actions that are clearly GATT-authorized. Thus, for example, antidumping or countervailing duties are not normally called "unilateral restrictions" because, even though they are taken without asking anyone's permission, GATT expressly authorizes national governments to impose antidumping or countervailing duties on the basis of the government's own investigation and decision.

161. *See* text accompanying notes 40 and 46 above.

162. It is sometimes argued that trade restrictions against harm-causing products have *only* the purpose of protecting one's own citizens against the moral discomfort of participating in the harmful commerce, and thus should be regarded as domestic policy measures rather than attempts to coerce other governments. This is sometimes called the "tainted-goods" model. The accuracy of such a characterization is an empirical question. One of the reasons for questioning the nonpunitive character of such measures is that their effect—stopping all trade in the product—seems far more restrictive than necessary merely to protect those who in fact have moral objections.

163. U.S. threats or actions seemed to have had some effect on Japan and others with regard to turtles, driftnetting, and the first whale moratorium for conservation purposes. For a general overview of such effects, see Charnovitz, *Environmental Trade Sanctions*, note 14 above; McDorman, note 19 above. *See also* Skare, note 35 above; Emert, note 38 above; Charnovitz, *Taxonomy*, note 3 above, at 30–31.

The August 19, 1994, U.S. action against Taiwan with regard to Tiger Parts and Rhino Horns (see text at notes 17–20 above) seems to have stimulated a number of high officials to press for more rapid passage of an already pending bill increasing penalties for dealing in contraband animal products. "Taiwan President Says Some Violate Conservation," Reuters, Aug. 25, 1994, available in LEXIS, News Library, Allnws File (statement by Speaker of Taiwan's Parliament).

The EC import ban on the fur of seal pups was followed shortly thereafter by Canada's adoption of a regulation prohibiting the commercial harvesting of seal pup fur. *See* HUDEC, ENFORCING INTERNATIONAL TRADE LAW, note 93 above.

164. For example, the current threats against Norway and Japan with regard to the resumption of commercial whaling have thus far been met with defiance by Norway, and it is not clear that Japan will yield to them. *See* text accompanying notes 30–35 above. For the view that fears of a similar result prompted the Clinton Administration's decision not to impose sanctions on China for trading in rhinoceros horns and tiger parts, *see* sources cited in note 137 above.

165. What one sees in the case of the conflicting positions taken by the EU is apparently another example of the point made in section 3.3 of this chapter concerning the tendency of different bureaucracies to operate in conflict with each other.

166. To be sure, parliamentary forms of government do not have the need to use legislation as a vehicle for policy dialogue between legislators and administrators.

167. *See, e.g., USTR Official Examines Conflicts Between Trade, Environment Pacts,* 11 Int'l Trade Rep. (BNA) 913 (1994).

168. *See* text accompanying note 55 above.

169. Rio Declaration on Environment and Development, Principle 12, U.N. Doc. A/Conf.151/5/Rev.1 (June 13, 1992).

170. Article XXI provides that:

Nothing in the General Agreement shall be construed ... (b) to prevent any contracting party from taking any action which it considers necessary for the protection of its essential security interests ... (iii) taken in time of war or other emergency in international relations.

GATT has no effective way to challenge a government's assertion that an outbreak of political hostility is an "emergency in international relations."

171. The principle of no legal review was established in a 1985 GATT complaint brought by Nicaragua against a trade embargo declared by the United States. The United States succeeded in obtaining GATT agreement to terms of reference expressly denying the panel the ability to adjudicate the legal validity of the U.S. Article XXI defense. *See* GATT Doc. C/M/192 (GATT Council meeting of Oct. 10, 1985).

172. The use of National Security restrictions on the export side has been rather extensive, through devices like the COCOM list. As a political matter, however, export restrictions have never figured very largely in the political balance underlying the system of reciprocal market access commitments.

A complete survey of activity under Article XXI is contained in GATT, ANALYTICAL INDEX: A GUIDE TO GATT LAW AND PRACTICE 553−64 (6th ed. 1994). For information on the U.S. oil restrictions, which seem never to have generated a GATT document, see JOHN H. JACKSON, WORLD TRADE AND THE LAW OF GATT 752 (1968).

173. *See, e.g.,* Steve Charnovitz, *GATT and the Environment: Examining the Issues,* 4 INT'L ENVIR'L AFF. 203, 218−20 (1992).

174. *See* note 137 above.

175. The same fate would apply to almost any "necessary" standard attached to an undefined seriousness standard. *See, e.g.,* the proposed standard in Erik C. Luchs, *Maximizing Wealth with Unilaterally Imposed Environmental Trade Sanctions under the GATT and the NAFTA,* 25 LAW & POL'Y INT'L BUS. 727, 760 (1994) (Article XX exception for unilateral measures "Necessary for the protection of the integrity of the global ecosystem").

176. Earlier it was explained how the terms of Article XX become relatively easy to satisfy in the context of externally-directed trade measures. *See* text accompanying note 131 above.

177. *See* text accompanying notes 44−66 above.

178. *See* text accompanying note 136 above.

179. For example, the United States acceptance of the Uruguay Round rules on dispute settlement was made with a rather large reservation as to the use of its Section 301 powers in cases not covered by mandatory GATT rules.

180. The WTO waiver procedure provides that waivers may be for more than one year, must have a definite termination date, and shall be reviewed each year if granted for more than a year. WTO Agreement, note 152 above, art. IX:4.

181. *See* note 108 above.

182. One indication of a division of U.S. opinion on the matter was the opposition in the U.S. Congress, in 1994, to adoption of "fast-track" legislation containing the power to

conclude environmental agreements as a part of future trade agreements. *See, e.g., All 44 Republican Senators Oppose Administration's Fast-Track Proposal,* 11 Int'l Trade Rep. (BNA) 1026 (1994).

183. *See* text accompanying note 119 above.

184. 22 U.S.C. § 1978(a)(1) (1988).

185. *See* text accompanying note 55 above.

186. Daniel Esty makes this argument with respect to certain classes of environmental problems. *See* ESTY, note 132 above, at 120 ("moral" environmental policies).

187. *See* note 138 above and accompanying text.

188. For examples of the role of political influence in the U.S. administration of altruistic trade sanctions, see note 137 above.

III   Labor Standards

4

Workers' Rights and International Trade: The Social Clause (GATT, ILO, NAFTA, U.S. Laws)

Virginia A. Leary

4.1   Introduction

Demands for the inclusion of a "social clause" in international trade agreements—a clause linking workers' rights to trade concessions[1]—is a major issue bedeviling current efforts to liberalize international trade. The adoption of a supplemental agreement on labor cooperation appended to the North American Free Trade Agreement (NAFTA) resulted from such demands. The issue of workers' rights was raised repeatedly during the Uruguay Round of trade negotiations and will continue to be raised at the new World Trade Organization (WTO). The International Labor Organization (ILO), after years of hesitation, has set up a working party to discuss the ILO response to demands for linking workers' rights to trade agreements. A number of U.S. laws condition trade preferences on the existence of adequate labor standards in beneficiary nations.

The issue of a social clause, or more generally the linkage of workers' rights with international trade, is highly controversial, as is evident from the most superficial perusal of government interventions at the Marrakesh meeting concluding the Uruguay Round.[2] Opponents of the linkage argue that conditioning international trade on non-trade-related matters, such as workers' rights, is detrimental to the promotion of welfare-enhancing free trade; that linkage is inimical to the economy of developing countries since increased export trade is one of the best methods of improving the economy of such countries; and that the argument for workers' rights is simply disguised protectionism. Opposition to the linkage comes primarily from governments of developing countries, free trade economists—in fact, the majority of economists—and many private enterprises in developed countries. The government members of GATT, as well as the government and employer representatives at the ILO, have been successful, until recently, in keeping the issue of a social clause off the agenda of these organizations.

Proponents of a link between labor standards and trade, on the other hand, argue that the export of goods which are produced under exceptionally bad working conditions is "unfair" competition which will negatively affect the working conditions in countries with high labor standards, resulting in a "race to the bottom" and the deterioration of working conditions in developed countries. Other proponents appear primarily concerned over the appalling condition of workers in many developing countries. The proponents of linking workers' rights and trade contend that the fundamental principles of workers' rights should be followed by all countries engaged in international trade, and that incorporation of a social clause in trade agreements will ultimately benefit workers both in developed and developing countries.

The major proponents of linking labor standards with trade are the United States government, some government members of the European Union, trade unions in Europe and the United States, as well as some unions and workers' organizations in developing countries. A new constituency—the human rights movement—has recently become active in urging a link between workers' rights and trade; human rights activists and organizations both in the North and South have joined with trade unions in promoting the social clause.

The strong emotions on both sides of the issue of linking workers' rights and international trade have led many to believe that compromise and political resolution is unlikely. The continued impasse over this issue, however, is detrimental to the promotion of international trade, to harmony in international relations, to the improvement of labor standards, and to furthering the work of international organizations. An effort should be made by all concerned to arrive at a satisfactory resolution. A better appreciation of the important problems raised by opponents of a social clause, on the one hand, and, on the other hand, a clearer understanding of what proponents of the clause mean by "labor standards" or "workers' rights" (to be included in such a clause) may contribute to a resolution of the issue.

Discussions concerning a social clause are often confused and the terminology employed is often unclear. The representative of Netherlands at Marrakesh pointed out that

[t]he fact that some speak of workers' rights and others of social rights or even social dumping is illustrative of the obscurity and confusion surrounding this issue. No one really knows at this stage what the issue is.... But first more clarity, analysis and dialogue are needed to establish if there is a need for the WTO to get involved.[3]

This study is an effort to provide clarity and analysis to the subject with the hope that it may lead to a more informed dialogue. While occasionally referring to political and economic aspects of linkages between workers' rights and international trade, the study focuses primarily on legal aspects. Such aspects are many: a number of legal instruments link labor standards and trade (U.S. legislation on preferences, Caribbean Basin Initiative, European Social Chapter of the Maastricht Agreement, Labor Cooperation Agreement of NAFTA); the study includes sections on these texts. But the role of law is not confined to focusing on existing texts, but also involves evaluation of opposing positions on issues, attempting to reconcile conflicting norms and interests and proposing solutions. The sections of the paper on the "problematique" of a social clause, the meaning of the concept of "internationally recognized labor standards," and the final chapter relating to the search for common ground are an attempt to fulfil this second important contribution which the law can make to the issue of the linkage between labor standards and trade.

A word about terminology. References are made throughout the essay to "social clauses," "internationally recognized workers' rights," and "minimum international labor standards." These terms concern basically the same issues and the phrases will be often used alternatively in this paper; where a distinction between the various phrases is necessary, the difference in meaning will be pointed out.

Section 4.2 presents the "problematique" of a social clause or the linkage of trade and labor standards. The problems which have been raised concerning such linkages are briefly presented in this section, leaving more detailed discussion to later sections. Section 4.3 outlines the long history of the link between international competitiveness and labor standards. Present controversy may obscure the fact that the issue is a long-standing one that dates from the middle of the last century.

The next four sections concern the forums in which the linkage between trade and labor standards has been raised. The International Labor Organization is the focus of Section 4.4. As the UN specialized agency with a mandate for labor issues, it is an appropriate forum for a discussion of the linkage of labor and trade. In its early history, the ILO drew attention to the relationship between international labor standards and competitiveness in international trade, but in subsequent years rarely focused on the problem. The present international concern with the issue has resulted in the active reinvolvement of the ILO in questions relating to a social clause.

The GATT is the other international forum where the issue of a social clause has been frequently raised—but never seriously debated. The creation of the World Trade Organization (WTO) and the inclusion of intellectual property, environment, and investment issues on its agenda, make a WTO debate on the social clause more likely in the foreseeable future. Section 4.5 discusses consideration of the issue in the context of the GATT and the WTO.

Sections 4.6 and 4.7 discuss, respectively, the Agreement on Labor Cooperation appended to NAFTA and U.S. legislation linking workers' rights and trade.

A major issue which underlies all aspects of this subject is examined in Section 4.8: the definition of "internationally recognized labor standards" (or "workers' rights"), a term frequently employed in referring to social clauses. Much of the confusion concerning this issue results from a failure to adequately address what is meant by "internationally recognized labor standards" in this context. The term is generally used to refer not to all the many international labor standards adopted, for example, by the ILO, but to refer rather only to the most fundamental "human rights" standards such as freedom of association, forced labor, and discrimination in employment.

Section 4.9, The Search for Common Ground, raises the question of whether any compromise or agreement is possible between proponents and opponents of linking workers' rights and trade and suggests that, despite the seeming irreconcilable views on the subject, a surprising amount of agreement on the issue can be discerned. It is suggested that an appreciation of the common ground accepted by both the proponents and opponents of linking workers' rights to trade may contribute to resolution of this difficult and contentious problem which is currently frustrating efforts both to enhance international trade and to improve the lot of workers worldwide.

4.2 The "Problematique" of Linking Trade and Workers' Rights

This section sets the stage for the remainder of the paper by citing, in abbreviated form, some of the main problematical aspects which are raised concerning the linkage of international labor standards and trade. These aspects underlie the discussion of the social clause in all domestic and international forums. Cited briefly in this section, they are discussed in more detail and evaluated in the succeeding sections on ILO, the GATT, NAFTA, U.S. legislation, the meaning of the "internationally recognized labor standards," and, particularly, in the final section of the paper suggesting possible areas of agreement concerning a social clause.

4.2.1   The Broader Perspective

The persistence of poor working conditions in many parts of the world should be viewed from a broader perspective than simply the enforcement of labor standards, many commentators have noted. They result from poverty, terms of trade unfavorable to poor countries, difficulties in accessing markets, and world trade policies. They thus cannot be resolved solely by legal mechanisms enforcing workers' rights or by the mere expansion of world trade.

Alston has pointed out that calls for increased respect for human rights (including workers' rights) "must be accompanied by the adoption of appropriate policies in the fields of international trade and related areas which offer adequate support for efforts aimed at achieving a more equitable internal order."[4] Van Liemt has asked:

Why is the question of labour standards brought up in isolation from the broader issues of imbalances in the world trade structure—including the issue of greater market access through accelerated restructuring of developed country economies, and that of raw material prices, many of which are at a low level and continue to fluctuate wildly.... why [should] the social clause ... be linked only to trade: would action not be more effective if it was also linked to public capital flows (such as official lending and aid flows) and strategic relations such as defence treaties?[5]

4.2.2   The Meaning of "Workers' Rights"

There is much confusion in the literature concerning the content to be given the phrases "internationally recognized workers' rights" or "minimal international labor standards" and precisely which standards are being referred to in the debate over linking them with trade. The ILO has developed an extensive code of labor standards consisting of over 170 conventions and many more recommendations that include fundamental human rights standards on freedom of association, forced labor, discrimination in employment and child labor, as well as very detailed standards relating to specific industries, such as hours of work in glass factories. Hence the term "labor standards" covers a very wide range. Legislation linking trade and workers' rights generally specifies a few fundamental standards but without clarifying whether the standards will be defined and interpreted in accordance with application and interpretation by ILO organs. These questions of definition will be discussed at more length in Section 4.8.

4.2.3   Unilateralism versus Multilateralism

The inadequacies of a unilateral approach to linking trade and workers' rights have been abundantly criticized. A unilateral approach, such as U.S. legislation on GSP or the Caribbean Basin Initiative (see section 4.7 on U.S. legislation), can too frequently reflect the political orientation of the country invoking violation of workers' rights or reflect protectionist pressures, rather than an objective determination concerning labor standards in the particular country. A multilateral approach is more likely to refer to generally accepted international norms and to avoid a partisan approach.

4.2.4   Reciprocity

Accusations of violation of workers' rights by particular countries raise the issue of reciprocity. It is argued that a country should not invoke violations of workers' rights which it does not itself support, i.e., by ratification of relevant ILO conventions. One of the frequent criticisms leveled against the United States efforts with regard to the linkage of trade and workers' rights is its own failure to ratify ILO conventions and thus contribute to a multilateral approach to the improvement of labor conditions.

4.2.5   Reaction of Developing Countries

The reaction of developing countries to the linkage of workers' rights and trade is well known. Van Liemt has pointed out that

Developing country governments ... feel that developed countries' concern about working conditions in their countries is due above all to their export success, and to the growing pressure for protectionism that has arisen from high unemployment in importing countries. They consider the social clause proposal to be disguised protectionism that could obstruct their industrial development and deprive them of one of their key comparative advantages: the ability to use low-cost labour productively. They object to what they consider to be interference in their domestic affairs and resent the fact that they appear to be asked for reciprocity in social obligations in return for trade concessions.[6]

4.3   An Issue That Won't Go Away: The History of the Linking of Workers' Rights to International Trade Issues

Current discussions relating to workers' rights and trade may lead to the perception that the linkage between workers' rights and trade is a new issue, but recognition of the relationship between the condition of workers and international competitiveness is a century and a half old, dating from the earliest concern about the conditions of workers during the Industrial Revolution in Europe. Harmonization of national labor laws was perceived as necessary in order to improve the condition of workers in any one European country; it was difficult to adopt laws regulating child labor, hours of work, or safe working conditions if such laws were not also adopted by competing countries.

Linkage of workers' rights and trade has been a recurring issue for 150 years. It is an issue that must still be taken seriously. The same issues that were being discussed a century and a half ago in Europe are being re-hashed today in the United States. Unlike issues involving subsidies and dumping, the issue of workers' rights and trade has not always been couched in the terms of what is "fair" in matters of trade; the emphasis has rather been on improvement of workers' rights and whether international trade linkages are an effective means of doing so.

4.3.1 Early Developments in Europe

The relationship between the treatment of workers and international trade was first raised in Europe in the middle of the 19th century—a time when the condition of workers was appallingly bad in all the industrializing countries of Europe. Labor law reformers in Europe ran up against the concern that the enactment of domestic laws prohibiting child labor or shortening hours of work would result in a competitive disadvantage in relation to other countries with lower standards. Their response was to urge the adoption of treaties establishing common labor standards which, it was hoped, would be ratified by all European industrialized countries, as well as the establishment of an international organization to supervise the treaties.

Today, the concern is basically the same, but the situation is reversed. Labor organizations and human rights activists in the United States and other industrialized countries are concerned that free trade may result in high labor standards in their own country being lowered to the level of newly competitive importing countries with inadequate labor standards and practices. The present-day concern lends itself to suspicions that the invocation of workers' rights is a disguised means of protection of domestic industries. The 19th-century concern is free of that taint—it appears to have been a genuine concern over the sad conditions of national workers and was not directed at limiting international trade but at the establishment of common international labor standards to overcome the problem of competitiveness.

In 1833, Charles Frederick Hindley, a member of the British Parliament, proposed an international treaty on hours of work as a means of promoting such legislation in England. He has been referred to as the founder of the idea of international labor legislation and as having "a clear insight into the interdependence between nations that was created by foreign trade and international competition."[7] In 1838–39, Jérome Blanqui, a French economist, wrote of the need for harmonization of labor legislation in European countries,

There is only one way of accomplishing it [the reform] while avoiding its disastrous consequences: this would be to get it adopted simultaneously by all industrial nations which compete in the foreign market.[8]

Daniel Legrand, an Alsatian manufacturer, has also been referred to as "the principal originator of the idea of international labour legislation, and precursor of the work of the International Labour Organisation." Between 1838 and 1855 he addressed a stream of memoranda to the governments of industrialized countries urging "an international factory law."

In the latter half of the 19th century a series of European congresses, promoted by different organizations of labor leaders, socialists, reformers, professors, and economists, took up the issue of labor laws reform, with many pointing out that labor reform was not solely a national issue.[9] The main concerns of these congresses related to child labor, hours of work, weekly rest for children and adult female workers, and, eventually, what we would refer to today as occupational safety and health—referred to then as "hygiene in the workplace." Concern over international competitiveness was a recurrent preoccupation.

Two unsuccessful efforts to organize international labor conferences took place in 1888 and 1890. The Swiss government issued invitations to 13 European states to attend an international labor congress in 1889. The invitations were withdrawn when Germany decided to organize a similar conference in 1890. The latter apparently failed by considering too many aspects of the conditions of workers, many of which were highly controversial, and by inadequate preparation.

The seeds for the eventual adoption of international labor conventions and an international labor organization were more immediately laid in 1897. Delegates representing workers in 14 countries met at an International Congress on Labor Protection in Zurich in 1897 and urged the Swiss government to invite other governments to set up a labor office. Also, in 1897, a conference of professors, economists, and politicians in Brussels discussed various issues relating to labor legislation in the European countries and set up a committee to establish an international association for labor protection, aiming, *inter alia*, at the adoption of international labor legislation. Statutes of the International Association for Labor Legislation were adopted in Paris in 1900 and an International Labor Office was opened in Basel in 1901.

The newly founded International Association of Labor Legislation decided to concentrate its work on two relatively uncontroversial subjects: (1) the prohibition of the use of white phosphorous in industry, particularly in the manufacture of matches, and (2) the prohibition of night work for women. Conventions (treaties) on these two subjects were adopted in 1905 and were widely ratified by European countries, despite some opposition to the prohibition of the use of white phosphorous.

Hansson points out that in the pre–World War I period a number of bilateral agreements were also negotiated dealing with common conditions of work.[10] A Franco-Italian treaty of 1904 required Italy to regulate working conditions in line with conditions in France, and gave Italian workers in France the same treatment as domestic workers regarding compensation for industrial accidents and pensions. By 1914, 28 bilateral agreements were negotiated between European countries, mainly relating to the treatment of migrant workers.

In 1913, a conference in Berne adopted two new conventions, one relating to hours of work for minors and women, and the other relating to prohibition of night work for minors. Events overtook these developments when war broke out. The diplomatic conference at which the conventions were to be signed never took place, but postwar developments led to a new era in the development of harmonization of labor law with the founding of the International Labor Organization.

4.4   A Turning Point: The Establishment of the ILO

The founding of the International Labor Organization (ILO) in 1919 and the ensuing adoption of multiple international labor conventions by the Organization are turning points in the history of the relation between workers' rights and trade. The creation of the ILO was a logical development from the century-old concern about the relationship between international competitiveness and labor conditions. The founding documents of the ILO refer expressly to the link. The 175 ILO labor conventions (as of 1 July 1994) serve today as references for the meaning of "internationally recognized worker rights."

The ILO was established by Part XIII of the Treaty of Versailles, which contained a labor charter and the ILO Constitution. In retrospect it appears surprising that the Treaty, focusing on issues of peace after the war, included Part XIII, establishing a labor charter and the ILO. It is rare today to hear references to the link between peace and workers' rights. Yet the link between democracy and peace is often invoked—and freedom of association is an essential element of democracy. Given the situation in postwar Europe, the perception of the link between peace and labor is understandable. The Bolshevik Revolution, with its emphasis on the rights of workers, was very much on the minds of Western European diplomats. The Peace Conference appeared to be a logical moment for the establishment of the permanent international labor organization earlier recommended by labor reformers.

4.4.1   Link between Trade and Labor Standards in Early ILO History

The link between international competitiveness and labor conditions was in the forefront at the time of the founding of the ILO. The chairman of a Committee on International Labor Treaties in France spoke of the issue in 1917:

In questions such as hours of work, the regulation of dangerous trades, the prohibition of certain work for women and children, international competition may for a long time favor those countries which do not accept the highest standards of human conditions, to the serious detriment of more generous nations.[11]

Prefiguring present-day accusations of "unfair competition," a memorandum concerning internal discussions of the British delegation at the Peace Conference pointed out that "[a]ny State, therefore, which does not carry out a Convention designed to prevent oppressive conditions is guilty of manufacturing under conditions which create a state of unfair competition in the international market."[12] The Preamble of the ILO Constitution expressly refers to the link between the condition of workers and harmonization of labor conditions. It reads:

Whereas also the failure of any nation to adopt humane conditions of labour is an obstacle in the way of other nations which desire to improve the conditions in their own countries....

The method chosen by the ILO to establish a certain degree of harmonization of conditions of labor is the adoption of international labor conventions by the annual International Labor Conference to be accepted by states through ratification. Nonbinding recommendations are adopted containing more detailed standards.

At the time of the founding of the ILO, the focus was on the industrialized countries of Europe, which were then at a relatively equal state of economic development—few developing countries were independent at that time or active participants in the international community. Early ILO conventions made exceptions for states then at a different state of economic development—in particular India and Japan. Later, ILO conventions contained "flexibility clauses" which took account of the varying economic development of countries.

In the drafting of detailed technical labor conventions the ILO has been conscious of the need to take account of differences in economic development. At the same time, it has emphasized that differences in economic development should not excuse violation of the fundamental human rights conventions relating to freedom of association and collective bargaining, forced labor, discrimination in employment, and child labor.

Early ILO conventions related to conditions of work and not to fundamental human rights. After the establishment of the United Nations, human rights became an important international issue and the ILO in the postwar period adopted conventions on freedom of association and collective bargaining, a new convention on forced labor, and conventions on discrimination in employment and equal pay for work of equal value.

4.4.2   The U.S. and the ILO

The United States did not join the ILO until 1934, despite the active participation of the American Federation of Labor at the Peace Conference; Samuel Gompers chaired the commission on labor matters at the Conference. The famous AFL motto, "Labor is not a commodity or an article of commerce," was adopted as a basic principle of the newly established organization.[13] U.S. participation in the ILO has had its ups and downs. It withdrew from the ILO from 1977 to 1980, allegedly due to double standards and politicization, but perhaps more accurately due to the opposition of George Meany to U.S. membership in an organization in which the Soviet Union participated. At the present time, the United States is an active participant and has recently ratified several ILO conventions—most recently Convention No. 105 on Forced Labor and Convention No. 150

relating to labor administration—attempting to overcome its abysmal record in this regard.[14] By 1995, the United States had ratified only 12 of the 175 international labor conventions, a shameful record that places the United States among the countries that have ratified the fewest ILO conventions—a fact that has elicited national and international criticism in view of the strong advocacy by the United States of the linking of workers' rights and trade within the GATT and the U.S. legislation linking GSP benefits, etc., with workers' rights. The United States has not ratified the ILO conventions on freedom of association, collective bargaining, equal remuneration, or discrimination in employment.

4.4.3   ILO Reticence Concerning the Social Clause

In the recent past, most efforts by U.S. organizations and individuals to link trade and workers' rights internationally have focused on the GATT as the more appropriate organization and not on the ILO. However, in 1991, a report of the Economic Policy Council of the United Nations Association of the USA, headed by Ray Marshall, concluded that the ILO was also an appropriate forum to develop and administer a program linking workers' rights and international trade. The report recommended that

The U.S. government should convene a working group in the United States to assess the possibility of linking the ILO and GATT in a way that both promotes the raising of living standards and protects the fundamental human rights of workers in all corners of the world. Furthermore, the EPC panel believes that, based on the findings of this working group, the U.S. government should lead efforts within both the GATT and the ILO to develop cooperative measures— involving not only the GATT and ILO but other multilateral institutions, such as the World Bank and International Monetary Fund—for strengthening the linkage between workers rights and international trade. The panel notes that United States law already links labor rights with trade even though some in this country are opposed to such linkages.[15]

Labor unions have no direct voice in the GATT, but they are fully participating members in the ILO, which may indicate the emphasis on the ILO in a study chaired by Ray Marshall.

   Despite the initial emphasis on the relation between the conditions of workers and international competitiveness, the ILO in ensuing years has not emphasized the relationship and has not actively promoted the inclusion of a social clause in trade agreements. It has not ignored the issue entirely, but has been unable to take a forthright institutional stand. (See section 4.4.4 for current ILO consideration of the issue.)

Three Directors-General have discussed the concept of a social clause in annual reports to the ILO Conference: Wilfred Jenks in 1973, Francis Blanchard in 1988, and Michel Hansenne in 1994. The Governing Body has also discussed the issue at various periods. As early as 1973, it considered the question of linking trade and workers' rights and came to no conclusion—except to discontinue discussion for the time being. It again discussed the subject extensively in 1990 with the same lack of further action. Several articles on the social clause have appeared in the *International Labour Review*, an ILO publication.[16] Blanchard pointed out in his report to the Conference in 1988 that "The various discussions which have taken place in the ILO and elsewhere have, however, revealed a number of difficulties, both of principle and of a practical nature."[17] The perception that labor costs are only one aspect of international competitiveness may have accounted for past ILO hesitation. Another reason appears to be the conviction that the improvement of labor conditions is a complex issue, best resolved through multilateral negotiation between social partners and eventual agreement on common principles, rather than through sanctions.

In its original form, the ILO Constitution envisaged the possibility of sanctions for violation of standards, but this provision was replaced by an article which merely mentioned the possibility of "action deemed wise and expedient to secure compliance" (Article 33). According to Blanchard, "Reliance has been placed rather on various forms of persuasion and moral pressure, with emphasis also on the importance of assistance by the ILO in overcoming difficulties in the implementation of its standards. It has been observed that, in general, rather than resorting to sanctions, specialised international organisations have given preference to measures involving conciliation and a pragmatic approach to upholding the organisations' rules."[18] The most likely reason for ILO reticence is the lack of agreement among ILO constituencies regarding the linkage. Unlike other UN intergovernmental organizations, the ILO is tripartite—composed of representatives of workers' and employers' organizations as well as governments. It has been difficult—indeed, impossible thus far—for these three constituencies to agree on a common ILO approach to social clauses. In an article in *Le Monde* in 1993, Blanchard pointed out that all efforts in the past to open the debate on the social clause either in the ILO Governing Body or at the annual Conference had failed before "the lukewarm attitude of governments, the declared hostility of employer representatives and the ambiguity expressed by trade union representatives."[19] Unions are well-known proponents of the linkage between trade and workers' rights and at the 1991 meeting of the Annual Labor Conference, Mr. Kearney, representative of the International Textile, Garment and Leather Workers' Federation, after detailing the limited effectiveness of international labor standards in this industry, stated that "the Federation is convinced that the only effective means of enforcing minimum standards is to link trade to worker rights, whereby it would be a condition for a country participating in international trade to respect and enforce the minimum standards set down by the ILO."[20] Numerous other statements by trade union representatives, especially from the developed countries, in the ILO and other fora could be cited to support linking trade and workers' rights.

Most governments and some union representatives from the third world are opposed to conditionality in trade or aid. The United States and some European countries campaign actively for the linkage, but the majority of governments remain opposed. Employers' organizations are almost universally opposed to linking trade and workers' rights.

4.4.4 Current ILO Developments on Linking Workers' Rights and Trade

Proposals by the Director-General
The discussions concerning the inclusion of a social clause in GATT/ WTO, the addition of a supplemental labor agreement to NAFTA, and the linking of labor standards to GSP provisions in several countries exerted pressure on the ILO to contribute publicly to the current debate; the ILO Governing Body engaged in open discussion of the issue for the first time in 1994. The Governing Body discussion was preceded by proposals by Michel Hansenne, Director-General of the ILO. Eight pages of his report to the 1994 annual Labor Conference were devoted to a discussion of "The 'social clause' in the context of an increasingly global economy." Hansenne stated that the ILO should advocate neither restrictions on trade nor compulsory equalization of social costs since both would be contrary to the following premises on which the ILO is based: (1) that free trade is to be sought for its contribution to economic development, improvement of standards of life and work, and the creation of jobs and (2) that the ILO should rely on cooperation not coercion.[21] He expressed reservations concerning unilateral action by individual states or groups of states linking trade concessions to compliance with ILO labor standards, pointing out that such actions might affect the ILO's promotion of standards: "While there is nothing in the Constitution which forbids it, its utility to our Organization is by no means clear and our supervisory machinery could suffer if the conclusions that result from it are used in a context of coercion."[22] Hansenne envisaged the creation of a special procedure similar to

the ILO procedure on Freedom of Association[23] which would consider whether states were "taking sufficient measures to examine the possibility of ratifying ILO standards and applying them to the extent their situation and means allow, and, in particular, to the extent made possible by the economic growth resulting from the relaxation of trade barriers."[24] Two sets of conditions should be required of states: (1) a sufficient degree of freedom of association on the national level and (2) certain minimum provisions on social security proportional to the economic situation of the country. Hansenne also suggested that the right of developed countries to examine the social situation in developing countries under such a procedure should entail reciprocity—the renunciation on the part of the developed country of unilateral imposition of trade barriers.

Finally, Hansenne stressed that his proposed procedure would not be an attempt to control "social dumping" ("with the exception of such identifiable abuses as the exclusion of general social legislation from export-processing zones"), nor would it be an attempt to legislate a standardization of labor costs. He suggested that this comprehensive approach—to include technical assistance provided by the ILO—could be established by a consensus in the Governing Body and in the Conference and take the form of a declaration and program of action, or a new convention, which would involve collaboration with the GATT.

Hansenne's report to the Conference was written before the Marrakesh meeting ending the Uruguay Round and the establishment of the WTO and before discussion of his report at the June 1994 ILO Conference. In an article in Le Monde on 21 June 1994, after Marrakesh and the ILO annual Conference, he suggested that, if the international community decided that it would be useful to link social progress with trade liberalization, it would not be difficult to find technical means of doing so. While reiterating comments made in his report, he added a new suggestion—namely, that one means of ensuring respect of social aspects by all the contracting parties to the WTO would be to make their acceptance of ILO conventions on freedom of association and collective bargaining (among the most widely ratified ILO conventions) a condition for their membership in the new World Trade Organization. In addition, he suggested an ILO mechanism to discuss and analyze social progress by all states and to provide examples and suggestions for general improvement of social progress.[25]

Consideration by the ILO Governing Body
Following discussions of a social clause at the 1994 ILO Conference, the Director-General suggested that a Governing Body working party be set

up consisting of 20 government members, 10 employer members, and 10 worker members to examine the question of a social clause. The Governing Body decided, however, at its meeting in June 1994 to establish a working party open to all 56 members of the Governing Body to discuss "all relevant aspects of the social dimensions of the liberalization of international trade."[26] The Director-General was asked to submit a working paper on that subject in time for the next meeting of the Governing Body in November 1994. The report prepared by the ILO Secretariat for that meeting is the first comprehensive report on the issue by the International Labor Office.[27] With the Office paper before it, the Working Party met on 14 November 1994. Since only half of those who wished to speak on the subject were able to present their views in the two sessions allotted to the subject, it was decided that no conclusions were possible and that the Working Party should resume its discussion at the March/April 1995 Session when the remainder of the listed speakers would express their views.[28] Joaquin Otero, U.S. Deputy Under Secretary for International Affairs, was reported as delighted that the ILO had kept the relationship between labor rights and world trade on its agenda even though no other countries had lined up in support. It was also reported that the United States found support only from organized labor at the meeting and to a lesser degree from France in pushing for inclusion of workers' rights in the work program of the new World Trade Organization.[29] Asked whether the recent Republican victory in U.S. congressional elections would destroy support for a social clause, Otero replied that it was too early to tell.[30] The employers and nearly all the governments presenting views were opposed to linking trade and workers' rights. India and Indonesia were reported to have argued strongly against linkages.

Office Working Paper re GATT/ILO Collaboration
The 27-page working paper presented by the International Labor Office for discussion by the Governing Body entitled "The Social Dimensions of the Liberalization of World Trade" stated that the term "social clause" had been deliberately avoided in setting up the Working Party since

all associate it with the idea of imposing a certain uniform basis of social protection as a condition of participating in the multilateral trade system. The approach taken during the debate at the Conference and that of the Director-General's report on which it was based are different: the question they raise is not whether it is appropriate and possible to impose a certain minimum social protection on everyone, but what conditions are likely to enable the persons concerned to enjoy an equitable share of the benefits resulting from the liberalization of international trade, each country designing in its own way the content of social protection that would be most appropriate to the conditions of each country.[31]

The Working Paper rejects the concept of equalization of social costs and points out that, while trade liberalization presupposes a minimum of social harmonization, equalization of wages and social protection should not be sought as an end in itself. Rather, the extent of social protection should correspond to the particularities of each country and should "as far as possible" reflect the free choice of *social partners* rather than dictation by the international community. Implicit in the reference to "social partners" is an emphasis on the importance of freedom of association for workers in the determination of social policies. The Office paper points out that nearly all the member States of the ILO are or will be members of the GATT:

Unless it proceeds from a certain schizophrenia, this membership of both organizations means that the States concerned endeavour in good faith to take account in each of these organizations of the objectives and obligations they have undertaken in the other. Once this observation has been made, the logical next step is to attempt to define the content of the social dimension that the community of these States may legitimately introduce in the trade system to guarantee the possibility (and not the content) of social progress from two different standpoints.[32]

The Working Paper then proceeds to discuss possible means by which a social dimension might be included in GATT/WTO. It refers to the difficulty in incorporating a social dimension in GATT which would involve a major new amendment of the texts. Such amendment would be unlikely given the recent substantial modifications of the international trade system and the need for a near universal consensus. The better procedure would appear to be the incorporation of the social dimension in the existing GATT order:

(1) perhaps by considering that abnormally low social conditions might be considered a subsidy under Article XVI of the GATT (denial of freedom of association giving rise to the presumption that working conditions are being maintained at an abnormally low level);

(2) perhaps by extending the general exceptions provided for any Contracting Party by Article XX of the GATT to include workers' rights which have a direct bearing on human dignity. (Article XX allows a Contracting Party to adopt or enforce measures restricting trade justified by public

order or economic considerations, in particular measures necessary to protect human or animal life or health, as well as measures relating to products
of prison labor.)

(3) perhaps through the nullification and impairment clauses of Article
XXIII. (This Article lays down general provisions aimed at remedying
failures to meet obligations under the Agreement resulting in the objectives being nullified and impaired.)

As explained below, the Working Paper develops the possibility of enforcing a social dimension through Article XXIII on nullification and impairment in preference to the GATT Articles referred to in (1) and (2)
above.

The Working Paper points out that the "GATT enforcement system
was designed along very specific lines which are not necessarily adapted
to the nature and aims of the 'social rules of the game'" which the ILO
supports. The enforcement procedures which would apply to issues of
subsidies under Article XVI of GATT, for example, would permit the
injured party to mete out justice itself and to redress the imbalance by
applying restrictions which it would not normally be allowed to apply;
such a decentralized system would not guarantee uniformity or proportionality. Thus, proceeding under Article XVI on subsidies would not be
the most appropriate approach, according to the Paper. Similar objections
could also be raised concerning the application of Article XX (on general
exceptions).

The Working Paper considers the provisions of Article XXIII on nullification and impairment to offer a more appropriate approach to linking a
social dimension to the GATT. Under Article XXIII, if a contracting party
feels that any benefit accruing to it is being nullified or impaired or that the
objective of the Agreement is being impeded by the failure of another
party to carry out its obligations under the Agreement, it may make
written proposals to the other contracting party. If no satisfactory result is
obtained, the matter may be referred to the Contracting Parties, who will
investigate and make appropriate recommendations or give a ruling. Paragraph 2 of Article XXIII provides that "[t]he Contracting Parties may
consult with Contracting Parties, with the Economic and Social Council of
the United Nations and with *any appropriate intergovernmental organization
in cases where they consider such consultations necessary*" (emphasis added).
If the circumstances are considered serious enough by the Contracting
Parties they may authorize Contracting Parties or parties to suspend the

application to any other Contracting Party of such concessions or obligations under the Agreement as they may determine to be appropriate in the circumstances. The procedure under Article XXIII thus has the advantage over the procedures under Article XVI and XX in not permitting unilateral enforcement. It is also suggested in the Working Paper that it opens up the possibility of the involvement of the ILO as an "appropriate intergovernmental organization" in issues arising under Article XXIII:

> It would be interesting to explore further, in consultation with the competent services of the GATT, the possibility of applying it [Art. XXIII] to the rules of the game in the social field, on which a consensus may be reached, by including compliance with relevant ILO Conventions among the obligations attaching to membership of the GATT and the WTO. . . . [T]he limited amendment necessary to establish the content of the 'rules of the game' by which the Contracting Parties would be bound in the social field could be accompanied by a sufficiently flexible structure for collaboration between the WTO and the ILO aimed at affording the most appropriate response to violations of specified ILO standards.[33]

The relevant ILO standards would presumably be those on freedom of association and collective bargaining contained in Conventions Nos. 87 and 98, those on forced labor in Conventions Nos. 29 and 105, and possibly standards relating to child labor organized in conditions that are tantamount to slavery.[34] The Working Paper suggests that if a new provision were to be incorporated in the Agreement stipulating that membership in the WTO *ipso jure* subjects the party to the obligations resulting from specific ILO conventions, "the establishment of a violation of these Conventions would make it possible to undertake the measures aimed at remedying it" since a violation of an obligation specifically laid down in the Agreement creates a presumption that a benefit has been nullified or impaired.[35] ILO procedures, in particular the relevant complaints procedures under Article 26 of the ILO Constitution, could be utilized to determine violations of the obligations of the standards in relevant ILO conventions. Article 26 provides that a State which has ratified a particular convention may file a complaint that another ratifying State is not effectively observing the provisions of the convention. The Governing Body may appoint a Commission of Inquiry to investigate the complaint if it sees fit. The Governing Body may also appoint Commissions of Inquiry on its own motion or on receipt of a complaint from a delegate of the Conference. States have rarely filed complaints under this Article although in recent years several complaints have been filed by Conference delegates.[36] According to the Office Working Paper, the Article 26 procedure contains safeguards against frivolous claims "in particular because of the required intervention of the Governing Body on a tripartite basis, *inter alia*, to decide whether or not to appoint a Commission of Inquiry."[37] If under the ILO procedures a violation were found, it would be up to the Contracting Parties to take any action considered appropriate under Article XXIII in the light of the conclusions of the Commission of Inquiry transmitted by the ILO Governing Body. It was noted that the ILO complaints procedure may be set in motion by a nongovernmental delegate to the Conference which would afford a possibility that does not exist under the purely intergovernmental framework of the WTO.

While the International Labor Office paper develops a procedure for linking international labor conventions and the ILO enforcement procedures with the GATT/WTO under the nullification and impairment provisions of Article XXIII, it would seem to be more logical to include provisions regarding workers' rights as an exception under Article XX, which relates to various questions of social policy. The problem of unilateral enforcement and of objectivity in determination of violations could possibly be taken care of under Article XX. The inclusion of some workers' rights under the exception provisions of Article XX is discussed at more length in the following section on the GATT.

Since the ILO Governing Body had not completed its discussion of the Office paper by the date of writing (March 1995), it remains to be seen whether the Governing Body will approve the suggestions contained in the Working paper and whether the WTO is interested in exploring with the ILO the question of including any provision on the social dimension of the liberalization of trade in the GATT.

Other international organizations have contacted the ILO in connection with the possible linkage of trade and labor standards. The European Community, in the process of adopting a new General Scheme of Preferences, asked the ILO for assistance in drafting the clauses relating to the linkage of labor standards with GSP. In June 1994, the OECD Council at Ministerial Level decided to adopt a work program involving cooperation with all relevant international organizations on, *inter alia*, "trade, employment and internationally recognised labour standards, including basic concepts, empirical evidence in trade and investment patterns, and current mechanisms for promoting higher labour standards worldwide" leading to a report to Ministers in 1995.[38] Representatives of the OECD visited the ILO in July 1994 to discuss the linkage of trade and labor standards. The ILO is thus at the center of international discussions concerning a social clause; it is being urged, from many sides, to clarify, willingly or not, the issues involved in the consideration or adoption of such a clause.

Reformers in the 19th century saw international conventions establishing common labor standards, and an international organization to monitor those standards, as the solution to the problem of working conditions and international competitiveness. There are now over 170 labor conventions adopted by International Labor Conferences and the ILO has an admired monitoring system to supervise the application of the Conventions, but the problem of labor standards and international trade has not been resolved; it remains an international concern. While progress has obviously been made in the improvement of labor conditions in the 150 years since the relation between labor conditions and international competitiveness was first discussed, it is also obvious that the setting up of the ILO and the adoption of 175 international labor conventions is not the solution to difficulties in the condition of labor which was once thought. Thus, the continued call for further linkages between trade and workers' rights.

Francis Blanchard, former ILO Director-General, writing in *Le Monde* in June 1993, pointed out that, for far too many countries, membership in the ILO simply salves their conscience. He noted that the scandal of child labor, slavery, and exploitation of workers—situations which shock the conscience—still continue and cited the failings of industrial countries as well as developing countries: the few ILO conventions ratified by the United States, the refusal of the United Kingdom to accept the social dimension of the European community, and the need for Japan to raise its labor law and practice to the same level as that of its Western partners. He concluded by urging the ILO, in consultation with GATT, to go beyond its present procedures and promote the social clause.[39] The demand for a social clause in trade agreements is, in some sense, a result of frustration that the efforts of the ILO have not been more successful. The limitations of the ILO effort to promote social justice, however, may be due less to deficiencies in that organization than to the failure of other international initiatives such as UN development programs, IMF structural adjustment programs, and trade liberalization efforts to include a social justice dimension in their programs.

4.5   The GATT, the WTO, and Workers' Rights

The 1948 draft Havana Charter of the ill-fated International Trade Organization included an article on fair labor standards as well as articles, *inter alia*, on restrictive business practices, commodity arrangements, and domestic employment practices.[40] The argument for linking these issues with international trade was the conviction "that the failure of interwar attempts to secure international agreements liberalizing trade was largely due to the practice of taking up trade questions in isolation instead of putting them in the more complex setting of economic policy as a whole."[41]

The General Agreement on Tariffs and Trade (GATT)[42] and the Havana Charter were both negotiated during the period 1946–48, but, while the ITO never entered into force, the GATT has been provisionally applied since 1948. The GATT was limited to traditional commercial aspects of trade in goods and did not include an article on fair labor standards, nor on most of the other trade-related issues included in the Havana Charter. Following the decision of the American administration not to submit the Havana Charter to the U.S. Congress, the ITO was effectively dead, but the GATT survived as a separate agreement—not an organization. In the form of a provisionally applicable agreement, it has continued for almost 50 years. The new World Trade Organization (WTO), established at Marrakesh in April 1994, incorporates the updated (to 1994) General Agreement on Tariffs and Trade, as well as the Uruguay Round agreements on agriculture, services, intellectual property (TRIPS), and investment, and it includes more substantial dispute settlement provisions than existed in the GATT.[43] The provision on fair labor standards in the 1948 draft Havana Charter (Ch. II, Art. 7) reads

1. The Members recognize ... that all countries have a common interest in the achievement and maintenance of fair labour standards related to productivity, and thus in the improvement of wages and working conditions as productivity may permit. The Members recognize that unfair labour conditions, particularly in production for export, create difficulties in international trade and, accordingly, each Member shall take whatever action may be appropriate and feasible to eliminate such conditions within its territory.
2. Members which are also members of the International Labour Organisation shall co-operate with that organization in giving effect to this undertaking.
3. In all matters relating to labour standards that may be referred to the Organisation ... [under dispute settlement provisions or the Charter] ... it shall consult and co-operate with the International Labour Organisation.[44]

No similar provision was included in the GATT, and with the demise of the proposed ITO the linkage of trade and workers' rights was no longer explicit in an international instrument. Nevertheless, the demand for the inclusion of a provision on labor standards in the GATT has been raised repeatedly during intervening years, and surfaced especially during the concluding negotiations of the Uruguay Round.

As Charnovitz has pointed out, the United States (joined at times by some European countries) unsuccessfully argued as early as 1953, and as recently as the Uruguay Round, for the inclusion of a provision on labor standards in the GATT.[45] The Nordic countries had also unsuccessfully attempted to raise the issue of a social clause during the negotiations of the Tokyo Round. Developing nations have blocked efforts within GATT to establish a Working Party to discuss the relation of international labor standards and trade. They have argued that the demand for a social clause is disguised protectionism, that it would erode their comparative advantage in labor costs, that the best method of improving labor standards is export-led growth and development (the "trickle-down" theory).[46]

During discussions at Marrakesh in April 1994, the United States and a few other countries argued forcefully for an explicit recognition of the relationship of labor standards (and environmental concerns) in the Final Act of the Conference.[47] In the event, the developing countries argued more effectively against any explicit recognition of the link of labor standards and trade. The only concession made by the opponents of the link was the acceptance of the following reference in the Concluding Remarks of the Chairman of the Trade Negotiations Committee:

In the statements which they made in the course of this meeting, Ministers representing a number of participating delegations stressed the importance they attach to their requests for an examination of the relationship between the trading system and internationally recognized labour standards. . . .[48]

But the impact of this mention was diluted by the inclusion in the same statement of a lengthy litany of requests for the examination of the relationship of other issues to trade: immigration policies, competition policy, rules on export financing, restrictive business practices, investment, regionalism, financial and monetary matters, debt and commodity markets, company law, compensation for erosion of preferences, political stability, alleviation of poverty, unilateral and extraterritorial trade measures. Some of these issues were urged by developed countries and some by developing countries. Proponents of a link between labor standards and trade may take small comfort in the fact that the relationship between trade and "internationally recognized labor standards" headed the long list.

Environmental issues fared better than labor standards at Marrakesh. Ministers at the meeting decided to direct the first meeting of the General Council of the new WTO to establish a Committee on Trade and the Environment.[49] The failure to adopt a similar decision at Marrakesh concerning labor standards does not foreclose consideration of the issue by the WTO. The Preparatory Committee set up to establish the WTO will discuss suggestions for the inclusion of additional items in the agenda of the WTO's work program and it appears likely that this will include issues of labor standards and trade.

The GATT is the remnant of a more comprehensive effort to consider trade in the wider context of economic policy and development. As mentioned earlier, the draft Havana Charter for the still-born ITO included provisions on investment, economic development of "underdeveloped countries," full employment, fair labor standards, cartels, and commodity agreements. While the GATT was intended to be limited to trade in goods, it has not been possible to keep issues of general economic policy and development—and even justice and ethical issues—from finding a place within the Agreement. Preferential treatment for developing countries is permitted by the Agreement and Article XX provides for exceptions from provisions of the Agreement for, *inter alia*, protection of human, animal and plant life, and health and prison labor. The recently concluded Uruguay Round brought services, agriculture, and intellectual property issues into GATT negotiations.

It is argued that only "trade-related" issues, and not issues such as workers' rights, should have a place in trade negotiations (i.e., note the use of the term "trade-related" intellectual property to justify the inclusion of intellectual property issues in Uruguay Round negotiations).[50] The categorization of "trade-related issues," however, appears to depend on the eyes of the beholder. Labor conditions in export industries are clearly "trade related." To the United States, commerce in the audio-visual sector (films, videos) is a trade issue which should be regulated by the GATT; the French argued successfully at the conclusion of the Uruguay Round that trade in films and other audio-visual aspects is a "cultural issue" which should be kept out of the Uruguay Round negotiations.

It is difficult to separate purely trade issues from any other issues that a substantial segment of the international community would like to have linked to trade. To the despair of free trade economists, political negotiations make it abundantly evident that the economic advantages from liberalization of trade are not always perceived as the only important issues in trade negotiations. Trade and other issues of economic policy are closely linked.

That the agreements during the Uruguay Round and at Marrakesh recognized the relationship of intellectual property, services, and the environment to trade make it increasingly difficult to argue that trade-related labor standards have no place in trade agreements. Pandora's Box has been opened, as demonstrated by the litany of other issues raised in the context of trade and referred to in the Concluding Remarks of the Chairman of the Trade Negotiations Committee demonstrate. The acceptance of an expressed link between trade and other economic issues within the new WTO will likely depend in the future not on the perceived intrinsic link or lack of link to trade (since nearly every economic issue has a relationship with trade), but on political bargaining between the parties.

Some have contended that the ILO and not the GATT is the appropriate international forum for consideration of labor rights and trade. As pointed out in the preceding section on the ILO, that organization has, until recently, shown as little enthusiasm as the GATT for consideration of the issue. The United States has focused its efforts in relation to the social clause on the GATT, as have other advocates of a social clause who perceive the use of trade sanctions as a more effective enforcement mechanism than ILO procedures.

Issues should be raised within the appropriate international organization—the ILO's mandate is labor issues. Nevertheless, a number of issues concern the activities of more than one organization. The subject of intellectual property has now become a concern of the WTO insofar as it is trade related, although the World Intellectual Property Organization (WIPO) is the organization specializing in such issues; environmental issues will now be considered in the GATT, despite the mandates of the United Nations Environmental Program and the Commission on Sustainable Development. The issue of the relationship of labor standards to trade touches the mandate of both the ILO and the WTO. Organizations concerned with the same issue should collaborate and avoid working at cross-purposes. While the ILO, for example, has pushed for higher labor standards, IMF-imposed structural adjustment programs have been perceived as leading to a lowering of such standards. Liberalization of trade, it is feared, will have a similar effect. Issues of the relationship of trade and workers' rights are thus the proper domain of both the WTO and ILO and should involve collaboration between the two organizations.

Proponents of linking labor standards and trade have not always clarified how the link could be made within the GATT or the WTO. Most proposals are limited to a request for a working group to study the issue—certainly a preliminary step which may or may not eventually lead to an explicit link. A working paper prepared by the International Labor Office—described at length in the preceding section on the ILO—has suggested a possible means of linking ILO labor standards with the GATT/WTO. Despite a certain degree of repetition, the main points of the ILO paper will be briefly reiterated.

The Office paper points out that nearly all member states of the ILO are or will be members of the WTO and that "this membership of both organizations means that States concerned endeavour in good faith to take account in each of these organizations of the objectives and obligations they have undertaken in the other."[51] The paper then examines the various provisions of the GATT with a view to perceiving in what manner a social dimension might be integrated into the economy of the GATT/ WTO. It discusses the possibility of considering abnormally low social conditions as a subsidy under Article XVI of the GATT or adding workers' rights to the exceptions to GATT provisions permitted under Article XX. The paper suggests that neither of these two solutions is appropriate since unilateral determination concerning the alleged subsidy or exception would be permitted under these articles, without objective determination.[52] It suggests that the better solution would be enforcing a social dimension through the nullification and impairment provisions of Article XXIII, which provide for a multilateral consideration of the questions raised under that Article, and also makes possible consultation with "any appropriate intergovernmental organization," in this case, the ILO. The ILO paper suggests that compliance with the main ILO conventions (freedom of association, the right to collective bargaining, forced labor, and possibly standards relating to child labor) could be made obligations attaching to membership in the GATT/WTO. Complaint procedures under the ILO Constitution could be utilized to determine violation of the provisions of these ILO conventions. If a violation were to be found, the GATT/WTO Contracting Parties would then be free to take any action they considered appropriate in the light of the ILO conclusions.

The International Labor Office paper, incorporating the above suggestions for ILO/WTO collaboration, is presently (March 1995) under discussion by the ILO Governing Body and thus has not yet been adopted as the formal suggestion of the Organization. In earlier Governing Body discussions, considerable opposition to any linkage of trade and workers' rights was expressed by many governments and representatives of employer organizations.

Another suggestion for linking labor standards with trade issues through WTO/ILO collaboration was made by several major trade union federations during Uruguay Round negotiations. The International Confederation of Free Trade Unions (ICFTU), the World Confederation of

Labour (WCL), and the European Trade Union Confederations (ETUC) prepared a joint statement on the social dimensions of international trade which delineated in detail a proposal for a social clause.

The statement pointed out that, while the Uruguay Round agreement has the potential to be a positive force for world economic development, it would only be translated into jobs and increased income if linked to respect for minimum international labor standards as defined by the ILO. The ICFTU, WCL, and ETUC stated that they would like to see included in a social clause ILO standards contained in its conventions relating to freedom of association and the right to collective bargaining, minimum age for employment, discrimination and equal remuneration, and forced labor. It pointed out that these standards contain principles that governments of all countries regardless of their stage of development should legitimately be expected to observe. It was suggested that a Joint Advisory Committee of the ILO and the GATT/WTO should specify a list of minimum standards to be included in a social clause and oversee their implementation, operating in cooperation with the ILO Committee on Freedom of Association and its Committee of Experts on the Application of Conventions and Recommendations. They suggested that, on the basis of specific complaints from the tripartite constituents of the ILO (governments, employers, and unions), the Joint Advisory Committee would examine the extent to which the contracting parties were meeting their obligations under the social clause and make recommendations accordingly:

When a country was found to be falling short of its obligations, the Joint Advisory Committee would recommend measures to be taken within a specified period that should not exceed two years. The ILO would also offer technical assistance to the country concerned, perhaps funded by a new international social fund.

At the end of the specified period, a further report would be prepared which would either state that the country was now fulfilling its obligations, or that progress was being made, specifying the additional time needed to deal with the problem, or that the government had failed to make adequate efforts.

In the latter case trade sanctions would be applied. These sanctions could consist of increased tariffs to be levied by all GATT/WTO Members on the offending country's exports.[53]

The proposal is similar to the International Labor Office paper in recommending collaboration between the two organizations and the use of ILO major labor conventions as a standard for judging respect for workers' rights. It lacks the specificity of the Office proposal regarding the incorporation of such a provision into the GATT/WTO order.

Despite the suggestion in the ILO Office paper concerning linking international labor standards and trade through the Article XXIII nullification and impairment provisions of the GATT, it would appear at first blush that Article XX on exceptions to the Agreement would be the more logical Article for such a link. Article XX permits a state to impose barriers to trade—not otherwise permitted under GATT—for certain reasons relating to social policy. States may impose barriers to trade as an exception under GATT for measures "necessary to protect human, animal or plant life or health" (Article XX(b)) or measures pertaining to conservation of exhaustible resources (Article XX(g)) or to prohibit import of articles produced by prison labor (Article XX(e)).

The logic supporting the right to bar imports produced by prison labor, for example, could also support the addition of language permitting the barring of imports produced by forced labor.[54] Commentators normally skeptical of or opposed to the linking of workers' rights to trade issues in general have remarked that, nevertheless, it should be considered unacceptable to obtain a comparative advantage through the use of forced labor.[55] There would seem to be an agreement, as Charnovitz has stated, that "there are some government policies that are beyond the pale"—and the use of forced labor would appear to be one of them.[56] The 'Leutwiler Group' report to the Director-General of GATT found that "there is no disagreement that countries do not have to accept the products of *slave* or *prison* labor" (emphasis added).[57] The exceptions under Article XX could also possibly be expanded to include goods produced under conditions which violated other "internationally recognized labor standards," in particular, such a fundamental human right as freedom of association. (See Section 4.8 for discussion of the definition of "internationally recognized labor standards" in this context.)

Nevertheless, the objections raised in the ILO paper concerning the use of Article XX are important. The paper correctly signals that Article XX permits countries unilaterally to impose barriers to trade on the basis of their own assessment. This opens the door to possible abusive use of trade barriers for protectionist reasons allegedly on the basis of the exceptions permitted under Article XX. The Preamble to Article XX contains an injunction against trade restrictions that are a "disguised restriction on international trade." If an exception were added to Article XX for the serious violation of a limited number of fundamental labor standards, a clause could be added requiring reference to the ILO conventions and monitoring bodies for interpretation and application of the exception in a concrete case. A GATT panel could then assess whether the claimed exception was permissible under Article XX.[58] John Jackson has pointed out that the new World Trade Organization, with a better institutional structure than GATT and improved dispute settlement provisions, would be more able to deal with certain contentious issues of international economic policy. Although Jackson did not mention the link between labor standards and trade, his comments would seem to have special pertinence to that issue. In remarks prepared for a hearing of the U.S. Senate Finance Committee in March 1994, he stated:

More and more governments find themselves frustrated in trying to regulate appropriately in situations where international economic behavior crosses borders, because the perpetrators of such behavior can sometimes play one nation off against another, develop rival or competitive 'reductions in regulation rigor' (sometimes called 'race to the bottom'). Thus an institutional structure that has the potential to meet these problems and to deal with them in an appropriate and balanced way through mutual cooperation is extremely important.[59]

It remains to be seen whether the new WTO will be able to deal with the issue of a social clause in a more balanced way through "mutual coopera- tion" than the pre-WTO/GATT.

4.6   NAFTA and Workers' Rights

On August 12, 1992, the United States, Canada, and Mexico announced the conclusion of negotiations for a free trade agreement. During the negotiations and following their completion, extensive opposition was voiced in the United States and Canada over the failure to consider the environmental and labor impact of NAFTA. While approval of the Agree- ment was assured in Canada and Mexico, it was subject to approval of the American Congress. During the presidential campaign in the fall of 1992, candidate Clinton, responding to the criticisms of labor unions and envi- ronmentalists, spoke of the need to consider means of taking these issues into account. After his election, when it became clear that renegotiation of the entire Agreement was not feasible, the administration decided to adopt supplementary agreements on labor and the environment.

The North American Agreement on Labor Cooperation (NAALC)[60] and a supplementary agreement on the environment were completed on August 13, 1993 and signed in Mexico City, Washington, and Ottawa in early September 1993.[61] On December 8, 1993, President Clinton signed into law the NAFTA Implementation Act and NAFTA Worker Security Act, incorporating the labor cooperation agreement and permitting the President to enter NAFTA into force on or after January 1, 1994.[62] The

AFL-CIO was a leading proponent of the need for some type of labor guarantees in NAFTA. "The AFL-CIO estimates that if Congress approves NAFTA, 73 percent of U.S. workers will suffer annual wage losses of approximately $1,000 and 500,000 to 600,000 workers will lose their jobs to lower-paid Mexican workers over 10 years."[63] The fear of loss of U.S. jobs centered on the belief that the Agreement would cause additional U.S. businesses to relocate to low-wage Mexico. Labor advocates cited the increasing tendency of American businesses to move to *maquiladora* production goods in special zones on the Mexican border where parts imported from the United States are assembled with low-wage Mexican labor and exported to the United States. It was also argued that companies competing in the United States with imports from Mexico would be placed at a competitive disadvantage.

Proponents of the parallel labor agreement also argued that it was necessary in order to assist the poor labor conditions of the Mexican worker. Mexican labor laws are generally good and Mexico has ratified a relatively large number of ILO conventions—far more than the United States. Criticism of the situation of workers in Mexico, however, have focused on limitations on freedom of association and on the failure to enforce the laws on the books.[64] While Mexico has good occupational safety and health laws and child labor laws, enforcement has been uneven and much less satisfactory in the nonunionized maquiladora plants. It is reported:

Yet many employers in the maquiladora sector provide their workers with a wide range of benefits and a safe working environment, and they adhere closely to strict environmental standards. However, these favorable conditions are not universal. Reports in newspapers such as the Wall Street Journal describe a perilous disregard for worker safety, substandard living and working conditions ... in communities on both sides of the U.S.-Mexican border....[65]

Proponents of NAFTA argued, on the other hand, that a supplementary agreement was not necessary since NAFTA would be highly beneficial to American companies—and thus, in the long run at least, aid the American and Mexican economies and both American and Mexican workers.[66] The primary objectives of the NAALC are stated in Article 1 to be the improvement in each party's territory of "working conditions and living standards" and the promotion of "compliance with and effective enforcement by each Party of its labor law." The focus of the Agreement is on the enforcement of each country's own labor laws and not the application and enforcement of internationally recognized labor standards or workers' rights. The phrase "internationally recognized labor standards" is nowhere found in the Agreement. It provides that each country should promote compliance with and effectively enforce its *own* labor law, through inspection, recordkeeping, and sanctions for violations, and refers to the most important internationally recognized labor standards (namely, freedom of association, the right of collective bargaining, and the right to strike) not as obligations of the Parties, but only as

guiding principles that the Parties are committed to promote, subject to each Party's domestic law, but [which] do not establish common minimum standards for their domestic law. They indicate broad areas of concern where the Parties have developed, each in its own way, laws, regulations, procedures and practices that protect the rights and interests of their respective workforces. (Annex I of NAALC)

The Agreement sets up a formal dispute settlement procedure for resolution of disputes relating to the enforcement of each Party's labor law concerning occupational safety and health, minimum wage, child labor, and technical labor standards, but provides *no* formal dispute settlement procedure relating to enforcement of laws concerning freedom of association, the right to bargain collectively and the right to strike.

The Agreement establishes a trilateral Commission on Labor Cooperation to promote joint cooperative activities relating to labor issues, through the organization of seminars, joint research, technical assistance, and conferences. The Commission is comprised of three elements:

1. a Ministerial Council, comprising cabinet-level representatives from each country to direct the implementation of the Agreement;
2. a small International Coordinating Secretariat (ICS) directed by the Council to prepare background reports, to carry out the co-operative work program and to support committees set up to evaluate enforcement problems; and
3. National Administrative Offices (NAO) in each country to compile and transmit information to the Secretariat and to receive and register complaints of non-enforcement of labour laws.[67]

The U.S. Secretary of Labor established the National Administrative Office (NAO), required by the Labor Cooperation Supplementary Agreement, on December 30, 1993.[68] The NAO is in the department's Bureau of International Labor Affairs and will serve as the central point of contact for all NAFTA labor-related issues. Similar offices have been established in Canada and Mexico.

Proceedings may be begun by any of the three countries against one of the others that has demonstrated a "persistent pattern of failure" to enforce its occupational safety and health, child labor, or minimum-wage technical standards. A Party can defend its failure to act if it "reflects a reasonable exercise of ... discretion ... or results from bona fide decisions to allocate resources to enforcement in respect of other labor matters determined to have higher priorities.[69] The Labor Commission, composed of the Ministerial Council and supporting Secretariat, oversees any such proceedings. Ministerial consultations may be requested, and if they do not resolve the dispute, the Council of Ministers may appoint an Evaluation Committee of Experts at the request of any Party to investigate the labor law enforcement and practices of each Party to the disagreement. If that further fails to lead to a settlement, the Council may appoint an Arbitral Panel by a two-thirds vote.

Five experts representing all three nations sit on the Arbitral Panel. If convened, the Panel must submit a final report to the Council within 240 days of initial formation summarizing its findings of fact and evaluation as to whether there has been a "persistent pattern of failure" and its recommendations for the remedying of the failure. If it is felt that the violating nation has failed to implement the recommendations, the Panel may be reconvened and eventually assess a monetary fine. The Council may use any monies collected "to improve or enhance the labor law enforcement in the Party complained against, consistent with its labor law." If the fine is not paid into the Council's fund, the complaining party may suspend the other party's tariff benefits by a duty increase, but only long enough to collect the amount of the fine or until an action plan is implemented. There is no provision for compensatory or punitive damages for the unions or workers whose rights are violated.

The procedure just outlined is many tiered and complicated; it relates only to enforcement of a country's *own* laws and does not concern the failure to uphold "internationally recognized labor standards." Issues of persistent failure to enforce freedom of association—the most fundamental of all labor standards—may not be raised through the dispute settlement procedure. Complaints concerning these issues are reviewed only by the NAO's and ministerial consultations.

Although the Agreement addresses the failure of Mexico to enforce its own relatively good labor laws relating to occupational health and safety, child labor, and certain technical labor standards, it does not address the major concern in Mexico, namely, limitations on freedom of association. The first public complaint addressed to the U.S. NAO related to such limitations in the maquiladora plants of U.S. companies in Juarez, Mexico. Allegations of violations of freedom of association, as mentioned above, are not subject to the complex dispute settlement procedure, but may be raised by an NAO in a request for ministerial consultations.

The U.S. Secretary of Labor's Notice of Establishment of the NAO stated that the Office would accept public submissions on labor law matters arising in the territories of the other Parties. Under the NAALC, only governments may ask for consultations with another government regarding issues in the Agreement, but under U.S. regulations an American individual or concerned group may raise relevant issues before the NAO. Further proceedings or consultations with the government alleged to violate the Agreement would depend on the U.S. government's taking up the issue with the other government.

In early 1994, two petitions were presented to the U.S. NAO relating to the actions of American companies operating in Mexico. The United Electrical, Radio and Machine Workers of America (UE) filed the first submission to the NAO alleging that General Electric had violated rights of association of its Mexican employees and had jeopardized the health and safety of employees at the company's Juarez motor plant, known as Compania Armadora or CASA. The petition alleged that General Electric had obstructed union organizing efforts by firing a number of workers active in organizing or by forcing voluntary resignations by such employees. A petition was also filed by the International Brotherhood of Teamsters charging that Mexican workers were fired for attempting to organize workers at a Honeywell electronics factory in Chihuahua, Mexico.

After a hearing in Washington, the NAO issued a report in October 1994 concerning the two petitions.[70] It found that Mexico had not failed to enforce its labor laws as the employees had the option of continuing their complaints about the companies under Mexican law or accept severance pay. In accepting severance pay they exercised their option and it was not possible, therefore, for Mexican authorities to determine whether their dismissals were for union organizing. The NAO thus did not recommend that the petitions be sent on for ministerial review under NAALC.

Later in 1994 another petition was filed by U.S. and Mexican human rights organizations charging that the SONY Corporation subsidiary in Nuevo Laredo, Mexico had infringed freedom of association by firing union activists.[71] At the time of writing (March 1995), NAO hearings on the petition had just been concluded in San Antonio, Texas.

While the important issue of freedom of association is not subject to the complex dispute settlement proceedings laid out in NAALC, the NAO hearings, at a minimum, make it possible to raise issues concerning freedom of association before the U.S. body and are obviously being used to do so. Unions and human rights organizations may well become disillusioned, however, by decisions of that body which fail to forward complaints for ministerial consideration. In January 1995, the Electrical Workers Union withdrew from further hearings on its charge against General Electric calling the October 1994 NAO report "blatantly inadequate" and charging that the NAO reviewed the testimony in "an extremely cursory fashion [and] generally ignored the evidence presented."[72]

In the year since NAFTA came into force, the political and economic problems of Mexico and the resulting need for major assistance from the United States and international financial institutions have blunted the perception of the bright prospects predicted by some to follow from NAFTA and—as commentators have noted—have created even more concern about the situation of workers in that country. Robert Kuttner reported in The Washington Post:

As part of the Mexican government's new austerity pact, wage increases will be held to 7 percent, although inflation is expected to run at 15 to 20 percent. In other words, real Mexican living standards ... will fall by at least 8 percent this year. It is ironic indeed that this journey to a free global market place is leaving Mexico with U.S. sponsored bailouts, currency stabilization deals and austerity pacts—hardly a free market.[73]

Most commentators studying the NAFTA Agreement on Labor Cooperation have found it wanting as a means of protecting labor in the three countries. Its failure to refer to internationally recognized labor standards, its minor reference to the ILO, its emphasis on enforcement only of each nation's own labor laws, and its complex and time-consuming dispute settlement procedures are generally perceived as a weak instrument for protecting workers.[74]

4.7 U.S. Legislation Linking Trade and Workers' Rights

At the present time a number of U.S. trade and aid programs are conditioned on the granting of "internationally recognized worker rights." Worker rights provisions have been included in legislation on the Generalized System of Preferences (GSP),[75] the Caribbean Basin Initiative,[76] the Overseas Private Investment Corporation,[77] and the Omnibus Trade and Competitiveness Act of 1988 (amending Section 301 of the Trade Act of 1974).[78] It is generally stated that the aim of these laws is to improve the condition of workers in countries that do not accord workers' rights and to counter "social dumping"—economic advantage resulting from producing products under poor labor conditions. In the eyes of many, however, the aim is primarily protectionist.

The GSP, adopted by Congress in 1974, amended in 1984 and recently continued for one year on a provisional basis, provides temporary duty-free treatment to certain products from developing countries. Under this program the President may not designate a country as a GSP recipient if it "has not taken or is not taking steps to afford internationally recognized worker rights to workers in the country," defined to include

(1) the right of association,

(2) the right to organize and bargain collectively,

(3) a prohibition on the use of any form of forced or compulsory labor,

(4) a minimum age for the employment of children, and

(5) acceptable conditions of work with respect to minimum wages, hours of work, and occupational safety and health.[79]

The legislation provides a rather complicated procedure for determining whether a country is "taking steps" to afford workers' rights, which include the opportunity to file petitions for review of a beneficiary country's conformity with the legislation and public hearings on such petitions. The Committee examining these petitions has recourse to information concerning workers' rights in the State Department annual *Country Reports on Human Rights Practices*, findings of the ILO, reports from U.S. embassies and consulates, and U.S. International Trade Commission reports on the economic effects of GSP decisions. Decisions concerning eligibility are decided each year and the GSP status of a country is suspended, terminated, or continued.

During debate on the renewal of the GSP, the 1984 House Ways and Means Committee Report stated:

It is not the expectation of the Committee that developing countries come up to the prevailing labor standards of the United States and other highly-industrialized developed countries. It is recognized that acceptable minimum standards may vary from country to country. However, the Committee does expect the President, in granting duty-free access to the U.S. market, to require that any developing country specifically demonstrate respect for the internationally recognized worker rights of its workers.[80]

Prior to 1987, the GSP status of Nicaragua and Romania were terminated, while a number of other countries in which the protection of workers' rights appeared in doubt were continued as GSP beneficiaries. These decisions led to criticisms that the program was politically biased.

In 1990, the Washington-based International Labor Rights Education and Research Fund, several labor unions, and human rights groups filed a complaint in the U.S. District Court for the District of Columbia alleging that the President had failed to adequately enforce the GSP worker rights provisions. The complaint was dismissed by the Court on the grounds that the controversy was not justiciable, given the discretion provided in the GSP statute and the President's authority in the field of foreign affairs. The Court's decision stated, "The Court cannot interfere with the President's discretionary judgment because there is no law to apply."[81] In October 1991, the District Court's judgment dismissing the action was affirmed by the United States Court of Appeals, District of Columbia Circuit, with concurring statements by two judges expressing separate reasons for the decision and a dissenting opinion by Judge Abner Mikva.

The Lawyers Committee for Human Rights, a New York-based human rights organization, examining the GSP legislation reported:

The question of what constitutes adequate "steps," then, is at present a very subjective one.... Critics argue that Congress intended that all petitions be reviewed but that the GSP Subcommittee has exercised too much latitude in deciding whether to accept or reject petitions. Critics further charge that the Administration's decisions are politically motivated, often relating directly to the state of United States' relations with the particular country.[82]

The U.S. workers' rights legislation has been sharply criticized by a human rights scholar as "aggressive unilateralism" (a term used by Jagdish Bhagwati to refer to U.S. trade legislation in general). In an article entitled "Labor Provisions in U.S. Trade Law: 'Aggressive Unilateralism'?", Philip Alston writes:

The policy assumptions embodied in current U.S. "international worker rights" legislation ... as well as the manner in which that legislation is being implemented are highly questionable from an international law perspective. Specifically, there are several matters which warrant careful examination by proponents of an international rule of law in relation to both trade and human rights matters. They include: the use of rhetoric but not the substance of "international standards"; the application to other countries of standards that have not been accepted by those countries and which are not generally considered to be part of customary international law.[83]

Alston is particularly critical of the failure of the legislation and the practical application of the legislation to take sufficiently into account the ILO interpretation of relevant international labor standards.

In October 1994, the Office of the United States Trade Representative announced that petitions to review the compliance of five countries with the workers' rights provisions of the GSP law remained under review: the Dominican Republic, Guatemala, Maldives, Pakistan, and Thailand. A number of other countries were certified for GSP since they were perceived as having "taken steps" to grant internationally recognized labor standards.

In July 1994, the U.S. Trade Representative Mickey Kantor had ruled that, despite legal recognition of unions in the Dominican Republic's export-processing zones, labor conditions in the zones required further investigation. The AFL-CIO, working with Dominican unions, had petitioned the Trade Representative to withdraw preferential treatment from products assembled in the Republic, alleging that they did not meet the standards set by U.S. laws. It was reported that, following the ruling, the Dominican government suspended the export license of a Korean-American firm and threatened to suspend the licenses of several other labor-law violators.[84] Union recognition in the threatened companies followed. David Jessup, the AFL-CIO's director of Human and Trade Union Rights, called the gains a "historic development." He said the AFL-CIO petition and assistance from other U.S. unions were key factors in the victory."[85] In February 1994, the U.S. Trade Representative had announced that review of Indonesia's workers' rights would be "suspended" for six months, a period that coincided with the eve of the meeting of the Asia-Pacific Economic Conference (APEC) in Jakarta. Indonesia's conformity with workers' rights and the Kantor decision to suspend the review have been widely criticized by human rights organizations.[86] In November 1994, Indonesia announced a series of measures to improve workers' rights, following a meeting between Kantor and the Indonesian Minister of Labor. Kantor referred to the measures as steps in the right direction. Earlier problems had related to recognition of a single trade union by the government and military and policy interference in labor disputes. The European Union has also adopted a GSP program which includes a provision requiring recipient countries to conform to certain internationally recognized labor standards. The reactions of Indonesia and the Dominican Republic suggest that the threat of removal of GSP has acted as an incentive for countries taking steps toward granting workers' rights.

Both the U.S. legislation and the European Union GSP will become less important in the post-Uruguay Round period. With the general lowering of tariffs as a result of Uruguay Round agreements, according preferential tariff treatment to developing countries has become less important to those countries.[87] In February, Congressman George E. Brown, Jr. introduced a bill in Congress labeled the Child Labor Deterrence Act of 1993, which would prohibit the importation of any product made in whole or in part by children under the age of 15 who are employed in industry or mining. The Bill, commonly referred to as the Harkin Bill, is now pending before Congress. It would require the Secretary of Labor to compile and maintain a list of industries in foreign countries that use child labor in the production of exports to the United States. When such foreign industry was identified, the Secretary of Treasury would be instructed to prohibit the importation of the project from an identified industry. The prohibition would not apply if a U.S. importer signs a certificate of origin affirming that it took reasonable steps to ensure that products imported from identified industries are not made by child labor. In addition, the President is urged in the Bill to seek an agreement with other governments to secure an international ban on trade in the products of child labor.

4.8   Definition of "Internationally Recognized Workers' Rights": A Key Problem in Linking Trade and Workers' Rights

The linking of trade and workers' rights in legislation or trade agreements requires a clarification of the concepts of "internationally recognized workers' rights" or "minimum international labor standards," common terminology employed in these instruments. What precisely are these minimum standards or internationally recognized rights? Despite the frequent use of these terms, it is not easy to define their essential core.

Should "internationally recognized workers' rights" be defined by reference to ILO conventions? Or to standards in international human rights treaties? Or to specification in U.S. legislation and in other national legal provisions? While there is substantial overlap in definition of the concepts in these various instruments, there is not total consistency.

Standards adopted by the ILO are the best reference for defining "internationally recognized worker rights" since they have been agreed to in a multilateral forum and the major ILO conventions are widely ratified. However, the ILO has adopted 175 conventions establishing labor standards on a multitude of issues ranging from the most general (freedom of association) to the very specific relating to working conditions in particular industries (road transport, seafaring, glassmaking, etc.). In addition to conventions, the ILO has adopted hundreds of recommendations, codes, and guidelines laying down labor standards. It is clearly inappropriate to consider all of these standards as "minimum international labor standards." Charnovitz has pointed out that

One could define unfair conditions to be any which do not meet the standards of the ILO. But such a definition has the undesirable consequence of putting just about every nation in the doghouse on at least one of the ILO's 161 [now 175] Conventions.[88]

The ILO itself has established a priority among its many standards by referring to conventions on freedom of association and collective bargaining, on forced labor, on equal remuneration, and on discrimination in employment as "basic human rights conventions" which should be accorded priority in ratification and implementation.[89] These conventions are the most widely ratified of all ILO conventions and those to which the ILO devotes the most attention.

Workers' rights are enshrined not only in ILO conventions, but also in the Universal Declaration of Human Rights and the International Covenant on Civil and Political Rights and the International Covenant on Economic, Social and Cultural Rights. The rights relating to labor in these instruments are more extensive than those in the ILO basic human rights conventions. They include rights

(1) to work;

(2) to just and favorable conditions of work, including fair wages, and safe and healthy working conditions;

(3) to protection against unemployment;

(4) to equal pay for equal work;

(5) to form trade unions;

(6) to rest and leisure and reasonable limitation of working hours; and

(7) the prohibition of forced labor.

Given the current important emphasis on human rights, should all of these rights be considered "minimum international labor standards" or the common core of "internationally recognized workers' rights" despite the fact they do not entirely coincide with the listing of rights in ILO basic human rights conventions and despite the generality of the provisions?

"Internationally recognized workers' rights" have been specified in U.S. legislation and also in the annual State Department Reports on Human Rights. In the latter, internationally recognized workers' rights are considered to be those defined in section 502(a) of the Trade Act of 1974 (as amended), namely,[90]

(1) the right of association;

(2) the right to organize and bargain collectively;

(3) prohibition on the use of forced or compulsory labor;

(4) a minimum age for the employment of children; and

(5) acceptable conditions of work with respect to minimum wages, hours of work, and occupational safety and health.

There is consistency as to the first three rights in nearly all lists of fundamental workers' rights, but not regarding child labor (4) or acceptable conditions of work (5). Conventions on child labor are not included among ILO "basic human rights conventions"; however, the ILO Committee of Experts has considered certain serious cases of the use of child labor as bonded or forced labor and directed comments to states which have ratified Convention No. 29 on Forced Labor concerning such cases.[91] The rights referred to in (5) are stated so generally as to be nearly meaningless—difficult to apply in practice without further specificity and thus subject to arbitrary application. ILO conventions on these subjects are complex, detailed, and applicable to various kinds of work. For example, 14 ILO conventions have been adopted since 1949 on various aspects of worker safety and health, relating to such diverse issues as the use of benzene, protection against radiation, safety and health in construction, occupational cancer, etc. Should the concept of "adequate conditions of work with respect to ... occupational safety and health" follow the detailed provisions of ILO conventions and recommendations on the subject? If not, what criteria can be used to determine adequate standards relating to safety and health? What are adequate "minimum wages"? And it is exceptionally complex to determine what constitutes adequate minimum wages in any particular country or industry.

U.S. legislation on the Caribbean Basin Initiative is even more general, providing that in determining whether to grant duty-free treatment to the country concerned, the President may take into account the extent to which workers are afforded "reasonable workplace conditions and enjoy the right to organize and bargain collectively."[92] In the 1993 article referred to previously, Alston has extensively criticized the labor rights provisions in U.S. law for failing to make explicit reference to ILO standards, since they purport to refer to "internationally recognized" standards, and for failing to include the important issue of non-discrimination in employment.[93] He states that

the US legislation does not contain any detailed standards at all. It simply misappropriates some of the terminology developed by the ILO, without involving any commitment whatsoever to make use of the specific standards that have been drawn up, after very careful negotiations, within the ILO framework.[94]

Alston also criticizes the inclusion of "minimum age for the employment of children" as an internationally recognized worker right. He points out that the standards in the relevant ILO convention (No. 138) are complex, detailed, and provide for the possibility of different minimum ages in different occupations and under different circumstances and require the adoption of measures aimed at eliminating exploitative child labor. As pointed out above, ILO supervisory organs consider that certain serious use of child labor may be considered bonded or forced labor and thus contrary to ILO forced-labor conventions.

A particularly perceptive effort to define "minimum international labor standards" was undertaken in the Netherlands in the mid-1980s. The Dutch Minister of Development Cooperation requested the Netherlands National Advisory Council for Development Cooperation to give its views regarding the advisability of incorporating a provision concerning "minimum labour standards into international agreements" on economic cooperation and trade policy. The resulting report is a thoughtful and thorough discussion of the issue of the linkage of trade and international standards and is particularly useful in the effort to determine what rights might constitute "minimum international labor standards."[95] The report should be compulsory reading for all concerned with workers' rights and trade.

The report defines minimum labor standards, in an "absolute sense," as those which "all countries ought to introduce and observe under all circumstances" and, in addition, points out that there are minimum standards "in a relative sense which develop more or less in line with economic growth."[96] The Advisory Council had recourse to ILO standards to define the content of "minimum internationally recognized labor standards," concluding that the standards in eight ILO conventions—two conventions on freedom of association; two conventions on forced labor; and conventions on discrimination in employment, equal remuneration, employment policy, and minimum age for employment—constituted a minimum package of international labor standards that might be incorporated in international agreements.

In reaching this conclusion, the council applied three criteria: (1) a social criterion, (2) a political and legal criterion, and (3) an economic criterion. The social criterion limited the choice to standards related to basic human needs and human rights. The second, the political and legal criterion, related to the degree of international acceptance of the standard. The Council checked whether the relevant convention was ratified by a geographically and economically diverse group of states. The final, economic, criterion was applied to ensure that the standard would not impose economic hardship or impair economic development. Applying these criteria, the Council arrived at the decision that the standards in the eight ILO conventions previously mentioned constituted the minimum package of international labor standards.

The Council also recommended that this minimum package of labor standards should be included in international agreements only if certain conditions were met: (1) the agreement itself must first contribute to the conditions needed to facilitate observance of the minimum international labor standards, (2) it must provide for a satisfactory procedure for the settlement of disputes by an independent body, and (3) the enforcement of minimum international labor standards must be based on reciprocity, that is, must not be used by countries which have not themselves accepted the standards.[97] It should be noted that the ILO suggestions for incorporating reference to certain labor standards in the GATT would meet these criteria. (See preceding sections on the ILO and on the GATT.)

The careful examination of the issue of workers' rights and trade in the Dutch report may be contrasted with the approach in the U.S. legislation. The U.S. legislation has not sufficiently linked the concepts of workers' rights with ILO standards and has failed to use the criterion of reciprocity in its criticisms of other countries (the U.S. has not ratified most of the relevant ILO conventions). The inclusion of the standards of minimum age for employment and employment policy in the Dutch list may be controversial, but their examination of the issues involved in the linkage of workers' rights and trade is persuasive.

There has apparently been no practical followup within the Netherlands to the conclusions reached by the Dutch Advisory Council, although there is a suggestion of renewed interest in the subject by the Present Minister of Development Cooperation.[98]

In view of the diversity in the rights included in the concept of "internationally recognized workers' rights," a minimal approach to the meaning of this concept is appropriate *in the context of international trade and economic agreements*. The wisest approach in this context would appear to be to limit the term "internationally recognized labor standards" or "workers' rights" in this context to freedom of association and the right to collective bargaining, the prohibition of forced labor (deemed to include serious abusive use of child labor), and discrimination in employment. These standards are all basic "human rights" included in major human rights instruments that have been widely ratified and not simply technical labor standards. As other basic human rights, they should not be denied for reasons of economic development or lack of resources. In addition, enforcing them would not entail excessive expenditure of national resources. Nearly all countries have pledged commitment to these rights either through membership in the ILO or ratification of human rights treaties.

There is less international agreement about the normative value and the interpretation of rights relating to equal remuneration, minimum wages, working hours, occupational safety and health, and the technical standards relating to child labor in various industries (which do not amount to serious or abusive use). The use of the lowest common denominator in this context may be the wisest course for advocates of linkage between workers' rights and trade; many of the frequent arguments against the linkage of trade and workers' rights would have less force if the definition of internationally recognized workers' rights were limited as suggested.

Freedom of association—the right of workers to form and join trade unions for the protection of their interests—is the most fundamental of all workers' rights. It is mentioned in the 1919 ILO Constitution, reaffirmed in the 1944 ILO Declaration of Philadelphia, and codified by the adoption of two major ILO conventions. Membership in the ILO implies a commitment to freedom of association, regardless of whether the relevant ILO conventions on freedom of association have been ratified. This commitment is explicit in the basic documents of the organization and has been restated in comments by various bodies of the ILO (Governing Body Committee on Freedom of Association, Annual Conferences, Committee on Application of Conventions and Recommendations) and is recognized even by member States that have not ratified the relevant ILO conventions (including the United States), but that, nevertheless, routinely respond to allegations of violations of freedom of association brought before the ILO Governing Body Committee on Freedom of Association.

Ratification of the two major ILO conventions on freedom of association and collective bargaining add little to the commitment to the concept of freedom of association for ILO members, but they add an element of accountability by requiring the submission of regular reports to ILO supervisory bodies.

It has been pointed out that, despite the failure to fully achieve freedom of association in most countries of the world, if the country is a democratic country which gives voice and participation to its workers, the fundamental obligations of freedom of association are being fulfilled.

4.9   Conclusion: The Search for Common Ground

Can common ground be found between the advocates and opponents of a social clause which would enable negotiation and compromise to resolve the issue of the inclusion of a social dimension in trade agreements, specifically in the GATT/WTO? It is important that such common ground be sought. The current controversy over the linking of trade and labor standards is unhealthy—it impacts negatively on the liberalization of trade, exacerbates international tension, and fosters North-South division. The failure to arrive at a satisfactory political solution at the multilateral, international organization level will almost inevitably lead to increased unilateral protectionist threats of action by individual states restricting trade on the allegation of violation of labor standards—an unfortunate tendency.

Examination of the opinions of the major protagonists on this issue suggests that they share more common ground than is generally assumed and that negotiation and compromise may be possible. As mentioned earlier in the paper, much of the controversy over the issue arises from lack of clarity about terminology and failure to specify precisely what form a social clause might take.

As is evident from the material discussed in the body of this essay, most serious advocates, as well as opponents, of a social clause agree that liberalization of trade, in general, provides economic benefits, that obstacles to trade should not result from protectionism, but that certain limitations on trade (or withdrawal of trade benefits) are justifiable in particular circumstances (failure to protect intellectual property, various exceptions listed in Article XX of the GATT), and that freedom of association, prohibition of child labor, and discrimination in employment are fundamental human rights standards which have been nearly universally accepted and should be upheld by all countries regardless of economic status.

With some exceptions, there is general agreement that a multilateral approach to issues involving workers' rights is much preferable to "aggressive unilateralism." There is also considerable agreement that harmonization of detailed technical labor standards involving wages, hours of work, occupational safety, and health should be encouraged through the moral persuasion of the ILO procedures but not be among those linked to trade concessions or benefits. There also appears to be much common agreement that if labor standards are to be linked with trade, they should not impact on the comparative advantage of developing countries—unless such trade is based on violation of the most fundamental workers' rights.

While liberalization of trade is generally perceived as a positive economic development, nevertheless, there is also a recognition—in the words of Charnovitz—that "there are some government policies that are beyond the pale"[99] and that comparative advantage in trade should not be based on such policies. Few would argue that international trade agreements should prevent a country from barring imports produced by slavery or forced labor. While slavery may be rare today—but not unknown—there is often failure to recognize that other egregious violations of the human rights of workers continue to exist; murder, torture, and arbitrary imprisonment of trade unionists, for example, are widespread practices in some countries, as is evident from ILO documentation and reports of human rights organizations. In urging the ILO to support a social clause, Francis Blanchard, former Director General of the ILO, noted that the scandal of child labor, slavery, and exploitation of workers—situations which shock the conscience—still continue.[100] Limiting obligations of a social clause only to very serious violations of fundamental workers' rights, coupled with a procedure for impartial and objective determinations of such violations, may be acceptable to all who recognize that some limitations on free trade are acceptable for moral reasons. It is suggested that a social clause should be limited to the minimal international labor standards of freedom of association, the right to collective bargaining, and the prohibition of forced labor (considered to include egregious use of child labor) and discrimination in employment. These labor standards are the basic human rights standards of the ILO, they are incorporated in the two main international covenants on human rights, and they are moral standards that few countries would contest and that most have accepted by virtue of membership in the ILO or ratification of human rights conventions. The acceptance of these fundamental standards should not result in economic difficulty for developing countries and, as ILO monitoring organs have emphasized, "standards on fundamental human rights ... must be observed regardless of economic circumstances or fluctuations."[101] Much of the literature in opposition to a social clause focuses on the economic problems and disadvantages of attempting to harmonize labor costs relating to wages or hours of work or other technical labor standards. The proponents of linking trade and workers' rights, however, have, in general, agreed with this criticism and have mainly urged only the inclusion of the previously mentioned fundamental human rights labor standards in a social clause rather than harmonization of labor costs. In the joint presentation of the ICFTU, the WCL, and the ETUC to the GATT concerning the social clause, it was clearly stated that the labor standards included in a social clause should be limited to basic human rights labor standards.[102]

A legitimate concern of opponents of a social clause is the fear that standards included in a clause will be interpreted and applied to limit trade arbitrarily and unilaterally for protectionist purposes. To avoid such a result, the adoption of a social clause and its interpretation and application to specific cases should be through multilateral institutions: the WTO and the ILO. While it may not be politically feasible to *demand* that unilateral linkages of trade and workers' rights in national legislation should be dropped as a concession for the acceptance of a multilateral link, such unilateral legislation should be discouraged.

The highly respected monitoring organs of the ILO have had frequent occasion to apply the fundamental human rights standards to concrete cases and to interpret their meaning; ILO interpretations of the implications of the rights should serve as a guide in the application of a social clause. ILO procedures might also be used jointly with the WTO in determining the degree of compliance with a social clause to be included in the GATT, as suggested recently in the International Labor Office paper referred to in previous sections.

In summary, agreement on the concept of a social clause might be reached, based on the perception that some egregious violations of workers' rights are indeed "beyond the pale" if

(1) a multilateral approach is stressed and unilateral use of such clauses discouraged.

(2) there is collaboration between the ILO and GATT/WTO in considering the social aspect of trade liberalization and how such an aspect might be included in the GATT. The ILO Working Paper on the Social Dimensions of the Liberalization of Trade is an important contribution to discussion of the issue. A first step should be the organization of a joint ILO/WTO working group to consider the issue.

(3) the labor standards to be included in a social clause are limited to fundamental workers' rights or minimal international labor standards (freedom of association, right to collective bargaining, prohibition of forced labor (including serious violations of the use of child labor), and discrimination in employment).

(4) the ILO interpretation of these standards is taken as a guide in determining their implications in specific cases.

(5) a procedure is created by the WTO and the ILO for examining complaints regarding the conformity of a country with the social clause. ILO

procedures might serve as a guide, with the possibility of complaints being presented by any one of the ILO constituencies (governments, employer organizations, or workers' organizations). Such a procedure should have more transparency than present GATT dispute panel decisions. The procedure should emphasize fact finding, dialogue, conciliation, and moral persuasion.

Despite the many areas of agreement among proponents and opponents of a social clause, there is considerable pessimism expressed by many over the possibility of incorporating any provision concerning workers' rights or labor standards in GATT given the strong opposition of many countries. Yet, as we have learned in recent years, governmental positions are rarely permanently fixed in stone. Economic and political developments change states' perceptions of their best interests.[103] Political negotiations involving exchange of concessions may lead to surprising results. The issue of linking trade issues with minimum internationally recognized workers' rights will not go away—it is an aspect of the strong contemporary international movement to protect fundamental human rights. Linkage of trade and workers' rights is a political issue with economic implications, and political issues are resolved primarily by negotiation and compromise. A better perception of agreed positions will assist ongoing negotiations.

Postscript

Following the March/April 1995 meeting of the ILO Governing Body, an ILO Press Release reported that the Working Party on the Social Dimension of the Liberalization of International Trade would

convene again in 1995 on the understanding that it would not pursue the question of trade sanctions and that any further discussion of the link between international trade and social standards through a sanctions-based social clause mechanism would be suspended. The Working Group [sic] will focus its energies on three broad areas: Shared values that will give political direction to the effort to promote social justice and economic progress; an examination of the ILO role in helping member states achieve social development through economic growth; and a broad discussion of different ways in which to improve the effectiveness of and strengthen the ILO standards supervisory system.[104]

NOTES

Virginia A. Leary is the SUNY Distinguished Service Professor, Faculty of Law, SUNY/ Buffalo.

1. A social clause has been defined as a clause that

... aims at improving labour conditions in exporting countries by allowing sanctions to be taken against exporters who fail to observe minimum standards. A typical social clause in an international trade arrangement makes it possible to restrict or halt the importation or preferential importation of products originating in countries, industries or firms where labour conditions are inferior to certain minimum standards.

Gijsbert van Liemt, *Minimum Labour Standards and International Trade: Would a Social Clause Work?* 128 INT'L LABOUR REV. (1989), No. 4.

2. *See* D. Shark (untitled, unpublished document prepared for U.S. Embassy, Geneva, WRST.MIA. 1994) for comments by government ministers at Marrakesh on linking labor standards and trade in the GATT.

3. *Id.*

4. Philip Alston, *International Trade as an Instrument of Positive Human Rights Policy,* 4 HUMAN RIGHTS Q. 155 (1982).

5. Van Liemt, note 1 above, at 435, 447.

6. *Id.* at 435.

7. GÖTE HANSSON, SOCIAL CLAUSES AND INTERNATIONAL TRADE 12 (1983).

8. JEROME A. BLANQUI, COURS D'ECONOMIE INDUSTRIELLE, 1838–1839 (1839), quoted in HANSSON, note 7 above, at 12.

9. The information regarding the early history of the linkage of labor reform and trade issues is primarily taken from HANSSON, note 7 above.

10. *Id.* at 18.

11. Charles Picquenard, *French Preparations, in* 1 THE ORIGINS OF THE INTERNATIONAL LABOR ORGANIZATION 83, 86 (James T. Shotwell, ed., 1934).

12. Quoted in HANSSON, note 7 above, at 19.

13. For the history of the founding of the ILO, see articles and documents in volumes 1 and 2, THE ORIGINS OF THE INTERNATIONAL LABOR ORGANIZATION (James T. Shotwell, ed., 1934).

14. Among countries that have been members of the ILO as long as the U.S., only El Salvador has ratified fewer conventions than the U.S.

15. THE INTERNATIONAL LABOR ORGANIZATION AND THE GLOBAL ECONOMY: NEW OPPORTUNI-TIES FOR THE UNITED STATES IN THE 1990S, 49 (Report of the Economic Policy Council of the United Nations Association of the USA, 1991). Kevin Cornacchio, Manager of Labor Affairs, U.S. Council for International Business, and member of the Panel, strongly dissented from the recommendations of the Report concerning linking labor standards with trade. *Id.* at 52–53.

16. *See* Van Liemt, note 1 above.

17. HUMAN RIGHTS—A COMMON RESPONSIBILITY 58–59 (Report of the Director-General, Int'l Labour Conf., 75th Sess., 1988).

18. *Id.* at 59.

19. Francis Blanchard, *La clause social et l'OIT*, LE MONDE, June 30, 1993, at 31 (author's translation).

20. INTERNATIONAL LABOUR CONFERENCE, PROVISIONAL RECORD (78th Sess., 24th sitting, June 21, 1991).

21. DEFENDING VALUES, PROMOTING CHANGE: SOCIAL JUSTICE IN A GLOBAL ECONOMY: AN ILO AGENDA (Report of the Director-General, Int'l Labour Conf., 81st Sess., 1994).

22. *Id.* at 59.

23. For a description of the ILO procedure on Freedom of Association, see Virginia A. Leary, *Lessons from the Experience of the ILO, in* THE UNITED NATIONS AND HUMAN RIGHTS: A CRITICAL APPRAISAL 604–11 (Philip Alston, ed., 1993).

24. DEFENDING VALUES, note 21 above, at 60.

25. Michel Hansenne, *Comment appliquer la clause sociale*, LE MONDE, June 21, 1994.

26. ILO Doc. GB.260/205 (June 1994).

27. *The Social Dimensions of the Liberalization of World Trade*, ILO Doc. GB.261/WP/SLD/1 (Working Party on the Social Dimensions of the Liberalization of International Trade, Int'l Labour Office, Governing Body, 261st Sess., 1994) [hereinafter *Social Dimensions*].

28. *Progress Report of the Working Party on the Social Dimensions of the Liberalization of International Trade*, ILO Doc. GB.261/11/31 (Nov. 1994) (Int'l Labour Office, Governing Body, 261st Sess.). A "reasonably" full account of the interventions is to be distributed at a later date, according to the Governing Body document.

29. Int'l Bus. & Fin. Daily (BNA) (Nov. 17, 1994).

30. *Id.*

31. *Social Dimensions*, note 27 above, ¶ 5.

32. *Id.* ¶ 25.

33. *Id.* ¶ 37.

34. *Id.* ¶ 29.

35. *Id.* ¶ 36.

36. THE REPORT OF THE COMMITTEE OF EXPERTS ON THE APPLICATION OF CONVENTIONS AND RECOMMENDATIONS (Int'l Labour Conf., 81st Sess., 1994) [hereinafter Report of the Committee of Experts] referred to complaints against Sweden and against Côte d'Ivoire submitted respectively by the employers' delegate of Sweden to the 1991 International Labour Conference and by the Workers' delegates to the 1992 Session of the Conference. *Id.* at 21, ¶¶ 62–63. For detailed information about ILO constitutional procedures, see Leary, note 23 above, at 609–11.

37. *Social Dimensions*, note 27 above, ¶ 43.

38. *OECD Press Release*, OECD Doc. SG/Press (94) 41 (June 8, 1994).

39. Blanchard, note 19 above.

40. For information concerning the ITO, see Percy W. Bidwell & William Diebold, Jr., *The United States and the International Trade Organization*, 449 INTERNATIONAL CONCILIATION (Mar. 1949); WILLIAM A. BROWN, JR., THE UNITED STATES AND THE RESTORATION OF WORLD TRADE (Brookings Inst., 1950); WILLIAM DIEBOLD, JR., THE END OF THE ITO (Princeton Univ., Essays in International Finance, No. 16, 1952); Jacob Viner, *Conflicts of Principle in Drafting a Trade Charter*, 25 FOREIGN AFF. 612 (1947); CLAIR WILCOX, A CHARTER FOR WORLD TRADE (1949); *Membership and Participation by the United States in the International Trade Organization*, H. J. Res. 236, 81st Cong., 2nd Sess. (1950).

41. Bidwell & Diebold, note 40 above, at 214.

42. General Agreement on Tariffs and Trade, *opened for signature* Oct. 30, 1947, 61 Stat. A3, T.I.A.S. No. 1700, 55 U.N.T.S. 187; 4 GATT BASIC INSTRUMENTS AND SELECTED DOCUMENTS (1969).

43. Final Act Embodying the Results of the Uruguay Round of Trade Negotiations, Apr. 15, 1994 (Done at Marrakesh), reprinted in 33 INT'L LEGAL MAT. 1125 (1994).

44. *Havana Charter for an International Trade Organization*, Dep't of State Pub. No. 3117, Commercial Policy Series 113 (1948). Also published with commentary: R. P. Terrill, *Havana Charter for an International Trade Organization, March 24, 1948, Including a Guide to the Study of the Charter*, U.S. Dep't of State Pub. No. 3206, Commercial Policy Series 114 (1948). See also WILCOX, note 40 above (text of Charter and commentary).

45. Steve Charnovitz, *The Influence of International Labour Standards on the World Trading Regime*, 126 INT'L LABOUR REV. 565, 574–75 (1985).

46. *See* QUAKER COUNCIL FOR EUROPEAN AFFAIRS, AROUND EUROPE (1994) (reporting on a public hearing on the social clause held by the European Parliament External Relations Committee).

47. *See* statements by J. P. Delamuraz (Switzerland), Michael Kantor (USA), Theodore Pangalos (on behalf of Presidency of the Council of the European Communities), Sir Leon Brittan (Commission of European Communities), Vice President Al Gore (USA), GATT Doc. MTN.TNC/MIN(4)/ST/74, 4, 107 (April 12–14, 1994).

48. *Concluding Remarks of H. E. Sergio Abreu Bonilla, Chairman of the Trade Negotiations Committee, Multilateral Trade Negotiations of the Uruguay Round at Marrakesh*, GATT Doc. MTN.TNC/MIN(94)/6 (April 15, 1994).

49. GATT Doc. MTN.TNC/W/14, contained in GATT Doc. MTN.TNC/MIN(94)/1/ Rev.1. Environmentalists from developed countries, especially the United States, had been appalled at the *Tuna/Dolphin* decision of the GATT panel in 1992 and had engaged in extensive publicity about the perceived anti-environmental role of the GATT.

50. Ian Robinson, a Canadian political scientist, writing during Uruguay Round negotiations on intellectual property issues, remarked:

Curiously, while talk of including worker rights in a trade agreement provokes cries of dismay from those who see themselves as free trade champions, no similar cry is raised when the United States seeks to tack property rights onto what is ostensibly a trade liberalization package. This is so even though the effect of these rights is to restrict rather than enhance the free flow of ideas across national boundaries and, with it, the more rapid adoption of new technologies to TNCs. [notes omitted]

Robinson points out, however, that Jagdish Bhagwati, one of the leading trade economists, agreed that intellectual property issues were only "tangentially related" to trade, but, as a realist, accepted their inclusion in the Uruguay Round negotiations. IAN ROBINSON, NORTH AMERICAN TRADE AS IF DEMOCRACY MATTERED 22, 64 n. 162 (Canadian Centre for Policy Alternatives & Int'l Labor Rights Education & Research Fund, 1993).

51. *Social Dimensions*, note 27 above, ¶ 25.

52. For a discussion of similar problems inherent in unilateral determinations under Article XX if extended to environmental issues, see Robert E. Hudec's article at Chapter 4 in this volume.

53. *The Social Dimension of International Trade: Joint Statement by World and European Trade Unions Confederations, ICFTU, WCL and ETUC*, 43/94 (Feb. 2, 1994) (World Confederation of Labour, 33, rue de Treves, B-1040, Brussels, Belgium) [hereinafter *Trade Union Joint Statement*].

54. The ILO Committee of Experts on the Application of Conventions and Recommendations cited a number of countries in its 1994 Report for failure to implement Convention No. 29 on Forced or Compulsory Labor due to their use of bonded child labor. REPORT OF THE COMMITTEE OF EXPERTS ON THE APPLICATION OF CONVENTIONS AND RECOMMENDATIONS 28, 89–148 (Int'l Labour Conf., 81st Sess. 1994).

55. *See, e.g.*, T. N. Srinavasan, *International Labor Standards Once Again!*, in INTERNATIONAL LABOR STANDARDS AND GLOBAL ECONOMIC INTEGRATION: PROCEEDINGS OF A SYMPOSIUM 35 (U.S. Dep't of Labor, Bureau of Int'l Labor Aff., July 1994).

56. Steve Charnovitz, *Promoting World Labor Rules*, J. COMMERCE, Apr. 19, 1994, at 8A.

57. Quoted in Steve Charnovitz, *Fair Labor Standards and International Trade*, 20 J. WORLD TRADE L. 61, 68 (1986). The prohibition of prison labor was probably included in the exceptions provision because of long-standing national legislation such as that in the United States barring the importation of goods made with prison labor. In origin, the reason for such prohibition was clearly protectionist—to protect national industries from "unfair competition"—and not for moral or ethical reasons since it is acknowledged that providing work for prisoners is helpful to their rehabilitation. Prison labor imposed under a valid judicial sentence and not imposed, *inter alia*, as a punishment for political views is an exception to the prohibition of forced labor in ILO Conventions Nos. 29 and 105 concerning the abolition of forced labor. In recent years, however, the prohibition of imports made by prison labor has taken on moral or ethical implications since prison sentences involving hard labor have been imposed on political opponents in China and in the former USSR.

58. *See* Robert E. Hudec's article at Chapter 4 in this volume for a discussion of the decision of the panel in the *Tuna/Dolphin* case and an extensive consideration of proposals relating to the inclusion of environmental aspects as exceptions in Article XX.

59. Testimony prepared for the U.S. Senate Finance Committee Hearing, March 23, 1994, on Uruguay Round Legislation, by John H. Jackson, Hessel E. Yntema Professor of Law, University of Michigan (Mar. 18, 1994).

60. North American Agreement on Labor Cooperation, Final Draft, Sept. 13, 1993, U.S.-Mexico-Canada, reprinted in 32 INT'L LEGAL MAT. 1499.

61. H.R. REP. No. 1003-361, 103rd Cong., 1st Sess., pt. 3, at 1 (1993), reprinted in 1994 U.S.C.C.A.N. 2731.

62. Pub. L. No. 103-182, 107 Stat. 2057 (1993).

63. Bill Day, *The NAFTA Nightmare*, MULTINAT'L MONITOR, Oct. 24, 1992.

64. *See* DAN LA BOTZ, MASK OF DEMOCRACY: LABOR SUPPRESSION IN MEXICO TODAY (1992).

65. *The Social Charter Implications of the NAFTA*, 3 CANADA-U.S. OUTLOOK (Aug. 1992).

66. *See* GARY C. HUFBAUER & JEFFREY J. SCHOTT, NORTH AMERICAN FREE TRADE: ISSUES AND RECOMMENDATIONS (1992).

67. Government of Canada, Highlights of the Labour and Environmental Agreements (Aug. 1993), quoted in Robinson, note 50 above, at 51.

68. United States Department of Labor, News Release, 93–584, December 30, 1993; 58 Fed. Reg. 69410-11 (1993).

69. North American Labor Cooperation Agreement, art. 49.

70. U.S. National Administrative Office's Public Report of Review on Submission Nos. 940001 and 940002, 197 Daily Lab. Rep. (BNA) (Oct. 14, 1994), at D-23.

71. The petition was filed by the Washington-based International Labor Rights Education and Research Fund, the American Friends Service Committee, and the National Association of Democratic Lawyers.

72. *NAFTA: Electrical Workers Drop Petition: Lambastes NAO for 'White Wash' Probe*, Daily Lab. Rep. (BNA) (Feb. 2, 1995).

73. Robert Kuttner, *Cheerleaders Down in Their Hole Without a Ladder*, reprinted in INT'L HERALD TRIB., Jan. 21–22, 1995, at 8. Kuttner cited the study by Gary Hufbauer and Jeffrey Schott of the Institute for International Economics, note 66 above, predicting that NAFTA would result in increased wages in Mexico and more jobs in the U.S., and contended that NAFTA caused just the opposite to occur. "Both the politics and the economics of NAFTA encouraged Mexico to keep its peso overvalued, to the point where a crash was just a matter of time." *Id.*

74. For comments concerning the Labor Cooperation Agreement, see Stanley M. Spracker & Gregory J. Mertz, *Labor Issues Under the NAFTA: Options in the Wake of the Agreement*, 27 INT'L LAWYER 737 (1993); Katherine A. Hagen, *Fundamentals of Labor Issues and NAFTA*, 27 UNIV. CALIF. DAVIS L. REV. 917 (1994); Elizabeth C. Crandall, Comment, *Will NAFTA's North American Agreement on Labor Cooperation Improve Enforcement of Mexican Labor Laws?*, 7 TRANSNAT'L LAWYER 165 (1994); Charles W. Nugent, Comment, *A Comparison of the Right to Organize and Bargain Collectively in the United States and Mexico*, 7 TRANSNAT'L LAWYER 197 (1994); Jerome I. Levinson, THE LABOR SIDE ACCORD TO THE NORTH AMERICAN FREE TRADE AGREEMENT: AN ENDORSEMENT OF ABUSE OF WORKER RIGHTS IN MEXICO 11 (1993); ROBINSON, note 50 above; Mark E. Czajkowski, J. D. 1995, Labor and the Aftermath of NAFTA (unpublished manuscript, International Labor Law Seminar, SUNY/Buffalo, on file with author).

75. Enacted as Title V of the Trade and Tariff Act of 1984, Pub. L. No. 98-573 § 503, 98 Stat. 2948, 3019 (codified as amended at 19 U.S.C. § 2462 (1988).

76. Caribbean Basin Economic Recovery Act, 19 U.S.C. § 2702(c)(8) (Supp. IV 1986).

77. Overseas Private Investment Corporation Amendments Act of 1985, Pub. L. No. 99-204, § 5, 99 Stat. 1669, 1670 (codified as amended at 22 U.S.C. § 2191a (1988)).

78. Omnibus Trade and Competitiveness Act of 1988, Pub. L. No. 100-418, § 301, 102 Stat. 1107 (1988) (codified at 19 U.S.C.A. § 2411(a) (1988)).

79. *See* Section 4.8 concerning the definition of "internationally recognized workers' rights" for a critique of these criteria.

80. House Committee on Ways and Means, Generalized System of Preferences Renewal Act of 1984, H.R. REP. No. 1090, 98th Cong., 2d Sess., reprinted in 1984 U.S. CODE CONG. & ADMIN. NEWS 5101, 5112.

81. International Labor Rights Education & Research Fund v. Bush, 752 F. Supp. 495 (D.D.C. 1990).

82. LAWYERS COMMITTEE FOR HUMAN RIGHTS, PROTECTION OF WORKER RIGHTS: A REPORT ON LEGAL MECHANISMS TO PROTECT WORKER RIGHTS 10, 15 (Human Rights and U.S. Foreign Policy Project, Oct. 10, 1991).

83. Philip Alston, *Labor Rights Provisions in US Trade Law: "Aggressive Unilateralism?"*, 15 HUMAN RIGHTS Q. 1 (1993).

84. Karl Berman, *Labor Solidarity Brings Change in the Dominican Republic*, NAT'L CATHOLIC REP., Feb. 24, 1985, at 12. Berman reported:

The Dominican Republic ships more than $2 billion in products to the United States annually. Among latin nations it is second only to Mexico in the importance of its export-assembly manufacturing sector. But, in spite of this profitable market demand, Jimenez [a worker in the export zone] said most workers in the Dominican export-processing zones still face deplorable conditions. They earn a mere 50 cents an hour, often working in sweatshop conditions. Not uncommon in factories, Jimenez added, are 'lock-ins,' where workers are bolted inside buildings to force them to work overtime.... Occupational safety is commonly absent from the workplace, Jimenez said. There are few protective devices and ventilation is deficient; consequently workers are frequently exposed to hazardous and toxic substances.

85. *Id.* col. 4.

86. *See Indonesia: Charges and Rebuttals over Labor Rights Practices, Analysis of Submissions to the U.S. Trade Representative*, ASIA WATCH (division of Human Rights Watch), Jan. 23, 1993.

87. T. N. Srinavasan, the Samuel C. Park, Jr. Professor of Economics at Yale University, has commented:

I view GSP as no more than crumbs from a rich man's table. The developing countries would be far better off under a liberal trading system than under one in which they get special and differential treatment in return for their acquiescing in the illiberal trade policies of the rich. By attaching undue significance to GSP and other measures of special and differential treatment, the developing countries have opened themselves to being pressured on imposing unsustainably high labor standards.

Srinavasan, note 55 above, at 37.

88. Steve Charnovitz, *Fair Labor Standards and International Trade*, 20 J. WORLD TRADE L. 61, 68 (1986).

89. The main ILO human rights conventions are Freedom of Association and Protection of the Right to Organise Convention, 1948 (No. 87); Right to Organise and Collective Bargaining Convention, 1949 (No. 98); Forced Labour Convention, 1930 (No. 29), Abolition of Forced Labour Convention, 1957 (No. 105); Discrimination (Employment and Occupation) Convention, 1958 (No. 111), Equal Remuneration Convention, 1951 (No. 100). *See* ILO CLASSIFIED GUIDE TO INTERNATIONAL LABOUR STANDARDS (ILO, Geneva).

90. Trade Act of 1974, Pub. L. No. 93-618, § 502, 88 Stat. 2066 (1975) (codified at 19 U.S.C.A. § 2462(b)(1)–(6) (1980)).

91. *See* REPORT OF COMMITTEE OF EXPERTS, note 36 above, at 89–148, relating to application of Convention No. 29. See especially comments concerning child labor in Bangladesh, Brazil, Haiti, Mauritania, Pakistan, Peru, Sri Lanka, Thailand, and particularly India.

92. Caribbean Basic Economic Recovery Act, 19 U.S.C. § 2702(c)(8) (Supp. IV 1986).

93. Alston, note 83 above, at 7–8.

94. *Id.* at 8.

95. National Advisory Council for Development Cooperation, *Recommendation on Minimum International Labour Standards* (Ministry of Foreign Affairs, Plein 23, The Hague, Netherlands, Nov. 1984). The Working Group which prepared the report consisted of the following members of the National Council: Professor L.J. Emmerij (Chairman), K. Fibbe, H. Hofsted, Mrs. M.J. 't Hooft-Welvaars, Mrs. E. Postel-Coster, Professor P.J.I.M. de Waart, Dr. Y.B. de Wit.

96. *Id.* at 17.

97. *See also* a recent similar analysis by Louis Emmerij, a member of the Dutch Advisory Council referred to in the text, former ILO official and presently Special Advisor to the President, Inter-American Development Bank. Louis Emmerij, *Contemporary Challenges for Labor Standards Resulting from Globalization, in* INTERNATIONAL LABOUR STANDARDS AND ECONOMIC INTERDEPENDENCY, ESSAYS IN COMMEMORATION OF THE 75TH ANNIVERSARY OF THE DECLARATION OF PHILADELPHIA (Int'l Inst. Labour Stud., 1994).

98. Telephone discussion of author with Professor Paul de Waart, member of the Advisory Council, Mar. 19, 1993.

99. Steve Charnovitz, *Promoting World Labor Rules*, J. COMMERCE, Apr. 19, 1994, at 8A.

100. Blanchard, note 19 above.

101. Report of the Committee of Experts, note 36 above, ¶ 21.

102. *Trade Union Joint Statement*, note 53 above.

103. *See* in this regard an article suggesting that India should reconsider its opposition to the linking of labor standards and trade: "The acceptance of universal labour standards would thus not only improve the relative attractiveness of India for foreign capital but would also reduce the disadvantage of competing with less democratic competitors." Narendar Pani, *Who's Afraid of Labour Standards?*, INDIAN ECONOMIC TIMES, Apr. 4, 1994.

104. ILO Press Release, 7 April 1995, ILO/95/8. See Also *Summary presented by the Chairperson, Ms. Hartwell*, Working Party on the Social Dimensions of the Liberalization of International Trade, ILO Governing Body GB.262/WP/SDL/12, 262nd Session, Geneva, March–April 1995.

5

General Reflections on the Relationship of Trade and Labor (Or: Fair Trade Is Free Trade's Destiny)

Brian Alexander Langille

Poverty anywhere constitutes a danger to prosperity everywhere.

ILO Declaration (Philadelphia)

The misery of being exploited by capitalists is nothing compared to the misery of not being exploited at all.

Joan Robinson, *Economic Philosophy*

5.1   Introduction

Leading practitioners of international trade theory have recently announced that their discipline is in a state of intellectual disarray and crisis. The concepts of harmonization, social charters, level playing fields, and, most recently, the slogan "fair trade" have come to dominate the agenda of trade theory. As Bhagwati has written:

... the true and greater crisis that we face in regard to the theory and policy of Free Trade comes, not from the theoretical modelling of imperfect competition and other conventional market failures, but from the growth demand for "level playing fields", "harmonization", "fair trade," etc. These demands undermine insidiously the legitimacy and feasibility of Free Trade, since it is virtually impossible to harmonize everything so that playing fields are truly level in every way.[1]

Later Bhagwati refers to "fair trade" as a "Pandora's box" which has "grown out of hand."[2] The immediate precipitating cause of this phenomenon appears in large part to be the aggressive tendency of the United States to justify protective measures in the name of some governmental policy established, or not established, by a trading partner. In this connection Hudec[3] has distinguished between what he calls claims of "offensive unfairness," which are claims against foreign governments that their policies have given unfair advantage to "their" firms selling in other markets, and "defensive unfairness," which is the idea that actions or policies of foreign governments may defend their own domestic producers from external competition.

Our leading theorists take, for the most part, a robustly cynical view of unfairness claims. This cynicism may well be completely justified in the context of the American political and trade system, where many claims of unfair competition often appear to be "bald faced protectionism" parading under a different name.[4] This realpolitik analysis is given support by academic analysis, which offers an economic model of this aspect of the political process.[5]

Vital questions remain, however, in spite of the fact that the arguments for "fair trade" lie ill in the mouth of many who utter them, and in spite of the fact that the realpolitik motivations of many "fair traders" are transparently self-interested ones. These vital questions are the following:

1. Is there anything of principle at stake in these claims? That is, ignoring the *ad hominem* arguments about who is putting forward these sorts of claims in many circumstances, are these claims valid?

2. Can trade theory ignore these claims and the issue of their validity, or is trade theory necessarily implicated in this debate?

3. If trade theory is forced to take these issues seriously as a matter of principle, how should it go about thinking about them?

These three issues are bound up together and it seems that trade theory is, from the point of view of many leading theoreticians, too radical for its own good. This paper argues that the question is not whether trade theory is too radical for its own good, but whether trade theory has the courage of its convictions. I will argue the view that while free trade theory leads to a fair trade debate, this is not unfortunate, but merely inevitable. I will also suggest that the general principles required for the resolution of this debate are already in place in the bedrock of the world trade system.

There is, however, a real risk that trade theoreticians will avoid real engagement with the fair trade debate, for at least two reasons. First, the overpowering cynicism arising from the realpolitik of the fair trade debate may forestall further inquiry. Second, if the idea of fair trade is debated on its merits, it may well be shunted into a very familiar yet inadequate set of rules for the conduct of that debate. That is, there is a significant risk that the fair trade debate will be forced onto territory which preempts discussion of the real issues at stake. If this occurs there will be no resolution of the fair trade/free trade debate. The result will be continued political posturing and avoidance. And from a theoretical point of view, those interested in free trade and those interested in fair trade will continue to occupy "two solitudes."

This paper is very general and does not attempt detailed legal resolution of the issues involved. It is a preface to that sort of detailed work. It presents a general way of seeing the fair trade/free trade debate and suggests, in the most general terms, the *sort* of resolution required.

5.2   The Old World Order

The origins of modern trade theory in Smith and in Ricardo[6] centered upon the gains to be secured from an international division of labor in the creation of products for trade. Adam Smith wrote:

What is prudence in the conduct of every private family can scarcely be folly in that of a great kingdom. If a foreign country can supply us with a commodity cheaper than we can make, better buy it of them with some part of the produce of our own industry.[7]

The theory centers upon a world in which producers are domesticated in a nation-state and produce goods for export. The economic logic of trade for Smith and Ricardo made out the case for unilateral free trade—an idea not commonly followed since and not a significant part of the world trade system as we know it.[8] The central ideas of the modern world trade system are multilateralism, reciprocity, negotiation, and neutral enforcement. In a world of nation-states with national producers making goods for export, the theory of trade is focused upon the movement of goods and, in particular, upon barriers to their mobility in the form of tariffs. The world trade system's great accomplishment has been the reduction of tariffs, among OECD countries to "almost negligible levels."[9] The resulting gains from trade have been impressive.[10] The focus of the world trading system has shifted to the resolution of non-trade barriers, including subsidies. This is the rabbit hole down which the free trade movement has fallen. Yet even here the intellectual case for free trade is said to be undiminished, and the "illogic" of countervailing and anti-dumping laws is as obvious as ever. Referring to antidumping law, Michael Trebilcock put this point as follows:

... why citizens in the importing countries should be concerned that they are able to buy goods at lower prices than citizens in the exporting country e.g. because of some form of monopoly a firm enjoys in the country of origin, has remained an impenetrable mystery."[11]

And Trebilcock also pithily makes the point about countervailing duty laws in similar terms:

Even in the case of an explicit export subsidy one can reasonably argue that consumers in the export market are better off as a result of the foreign subsidy and that it should be viewed as a form of foreign aid that on balance increases the welfare of citizens in the importing country and that our reaction ought to be to send a thank you note to the foreign government, noting only our regret that its subsidies are not larger and timeless.[12]

Under the classic formulation of the free trade problem, of national producers of goods for export, the logic of an internationalization of the division of labor and the gains from specialization necessitated an internal, domestic adjustment process. This is because the gains to domestic consumers from foreign trade will almost always be greater than the additional gains to domestic producers from purely domestic trade.[13] The cost estimates of protecting domestic producers and workers in such situations are both staggering and illuminating. The policy choice for any individual state is, on the logic of the theory, clear—protectionism is not worth it. The only issue is the residual one of how to distribute the gains from trade and in particular whether and how to compensate the losers, such as those formerly employed in industries losing out to producers located elsewhere. These issues are central political issues which are settled through domestic democratic political processes in which all relevant constituencies have a voice. There is, to be sure, a highly contested political debate about these questions, but the best advice in such circumstances is to redirect some of the gains from trade to the "losers" in the form of adjustment and retraining programs for those displaced.[14] This is, however, advice that, for example, Canada has not followed terribly well.[15] Here international competition does put pressures upon domestic producers, consumers, and workers. But the resolution of the issue is one undertaken by those same consumers, producers, and workers. The rational decision to take the gains and compensate the losers, within domestic politics, is made by the producers, consumers, and workers who are faced with the policy dilemma. The legitimacy of that decision follows from their equal access to the democratic political forum.[16]

The world, then, as perceived in this sketch is one in which domestic producers export goods to other nation-states. The basic policy question within each state is whether to erect tariff barriers to foreign goods. The liberal theory of trade predicts gains from trade and costs of protectionism. The decision to engage in trade is legitimated by the domestic democratic decision-making process within each state and that decision will rest in turn upon the resolution of the residual issue within each state—how to distribute the gains from trade among the winners and losers: domestic firms and workers. The legitimacy of that decision, in this sketch of the world, flows from the equal voice of those constituencies in the domestic political forum.

In this world the liberal theory of trade provides a compelling policy prescription.[17] The problem is that this is no longer an accurate description of the world or its policy dilemmas.

5.3   New Developments

The crisis in modern trade theory may be seen as being precipitated by two concurrent phenomena which change this terrain of debate—one intellectual and one worldly.

The conceptual point is the following one. The world trading system's great accomplishment has been the removal of tariff barriers to trade. It is not just a pragmatic or programmatic sensibility that has posited nontariff barriers, especially subsidies, as the new terrain for the campaign of trade liberalizers. The requirement of logical consistency has informed this shift of emphasis. From a global and abstract point of view there is no relevant distinction between a tariff on imported goods to protect domestic producers from foreign produced competing goods, on the one hand, and a subsidy to domestic producers which achieves the same result and/or objective. Once the logic of the project of eliminating tariffs is accepted, the subsidies project cannot be avoided. Subsidies can and are just as effective a "barrier" to trade as tariffs. This insight cannot be cabined or mediated by ideas such as "specificity."[18] Furthermore, this insight must be tied to another that flows from it. Within the notion of a subsidy itself there is no relevant distinction between a positive subsidy and a negative subsidy. A governmental policy choice to fund out of general tax revenues a maternity leave requirement, or the purchase of pollution-abatement equipment, may be viewed as a subsidy by foreign producers on either "offensive" or "defensive" grounds. But the equally obvious point is that the failure of the government to impose the maternity leave or pollution-abatement requirement in the first place, that is, governmental nonaction, may just as well be viewed as a subsidy from the point of view of competing producers in other jurisdictions who are bound by such (costly) requirements. The path here is from tariffs to subsidies and from subsidies to negative subsidies. This is, more precisely, the rabbit hole down which trade theory has fallen. It is this combination of insights which is currently driving international trade theorists to distraction.

Lurking here is the insight, to which some of our theorists allude,[19] that traditional trade theory has made its way in the world (and avoided the problem within the idea of subsidies) by avoiding insights which are accepted as commonplace elsewhere. This is true in spite of the fact that this point has been near the surface of trade theory for years.[20] The assumption is that there is a natural or genuinely noncontroversial mode of economic ordering and that distortions or perversions of this "normalcy"[21] can be detected, measured, and taken into account by trade theory. But this is not the case. The case for regulation of productive activities by means of the private marketplace is always and everywhere genuinely controversial, and not just controversial in the sense that self-interested economic actors may position themselves to their advantage in any debate over the question.

This is why the debate over fair trade is so intractable. There is no way for trade policy or its economic principles to be insulated from the political issues at stake. Fair trade is free trade's destiny. That is, once governmental action or nonaction in labor policy (for example) is problematized as a potential subsidy, then there is no alternative to engaging in the debate about the appropriate scope of market regulation (of labor relations, for example).

These insights within trade theory are given an even greater life force by a series of developments in the international economy which have pushed these regulatory policies to the forefront of national and international politics. These developments taken together are often referred to as "globalization" or the internationalization of the economy. In this international economy domestic producers are increasingly subject to foreign competition and a number of new economic forces. Investment, services, ideas, and other factors of production have become increasingly mobile. In this world multinational manufacturing companies

seeking to cut costs in the "struggle for the world product" have divided their operations into separate units: raw materials, processing, manufacture of components, assembly and distribution. On the basis of worldwide searches they have sought to situate units in locations that will yield the lowest total production costs. Nations are struggling to attract investment operations that will add value to their economies and strengthen their position in international trade.[22]

In this world governmental regulatory policy is another "factor endowment," albeit a created one,[23] and regulatory competition is to be expected as the norm. This is the "indirect" impact of trade liberalization and glob-alization on the economy.[24] This regulatory competition actually mani-fests itself as a series of phenomena which should be unpacked, although they are related. In the internationalized global economy the traditional model of trade theory has been significantly altered. Classical discussions naturally centered upon domestic and foreign producers with goods in international circulation. The problem was trade in goods. We now have a world in which most, but not all, factors of production are highly mobile. The relative immobility of labor, and nation states (or jurisdictions), is critical in understanding the world as we now know it. For labor lawyers the especially critical factors are labor and capital. In the modern world capital is relatively mobile, and labor immobile.[25] In this world capital has now obtained the threat of exit, labor has not.[26]

The state is also immobile, by definition. Theory predicts that the mo-bile factors will be able to engage in regulatory arbitrage—playing off one jurisdiction against another. The net result is that the classical model of the political economy which rationalizes free trade no longer captures all the important dynamics in play.[27]

The most obvious impact of regulatory competition is loss of market share, here or there, or in third-party markets, by domestic producers, with the resulting loss of employment. This is not distinguishable from the situation described above under classically understood free trade. But the impact can now be seen to flow from governmental policy in the other jurisdiction. The further phenomena which are directly related to the new internationalization of the economy are

(1) the relocation of "domestic" firms, in search of regulatory advantage, to other jurisdictions;

(2) domestic firms threatening relocation (exit) in their bargaining with local employees and trade unions, demanding lower negotiated standards (concessions);

(3) domestic firms threatening relocation (exit) in the political process, resulting in an alteration in regulatory standards or a resistance to higher standards; and

(4) firms engaging in jurisdiction shopping for positive or negative sub-sidies, with resulting regulatory subsidy contests by jurisdictions.

In this context capital exercises a new ability to exit, or threaten exit, to extract regulatory benefits. These benefits may take the form of general externalization of some cost, or selective externalization of some costs, to labor.[28] This is simply another way of saying that the existence of the exit option affects the distribution of power between capital and society at large or between capital and labor. The logic here is compelling. The question is: What can we make of that? Is such regulatory competition good or bad?[29]

This confluence of these two forces, one intellectual and one worldly, has precipitated the problematic circumstance which so bedevils our leading trade lawyers and economists. The issue of subsidies is unavoidable, and increased regulatory competition (competition among subsidies) has forced these issues to the forefront in trade negotiations. We are at a point where, in effect, labor and other social policies are increasingly, to some extent, being set internationally—that is unavoidable; the question is how will they be set—by what mechanism? The obviously available options are within the international marketplace or the international political arena. Leaving Europe aside, the most significant international political arenas have recently turned out to be the GATT and NAFTA negotiations.[30]

If trade theory is to tackle this question of the value of regulatory competition and not avoid it, then it is necessary to examine the nature of the politics of that question. If fair traders are to be dealt with honestly and completely—if they are ever to be convinced—then their view of the world must be engaged, debated, and a resolution brought about. Otherwise the world trading system will be forever at risk—not from unprincipled manipulation, but by valid arguments about its inability or unwillingness to face the issues it is forced to confront.

5.4   The Politics of Labor Law

Labor policy is a useful vehicle by which to expose these issues which are so central to trade theory's agenda. An understanding of how North American labor lawyers commonly think about our regulatory labor policy will reveal that the debate about the appropriate scope of regulatory competition in labor policy is more deeply problematic than is commonly thought. Labor lawyers who are fair traders are not self-interested hypocritical manipulators, nor are they making a conceptual mistake. Rather, they represent a well-known and perhaps dominant view within our political theory—that the relationship between markets and politics is complex and as a matter of principle contestable.[31] By contestable I do not mean irresolvable. Liberalism is not another word for skepticism.[32]

There are important lessons to be learned here, at least at a general level of debate. The most important of these lessons is that the standard response of free traders, certainly as manifested in the Canadian debate over free trade,[33] is unsatisfactory both as a matter of principle (because it avoids the issues) and as a matter of political pragmatism (because the issues will not go away).

Canadian and, I believe, American labor lawyers have a common way of analyzing the content of our labor policy. This common understanding is a way of conceptually organizing the field of labor law and it comes in the form of a rough quasi-chronological ordering of the major components of our labor law as "events" on a historical continuum. The chronology is inaccurate,[34] but this is of little or no importance. What is important is the setting out of the various elements of our labor law in relation to one another and the providing of an account of those interrelationships.

This shared way of organizing their field of endeavor is passed down at the law schools and by those immersed in this aspect of legal practice. This received wisdom contains many controversial aspects. Nonetheless, part of the utility of the resulting map of the field is precisely that it provides a way of charting our disagreements and controversies. It is a way of perceiving the world, problematic and controversial as it is. What I am about to set out then is what, literally, goes without saying among practicing labor lawyers and academics.

It may be observed that appealing to what labor lawyers commonly think will be of no assistance in a rigorous critical and normative analysis of labor relations and labor law. After all, this might simply be a description of mass delusion or unreflective and inertially guided quiescence. The proof of this pudding is in the eating, but there is at least one point which cannot be avoided. The appeal here is to what we know to be our labor law: It takes the world we actually live in and attempts to make sense of it. It is not a creation of an overactive imagination. It may then of course be said that our labor law is simply misguided policy. But this depends upon the account which can be given of it. This is what the "received wisdom" purports to do and in my view generally succeeds in doing.

We can begin by pointing out a confusion about the terms "labor law" and "employment law," terms which I will use interchangeably throughout this essay. Historically, in North American legal education "labor law" referred to the law relating to the processes of collective bargaining—that is, the law for and about unionized workplaces. The term "employment law" was reserved for everything else bearing upon work relations. In Canada and in North America "everything else" basically means, first, the common law of the contract of employment and, second, a host of statutory instruments represented in Canada by omnibus Employment Standards

Acts, human rights codes, occupational health and safety acts, etc. There has been a recent movement in North America legal thinking from the historically favored emphasis on collective bargaining law ("labor law") to a broader subject embracing all three of the regimes—common law, collective bargaining, and direct statutory intervention as I shall refer to them. There is not much doubt that in the U.S. this movement is in part pragmatically related to the decline in union density rates.[35] But in Canada there has not been a precipitous decline in union density, and the reasons for the change are pedagogical and conceptual rather than pragmatic.[36] The basic case for expanding the field of vision is not simply the pragmatic one that there is more relevant law out there that law students and lawyers should know about, but rather the important pedagogic insight that the relevant merits and demerits of the three primary modes of regulation cannot be fully understood until comparisons can be made between them. It is also the case that many, if not most, of our "hard cases" resolve around the relationship, both procedural and substantive, among these three regimes. That is, the objective set by labor law courses in North American law schools is to search for critical understanding of the alternative modes of regulation, and their vices and virtues. Clearly, this is a normatively controversial but unavoidable project.[37] The underpinnings of the common law, collective bargaining, and direct statutory intervention are politically diverse and in tension—if not contradiction.

How is it then that Canadian and North American labor lawyers in general understand this newly expanded field of study? They do so by telling themselves the following story.

Labor lawyers conceptually begin their story with the idea of productive relations conceived of as a series of contractual relationships. They understand that productive relations can be organized, and historically have been organized, by different principles. Nonetheless, they accept that the overwhelming mode of engaging in productive relations in North American society is through the mechanism of contract and specifically the contract of employment. They understand, too, and take for granted, that the common law's method of analyzing the employment relationship through the lens of contract law has been much debated in the employment law literature, but it is clearly accepted that the dominant mode of analysis is the contractual one. Employees and employers are viewed as participants in a labor market engaged in the exercise of contracting, that is, the formation of individual contracts of employment. Here all the conceptual apparatus of private market ordering is understood to apply. So, too, is it well understood that the standard rights-based[38] and efficiency-based arguments conjoin to offer the familiar defenses of this method of regulating the employment relationship.

Nonetheless, labor lawyers see the development of labor law, certainly in this century, as one of elaborating and remedying a series of disenchantments with this method of analysis and its normative underpinnings. Labor lawyers understand that while the market paradigm for ordering productive relations is in some sense primary, the actual development of modern labor law has been to (at least partially) reject that method of regulation and to vary it in distinct ways.[39] In fact, labor lawyers understand the two other modes of regulation (collective bargaining and direct statutory regulation) as two methods of responding to the inadequacies of market regulation. Not all labor lawyers agree with the content of our labor law or think it is (all) a good idea. Nonetheless, they agree that in order to understand what clearly is our labor law we must understand it in this way.

Thus, labor lawyers have, first, an understanding that market regulation is primary but inadequate, and that the inadequacy of market regulation has been addressed in two distinct ways. For labor lawyers the perceived inadequacies of market regulation are often summed up in the slogan "inequality of bargaining power." It may be true that for some labor lawyers the invocation of this phrase is unreflective and unrefined. Nonetheless, most labor lawyers, academics, and judges who make reference to this idea use it as a shorthand way of capturing a complex set of arguments and disagreements about the idea of market ordering of employment. Essentially, labor lawyers (like lawyers in other areas of practice and theory) understand labor law as that portion of our law which seeks to secure justice in the employment relationship. By justice most labor lawyers have a rough idea of achieving fairness and efficiency within productive relations. The slightly more sophisticated will draw upon ideas, such as those elaborated by John Rawls or Ronald Dworkin, about a liberal theory of justice containing two elements, sometimes expressed as "concern" and "respect." It is the dilemma of a liberal labor law to reflect both the need to respect individuals as autonomous (including autonomous economic) actors and at the same time to express concern for them as human agents and for their ability to lead flourishing lives and indeed act as independent (economic) actors.[40]

In the common story, then, the next step is as follows. Justice, in this rough sense, in the employment relationship will not be secured because the common law analyzes the employment relationship as a contractual one and employees will not secure a just contract of employment because of "inequality of bargaining power." The response to this is, as I have said, twofold. First, there is a *procedural* response. The basis of this response is straightforward: *If* the object is to secure justice in productive relations, and the reason that justice will not be secured is because the common law analyzes employment as a contractual relationship and employees will not secure a just result because of "inequality of bargaining power," *then* the answer is to redress this inequality of bargaining power by permitting labor to bargain collectively and thus increase its bargaining power. Of course there is no guarantee that employees will be able to secure much benefit by acting collectively, but the essence of collective bargaining is to remove legal obstacles to collective action and to compel the employer to deal with the union as the collective representative of the employees. The accepted wisdom concerning collective bargaining is that it is entirely *procedural* and that the *substance* of the bargain is still left to the parties to determine through the exercise of their now slightly restructured bargaining power relationship. The employer's freedom *to* contract with whom it wishes is taken away and it is compelled to bargain with the collective representative. But the employer's freedom *of* contract is maintained. This is a deeply problematic condition to sustain. It is so problematic that American labor law, for example, and Canadian labor law to a lesser extent, has failed to maintain the validity of the process.[41]

The other part of the received wisdom is that there is a second sort of response to the inadequacy of common law contractual analysis. This is substantive intervention. If the perceived problem is that the common law analyzes the employment relationship as a contractual one, and because of "inequality of bargaining power" employees in general would not receive a just bargain, then the appropriate response is simply to rewrite that bargain by means of direct legislative action. This is the "new wave" of labor law and is reflected in a wide series of legislative enactments aimed at general labor standards (minimum wages, vacation entitlements, maternity leaves, etc.), human rights legislation and occupational health and safety legislation, pay equity, and employment equity laws, although this list is not complete.

That is the common way of conceptually organizing the field. Now turn for a moment to the critical and normative questions which this way of organizing the field exposes. Remember, too, that the pedagogic case for the expansion or notion of "labor law" is precisely that these normative issues are revealed for analysis.

Every part of the received wisdom is controversial. It is historically controversial in its claims to represent a chronology of events. More obviously, while the claim that labor law aims at securing justice in employment relations may be a common one, theories of justice have a way of disagreeing with one another. In this regard, perhaps the most controversial aspect of our labor law is precisely that it invites an analysis of the virtues of market ordering in this particular concrete context. The slogan "inequality of bargaining power" is a red flag for many economists and defenders of the market models and its virtues. For them this slogan is a meaningless and empty one.[42] They see this as a conceptual, rather than a normative, point. This is a bit unfair, because I think it is clear that on the neoclassical model a significant part of what goes under the broad rubric of "inequality of bargaining power" can find a home. That is, defenders of reregulation of the labor market are often on common ground with market theorists. Analysis of intervention in labor markets in terms of "market-defect analysis" (information asymmetries, for example, to defend the "right-to-know" provisions in occupational health and safety laws) are not uttering what is, even from the economists' point of view, an empty slogan.

But defenders of reregulation of the common law contract of employment (that is, those who accept the normative case for collective bargaining and direct statutory intervention) are not, when they move beyond "market-defect analysis," merely uttering an "empty slogan." It may be wrong, but it is not empty. The reason that economists are driven to distraction by those invoking the phrase "inequality of bargaining power," insofar as the phrase goes beyond "market-defect analysis," is that they believe the phrase "inequality of bargaining power" to be uttered or put forward as a meaningful one *within economic theory*. And economists can quickly, decisively, and derisively point out that this is a form of nonsense.[43] So, for example, Alchain and Allen wrote:

Buyers and sellers often restrict others from the market as competitors. And the buyers and sellers of labor services are no exception. Now labor markets will be analyzed in an effort to detect the constraints that work to change money wages from the open-market levels. First, we expose a fallacy. Restrictions on the market are often advocated to protect employees from the employer's superior bargaining power. Proponents say that individual workers are helpless against the powerful employer. An employee, acting alone, can readily be replaced if he asks for higher pay; his alternatives are limited. But, united, employees can prevent the employer from playing one against the other. To further protect the laborer minimum-wage, fair-employment, and working-condition laws are proposed.

Whatever one's impression about the plight of employees, the fact is that the price anyone can get is limited by the offers made to him by potential buyers. General Motors is also limited. What, for example, limits its ability to keep wages down? The answer is that if General Motors offers less pay than other employers, it will get fewer employees. Any employee can get a salary that is at least as high as his services are worth to some other employer.... What "bargaining power" may mean, therefore, is simply the highest salary one can get from other jobs. If that is a great deal less than he is now getting, the employee will be reluctant to press for higher wages and may even accept some impositions or a wage cut rather than quit.

It may be said that the employer who loses an employee loses only one employee, while the employee loses his entire income. In fact, the employee does not lose his entire income; he loses the premium he was getting in his former job over the next best alternative adjusted for moving and job-exploration costs. Of course, if the employee quits, his losses can be greater than those imposed on the employer; but such a comparison is irrelevant. Employers hire employees because the employer gains by doing so, not because the employee gains less.

Do not mistake the purpose of the preceding remarks. They are not anti-employee, antiemployer, or antiunion; they are anticonfusion.[44]

Of course, *if* the phrase "inequality of bargaining power," insofar as it goes beyond market-defect analysis, is meant as a comment *within* economic theory, it *is* a form of nonsense. The point is, however, that it is not meant to be an observation from within economic theory, but rather a comment *about* neoclassical economic theory. It is rather like another famous slogan: "Property is theft." When Proudhon offered this suggestion he did not set out to make a comment which was meaningful *within* property law. If a first-year property law student says "Property is theft" meaning it as a statement within property law theory, then the student has obviously made some serious conceptual errors and is headed for a poor grade. It is not possible for property to be theft *within* the theory. But the whole point of Proudhon's comment, and a large part of the point about "inequality of bargaining power" (insofar as it goes beyond market-defect analysis), is to make a critical comment external to property or contract law. As John Searle has pointed out,[45] an interesting aspect of the slogan, and whence it derives its rhetorical force, is that it uses concepts from *within* the theory in order to make a criticism *of* the theory.[46] That is why it is a catchy slogan, regardless of its other claims to usefulness.

If this point is well taken then the ground of controversy shifts. The issue then becomes what sort of claims can be made about, and external to, contractual ordering, and how can they be usefully organized along with the internal claim about defects in the structure of the underlying market to which economists are attuned. There are in fact two sets of further claims made by critics of market ordering generally, and in the labor law context specifically. These two further sets of claims can be understood as follows.[47] There is a set of claims which in essence accepts the normative defense of market ordering by, for example, agreeing that the promotion of liberty and autonomy is a worthwhile and fundamental ideal. But the concepts of liberty and autonomy are contestable ones and there is an enduring debate in our political theory and our labor law as to whether market ordering will actually secure autonomy, especially for workers.[48] Thus the content of Employment Standard Acts (for example, maximum hours, minimum wages, abolition of the "truck" system of payment, abolition of "yellow dog" contracts) can be seen as a rejection of the assumptions of market theories about "consent" when circumstances of contracting result in such contracts. The fact such contracts are the result of decisions made by others in similar circumstances is seen as problematic, not saving, as Alchain and Allen would have it.

But there is yet another set of claims which either reject the normative underpinnings of market ordering or call in aid other normative standards as trumping or countervailing the values of the market ordering. Thus, we do not permit child or indentured labor, and we do not have a market in babies or, in Canada, in health care, not necessarily because of the defects in the markets or their normative defenses, but rather because of countervailing and other moral concerns, such as "respect" for human dignity and the fundamental idea of equality.

The normative and political struggle for our labor law thus revolves around three sets of claims—first, claims about whether the pre-conditions for a properly ordered market exist (market-defect analysis); second, claims about whether markets can actually deliver on their often cited normative justifications; third, claims about the inadequacy of the normative defense or the invocation of other normative ideals in this aspect of our lives. All three levels of debate are implicated in our labor law, and must be kept in mind in assessing the development of our law from one centered upon private contract to the process of a restructured collective bargaining process and to the substitution of private preference by public policy through direct statutory intervention.

The critical point here remains, however, that much of our labor law is driven by, can only be understood as, and is normatively grounded in a (controversial) view of the appropriate scope of market ordering. This debate cannot be solved by simply pointing out that from within the theory of market ordering the debate makes no sense, as critics of "inequality of bargaining power" often attempt to do. The point is that the contested ground of labor law is just the contested ground of the theory of market ordering. *"Fair trade" and "free trade" sloganeering reflects just the same level of conceptual error and resulting frustration.* Those advocating fair trade are like those using the slogan "inequality of bargaining power." The response of many free traders is also often similar to those criticizing that slogan. But that response assumes the answer to the real issues at stake. The ground of the debate is elsewhere—in evaluating the justifications of certain forms of political and economic ordering—not pre-empting that debate by appealing to one possible resolution of it. Of course this is ground ripe for disagreement but from this there is no escape. To para-phrase Keynes, those who think they can avoid this sort of theorizing are simply in the grips of another theory.

If that debate is joined, and it often is by labor lawyers and economists, then it is clear that economists have much to say and much to defend. But simply because our labor laws still provide for a minimum wage in the teeth of economists' predictions of an undesirable unemployment effect, or because our labor laws still forbid racial discrimination in hiring when some economists predict that the market would provide the desired remedy, or because our public policy still favors unionization and collec-tive bargaining in spite of "economic logic," does not mean that people have failed to understand something conceptually basic or obvious or are making a clear mistake. Two other possibilities are available. First, that economic theory does not fit the data[49] and, second, that the economic theory is inadequate to the normative task at hand either because its own normative underpinnings are suspect or because other values are more robust.

A clear example of this is the misunderstanding of collective bargaining law. The standard defense of collective bargaining in Canada is threefold: first, that collective action by workers opens the possibility of a better contract for workers; second, it introduces the notion of the rule of law into the workplace; and third, and most important, it is an exercise in self-government.[50] On this view the workplace is an institution in need of democratization. This claim cannot be solely evaluated or answered from within economic theory.

It might be said that all of this is too complex. Complex it is, but also unavoidable. Those who fail to take account of this complexity will fail to understand our labor law. One further comment might clarify our thinking about labor law. For many the disputes between defenders of reregulation of the labor market and defenders of pure market ordering are seen as one between allocative efficiency on the one hand and distribution on the other. This is much too crude an analysis. Our labor law would be much less intractable if this were the only issue on the table. Rather, the dispute is often a deeper one about what it is that is worth maximizing in the first place. Is a world of more bargains of this sort, created under these conditions of choice, better than the alternatives?

The problem then is one of resolving this political debate, which is so central to North American politics, of the appropriate use of private ordering as the policy instrument of choice. The democratic process is the preferred forum for this debate and its resolution. Since these are political issues, their resolution can derive legitimately only through a process in which all relevant constituencies are represented and have an equal and effective voice.

5.5   The Current Dilemma

An account of the world as we now know it (and which creates the burden with which trade theory is now strapped) would, then, highlight the following points. Trade theory has found itself unable to limit its concepts of trade barriers or distortions and has found itself sliding down the slippery slope of governmental regulation with no intellectually sustainable stopping point. In a world characterized by an internationalized economy and increased mobility of factors of production (other than labor and the nation states which generate regulation), a natural result is the creation of an international market in labor policy. This is problematic given that the nature of labor law is just to question the proper relationship of politics and markets, that is, to establish the proper scope of market regulation. As a result, a political or democratic deficit is created and the increased pressure put upon trade negotiations, such as NAFTA, to resolve at the level of international political agreement issues such as labor policy, is pressure to take up this political or democratic slack.

Faced with this situation, there are a number of possible policy responses. The Canadian federal election of 1988 was fought dramatically and overtly on precisely which of these responses was most appropriate in the context of the United States/Canada Free Trade Agreement which was then proposed. That debate is not over and remains instructive. The failure of those engaging in that debate to acknowledge what was at stake still resonates down the years of subsequent Canadian politics, and, moreover, exactly the same debate replayed regarding NAFTA.

During the debate which preceded the Canada/U.S. Free Trade Agreement, and which dominated the 1988 Canadian Federal election, two of the most important issues were (1) the direct impact upon Canadian jobs, especially in the manufacturing sector, and (2) the indirect impact of the agreement upon Canadian labor and social policy. On the direct employment effects the Report of the Economic Council of Canada entitled *Venturing Forth*[51] came to play the role assumed by the Cechinni Report in Europe. In particular, a small positive net impact on job creation over the medium term was predicted, but with significant and predictable adjustment and restructuring effects. The actual direct impact on jobs of the Free Trade Agreement is still extremely controversial and, for the time being, unknowable. Given the complications caused by high interest rates, a high dollar, the recession, and the other elements of internationalization, all that is certain is that Ontario's manufacturing sector has been "hammered," to use a word invoked by Ontario Premier Bob Rae.[52] But by far the most dramatic moments during the 1988 election, and in particular the debate between Prime Minister Mulroney and then Liberal leader John Turner, did not revolve around the *direct* impact of the proposed Free Trade Agreement, but rather the *indirect* impact upon Canadian social (including labor) policy. The argument was that putting, among other things, Canada's more generous labor policy (on virtually every issue from minimum wages to pay equity to collective bargaining laws resulting in much higher union density) into competition with the "deregulated" market of America would put inevitable pressure on the Canadian lawmakers to follow suit in order for firms in Canada to remain "competitive." For some this was the very reason for the Free Trade Agreement, not an undesirable side effect. But the main defenders of the Free Trade Agreement denied that these policies were "on the table" or likely to be affected.[53] It cannot escape our attention, however, that since the signing of the agreement we have had, for example, a strident[54] outcry over proposed amendments to Ontario's labor laws on precisely the grounds of competitiveness with U.S. firms operating under the slacker labor regime there.[55]

What is striking about the 1988 debate, however, is that overwhelmingly the perceived public policy choice was all or nothing—either accepting or rejecting the agreement. The two main positions staked out in the debate I have identified as "status quo/nationalist" and "classic free trade":

The big business community in Canada, represented by the Business Council on National Issues, and the Mulroney government, argued for free trade on the neo-classical economic lines. They argued that economies of scale, the theory of comparative advantage, and heightened competition with U.S. firms will create jobs and wealth for Canada. As part of this view little attention was paid to the adjustment costs of the move to the free trade regime. Although lip service was paid to adjustment policy, nothing is said about such policies in the FTA and indeed there may be real problems with certain adjustment policies under U.S. trade law and the subsidies negotiations. And a very clear subtext here concerned the virtues of market ordering and renewed competition on labour market issues which Canadian labour law had taken out of competition or for which it established significant normative baselines.

The status quo/national position was articulated by broad coalition interest groups (the Pro Canada network), the NDP, the Liberal Party of Canada and the labour movement ... [t]hose opposed to the FTA focussed upon its indirect effects. They noted that inherent in the pro-FTA agreement, in its celebration of the gains from competition and a much larger marketplace, was the essential idea of putting Canadian labour and social policy into competition with those of America. In this purely competitive exercise, the pressure to lessen the burden of the Canadian regulatory state upon business was said to be straightforward. However, the status quo/nationalist argument, while attending to the direct and indirect costs of trade liberalization, ignored the cost of the status quo protectionist policy. No effort was made to assess whether the costs per job saved from protectionist measures was actually a wise investment.[56]

There was a third, much less well publicized, but better position staked out during the U.S./Canada Free Trade debate. In the main it was made out by academic commentators and is best exemplified in the work of Michael Trebilcock. I have characterized this position as "adjustment for losers":

This position is constituted by three elements. First, that the best evidence is that the gains predicted by trade theory will be real. Second, the cost annually per job saved by protectionist measures are astonishingly high and represent, in general, a bad investment. Third, that the gains from trade and savings from foregoing protectionism enables us to compensate the losers in the form of adjustment policies, and in addition finance the social programmes which are distinctively Canadian. This position does not, however, answer adequately the general argument about the adequacy of (international) market ordering nor the problem of the indirect and downward pressure on Canadian labour and social policy in the absence of baseline norms.[57]

Canadian debate in 1988 was dominated by the first two of these three positions and the idea of a social charter or "side" agreements played virtually no role. That is, the idea of accepting trade liberalization but with agreement on fundamental social or labor policy, or at least baseline minima, never seriously emerged as a possible option. This idea has now had increased exposure as a result of the NAFTA negotiations to which Canada appended itself.[58] Moreover, the very fact that Canada appended itself to the U.S./Mexico negotiations and the universally accepted explanation for that intervention on our part—that we need to be at the table to ensure the alleged FTA gains are not undermined[59]—point to our commitment, at least sometimes, to the idea that the whipsawing and the

bargaining down which results from international marketplace negotiations have to give way to multilateral agreements and structures limiting
isolated bilateral bargaining outcomes. Put crudely, we perceive in this
instance that it is not in our interest to bargain individually and be played
one off against the other.[60]

There are clear answers to the positions staked out by the defenders of
free trade and their strong opponents in the Canadian debate. The free
trade position as argued in Canada simply denies what is theoretically
obvious and often observed—that there will be increased pressure upon
Canadian labor law policy (both legislated and negotiated) to conform to
the lower standards set elsewhere. The status quo/nationalist response
accurately perceives the theoretical and real-life points, but then provides a
remedy which is worse than the cure. The problem with that position is
not only the effort to make Canada an economic island, but a democratic
one.

The position staked out by Michael Trebilcock is clearly much more
attractive—it is sensitive to the economic gains from trade and the economic costs of protectionism. It is a position endorsed by others.[61] Nonetheless it is insufficiently sensitive to the real crisis in trade theory brought
about by the democratic deficit in the establishment of labor and social
policy. To excavate this point we must recall the scenario presented by
traditional trade theory. In the traditional picture, Bhagwati says, "Governments played no role."[62] Now the subsidy idea has captured all governmental activity or inactivity and this is the crisis that trade theory is now
confronting. On the other hand, before this crisis governments did have a
function which did attract the interests of some trade lawyers:[63] the appropriate distribution of the gains from trade among the members of the
nation-state in question. This issue was residual and, although controversial, not conceptually difficult to accommodate. The issue was simply one
of distribution of gains between winners and losers and the appropriateness of the policy of "adjustment for losers." The issue of what policy
stand to take on this distributional issue has been well argued elsewhere.[64]
But this debate takes place on familiar terrain: the background of political
normalcy within a nation-state. That is, the residual issue of distribution of
gains and losses is simply one that will, again, be resolved within the
nation-state among the relevant constituencies of capital, labor, and consumers. In this world view governmental action *elsewhere* is irrelevant
because it does not enter the causal chain of trade theory. And governmental action *here* is completely legitimated by the presence of the relevant constituencies and their equal access to a voice in the political

process. Labor and capital were, within the nation-state view of the world, partners in a bilateral monopoly, each with the power of voice, but not, critically, of exit. In this picture then there was a two-way street of democratic legitimacy—the irrelevance of the political processes elsewhere and the legitimacy of resolution of labor policy issues domestically.

There is now a breakdown of this claim to democratic legitimacy—and it too runs in both directions. Governmental activity *elsewhere* is now clearly understood as bearing upon domestic politics. This perception has found expression in the notion of subsidy, level playing fields, and found an outlet at the international trade negotiating table. Furthermore, the mobility of capital and (relative) immobility of labor have broken the traditional mode of understanding of the legitimacy of the resolution of labor law issues in two ways. First, the result is that within any particular state the ground of political legitimacy is shifted. Labor and capital are no longer in a bilateral monopoly within a nation state with equal access to the political processes. Capital has slipped the moorings of the nation-state, labor has not done so. Capital has acquired the option of exit, labor has not done so.

Second, the result is the creation of an international market place in (labor) regulatory policy. Regulatory arbitrage is the expected and observable norm. The primary political task of delimiting the relationship of markets and nonmarket regulation has been usurped. The fundamental understanding of labor law is directly challenged—it is a dialogue about the appropriateness of market regulation. One view is that the outcome of this debate will be determined by the market. That is, however, to beg the question.

Some observers have commented that this sort of internationalization "erodes a people's capacity to control its own affairs."[65] This is correct, but only goes part of the distance required. The problem is that such phenomena erode, to some extent, *any* people's capacity to control its own affairs, critically so when those affairs are precisely about the scope of market regulation. To claim that this issue should now be settled by the international marketplace is as deep a misunderstanding of the problem involved as we saw with the misunderstanding the "inequality-of-bargaining-power" idea.

At this point in the debate proponents of the international market in labor policy may then invoke an argument from "democracy" or, more likely, "sovereignty" of their own.[66] Invoking ideas familiar from several contexts, they point out that what pressures Nova Scotia (in the Michelin example) or Ontario (in the reform of The Labour Relations Act) or the

United States (in its relationship to Mexican labor law) are simply the choices made by other players in the market for labor policy. Other states make different political decisions (and on the negotiation side, other workers sign different sorts of collective agreements) but that cannot be problematic, as we have seen Alain and Allan note.[67]

This overlooks the first aspect of our problem—that we are now dealing with an internationalized market in which, from a domestic perspective, only one player has the exit option. Leaving this point aside for the moment, however, there are other very problematic implications here.

As in standard normative defenses of market ordering, the choices made elsewhere (in order to legitimately constrain choices here) must be capable of being characterized as free, among other things.[68] The argument is really of the following sort. What is wrong with the people of Mexico, or Malaysia, or Thailand deciding upon a different mix of labor market policies which are attractive to investors? But this rhetorical mode puts extreme pressure upon the validity of the choices made elsewhere by, for example, the Mexican people. On the legislative side it assumes a democratically elected government which is the precondition of a legitimate choice elsewhere. On the negotiation side, it assumes an independent and free labor movement. Both of these assumptions are problematic, not only in many of the states commonly brought to mind in these sorts of debates—Malaysia,[69] Thailand[70]—but in Mexico as well.[71] To the extent that undemocratic regimes maintain standards which undermine ours, they are externalizing their own democratic deficit to our shores. Those arguing for the legitimacy of the constrained choice here (by a legitimate choice elsewhere) have, in many real-life circumstances, a difficult task.

The claim that "fair traders" insult the "sovereignty" of other peoples is also a shallow one for a deeper reason. The essence of the claim is that issues which should be decided in Ottawa or Mexico City are now being settled at international trade negotiations in Washington. This insult to the right of self-determination is meant to shame "fair traders" and to tell them to keep domestic labor law issues on the domestic table, and not risk losing control of them. But this may be a very bad bit of advice. The point that fair traders argue is that Canada (Ottawa) already has, to some extent, lost "control" of the regulation of labor policy and the reality is that international trade talks provide a forum for regaining some measure of political control over those issues. To put this point another way, our ability to establish our own domestic labor standards has been eroded. These standards will, to some extent, be established internationally. The issue is how, not whether, they will be established internationally. The issue is whether they should be established by the international market-place in labor policy or via international agreement.

This point was made recently in *The Economist*. In discussing the challenge to NAFTA successfully issued by environmentalists who wished to "shoot down" the treaty altogether, *The Economist* observed,

> But wait. American firms can relocate to Mexico now, and presumably will always be able to do so. Without a trade agreement, they can be as environmentally unsound as they like, subject only to the sporadic enforcement of domestic Mexican law. With the trade agreement, the enforcement of that Mexican law would be something to which Mexico was bound by international treaty, with all the American interest groups watching. In other words, what good to the environment, precisely, is killing NAFTA supposed to do?[72]

Although made in the context of environmental policy, this argument is at least as persuasive regarding labor policy. From the labor lawyer's perspective, the choice is even clearer: One choice (international political agreement) is congruent with the fundamental nature of labor law, and one (the international marketplace) is not. And implicit in The Economist's observations is another valid point that the *causal* argument is not a crucial one. Trade liberalization is not the sole determinant or cause of an international market place in labor policy (to the extent that it exists). But the crucial fact is that international negotiations often are the only real and immediate political outlet for these political issues.

The problematics of the new political order are not, however, exhausted by the points about democratic illegitimacy or externalization. There is a further and more fundamental flaw in the globalized labor market. Assuming away for the moment concerns about democratic accountability, nations faced with a marketplace for labor policy will confront the following dilemma. If each nation democratically decided upon the same optimal set of labor regulatory policies (regarding, say, occupational health and safety protection against hazardous working conditions or protection of collective-bargaining rights), then the internationalization phenomenon would nevertheless systematically operate to dismantle or subvert that result. This is because of the pervasiveness of collective-action problems in such circumstances.[73] The much rehearsed argument is as follows: In spite of the fact of agreement upon the optimal set of labor policies, the rational strategy for any single nation is to defect from this strategy in order to gain competitive advantage in the attraction of investment, and this is so regardless of the strategies adopted by other nations. If the other nations maintain their regulatory regime, it may well be in the self-interest of any particular nation to lower its standards to secure the gains from additional investment, and certainly the political pressure will exist not to forgo obvious gains. If the other nations lower their standards, then *a fortiori* the first nation must follow suit. This is the rational strategy for all players. But it is a mutually destructive strategy in terms of the optimal labor regime, which, by hypothesis, had been agreed upon. The result of this prisoner's dilemma has been called the "race to the bottom," "the race to laxity," "Regulatory Meltdown," and, in Europe, "social dumping."[74]

It is, of course, controversial just how significant a factor labor regulation, or environmental regulation, is in investment decisions. However, even without systematic and empirical study we do have systematically observable phenomenona[75] and the dictates of theory. I do not make any claims other than these. The logic of a prisoner's dilemma is that an optimal strategy for all players can be subverted because it is in the self-interest of no single player to pursue that goal, regardless of what the other players do. Labor law contains a series of prisoners' dilemmas— within firms, between firms, between states or provinces in federal jurisdictions, and now internationally.[76] The solution to prisoners' dilemmas lies in securing avenues of discussion and negotiation, cooperation and agreement, i.e., enforceable agreements against defection and opportunistic cheating.

Some have suggested that the world trading system, as we know it, reflects the same logic. Thus, Stein writes:

Collective goods issues are not the only problems characterized by prisoner's dilemma preferences for which international regimes can provide a solution. The attempt to create an international trade regime after World War II was, for example, a reaction to the results of the beggar-thy-neighbour policies of the depression years. All nations would be wealthier in a world that allows goods to move unfettered across national borders. But any single nation or group of nations could improve its position by cheating—erecting trade barriers and restricting imports. The state's position remains improved only so long as other nations do not respond in kind. Such response is, however, the natural course for those of that nation. When all nations pursue their dominant strategies and erect trade barriers, however, they can engender the collapse of international trade and depress all national incomes. That is what happened in the 1930s and what nations wanted to avoid after World War II.[77]

Howse and Trebilcock elaborate upon this general point, that there are collective-action problems in the path of classical free trade's prescription of universal and unilateral free trade which explain the contours of our actual world trading system:

While classical trade theory emphasized the advantages of unilateral trade liberalization over the protectionist base case, taking the trade policies of trading policies as a given, it is obviously the case that the country is likely to realize additional economic advantages from trade liberalization if it can persuade its trading partners also to liberalize their trade policies, thus generating benefits on both the import and export sides. This raises complex strategic issues for the first country. The modern trade literature distinguishes two kinds of reciprocity—passive and aggressive reciprocity. Pursuing a strategy of passive reciprocity, a country might simply decline to reduce any of its existing trade restrictions until its trading partners agree to reduce some of their trading restrictions. However, if the trading partners appreciate that it is in the first country's interests to liberalize trade whatever the former do, they may choose to withhold any concessions in the hope of gaining the benefits of the first country's trade liberalization for free. This is a classic Prisoner's Dilemma problem, which may inhibit trade liberalization and lead to inefficient outcomes in which everyone is worse off. On the other hand, the trading partners may realize that it could be difficult from a political standpoint for the first country to liberalize on the import side without being able to enlist the support of its export-oriented producers and moderate the effects of contraction in its import-sensitive industries with growth in its export industries. In this case the strategy of passive reciprocity may produce a mutual agreement on trade liberalization.[78]

It may well be, then, that the notion of fair trade is inherent in the basic structures of the world trading system: We do not observe an international market in trade policy, but rather the basic ingredients of that system are the basic ingredients required to solve all prisoners' dilemmas.

Discussions of prisoners' dilemmas and "races to the bottom" are bound to raise agitated opposition and debate. The literature here is large, and it is particularly well developed in legal circles in connection with the "Delaware phenomenon": the competition among American states[79] corporate law with the aim of attracting corporate registrations. As Charny summarizes it:

Both European and U.S. legal history support the view that the laws offered by jurisdictions led them to emerge as favoured sites of incorporation because of the laws that they offer. In the United States New Jersey came to the fore during the first great merger wave of the last 19th century with a set of rules that favoured the formation of "trusts." New Jersey's corporate doctrine emerged from an active—and, at least from a business viewpoint, fruitful—collaboration among entrepreneurs (affectionately known as "robber barons"), the New York Bar, and the New Jersey legislature, which adopted laws drafted by the Bar and collected enormous revenues from incorporation fees.

The second wave of incorporation carne in the second and third decade of the 20th century. After New Jersey's progressives, led by Woodrow Wilson, tightened that state's corporate law, corporations in large numbers reincorporated in

Delaware, whose law—drafted under the auspices of the Dupont family to protect their managerial and shareholder interests—appeared relatively favourable to managers-shareholders of other corporations as well. Delaware remains to this day the leading state of incorporation. Over 40% of New York Stock Exchange listed companies and over 50% of the Fortune 500 companies are incorporated in Delaware. Eighty-two percent of the firms that reincorporate move to Delaware.[80]

The debate among corporate law theorists is not about whether there is a race (the existence of regulatory competition)—that is taken as a theoretical given—but whether the race is to the bottom, the top, or the optimal.[81] This debate seems inconclusive in its own terms, and based upon suspect methodologies. It is also irrelevant for labor law.[82] The idea is that investors can discipline managers through various devices including the market for corporate control. This disciplinary phenomenon depends upon diversification and an easy exit option for shareholders—these conditions do not hold for workers domestically, let alone internationally.

But these points about the relevance of the corporate law debate obscure the basic point at stake. At its most basic level, the debate about whether the competition among jurisdictions in corporate law is beneficial or not is really a debate about whether there is a prisoner's dilemma involved or not. Where some observers report the sighting of a prisoner's dilemma, other observers note simply the operation of an invisible hand. The debate here is whether there is some socially optimal policy which can be undermined by unbridled competition as in the classic prisoner's dilemma. Economists who deny the existence of the race to the bottom may, in the end, only be denying that there is a standard other than the market standard for determining the socially optimal.

There is of course much to be said within market theory about the benefits of competition, and transaction-costs economics can be applied to states. Analogizing them to firms, the question posed is whether it is more efficient to rely upon competition in contracting as opposed to institutionalizing policies in the firm or governmental policy. A particularly useful example of this type of analysis is contained in Trachtman's "International Regulatory Competition, Externalization, and Jurisdiction."[83]

The virtue of Trachtman's analysis is that he recognizes that "regulatory competition is an extremely complex game."[84] Included in his analysis is the question of the ability of firms and states to externalize costs. It is a quirk of the American conflict-of-laws rules that the law governing corporations is the law of the place of registration, not the law of the place where the corporation actually does business. Thus, Delaware externalizes the impact of its laws. This situation is distinct from labor regulation which regulates activity within the jurisdiction where business is done. However, also included in Trachtman's analysis is the notion of the relative mobility of resources, a concept he elucidates in connection with the problem of fiscal competition, where he notes that

On this basis, regulatory competition is the "competition of the immobile factors for the mobile factor."

This observation leads to the possibility that states will seek to tax relatively immobile factors more harshly in response to regulatory arbitrage effected through the manipulation of mobile factors.[85]

Unlike the Delaware example, workers are not like shareholders, they are not able to cross jurisdictional lines either for *de facto* or *de jure* reasons. In Trachtman's terms the idea of externalization is effectively large enough to capture the transfer to capital from labor brought about by this relative differential in mobility. He is also sensitive to the democratic condition required for the legitimate establishing of social policy. He writes:

... both the firm and the state have multiple interests and multiple constituents. There are many customers for law as a product, each with a role in any "purchase" decision. In order to analyze the firm's mobility and the extent to which the market will limit mobility to jurisdictions with lax regulation, it is necessary to consider the influence of all the constituents and factors important to the firm. In order to analyze the state's conduct it is necessary to consider all of its constituents.

Private factors that we have referred to as selective domestic externalization implicate the concept of law as a product. It is necessary to broaden the classic consumers of law as a product to include not just taxpayers, managers, and shareholders, but also the full range of persons protected by regulation. These consumers of law may not pay through taxes and may not be consumers of real products; they may be workers, financiers, or residents. Each will vote with her feet to the extent that ... she is informed and mobile.[86]

Trachtman concludes:

Assuming that a particular theoretical level and type of regulation is appropriate to address domestic social goals, regulatory competition that reduces regulation below such level will obviously be sub-optimal from a domestic policy perspective. Deregulation below this optimal level is a means of providing advantages to particular firms at the expense of either society at large (broad-based domestic externalization or a particular segment of society (selective domestic externalization). Such deregulation amounts to a regulatory subsidy.[87] (emphasis added)

... There can be little doubt that mere differences in economic regulation, regardless of intent to subsidize, result in differences in competitiveness among the industries of different states, thereby distorting trade.[88]

The key word here is "assuming." This is the real dilemma which trade theory faces. There is no prisoner's dilemma if there is no basis far establishing a baseline of social policy as optimal other than through regulatory competition. This is the question, and it is a question that labor law, within all the developed nations, has answered in the affirmative. The market is not seen as a complete guarantee of a just labor law. International competition in labor policy is, on this view, an invitation to a prisoner's dilemma.

Tarullo has written in the context of a federal system, but in a way which applies to the international competitive situation, as follows:

In a federal system business may play off one regional government against another. In most federations a regional government may not limit commerce; a company that invests in one state can sell freely to others. Regional governments, accordingly, often compete to attract investments for economic and employment growth. Such competition is desirable where regions vie to offer better schools or transport systems or otherwise to enhance economic growth. But other forms of competition among regions to attract private investment can erode social standards—competitive tax abatements, wasteful subsidies or weakened environmental, health or employment regulation opposed by business interests.[89]

Tarullo's most important insight is the one that is left implicit in these remarks—that competition is sometimes beneficial and in other circumstances not. The only method of making such distinctions is by taking the political issues presented and designing institutions to cope with those issues and the collective action problems inherent in their solution. There are both substantive and procedural issues at stake here. These are not issues which trade law can avoid. Furthermore, trade law has already saddled itself with this project, because trade law cannot, on a principled basis, distinguish its efforts and accomplishments relating to other regulatory policies. Trebilcock and Howse write:

In our view, having brought into the GATT and to some extent legitimized the fair trade approach with respect to intellectual property and services, it is impossible to sustain principled resistance to consideration of environmental and labour standards—related claims as well. What is important at the outset is to distinguish the various concepts of fairness at issue and the different kinds of claims and then to consider their consistency with both the liberal theory of trade and most importantly with the basic multilateral framework for liberal trade—both norms and institutions. Are these claims simply indeterminate or open ended, or can new benchmarks be found, or new institutional avenues established, to develop means of distinguishing legitimate from illegitimate claims and thereby constraining purely unilateral approaches?[90]

The case of European economic integration is even more striking. There the harmonization of much of the legal and regulatory background makes the "social dimension" an anomalous exception which cannot be explained away in neutral political terms.

What then is the appropriate response to this series of predicaments, precipitated by the internationalization of the economy of which trade liberalization is a part?

5.6   Prolegomena to Any Reform

The argument presented here is that there is a requirement that trade theory come to grips with the problem of an international market in labor policy. This requires the design of institutions and substantive solutions to the democratic and collective action problems posed. The most fundamental problem is that of establishing political dialogue between capital, labor, and the state at the international level. These arguments are not likely, however, to win immediate support from free traders. Free traders will continue to seek the rhetorical high ground (who can be against "diversity"?) and to be relentlessly skeptical of fair trade claims both as a matter of political analysis and moral philosophy ("fairness is in the eye of the beholder").[91] It is also the case that arguments about the benefits and costs of harmonization will continue to assume away the problem which mobile capital poses[92] or take the phenomeon of mobile capital essentially as a given and treat choices made by "sovereign states" elsewhere as inscrutable and independent rather than interactive. While I believe that this paper has addressed these concerns, it should also be borne in mind that the arguments presented in this paper in favor of "fair trade" are based upon an appeal to the nature of labor law and its relationship to market ordering of labor, ideas internal to trade and economic theory, the concept of a democratic deficit, and the logic-of-collective-action problems. While these are important and obviously debatable elements in the arguments for linking trade and labor issues, they are also not the most powerful arguments. We should not lose sight of the fact that the fundamental reason for wishing fair labor standards elsewhere is that it is the right thing to do. The arbitrary arrest, torture, and murder of trade union organizers or the locking of doors in Thai garmet factories resulting in hundreds of workers burning to death are not matters that are to be thought about mainly in terms in which the debate has been conducted in this essay. And they are not issues which are much affected by issues of sovereignty, the subjectivity of value judgments, or claims of comparative advantage. Of course many labor law issues are not as easy as matters of morality—but many are.

However, based upon the sorts of arguments presented in this paper, unilateral trade action in response to labor regimes elsewhere is, *prima facie*, methodologically unsound and is an invitation to more trauma for free trade. In the absence of agreement, there is no natural baseline of governmental labor law regulations which is then objectively analyzable as being subsidized by state action or inaction. Mutual and continued guerilla warfare, incited by protectionist interests, is the outcome of such processes.

Unilateral refusal to enter trade negotiations is a poor strategy not only for free traders, but for fair traders. In addition to forgoing the gains from trade, it is the case that the existing dynamics of an internationalized labor policy market will continue unmediated.

Thus the two most favored strategies of the fair trader[93] are poor policy options.

The resolution of our dilemma must be based in multilateral negotiation, agreement, and enforcement which aims at securing the gains from trade while permitting political negotiation of the proper scope of the market in labor. This respects the logic of labor law and avoids collective-action problems. The dialogue about labor law breaks down when capital acquires the unilateral exit option. The idea is to re-establish the conditions of political equality. Thus, the institutional process must be a tripartite one. If one examines the world for a model of multilateral, tripartite negotiated labor law, one is immediately drawn to the examples of the European Union and the ILO. The problem within the ILO process is that it lacks direct connection to the trade issue. The key is to connect the two.[94]

Multilateral trade negotiations act as a magnet for labor law issues precisely because they also act not only as a focus for concern, but as an effective political forum with effective remedies. Although multilateralism is the preferred avenue, this is not to deny that trade action against "holdouts" may be the most efficacious method of proceeding in certain circumstances.[95]

This leaves many other labor issues which will have to be debated. There are the problems of giving concrete form to any norms and of adjusting norms to differing cultural, economic, and social circumstances. In this connection, the distinction between labor standards and labor rights[96] may be crucial. So may be the idea of tying these issues to broader economic development agendas. The central point, though, is that there are concrete existing models of the possibility of putting processes in place which will generate determinate and mutually agreed but sufficiently flexible norms in place in these circumstances.

The point of this paper is, however, not to undertake the detailed arguments about substance and institutional design, but to show that that task is necessary.

NOTES

Brian Alexander Langille is a Professor at the Faculty of Law, University of Toronto.

1. Jagdish Bhagwati, *Fair Trade, Reciprocity and Harmonization: The New Challenge to the Theory and Policy of Free Trade*, in ANALYTICAL AND NEGOTIATING ISSUES IN THE GLOBAL TRADING SYSTEM 548 (Alan V. Deardorff & Robert M. Stern, eds., 1994).

2. *Id.* at 582–83.

3. Robert E. Hudec, *"Mirror, Mirror on the Wall": The Concept of Fairness in the United States' Trade Policy*, in CANADA, JAPAN AND INTERNATIONAL LAW 88 (1990 Proceedings, Canadian Council on Int'l Law).

4. *Id.* at 4 (citing J. Michael Finger, *The Meaning of "Unfair" in United States Import Policy*, 1 MINNESOTA J. GLOBAL TRADE 35 (1992).

5. For a discussion of this "public-choice" theory of politics, see Michael J. Trebilcock and Robert Howse, THE RESULATION OF INTERNATIONAL TRADE 14 (1995).

6. For a general discussion, see *id.*

7. Adam Smith, THE WEALTH OF NATIONS 424 (Modern Library Edition, 1937) (1776), as cited in Trebilcock & Howse, note 5 above, at 2.

8. *See* Jagdish Bhagwati, THE WORLD TRADING SYSTEM AT RISK 3–4 (1991).

9. *Id.* at 5.

10. Richard B. Stewart, *Environmental Regulation and International Competitiveness*, 102 YALE L. J. 2,039, 2,042 (1993); Michael J. Trebilcock, *The Case for Free Trade*, 14 CANADIAN BUS. L. J. 287 (1988); JAGDISH BHAGWATI, PROTECTIONISM 79 (1988); MICHAEL J. TREBILCOCK, MARSHA A. CHANDLER, & ROBERT HOWSE, TRADE AND TRANSITIONS (1990).

11. Michael J. Trebilcock, *The Future of the World Trading Regime: Multilateralism or Regionalism? Free Trade or Fair Trade* (unpublished manuscript) at 20.

12. *Id.* at 21.

13. Trebilcock & Howse, note 5 above, at 5.

14. TREBILCOCK, CHANDLER, & HOWSE, note 10 above.

15. Brian A. Langille, *Canadian Labour Law Reform and Free Trade*, 23 OTTAWA L. REV. 581 (1991).

16. *See, e.g.*, JOHN RAWLS, A THEORY OF JUSTICE 226 (1971).

17. Although not a complete one. There is still room here for us to eschew gains from trade that flow from immoral practices (indentured labor, for example) or that affect national-security interests.

18. Daniel K. Tarullo, *Beyond Normalcy in the Regulation of International Trade*, 100 HARVARD L. REV. 546 (1987).

19. Trebilcock, note 11 above, at 21.

20. Warren F. Schwartz & Eugene W. Harper, Jr., *The Regulation of Subsidies Affecting International Trade*, 70 MICHIGAN L. REV. 831 (1972).

21. Tarullo, note 18 above.

22. Stewart, note 10 above, at 2,042.

23. Joel P. Trachtman, *International Regulatory Competition, Externalization, and Jurisdiction*, 34 HARVARD INT'L L. J. 47, 59 (1993).

24. I refer here to the "direct" impact on jobs and "indirect" impact upon policy.

25. FREE MOVEMENT: ETHICAL ISSUES IN THE TRANSNATIONAL MIGRATION OF PEOPLE AND OF MONEY (Brian Barry & Robert E. Goodin, eds., 1992).

26. Albert O. Hirshman, EXIT, VOICE, AND LOYALTY (1970). *See also* Albert O. Hirshman, ESSAYS IN TRESPASSING (1981), especially Ch. 11, 66 *Exit, Voice, and the State*.

27. Trachtman, note 23 above, at 52–53. For examples of this phenomenon in a labor law and social policy context, see the debate in Ontario about proposals to reform the Ontario Labour Relations Act in 1991–93. *See also* Brian Langille, *The Michelin Amendment in Context*, 6 DALHOUSIE L. J. 523 (1981); PAUL E. PETERSON & MARK C. ROM, WELFARE MAGNETS (Brookings Inst. 1990).

28. Trachtman, note 23 above.

29. *See* text accompanying notes 89–90 below.

30. The magnetlike effect of trade negotiations upon labor and environmental policy issues is independent of any argument about whether trade liberalization is or is not the key factor in the internationalization of the economy. Trade negotiations may be simply the only game in (or out of) town.

31. Will Kymlicka, AN INTRODUCTION TO POLITICAL THEORY (1991).

32. On this point see Stephen A. Gardbaum, *Why the Liberal State Can Promote Moral Ideas After All*, 104 HARVARD L. REV. 1350 (1991).

33. *See* Langille, *Canadian Labour Law Reform*, note 15 above.

34. Barry J. Reiter, *The Control of Contract Power*, 1 OXFORD J. LEGAL STUD. 347 (1981); KARL POLANYI, THE GREAT TRANSFORMATION (1944); E. Merrick Dodd, *From Maximum to Minimum Wages: Six Centuries of Regulation of Employment Contracts*, 43 COLUMBIA L. REV. 643 (1943).

35. *See* Pradeep Kumar, *Industrial Relations in Canada and the United States: From Uniformity to Divergence* (Queen's Univ., Industrial Relations Centre, Working Papers 1991–92) at 1; Douglas R. Leslie, *Retelling the International Paper Story*, 102 YALE L. J. 1,897 (1993).

36. Brian A. Langille, *Labour Law is a Subset of Employment Law*, 31 UNIV. TORONTO L. J. 200 (1981).

37. *See* Symposium, *The Conceptual Foundations of Labor Law*, 51 Univ. Chicago L. Rev. 945 (1984); Symposium, *Economic Competitiveness and the Law*, 102 Yale L. J. (1993); Paul C. Weiler, Governing the Workplace (1990).

38. Milton Friedman, Capitalism and Freedom (1962); Robert Nozick, Anarchy, State, and Utopia (1974).

39. And it has always been so. *See* Polanyi, note 34 above; Reiter, note 34 above. *See also* P. S. Atiyah, The Rise and Fall of Freedom of Contract (1979).

40. Thomas M. Scanlon, *Liberty, Contract, and Contribution, in* Markets and Morals 43 (Gerald Dworkin, Gordon Bermant, & Peter G. Brown, eds., 1977); Thomas Nagle, Book Review, *Libertarianism Without Foundations*, 85 Yale L. J. 136 (1975) (reviewing Nozick, note 38 above).

41. Brian A. Langille & Patrick Macklem, *Beyond Belief: Labour Law's Duty to Bargain*, 13:1 Queen's L. J. 62 (1988).

42. Leslie, note 35 above.

43. Here I use 'nonsense' in a formal Wittgensteinian sense. What economists point out here is that people are trying to say something which cannot be said, something which shows that you have not mastered the basic concepts involved.

44. Armen A. Alchian & William R. Allen, University Economics: Elements of Inquiry 407 (1972).

45. John R. Searle, Speech Acts: An Essay in the Philosophy of Language 168 (1969).

46. Brian A. Langille, *Revolution Without Foundation: The Grammar of Scepticism and Law*, 33 McGill L. J. 451 (1988).

47. Here I think I part company with most labor lawyers, not in that they disagree, but in that this is a refinement of the common understanding which makes explicit sense of what is implicit.

48. *See* Friedman, note 38 above; C. B. Macpherson, *Elegant Tombstones: A Note on Friedland's Freedom, in* Democratic Theory: Essays in Retrieval 145 (1973); Max Weber, Law in Economy and Society 188–91 (1954).

49. Ian Ayres, *Fair Driving: Gender and Race Discrimination in Retail Car Negotiations* 104 Harvard L. Rev. 817, 867 (1991); Leslie, note 35 above; Richard B. Freeman & James L. Medoff, What Do Unions Do? (1984). *See also* the response of Posner in Richard A. Posner, *Some Economics of Labor Law*, 51 Univ. Chicago L. Rev. 988, 1,000 (1984).

50. *See, e.g.*, Paul C. Weiler, Reconcilable Differences 15 (1980).

51. Economic Council of Canada, Venturing Forth (1988). *See also Open Borders* (background discussion paper #344, Economic Council of Canada, 1988).

52. *See* Langille, *Canadian Labour Law Reform*, note 15 above.

53. *See, e.g.*, D'Aquino, *10 Myths About the Deal*, Policy Options, Dec. 1990, at 35. *See also* the Canadian government ad campaign for example, Globe & Mail, Nov. 3, 1988, at A10.7.

54. For some flavor of the high-profile public debate, *see Big Three Assail Changes to Ontario's Labour Laws*, GLOBE & MAIL, Jan. 15, 1992, at B1 (containing a chart entitled "Competition in Labour Policy" comparing, among other things, rights to statutory termination or severance pay in Ontario and jurisdictions such as Tennessee); *Union Criticizes "Scare Tactics*," GLOBE & MAIL, Jan. 16, 1992, at B5; Robert Shepard, *Let's Have a Debate, Not Scare Tactics*, GLOBE & MAIL, Feb. 5, 1992.

55. *See, e.g., Try Offering Suggestions Rae Tells Lobby*, GLOBE & MAIL, Feb. 5, 1992, at A5.

56. Langille, *Canadian Labour Law Reform*, note 15 above, at 599–600.

57. *Id.* at 600–01.

58. *See, e.g.*, Michael S. Barr, Robert Honeywell, & Scott A. Stofel, *Labour and Environmental Rights in the Proposed Mexico-United States Free Trade Agreement*, 14 HOUSTON J. INT'L L. 1 (1991).

59. Langille, *Canadian Labour Law Reform*, note 15 above, at 21; Stephen Zamora, *The Americanization of Mexican Law: Non Trade Issues in the North American Free Trade Agreement*, 24 LAW & POL'Y INT'L BUS. 391 (1993).

60. *See* Trebilcock, note 11 above.

61. Tarullo, note 18 above; ROBERT B. REICH, THE WORK OF NATIONS (1991); A. Jean DE GRANDPRÉ, ADJUSTING TO WIN (1989); PREMIER'S COUNCIL, PEOPLE AND SKILLS IN THE NEW GLOBAL ECONOMY.

62. Bhagwati, *Fair Trade, Reciprocity and Harmonization*, note 1 above, at 584.

63. TREBILCOCK, CHANDLER, & HOWSE, note 10 above; Tarullo, note 18 above.

64. TREBILCOCK, CHANDLER, & HOWSE, note 10 above.

65. PAUL KENNEDY, PREPARING FOR THE 21ST CENTURY 53 (1991). *See also* Daniel K. Tarullo, *Can the European "Social Market" Survive 1992?* AMERICAN PROSPECT, Spring 1991, at 61.

66. *See* Zamora, note 59 above.

67. *See* text accompanying note 44 above.

68. *See* FRIEDMAN, note 38 above.

69. Amii Larkin Barnard, *Labour Law in Malaysia: A Capitalist Device to Support Third World Workers*, 23 LAW & POL'Y INT'L BUS. 915 (1991–92).

70. W. Gary Vause & Nikom Chandravithun, *Thailand's Labor and Employment Law: Balancing the Demands of a Newly Industrializing State*, 13 NORTHWESTERN J. INT'L L. & BUS. 398 (1992).

71. Peter Morici, *Implications of a Social Charter for North American Free Trade Agreement*, *in* TIES BEYOND TRADE (Jonathan Lemco & William B. P. Robson, eds., 1993).

72. *Free Trade: Side-Swiped*, THE ECONOMIST, July 3–9, 1993, at 27.

73. JON ELSTER, NUTS AND BOLTS FOR THE SOCIAL SCIENCES (1989); ROBERT M. AXELROD, THE EVOLUTION OF COOPERATION (1984); Tarullo, *Can The European "Social Market" Survive 1992?*, note 65 above.

74. Hugh G. Mosley, *The Social Dimension of European Integration*, 129 INT'L LABOUR REV. 147 (1990); LOUKAS TSOUKALIS, THE NEW EUROPEAN ECONOMY: THE POLITICS AND ECONOMICS OF INTEGRATION (1991).

75. *See* Langille, *The Michelin Amendment*, note 27 above; Langille, *Canadian Labour Law Reform*, note 15 above (discussing the controversy surrounding the O.L.R.A. amendments).

76. Langille, *Canadian Labour Law Reform*, note 15 above, at 621–22.

77. ARTHUR A. STEIN, WHY NATIONS COOPERATE 35–36 (1990). *See also id.* at 208 (arguing that the international trade agreements' adoption of unconditional most-favored-nation clauses is in effect constructing "collective goods" from which other later signatories cannot be excluded); FRANK R. FLATTERS & R. G. LIPSEY, COMMON GROUND FOR THE CANADIAN COMMON MARKET (Inst. for Research on Public Policy, 1983); AXELROD, note 73 above, at 7.

78. Trebilcock & Howse, note 5 above, at 7. Later, Trebilcock and Howse add the following insight: "Reciprocity, of course, is a fundamental principle that has pervaded both multilateral and regional efforts that trade liberalization in the post-war period, even though—as we have discussed at various points in this book—it is at odds with the logic of the economic theory of the gains from trade, which suggests the rationality of unilateral liberalization, i.e. the removal of trade barriers even in the absence of reciprocal concessions by trading partners. Nevertheless, reciprocity is in a certain sense rational, for it may be entirely rational to insist on being paid for doing something that it is in one's own interests to any how."

79. In Canada, too. *See* Ronald J. Daniels, *Should Provinces Compete? The Case for a Competitive Corporate Law Market*, 36 McGILL L. J. 130 (1991).

80. David Charny, *Competition Among Jurisdictions in Formulating Corporate Law Rules: An American Perspective on the "Race to the Bottom" in the European Communities*, 32 HARVARD INT'L L. J. 423, 427–28 (1991).

81. For a summary, see *id.*; Trachtman, note 23 above.

82. Langille, *Canadian Labour Law Reform*, note 15 above.

83. Trachtman, note 23 above.

84. *Id.* at 77.

85. *Id.* at 73.

86. *Id.* at 78.

87. *Id.* at 81.

88. *Id.* at 83.

89. Tarullo, *Can the European "Social Market" Survive 1992?*, note 65 above, at 63.

90. Trebilcock & Howse, note 5 above, at 411. *See also id.*, ch. 9 at 20 (Prisoners' Dilemma in services regulation).

91. Jagdish Bhagwati, *The Demands to Reduce Domestic Diversity Among Trading Nations*, (unpublished manuscript, 1994) at 1–2.

92. For example, see Richard L. Revesz, *Rehabilitating Interstate Competition: Rethinking the "Race to the Bottom" Rationale for Federal Environmental Regulations*, 67 NEW YORK UNIV. L. REV. 1,210 (1992).

93. Langille, *Canadian Labour Law Reform*, note 15 above.

94. Harlan Mandell, Note, *In Pursuit of the Missing Link: International Worker Rights and International Trade?* 27 COLUMBIA J. TRANSNAT'L L. 443 (1989).

95. For example, see Howard Chang, *Trade Measures to Protect the Global Environment* (unpublished manuscript, 1994).

96. ECONOMIC POLICY COUNCIL OF THE UNITED NATIONS ASSOCIATION OF THE U.S.A., THE SOCIAL IMPLICATIONS OF THE NORTH AMERICAN FREE TRADE AGREEMENT (1993).

IV

Competition Policies

6   Antitrust or Competition Laws Viewed in a Trading Context: Harmony or Dissonance?

Daniel J. Gifford
Mitsuo Matsushita

6.1   Relation of International Trade Issues to Antitrust and Competition Policies

6.1.1   Our Focus

Under the General Agreement on Tariffs and Trade (GATT)[1] the major trading nations have agreed to eliminate nontariff barriers to trade, and through several rounds of negotiations have drastically reduced tariffs. Recently, the trading nations have agreed (in the Uruguay Round of negotiations) to an expansion and strengthening of this trade-facilitating international structure.[2] If trade is nonetheless hindered by invisible barriers, the objectives of the GATT and its new successors—the General Agreement on Tariffs and Trade 1994 (GATT 1994) and the World Trade Organization (WTO)—are being partially frustrated. This chapter addresses the concern that barriers to trade arise from the actions of private cartels, with or without government approval.

The claim that private cartel-like behavior and exclusionary practices are impeding trade has been made with increasing frequency by critics in the United States, by the United States government,[3] and officials of the European Community[4] with reference to sales of foreign companies in Japan. As a result, the question of whether cartel behavior is impeding foreign sales in Japan has been the focus of major international attention. Similar questions about cartel behavior impeding foreign access, however, have arisen in connection with other markets as well.

In this chapter we address the broad subject underlying these particular trade disputes: the relation of competition policy to international trade. We are concerned with the ways that domestic competition laws may act as an impediment to trade. Our particular focus thus brings us to the core concern of most competition laws: private arrangements erecting barriers to market entry. Generally, the erection of artificial barriers to market entry is at least formally illegal under most domestic competition laws. We will argue that when private agreements result in the erection of barriers to entry into national markets, that behavior undercuts government action in removing official barriers to trade and, in so doing, becomes a matter of international (as well as of national) concern. In the following pages we attempt to develop a format for a dialogue about the relationship between trade and competition policies. We believe that a carefully structured dialogue carries substantial promise of progress in furthering understanding and consequently in reducing the number of trade disputes.

We are aware, however, that the subject is a complex one: that although the major trading jurisdictions share a goal of furthering trade through the reduction of trade barriers, including barriers erected through private agreements and behaviors, several factors may sometimes interfere with this goal. First, competing policies sometimes override this goal. Second, customary methods of doing business which may be exclusionary in fact are sometimes difficult to modify. Third, verbal similarities in the competition laws of the trading jurisdictions may obscure differences in their operation and differences in the ways their provisions are understood. For these and other reasons, progress towards substantive and procedural harmonization of competition laws is impeded by immense difficulties whose roots lie not only in differing national policies but in culture, traditional business practices, and in linguistic impediments to communication.

We believe that the first step towards the needed core harmonization of competition laws consists in facilitating an effective dialogue. So far, dialogue on this topic has been mired in misunderstanding. In the material that follows, we identify broad parameters for a successful dialogue. We acknowledge that participants in the dialogue may be starting from different points and may hold significantly different views about the content of competition laws and the ways in which they interact with competing national policies. We also start with the simplifying assumption that the initial dialogue is among the major trading jurisdictions: the United States, the European Community, and Japan.

In attempting to lay the groundwork for a dialogue on harmonizing competition policies, it is necessary, first, to identify the commonalities of the major trading jurisdictions in their approach to this subject. For despite significant differences in method, they share much[5] and that which is shared provides a potential framework for dialogue. Second, it is necessary to identify the places in which these jurisdictions differ on competition policy, its goals, or methods of implementation in ways that cause international tensions and, to the extent possible, to identify the reasons or concerns which underlie these differences. A dialogue focused upon reducing the places where inconsistencies in competition laws or other characteristics of those laws give rise to trade disputes has immense potential for improving the climate of the trading environment. Moreover, such a dialogue carries the potential for stimulating each of the trading jurisdictions to reform their competition and related laws, even in those areas which affect primarily domestic commerce.[6]

A synopsis of our analysis is as follows: First, the major trading jurisdictions broadly accept an efficient allocation of the world's resources as a goal. Through a variety of behaviors, they also share a common failure to live up to the standards which this goal implies. These failures are, in some cases, predictable responses to perceived domestic economic concerns such as a desire to assist a domestic industry to restructure, to stimulate the growth of an "infant industry," to foster the growth and prosperity of a commercially important industry, and so forth. Second, taking a contextual approach, we argue that trading barriers impair an efficient allocation of resources, whether they are erected by governments or private business firms. Third, we argue that the original GATT, GATT 1994, and the new WTO themselves are guides to some aspects of an ideal competition law, in that competition law ought not to permit privately erected market barriers which governments would be forbidden to erect. These are the major guideposts of a dialogue. The shared commitment to efficient resource allocation is strong enough to justify an expectation that domestic competition laws in each trading jurisdiction will ensure that the markets of each jurisdiction are open and free from cartel or cartel-like restrictions. In the cases in which this expectation of an open market is disappointed, the responsible jurisdiction has a moral obligation to justify the exception or at least to explain it. A dialogue under these ground rules, we believe, carries the potential for significant long-term movement in the direction of freer trade. This movement will come as the participants in the dialogue reflect upon their own competition laws, those of the other jurisdictions, the benefits of freer trade, and the justifications raised for exceptions to freer trade.

Before developing our format for dialogue on improved harmonization, we first direct our readers' attention to the many occasions since the end of World War II in which the international community has recognized the close relationship between competition policy and international trade. A brief review of this history confirms the importance of this relationship and at the same time shows the difficulties inherent in achieving success in harmonization.

6.1.2   Historical Connection between Issues of International Trade and Antitrust and Competition Policies

Havana Charter

The Havana Charter provided the background for the creation of the original GATT and thus indirectly for GATT 1994 and the new WTO.[7] The impediments to international trade which can arise from cartel and cartel-like behavior have been widely recognized internationally, at least since the negotiations which gave rise to the General Agreement on Tariffs and Trade in the years following World War II. The immediate background to the formation of the GATT was the United Nations Conference on Trade and Employment held at Havana, Cuba from November 21, 1947 to March 24, 1948. That Conference produced a Charter for a proposed International Trade Organization (the "Havana Charter").[8] Article 1 of the Charter set forth the purposes and objectives of the Charter, which included a commitment to "increase the production, consumption and exchange of goods,"[9] equal "access to markets,"[10] and "the reduction of tariffs and other barriers to trade."[11]

Chapter V of the Charter (Articles 46–54) contained provisions designed to prevent restrictive business practices from interfering with international trade. Paragraph one of Article 46 provided:

Each member shall take appropriate measures and shall co-coperate with the Organization to prevent, on the part of private or public commercial enterprises, business practices affecting international trade which restrain competition, limit access to markets, or foster monopolistic control, whenever such practices have harmful effects on the expansion of production or trade and interfere with the achievement of any of the other objectives set forth in Article 1.[12]

Other provisions in Chapter V provided for investigation of complaints about restrictive business practices and means of obtaining redress for such practices.[13] Article 50 imposed an obligation on member states "to take all possible measures by legislation or otherwise, in accordance with its constitution or system of law and economic organization, to ensure, within its jurisdiction, that private and public commercial enterprises do not engage in [restrictive business] practices...."[14] Among the practices defined as restrictive was "excluding enterprises from ... any territorial market."[15]

The attention of the drafters of the Havana Charter was probably fo-cused upon international cartels interfering with world trade through mar-ket allocations and boycotts rather than upon domestic cartels of a single nation impeding access to their home market. Such a focus was a proper one—at the time international cartels were in fact allocating world mar-kets in a number of industries. Thus the practices which were made subject to complaint are only those in which the enterprises "possess effective control of trade among a number of countries in one or more products."[16]

When it appeared that the U.S. Congress would not accept the ITO Charter, the United States, the United Kingdom, and other nations pro-posed the General Agreement on Tariffs and Trade (the GATT) as a means of salvaging some part of the ITO Charter.[17] Thus the present set of international trade rules (the GATT) originated in a context in which the negotiating parties had shown a public awareness that arrangements among governments designed to foster trade could be undermined when commercial enterprises engaged in cartels or other restrictive business practices and in which the negotiating parties had proposed treaty provi-sions to ensure that competition policy would reinforce government mea-sures designed to promote international trade.

The United Nations
During the 1950s, the Economic and Social Council of the United Nations (UNESCO) took up the matter of controlling restrictive business practices through an international agreement. Although the UNESCO efforts ulti-mately were unsuccessful, in 1980 the United Nations General Assembly adopted a set of principles on restrictive business practices.[18]

The Organization for Economic Cooperation and Development
The program of controlling restrictive business practices was also taken up by the Organization for Economic Cooperation and Development (OECD). The OECD entered the competition policy field in 1967 when it estab-lished procedures for coordination of action and exchanges of information among member states as well as a procedure for notification when compe-tition-law enforcement activity of a member state affected interests of another state.[19] Its current recommendations on information exchanges were issued in 1986.[20] In its 1976 Declaration on International Investment and Multinational Enterprises, the OECD included a section on compe-tition policy. The section on competition, however, is cast in general language, somewhat less specific than the UNCTAD set of principles.[21] At present, the OECD pursues issues of restrictive business practices through

its Competition and Consumer Policy Division and its Committee on Competition Law and Policy. The OECD hosts periodic meetings in which officials in charge of the enforcement of competition laws of the member nations meet and discuss common international issues. The OECD also sponsors joint studies of competition-law issues that are of common interest to the enforcement agencies of the member nations. Although the OECD has assisted the enforcement agencies of member nations in coordinating their activities and has promoted the understanding of underlying international competition law issues, its role has remained in the area of coordination and adjustment.

The GATT in the Post–Uruguay-Round Future
The GATT has undergone extensive revision and expansion. The agreement reached in the recently completed Uruguay Round (the UR) of negotiations is awaiting ratification by the parties. It is expected, however, that when the next round of trade negotiations occurs the harmonization of competition laws will be an important part of the agenda. Pursuant to the widely shared belief that internal competition laws complement external trade obligations, many observers believe that the next round of negotiations is likely to produce agreement on, *inter alia*, harmonization of some substantive portions of competition laws, of enforcement procedures, of penalties, and of dispute settlement. For the reasons developed below, however, progress towards substantive and procedural harmonization of competition laws is impeded by real policy differences and by misunderstandings engendered by cultural and linguistic factors.

Other Harmonization Initiatives
The American Bar Association, through its Special Committee on International Antitrust, recently addressed the question of whether domestic antitrust or competition laws in the trading nations are needed as means of reinforcing the world's movement towards freer trade.[22] In its Report, issued in 1991, the ABA Committee asserted its belief that cartel behavior ought to be treated as criminal by every trading nation.[23] It considered the desirability of a limited anticartel code as a model for legislation for the trading world, noting pluses and minuses of such an approach to harmonization of competition laws.[24] The Committee also noted that while cartel behavior is widely treated as at least formally illegal, many nations in fact exempt designated types of cartels from their competition laws.[25] In the end, the ABA Committee concluded that no worldwide competition-law standards are feasible.[26] The apparently wide differences in policies to-

wards cartels and the widespread uses of a variety of industrial policies support the ABA position that international agreement on a competition code is not presently feasible.

In July 1993 a working group composed of twelve scholars meeting in Munich (the "Munich group") took a position diametrically opposite to that of the ABA when they released a draft International Antitrust Code, proposed as a GATT-MTO–Plurilateral Trade Agreement.[27] Although the drafters contended that no particular model of competition underlay their work, they freely acknowledged that their draft Agreement was designed to promote "free market entry," access to resources necessary to compete, and the prevention of unnecessary or inefficient restraints. In short, the draft Antitrust Code seeks to reinforce present and future GATT provisions reducing or eliminating official trade barriers with prohibitions directed against private behavior which might erect unofficial barriers or otherwise impede trade.

Like all actual or proposed antitrust or competition laws, the draft International Antitrust Code is subject to some criticism. For example, the Code subjects enterprises to sanctions under open-textured language and places ultimate interpretative authority in the hands of panelists holding office for six-year terms. Moreover, the structure of the Code is to use broad language in its prohibitions and then to place a burden of justification upon covered enterprises. This tendency of the draft Code towards overinclusiveness in its prohibitions has provoked criticisms by the OECD Committee on Competition Policy[28] and from the chief of the Foreign Commerce Section of the U.S. Department of Justice.[29] Thus if the ABA Committee was too sensitive to policy differences among the nations on competition policy, the Munich group appeared to err in the opposite direction. By glossing over legitimate policy concerns and ignoring the extent to which its code itself possesses the potential for imposing market inefficiencies, the Munich group produced a draft Code which is doomed from the start.

6.1.3   Bilateral International Efforts towards Coordinated Approaches to Competition Policy

U.S.–European Community
In September 1991 the United States and the European Community entered into an agreement on cooperation and coordination on competition law.[30] Under the agreement, the two jurisdictions have agreed to notify each other about relevant enforcement activities, to exchange information on enforcement, and to cooperate in enforcement activities. Most

important, from the perspective of this chapter, the two jurisdictions agreed to cooperate in approaching anticompetitive activities within one jurisdiction adversely affecting the other party. Most recently, the Department of Justice and the European Economic Commission cooperated in their investigations of Microsoft Corporation, developed a common position, and entered into simultaneous consent agreements with that company.[31]

U.S.–Japan

Negotiations between the U.S. and Japan over competition policy have been going on for a number of years. During the late 1980s, the United States and Japan engaged in talks known as the Structural Adjustment Dialogue. These were focused upon the prospect of increased harmonization of the domestic institutions of the two nations.[32] The Structural Impediments Initiative Negotiation (the SII) between the United States and Japan began in 1989 and continued until the early 1990s.[33] In these negotiations, both governments recognized the importance of competitive markets to the facilitation of trade. Thus, for example, in its Interim Report of April 5, 1990, the Japanese Delegation stated:

Maintenance and promotion of fair and free competition is an extremely important policy objective, which not only serves the interest of the consumers but also increases new market entry opportunities including those of foreign companies.[34]

Both governments agreed that barriers which impeded market penetration by foreign enterprises in the Japanese market are not formal governmental measures such as tariffs and quotas but "structural impediments." They include such items as business customs and restrictive business practices. To deal with such issues, the Japanese government agreed to increase the enforcement of the Japanese Anti-Monopoly Law (the AML).[35] Resulting reforms of the AML include an increase of the administrative surcharge, an increase of criminal fines on corporations, and an announcement of enforcement guidelines.

In 1993, the Structural Impediments Initiative was replaced by a new negotiation format, The United States–Japan Framework for a New Economic Partnership (Framework). One of the important premises of the Framework negotiations is a shared interest of both nations in "open markets."[36] On the issue of foreign access to the Japanese market, Japan agreed to pursue "the medium-term objectives of ... increasing the market access of competitive foreign goods and services...." Again, the two nations identified as matters of mutual interest and the subject of negotiations:

measures ... [to] address reform of relevant government laws, regulations, and guidance which have the effect of substantially impeding market access for competitive foreign goods and services, including ... competition policy, transparent procedures and distribution.

Although negotiations between the two nations are currently at an impasse in a number of areas, it is important to identify the broad underlying areas in which the U.S. and Japan either agree or share similar views in order adequately to appreciate the focus of the actual disagreements. As the preceding paragraphs make abundantly clear, both nations publicly accept the need for competitive markets as a corollary to freer trade. Both governments publicly recognize the possibility that government actions in eliminating or reducing trade barriers could be offset in fact by cartel or cartel-like restrictive business practices.

The present differences between the U.S. and Japanese governments result from different interpretations of the facts and judgments about their implications. The U.S. government believes that although the Japanese government has eliminated or reduced most official trade barriers, access to the Japanese market is impeded by unofficial barriers, especially cartel-like action of Japanese business firms. Further, the U.S. government believes that the AML so far has not been effective in ending unofficial trade barriers erected by private companies. As a result, the U.S. government has been insisting upon some form of quantitative measure by which openings in the Japanese market could be measured. By contrast, the Japanese government, although acknowledging the existence of unofficial trade barriers, believes that these consist largely in customary methods of doing business which are often not in fact anticompetitive. The Japanese government further believes that its domestic market is gradually becoming more open as traditional business practices evolve, but that the process requires time. The American proposals for quantifiable measures or targets thus are perceived as the substitution of government intervention for private choice and, as such, antithetical to the competitive process that both governments support.

6.2   The Argument

6.2.1   The Commonalities

Most of the major trading jurisdictions possess an antitrust law in one form or another. The leading trading nations—the United States,[37] the European Community,[38] and Japan[39]—all have antitrust laws. The trading nations (again including the U.S., the EC, and Japan) also adhere to the General Agreement on Tariffs and Trade (GATT)[40] and they have reached agreement on a broad revision and successor, GATT 1994 and the WTO.[41] All three jurisdictions, through their domestic antitrust legislation and commitment to the GATT, GATT 1994, and the WTO broadly recognize the benefits of free, open, and competitive markets and the benefits of efficient allocations of resources. All three jurisdictions qualify that commitment through their antidumping and other trade legislation which is widely criticized as anticompetitive and protectionist.[42] The U.S. and the EC have employed antidumping, countervailing duty, and other similar official trade barriers vastly more than has Japan.[43]

These common basic approaches of the three major trading jurisdictions provide a promising framework for examining trading problems, especially those possessing a competition-law dimension. We propose to develop this framework by employing (1) a contextual (or problem-oriented) approach, (2) an efficiency norm as a tool for analysis and evaluation, (3) a focus upon the spheres allocated in the several jurisdictions, respectively, to the government and to the market, and (4) a use of the GATT, GATT 1994, and the WTO as partial guides to the proper content of competition laws.

Using a Contextual (or Problem-Oriented) Approach as the Focus
Antitrust harmonization is on this conference's agenda because antitrust or competition policy has been increasingly implicated in trade disputes. Indeed, emerging trading issues are growing more complex, involving the domestic trade and antitrust laws of both disputants and their international commitments to the GATT, GATT 1994, the WTO, and to other bilateral and multilateral arrangements. While there are benefits to analyzing a problem solely from the point of one set of laws—as, say, from the exclusive perspective of antitrust law or of antidumping law—it is more useful for us to put trade problems in a larger context in order to appreciate the possibilities inherent in antitrust and competition law for shedding light on the problems and for redressing the underlying causes of the disputes.

Taking a problem-oriented approach to trade disputes that impinge upon national competition policies assists in avoiding unhelpful rhetoric and overstatements, and in limiting and confining the dimensions of disputes. Thus most trade disputes involve charges of lack of market access: that foreign suppliers are being excluded from a national market, if not by the government, then by a private cartel. We contend that exclusion is exclusion[44]; and that by focusing initially on the problem from a broad normative perspective, the thoughts of the disputants and of onlookers like ourselves will be clarified and the chances for resolving differences will be improved. We suggest, therefore, that we use efficient resource allocation as a normative standard for looking at, and talking about, trade disputes, especially those that may have antitrust or competition-law dimensions.

An Efficiency Norm as a Tool for Analysis and Evaluation
The use of an efficiency norm is especially appropriate in discussing issues that may trigger competition-law concerns, because competition law bears a close connection with an efficiency norm. In the United States the dominant view[45] is that efficiency is the sole objective of the antitrust laws and even the dissenters accept efficiency as the law's most important objective.[46] In Europe and Japan, efficiency is not the only purpose of their respective competition laws,[47] but it surely does constitute one important purpose because that is what competition in fact does, i.e., it promotes efficiency. Second, as noted previously, the adherence of the three jurisdictions to the GATT, GATT 1994, and the WTO again demonstrates their recognition of the broad benefits of efficiency and their acceptance of efficiency as an aspirational norm. Finally, it is relevant to observe that the United Nations General Assembly has adopted a set of principles on restrictive business practices which, if followed, would further the efficient allocation of the world's resources.[48]

In short, the efficiency principle is embodied in the internal law of the three major trading jurisdictions; it is embodied in the GATT to which all three such jurisdictions adhere; and it is embodied in principles adopted by the U.N. General Assembly. With such universal support, that principle may carry sufficiently strong normative characteristics to require that departures from it be justified or at least explained.

Focusing on the Spheres Allocated in the Several Jurisdictions
Despite broad agreement among the major trading nations on the beneficial effects of market allocation of resources, trade disputes nonetheless arise. They arise, in significant part, from differing views about the role and scope of government and the role and scope properly allocated to markets. These are really definitional differences: Exactly what is the range of behavior which should be regulated by the market alone? What is the proper role of government in the generation and supervision of business behavior?[49] To what extent should private business concerns be free to engage

in restrictive behavior? To what extent should government tolerate, encourage, or suggest restrictive behavior by business firms? As nations answer these questions differently, trade disputes are likely to arise. Some, but not all, of these disputes are likely to relate to the antitrust laws and competition policies of one or both of the disputants.

In short, thinking about the role of government and the role of business involves a continuum of behavior about whose structure there is almost universal agreement: At one end of the continuum government acts in its essential role as a provider of public order and at the other end lies the core area of marketplace competition which is normally the sole preserve of private business firms. In the midranges of the continuum, where the purely governmental and the purely private business blend into a range of government-business cooperation and regulatory interaction, the boundaries are imprecise and different nations take a variety of views on the appropriate boundary lines separating government from business.

The Market-Failure Explanation   A common way of describing the spheres of resource allocation committed to, or fully or partially removed from, market determination is to use the language of market failure[50] and public goods.[51] In all nations, government carries out basic tasks like providing for the safety and well-being of its citizens and maintaining order, including commercial order. Governments provide education and support research (especially pure and theoretical research). In most trading nations, governments establish and maintain an environment broadly hospitable to business behavior. All or most of these activities can be described as the provision of "public goods": those goods which the market by itself would not supply adequately or at all, generally because of free-rider problems. There is broad agreement in theory that the governmental function extends to the provision of "public goods."

Again, it is commonly agreed that nations properly remove resource allocation from the free market or modify the market's result in those areas in which they determine that the market produces a socially undesirable or less-than-optimal result. Such circumstances may arise when social costs (as, for example, costs of worker injuries or environmental damage) are not internalized by business enterprises. Not only do governments intervene directly by regulation into some business behavior, governments sometimes also establish systems of private interaction or of industry self-regulation that might not have developed by themselves.[52] Most nations, for example, have established government-supervised systems for labor-management bargaining.[53] The circumstances in which governments modify, supplement, or replace the action of the market because of the socially suboptimal results which the market alone would produce are commonly referred to as cases of "market failure." Each nation generally determines for itself the degree to which the market fails to produce socially optimal results and hence the circumstances of market failure.

While there is probably broad agreement about the concepts of "public goods" and "market failure" and how those concepts relate to the role of government involvement in the markets, nations often take different views about applying these concepts. For example, as noted previously, some types of research can be viewed as a public good: It would not be generated by the market; it produces substantial economic benefits; and, once created, its use is costless. This is the classic definition of public good.[54] Yet some nations may treat a particular type of research as a public good and other nations may not.

Trade disputes involving both antitrust law and the language of market failure can arise when exceptions to an antitrust law are justified on the ground of market failure: that enforcing an open and freely competitive market would impede the provision of a socially required good or service. For example, the provision of a defense-related good by a domestic producer might be impossible in a free and open marketplace, because the domestic producer cannot compete on cost with foreign suppliers. And for reasons of national defense, a domestic supplier may be deemed essential. In such circumstances, the domestic producer would require support; and given certain legal, political, and market conditions, that support might come from a cartel-like restraint through which importers would not handle competitive goods. We will raise other more problematic cases below.

For the moment, we merely suggest that an exception to the general competitive mandate of antitrust law ought to be justified on grounds which are related either to the norm of allocative efficiency or to the common practice of the trading nations.

Public-Choice Theory Theoretical developments during the last 30 years have shown how cohesive interest groups, often sharing a substantial economic stake, bring pressure to bear on government for special favors,[55] one of which may be to protect them from the rigors of the marketplace. Such legislative favors accorded to producers, of course, injure their customers. But when the customers are scattered and few of them purchase in quantities sufficient to be individually salient, then the customers are likely to be less effective in opposing the release of their suppliers from competitive pressures.[56] The industrial interest groups experience smaller organizational impediments and free-rider problems of vastly less magnitude. The industrial interest groups who seek government support are not unlikely to do so using the rhetoric of "market failure." There is often, therefore, a question as to whether legislation substituting government regulation for the market is genuinely a response to market failure or to the pressures of interest groups. More accurately, the question is often how (or to what extent) has the perception of market failure been skewed by the pressures of organized interest groups.

Whether or not skewed by interest-group pressures, most government involvements in their economies have little potential for engendering international disputes. Whether governmental intervention is perceived as improving or worsening a nation's allocation of its resources depends upon one's view of the way the unaided market would have responded to the perceived problem. To the extent that government intervention has misallocated its society's resources, that problem generally is the primary concern only of the citizens of the affected nation. The same may be said about exceptions to antitrust laws. Most exceptions to antitrust laws will produce principally domestic effects, exposing citizens to cartel-like exploitations. When exceptions to antitrust laws facilitate the exclusion of market entry by foreign suppliers, however, then the exceptions may engender trade disputes.

Industrial Policy   "Industrial policy" is a general term and amenable to different interpretations. It is sometimes used to refer broadly to policies followed by a government towards industry generally as well as to specific policies directed to particular sectors of the economy. Broad government policies directed towards all or most sectors (such as across-the-board tax rates or programs for training in basic skills) rarely are the source of trade disputes.

In its narrow meaning the phrase is generally understood to refer to a policy of the government with regard to a specific sector of the economy in an effort to promote, reorganize, or protect that sector.[57] This kind of industrial policy, therefore, may conflict with the goals of competition policy, especially when a specific industrial sector is being reorganized or protected.

As developed in more detail following, the most frequent and widely experienced conflicts between industrial policy and competition policy occur in circumstances in which a domestic industry, having lost its international competitiveness, is under heavy pressure from foreign competitors. In these circumstances, governments often take steps to encourage the modernization and/or restructuring of the domestic industry and to protect the industry temporarily from foreign competition. In the EC and Japan this restructuring has been carried out with the assistance of a domestic cartel. The protection incident to this restructuring in most cases probably falls within the scope of GATT Article XIX, and for reasons developed more fully below thus is properly tolerated by the international community.

Other examples of a conflict between industrial policy and competition policy relate to promotion of an industrial sector in circumstances which fall outside of GATT Article XIX cognizance. When the promotion consists primarily of governmental aid (financial and otherwise) to domestic producers, the result is an excess of supply, a condition not normally addressed by competition laws and hence outside the scope of this paper. It is when the promotion of an industrial sector involves protection from competing imports (and hence a restriction on supply) that a conflict between industrial policy and competition policy arises. When such protection is involved and when it is carried out, in whole or in part, through the action of private cartels, then this subordination of competition policy becomes a matter of concern and, under the rules of the dialogue, requires justification and/or explanation.

6.3   Trade Problems Related to Underlying Differences in Competition Law and Policy

Problems of international cognizance arise when a government, in its efforts presumably intended to assist its own citizens or some of them, takes, compels, permits, or induces action which has significant adverse consequences on business firms in other nations. Some such government action falls outside the potential range of antitrust discourse and presents problems solely of a political nature which must be resolved through international negotiations. Some such government action falls within the traditional scope of trade laws which themselves often produce consequences at variance with efficient resource allocation, and often at variance with the principles underlying the antitrust laws of the reacting state.[58] Some of the resulting business behavior, however, is analogous to behavior with which antitrust law has traditionally been concerned. It is this behavior and the problems that it presents for antitrust law which are addressed below.

There are a number of ways in which government intervention can give rise to a trade dispute. The history of the GATT and its successive evolutions[59] have grappled with the most obvious: The GATT itself was designed to transform all trade barriers into tariffs, which have been thought to be the most visible of trade barriers.[60] Through periodic multilateral negotiations those tariffs have been substantially reduced over time. Of the nontariff barriers to trade, cartels, boycotts, and concerted refusals to deal constitute a new focus for attention. Government involvement here can take the form of an official approval of a cartel, so that the cartel becomes, in effect, an act of government. Somewhat more interesting are the cases in which government action takes the forms of nonenforcement of an existing antitrust law or of suggesting or encouraging cartel-like behavior. In jurisdictions lacking effective private enforcement mechanisms, government nonenforcement has the same effect as government approval. In jurisdictions in which private enforcement is possible but burdensome,[61] government nonenforcement may not be quite approval but it may approach the effect of an approval.

Much, if not all, of the exclusionary or restrictive behavior listed below may be protected because it falls within the ambit of a government's industrial policy. This is not surprising: Industrial policy—which tends to be sector specific—is likely to override economy-wide competition policy. While we identify a variety of exclusionary practices below and describe our approaches to each of them, we will also address ourselves broadly to the intersection of industrial policy and competition policy as a special subject of concern.

Cartel-like behavior—either with or without overt government support and approval—can affect trade in ways capable of generating international problems. The principal varieties are the following[62]:

(1) Through the formation and operation of crisis cartels whose objective is the rescue and restructuring of industries in distress.

(2) Through the maintenance of permanent or long-term barriers to market entry. These activities deny markets to foreign producers. As distinguished from the crisis cartels referred to above, the restraint referred to here involves long-term protection to one or more domestic industries, through the exclusionary behavior of domestic business firms controlling the import trade (with or without government assistance).[63]

(3) Through combinations of domestic exclusions and predatory behavior abroad.

(4) Through facilitating extensive and long-term supplier-customer relationships, thus denying market access to foreign suppliers.

(5) Through voluntary export restraints with or without the participation of the governments in the exporting or importing nations.

(6) Through voluntary import expansions with or without the participation of the governments in the exporting or importing nations.

Because the activities identified here involve cartel activity, that is, the cooperative behavior of private business firms, they are *prima facie* the subject of domestic competition law. To the extent that the law extends to the behavior in question, the law is enforced and the cartel behavior ended, there is no occasion for an international trade dispute to arise. To the extent that the cartel behavior is not covered by the domestic competition law, either because the law's terms do not extend to such activity or because an exemption has been granted or because the law is unenforced, then the reasons for the inapplicability or nonenforcement become the subject for dialogue between or among the trading partners.

In the material immediately following we address the restraints listed above and attempt to identify for each the points of likely concern:

Items 1 and 2:   We will take items 1 and 2 together for discussion. They each involve import limitation in the interest of aiding a domestic industry. Permanent limitation of imports by government violates the GATT and no exception is available. From the perspective we are developing here, nations have a right to expect that the competition laws of their trading partners will preclude the imposition of an import barrier through a private cartel at least in circumstances in which the erection of an equivalent barrier by government would constitute a GATT violation. Permanent or long-term exclusion of imports through cartel restrictions is, from this perspective, *prima facie* unacceptable.

Limitation of imports in connection with an industrial policy which seeks to rescue and/or restructure a distressed domestic industry is a different matter; it is an activity which all three trading jurisdictions have engaged; and it is an activity which the GATT itself contemplates.[64] The situation which gives rise to an attempt at restructuring is generally characterized by excess capacity and obsolescent plants. This excess capacity is not merely cyclical. Many industries experience excess or unused capacity in the bottom of the business cycle. Such excess capacity is anticipated and generally is built into the industry's cost structure. More serious is excess capacity which will not be employed even at the upturn of the business cycle. Continuing, chronic overcapacity may be the result of shifting patterns of long-term demand and/or of overly optimistic predictions of the industry managers responsible for the overbuilding of plants.

Left to itself the market will bring about a downward adjustment of capacity as prices fall to levels which make the operation of the least efficient plants unremunerative. Those plants will then cease operation. New investment in the industry will be discouraged until the prospects for profits return. Eventually, then, capacity will be reduced as a result of the abandonment of inefficient plants and the absence of new investment. Market pressures will be most severe on those firms experiencing high variable costs/low fixed cost combinations as opposed to those experiencing a low variable cost/high fixed cost mix until the time comes for capital replacement, even though the former may be more efficient.

All three of the trading jurisdictions have been unwilling to wait for the market to readjust capacity in the manner described or to accept its results. Both Europe and Japan have opted for an alternative method of adjusting capacity to a fallen demand through industry agreement. In common parlance, these agreements are often referred to as "crisis cartels." Generally the firms in the industry allocate the existing demand among themselves pursuant to a system of quotas, as apparently was the case with the Japanese petrochemical industry.[65] Alternatively, they collectively decide which plants to shut down, as was the case in the European synthetic fiber industry.[66] Significant restructuring in Japan has been carried out under the Law on Temporary Measures for the Stabilization of Specified Industries. Administered by the Ministry for International Trade and Industry (MITI), the law has facilitated cartel-administered production restrictions and import restrictions through so-called administrative guidance.[67] (Its successor, the Specific Industries Reorientation Law, has shifted this focus to one of facilitating exit from structurally depressed industries.[68]) Sometimes a new and more efficient plant replaces some (but not all) of the removed plant.[69] This has been the case under the Temporary Measures Law and was the case with the European synthetic fiber industry agreement.[70] The latter arrangement anticipates some of the results which the unaided market would eventually achieve, and it may reach that result with less pain to the participants.

Indeed, a crisis cartel could be defended on the ground that it acts as a surrogate for the market, reducing capacity and replacing inefficient with efficient plants, thus replicating the results which the market would eventually reach, but more quickly.[71] A danger of accepting such a justification, of course, is that efficiency justifications for crisis cartels are easier to assert than to back up with results. In short, efficiency justifications for crisis cartels should be received with skepticism.

One objective of such a crisis cartel is the rescue of the domestic industry. The point of replacing some of the obsolescent plants with modern and efficient plants is to enable the domestic industry to survive. Without the crisis cartel and with free trade facilitating a laissez-faire market solution, the surviving firms might have all come from abroad. The crisis cartel preempts the market's determination as to the identity of the surviving firms and helps to ensure the continuance of the domestic industry.

Even with a collaborative arrangement allocating quotas among domestic producers and/or for reducing and replacing plants, a crisis cartel in internationally traded goods is likely to be unsuccessful without control over imports.[72] Sometimes a domestic cartel relies on government to restrict imports; sometimes imports are already restricted pursuant to international agreement.[73] It is possible in some cases for imports to be restricted or blocked by cartel action itself, if the cartel or its allies control importation. Imports are sometimes limited by voluntary export agreements, thus in effect extending effective cartel participation to foreign suppliers.

There are no formal arrangements for "crisis cartels" in the United States, although results similar to those achieved by such cartels can be recognized in a number of industries. The American version generally involves import control, usually through a negotiated voluntary export restraint (VER) and oligopolistic domestic pricing.[74] U.S. antidumping laws often play a major role in pressuring foreign suppliers to acquiesce in a VER. Generally the U.S. government does not attempt to pressure the domestic industry to reduce capacity, although it has (in the case of the steel industry[75]) pressed the industry to modernize its plants during the period of import relief.

Viewed in the light of ensuring the survival of a domestic industry, crisis cartels and associated import restrictions seem to be tolerable interferences in the free market. The EC, Japan, and the United States engage in activities designed to provide relief for domestic industries. While all of these activities can be criticized as preempting the free-market solution to the overcapacity problem, they carry a practical legitimacy in the sense that every nation engages in them in some form.[76] Good-faith dialogue directed towards reducing trade disputes related to competition laws cannot object to behavior which, in one form or another, is common to all of the trading states. Accordingly, measures which are designed as ad hoc efforts to rescue a troubled domestic industry with the ultimate objective of restoring marketplace competition cannot be seen as engendering substantial trade problems.

Item 3:   Next we address a model of behavior involving a complex interplay between exclusion of foreign suppliers from a domestic market and the exploitation abroad of advantages attained from that exclusion. In the version raising most acutely competition-law dimensions, foreign suppliers are excluded from the domestic market by domestic cartels. Domestic firms, freed from foreign competition in their home market, attain scale economies and advance on the industry-learning curve. When domestic firms have attained a high degree of efficiency, they begin to export, including exporting to the home markets of excluded foreign suppliers and into third-country markets.

Thus far described, the model resembles a typical infant-industry scenario.[77] Where it differs from the infant-industry scenario is that the exclusion of foreign suppliers from the domestic market continues even after the domestic industry has attained levels of efficiency comparable to its foreign rivals. It is the continuance of the exclusion when the exclusion can no longer be justified as essential to the survival of the domestic industry that marks this model as qualitatively different from the protection afforded by government under an infant-industry rationale. Beyond that point, the exclusion confers differential cost advantages on the home industry which are then exploited abroad. Conversely, foreign suppliers are *pro tanto* less efficient than they would be in the absence of the exclusion. The efficiency advantage is thus in part directly attributable to the market exclusion.[78]

In the circumstances described, the exclusion of foreign suppliers from their domestic market isolates the domestic market from the trading world, enabling the members of the cartel to price at home at higher levels than the generally prevailing world price. A situation is then presented in which these firms may be able to cover their fixed costs from domestic sales while pricing at below-average-total-cost levels abroad. Moreover, they can maintain these prices indefinitely while earning positive profits from them. The result then can be that equally efficient foreign sellers withdraw from the industry, since their continuance in the market will require that they eventually replace their capital. They cannot perform that task in an economically rational manner unless they can recoup their capital costs from their revenues, an impossible feat so long as prices remain at less than average-total-cost levels.

If the industry is such as to embody extensive scale economies or continuously falling learning curves, the withdrawal of the foreign rivals can confer a further advantage on the sellers from the protected home market. The additional volume which they achieve further lowers their costs. At this point the survivors have advanced so far on their learning curves that new entry is virtually impossible. The world's public cannot complain too much that their supplies now come from an oligopoly or cartel because costs have dropped so much that consumers are clearly better off in the latter stage than they were in earlier stages. Yet the determination of the survivors was not made on the basis of productive efficiency; in the model described it was the exclusion from their home market which provided the critical advantage.[79]

Item 4:   Extensive and long-term supplier-customer relationships built up over the years between domestic firms have the potential for denying market access to foreign suppliers. Vertical relationships between suppliers and customers have had a checkered antitrust history.

American law has always recognized that long-term exclusive supplier-customer relationships benefited from a number of efficiencies.[80] Nonetheless, exclusive supply contracts were subjected to antitrust scrutiny under both section one of the Sherman Act and section three of the Clayton Act on the theory that they "foreclose" other suppliers from the market and foreclose customers from alternative sources of supply. The traditional test for evaluating these arrangements is whether a "substantial share" of the market has been foreclosed to suppliers or to customers.[81] The underlying rationale was that this foreclosure acted as an entry barrier, forcing an entrant into the market at one level (the input or output level) to incur the costs of entry at two levels (both the input and output levels). More recently, the Department of Justice employed this type of analysis in its Vertical Restraints Guidelines.[82] Yet to recognize that some supplier/customer relations may operate as barriers to entry into the input market is not necessarily to conclude that they are unlawful. Whatever barriers they may erect may be justified by their efficiencies. Indeed, as indicated, this has been the approach that the U.S. law has taken, however hesitatingly.

At least since the publication of Oliver Williamson's *Markets and Hierarchies*,[83] antitrust scholars have developed a growing awareness of the efficiencies which vertical integration can generate.[84] The courts also have shown an increasing tolerance of vertical integration. Moreover, this growing acceptance of vertical integration is supported by the powerful argument that vertical integration which turns out to be inefficient will ultimately be penalized in the final-product market. In recent years, American business firms have become increasingly aware of the efficiencies which can result from close supplier-customer cooperation.[85] That cooperation is furthered when suppliers and customers can deal with each other with confidence that their plans and other confidential information will not be unfairly exploited by the other. Long-term supplier-customer relations help to establish and foster this necessary trust.[86]

The approach of U.S. law to long-term exclusive supplier-customer relations is nonetheless complex. There is at least a question whether long-term, but noncontractual, relationships between suppliers and customers fit the language of either section one of the Sherman Act or section three of the Clayton Act. Passing over that largely technical hurdle, U.S. law governing long-term exclusive supply contracts has undergone substantial change over the decades since the Supreme Court last addressed their lawfulness in 1961.[87] Under the broad approach of the Court's *GTE Sylvania* decision[88] to nonprice vertical restraints, exclusive supply contracts would be evaluated under a rule of reason. In effect, this means that normally such contracts would be treated as lawful unless it could be shown that they were responsible for decreasing supply in the general (or interbrand) market for the goods in question. No such restraint could be so found unless one of the parties to the restraint possessed market power, i.e., controlled a significant portion of overall supply. During the period from 1985 to 1993, the Justice Department codified its approach to exclusive supply contracts in its Vertical Restraints Guidelines. Under these Guidelines, the Department reviewed the restraints under a two-step analysis[89] designed to provide a safe harbor for most exclusive supply contracts by identifing only those which posed a substantial exclusionary potential. Exclusive supply contracts employed by firms with 10 percent or less of the relevant market and those which did not extend to codified shares of the input or output markets were generally cleared under the initial step. Those exclusive supply contracts which were not cleared under the mechanical tests of step one were evaluated more intensively under step two to determine whether they appeared as substantial entry barriers by unduly raising the costs of entry.

The Vertical Restraints Guidelines were criticized by some who regarded them as too tolerant towards vertical restraints. Partly as a result of this criticism, the Department revoked them in 1993. The result is that the lawfulness of exclusive supply contracts is now assessed without the assistance that the Guidelines previously offered. What can be said with confidence is that exclusive supply contracts become more problematic as their duration increases and as one or both parties to the contract occupy increasingly large shares of the market. Moreover, the use of similar contracts by others is taken into account in their evaluation.[90] Yet these concerns over breadth and duration are, to a large extent, residues of an earlier age of analysis which undervalued their potential efficiencies. In any event, even a long-term exclusive supply contract is innocuous when entered into by a firm with a relatively small market share. And even under traditional antitrust approaches industry-wide use of exclusive supply contracts of several years duration can be affirmatively justified on an efficiency basis, as for example when long-term commitments are neccessary to facilitate capital or other investment in providing the goods under the contract.

European Community law on exclusive supply (or requirements) contracts resembles that of the U.S. law. The principal vice attributed to these arrangements consists in foreclosure of suppliers from outlets for their goods, but, as in U.S. law, their potential efficiencies are also recognized. Indeed, Regulation No. 1984/83[91] governing most exclusive supply contracts between suppliers and distributors makes explicit reference to such efficiencies. Regulation No. 1984/83 limits the duration of such contracts to a five-year term. Exclusive supply contracts involving goods used by the customers as inputs in the manufacture of a final product fall outside the block exemption of Regulation No. 1984/93 but are governed by similar considerations. As in U.S. law, the cumulative exclusionary impact of the vertical arrangements of numerous suppliers and/or customers is taken into account in evaluating their lawfulness.[92]

Long-term relations between suppliers and customers have been the subject of trade disputes between the United States and Japan, the U.S. claiming that these so-called "keiretsu" relationships operate to exclude U.S. and other foreign suppliers from the Japanese market.[93] It is probably true that U.S. and other foreign suppliers are not being differentially excluded because of their nationality: All suppliers (Japanese and foreign which do not belong to the customer's keiretsu) are excluded.[94] Moreover, the Japanese government correctly argues that these extensive keiretsu relationships in principle are consistent with interbrand competition in the final-product markets and so are not obviously anticompetitive. Yet it is their exclusionary effects which give rise to the trade disputes; and it is the possible relevance of competition law to this exclusion which has been raised by the U.S. government.

The perspective of allocative efficiency proposed by the authors possesses immense potential for resolving these keiretsu-related disputes. First, because the supplier-customer keiretsu relations are forms of vertical integration, they cannot be less objectionable from a foreclosure-of-suppliers perspective than full vertical integration. Gary Saxonhouse points out that General Motors or its wholly owned subsidiaries provide 70 percent of the final value of a GM automobile.[95] The foreclosure of suppliers is the same when GM produces the input itself as when Toyota obtains the input from a supplier with which it maintains a long-term (keiretsu) relationship. The determination of whether to produce the input in house or from a contractually related supplier or on the open market is a question for the final-product producer, which it determines on an evaluation of cost and quality. Indeed, the contribution of Oliver Williamson was precisely to point out that the choice of a business firm to integrate fully or through contract or to rely on the market for its supplies is governed by that firm's assessment of the relative costs of the several alternatives. This basic insight, while widely recognized, is not necessarily fully incorporated into the competition laws of the U.S., the EC, or Japan. Accordingly, in a trade-focused dialogue, the emphasis ought to be not on the technical requirements of the laws of any of these nations but upon whether the keiretsu relationships unnecessarily exclude without offsetting efficiency effects.

The authors thus suggest two different but parallel approaches on the keiretsu issues. First, since final-product competition ensures that long-term customer-supplier relations do not inefficiently exclude other inputs, disagreements over the exclusionary effects of keiretsu on the input market appear to be resolvable in principle by reference to the final-product market. If both sides can be satisfied that foreign suppliers possess relatively easy access to the relevant final-product markets, then competition in those final-product markets provides the needed assurance that keiretsu relationships are indeed justified by their inherent efficiencies and that competition in the final-product markets will discipline any final-product producer who maintains inefficient relations with suppliers.

This approach appears particularly promising as a way of dealing with the complaints of the U.S. government that American parts suppliers have been excluded from supplying inputs to Japanese final-product producers by keiretsu relationships. Here the suggested focus on the final-product market would help to resolve questions about the efficiency basis of these keiretsu relationships. Japanese auto producers compete with American and other non-Japanese auto producers in numerous markets outside Japan.[96] Competition in these final-product markets helps to provide objective assurance that parts procurement is done efficiently.[97]

Second, the standards for admission to keiretsu could be made more transparent. Although competition in the final-product market discourages all inefficient procurement practices, increased transparency would provide additional—and confirming—assurance that output producers are purchasing inputs on an objective price/quality basis. Foreign suppliers and foreign governments need to be reassured that admission is possible; they need to learn the timeframes involved and the quality standards being employed. These factors undoubtedly vary from firm to firm and from industry to industry, and the mechanics of conveying this information may be complex. Nonetheless, the advantages of increased transparency are apparent: Foreigners then have a more objective basis for assessing the openness of input markets and the justifications for such barriers as do exist.[98] This latter approach would accord more closely with the substantive competition law of the U.S. and EC where substantial barriers to entry resulting from the aggregate effects of long-term vertical relationships ultimately are a matter for judicial evaluation under more or less objective criteria.[99]

Items 5 and 6: Voluntary export restraints are, in effect, cartel arrangements between the suppliers in the exporting state and those in the importing state. By limiting supply in the importing state, prices are maintained at artificially high levels and the exporters are compensated for cooperating in the arrangement by being able to sell their quota at inflated prices. VERs, however, do not carry a significant potential for trade friction because they are usually negotiated with the participation of the governments of both the importing and exporting states.

VIEs—or voluntary import expansions—have been sought by the United States in negotiations with Japan as a remedy for what the U.S. has perceived as market barriers. The U.S. sees VIEs as targets approximating what the foreign market share would be in the absence of these barriers. The Japanese side criticizes VIEs as "managed trade." VIEs clearly are a second-best solution to a perceived market barrier. Whether they move in the direction of free markets or the opposite depends upon whether the U.S. perception of market barriers is accurate.

Both VERs and VIEs may soon cease to be sources of concern, since both types of arrangements are prohibited under the Uruguay Round Agreement on Safeguards.[100]

6.4   An Agenda

A review of trade issues from a competition-law perspective identifies several matters with development potential.

6.4.1   The Standards for Predatory Pricing in an International Context

One trade-related issue arising from time to time concerns the standards to be used in predatory pricing analysis in an international setting. The matter is a complex one whose untangling may provide the occasion for dialogue leading eventually to greater international understanding and possibly to greater harmonization of laws on a number of fronts. A consideration of the standards that ought to be used to evaluate predatory pricing raises two initial questions: (1) What ought to be the standards employed to evaluate predatory pricing generally? and (2) should the standards for evaluating predatory pricing in an international setting be different from the standards for evaluating it in a domestic setting? The latter question raises further questions about whether there are, or may be, factors at work in an international setting that are significantly different from the factors at work in a domestic setting.

Few people defend the practice of predatory pricing. Yet the concept itself is a remarkably open-textured one. Broadly speaking, predatory pricing is generally understood as pricing at levels which are unduly low and generally below cost for the purpose of injuring rivals. Such behavior makes sense only on the assumption that the predator has a longer-term goal beyond the short-term one of injuring its rivals. Accordingly, most theories of predatory pricing assume that the predator is attempting to injure its rivals as a means to an end: either of driving them out of the market entirely and succeeding to a monopoly or of coercing them to cooperate in explicitly or tacitly restricting output and pricing supracompetitively.[101]

There is no universal agreement on a more refined definition of predatory pricing. The position most widely followed in the United States is derived from the 1975 proposal made by Philip Areeda and Donald Turner in the pages of the Harvard Law Review.[102] There, Professors Areeda and Turner argued that marginal cost was the theoretically ideal line which, for antitrust purposes, should separate lawful from unlawful pricing, because so long as a firm priced at or above marginal cost, it could not drive an equally efficient rival from the market. Such pricing would be compatible with the dynamics of a competitive market: where more efficient firms eventually drive out and replace the less efficient firms. Pricing above marginal cost should therefore be deemed lawful and pricing below marginal cost should be deemed predatory and hence unlawful. Because marginal cost was impractical to calculate, however, they suggested average variable cost be employed as a "surrogate" for marginal cost in pricing analysis.[103]

The Areeda/Turner proposal generated a large quantity of scholarly literature.[104] Despite the various criticisms which have been leveled against it, the Areeda/Turner standard of marginal cost and its practical surrogate, average variable cost, have been accepted by most circuits as the governing one.[105] To be sure, the courts have not accepted the test in exactly the form proposed. Areeda and Turner wanted a simple test which could be used by judges to dismiss unmeritorious cases prior to trial. To that end, they tried to make the determination of variable cost a question of law. That aspect of their proposal has not been accepted; instead, the courts generally use the average-variable-cost standard to allocate burdens of proof.[106] Proof of sales below average variable cost shifts the burden to the defendant to prove that its prices were not predatory. If the plaintiff is unable to prove that the defendant's prices were below average variable cost, then the plaintiff retains the full burden of proving that the defendant's prices were predatory by proving, *inter alia*, that all necessary conditions for predatory pricing were present, i.e., that the market was protected by entry barriers, that the plaintiff was incurring present losses for the purpose of generating future monopoly profits, etc.

Although widely accepted, the Areeda/Turner standard has not attained universal acceptance, even within the United States. The Eleventh Circuit has rejected it in favor of an average-total-cost standard.[107] Judge Easterbrook for the Seventh Circuit[108] had asserted that for Robinson-Patman Act purposes a different standard seemed to be required by the Supreme Court's 1967 decision in the *Utah Pie* case[109]; that position, however, appears to have been undercut by the U.S. Supreme Court's most recent predatory-pricing decision.[110] Outside the United States, the Areeda/Turner standard seems to be followed in Canada, but it has been rejected in the European Community in favor of a less defined one and a test more open to proof of subjective intent.[111] And Japan has very little law on predatory pricing.[112]

Recently, a number of proposed bills in the Congress have employed an average-total-cost standard to be used in evaluating the prices of foreign suppliers selling in the United States. Without getting to the merits of these bills, it is important to the task of examining the sources of international trade tensions to identify why these bills have employed the average-total-cost standard. Actually, most of these bills apply the average-total-cost standard only to the U.S. pricing of firms whose home markets are closed to foreign suppliers or lack substantial competition. The behavior model underlying the bills involves a seller operating out of a closed home market which is able to earn monopoly profits at home (and thus more than cover its fixed costs from its home market revenue) while selling at close to marginal-cost prices abroad. Such a seller is able to sell abroad indefinitely at below average-total-cost prices, while those of its rivals who lack a protected home market cannot. They cannot because eventually they will have to replace their capital, an act which cannot be economically rational so long as there is no expectation that prices will reach average-total-cost levels.

The relation between the model of behavior described and the efficient allocation-of-resources norm generally assumed in models of competition and free trade is complex. The impact on the import market depends upon whether the exporters from the protected home market are likely to secure market power in the import market after the exit of the free-market sellers. This in turn depends partially on how easy reentry would be if prices later rise to monopoly levels. If the sellers based in the protected home market continue to sell indefinitely at marginal cost in the importing market, even after the exit of their rivals, then their behavior benefits consumers in the importing nation.[113] Nonetheless, the home-market protection which they received skewed the market's determination of the surviving firms, possibly away from those who were most efficient.

The model illustrates a type of behavior in which a protected home market is exploited offensively to drive rivals from the field, even rivals that are equally or more efficient. The incorporation of an average-total-cost standard in recent bills directed at international trade may, or may not, be a good idea. But the reason why that standard has been employed is as a defense against this model of behavior.

The model of behavior in which a seller operating out of a protected home market sells abroad at close to marginal-cost prices is not a new one. Its more recent incarnations contain some new elaborations,[114] but this is the basic model that underlay the enactment of antidumping legislation early in the 20th century.[115] This model thus describes a persistent source of trade tension. An examination of this model, its various manifestations, and the way the behavior it describes fit into the understandings underlying international trade may provide a basis for productive dialogue. Similarly, the examination of the standards of predatory pricing appropriate to the international-trade context and whether the presence of protected or otherwise uncompetitive home markets ought to justify different standards of predatoriness than are generally used to evaluate pricing in domestic markets provides another approach to an examination of this same type of behavior, and one that is potentially capable of producing a productive dialogue.

6.4.2   International Harmonization of Competition Laws

Approaching trade problems from a perspective of antitrust harmonization provides an opportunity to transcend the particular antitrust law of a single jurisdiction. By providing a stimulus for examining trade problems contextually, this approach focuses attention upon internal—as well as external—harmonization. Indeed, to the extent that a nation's trade laws embody policies which are inconsistent with those underlying its antitrust or competition laws, the occasion for exploring the issue of harmonizing competition laws among nations almost compels a consideration of internal harmonization, i.e., harmonizing the trade and antitrust laws within each jurisdiction. For how can a nation complain about the lack of harmony between its antitrust law and those of a trading partner when there is a lack of harmony between its antitrust law and its own trade laws? Certainly if a nation were serious about competition policy and the efficient allocation of resources, it would ensure that its trade laws embodied the same efficiency standard as its antitrust law does.

The harmonization of trade laws with antitrust laws is not so radical an idea as it may at first appear.[116] Modern antidumping and countervailing-duty laws are related to U.S. laws which preceded those of most other nations. Canada had enacted antidumping legislation prior to 1916, when the first U.S. antidumping legislation was enacted.[117] The 1916 act was designed as an antitrust law and required the proof of a predatory intent.[118] The behavior targeted by the 1916 act was the international analogue of domestic behavior targeted two years earlier in section two of the Clayton Act.[119] In the Clayton Act, the Congress sought to eliminate predatory pricing in various local markets which, Congress believed, were being subsidized out of monopoly revenues generated in other markets in which the predator held a monopoly. Although the 1916 legislation is couched in terms of price discrimination—sales prices in the home market exceeding the prices abroad—the context and legislative history show that the law was directed at a narrower target than mere price discrimination. It was directed at cartel pricing in an exporter's home market combined with below-cost pricing abroad.[120]

The 1916 act has not been extensively used. Indeed, potential plaintiffs have generally been unable to prove the predatory intent which the act requires. This practical difficulty in employing the 1916 act was the reason why Congress enacted entirely new antidumping legislation in 1921, legislation whose provisions still form the core of the operative U.S. antidumping machinery.[121] The 1921 legislation resembles the 1916 act in a number of significant ways, but differs from the earlier act by dropping the predatory-intent requirement and by removing enforcement from the courts and substituting an administrative procedure under the control of a cabinet officer. The structure of the 1921 legislation and its background provide some support for the view that Congress wanted to control predatory pricing—just as it did in the 1916 act—but took a different procedural route to control it. It eliminated the requirement that intent be proved in the interest of effective enforcement but entrusted enforcement to a cabinet officer so that the easier proof standards would not be abused.[122]

Antidumping law has come to focus upon the protection of competitors rather than on the protection of the competitive process.[123] Yet if the trading nations broadly agree on efficient resource allocation as an objective, then they should be willing to consider reforming their domestic laws to conform to that objective. Their antitrust laws largely conform to this efficiency objective. Their trade laws do not conform to that objective. But the earliest of the trade laws of the three major trading jurisdictions plausibly can be viewed as an effort to conform international competition to the free-market norms of domestic competition law.[124] It is not impossible to rethink the premises of antidumping and countervailing duty laws.[125] Such a reexamination of premises carries the potential for a thorough revamping of current trade laws. Were new trade legislation designed with conscious attention to the efficiency norms which underlie antitrust laws, that legislation would be both revolutionary and paradoxically a return to the efficiency concerns implicitly underlying the predatory-pricing provisions of the 1916 antidumping act. It would also bring coherence into the laws governing domestic and international trade.

The premises of U.S. antidumping laws are that foreign suppliers ought not to sell at prices in the United States below those prevailing in their home markets or below cost. Putting aside the technical problems involved with the calculation of cost,[126] the obscure and partially hidden underlying principle is that of competition on a fair and nondiscriminatory basis, with the winners determined on the basis of quality and efficiency. At this abstract level, the underlying premises plausibly can be reconciled with competition law. Indeed, if the nondiscrimination provision of the antidumping law were restated in a norm forbidding protected markets, the concern of the antidumping law would be met and those laws could be effectively repealed.

In September 1992, the Judiciary Committee of the U.S. Senate reported favorably on S.2610, a proposed International Fair Competition Act of 1992.[127] That bill was one of a number of similar bills which have been pending in the Congress over the last several years. S.2610 would have amended the 1916 antidumping act to provide an antitrust cause of action in cases in which an exporter from a foreign nation commonly and systematically sells goods in the U.S. at a price less than average total cost when the market in the foreign nation for the goods in question lacks effective competition or is substantially closed to effective international competition. The bill further provided an affirmative defense for a defendant who showed that the lack of domestic or international competition in its home market was not a factor in its U.S. price.

As its provisions show, S.2610 was directed at the model of behavior in which foreign suppliers sell from a protected home market, enabling them to price indefinitely abroad without the need to recoup their capital costs and with other advantages which a closed home market provides them. This model underlay the antidumping legislation of 1916 and 1921. The particular significance of bills like S.2610 lies in the conceptual framework in which the Senate Committee operated. The Report shows a renewed focus upon antitrust-type concern with open markets and away from a focus upon protection. These bills provide a new opportunity for rethinking and revamping existing antidumping legislation by switching the focus from protection to efficiency and open markets as the guiding principles.

The Department of Justice opposed the bill on the grounds (1) that the provisions of the bill would provide a tactical weapon for U.S. firms to chill price competition from foreign rivals; (2) that the bill is unnecessary because predatory pricing is covered by existing antitrust law and existing administrative antidumping machinery is adequate to protect U.S. industry from injury; (3) that the bill may be inconsistent with the GATT; and (4) that the bill would be likely to engender foreign hostility to U.S. antitrust laws.[128] An ABA Committee[129] also opposed the bill on the grounds that the bill (1) employed an average-total-cost standard which was different from the average-variable-cost standard generally employed in domestic antitrust; (2) failed to define a number of terms such as, e.g., "average total cost" or failed to articulate the standards of proof for a number of issues such as showing the foreign market was "closed" or that it "lacked effective price competition"; and (3) may conflict with the GATT. Not emphasized in the criticisms of S.2610 was the requirement that the sales below average total cost requisite for a violation had to occur "commonly and systematically,"[130] a change in emphasis from the provisions of current antidumping law which have been criticized for employing measures of cost which are skewed by short-term events.[131]

This is not the place to examine the pros and cons of S.2610. What is important for present purposes about S.2610 and similar bills is the focus on open markets. True, S.2610 is evidence of a substantial feeling in the United States that protected foreign markets provide, or are capable of providing, advantages to foreign producers which are "unfair." That sense was behind the antidumping legislation enacted in the United States in 1916, in 1921, and supplemented periodically thereafter. But the historic focus of the antidumping laws has been on protection—a focus generally unhelpful to all parties: Foreign exporters and domestic consumers lose from protection and (unless the protection is temporary) even the protected domestic industries ultimately lose, as they become increasingly less competitive. Bills like S.2610, therefore, provide a new focus for debates about issues of fairness, shifting the emphasis from market protection to market expansion. Indeed, all of the problems represented by existing antidumping legislation and proposals like S.2610 could be removed by effective prosecution (under the domestic-competition laws of the exporting nations) of foreign cartels which exclude suppliers from abroad.

For the United States—and indeed for each trading nation—there is an urgent task to take steps to harmonize its trade laws with its competition laws. Each jurisdiction can pursue this task unilaterally, pending further international harmonization of competition laws.

Within the United States, a start could be made by comparing present antidumping legislation with the Robinson-Patman Act. Even that Act (which is widely considered to be an anticompetitive anomaly among the U.S. antitrust laws) provides a "meeting competition defense," allowing a seller to lower its price differentially in order to meet lower prices offered by rivals.[132] Yet a meeting-competition defense is not explicitly recognized under either U.S. antidumping legislation or the international antidumping code.[133] Since an exporter cannot compete in a foreign market unless it meets the prices prevailing in that market, the introduction of a meeting-competition defense into current antidumping law would move that law minimally in the direction indicated by the efficiency goals embodied in antitrust laws.

We suggest, however, a much broader revision of the antidumping legislation in the direction of the efficiency goals underlying the antitrust laws, the GATT and the WTO. Thus if the concerns which have underlain antidumping legislation could be rethought and readdressed in antitrust law under efficiency standards, we would begin domestically with a reform which could be a model and a stimulus for effective reform abroad. We are suggesting replacement of existing antidumping legislation with antitrust provisions which are directed against systematic and long-term exploitation of advantages derived from closed foreign markets.

We believe that this approach is generalizable. Following that approach, the United States would be more true to its own proclaimed free-trade/ free-market standards and would attain greater credibility abroad as it seeks removals of impediments to trade. But other trading jurisdictions (such as the EC and Japan) would benefit themselves and others by abolishing their own antidumping legislation and replacing it with competition-law provisions directed against systematic and long-term exploitation of advantages derived from closed foreign markets. Not only would the new provisions be more consistent with the efficiency goals of competition laws, GATT, GATT 1994, and the WTO, but they would also exert a healthy change of emphasis from a concern with protecting domestic industries (a concern underlying present antidumping laws) to an emphasis upon opening markets.

6.4.3 Using Efficiency to Reassess Other Restrictive Domestic Laws

In all three jurisdictions various forms of legislation imposing inefficient constraints on distribution have been enacted. For the most part, these laws are not the sources of trade disputes because the burden of the inefficiency is borne by the citizens of the nation concerned and foreign suppliers are able to cope with the inefficiencies in the same way that domestic suppliers are.

As examples of legislation imposing inefficient constraints on distribution, we will take a common form of state legislation in the United States which provides that a motor vehicle manufacturer may not establish a new dealership within a specified number of miles of an existing dealership without the consent of the existing dealer. If such consent is withheld, then the manufacturer must make a showing of "need" before it is authorized to establish the new dealership. Such laws have been enacted in many states, including Minnesota[134] and California.[135] These laws bear a superficial resemblance to Japan's Large Scale Retail Stores Law.[136]

Japan's Large Scale Retail Stores Law makes it extremely difficult to establish large stores as governmental approval is required and the process of approval employs a screening committee of local merchants. Since the latter are likely to be adversely affected by the competition of a large retail store, they are likely to approach the application with hostility. The result is that most retailers are small.[137] This in turn produces a negative impact on foreign suppliers of consumer goods, since small stores tend to have limited inventories, handling only Japanese brands.

Although the Large Scale Retail Stores Law resembles the Motor Vehicle Dealership Law in that permission of rival dealers is required in order to establish the new retail outlet, the effects seem to vary considerably. The Large Scale Retail Stores Law is widely criticized, in the context of other aspects of Japanese retail distribution, as impeding the entrance of foreign suppliers into the Japanese market. The motor vehicle distribution laws do not appear to have inhibited the entry of Japanese motor vehicle suppliers into the U.S. market at all. Indeed, during the 1970s when Japanese motor vehicles were first entering the U.S. market, they were distributed principally by U.S. dealers handling domestic brands. Many of those dealers could carry the then-smaller Japanese vehicles as an adjunct to their sales of the then-larger U.S.–manufactured vehicles. Moreover, during the 1970s, the U.S. antitrust laws were interpreted to preclude the U.S. suppliers from barring their dealers from handling competing brands.

Both the motor vehicle distribution laws in the U.S. and the Large Scale Retail Stores Law in Japan promote inefficient distribution systems. Both nations would be better off by repealing those laws. The repeal or substantial modification of the Large Scale Retail Stores Law, in addition to benefiting Japanese society, would remove a source of trade friction between the U.S. and Japan. Indeed, the Large Scale Retail Stores Law was one of the focal points in the Structural Impediments Initiative negotiations between the United States and Japanese governments where it was agreed that this law would be relaxed. A partial relaxation was in fact achieved through the introduction of a provision allowing a supermarket to add new floor space (to the existing store) without a license, so long as the additional space is devoted exclusively to the sale of imported commodities. The governments also agreed that the law would be reexamined in five years with a view to abolishing it. Subsequently, a number of proposals have been made by advisory councils attached to the Japanese government for the abolition of this law. At present, however, there is no clear prospect for the complete abolition of this law, due to political pressures. Nonetheless, the trend for the future is clearly towards more liberalization in the law and ultimately its abolition.

6.4.4 Using the Government/Industry Relation as a Model for Evaluating Competition Laws

The GATT constrains governments from imposing nontariff trade barriers and tariffs in excess of so-called "bound" rates, except in certain limited cases: under the Article XIX "escape-clause" provisions where a domestic industry is threatened and under the Article VI antidumping and countervailing duties code where duties are authorized to offset dumping and subsidies. These exceptions to the normal obligations of governments under the GATT are temporary: The escape-clause provisions apply only so long as is necessary to remedy the injury to the domestic industry. And the antidumping or countervailing-duties provisions apply only so long as the dumping or subsidies continue. In addition, Article XVIII recognizes the appropriateness of an infant-industry exception for the developing countries but refers to that exception as a temporary one.

In the circumstances of crisis cartels and infant-industry protection, governments might plausibly justify their protectionist and other market-distorting behavior on the ground that they are merely seeking an objective which is broadly consistent with that which the unaided market would generate: industries operating at high levels of efficiency with capacity adjusted to demand.[138] That the ultimate objective—and the reason for the intervention—is the existence of a thriving domestic segment of that industry might be viewed as not significantly detracting from that justification, even if a laissez-faire worldwide marketplace would have directed productive resources elsewhere.

A view that government intervention can be justified so long as it merely anticipates the broad results which the market alone would generate is related to the justification for government intervention to correct market failure. In the latter case, government intervenes to bring about a result which the market would produce in the absence of impediments like information scarcity or high transactions costs. As previously observed, however, despite widespread agreement about the desirability of free markets, governments may make different judgments about the existence of market failure and the propriety of intervention in particular settings.

In a variety of circumstances, restrictive private agreements can interfere with trade. Indeed, the universally recognized purpose of competition laws is to prevent private agreements from interfering with trade and thereby derogating from the social benefits which a free and open marketplace generates. Trade tensions are engendered when nations expect the competition laws of their trading partners to facilitate trade by eliminating private barriers to trade, especially those which are imposed by cartels or monopolies, and those expectations are disappointed.

Yet in our heterogenous world it is likely that nations will have developed different views as to the proper content and scope of competition laws. Many of these differences of view are likely to be embodied in a nation's "industrial policy," under whose auspices sector-specific exclusionary activity is most likely to occur. It is desirable that all of these differences be narrowed, so that trade tensions will be reduced. Dialogue is, of course, a promising route to long-term harmonization. Dialogue, however, is furthered the more that nations can identify common points of reference. We suggest that the trading jurisdictions look to their GATT obligations as a reference for rethinking the content of their competition laws generally and including whatever modifications of those laws are exerted by sector-specific industrial policies. The GATT imposes severe limitations on the trade barriers which governments may impose. *Prima facie*, a nation ought not to permit a monopoly or cartel to erect a trade barrier which the government is forbidden to impose.

Thus the restrictions on government mandated by the GATT may provide a model for the minimum requirements of national-competition laws. By its adherence to the GATT, the trading jurisdictions have publicly disavowed a wide range of trade barriers. This public testimony arguably provides a set of initial referents for evaluating each jurisdiction's competition laws and should carry sufficient moral weight that departures should be justified or explained. Thus, if a government is constrained to a temporary period under Article XIX in granting import relief to a distressed industry, then cartel agreements limiting imports should also be limited to the same maximum period as the government. Indeed, since almost all exceptions applicable to governments are temporary ones, competition law should not recognize permanent exceptions. Finally, since the GATT limits the infant-industry exception to developing countries, the competition law of each of the major trading jurisdictions should not tolerate cartel-imposed import barriers which are justified on grounds of assisting the growth and development of fledgling industries.

6.5   Particular Potential for Productive Dialogue on Industrial Policy: Interplay among Industrial Policies, Competition Policies, and Trade Policy

6.5.1   The Intersection between Industrial Policy and Competition Law

The intersection between industrial and competition policies underlies most of the trade issues highlighted in Section 6.4. It is this intersection that is the subject of current and recent disputes between Japan and the United States. Many U.S. complaints in the SII negotiations were complaints about business behavior allegedly encouraged or tolerated by the Japanese government, despite questions about their compatibility with competition law: horizontal exclusions pursuant to cartel arrangements or exclusions pursuant to vertical keiretsu relationships. While the latter can be evaluated from a purely competition-law standpoint as shown above, market-entry barriers erected in connection with cartel arrangements exempted from, or not challenged under, the AML do appear to involve this intersection between industrial and competition policies.

A major step in reducing the number and frequency of those disputes could be taken by identifying the industrial policies pursued in each of the several trading jurisdictions and the factors which each jurisdiction employs in resolving internally and in its own domestic-market conflicts between its industrial and competition policies. Once these policies are articulated, the basis is set to refine the trade/competition-policy dialogue on the critical intersection of competition and industrial policy: the point where most policy differences probably lie.

Since all of the major trading jurisdictions have enacted competition laws and recognize efficiency as at least an aspirational norm, it is to be expected that when competition laws are subordinated to conflicting industrial policies, that subordination will often be justified on the ground of market failure.[139] Thus in the dialogue we visualize each participating jurisdiction would be expected both to identify its industrial policies which override competition law and to provide a justification (or at least an explanation) for the subordination of competition law. We expect that in most cases the tendered justification will be grounded in an asserted market failure. Ultimately, the dialogue will thus tend to focus upon the validity of the market-failure justifications proffered. Since all of the trading jurisdictions recognize market failure as a ground for market intervention, focusing the dialogue on market-failure issues carries a promise of increasing international understanding and decreasing disputes.

Conversely, by bringing to light industrial policies that cannot be justified on a market-failure basis, such a structured dialogue would disclose to the world the absence of any such justification. While each jurisdiction would be free to offer other justifications or explanations, sometimes the dialogue would effectively reveal that the industrial policy was merely the result of a capitulation of the government to private interests—the likely conclusion in the absence of an objectively plausible market-failure justification. Increasing the visibility of industrial policies which cannot be justified on a market-failure basis would engender pressures for ending or modifying them in ways which would reduce their overall inefficiencies.

Indeed, to the extent that competition policies are subordinated to "industrial policies" lacking an objective market-failure rationale because of political pressures exerted on a government by powerful domestic industries, a dialogue that centered international attention on these industrial policies would itself help to offset the political pressures exerted by these domestic industries. Transparency has been recognized as a useful device in other settings: Here the obligation to justify an apparently inefficient industrial policy would help to reveal either a plausible market-failure rationale or a rationale based upon political pressures exerted by the beneficiaries of that policy.

Finally, for the following reasons, we believe that the commencement of a dialogue such as we have described—under properly structured ground rules—would provide a special stimulus to the United States to reexamine its own chaotic set of policies that constitute its "implicit" industrial policy and, in the process, to reevaluate its antidumping machinery and the socially perverse results which it produces.

6.5.2 Coherence of Industrial Policy in the Several Trading Jurisdictions

Industrial policy in the sense of government policy which seeks to reorganize, stimulate, or protect a specific sector of the economy is carried on in the European Community[140] and in Japan.[141] As noted above, industrial policy in the United States is widely disavowed but the operation of a number of U.S. laws and programs could be described as the equivalent of an industrial policy, even if in fact a contradictory and incoherent one.

The European Economic Commission is the primary institutional body overseeing competition policy. It is in this role that it also supervises restructuring and rationalization agreements. These agreements come before the Commission for exemption from Community competition law under Article 85(3) of the Rome Treaty.[142] Since the Commission both enforces the competition law and provides exemptions to that law, it is to be expected that industrial and competition policies are administered in such a way as to minimize conflicts between them.

Japanese industrial policy appears to result from several identifiable sources: The Ministry of International Trade and Industry (MITI) and, to a lesser extent, the Ministry of Posts and Telecommunications (MPT) play major roles in the development of such policies. But MITI and MPT do not act alone. MITI and MPT act on the basis of extensive consultation with industry. The Japanese Fair Trade Commission (FTCJ) is the prime institutional body concerned with the maintenance of domestic competition. Since the industrial policies furthered by MITI or MPT may run into conflict with competition policy, these ministries must often negotiate aspects of industrial policy with the FTCJ. Although there are several players in the development of industrial policy, the policy which is implemented is coherent and seeks identifiable goals designed to further the economic welfare of Japan, as that welfare is perceived through the eyes of the participating ministries.

Outside of military procurement and defense-related areas,[143] the United States has not had an avowed industrial policy. European critics have asserted that a number of U.S. industries (especially aircraft and high technology) have benefited commercially from defense contracting. Any such benefits, however, appear to have been unintended and thus not the result of a conscious industrial policy. Other critics, in particular Robert Reich, have contended that the U.S. does in fact have an industrial policy, albeit in the broad sense. That is, the U.S. government and laws do advantage some industries over others, but do so in response to interest-group pressures or isolated concerns of particular parts of the bureaucracy, failing completely to shape actual policy in accordance with national interest.[144] Reich terms this aggregation of laws and other government action an "implicit industrial policy." In his words, "the resulting [implicit] industrial policy has lain fragmented and hidden from view while the larger choices it embodies have never been clearly posed."[145] Laura Tyson also refers to "several occasions [in which] the United States has had a haphazard and inefficient industrial policy in the form of costly protectionist measures,"[146] employing antidumping machinery or VERS for the protection of "such diverse industries as textiles, footwear, color televisions, steel, machine tools, and automobiles."[147] Reich and Tyson, both currently (1995) playing important roles in the Clinton Administration, thus identify an implicit industrial policy in the commercial markets, one which is often patently at odds with the overall U.S. national interest (perceived as an increase in economic well-being), and which from the perspective of the U.S. economy as a whole is incoherent and contradictory.

Reich and Tyson have provided various examples of government actions having sectoral impact and which are not evaluated from the broad perspective of their effects on the U.S. economy. Reich refers to the downsizing of Bell Laboratories, a major center of research, as a result of the AT&T antitrust litigation pursued by the U.S. Department of Justice. Tyson refers primarily to the workings of antidumping machinery and VERS, both protectionist devices, as examples of this decentralized industrial policy. Their examples point to the apparent fact that because the U.S. fails to acknowledge the existence of an industrial policy, various governmental units act in uncoordinated ways to advantage or disadvantage particular segments of the economy. Reich is surely correct in suggesting that the AT&T divestiture was approved by the Department of Justice from the point of view of enforcing competition law and with no special concern for preserving the integrity of Bell Laboratories as a national asset. Indeed, there is no government unit whose responsibility embraces such a concern. Similarly the antidumping laws are structured to maximize interested private input and to minimize concern with competition in the administration of those laws. The antidumping laws are administered by the Commerce Department and the (independent) International Trade Commission (ITC) with little or no concern about marketplace competition or the maintenance of a competitive market structure. At the same time, the Justice Department enforces the antitrust laws, generally focusing single-mindedly upon marketplace competition and often pursuing policies in opposition to those of the Commerce Department. We are not criticizing the Justice Department, the Commerce Department, the ITC, or any other government unit. Each of these units is pursuing its responsibilities as well as it can. The point is rather that these government units are acting in uncoordinated and often contradictory ways.

It is likely that the industrial policies of the European Community and Japan possess a greater degree of overall coherence than does the "implicit" and decentralized U.S. industrial policy, because the former "explicit" industrial policies are supervised by a single agency and are at most modified in intragovernmental negotiations. The dialogue which we are suggesting carries trade-engendering potential in both the jurisdictions (such as the European Community and Japan) which have adopted coherent industrial policies and in the United States, which has not adopted a coherent industrial policy.

In Europe and Japan, the very coherence of their industrial policies suggests that they are less likely to be responsive to the ad hoc requests of particular industrial interest groups. At least a coherent industrial policy would be expected *prima facie* to establish criteria or standards for subordinating competition policies to cartel-like restrictions for a particular industrial sector. At the same time, from the point of view of a general (albeit aspirational) norm of efficient allocation of resources, general standards for subordinating competition policy are *prima facie* suspect and require substantial justification.

For the United States, the kind of dialogue we are proposing carries an immense potential for stimulating a reexamination of its array of uncoordinated government sector-specific actions and policies. Even without a trade agenda in the background, the United States needs to undertake such a reexamination, just for the purposes of improving its own domestic economic well-being. An overall examination of its unacknowledged array of contradictory industrial policies would provide a basis for reorganizing those policies in a coherent way and, of course, modifying some or all of them when required to carry out whatever new, but coherent, policy objectives the U.S. government adopts.

Laura Tyson has identified many of the self-defeating U.S. industrial policies as embodied in the U.S. antidumping laws, their operation, and the VERS to which they often give rise. We have argued above that a renewed focus upon efficiency as a governing norm for evaluating trade disputes and domestic laws affecting trade could play a role in the reform of U.S. antidumping legislation. Evaluating antidumping legislation in the format of an overall examination of all of U.S. industrial policies for their coherence and effectiveness in furthering the U.S. national interest would heighten the probabilities for their reform. Those probabilities would be further raised if this examination were to take place in a context in which the industrial policies of the other major trading jurisdictions—including their antidumping and other like protectionist devices such as import barriers connected with recession cartels, etc.—were also in the process of reevaluation and reform.

APPENDIX A   THE JAPANESE ANTI-MONOPOLY LAW

Mitsuo Matsushita

A.1   Competition Law and Trade Issues

A.1.1   The Problem

Harmonization of competition law and policy is important in trade relationships between Japan and its major trading partners, especially with the United States and the European Community. Although Japan has lowered both tariffs and nontariff barriers and has taken many other trade-liberalizing measures, its trade surplus has stubbornly remained and constitutes a major economic and political issue in international trade.

Political leaders and trade negotiators in the United States, the European Community, and Japan have come to a realization that the core of the problem in Japan is not trade barriers in the traditional sense of the term, such as tariffs and quantitative import restrictions. Rather, in their view, the core of the problem lies in certain structural features of Japanese business systems, such as exclusive business customs, cartels, "keiretsu" systems, continuous transactional relationships among Japanese companies, mutual ownership of stock and the like. It is these structural aspects of the Japanese business system that have sometimes been asserted to constitute the major impediments to market access in Japan by foreign enterprises.

If market access in Japan were denied by formal governmental measures such as tariffs or import quotas, the remedy would lie in a reduction or removal of such measures and could be dealt with through traditional trade negotiations. If, however, peculiar structural aspects of business systems are at issue, different measures must be applied to resolve the problem. Since a nation's business systems are deeply rooted in its history, tradition, political and economic climate and related matters, it is often difficult to change it overnight. Also business systems are highly complex and reflect the totality of many complex economic and social elements in a society. It may not, therefore, be sufficient to apply just one uniform measure to deal with such problems. Rather, the identification of effective solutions for these structural problems is much more difficult than identifying the solutions to traditional trade problems such as tariffs and import quotas.

A.1.2   The Structural Impediments Initiative (the SII)

The SII negotiated between the United States and Japan attempted to deal with problems of the above nature. Negotiators of the United States and Japan in the SII agreed that problems in Japan lay in such factors as high savings rates, high land prices, exclusive business practices, keiretsu issues and price differentials between the United States and Japan. Among those, however, issues connected with exclusive business practices and the keiretsu were regarded as critical for the purpose of increasing market access.

In the SII, the United States and Japan agreed that the Japanese government would increase the enforcement of the Antimonopoly Law in Japan (the AML) and thereby reduce exclusivity in business systems. Several reforms resulted from this agreement. First, the rate of administrative surcharge, which applies to participants of a price cartel, was raised from 2 percent of the total sales of a participant of a cartel (in manufacturing) to 6 percent. Second, the criminal fine to be imposed on a corporation was raised from the maximum of 5 million yen to 100 million yen. Third, the Fair Trade Commission of Japan (the FTCJ) announced a program to assist a private plaintiff who brings an action for the recovery of damages sustained as a result of a violation of the AML.

These are the major changes made to the AML. Beside these changes, the FTCJ in 1991, announced, "The Guidelines on Distribution and Trade Practices" (1991 FTCJ Distribution Guidelines) in which it laid out details of regulation that it would apply to restrictive practices and keiretsu relationships. Details of the 1991 FTCJ Distribution Guidelines will be explained later.

More recently, a task force commissioned by the FTCJ to study activities of trade associations identified problem areas connected with trade associations. This is also an important aspect of the AML in relation to trade issues since there have been complaints by foreign enterprises that some activities of trade associations are exclusive and they have impeded access to Japanese markets.

It is too early to evaluate the effectiveness of these reforms of the AML. They have had very little effect, if any, on the reduction of the bilateral trade imbalance between the United States and Japan. In this respect, there is disappointment on the part of the United States government under President Clinton with the SII. It is rumored that the Clinton Administration would discontinue the SII and initiate a new program in which the United States government requests the Japanese government to establish "target market shares" in the Japanese market for designated foreign products such as semiconductors, auto parts, supercomputers and others.

It should, however, be emphasized that the effect of reforms in the AML as a result of the SII should be evaluated in a long-term perspective. Those reforms are an attempt to harmonize the rules of conduct which the United States and Japan apply to enterprises and, in this sense, should be regarded as an example of harmonizing competition laws and policies.

A.2   An Outline of the Anti-Monopoly Law

It is useful to provide an outline of the AML in order to facilitate understanding of the analysis of the problems. There are three categories of conduct that are governed by the AML: (1) private monopolization, (2) unreasonable restraints of trade (cartels and trade associations), and (3) unfair business practices.

A.2.1   Private Monopolization

A private monopolization, which is defined in Article 2(5) and prohibited by Article 3 of the AML, is an exclusion or control by a powerful enterprise of the business activities of another enterprise which brings about substantial restraint of competition in a market. Examples would include an acquisition by a powerful enterprise of shares in competing corporations that would eliminate competition in a market. The provisions governing mergers and acquisitions (Articles 10 and 15 of the AML) are regarded as supplementing the provisions governing private monopolization (Article 3).

A.2.2   Unreasonable Restraint of Trade (Cartels)

Activities of cartels and trade associations which restrain competition are called "unreasonable restraint[s] of trade." They are defined in Article 2(6) and are prohibited by Article 3 of the AML. Also Article 8(1) (i)–(iii) of the AML prohibits trade associations from engaging in activities that restrain competition substantially and otherwise restrict the freedom of member enterprises. As touched upon later, however, there are a number of laws exempting joint activities of enterprises from the application of the AML including depression cartels, rationalization cartels, export cartels, small business cartels, and others.

A.2.3   Unfair Business Practices

The third category of conduct under the control of the AML is collectively called "unfair business practices." They are defined in Article 2(9) and prohibited under Article 19 of the AML. The FTCJ is authorized to designate unfair business practices within the framework of Article 2(9). Unfair business practices designated by the FTCJ include conduct such as refusals to deal, boycotts, discriminatory treatment, price discrimination, sales below cost of production, sales with excessive premiums, false and misleading advertisements, exclusive dealing, tie-in sales, resale price maintenance, vertical territorial and customer allocations, and abuses of dominant position.

A.2.4   The Enforcement Agency and Process

The primary enforcement agency of the AML is the FTCJ. There are three types of actions against a violation of the AML. First, the FTCJ is authorized to initiate an administrative proceeding when there is sufficient evidence to support an initiation of the proceeding. If, as the result, it is proved that a violation has been committed, the FTCJ issues an elimination order (cease-and-desist order) requiring the party in violation to discontinue the violation. An order by the FTCJ is appealable to the Tokyo High Court and to the Supreme Court.

If enterprises have established a price cartel or a cartel which affects price, the FTCJ must impose an administrative surcharge on the parties in violation for the period in which the cartel was effectively enforced. As mentioned previously, under the 1991 amendment, the rate of administrative surcharge is 6 percent of the total sales of the product involved by a party to a cartel during the life of the cartel. Administrative surcharges can be applied retroactively for a three-year period beginning from the time when a cartel in question was terminated.

Some violations of the AML such as a cartel and a private monopolization are punishable by a criminal penalty. The maximum penalty on individuals is an imprisonment of three years or a fine of 5 million yen or both and that for corporations is a fine of 100 million yen.

Parties who have suffered damage in property can bring a suit against a party in violation of the AML for the recovery of damage. This can be done either under Articles 25/26 of the AML or Article 709 of the Civil Code which provides for the recovery of damage caused by a tortious conduct.

A.3   Distribution and Trade Practices

Exclusivity in distribution sectors and subcontractor's systems in Japan have been alleged by foreign enterprises and governments (especially the United States government) to constitute important structural impediments. There are counter-claims on the part of the Japanese government and industries that Japanese business systems are basically open and that no discriminatory measures *vis-à-vis* foreign enterprises are applied. Although we must refrain from a full scale assessment of merits and defects of such claims and counterclaims, they certainly raise important issues of market access.

As mentioned before, the FTCJ announced the 1991 Distribution Guidelines to deal with these problems. The 1991 Distribution Guidelines are divided into three parts: (1) provisions on continuous and exclusive dealings, (2) those on restrictive activities in distribution sectors, and (3) those on sole agencies. Among those, (1) is primarily concerned with restrictive activities in the sale and purchase of capital goods and raw materials, (2) with those in distribution of goods from manufacturers to retailers and (3) with restrictive activities of sole agencies including sole import agencies. They include detailed provisions on activities of enterprises in those three areas. Although it is not necessary and useful to explain all of them, we will briefly touch on some major items.

A.3.1   Resale Price Maintenance

Although there are exemptions from the application of the AML to resale price maintenance in the fields of books and publications (as provided for in Article 24-2 of the AML) and cosmetics and pharmaceuticals (as designated by the FTCJ as candidates for exemptions), resale price maintenance is generally regarded as unlawful under the AML. There are several Supreme Court decisions (such as the *Meiji Shoji* case and the *Wakodao* case) which declared that resale price maintenance was unlawful unless it was exercised with regard to commodities exempted under Article 24-2 or designated by the FTCJ as candidates for exemptions. There are many cases in which the FTCJ has proceeded against resale price maintenance and has held it unlawful.

The 1991 FTCJ Distribution Guidelines repeat this position and provide that, not only resale price maintenance exercised through an explicit agreement or coercion, but also, resale price maintenance enforced through an informal threat of retaliation by a manufacturer against distributors and retailers in the absence of explicit agreement is unlawful.

With regard to the prohibition of resale price maintenance, there is a substantial degree of similarity among United States antitrust laws, EEC competition rules, and the AML in Japan.

A.3.2   Exclusive Dealings, Vertical Territorial, and Customer Restrictions

Exclusive dealings and vertical territorial and customer restrictions are not unlawful in principle. However, they are held unlawful if they are employed by a "powerful enterprise" and thereby price is maintained at a high level. The threshold of a "powerful" enterprise is defined to be a market share of 10 percent or a ranking in terms of market share being within the top three. Even though an enterprise exceeds this threshold, it is not automatically treated as a powerful enterprise. In order to decide whether an enterprise is powerful or not, factors such as market concentration, peculiarities of the product in question, product differentiation, ease of new entry, the position of the party in question and all other related factors are taken into consideration.

A.3.3   Refusals to Deal and Boycott

Refusals to deal by a single enterprise are held lawful unless exercised as part of a program to exclude competition and thereby to achieve a monopoly or as means to accomplish an unlawful purpose (such as resale price maintenance).

On the other hand, a collective refusal to deal (boycott) is generally held unlawful. The 1991 FTCJ Distribution Guidelines cite, as an example of such an unlawful boycott, an agreement among manufacturers that they notify their distributors that, if a distributor sells an imported product which competes with those produced by the manufacturers, a sale to that distributor will be stopped.

A.3.4   Reciprocal Dealings

If a powerful enterprise sells or purchases commodities or services on the condition that the other party to the transaction purchases or sells (as the case may be) commodities or services in return, such a reciprocal condition may be held unlawful when business opportunities of competing enterprises are unduly restricted.

A.3.5   Effectiveness of the Anti-Monopoly Law in Dealing with Exclusivity in Distribution

The 1991 FTCJ Distribution Guidelines are a restatement of the existing legal principles with regard to distribution and trade practices rather than an announcement of new rules. As such, however, they have had "announcement effects" on corporate behavior in Japan. Many companies have taken them seriously and incorporated them in their antitrust compliance programs.

There is, however, a limit to the effectiveness of the application of the AML *vis-à-vis* such problems. First, many of so-called "keiretsu" relationships are factual and sociological combinations rather than ones based on contract. For example, in auto distribution systems, there is generally no language in the distribution agreements between manufacturers and dealers that the dealers must not sell competing cars. However, dealers usually do not sell competing cars because of such factors as long-standing relationships between the manufacturer and the dealer, subsidies and assistance given by the manufacturer to the dealer in times of depression, a general reluctance on the part of the dealer to engage in business that may be adverse to the relationship between the manufacturer and the dealer and similar socio-psychological reasons.

Secondly, in many industries in Japan, there is strong "inter-brand" competition between different keiretsu systems. Again, in the auto distribution area, there are several vertically integrated systems such as Toyota, Nissan, Honda, and Mitsubishi and they engage in both price and nonprice competition with each other. Although each system may be exclusive and difficult for outside parties to penetrate, there is little antitrust problem in the context of the 1991 FTCJ Distribution Guidelines as long as there is intensive inter-brand competition. Under the *Sylvania* doctrine, the legal situation is not so different in the United States. This situation may make it difficult for foreign enterprises to penetrate Japanese distribution systems and thereby may constitute a structural barrier to entry. But it does not raise antitrust issues. It is important to note that, even though it may be a trade issue, it is not necessarily an antitrust issue. Seen in this context, although an increase of enforcement of the AML in Japan will have a long term effect of leveling the playing field between Japanese enterprises and U.S. enterprises, there will be no immediate effect of increasing the penetration of the Japanese market by U.S. enterprises, as far as distribution and production keiretsu are concerned.

For the immediate purpose of easing market access by foreign enterprises, some other prescriptions may be more effective, at least in the short run. For example, a government agency like the Ministry of International Trade and Industry (the MITI) can formulate policies to encourage new entry into a market. In the auto distribution area, there are potential entrants such as large lease companies, department stores and large supermarkets. They are large enterprises and they are not under the control of keiretsu systems of any manufacturer. Also department stores and supermarkets may tie up with credit companies so that the latter can finance purchasers while the former engage in selling cars of various manufacturers including foreign cars.

The MITI can assist them by means of, for example, reduction of taxes and preferential finance by industrial banks and other financial institutions. The MITI can announce an indicative program oriented toward encouraging entry of such kinds and a mere announcement will have a great impact on the existing keiretsu. Although such a governmental measure is characterized as a "guidance principle" rather than a "competition principle," it has a more immediate effect of breaking keiretsu systems.

Recently some Japanese manufacturers have entered into agreements with foreign competing enterprises whereby the former import products into Japan from the latter and sell them through their domestic distribution networks. A prime example is the agreement between Toyota and Volkswagen whereby Toyota would import VW cars and distribute them through its distribution networks. Such a measure may be regarded skeptically and even suspiciously by antitrust advocates. Prescriptions depend on the question: "Do we want competition or a quick access in the Japanese market and an increase of import?"

A.4   Cartels and Trade Associations

Some activities of cartels and trade associations have restricted the entry of foreign enterprises into the Japanese market. In this section, major problems involving cartels and trade associations are examined in the context of international trade.

A.4.1   Import Cartels

There are several important cases in which import cartels entered into among Japanese enterprises were at issue under the U.S. antitrust laws. One is the *Tanner Crab* case, in which the U.S. Justice Department challenged the activities of Japanese importers of crabs produced in the United States and exported to Japan. Japanese importers formed an import association in which the members "exchanged" price information for the purpose of holding down import prices. The case was resolved by a consent decision and the Japanese defendants were ordered, *inter alia*, to refrain from exchanging price information in Japan with regard to crabs imported from the United States to Japan and related matters.

In the *Daishowa* case, a private case in which a U.S. export association challenged activities of Japanese importers as a "boycott," a U.S. court held that the activities of Japanese importers in excluding a U.S. export association were not immunized from the application of United States antitrust laws, although the U.S. export association was immunized under the Webb-Pomereme Act.

In 1992, the U.S. Justice Department, citing these two cases, announced that it would challenge foreign country enterprises that would impede U.S. exports to that country. The FTCJ announced that such a move by the U.S. Justice Department would be an infringement of Japanese sovereignty and that anticompetitive activities in Japan should be controlled by the AML of Japan.

In some cases, the U.S. government has notified the FTCJ of the behavior of Japanese enterprises which have impeded imports into Japan. One of the well-known cases is the *Soda Ash* case in which Japanese manufacturers of soda ash organized a program of jointly restricting the import of soda ash from the United States. Upon notification by the U.S. government, the FTCJ challenged the enterprises in question and held the activities unlawful.

There are at least two cases in which the FTCJ challenged bid-rigging activities of Japanese construction companies with regard to construction works in U.S. Naval and Air Force bases in Japan. In one of them, the *Yokosuka Naval Base* case, the U.S. government announced that it would bring an antitrust action for the recovery of damages (treble damage suit) under United States antitrust laws against the Japanese construction companies. The companies settled the case and paid a large amount of money to the U.S. government.

Unlike keiretsu issues, it is clear that import cartels in Japan have more direct effects on exports from the United States to Japan. From the antitrust standpoint, it should be recommended that the Japanese government increase the enforcement of the AML *vis-à-vis* import cartels stringently.

However, a provision in the Export and Import Transactions Law permits importers to enter into an import agreement if foreign exporters to Japan monopolize the export market or engage in an export cartel, although this provision is hardly used. In this sense, Japanese import cartels are countervailing cartels. Therefore, if Japanese import cartels are to be abolished and prohibited altogether, it is necessary to reduce or abolish export cartels in trading nations.

A.4.2   Activities of Trade Associations

Trade associations play a vital role in Japanese business. To enumerate a few of their activities, they play the role of information centers for business data, promote improvements of management and production, carry out testing and approving of products and act as the representative of industries in petitioning the government. Often it is essential for enterprises to join trade associations in order to carry on business successfully. Activities of trade associations are regulated under Article 8(1) (i)–(v) of the AML.

In view of the importance of the activities of trade associations in the context of trade, the FTCJ organized a task force to investigate these activities and the task force announced its report on March 5, 1993. The report contains detailed accounts of activities of trade associations. It states that the following principles need to be observed by a trade association. It is necessary to:

(a) allow entry of any enterprise to the trade association when it is vitally important to be a member of the trade association in order to carry on business in the area concerned (openness);

(b) provide services to outside parties for a reasonable cost if it is essential to utilize services of the trade association (nondiscrimination);

(c) allow the freedom of activities of members of the trade association (freedom);

(d) take into account views of consumers and outside parties in the trade association's activities (views of consumers and outside parties);

(e) maintain the transparency of the decision-making process of the trade association (transparency);

(f) comply with international standards and harmonize its activities with those of trade associations in foreign countries (international standards); and

(g) make certain that its activities do not constitute anticompetitive activities.

In light of these requirements, if a trade association restricts the entry of a foreign enterprise into its membership, it may constitute a violation of the AML. Often a trade association performs product testing and approving and the approval of the trade association may be a prerequisite to an approval by the government. In this situation, if a trade association refuses entry by a foreign enterprise, it would constitute a violation of the AML.

A.4.3   Exemptions

For a variety of reasons, there were 42 laws that exempted cartels from the application of the AML according to a report published by the FTCJ in 1991. The number of laws may have been reduced a little since then. However, there is little difference between 1991 and now. Authorized cartels under those laws include, *inter alia*, depression cartels, rationalization cartels, export/import cartels, medium and small business cartels, shipping conferences, international agreements on tariffs and other terms of business in aviation, activities of insurance associations, and some others.

The report of the FTCJ mentioned above states that there were 247 cartels authorized under those laws in 1991. The number of authorized cartels in 1965 was 1,079. Therefore, the number of authorized cartels has been reduced drastically in the past 25 years. However, it is still true that there are many authorized cartels operating.

Not all of these cartels are intended to exclude activities of foreign enterprises from the Japanese market. However, widespread cartelization under the authority of various laws creates opportunities for enterprises to discuss and to coordinate business terms among themselves. This, in turn, may create an "in-group feeling" among enterprises and exclusivity. In this respect, therefore, it is important to reduce the number of authorization laws and to create a climate favorable to a more stringent enforcement of the AML.

Even if we set aside the impact of cartelization on the difficulty of market access in Japan, it is reported that efficiency is lacking and consumer prices are generally high in those areas in which cartelization is allowed. The Temporary Administrative Reform Promotion Council announced in 1988: "The AML is the most universal rules of competition in market and exemptions from it should be limited to its minimum necessity. Although the number of exemption laws are more than 40 at present, it is necessary to review the need for maintaining the existing exemptions from the competition policy viewpoint."

The Temporary Administrative Reform Promotion Council announced its third report in 1992 in which it proposed that, in light of the fact that the Japanese economy enjoyed a high level of international competitiveness, it was necessary to introduce openness to the Japanese market and to reform the economic structure so that it would be more compatible with those of other major nations. In order to promote this compatibility, it proposed that the Japanese government reconsider the total legal system with regard to exemptions of cartels from the application of the AML, including the abolition of some of such exemptions. With regard to exemptions of cartels from the application of the AML, the Council stated that whereas there were numerous laws and various types of cartels exempted under those laws, the number of such laws and cartels could be reduced more and it recommended that the Japanese government initiate an extensive program to reduce the numbers of exemption laws and cartels.

The Third Report of the Temporary Administrative Reform Promotion Council urged that with regard to the review of exempting laws, the FTCJ and the ministries in charge should engage in consultation and the Japanese government should come to a conclusion by the end of 1995. It is expected, therefore, that the number of authorized cartels in Japan will be drastically reduced in the future.

A.5   "Managed Trade" and Antitrust Policies

The Clinton Administration may propose a trade policy in which the United States government negotiates with the Japanese government to conclude a series of agreements that would contain "target market shares" for foreign products in some designated areas such as semi-conductor chips, auto parts, automobiles, and supercomputers in the Japanese market. Such an agreement would involve a commitment by the Japanese government that the market share of a foreign product in the Japanese market would be, for example, 20 percent. The Japanese government would be under obligation to achieve this market share.

An attempt to enforce VIEs gives rise to antitrust issues, as VERs would. In this respect, VIEs are similar to VERs. However, there is an important difference between them. In VERs, the Japanese government has the ultimate authority to control export by means of the Foreign Exchange and Foreign Trade Control Law. The Japanese government generally uses administrative guidance with this law in the background. This would make it possible for exporters to invoke the act of state doctrine or the foreign government compulsion doctrine when challenged in the United States.

However, in VIEs, the Japanese government has no ultimate legal authority to order enterprises to purchase foreign products. Therefore, the government has to rely more heavily on "voluntary compliance" by purchasers and coordinated activities among them in order to bring about the market shares that have been agreed upon. Such an agreement for "managed trade" seems to involve a high degree of risk under the AML and also under the United States antitrust laws, since the Japanese government has no legal means of enforcing such an agreement and of achieving the target market share. The government, accordingly, would have to utilize a *de facto* pressure on importers and users of a designated product to purchase a predetermined amount. It will inevitably involve coordinated activities among Japanese enterprises under "administrative guidance" by the government, as to the amount of purchases that each enterprise must make with regard to the product involved.

To fulfil the promise that the market shares agreed upon would be attained, there would be "import cartels" or similarly coordinated activities among enterprises. As noted previously, this would create a significant legal risk under the AML and also under the United States antitrust laws.

NOTES

Daniel J. Gifford is the Robins, Kaplan, Miller & Ciresi Professor of Law, University of Minnesota Law School.

Mitsuo Matsushita is a Professor of Law, Seikei University, Tokyo.

1. General Agreement on Tariffs and Trade, *opened for signature* Oct. 30, 1947, 61 Stat. A3, T.I.A.S. No. 1700, 55 U.N.T.S. 187.

2. *See* Final Act Embodying the Results of the Uruguay Round of Multilateral Trade Negotiations, Apr. 15, 1994 (Done at Marrakesh), which includes the Agreement

Establishing the World Trade Organization [hereinafter WTO Agreement] and the General Agreement on Tariffs and Trade 1994 [hereinafter GATT 1994].

3. Thus, for example, Assistant Attorney General Anne K. Bingaman in a press conference of November 23, 1993 expressed concern about privately erected barriers to entry in the automobile and glass markets and noted that the United States was urging the Japanese government to increase criminal enforcement of the Anti-Monopoly Law, to expand private rights of action, to increase access to trade associations, and to repeal the premiums law. *See U.S. Officials Urge More Activity by Japanese in Antitrust Enforcement*, 65 Antitrust & Trade Reg. Rep. (BNA) 717 (1993). Under the Structural Impediments Initiative (SSI) talks, competition law concerns were a focus of U.S./Japanese discussion. *See, e.g., Interim Reports of U.S. and Japanese Delegations on Talks Under Structural Impediments Initiative, Released April 5 [1990]*, 7 Int'l Trade Rep. (BNA) 527, 536 (1990) [hereinafter *SII Interim Reports*].

4. *See, e.g.*, remarks of EC Competition Commissioner Karel van Miert at a Tokyo competition conference, stating that trade barriers are created "by various forms of private restraints and collusion." He further complained that European companies encounter difficulties in entering Japanese markets "because the distribution system is not very open and often tied up by preferential arrangements with local manufacturers." *Van Miert Displays EC Competition Policy as Model To Be Emulated by Japanese FTC*, 65 Antitrust & Trade Reg. Rep. (BNA) 668 (1993).

5. The shared approaches of the U.S., the EC, and Japan are bearing fruit in a number of recent developments: The U.S./EC Agreement on Antitrust Cooperation and Coordination (Sept. 23, 1991), reprinted in 61 Antitrust & Trade Reg. Rep. (BNA) 382 (1991); the Japan FTC's Enforcement Guidelines under the Anti-Monopoly Law (July 11, 1991). See also the call by Noboru Hatakeyama, MITI's Vice-Minister for International Affairs for harmonization of competition policy, particularly with the European Community. 64 Antitrust & Trade Reg. Rep. (BNA) 156 (1993).

6. *See* Mitsuo Matsushita, *The Japanese Antimonopoly Law*, Appendix A to this chapter [hereinafter Matsushita, Appendix A]. Professor Matsushita reports a concern in Japan that cartels may be eroding efficiency and inflating consumer prices. As a result, the Temporary Administrative Reform Promotion Council indicated that exemptions from the Anti-Monopoly Law should be minimized.

7. The WTO succeeded the GATT on January 1, 1995.

8. United Nations Conference on Trade and Employment held at Havana, Cuba from November 21, 1947 to March 24, 1948, Final Act: Havana Charter for an International Trade Organization, reprinted in Dep't of State Pub. No. 3117, Commercial Policy Series 113 (1948) [hereinafter Havana Charter].

9. *Id.* art. 1(1).

10. *Id.* art. 1(3).

11. *Id.* art. 1(4).

12. *Id.* art. 46(1).

13. *Id.* arts. 48, 50(2), 50(3), 50(4), 50(5).

14. *Id.* art. 50(1).

15. *Id.* art. 46(3)(b).

16. *Id.* art. 46(2)(c).

17. *See, e.g.,* KENNETH W. DAM, THE GATT LAW AND INTERNATIONAL ECONOMIC ORGANIZA-TION 10–12 (1970).

18. UNCTAD, The Set of Multilaterally Agreed Equitable Principles and Rules of the Control of Restrictive Business Practices, UN Doc. TD/RBP/Conf/10 (May 2, 1980) [hereinafter UNCTAD Principles], adopted by UN General Assembly on November 12, 1980, UN Doc. A/C.2/35/L.75. The UNCTAD principles are extensively reviewed in 2 BARRY E. HAWK, UNITED STATES, COMMON MARKET AND INTERNATIONAL ANTITRUST 990–1003 (2d ed., Supp. 1990).

19. 1967 OECD Council Recommendation [C(67)53(Final)]. See also its subsequent report, *Report on the Operation of the 1967 Council Recommendation Concerning Cooperation Between Member Countries on Restrictive Business Practices Affecting International Trade [C(67)53(Final)] During the Period 1967–1975,* reprinted in 22 ANTITRUST BULL. 459 (1977).

20. See discussion in Sabrina Haake, *Antitrust in the United States and European Community: Toward a Bilateral Agreement,* 2 INDIANA INT'L & COMP. L. REV. 473 (1992).

21. *See* HAWK, note 18 above, at 1021–22. The OECD competition guidelines are discussed in Joel Davidow, *Some Reflections on the OECD Competition Guidelines,* 22 ANTITRUST BULL. 441 (1977).

22. AMERICAN BAR ASSOCIATION, REPORT OF SPECIAL COMMITTEE ON INTERNATIONAL ANTI-TRUST (1991) [hereinafter ABA REPORT].

23. *Id.* at 36.

24. *Id.* at 288–94.

25. *Id.* at 37, 289.

26. *Id.* at 294.

27. 64 Antitrust & Trade Reg. Rep. (BNA) No. 1628 (Special Supp.) (1993).

28. According to one OECD official, the draft's provisions governing both horizontal and vertical relationships were "far too restrictive." *See OECD Committee Lacks Enthusiasm for Draft International Antitrust Code,* 65 Antitrust & Trade Reg. Rep. (BNA) 771 (1993).

29. *Antitrust Division Official Predicts Scant Prospect of International Code,* 11 INT'L TRADE REP. (BNA) 220 (1994) (reporting remarks of Charles S. Stark, Chief of Foreign Commerce Section, Dep't of Justice).

30. *See U.S., EC Commission Forge Antitrust Cooperation Accord,* 61 Antitrust & Trade Reg. Rep. (BNA) 375 (1991).

31. *See Microsoft Settles Accusations of Monopolistic Selling Practices,* 67 Antitrust & Trade Reg. Rep. (BNA) 106 (1994).

32. *See* Gary R. Saxonhouse, *Japan, SII and the International Harmonization of Domestic Economic Practices,* 12 MICHIGAN J. INT'L L. 450, 455 (1991).

33. *See generally* Mitsuo Matsushita, *The Structural Impediments Initiative: An Example of Bilateral Trade Negotiation,* 12 MICHIGAN J. INT'L L. 436 (1991). *See also* Y. S. Lanneaux, Recent Development, *International Trade: Joint Report of the United States-Japan Working Group on the Structural Impediments Initiative, June 28, 1990,* 32 HARVARD INT'L L. J. 245 (1991).

34. *SII Interim Reports*, note 3 above, at 536.

35. *Id.*

36. *Joint Statement [of U.S. President Clinton and Japanese Prime Minister Miyazawa] on the United States-Japan Framework for a New Economic Partnership, issued July 10 [1993] in Tokyo,* 10 Int'l Trade Rep. (BNA) 1185 (1993).

37. Sherman Act, 26 Stat. 209 (1890) (codified as amended at 15 U.S.C. §§ 1–7 (1988)); Clayton Act, 38 Stat. 730 (codified as amended at 15 U.S.C. §§ 12–27 (1988)). The Federal Trade Commission Act, 38 Stat. 717 (1914) (codified as amended at 15 U.S.C. §§ 41–77 (1988)), does not fall within the Clayton Act's definition of "antitrust laws" but nonetheless forbids the same behavior as do the Sherman and Clayton Acts.

38. TREATY OF ROME, arts. 85 & 86.

39. Antimonopoly and Fair Trade Maintenance Act (Law No. 54, 1947) (Shiteki Dokusen no Kinshi oyobi Kosei Torihiki no Kakuho ni kansuro Horitsu). The Japanese Anti-Monopoly Law is discussed in MITSUO MATSUSHITA, INTERNATIONAL TRADE AND COMPETITION LAW IN JAPAN 74–169 (1993); MITSUO MATSUSHITA, INTRODUCTION TO JAPANESE ANTIMONO-POLY LAW (1990); MITSUO MATSUSHITA & THOMAS J. SCHOENBAUM, JAPANESE INTERNATIONAL TRADE AND INVESTMENT LAW 139–71 (1989); and in Matsushita, Appendix A, note 6 above.

40. GATT, note 1 above.

41. *See* WTO Agreement, note 2 above; GATT 1994, note 2 above.

42. *See, e.g.,* Angelika Eymann & Ludger Schuknecht, *Antidumping Enforcement in the European Community, in* ANTIDUMPING: HOW IT WORKS AND WHO GETS HURT 221, 222 (J. Michael Finger, ed., 1993); J. Michael Finger & Tracy Murray, *Antidumping and Counter-vailing Duty Enforcement in the United States, in id.,* 241, 249.

43. *See* Gary Saxonhouse, *Antidumping Law in Japan, in Antidumping Law: Policy and Imple-mentation,* 1 MICHIGAN Y. B. INT'L LEGAL STUD. 245 (1979). *See also* Finger & Murray, note 42 above, at 251–54; Eymann & Schuknecht, note 42 above, at 223–24.

44. *Cf.,* GERTRUDE STEIN, SACRED EMILY (1913); WILLIAM SHAKESPEARE, ROMEO AND JULIET, act 2, sc. 2.

45. ROBERT H. BORK, THE ANTITRUST PARADOX 405 (1978); RICHARD A. POSNER, ANTITRUST LAW 19–20 (1976). The U.S. Supreme Court has several times declared that the purpose of the antitrust laws is the furtherance of consumer welfare. *See, e.g.,* National Collegiate Athletic Ass'n v. Board of Regents of Univ. of Okla., 468 U.S. 85, 107 (1984); Reiter v. Sonotone Corp., 442 U.S. 330, 343 (1979). In the antitrust legal literature, consumer welfare has been used as synonymous with both the combination of productive and allocative efficiency and the sum of producer and consumer surplus. The most articulate spokesperson for this position is Robert Bork. *See* Bork, above, at 105–15, 405. Bork's position on efficiency draws heavily from Oliver Williamson. Oliver Williamson, *Economies as an Anti-trust Defense: The Welfare Tradeoffs,* 58 AMERICAN ECON. REV. 18 (1968). *See also* Oliver Williamson, *Economies as an Antitrust Defense Revisited,* 125 UNIV. PENNSYLVANIA L. REV. 699, 711 (1977).

46. *See, e.g.,* Eleanor M. Fox, *The Modernization of Antitrust: A New Equilibrium,* 66 CORNELL L. REV. 1140, 1176–90 (1981). *See also* Eleanor M. Fox & Lawrence A. Sullivan, *Antitrust—Retrospective and Prospective: Where Are We Coming From? Where Are We Going?,* 62 NEW YORK UNIV. L. REV. 936, 945, 955–59, 963 (1987).

47. On the relation between efficiency and other concerns in European Community competition law, see, e.g., HAWK, note 18 above, at 5–14. On these factors in the administration of the Japanese Anti-Monopoly Law, see, e.g., MITSUO MATSUSHITA, INTERNATIONAL TRADE AND COMPETITION LAW IN JAPAN 74, 135, 273 (1993). On the universally recognized importance of efficiency as a guide to the administration of competition law and yet the controversial nature of its use as a sole criterion, see the action of the OECD Secretariat in releasing the report COMPETITION POLICY AND VERTICAL RESTRAINTS: FRANCHISING AGREEMENTS (Jan. 13, 1994) and the failure of the OECD Competition Law and Policy Committee to adopt the report. *Divisive OECD Report Stresses Efficiency as Goal of Enforcement*, 66 Antitrust & Trade Reg. Rep. (BNA) 128 (1994).

48. UNCTAD Principles, note 18 above.

49. See JAGDISH BHAGWATI, PROTECTIONISM 94–101 (1988).

50. *See* A. C. PIGOU, THE ECONOMICS OF WELFARE (1920). *See also* STEPHEN G. BREYER, REGULATION AND ITS REFORM 23–26 (1982); RICHARD A. POSNER, ECONOMIC ANALYSIS OF LAW 156–65 (1972).

51. ARMEN A. ALCHIAN & WILLIAM R. ALLEN, EXCHANGE AND PRODUCTION: COMPETITION, COORDINATION, AND CONTROL 122–24 (2d ed., 1977).

52. Within the United States, the securities industry is the subject of an extensive system of self-regulation overseen by government but operated on a day-to-day basis by private business firms. See the description of such self-regulation in Silver v. New York Stock Exchange, 373 U.S. 347, 349–57 (1963).

53. *See, e.g.*, ROBERT A. GORMAN, LABOR LAW (1976); Robert J. Flanagan, *Efficiency and Equality in Swedish Labor Markets, in* THE SWEDISH ECONOMY 125–84 (1987). An insightful comparison of differences in the regulation and operation of labor/management relations in Japan and the United States is contained in WILLIAM B. GOULD, JAPAN'S RESHAPING OF AMERICAN LABOR LAW (1984).

54. *See, e.g.*, Alchian & Allen, note 51 above, at 122.

55. *See* MANCUR OLSON, JR., THE LOGIC OF COLLECTIVE ACTION 14–16 (1965). *See also* DENNIS C. MUELLER, PUBLIC CHOICE 13 (1979).

56. *See, e.g.*, DANIEL A. FARBER & PHILIP P. FRICKEY, LAW AND PUBLIC CHOICE 23 (1991).

57. A leading Japanese text on industrial policies describes them as including measures to deal with externalities, anticompetitive structures and conduct, promotion of economies of scale, infant industries, basic research and development, and the elimination of uncertainty in industrial development. NIHON NO SANGYO SEISAKU [Industrial Policy in Japan] (Komiya, Okuno, & Suzumura, eds., 1984), described in MITSUO MATSUSHITA, INTERNATIONAL TRADE AND COMPETITION LAW IN JAPAN 273 (1993).

58. See discussion in text accompanying notes 111–119 below.

59. On GATT evolution, *see* ROBERT E. HUDEC, DEVELOPING COUNTRIES IN THE GATT LEGAL SYSTEM (1987).

60. *See, e.g.*, DAM, note 17 above, at 25–27. *See also* ROBERT E. HUDEC, THE GATT LEGAL SYSTEM AND WORLD TRADE DIPLOMACY 10, 15, 23, 50 (2d ed. 1990).

61. In Frank K. Upham, *The Legal Framework of Japan's Declining Industries Policy: The Problem of Transparency in Administrative Processes*, 27 HARVARD INT'L L. J. 425, 444–45

(1986), it was reported that as of 1986 no private action had ever been successful under the Japanese Antimonopoly Law. Professor Upham attributes this lack of success to stringent causation standards imposed by the courts for establishing injury. He relates, however, difficulties experienced by indirect purchasers in establishing injury and explains that direct purchasers are likely to be deterred from suing because they are likely to wish to preserve their relations with their suppliers. In 1993, however, the plaintiffs successfully recovered damages sustained due to violation of the Antimonopoly Law in the Toshiba Elevator Case. Decision of Tokyo High Court, July 30, 1993, HANREI JIHO (Current Cases Reporter) No. 1479, at 21 et seq. This may be a sign that private suits for damage under the Antimonopoly Law may increase in the future.

The considerations affecting antitrust suits identified by Professor Upham are not unique to Japan. Indirect purchasers lack standing to sue under U.S. antitrust law. *See* Kansas & Missouri v. Utilicorp United, Inc., 497 U.S. 199 (1990); Associated General Contractors of California, Inc. v. California State Council of Carpenters, 459 U.S. 519 (1982); Illinois Brick Co. v. Illinois, 431 U.S. 720 (1977). And direct customers often are reluctant to sue their customary suppliers in the U.S. also. *See* Stuart Macaulay, *Non-contractual Relations in Business: A Preliminary Study*, 28 AMERICAN SOC. REV. 55, 59 (1963).

62. In addition to the listed acts of cartels, Akinori Uesugi has suggested that cartel activity can be thought of as involving subsidies to business firms much as governments sometimes subsidize industries or business firms: By restricting output and raising prices, cartels provide transfer payments from customers to cartel members; the receipt of these payments by the more inefficient members of the cartel subsidizes their continued operation. Akinori Uesugi, *Japan's Cartel System and Its Impact on International Trade*, 27 HARVARD INT'L L. J. 389, 395 (1986). This kind of subsidy, however, ought not to generate serious trade disputes, because the "subsidy" passes through the cartel and can be as easily visualized as a subsidy from the more efficient to the less efficient members of the cartel. The harm to foreign suppliers comes not from the subsidy but from the import barriers which make the cartel's monopoly pricing possible. Moreover, even if the inefficient firms kept in operation through this subsidy also engage in the export trade, they would not appear to increase the challenge to foreign rivals in external markets.

63. *See* Matsushita, Appendix A, note 6 above.

64. GATT art. XIX.

65. *See* Upham, note 61 above, at 457–58; CLYDE V. PRESTOWITZ, JR., TRADING PLACES 276 (1989 ed.).

66. Synthetic Fiber Agreement, Commission Decision of July 4, 1984, Common Mkt. Rep. (CCH) ¶ 10,606 (1984).

67. *See* K. Sato, *Trade Policies in Japan, in* 2 NATIONAL TRADE POLICIES, 109, 123–24 (Dominick Salvatore, ed., 1992). Mr. Sato reports that as of May 1978, fourteen industries were designated as structurally depressed and therefore eligible for treatment under the Temporary Measures Law. These industries included steel, aluminum refining, fertilizers, textiles, synthetic fibers, and shipbuilding. *Id.* The restructuring of the Japanese shipbuilding industry under the Temporary Measures Law is described in Mototada Kikkawa, *Shipbuilding, Motor Cars and Semiconductors: The Diminishing Role of Industrial Policy in Japan, in* EUROPE'S INDUSTRIES: PUBLIC AND PRIVATE STRATEGIES FOR CHANGE 236, 241–43 (Geoffrey Shepherd, Francois Duchene & Christopher Saunders eds., 1983). *See also* Upham, note 61 above, at 453. Professor Matsushita has indicated that there are approximately 42 laws exempting cartels from application of the Anti-Monopoly Law. Matsushita, Appendix A, note 6 above, at 317. Writing in 1986, Akinori Uesugi identified 45 cartels "which would

not be authorized by comparable systems under United States law." Uesugi, note 62 above, at 408. Mr. Uesugi further identified five depression cartel systems, five rationalization systems, and eleven systems of excessive competition prevention cartels, all of which can function as adjustment mechanisms. *Id.* at 409.

68. MITSUO MATSUSHITA, INTERNATIONAL TRADE AND COMPETITION LAW IN JAPAN 285 (1993).

69. *Id.*

70. Sato, note 67 above, at 124; Synthetic Fiber Agreement, note 38 above.

71. *See, e.g.,* Uesugi, note 62 above, at 394 ("MITI has long argued that without cartels or some other form of government intervention excess capacity would not be eliminated in Japan, and that only with government encouragement can it be eliminated speedily and completely."). A similar type of government intervention which quickly brings about results similar to those which the unaided market would eventually produce is discussed with approval by Judge Posner in Omega Satellite Products Co. v. City of Indianapolis, 694 F.2d 119, 126–27 (7th Cir. 1982).

72. Prestowitz claims that the petrochemical arrangement allocated normal demand to domestic producers with excess demand allocated to imports. PRESTOWITZ, note 65 above, at 276.

73. Thus the European synthetic fibre agreement was possible only because imports were controlled by the Multifibre Agreement.

74. *See, e.g.,* Walter Adams & Hans Mueller, *The Steel Industry, in* THE STRUCTURE OF AMERICAN INDUSTRY 74, 94–97 (Walter Adams, ed., 7th ed. 1986); Walter Adams & James W. Brock, *The Automotive Industry, id.* at 159. Such restructuring as has occurred in the American steel industry, for example, has occurred in the presence of voluntary export restraints or other import controls. *Id.* at 93–97 (describing prolonged limitations on imports). This restructuring has taken place in the absence of cartel or government allocation of quotas and in the presence of the competition from the so-called minimills. Adams attributes modernization to the pressure of import and, to a lesser extent, minimill competition. *Id.* at 113.

75. *See* Trade and Tariff Act of 1984, Pub. L. No. 98-573, § 806, 98 Stat. 2948 (1984) (Steel Import Stabilization Act). *See also* GARY C. HUFBAUER & HOWARD F. ROSEN, TRADE POLICY FOR TROUBLED INDUSTRIES 72 (1986).

76. *Cf.,* Telex Corp. v. International Bus. Mach. Corp., 510 F.2d 894 (10th Cir.), *cert. dismissed,* 423 U.S. 802 (1975) (customary behavior helps to define the boundaries of the legitimate).

77. We have not discussed "infant-industry" protection because such protection is normally undertaken by governments. Since the GATT limits infant-industry protection to developing nations in Article XVIII, that kind of protection is not legitimately available to developed nations. Even if a cartel mechanism were used to limit imports in order to foster the development of a new industry, that behavior would be illegitimate in any developed nation under the approach we have taken in text, because we argue that competition laws should not permit private business firms to erect market barriers which governments are forbidden to erect. *See* discussion between notes 137–38 below.

78. *See* PAUL R. KRUGMAN, RETHINKING INTERNATIONAL TRADE 190–98 (1990); ELHANAN HELPMAN & PAUL R. KRUGMAN, TRADE POLICY AND MARKET STRUCTURE 173–74 (1989).

79. *See* KRUGMAN, note 78 above, at 190–98. Aspects of this model are discussed in a paper written for the same conference as those in this volume: Christopher Bliss, *Trade and Competition Control*. In his paper, Bliss points out that a competition policy which was focused naively upon maintaining the existence of large numbers of competitors in the domestic market would impede exports by preventing domestic firms from attaining the economies of scale which would advantage them in international competition. Indeed, such a policy would destroy domestic producers in their home markets unless they were protected from efficient foreign competition. Conversely, Bliss points out that a competition policy which permits domestic firms to attain the volume essential to reduce unit costs would advantage domestic firms in international competition. The model referred to in the text of this paper is one in which a coordinated domestic competition and trade law protects one or more domestic producers, enabling them to attain a level of output (and resulting efficiency) which would have been unattainable without the protection. The resulting low unit cost then confers an advantage in the export trade.

80. Standard Oil Co. (California) v. United States, 337 U.S. 293, 306–307 (1949); DOJ, Vertical Restraints Guidelines § 3.1 (1985, repealed 1993).

81. Standard Oil Co. (California) v. United States, 337 U.S. 293, 314 (1949); Tampa Elec. Co. v. Nashville Coal Co., 365 U.S. 320, 328–329 (1961).

82. DOJ, Vertical Restraints Guidelines § 3.22 (1985; repealed 1993). The evaluation of exclusive supply contracts under these guidelines involved the use of a "coverage ratio" and a vertical restraints index. The former was the percent of each market involved in the restraint. The latter was the sum of the squares of the market shares of each firm employing the restraint at the same vertical level. The use of these measures is described in note 89 below. The Vertical Restraints Guidelines were revoked in August 1993. *See* TRADE REG. REP. (CCH) No. 276 (Aug. 17, 1993).

83. OLIVER E. WILLIAMSON, MARKETS AND HIERARCHIES (1975).

84. *See, e.g.,* ROGER D. BLAIR & DAVID L. KASERMAN, LAW AND ECONOMICS OF VERTICAL INTEGRATION AND CONTROL (1983).

85. *See, e.g., Learning from Japan,* BUSINESS WEEK, Jan. 27, 1992, at 52. John McMillan, *Why Does Japan Resist Foreign Market-Opening Pressure?,* Chapter 14 of Volume I, describes the growing use of keiretsu relationships by U.S. companies.

86. Prestowitz, note 65 above, at 305.

87. Tampa Elec. Co. v. Nashville Coal Co., 365 U.S. 320 (1961). *See also* FTC v. Brown Shoe Co., 384 U.S. 316, 321, (1966).

88. Continental T. V., Inc. v. GTE Sylvania Inc., 433 U.S. 36 (1977).

89. Restraints would pass the Department's initial review if any one of the following conditions were satisfied: (1) the firm employing the restraint possessed a share of 10% or less of the relevant market; (2) the Vertical Restraints Index is under 1200 and the coverage ratio is below 60% in the same market; (3) the VRI is under 1200 in both relevant markets; or (4) the coverage ratio is below 60% in both relevant markets. DOJ, Vertical Restraints Guidelines § 4.1 (1985, repealed 1993). Restraints which were not cleared under the first step would be reviewed under a "structured rule of reason analysis" in step 2. *Id.* § 4.2, an analysis which explicitly focused largely on ease of entry, whether small firms and new entrants employ the restraints, efficiencies resulting from the restraints.

90. This is a two-edged sword. The existence of other exclusive supply contracts increases the foreclosure effect; but widespread use by many firms in the industry of exclusive supply contracts may also be evidence that these contracts are efficient ways of doing business.

91. Regulation No. 1984/83, reprinted in 2 Common Mkt. Rep. (CCH) ¶ 2733.

92. *See* Brasserie De Haecht S.A. v. Wilkin (No. 1) (23/76) [1967] E.C.R. 235, [1966] C.M.L.R. 26. *See also* discussion of "bundle" principle in Masterfoods Ltd. v. HB Ice Cream Ltd., [1992] C.M.L.R. 830 (Irish High Court).

93. *See, e.g.,* Joint Report of the U.S.-Japan Working Group on the Structural Impediments Initiative, ch. V (June 28, 1990) (Keiretsu Relationships).

94. *See* Matsushita, Appendix A, note 6 above.

95. Saxonhouse, note 32 above, at 467. See also Gary G. Saxonhouse, *A Short Summary of the Long History of Unfair Trade Allegations Against Japan,* Chapter 13, Volume I (discussing the Structural Impediments Initiative and exclusionary business practices: Part VIII(E)).

96. The question of whether the Japanese market in automobiles is open to foreign suppliers is irrelevant to the question of whether the keiretsu are efficient parts-procurement devices, because substantial competition between Japanese and non-Japanese auto manufacturers takes place in other markets.

Even though the foreign presence in the Japanese domestic market in finished automobiles remains small, however, it is expanding. BMW has apparently established its own independent distribution system in Japan, thus demonstrating the feasibility of foreign entry into the final-product market. Again, the sales of the Ford Motor Co. have been expanding rapidly, albeit from a small initial base. Ford also appears to be negotiating with Japanese banks for financing production of the right-hand-drive vehicles appropriate for Japanese roads. Chrysler Motors Corp. and General Motors Corp. are apparently also in contact with Japanese banks for similar financing. Chrysler has entered into two joint sales agreements for the distribution of Jeep Cherokees and other Chrysler vehicles.

97. Other Conference participants have concluded that the customer/supplier relationships of vertical keiretsu are most likely efficiency enhancing. *See* McMillan, note 85 above (comparing the efficiencies of vertical keiretsu with the inefficiencies of the Large Scale Retail Stores Law and the practice known as "dango"); Saxonhouse, *Short Summary,* note 95 above, at Part VIII(E).

98. OECD Working Paper No. 136, a study of the distribution system in Japan, has called for increased transparency for Japanese business transactions. *See OECD Studies Distribution in U.S., UK, Japan, France,* 65 Antitrust & Trade Reg. Rep. (BNA) 773 (1993).

99. As the text indicates, long-term supplier-customer relationships have long been recognized as potentially efficiency-generating. They have also been perceived as potentially exclusionary when such long-term exclusive relationships are maintained by a substantial portion of an industry. Because the exclusionary effect arises from the combination of many such relationships, the lawfulness of any one such relationship may depend upon whether that relationship is replicated by others in the industry. Under the now repealed vertical guidelines, the Justice Department employed coverage ratios and other measures to assess the probable aggregate effects of these relationships. When most firms in an industry enter into long-term exclusive supplier-customer relationships, that fact is likely to indicate that these relationships are efficient. When a supplier or customer entering into such a relationship either possesses market power or is a member of an oligopolistically structured

industry, however, the burden of affirmatively justifying that arrangement as efficient is likely to be imposed upon the parties.

100. Agreement on Safeguards, art. 11.

101. *See* Brooke Group Ltd. v. Brown & Williamson Tobacco Corp., 113 S. Ct. 2578 (1993) (holding that pricing cannot be predatory unless the predator has a reasonable basis for believing that it can recoup its losses from supracompetitive profits in the future).

102. Phillip Areeda & Donald F. Turner, *Predatory Pricing and Related Practices Under Section 2 of the Sherman Act*, 88 HARVARD L. REV. 697 (1975); 3 PHILLIP AREEDA & DONALD F. TURNER, ANTITRUST LAW 150–94 (1978).

103. *Id.* at 716–18.

104. A significant amount of this criticism is summarized and evaluated in Joseph F. Brodley & George A. Hay, *Predatory Pricing: Competing Economic Theories and the Evolution of Legal Standards*, 66 CORNELL L. REV. 738 (1981).

105. Kelco Disposal, Inc. v. Browning Ferris Indus., 845 F.2d 404, 407 (2d Cir. 1988), *aff'd,* 492 U.S. 257 (1989); C.E. Services, Inc. v. Control Data Corp., 759 F.2d 1241, 1245 (5th Cir. 1985), *cert. denied,* 474 U.S. 1037 (1985); Arthur S. Langenderfer, Inc., v. S.E. Johnson Co., 729 F.2d 1050, 1060 (6th Cir.), *cert. denied,* 469 U.S. 1036 (1984); Chillicothe Sand & Gravel Co. v. Martin Marietta Corp., 615 F.2d 427, 431 (7th Cir. 1980); Morgan v. Ponder, 892 F.2d 1355, 1360 (8th Cir. 1989); Marsann Co. v. Brammall, Inc., 788 F.2d 611, 616 (9th Cir. 1986); Instructional Systems Dev. Corp. v. Aetna Cas. & Sur. Co., 817 F.2d 639, 649 (10th Cir. 1987). *See also* Barr Laboratories, Inc. v. Abbott Laboratories, 978 F.2d 98 (3d Cir. 1992).

106. *See* Morgan v. Ponder, 892 F.2d 1355, 1360 (8th Cir. 1989); William Inglis & Sons Baking Co. v. ITT Continental Baking Co., 668 F.2d 1014, 1035–36 (9th Cir. 1981), *cert. denied,* 459 U.S. 825 (1982). *See also* DANIEL J. GIFFORD & LEO J. RASKIND, FEDERAL ANTITRUST LAW CASES AND MATERIALS 360–61 (1983).

107. McGahee v. Northern Propane Gas Co., 858 F.2d 1487 (11th Cir. 1988).

108. A. A. Poultry Farms v. Rose Acre Farms, 881 F.2d 1396 (7th Cir. 1989).

109. Utah Pie Co. v. Continental Baking Co., 386 U.S. 685 (1967).

110. Brooke Group Ltd. v. Brown & Williamson Tobacco Corp., 113 S. Ct. 2578, 7–10 (1993).

111. Commission Decision (85/609/EEC) (Dec. 14, 1985), relating to a proceeding under Article 86 of the EEC Treaty (IV/30.698-ECS/AKZO) O.J. (L 374) 1, 31.12.85, *aff'd,* AKZO Chemie BV v. EC Comm'n (Case 62/86) [1993] 2 CEC (CC 1-1) 115. The Areeda/Turner approach seems, however, to underlie the recently announced Canadian Predatory Pricing Enforcement Guidelines. *See* 62 Antitrust & Trade Reg. Rep. (BNA) 725 (1992).

112. *See* MATSUSHITA & SCHOENBAUM, note 39 above, at 162–63; MATSUSHITA, note 39 above, at 57–58 (discussing JFTC General Designation No. 6 and the Maruetsu-Haromato [the Milk Retail] case and the Chubu Yomiuri Shinbun case).

113. *See, e.g.,* JACOB VINER, DUMPING: A PROBLEM IN INTERNATIONAL TRADE 138–39 (1923).

114. *See* KRUGMAN, note 78 above, and text accompanying note 78 above.

115. *See* Daniel J. Gifford, *Rethinking the Relationship Between Antidumping and Antitrust Laws*, 6 AMERICAN UNIV. J. INT'L L. & POL'Y 277, 291–302 (1991) (describing the origins of U.S. antidumping legislation). The development of U.S. antidumping legislation is summarized in two chapters in these volumes: Ronald A. Cass & Richard D. Boltuck, *Antidumping and Countervailing Duty Law: The Mirage of Equitable International Competition*, Chapter 9 in this volume; Richard H. Clarida, *Dumping: In Theory, in Policy, and in Practice*, Chapter 9 in volume I.

116. *See* Gifford, note 115 above; Barbara Epstein, *The Illusory Conflict Between Antidumping and Antitrust*, 18 ANTITRUST BULL. 1 (1973); Diane P. Wood, *"Unfair" Trade Injury: A Competition-Based Approach*, 41 STANFORD L. REV. 1153 (1989).

117. *See, e.g.*, J. Michael Finger, *The Origins and Evolution of Antidumping Regulation, in* ANTIDUMPING: HOW IT WORKS AND WHO GETS HURT 13, 16 (J. Michael Finger, ed., 1993). Australia and New Zealand enacted antidumping laws shortly after Canada adopted its law. *Id.*

118. Act of Sept. 8, 1916, ch. 463, 39 Stat. 799 (1916), codified at 15 U.S.C. § 73 (1988). *See* discussion in Gifford, note 115 above, at 292–93.

119. Clayton Antitrust Act, 38 Stat. 730, ch. 323, § 2 (1914), codified as amended, 15 U.S.C. § 13(a) (1988).

120. *See* Gifford, note 115 above, at 291–93.

121. Antidumping Act of 1921, ch. 14, § 201, 42 Stat. 11 (1921). The 1921 Act remained the primary U.S. antidumping legislation until 1979 when Congress enacted the Trade Agreements Act of that year. Congress then repealed the provisions of the 1921 Act but substantially reenacted them as an amendment adding Title VII to the Tariff Act of 1930. Trade Agreements Act of 1979, 101 Pub. L. No. 96-39, §§ 101, 106, 93 Stat. 144, 162, 193. Title VII is codified at 19 U.S.C. §§ 1671–1677g (1988). *See* Gifford, note 115 above, at 297.

122. *See* Gifford, note 115 above, at 293–96.

123. The anticompetitive ramifications of antidumping law are discussed in a number of Conference papers. *See* Clarida, note 115 above; Cass & Boltuck, note 115 above; James Levinsohn, *Competition Policy and International Trade*.

124. The 1916 Antidumping Act clearly took the form of an antitrust law. Subsequent legislation, beginning with the 1921 antidumping act, has traceable roots in the earlier legislation. It is now time to reconsider the policies underlying the trade laws and to bring them into line with the efficiency norms underlying antitrust law.

In 1985, Susan Liebler, then Vice Chair of the U.S. International Trade Commission, unsuccessfully pursued that approach by attempting to incorporate the Areeda/Turner predatory-pricing standard into the administration of the antidumping determinations. *See* Certain Red Raspberries from Canada, USITC Pub. 1707, Inv. No. 731-TA-196 (final) (June 1985) (concurring opinion). That approach was later rejected by the courts. USX Corp. v. United States, 682 F. Supp. 60 (Ct. Int'l Trade 1988).

125. Laura Tyson has argued forcefully that both the antidumping and countervailing duty laws need drastic revision. *See* LAURA TYSON, WHO'S BASHING WHOM? 267–74, 280–86 (1992). Ideally, she would replace the antidumping laws with enforceable multilateral competition policies. *Id.* at 268.

126. *See, e.g.*, N. David Palmeter, The Antidumping Law: A Legal and Administrative Non-Tariff Barrier 9 (Paper presented to the Conference on Procedures & Methods in the

Commerce Department's Administration of the Trade Remedy Laws, Brookings Inst., Nov. 27, 1990).

127. SEN. REP. NO. 102–403, 102d Cong., 2d Sess. (1992), reprinted in Trade Reg. Rep. (CCH) No. 231 (1992).

128. *See* letters from the Department of Justice to Hon. Howard M. Metzenbaum, dated July 28, 1992 and to Hon. Joseph R. Biden, Jr., dated July 30, 1992, reprinted in SEN. REP. NO. 162–403, note 127 above, at 18–23.

129. *See* ABA, REPORT OF THE SECTION OF ANTITRUST LAW CONCERNING PENDING ANTI-TRUST/TRADE LEGISLATION (discussing S.2508, S.2610, H.R. 5348).

130. S.2610 § 3(b), adding (a)(1) to § 801 of the Act of Sept. 8, 1916, (presently codified at 15 U.S.C. § 72 (1988)).

131. *See* 19 U.S.C. § 1677b(b) (1988). *See also* Palmeter, note 126 above, at 9.

132. 15 U.S.C. § 13(b) (1988).

133. A seller which has met the prevailing market price in the export market might claim that its sales have caused no "injury" to domestic producers in that market. The success of such a claim might very well turn on whether the quantities sold by the exporter were sufficient to depress that price or whether, on the contrary, they were insignificant *vis-à-vis* the total supply, so that they could exert no appreciable effect on price. Attempting to assert a "meeting-competition" defense through the "injury" provision is, of course, more difficult than asserting such a defense directly.

134. MINN. STAT. § 80E.14 (1994).

135. CALIF. VEH. CODE ANN. § 507. This statute was upheld against an antitrust-based challenge in New Motor Vehicle Bd. v. Orrin W. Fox Co., 439 U.S. 96 (1978).

136. *See* MITSUO MATSUSHITA, INTRODUCTION TO JAPANESE ANTIMONOPOLY LAW 95 (1990); Sato, note 67 above, at 126; TAKATOSHI ITO, THE JAPANESE ECONOMY 394–97 (1992). The Large Scale Retail Stores Law is also discussed in Chapter 14 of Volume I by McMillan, note 85 above.

137. *See* Sato, note 67 above, at 126.

138. *See* text accompanying note 71 above.

139. Thus, for example, a standard work on Japanese industrial policies defines them as "designed to cope with the market failure in the allocation of resources." NIHON NO SANGYO SEISAKY [Industrial Policy in Japan] (Komiya, Okuno & Suzumura, eds., 1984), quoted in MITSUO MATSUSHITA, INTERNATIONAL TRADE AND COMPETITION LAW IN JAPAN 273 (1993).

140. In the European Community, industrial policy has sought to stimulate a number of industries—aircraft, aerospace, electronics, semiconductors—through the financing of pan-European ventures. TYSON, note 125 above, at 288. These ventures include Ariane (aerospace), Eureka (electronics), Jessi (semiconductors), and Airbus (aircraft). *Id.* As previously observed, however, sector-specific government financing raises issues outside of the framework of this paper. Our focus is upon entry barriers effected through cartel behavior, the government role taking the form of actual approval through formal exemptions from competition laws or failures to enforce them. The restructuring, downsizing, and re-capitalization of overextended European industries has already been described. This restructuring has been effected through rationalization agreements and crisis-cartel arrange-

ments, under the supervision of the European Commission as the synthetic fiber agreement illustrates. Insofar as entry barriers form a constituent part of this restructuring, the EC industrial policy runs into conflict with competition and trade policies.

141. *See generally* MITSUO MATSUSHITA, INTERNATIONAL TRADE AND COMPETITION LAW IN JAPAN 48–50, 272–95 (1993).

142. Article 85(1) prohibits agreements preventing, restricting, or distorting competition within the Community but the Commission has authority under Article 85(3) to exempt certain kinds of agreements from the Article 85(1) prohibition.

143. In the defense arena, "[t]he United States has had a coordinated and far-reaching industrial policy to direct resources to particular technologies, industries, and producers for defense purposes." TYSON, note 125 above, at 289.

144. *See, e.g.*, ROBERT B. REICH, TALES OF A NEW AMERICA 230–31 (1988).

145. *Id.* at 231.

146. TYSON, note 125 above, at 288.

147. *Id.* at 289.

7   Competition Law and the WTO: Alternative Structures for Agreement

Brian Hindley

7.1   Introduction

Some accounts of a possible WTO agreement on competition law and policy treat governmental sins of omission—their failure to pursue private anticompetitive practices with sufficient vigor—as the only possible subject matter for agreement. But anticompetitive practices often require governmental sins of commission—without the active support of a government, the practice would vanish. In assessing the legal structures that might emerge from intergovernmental negotiations, the activities of the participating governments themselves cannot sensibly be neglected.

A second reason for considering a broad range of anticompetitive practices and actions lies in the simple fact it *is* a negotiation that will determine the form of a WTO agreement. Some discussions of Trade-Related Aspects of Competition Law and Policy (TRACLAP) seem to assume that differences between governments about TRACLAP can be resolved by intellectual conversion, so that the prospective negotiation is viewed as a sort of intergovernmental seminar on antitrust economics. A negotiation, though, needs *quids* and *quos*, and in the case of negotiations designed to lead to an agreement on TRACLAP, the character of these *quids* and *quos* is not self-evident. To cast too narrowly risks a failure to identify potential exchanges.[1]

7.2   Role of Governments

An agreement on TRACLAP might deal with three broad categories of government involvement. First, national competition laws are structured and applied in ways that directly affect foreign residents. Second, some alleged anticompetitive practices (AACPs) are directly due to the actions of governments. Third, the survival of many "private" AACPs requires the active support of a government.

7.2.1 Aggressive Use of National Competition Laws

Exemption of Export Cartels from National Competition Law
Exemptions from national competition laws of cartels directed solely at foreign buyers provide a prime example of a direct effect on foreign residents of the way in which national competition laws are structured. Such exemptions are either given or made possible under, for example, the Webb-Pomerene Act in the U.S. and the Transactions Law in Japan. EU competition rules do not expressly exempt cartels formed solely for the purpose of exploiting foreign buyers. The target of Article 85 of the TEU (Treaty of European Union), however, is "concerted practices which may affect trade between the Member States and which have as their object or effect the prevention, restriction or distortion of competition *within* the common market" (emphasis added).

Some participants in a negotiation on TRACLAP will probably seek to eliminate such exemptions. In the present context, however, that target does not seem worth extended discussion. A WTO agreement on TRACLAP that allowed signatories to facilitate the exploitation of residents of other signatories through their competition laws would be a very strange beast. A willingness to include export cartels in the scope of national competition laws is more likely to be a first test of the seriousness of the participants in the negotiation than a bargaining chip. Countries whose law provides such exemptions are unlikely to be able to command a high negotiating "price" for removing them. It therefore seems likely that if there is an agreement on TRACLAP, the exemptions will go without playing any substantial role in other parts of the negotiation.

Extraterritoriality
Extraterritoriality, though, is a different matter. National laws facilitating the exploitation of foreigners by domestic cartels have raised less controversy in recent years than applications of the competition law of one country to alleged anticompetitive arrangements in another—that is, extraterritorial application of national competition laws.

An example of U.S. extraterritorial action (one of a considerable number) is provided by the *Tanner Crab* case, in which the U.S. Justice Department obtained a consent decree against an arrangement whereby Japanese purchasers of crabs exchanged information on prices offered by the U.S.

sellers. As Mitsuo Matsushita observes, "In so far as this order directed the Japanese companies to revoke the arrangement which had been enforced in Japan and to refrain from engaging in an exchange of price information in Japan, it had 'extraterritorial' effect."[2]

The United States is not alone in claiming extraterritorial jurisdiction. The EU competition authorities have prosecuted firms whose actions affect EU consumers, even when those firms have no production in the EU (for example, producers of wood pulp).[3] EU merger regulations, moreover, authorize the Commission to act against mergers that affect the EU, even though the companies involved have their headquarters and the bulk of their business outside of the EU.

Protection against extraterritorial action is likely to be a primary negotiating objective of some participants in a negotiation on TRACLAP. The price that users of extraterritorial action ask for giving it up is therefore likely to be a central issue in the negotiation.

Negotiation of explicit rules of jurisdiction, though, will be difficult. If the law and enforcement of country A produces higher probabilities of conviction and higher levels of penalty for an AACP than those of country B, a concession of jurisdiction by A to B amounts to a relaxation of A's competition law.

In principle, the problem could be solved by harmonization of national competition laws, enforcement, and penalties. But that also will be difficult to achieve. There are genuine differences of opinion about what practices should be vulnerable to the law and, more generally, about the appropriate level of penalties for offences.[4]

7.2.2   Government-Contrived Trade Restraints

When the governments of Australia, Canada, the U.S., and the EU were asked to provide examples of interaction between trade and competition policies for an OECD assessment, the bulk of the issues they listed did not involve private arrangements at all, but arrangements in which a government is an essential participant.[5] Leaving aside several cases that turn upon antidumping action and/or voluntary export restraints, the list includes government purchasing and distribution monopolies in tobacco (in Japan, Taiwan, and Thailand), alcoholic beverages (in Canada and Taiwan), and beef (in the Republic of Korea); the uranium cartel, supported by the Australian government; barriers to entry into retailing in Japan, blamed on the Large Scale Retail Store Law; marketing restrictions in Japan, administered by the Fair Trade Commission; sales of value-added telecommunication services to state-owned PTTs; procurement of heavy electrical equipment by state-owned EU utilities; exemption of export cartels from antitrust law; and "trade-policy-inspired industrial policy."

All of these are examples of government-contrived restraints on trade that might in principle be dealt with by an agreement on TRACLAP. Existing GATT articles and agreements, however, clearly apply to some of them—for example, Article XVII (State Trading Enterprises), which is the subject of a Uruguay Round understanding on interpretation; and the Uruguay Round agreement on government procurement. Others are not, or not obviously, the subject of existing articles and agreements— for example, the alleged effects of the Large Scale Retail Store Law in Japan.

Applicability of Article XXIII:1(b)

GATT articles and agreements are sometimes so broad, though, that it is difficult to know whether an issue is covered by them. Consider, for example, the crucial Article XXIII. Article XXIII:1 allows a WTO member to invoke the dispute settlement procedures if "... any benefit accruing to it directly or indirectly under this Agreement is being nullified and impaired or ... the attainment of any objective of the Agreement is being impeded as a result of:

(a) the failure of another Member to carry out its obligations under this Agreement, or

(b) the application by another Member *of any measure, whether or not it conflicts with the provisions of this Agreement*, or

(c) *the existence of any other situation* (emphasis added).

Parts (b) and (c) give very wide grounds for complaint—wide enough, perhaps, to apply to TRACLAP issues. The U.S., for example, complains that the Large Scale Retail Store Law (LSRSL) impedes entry into Japanese markets, and therefore limits U.S. exports to Japan. Without entering the merits of the U.S. case, could the U.S. use Article XXIII:1(b) to mount an action in the WTO against the LSRSL?

A principal legal barrier to such an action would be the existence of the LSRSL at the time concessions were made by Japan. The U.S., it would be argued, could anticipate the effects of the LSRSL on those concessions and therefore cannot now claim that those effects nullify or impair benefits that it reasonably expected.

Viewed with an economist's eye, however, that argument is not compelling. The effects of the LSRSL that the U.S. complains of would *not* have
been easy to foresee—and might have been impossible to foresee.

Even as matters now stand in the GATT, it might be possible to make
this case, so that, if other elements of its complaint were valid, the U.S.
could obtain a ruling against the LSRSL under Article XXIII:1(b).[6] That
outcome would be facilitated, however, by a very simple agreement on
government-contrived impediments to competition, which could take the
form of a Ministerial Declaration that:

Nullification and impairment of concessions may be caused by impediments to
competition deriving from national laws or acts of national governments. Such
effects, however, cannot easily be predicted. Thus, when a complaint under Article
XXIII:1(b) is based on an allegation that a law or an action of a government impedes
competition, the contention that the complaining member could have foreseen the
effect of the law or action on a concession will not constitute an adequate rebuttal.

Actions under Article XXIII:1(b), however, carry a difficulty that is relevant to thinking about a WTO agreement on TRACLAP. The Uruguay
Round understanding on the settlement of disputes calls for the withdrawal of a measure that is deemed to violate Article XXIII:1(a). If Article
XXIII:1(b) applies, however, the measure that is the subject of complaint
does not in itself violate any WTO agreement. In that case, the understanding allows the government to maintain a measure that is deemed to
fall foul of Article XXIII:1(b), though, if it does so, it must compensate
other WTO members for the adverse effects of the measure upon them.

This right to maintain a measure that is deemed to fall foul of Article
XXIII:1(b) can be viewed as a cost of the broad scope of that provision.
Members cannot know which of their policies or actions might be deemed
to fall foul of Article XXIII:1(b) and so are unwilling to commit themselves
in advance to terminate an action or policy that is found to nullify or
impair under that provision.[7]

The same problem may play a role in the negotiation of an agreement
on TRACLAP. Unless the policies or measures that are vulnerable to
action under the agreement are tightly defined, acceptance that those
deemed to fall foul of the agreement should be automatically terminated
might be difficult to obtain.

7.2.3 Law, Policy, and Private AACPs

Governments organize and orchestrate practices that are regarded as
anticompetitive by other governments. Private anticompetitive practices,

requiring only freedom from hostile government action to survive for substantial periods, probably do exist. Between these two extremes, though, there is a very broad range of possible public-private sector interactions.

The general issue that a substantive agreement on TRACLAP must address arises when an AACP in country B is perceived by the government of country A to harm residents of A. The relevant political problem appears when the A government registers its claim that A residents are harmed by the practice, but the government of B fails to remove the alleged harm.

The crux of the negotiating problem is captured by asking how an AACP in B manages to survive, either before or after the A intervention. There are at least five possible answers. It may survive because it:

(a) is required by B law; or

(b) is allowed by B law; or

(c) is actionable under B law but is subject to penalties too low to deter it; or

(d) is actionable under B law and is subject to penalties that will deter it, but enforcement of the law is given only low priority by the B government; or

(e) is actionable and subject to penalties that will deter it, but the government of B does not know about it or cannot legally prove its existence.

The difficulty of negotiating an agreement on TRACLAP is likely to depend on which explanation applies. If (e) applies, for example, A and B might agree that a practice merits roughly the same punishment, and each might believe that it can more efficiently acquire information about the practice by cooperating with the other. Under those circumstances, agreement might not be difficult to achieve. States of affairs (a) through (d), though, are consistent with a belief by the government of B that an AACP that is the subject of protest by the government of A is socially justified or has socially redeeming features.[8] Negotiating an agreement between parties with different views about appropriate levels of punishment, and/ or about the priority that enforcement should receive, is likely to be a quite different—and much more difficult—matter.

This more difficult matter, however, is likely to be at the heart of negotiations about TRACLAP. Claims that an agreement on TRACLAP will yield substantial economic gains presumably rest on the notion that many anticompetitive practices affecting the interests of foreign residents are not reached by national competition laws. But if many anticompetitive practices are not reached by national laws, the possibility that different jurisdictions have different views on appropriate enforcement and penalties must be faced.

Different views are not, of course, an insuperable barrier to agreement. Parties to a successful negotiation usually give up things that they would intrinsically prefer to keep—by giving them up, they obtain things of even greater value to themselves. A problem with the proposed negotiation on TRACLAP, however, is that the potential exchanges are not obvious. In particular, it is not obvious what the U.S. can offer, apart from cessation of extraterritorial action, to obtain its objectives in Japan.

7.3   Possible Forms of Agreement

Before turning to more complicated agreements, however, it should be noted that Article XXIII:1(b) might in principle be used to deal with an important class of intergovernmental complaints about private anticompetitive practices.

7.3.1   Article XXIII:1(b) and Private Anticompetitive Practices

Governments frequently complain that another government is failing to apply its own national competition law to anticompetitive practices in its private sector. A simple agreement to facilitate application of Article XXIII:1(b) to that problem might take the form of a Ministerial Declaration that:

Private anticompetitive practices can nullify and impair concessions. The failure of a member to apply its national competition law to a private anticompetitive practice that has the effect of nullifying or impairing a concession is a valid basis for complaint under Article XXIII:1(b). Such a failure will be construed as an "application" of a measure, as called for by Article XXIII:1(b). In such cases, it will be presumed that the failure to apply the national law could not have been foreseen by other members.

The practices to which an agreement in this form would apply are defined by the law of each jurisdiction (the scope of which, of course, could be a topic for negotiation). Beyond that, it uses existing dispute-settlement procedures and penalties.

Clearly, more complicated agreements are possible. An agreement to facilitate the use of Article XXIII:1(b), as sketched above, though, provides a useful benchmark for assessing these.

7.3.2   Issues for Negotiation

The essence of a WTO agreement on TRACLAP will lie in the answers it gives to four questions:

(1) To which anticompetitive practices does the agreement apply?

(2) What conditions must be satisfied before a government is required to act against an anticompetitive practice?[9]

(3) What action must it take?

(4) If the action taken is deemed insufficient by the complainant government, what recourse does that government have?

The issues raised by each question are discussed in turn.

Which Practices?
Broadly speaking, there are two approaches to determining which AACPs will be covered by an agreement. One is to provide a list of actionable practices. The second is to make actionable any practice that produces specified effects. Each approach has advantages.

Some anticompetitive practices *must* be covered if an agreement on TRACLAP is to have substance. Cross-border collusion between producers that has the effect or objective of raising prices or dividing markets, for example, *must* be targeted. A list can state that, more or less unambiguously.

Lists of practices may also be useful if the negotiating parties are hopelessly at odds on the social value of some AACPs. A list permits the exclusion of practices from the scope of the agreement. It therefore allows irreconcilable differences to be put on one side, possibly facilitating progress elsewhere.

If effects are used, an obvious trigger for the provisions of a WTO agreement is an effect on international trade and/or international investment. The problem lies in deciding what effect. Will any impact suffice, regardless of size or direction? Will an effect on international investment trigger the agreement? Will an anticompetitive practice in country B that affects residents of country A only if they travel to B be enough?

One way of answering such questions, within the GATT/WTO tradition, would be by reference to the benefits reasonably expected from other WTO agreements. With that trigger, the relevant question about an AACP is whether its effects reduce benefits that other WTO members might reasonably have expected from concessions under another WTO agreement. (This is, of course, also the question upon which the outcome of an Article XXIII action turns.)

These two approaches do not exclude one another. The TEU provides a good example of a combination of a list and an approach based upon effects. Article 85 requires the Commission to act against "... all agreements between undertakings, decisions by associations of undertakings and concerted practices which may affect trade between the Member States and which have as their object or effect the prevention, restriction, or distortion of competition within the common market...." That instruction is supplemented, though, by a list of practices which are considered *prima facie* contrary to this objective, and by a second list that gives grounds for defense of a concerted practice. Article 86 prohibits "any abuse by one or more dominant undertakings of a dominant position within the common market in so far as it may affect trade between the Member States," and contains a (nonexclusive) list of particular practices that are to be considered abusive *prima facie*. A combination of this kind must be a strong candidate for a WTO agreement on TRACLAP, though, for the reasons noted above, agreement on its contents might be difficult to arrive at.

Conditions for Action

The government of country A alleges that a targeted anticompetitive practice and/or effect occurs in country B, which the B authorities are not attacking. What must the A government do to get the B competition authorities to act?

Clearly, a first condition must be demonstration of the existence of the practice or effect, in the first instance, presumably, to the B authorities. But the B authorities may not be convinced—or may say that they are not convinced.

The prior failure of the B authorities to act may simply be due to lack of awareness of the practice and, in that case, action may promptly follow enlightenment. It is also possible, though, that the prior failure was due to internal B politics, and the A government may then find it more difficult to persuade the B authorities to concede that the practice does in fact exist. Failure of the B authorities to act after the intervention of A may also, of course, be because the A complaint is badly based.

The latter possibilities argue strongly for the ready availability of adjudication, independent of the governments of A and B. Such adjudication might take the form of a standard WTO dispute-settlement panel. Alternatively, an agreement on TRACLAP might establish a body through which all complaints of one government against the actions or inactions of another with respect to TRACLAP must pass. If so, that body could also act as adjudicator in the first instance, deciding whether the A government has established a *prima facie* case for the existence in B of a targeted practice or effect.

Action

When a practice and/or effect subject to the agreement has been shown to exist in country B, what action must the B government take? Clearly, if only a *prima facie* case has been established, all it can be expected to do, in the first instance, is to investigate whether prosecution under B law is feasible. Such an investigation will often provide opportunities for foot-dragging and delay on the part of B (and for A suspicion of foot-dragging by B even when B is acting as expeditiously as possible).

Once a sufficient basis for prosecution has been established, however, penalties become the central issue. The law of country B may provide insufficient penalties to deter the practice or sufficient only to change its form, not to fully remove the damage to A residents.

Two broad approaches can be visualized to deal with this situation. The first is for parties to the agreement to adopt similar penalties for targeted practices, whether by harmonizing penalties outright or by agreeing to minimum levels of penalty, with parties left free to exceed that minimum should they wish to do so. The second is to agree that governments must take whatever action is needed to remove the damage to the residents of other countries, without specification of what that action should be.

Given the likely difficulty of harmonizing penalties, the second approach has clear attractions. But it has its own difficulties. At one extreme, it might be interpreted to imply that if even the strongest action available under existing B law were insufficient to remove the damage caused by an anticompetitive practice, the government of B would be obliged to seek a strengthening of B law. At the other extreme, it might be taken to mean merely, *à la* Article XXIII:1(b), that B must compensate A for the impairment of its expected benefits.[10]

Recourse in the Event of Insufficient Action

When the A government has a valid complaint against an anticompetitive practice in B, but the B government does not act to remove the cause of the complaint, what recourse does the A government have? One possibility, clearly, is to authorize the use of trade-policy measures against B, as in a complaint under Article XXIII:1(a).

Extraterritorial action might also become an issue under this heading. When an anticompetitive practice in country B could be attacked either under the law of A, applied extraterritorially, or under a WTO agreement on TRACLAP, some priority between the two must be established. If the government of B fails to remove the cause of injury to A residents by action under the agreement, though, there is no evident reason why the A government should not be free to take extraterritorial action.

7.3.3   Difficulty of Obtaining Agreement

Obtaining an agreement that goes far beyond facilitation of Article XXIII:1(b) is unlikely to be easy. The difficulties center on the action required by such an agreement.

First, the actions required under existing national competition laws are the outcome of some process of national consensus. Attempts to change them through multilateral negotiations are bound to meet resistance.

Second, there is an obvious tension between the number of anticompetitive practices covered by an agreement—whether expressly, in the form of a list, or implicitly, in terms of effects—and the action required when the existence of a targeted practice is demonstrated. The stronger the required actions, the more difficult to obtain acceptance of anticompetitive practices as targets, and vice versa.

Third, between acceptance by a government of a *prima facie* case that a targeted practice or effect is occurring in its jurisdiction and construction by it of a sound case for presentation in the national courts, there is a long and variable lag. This situation is pregnant with possibilities for mutual distrust: for delay by the government that is supposed to act and of accusations of delay—even when action is taken as rapidly as possible— by the government making the complaint.

These difficulties are enhanced by the lack of mutually acceptable concessions. In most negotiations, each participant has something to give and something to gain—a tariff reduction in country A, for example, in exchange for a tariff reduction in country B. The *quids* that will balance the *quos* in a negotiation on TRACLAP, however, are unclear—apart from extraterritorial action. Without balance in available concessions, it is possible that attempts will be made to press the "negotiation" forward by the use of either persuasion or force. Neither alternative, however, suggests an easy passage.

7.3.4   The U.S.–EU Agreement

The U.S.–EU *Agreement on the Application of Competition Law* has been widely hailed as a major step forward in international coordination of competition policies. Sir Leon Brittan, the EU Commissioner responsible for competition policy when the Agreement was signed, is reported to have "... indicated that the agreement might serve as a basis for similar pacts with Canada and possibly Japan."[11] Nevertheless, it falls far short of the kind of agreement that would call for a WTO-type dispute-settlement system. In so doing, it suggests the difficulty of negotiating an enforceable WTO agreement.[12]

The principal elements of the *Agreement* are, first, to establish a framework within which the EU and U.S. can agree to coordinate action against anticompetitive practices that affect both of them. They are not obliged to coordinate activities, but, in considering whether they will do so, they must consider whether coordination will increase efficiency, make possible the collection of more or better information, or reduce the costs of persons subject to the enforcement activity.[13] Second, Article V permits the European Commission or the U.S. government to request legal action by the other when either believes that anticompetitive activities adverse to its interests are being carried out in the territory of the other. The notified party is not required to take action, but must inform the notifying party of its decision and of the outcome of any enforcement proceedings. Third, Article II requires notification when enforcement activities in one country affect important interests of the other, and Article VI commits each to take into account important interests of the other "[w]ithin the framework of its own laws and to the extent compatible with its own important interests...." It includes a list of factors to be considered "... in seeking an appropriate accommodation of the competing interests."

The *Agreement* is binding only in its procedural provisions, not in its substantive ones. It contains no binding rules on jurisdiction, and does not preclude extraterritorial action. The EU sought such rules, but the U.S. rejected them. That the *Agreement* has been hailed as a large step forward suggests the difficulty of the terrain that must be traversed to arrive at a WTO agreement on TRACLAP.

7.4   Economic Gains?

Assessment of the overall economic benefits of a WTO agreement on TRACLAP is peripheral to the main topic of this paper. Nevertheless, if a substantive WTO agreement will be difficult to achieve, large prospective economic gains might seem to be a precondition of enthusiasm for the effort to obtain one. In fact, however, advocacy of the project for an agreement on TRACLAP conspicuously lacks claims—or any substantial basis for claims—that private cartels or cartel-like activity are rife, have substantial effects on international trade and investment, and can be controlled only by a WTO agreement on TRACLAP. Evidence that such an agreement will directly give rise to large economic gains is missing.

The slate is not completely blank, of course. The complaints of U.S. exporters or potential exporters to Japan appear with some frequency, though usually without analysis of the economic plausibility of the alleged Japanese behavior. But even if every charge were true, it is reasonable to doubt whether ridding the world of soda-ash cartels and dango in the Japanese construction industry—assuming that such *would* be the effect of an agreement—will yield economic benefits commensurate with the difficulty of achieving that result through a WTO agreement.

In the economic case for an agreement on TRACLAP, indirect gains dominate direct ones. One asserted indirect effect is to end or limit the problems that antidumping laws raise for the international trading system. An agreement on TRACLAP is seen as a first step in positioning national competition laws to absorb or dominate antidumping laws. But while an end of antidumping abuse would be very valuable, no one is willing to say that it could soon be achieved as a result of an agreement on TRACLAP (advocacy of this crablike approach via competition law being itself a tribute to the strength of the pro-antidumping lobbies). Attempts to deal with antidumping by this means, moreover, may end with antidumping corrupting competition law rather than with competition law cleansing antidumping.

A second possible positive effect of an agreement on TRACLAP is prophylactic—preventing a return to the cartel-ridden state of the world economy of the 1930s. International cartels were, of course, common in the period prior to the Second World War.[14] According to a 1944 survey by the British government, 30 percent of British exports in 1938 were regulated by some form of cartel.[15]

But while the desirability of averting a return to that situation is widely accepted, the threat seems small and the role in averting it of an agreement on TRACLAP problematic. Possibly the most important factor in the decline of international cartels has been vigorous action against collusion in the U.S.—in many industries, an "international" cartel that does not include U.S. producers cannot succeed. U.S. antitrust action that deters the participation in international cartels of U.S. producers increases the costs and problems of organizing an international cartel.[16]

An agreement on TRACLAP does not seem to have much scope to improve on this situation, and might conceivably worsen it. Harmonization of competition laws is bound to become a topic in any negotiation on TRACLAP. United States antitrust laws, though, are in most respects stronger than those of other countries, so harmonization threatens to weaken them. That possibility is not reduced by recent pressures within the United States to weaken the antitrust laws so as to "increase United States competitiveness"—pressures that might be seen as urging, in effect, harmonization by the United States on the standard for competition law set by Japan—or at least the standard that Japan is alleged in the United States to set.[17]

7.5   Conclusions

At least three levels of international agreement on trade-related aspects of competition law and policy can be defined. They are:

(a) agreements on the application of competition law, following the lines of the U.S.-EU *Agreement on the Application of Competition Law*. Being procedural, application of the WTO dispute-settlement mechanism would not be needed and would not be appropriate. Moreover, since the number of essential participants is small (the U.S., the EU, and Japan; and possibly Canada and Australia), the negotiation of such agreements does not need the WTO as a forum.

(b) a WTO agreement (plurilateral or multilateral) to facilitate application of Article XXIII:1(b) to trade-related aspects of competition law and policy.

(c) a WTO agreement on TRACLAP with substantive provisions that go beyond facilitation of Article XXIII:1(b).

The first two are not mutually exclusive, and an agreement to facilitate application of Article XXIII:1(b) to competition law and policy does not exclude the possibility of an attempt by participants to negotiate agreement on standards for national competition law. Such an agreement on standards might be, but does not need to be, part of a WTO agreement.

To aim for an agreement to facilitate application of Article XXIII:1(b) to competition law and policy, moreover, may minimize the need for *quids* and *quos* in the negotiation. Such an agreement would create a procedure to assess whether past concessions have been eroded by anticompetitive practices, and to restore their value when they have been so eroded. Since the agreement would revive the effects of concessions that have already been made, negotiation of it may require fewer new reciprocal concessions than negotiation of more complicated agreements.

A great deal of commentary on a WTO agreement on trade-related aspects of competition law and policy, however, takes (c) to be the proper target for negotiation. But if exchanges of information can be obtained under (a), and intergovernmental disputes about inadequate enforcement of national competition laws can be achieved under (b), what is the target of (c)?

Only two answers present themselves. One is to obtain a greater coverage of practices than is provided by current national law. The other is to obtain a greater similarity of enforcement and punishment—in a word, harmonization. If (a) and (b) can be negotiated, however—and if they cannot be, there is little point in aiming for (c)—the *incremental* benefits of greater coverage or harmonization seem likely to be small. The value of an attempt to negotiate a WTO agreement that goes beyond facilitating application of Article XXIII:1(b) to issues of competition law and policy is open to doubt.

NOTES

Brian Hindley is with the Department of Economics, London School of Economics.

1. Of course, differences between the parties to the negotiation *might* be bridged by intellectual conversion—it is simply unwise to *assume* that outcome (especially in the light of academic differences over the appropriate treatment of alleged anticompetitive practices, well summarized in E. M. Graham & J. D. Richardson, *Summary of Project on International Competition Policy of the Institute of International Economics* (Inst. Int'l Econ., 1994)). It is also true that in a GATT/WTO round, concessions in one area by one member might be "paid for" by another member with concessions in another area. In assessing possible outcomes of a negotiation on TRACLAP, though, it is useful to know if such out-of-area exchanges will be necessary.

2. Mitsuo Matsushita, *The Role of Competition Law and Policy in Reducing Trade Barriers in Japan*, 14 WORLD ECON. 181, 190 (1991).

3. The defendants in *Wood Pulp* argued that the Commission had exceeded its jurisdiction in attacking alleged anticompetitive behavior that took place outside of the EC. The Court of Justice disagreed. "The producers in this case implemented their pricing agreement within the Common Market," it said. "Accordingly, the Community's jurisdiction to apply its competition rules to such conduct is covered by the territoriality principle as universally recognized in public international law." 1988 E.C. REP. 5193.

4. For a useful discussion of the *de jure* and *de facto* differences between the U.S. and the EU, see Phedon Nicolaides, *Towards Multilateral Rules on Competition*, 17 WORLD COMPETITION 5–48 (1994).

5. These submissions are summarized in OECD, *Cases of Interaction between Trade and Competition Policy*, OECD Doc. COM/TD/DAFFE/CLP(92)50 (1992).

6. The question of whether Article XXIII might in principle apply to anticompetitive practices has been debated in the GATT since at least 1958. For a valuable history and analysis of the issue, see Bernard M. Hoekman & Petros C. Mavroidis, *Competition, Competition Policy and the GATT*, 17 WORLD ECON. 121 (1994).

7. The potential impact of "the existence of any other situation" under Article XXIII:1(c) is even more difficult to accurately foresee. When the provisions of Article XXIII:1(c) apply, a panel may make only rulings and recommendations.

8. They are also consistent with the possibility that members of the government have some sort of alliance or relationship with those in the private sector who benefit from the structure of the law and/or its enforcement and/or the supportive actions of the government. Even in that case, of course, members of governments are likely to explain their action or inaction in terms of socially benefical consequences.

9. In some jurisdictions—notably the U.S.—private antitrust actions are possible. An agreement on TRACLAP, though, seems likely to be directed at the actions of governments.

10. The possibility of compensation raises a further issue. Almost all anticompetitive practices will permit a showing that some foreign residents have gained and others lost. A cartel in construction or office cleaning in country B, for example, might prevent the otherwise legal entry of an A resident into the cartelized industry. But it might be suggested in defense of the cartel that by raising the costs of production of B industries that use its services, the cartel benefits the competitors in A of those industries. Any sensible agreement will make clear that arguments based upon indirect effects have no weight: It will focus entirely on direct effects.

11. FINANCIAL TIMES, Sept. 24, 1991.

12. In the summer of 1994, the European Court of Justice declared the U.S.-EU Agreement void. At issue was a question of EU procedure (whether the Commission had the right to conclude the agreement without reference to the Council of Ministers). The argument of the following paragraphs is not affected.

13. Agreement on the Application of Competition Law (U.S.-EU), art. IV.

14. GEORGE W. STOCKING & M. W. WATKINS, CARTELS IN ACTION (Twentieth Century Fund, 1946).

15. D. C. Elliot & J. D. Gribbin, *The Abolition of Cartels and Structural Change in the United Kingdom*, in 2 WELFARE ASPECTS OF INDUSTRIAL MARKETS 345, 346 (A. P. Jaquemin & H. W. de Jong, eds., 1977).

16. An international cartel that fails to include EU producers will typically have poor prospects also. But the penalties for breaching EU competition law appear to be small, relative to the gains to be expected from a successful cartel. Patrick Messerlin, *Anti-Dumping Regulations or Pro-Cartel Law: The EC Chemical Cases*, 13 WORLD ECON. 465, 490 (1990). They may be too small to deter EU producers from forming or joining cartels. If so, EU competition law is a less effective bulwark to the formation of international cartels than U.S. law.

17. The reasoning behind such pressures, of course, is faulty. That the Japanese economy has been successful can neither support an inference that the alleged lack of effective antitrust law in Japan has contributed to the success nor an inference that a relaxation of U.S. antitrust law will improve the performance of the U.S. economy.

V   Fairness Concepts

8

Antidumping and Countervailing-Duty Law: The Mirage of Equitable International Competition

Ronald A. Cass
Richard D. Boltuck

8.1 Introduction

8.1.1 Discussing Trade: Linguistic Conventions

Discourse about international trade law, as with other areas of law, takes place among groups that, like Americans and Britons, are separated by a common language. One group, largely those in the political domain, converse mainly in the language of ethics. The critical concern expressed in their discussions is specification of fair rules for trade. This language is embedded in the formal texts governing offsets to certain forms of government subsidy for firms engaged in international trade (countervailing-duty law) and to price discrimination in international trade (antidumping law). These texts address "unfair trade practices."

Over the past two decades, the fairness label has been deployed with increasing frequency in discussions of varied aspects of international economic life. Nearly all trade practices that adversely affect import-competing industries, and nearly all policies of other governments linked to such trade practices, are said to constitute sources of unfair competition. While this label is predictable in political argument by potential beneficiaries of trade restraints, it has achieved much more widespread acceptance in the political domain.

The term "dumping" similarly has enjoyed growing popularity. Originally confined to international price differences thought to reflect predatory strategies, the term "dumping" has taken on a protean quality. Virtually all "unfair" acts now are said to result in some form of "dumping." The fact that workers in other nations earn lower wages, have less generous health and pension benefits, enjoy less stringent safeguards against industrial accidents, and so can provide lower labor costs for some products, has been said to be unfair. Trade in these workers' products has been termed "social dumping," in analogy to the dumping that occurs when products trade at different prices in two countries. The fact that costs of environmental protection differ across countries also has been labeled "unfair" and international trade in products from less protected environments has been called "environmental dumping."

Lawyers, used to taking their linguistic cues from the legal texts with which they work, have adopted the language of fairness in addressing international trade issues. They readily discuss the fairness not only of particular trade practices, but also of the administration of international trade law, borrowing in this context from "due process" jurisprudence.

Economists, for the most part, have employed a different argot, discussing not the fairness but the "efficiency" of international trade laws and possible alternative regimes. Efficiency can be a positive description or a prescriptive norm, based on the ethical constructs of utilitarianism. In its positive sense, efficiency is a description of the results produced by the operation of market forces unconstrained by certain "frictions" (such as costs of bargaining, of enforcing agreements, and so on). Depending on the market frictions abstracted away from and the baseline (including allocations of rights) from which movement is assessed, this concept may be fairly close to normative concepts of efficiency.

Economic writings using a normative concept of efficiency generally build on the notion of Pareto optimality, a state in which no move can make anyone better off without making someone worse off. A move *toward* Pareto optimality leaves no one worse off and hence is a decision that should garner unanimous consent of those affected. A weaker, and more controversial, form of the efficiency norm is increasing aggregate societal welfare, as in higher-valued Bergson-Samuelson social welfare functions. Many economists use efficiency in its normative sense in discourse on international trade policies. Normative efficiency (in almost any of its forms), if not synonymous with all concepts of "just" results, has at least some place in most accounts of just decisions. Other things equal, it is better to move toward just outcomes—however defined—through efficient processes. Normative efficiency also has strong congruence with many concepts of justice. (In this respect, it may be worth noting that many *non*-economists declare trade practices to be "unfair" *because* they are "inefficient.")

If not uniform in the meaning given to "efficiency," economists are very consistent in their assessment of the efficiency implications of a wide variety of international trade policies. While much has been made of the "new economics" of international trade, there has been a fairly steadfast consensus among economists for a century or more that the vast majority of trade restraints are efficiency-reducing, from either a national (importing nation) or global perspective. Abstract analysis, formal modeling of international trade, and empirical studies have presented a picture of remarkable uniformity for a profession not known for consensus. (The profession's reputation for disputation is most commonly reflected in the canard that if all the economists in the world were laid end to end, they still wouldn't reach a conclusion.) Recent work on strategic trade theory elaborates the manner in which certain types of trade restrictions under specified conditions can increase national welfare. Even ardent advocates of this theory, however, acknowledge the infrequency of encountering those conditions, and express major skepticism that existing trade policy mechanisms are invoked only when the sufficient conditions for trade restriction are identified. Whatever their prescription, economists writing about international trade tend to discuss its efficiency, not its fairness judged in other terms.

Finally, a more cynical set of commentators has attempted to divine what really accounts for trade laws and policies. These students of politics analyze the correlation of trade rules and decisions with factors such as the concentration of import-competing producers in the home districts of key congressmen. Theirs is an unabashedly positive enterprise—to find out what accounts for the way things are, rather than to tell us how things ought to be. This commentary has not found much systematic correlation of trade remedies with either efficiency or fairness. Still, this literature has had difficulty describing with any precision what accounts for the pattern of trade rules and decisions that exists.

8.1.2   The Inquiry Proposed

This paper does not harmonize these divergent vocabularies but looks critically at specific claims advanced in terms both of fairness and efficiency with respect to countervailing-duty and antidumping law. We do not, in the manner of the commentators described above who perform positive analyses of trade politics, endeavor to explain the forces that shape these areas of the law. Nor do we explore in great detail the various provisions of these laws or the mechanics of their administration. Rather, we take seriously the claims made in behalf of these laws, examine the analytic predicates that inform those claims, and ask how persuasive those rationales are, given the laws' current shape and implementation.

Our goal in this inquiry is not to engage directly the issue implicated in Professor Robert Hudec's observation that

[m]any students of U.S. trade policy insist that unfairness claims directed against import competition are simply a rhetorical convention, and have little or no substantive bearing on the protective measures adopted.[1]

It would, of course, be no surprise to students of politics if rhetorical conventions are adopted to promote public acceptance of policies that in fact are the product of the interplay of special interests.

If there is, however, some injustice that is rightly perceived in the practices labeled "unfair"—if unfair trade really is unjust trade (at least in some circumstances)—identification of the nature of the injustice and the circumstances in which it occurs can provide important insight into the proper ambit for trade laws and guidance for their administration. We pay particular attention to claims that the source of unfairness is interference with the operation of otherwise well-functioning markets; that is, that the unfairness is interference with efficiency.

The fairness claims cannot, however, be reduced to any definite, sustainable argument, much less to one that is consistent with the present structure of trade law as administered. Many of the fairness claims, on examination, depend on factual predicates that do not fit the trade context in which these claims arise. Some depend on differences in economic organization that are not readily turned into questions of justice or that do not reveal inefficiencies that would concern governments in other contexts. Extending core concerns about price-cutting—to instances of social dumping, environmental dumping, and the like—implicates arguments that are even further afield from readily cognizable ethical or efficiency claims.

8.1.3   Organization

The chapter is organized as follows. Section 8.2 begins with the analogy of the level playing field and considers the analytical components of the analogy. These analytical components point to differences between sports contests—the home turf of the level-playing-field analogy—and international trade, but the analysis focuses on only one question presented by this analogy. That is, What is the baseline of equitable competition (the level field)? Put differently, How do we conclude that a given action unfairly tilts away from equitable competition?

Section 8.3 describes the basic structure and operation of the antidumping and countervailing-duty (antisubsidy) laws of the United States. We explain the core cases that animated concern over dumping and subsidies and also discuss ways in which these laws have evolved, in some respects moving away from those core concerns.

Section 8.4 explores a series of possible unfairness claims that could be advanced to support antidumping and countervailing-duty remedies. In general, these are claims that in fact have been advanced by proponents of the current antidumping and countervailing-duty regimes, although the underlying precepts for such claims seldom are spelled out with care. This is especially true of arguments based on assumed differences in firms' access to capital. We expose the arguments supporting particular claims, working from those relevant to the core cases of dumping and subsidies—cases that give rise to widespread concern and that most plausibly justify remediation through antidumping or countervailing duties—to claims relevant to activities that only recently have been thought to raise concerns similar to core dumping and subsidy cases.

Finally, in Section 8.5, we ask whether a different sort of ethical claim than we examine in Section 8.4 might support these legal regimes. Section 8.4 looks narrowly at the possible unjustness of specific economic activity and at the potential for curing any unjustness through offsetting duties. Section 8.5, in contrast, looks at the broader context for trade policy and at possible "second-best" justifications for the laws derived from that context.

8.2   The Level Playing Field as Moral Imperative

8.2.1   Analogy as Analytical Framework

At the outset, it is important to understand the basis for the claims that practices addressed by the unfair trade laws are in fact unfair. As in much other regulation of commercial activity, the axiom that commonly is invoked as the embodiment of the state's moral imperative is the obligation to maintain a level playing field.

The analogy to sport, as it commonly is conceived, contains three features:

• First, the nature of the activity at issue is a *contest*;

• second, the outcome of the contest is affected not only by the contestants' skill and determination but also by externally imposed rules of the game and by "environmental" factors (weather, field conditions, and so on); and

• third, the goal of the external authority in charge of the contest should be to make the terms of the contest equal, to provide each contestant a fair opportunity to prevail.

The image of a tilted playing field conveys the unmistakable impression that one contestant has an advantage, conferred by some factor apart from his own endowments, that prejudices the game's outcome, perhaps even determines that outcome. No player, we all intuit, should constantly have to fight uphill.

There is a fairly ready acceptance of the sports analogy in international trade. The articulable principle that seems to animate disinterested observers in their concern about unfair trade is not an abstract notion of ethical entitlement to insulation from competition nor any particularized claim sounding in the ethics of justice; it is, instead, an equality principle of the sort that is inherent in the sports analogy.

On the surface, the dumping and countervailing-duty laws are efforts to apply the equality principle that the analogy suggests should govern to domestic firms that produce import-competing products. These laws protect domestic firms that are materially harmed, through imports, by "unfair" artificial advantages enjoyed by foreign competitors. The targeted advantages include subsidies to production or exportation, as well as protected home markets that generate dumping, i.e., lower prices for export-destined products than for home market-destined products. Intuitively, it seems unjust when the ordinary, commercial "rules of the game" are altered through foreign governmental intervention in the global marketplace, for the direct benefit of foreign competitors, and, as a consequence, domestic investors in human and physical capital suffer a financial reversal. Sometimes, as when a foreign government creates a new program that directly subsidizes exports from a given industry, losses to domestic competitors in that industry seem akin to losses from malicious destruction of property by foreign agents. You increase your efficiency and lower your costs, but I persuade my government to offset my higher costs for products I export to your markets—in such cases, the playing field does, indeed, seem unfairly tilted.

8.2.2 Baseline Questions

Despite the common intuition that we are on the right track searching for a level playing field for international trade, that intuition provides little assistance in devising a framework for identifying unfair competition and for assessing efforts to halt it or to remedy its effects. Any serious inquiry into the proper reasons for labeling trade practices unfair and the proper steps to combat the unfairness suggests that the sports analogy is problematic. Before we can begin leveling playing fields, three questions should be addressed:

• First, is it proper to view international trade as a *contest* between commercial rivals rather than as part of a larger arrangement that benefits society in general? To be sure, there are rivals engaged in competition, but international trade is not a spectator sport where the spectacle of the contest—especially a contest between competitors so evenly matched that the outcome is a matter of suspense—is what benefits others. As economists since Adam Smith have tirelessly preached (tirelessly, but not always—or often—effectively), international trade produces positive gains between traders and creates positive externalities in just the same way that competition within a domestic economy does.[2]

• Second, insofar as trade involves goods produced by commercial rivals, is it proper to identify the rivals by nation—in other words, is the competition rightly conceived as one between competitors with distinct national identities defined by the border across which trade takes place, a *foreign* exporter and a *domestic* rival? Increasingly, production is not sufficiently localized and corporate ownership is not sufficiently concentrated to provide a clear national identity to the competition that trade may be seen as encompassing. Imports may help a domestically-owned competitor more effectively confront a foreign-owned rival; imports also may have high domestic content, even when imported, and surely can be incorporated into goods that have high domestic content, while "domestic" products can be quite heavily infused with imported parts, research, design, or finance. Imports may in fact be less the clear product of any one country than of a single, multinational (or multinationally sourced) company.[3]

• Third, is *equality* between commercial competitors the right goal for a national governnnent to pursue? And, if so, what does it mean? Given the array of factors that influence the outcome of the competition, what does equality consist of? Or, if a *full* equality is not what we seek, what does a *fair* equality consist of?

We will not address the first or second question here. Suffice it to say that the answers to these questions are anything but self-evident. Plainly, the contribution that specialization can make to increased productivity is part of the driving force behind the globalization of business. This both increases the likely (beneficial) spillover effects from trade that responds to comparative advantage and makes more difficult isolation of commercial competitors that confidently can be said to be *American* (GM or Ford, with global production and investments in Europe and Asia?) or *foreign* (Honda of Ohio? Royal Dutch Shell? Unilever?).

Our attention, however, will focus on the third question—What does equality, or a "fair" equality, mean in the context of international trade laws? The natural corollary to this—What should be done when inequality, or at least an "unfair" inequality, has been found?—also is addressed.

The first part of this question, defining the sort of equality we seek in international trade, presents vexing questions. The assumption implicit in casting antidumping and countervailing-duty law as remedies to "unfair trade practices" is that some ascertainable standard of acceptable trade practices—from which these unfair practices derogate—exists. A world in which only fair trade practices are deployed is, then, one characterized by the sort of international commercial competition that *ought* to obtain, what we might label "equitable competition." The concept is not of a *perfectly competitive* market, in the sense of microeconomic texts—namely, one characterized by the absence of market power (capacity to set prices). Instead, equitable competition comprehends a different ideal, one that admits the possibility of differentiated products, strategic behavior, and other departures from the common economic model of a perfectly competitive market.[4]

The notion of equitable competition implicit in the level-playing-field analogy is that a set of rules exists that allows international commercial competition to be based on skill, determination, and permissible "natural" advantages; under these rules, so far as competitors differ, the more efficient competitors will prevail. As Professor Diane Wood frames the position, laws restraining or remedying unfair trade practices are intended to protect the benefits of such "natural advantages" as those that firms in the domestic economy "derive from sources like historical specialization, skills in the workforce, supply of laborers, natural resource endowments, and technological developments" and to offset "artificial" foreign advantages such as "targeted favorable tax laws, interest-free loans from the government, subsidized export credits, high tariff walls preventing competitive imports, [and] state-conferred monopolies."[5]

On this view, the unfairness to be remedied by international trade laws, such as antidumping and countervailing duty law, is the alteration of rules to the advantage of one competitor or the alteration of competitive conditions to advantage one and disadvantage another competitor in a way that derogates from the equitable competition baseline. Thus, dumping assertedly constitutes a distortion of equitable competition because one competitor enjoys a protected home market that allows the competitor to increase price in one market and offer the same product for less in the export market (without a protected home market, presumably, there would not be a division between two markets with goods priced differently in each market—an assertion we examine below).[6] So, too, subsidization assertedly distorts from perfect competition in altering one competitor's decisions—on export quantities and prices, on production, or on other matters—from those that would be reached under the constraints of the marketplace, even though other competitors are fully subject to market forces.

But the underlying concept of a baseline of perfect, undistorted competition that will serve as the test for equal treatment of competitors proves almost impossible to reduce to a set of concrete propositions similar to those that describe the economist's perfectly competitive market. The problem is not that something we might call equitable competition cannot be found in the real world—that would not distinguish the concept of equitable competition from the economists' concept of perfectly competitive markets, for in truth economists rarely find markets that are perfectly competitive. The difference, rather, is that, unlike the well-specified model of a perfectly competitive market, the baseline for equitable international competition lacks coherent definition. Put more strongly, the arguments currently at our disposal *cannot* provide coherence to the notion of equitable international competition.

This lack of a clear basis for setting the baseline also distinguishes trade law from the sports analogy so often invoked as a metaphor. Markets respond to such a variety of factors that identification of a set of conditions that constitute the fair rules of the game necessarily implicates judgments that are absent in sports contests. The entire array of differences in national laws, customs (using the term in its ordinary, nontrade sense), and resources (natural and human) will affect trade flows among nations. Isolation of a single source of inequality must be ventured with care, lest some differences take on undue importance. In the extreme, equality can mean the elimination of all sources of comparative advantage, a basic source of gains from trade. A more modest goal than assuring complete equality must inform the effort to address unfair trade practices. Specification of that goal is essential to definition of equitable international competition and to recognition of acts that violate the terms of such competition.

Even the identification of a set of conditions that constitute the grounds for equitable competition, and bases for identifying deviation from them, cannot end our inquiry or we risk the mistake identified by the late Professor

George Stigler. Professor Stigler insistently queried with what confidence we know that the cure is not worse than the disease—that is, that we can depend on government to act with perspicacity, integrity, and effectiveness to correct known failures of the marketplace's invisible hand.[7] In remediating injustice that arises from foreign state action (or any other source), the realm of corrective government action has practical limitations imposed by government's capacity to act with efficiency and precision. Government failure can result from honest errors of fact determination and inference—leading government too often or too seldom (or in the wrong mix of cases) to conclude that an injury is properly attributable to an unfair foreign practice. Government failure can also occur through conversion of the governmental process from the public interest, in pursuing valid fairness claims, to the private interest, where the process becomes captured and corrupted into an expansive instrument to serve one group within society at the expense of the general public. Our inquiry into the operation of the dumping and countervailing duty laws will in passing touch on the *feasible* alternatives to living with some unfairness.

In discussing the antidumping and countervailing-duty laws, we evaluate the degree to which the laws are triggered by conduct that seems to conflict with the hypothetical state of equitable competition (in contrast to conduct that would, in a domestic context, be deemed consistent with such competition). We also discuss the degree to which the laws can be said to impose restrictions that promote equitable competition. First, however, we review the laws and their operation.

8.3   Antidumping and Countervailing-Duty Regulation: Concepts and Implementation

Antidumping and countervailing duty laws, although written and implemented at the national level, generally are governed by the General Agreement on Tariffs and Trade (GATT). Debate within the negotiating rounds that have shaped the current GATT accords reveals substantial differences in the way nations view antidumping and countervailing-duty regimes. Some nations' spokesmen have described them as essential protections against unfair trade practices, while others have characterized them as simple protectionism masquerading in fairness garb. Outside the negotiating rounds, argument about these laws has focused on the instances of more aggressive application of them by governments sympathetic to the fairness claims. In this Part, we discuss some basic aspects of antidumping and countervailing-duty law in the United States, one of the most enthusiastic supporters of these regimes.

8.3.1 The Evolution and Expansion of Dumping Policy in the United States

The Historical Roots of Dumping Regulation
U.S. prohibitions against foreign dumping have their roots in antitrust policy and its concern about predatory pricing. As traditionally viewed, predatory pricing occurs when a firm attempts to drive its rivals out of business through low prices, with the intention and expectation of re-couping the lost revenue this strategy occasions by then exploiting the resulting increase in market power created by the lessening of competi-tion.[8] Predation reduces national welfare through excess costs imposed on consumers after competitors leave the market.[9]

The Sherman Antitrust Act of 1890, the basic charter of U.S. antitrust doctrine, broadly proscribes practices, including predation, that unduly restrain competition, in particular focusing on anticompetitive activities coordinated among firms.[10] The Act does not limit its focus strictly to domestic activities, prohibiting "[e]very contract, combination in the form of trust or otherwise, or conspiracy, in restraint of trade or commerce among the several States, *or with foreign nations.*"[11] Judicial decisions, how-ever, limited the application of this provision to foreign producers, who could evade its strictures in several ways.[12] Antitrust concerns with for-eign producers also were reflected in Section 73 of the Wilson Tariff Act of 1894, which expressly applied to foreign conspiracies and combinations intended to restrain trade or to raise US import prices. Subsequent court rulings severely limited the scope of this Act as well.

The Antidumping Statutes
In the early 1900s, the United States enacted two laws directed at low-priced sales by foreign producers. Both of these laws—the Antidumping Law of 1916[13] and the Antidumping Act of 1921, carried forward as Title VII of the Tariff Act of 1930 (the Smoot-Hawley Tariff Act)[14]—remain in effect today. The evolution of this statutory duplication reveals much about the political process that has generated the antidumping and coun-tervailable subsidy regulation that prevails today.

In response to the apparent legal impotence of the earlier antitrust policies, the Antidumping Law of 1916 created a private civil cause of action in federal court for victims of predatory dumping and provided for treble damages. Despite this incentive, only two cases have ever been pursued under the statute because it requires that the plaintiff prove that the act occurred

with the intent of destroying or injuring an industry in the United States ... or of restraining or monopolizing any part of trade and commerce in such articles in the United States.[15]

The "intent" provision established clearly that the law was narrowly targeted against predatory conduct carried out through sales in the U.S. market at illegally low prices, but it also imposed a burden of proof on the plaintiff that was extraordinarily difficult to satisfy.

Adoption of the Antidumping Act of 1921, which did away with the intent requirement and created an administrative process for resolving and remedying dumping complaints, responded to congressional concern that the prior law's provision for judical scrutiny of intent posed so high a hurdle that meritorious suits had been deterred.[16] By eliminating the intent provision, the 1921 law allowed the determination of dumping to be based solely on mechanical evidence, based on price comparisons between products destined for sale in the foreign producer's home market and products destined for sale in the United States.[17]

Dumping, under the 1921 Act, is the sale of merchandise destined for sale in an export market at a price below normal or "fair" value. "Fair value" is principally defined by the price of the same type of merchandise destined for sale in the foreign producer's home market, although, as will become evident, the question of measuring fair value has grown in complexity and slipperiness over the years.

The 1921 Act was administered by the Treasury Department, which had responsibility for reaching two determinations: first, that the merchandise under investigation is being or is likely to be dumped and, second, that a U.S. industry is being or is likely to be injured, or is prevented from being established, by reason of the subject imports. Since the law's recodification in 1979, the Commerce Department has been responsible for measuring the dumping margin, and since 1954 the U.S. International Trade Commission has been responsible for the injury test.

Expanding the Scope of Proscribed Foreign Practices: Theory Follows Law
Under the 1921 law and its 1979 successor, an international price disparity constitutes unfair competition even if it arises for reasons unrelated to predation or predatory intent.[18] Such disparities occur in many circum-

stances. These include situations that look similar to those that can give rise to predatory pricing, but they also include situations in which there is no serious prospect for driving rivals from the market and recouping losses through monopoly pricing.

Although rigorous explanations for nonpredatory dumping were not developed at the time the 1921 law was crafted, it now is understood that when a foreign producer enjoys greater market power in its home market than in its U.S. export market, the producer's most profitable course is to charge a lower price for export sales than for home market sales. Such international price discrimination constitutes dumping under the U.S. law.

Unlike the traditional predation model, the disparity in market power between home and export markets need not reflect any advantage for the exporter. Thus, for example, a similar price discrimination will occur (and dumping will be found) when foreign producers engage in promotional pricing (or temporal loss-leadership) to introduce to the U.S. market a brand of an experience good with which U.S. customers are unacquainted. The disparity in this instance can be purely a function of the time at which a brand good is introduced into different markets. Temporal loss-leadership is a common business practice when seeking sales in new markets, especially in very competitive markets where monopolization is utterly improbable. A familiar example of promotional pricing is discounted introductory magazine subscriptions; an extreme form of promotional pricing is the distribution of free samples, far more common in highly competitive product markets (soaps, detergents, toothpaste, shampoo, and similar consumer goods) than in less competitive markets.

That the 1921 law's approach to evidence necessarily captured nonpredatory foreign pricing practices was an unavoidable consequence of simplifying and redirecting the evidentiary requirement. The expanded coverage lacked any direct, articulate policy rationale other than an implicit acceptance of errors in application as the price of making the law practically accessible to aggrieved U.S. industries.[19] Indeed, the fundamental lack of comprehension among economists (whose discipline it is to study market processes) about why dumping occurs precluded any detailed policy basis other than predation for the 1921 law.[20]

Predation, however, provides weak support for the law, because it is not a credible explanation for the great bulk of actions that are the subjects of investigation and subsequent antidumping orders. In part, this assertion is a claim about economic theory: Standard microeconomic theory has discounted the initial suppositions supporting the likelihood of predatory pricing, and predatory-pricing claims have been dismissed as inherently implausible given economic understanding of markets developed over the half century following adoption of the antidumping law.[21] As traditionally conceived, the necessary conditions for predatory pricing to occur are so restrictive as to be improbable. Sales at predatory prices must foreseeably result in exit from the industry by one's competitors, permit recoupment of foregone profits through exercise of subsequent market power, and not be undermined during the recoupment period by induced entry of new firms or reentry of former firms. Putting aside industries in which physical capital that is idled when firms exit dissipates and cannot easily be re-assembled, induced reentry ordinarily poses an insurmountable obstacle to successful predatory pricing of the bankrupting-rivals variety.

Even so, this part of the critique of predation cannot be taken as conclusively proven, given the recent revival of predation as a theoretical explanation of business practices.[22] Economic writings based in game theory indicate the possibility that companies might engage in predatory pricing under conditions different from, and probably more common than, those that economists historically regarded as essential. The conventional account of predation depends on asymmetric access to capital, which precludes competitors that must borrow at comparatively high interest rates from remaining in a profitable market made temporarily unprofitable by one firm's predatory pricing. The more recent innovations, attributable largely to the pioneering work of Paul Milgrom and J. D. Roberts, focus on the information content of prices.[23] Under conditions that have been investigated in the theoretical literature, competitors (or those who finance them) cannot distinguish fully between "low" prices that reflect predation and "low" prices that result from comparatively low marginal costs on the part of a single firm. Competitors subjected to predatory pricing (or those on whom they depend for financial backing) may accordingly conclude erroneously that the market will be permanently unprofitable and hence that exit from the industry is the most rational strategy. The rewards of this strategy for the predator are the same as in the conventional account, i.e., a more concentrated industry and higher consequent prices beginning at some future date.[24]

The evolution of economic theory on this score qualifies, but does not reverse, the claim that predation cannot provide a suitable theoretical predicate for the present antidumping law. There is a question whether the work done respecting predatory pricing in domestic markets can be applied without qualification in international markets. The Milgrom-Roberts model of predation has been applied explicitly to international dumping,[25] but it is not clear whether the same signaling effects are effective in international markets or whether, insofar as government policies play an important role in structuring international competition, the same incentives can be imputed to key decision makers as in domestic markets. More important, as discussed later in this chapter, few actual investigations involve circumstances that resemble those in which predatory pricing is a likely prospect under the new theories, much less the old.[26] Finally, predatory pricing is not only less likely to occur in international markets than economic theory projected when the 1921 Antidumping Law was passed, even where it might occur such pricing strategies would be extremely difficult to distinguish from merely competitive low pricing.[27]

Between enactment of the present antidumping framework and the recent revival of economic interest in predation, an alternative theoretical explanation for antidumping law was developed that provides support for casting the antidumping net beyond predation.[28] The ability to charge a higher price in a protected home market creates a profit sanctuary that may permit a foreign firm, especially one that is characterized by high fixed costs, to survive in the global industry with adverse effects on competitors who otherwise would have survived in place of the price-discriminating foreign firm or who otherwise would have enjoyed higher prices and sales.[29]

With the development of economic theory respecting industrial organization in the period leading up to the Second World War, economists' concerns about the unfairness of dumping no longer focused on monopoly pricing following dumping but instead on the effects of a divided market on competitors. Absent home market protection and subjected to the equitable forces of unimpeded comparative advantage, the foreign competitor would be out of business. Therefore, the reasoning goes, it is unfair to compel American firms to compete with such foreign firms charging prices below those they charge at home—high home prices sustain foreign firms that would not otherwise be competitive, and the American firms (whose home market is more competitive) have no similar opportunity to charge those prices anywhere.[30]

Administrative Expansion: Measuring the Margin of Dumping
Current antidumping regulation and its administration is an imperfect fit with even the broader complaint about dumping. Although there are some instances in which the administration of antidumping law is narrower than the justification for it would support, by and large the administration errs

in the direction of applying antidumping constraints to situations outside the explanation for antidumping enforcement or of applying more substantial constraints than are justified by that explanation.

This asymmetric misfit is most apparent in decisions of the U.S. Department of Commerce's International Trade Administration on the magnitude (or margin) of dumping. Numerous aspects of the calculation of dumping margins by the administering authorities—the Treasury Department through 1979 and the Commerce Department since—lead to more antidumping orders and greater duty or cash bond collections than would be justified by a calculation of pricing differences that responded more to ordinary economic and accounting concepts or by an administrative procedure that less frequently translated burdens for producing information into fact inferences that significantly, even dramatically, influence the conclusion.[31]

For example, the Trade Act of 1974 extended a provision of the Antidumping Act of 1921 that permitted the administering authorities to exclude home market sales at prices below the cost of production from the data set in calculating normal (or fair) value.[32] (Normal value is compared to the factory-gate price of merchandise destined for sale in the United States to determine the dumping margin.) Thus, in effect, normal value was required to exceed foreign production cost in all cases.

This provision is not necessarily divorced from all economic accounts of markets. It could be based on a simple textbook notion of how perfectly competitive markets operate. In the textbook version, competitive industries that are in competitive equilibrium are characterized by a price that just equals average production cost. Hence the statute's authors might have concluded that prices below average cost could not be "normal" and thus should not form any part of a basis for measuring the dumping margin.

If this explanation helped sway those not responding only to the political pressure to expand the exclusion of below-cost home market sales from the dumping calculation, it may be chalked up as another demonstration that a little knowledge is a dangerous thing. For purposes of pedagogic clarity, the textbook version of perfect competition is stripped down and abstracts from significant features of markets that often result in prices below cost. Virtually all industries are subject to variations in demand, for instance due to a business cycle, and thus charge "low" prices at times, offset by "high" prices at other times. This phenomenon is fully consistent with perfect competition. The only theoretic requirement to remain in business is that the price at all times cover *variable*—not average—total cost. Many firms—most notably "startup" firms—often fail to cover fully-loaded costs for an extended period of time. For startups, this time is necessary to acquire production experience and customer acceptance, following which the successful firms become profitable and unsuccessful firms become history.[33]

A second significant methodological quirk in the Commerce Department's calculation of dumping margins is the "zeroing out" of negative margins. Typically, in dumping investigations, the Commerce Department has compared individual export prices for merchandise destined for the United States to an average home market value, and then averages the resulting margins for each export sale. Negative margins that arose when the export price was *greater than* normal value, however, were set to zero before the grand average was taken. This method—which only now has been specifically proscribed for most purposes—is arithmetically guaranteed to report a positive dumping margin whenever prices exhibit some dispersion and the distributions of prices of merchandise destined for the exporter's home market and for the United States are *identical*, i.e., when, by any sensible definition, *no dumping is taking place*.[34]

These two components of the Commerce Department calculation combine to generate a dumping margin that approximately equals the standard deviation of the price distribution (when the two price distributions are identical). Thus, when the standard deviation is 10 percent, the reported dumping margin is also approximately 10 percent, even though the "true" dumping margin (common sense confirms) is zero.[35]

To illustrate, suppose a foreign producer makes three home market sales, at $9, $10, and $11 respectively, and three export sales to the United States at the identical prices. Anyone not sufficiently educated would readily conclude that no dumping is taking place. Suppose further that the average cost of production is $10. The Commerce Department will thus disregard the home market sale at $9 since it is below the cost of production. Consequently, normal value is $10.50, the average of the remaining two prices. Now the three dumping margins are $1.50, $0.50, and −$0.50. Expressed as a percentage of the export price to the United States in each case, the margins are about 16.7 percent, 5.0 percent, and −4.5 percent. By setting the negative margin to zero, the average margin is 7.2 percent—and this in an example contrived deliberately to correspond to a true margin of zero!

Three other significant departures from common economic and accounting treatments of pricing comparisons also should be noted. First, in instances where the exporter's home market is deemed not to be viable as an independent market for the exported product—that is, home market sales account for less than five percent of production—the Commerce Department will rely on sales to a principal third-country market. Typically, however, no third-country market proves satisfactory, and Commerce falls back on "constructed value" as a basis for calculating normal value. Constructed value is a measure of fully-loaded average cost. Roughly half of all cases are based on constructed value, rather than price-to-price comparisons. The use of constructed value provides numerous opportunities to assign costs to the production of the exported product that would not, in ordinary market conditions, be reflected in the product's price, would not be reflected in price during the period Commerce looks at to set the product's cost, or do not in fact exist as real costs of the particular product.

Second, the statutory requirement to include minimum markups for general expenses and profits in computing constructed value (only recently repealed) not only introduces another unidirectional bias into Commerce's calculations—it also is inconsistent with U.S. obligations under Article 2.4 of the *Antidumping Code*.[36] Until 1995, U.S. law required that general expenses equal a minimum of ten percent of direct production costs, and that profits equal a minimum of eight percent of the combined sum of general expenses and production costs.[37] Article 2.4 of the *Code*, however, requires that any amounts added for profits be limited generally to "the profit normally realized on sales of products of the same general category in the domestic market of the country of origin." From an economic perspective, such minimums simply increase normal value during times when demand is generally depressed and prices are low.[38]

Finally, the Exporter's Sales Price cap on indirect-selling-expense deductions in establishing the home market price also significantly distorts measured dumping margins in many investigations. In seeking to compare prices at the factory gate, the Commerce Department generally deducts forward expenses from prices observed both in the home market and in export transactions. When the U.S. importer is related to the exporter, however, Commerce begins with the first sale to an unrelated party in the United States.

Among the adjustments that must be made both to these prices and to home market prices is the subtraction of indirect selling expenses. With little statutory guidance, but with judicial approval, Commerce limits the amount deducted from the home market price to no more than the amount deducted from the forward U.S. price. As a result, in any situation where home market indirect selling expenses exceed U.S. expenses, the home market ex-factory price will be overstated, and the dumping margin will be artificially inflated.

Expansion, Inconsistency, and Discretion: Assessing Material Injury
Administrative practice that may be at odds with apparent legislative command has not led simply to a straightfoward expansion of the scope of antidumping law. It also has introduced inconsistencies into the law. While the legislation apparently grants a measure of discretion to administrative officials to implement the terms of antidumping law in the United States, there has been significant variation over time in the way that discretion has been exercised and at times its exercise has been difficult to square with any coherent rationale for the antidumping law.

This is most apparent in the application of the injury test at the U.S. International Trade Commission, which has six presidentially-appointed and Senatorially-confirmed members and which functions in a relatively judicial mode. Members of the Commission have not only differed in their assessment of fact and inference from record evidence, but have adopted mutually inconsistent modes of analysis, which have been tolerated by the reviewing courts to one extent or another.

The distinction is dramatic and radical between the unitary "but for" test of injury and the bifurcated "trends" test, each accepted by some members of the Commission. The two approaches ask different questions, analyze information by different means, and suggest different understandings of the nature of dumping and the nature of the inquiry legally entrusted to the Commission in antidumping investigations. The two approaches, indeed, are conceptually orthogonal and will arrive at the same conclusion about material injury in merely coincidental instances.[39]

The unitary approach asks how much better off the domestic industry would have been but for the dumping. This question is typically answered with the assistance of economic-model-based analysis that performs a comparative statistics experiment. The analysis compares the price, volume, and industry revenue with and without dumped imports in the market.[40] While this approach has been developed more rigorously over the past decade, its roots can be found—and its essential precepts were followed—in U.S. antidumping administration from the inception of the injury test to the early 1980s.[41]

The bifurcated approach developed in the early 1980s and came to dominate Commission decisions by the mid–1980s. The most common version of the bifurcated approach asks two sequential, threshold questions: (1) is the domestic industry that produces the like product unhealthy or in declining health, so as to be materially injured; and (2) if so, have imports contributed more than negligibly to this quantum of injury? By contrast, the unitary approach ascribes the requisite material injury directly to the foreign unfair act by answering whether the domestic industry would be materially better off absent the foreign unfair trade practice.

A hybrid approach has been fashioned that attempts some synthesis of the trends and "but for" approaches by first assessing the industry's vulnerability to injury based on its overall health. A healthier industry is less subject to injury or, equivalently, requires a greater adverse impact to constitute the same magnitude of injury as would a less healthy industry. The central question in the hybrid approach is the same as in the unitary approach.

Both underlying approaches are founded on the statutory command that the Commission must find that a U.S. industry "is materially injured ... by reason of imports of that merchandise"[42]—referring to the "merchandise [that the Commerce department has determined] is being ... sold in the United States at less than its fair value."[43] A central issue in interpreting this language is whether the injury referred to in the statute is that done by *all* imports of the class or kind under investigation (in the sense of determining what harm all of those imports have done or how much better off the industry would be but for all of the imports) or, instead, if the injury to be analyzed is harm from the subject imports only in so far as they are sold at unfairly low prices (that is, harm from the unfair pricing). The bifurcated approach takes the former tack; unitary analysis generally takes the latter approach.

The bifurcated approach is predicated, in part, on the assertion that a valid unitary analysis is not practicable, particularly within the statutory time frame for completing an injury investigation and reaching a determination. Prior to the mid- to late 1980s, unitary analysis generally employed a "subtraction" methodology that accounted for the effects of all factors *other than* the dumped imports under investigation. The conclusion was that any residual "effect" must then be attributable to unfair import sales. This methodology is open to serious question, and faces considerable practical difficulties, given the factual record that is before the Commission.

Statistical tools such as regression analysis provide the means for coping with such problems in other settings where causation is an issue and many factors might contribute to the observable outcome. These tools have not been used by the Commission in antidumping investigations, perhaps because the data available to the Commission give insufficient degrees of freedom for meaningful deployment of such tools.[44]

Over the past decade, however, better economic methods for dealing with the causation problem in the presence of sparse data have been developed and implemented at the Commission. These allow the Commission to conduct economic comparative statistics analyses that (on a simulated basis) can isolate the adverse impact of dumping. Partially as a result of these innovations, an increasing number of Commissioners again have been receptive to the unitary approach in recent years.

While those who take analysis of trade issues seriously should applaud the improvement in Commission methodology, the relation of available analytical methods to actual Commission decisions presents more questions than it answers. Development of analytical tools designed specifically for the Commission's producer-injury-from-dumping inquiry may be recent, but similar analyses have been performed with much greater economic sophistication in other legal proceedings for many years.[45] Commentators have offered sharply differing views of the reasons such analysis largely has been eschewed in administration of the antidumping laws.[46]

What's Good for the Goose: The Lack of Symmetry between Domestic and International Price Regulation

Antidumping law's antipathy to international price discrimination finds no exact parallel in U.S. law respecting purely domestic business practices, although there is a restriction in antitrust law on some price discrimination. The 1936 Robinson-Patman Act, which amended the Clayton Act, constrains price discrimination within the United States. Robinson-Patman prohibits price discrimination whenever the effect

> may be substantially to lessen competition or tend to create a monopoly in any line of commerce, or to injure, destroy, or prevent competition with any person who either grants or knowingly receives the benefit of such discrimination, or with customers of either of them.[47]

This law dates from the time when economists began generally to view antidumping law as a constraint less on traditional predation than on price discrimination.

Robinson-Patman has been controversial, both as to its advisability and as to its effect. The law's critics contend that it inhibits much desirable business activity, even though over time judicial interpretation has limited its application to a narrower range of practices than it covered in its heyday and a considerably narrower range than the antidumping law.[48]

The essential problem for implementation of Robinson-Patman—the reason that critics object to it, that businessmen are concerned about it, and that its protagonists struggle to articulate clear tests for its application—is that price discrimination is a common and profitable business practice.

Price discrimination occurs in numerous domestic contexts. Promotional discounts are often offered in one part of the country (where a product is not well established) but not in another part of the country (where it is). Hotels charge different prices for the same room to different customers. Almost all of us encounter some form of price discrimination every day. Senior citizen discounts are a typical (now almost ubiquitous) example. Price discrimination is not confined to businesses that do not trade in international commerce. Indeed, in a recent antidumping investigation, *Aramid Fibers from the Netherlands*,[49] the U.S. petitioner, DuPont, alleged that dumping by Akzo *undermined* DuPont's ability to successfully "value price" in the United States—that is, to price discriminate among customers and thereby earn greater profits.

Why then does antidumping law, especially as applied, so sweepingly condemn price discrimination? Perhaps the common domestic practice of selling at different prices can be distinguished from international price discrimination. Some commentators have contended that differences between the conditions of domestic and international commerce may justify superficially different policies regarding price discrimination.[50] According to this argument, the lack of protected markets within the United States, assured by the Interstate Commerce Clause, obviates one of the key predicates to unfairness that underlies antidumping regulation in international trade. That argument, however, gains force only if the existence of protected markets is objectionable. We examine that proposition in Section 8.4.

8.3.2 The Regulation of Countervailable Subsidies

Development of U.S. Countervailing-Duty Law
The United States first enacted countervailing-duty legislation, targeted at imports of certain grades of subsidized sugar, in the U.S. Tariff Act of 1890. This legislation was followed by general provisions to countervail subsidized imports in the U.S. Tariff Acts of 1897, 1909, and 1913. The countervailing-duty provisions of these Acts were superseded by Section 303 of the Fordney-McCumber Tariff Act of 1922, which subsequently became Section 303 of the Tariff Act of 1930.[51] Only dutiable imports were subject to countervailing duties under these early enactments, the last of which (Section 303 of the Tariff Act of 1930) continued until 1995 to govern cases involving dutiable imports from nations that have not acceded to GATT's Subsidies Code.

Unlike the dumping laws, for many years there was no inquiry into the effect of a subsidy on U.S. industries prior to issuing countervailing-duty orders. Although there presently is an injury test in countervailing-duty cases involving imports from other GATT signatories (or imports that would have been duty-free), this test dates only from the 1974 Trade Act, when Congress expanded countervailing-duty law to allow imposition of duties on imports that were otherwise nondutiable (subject to a zero tariff rate).[52] GATT since 1947 has required an injury test in countervailing duty-cases generally, but the U.S. had obtained "grandfather" rights waiving that GATT requirement for imposing countervailing duties on dutiable imports.

Of Geese Again: Distinguishing Domestic Law
Also unlike the dumping laws, which had their origins in domestic anti-trust principles, the regulation of subsidized foreign merchandise has no domestic analogue. The Interstate Commerce Clause of the United States Constitution, which has been interpreted to prevent a variety of impediments to trade among the states, has been read as preventing the imposition of "tariffs" on sales of goods that receive subsidies from other states.[53] States and localities often subsidize industry, competing with tax abatements and other incentives to attract or retain particular businesses or, at times, particular industries. The political controversy over such state and local subsidies almost invariably is whether the price paid in a given case was too high, rather than whether a neighboring jurisdiction's subsidy should be offset.[54]

This asymmetry may well be validated, in part, by the general desire of domestic industry to encourage, rather than discourage, internal "subsidy wars" among subnational jurisdictions.[55] But both the asymmetry and the explanation for the domestic rule call into question the basis for regulation of subsidies in international trade. Neither the interests of domestic industry nor the welfare-reducing effects of subsidy wars would seem readily to distinguish the international and intranational contexts.

Core and Other Cases: Fitting Right with Remedy
The core of international subsidy concerns, however, addresses a subsidy that is deployed in international trade but not, to our knowledge, in intranational trade. The core case for countervailable subsidies—from the standpoint of economic theory, international agreement, or national law—is a subsidy, not for *locating* production in a given jurisdiction, but for *exporting* products from that jurisdiction. Export subsidies directly expand

sales and (except where the export market is perfectly competitive for the exported good) reduce the internal price of the imported product in the importing country.[56] Principally this follows from diverting sales of the subsidized product from other markets (commonly, the home market, but if an export subsidy applies to only selected export markets there will be diversion from other markets as well). That is why export subsidies are particularly troubling, whether the concern is safeguarding domestic markets that are efficient or insulating markets that are protected against the rigors of competition. The three different vantages of economics, international accord, and national legislation diverge in several respects, but they begin with the same central focus. For national law, one additional qualifier should be added in defining the core case: The export subsidy that is of special concern is one that effectively lowers prices on goods destined for *that* nation. For U.S. law, the prime concern (playing a role similar to predatory price-cutting for antidumping law) is an export subsidy targeted on merchandise destined for sale in the United States.

Both GATT and current U.S. law extend well beyond this core case, although both the fact of the extension and the exact boundaries of it are matters of controversy. Prior to 1974, the language of U.S. countervailing-duty law spoke not of "subsidies" but of goods that had received a "bounty or grant" from a foreign government. This language is retained in Section 303 of the Tariff Act of 1930. The term "subsidy" in Title VII of the Trade Act of 1974 is meant to be equivalent. But what does that include? The GATT defines countervailable subsidies to include any industry-specific "financial contribution by a government or any public body" or "any form of income or price support" that confer a benefit.[57] The United States, with GATT confirmation (prior to recent changes following the Uruguay Round), interpreted this to cover not only export subsidies but also general production subsidies to an industry, subsidies to production inputs, and even to inducements to locate in particular regions.[58]

Charles Goetz, Lloyd Granet, and Warren Schwartz have observed that the extension of countervailing-duty law to subsidies other than direct export subsidies transforms an entitlement to relief from harm when subsidies directly affect U.S. producers into a statute that looks as if its goal is deterring foreign governments from conferring subsidies on particular industries, regardless of their effect on U.S. national welfare or even on our producers' welfare.[59] Professor Richard Diamond has joined this critique of U.S. law as applied, urging an interpretation of the law that largely would avoid that problem.[60] Other commentators have disagreed with Professor Diamond on the interpretive question, although concurring in the desirability of an interpretation that would increase the coherence of U.S. trade subsidy law.[61] Judicial and administrative decisions have left Diamond's interpretation in the rough. Hence in addressing the fairness issues in countervailing-duty law below we treat the current, more expansive version of subsidy regulation.

In addition to satisfying the definition of countervailable subsidy, under both GATT and applicable U.S. law it must be shown that the subsidized imports, through the trade effects of the subsidy, also injure a domestic industry. The injury determination for countervailing-duty cases is similar to that under antidumping law, but there is a complication. The injury from the subsidy is more difficult to determine in many cases, as the subsidy's effect on export prices and volumes will be mediated through, and to some extent diffused by, other economic factors.

Another complication for countervailing-duty law involves calculation of the duty. The GATT 1994 *Subsidies Code* states that

[i]t is desirable ... that the duty should be less than the total amount of the subsidy if such lesser duty would be adequate to remove the injury to the domestic industry....[62]

Notwithstanding this provision, U.S. law *requires* that each countervailing duty be set equal to the subsidy determined by the investigation, which equals the average benefit to the recipient firm.[63]

It is difficult to line up economic arguments with the U.S. law's treatment of the calculation of countervailing-duty rates. A duty that would eliminate the effects of any identified subsidy on external markets typically would be considerably less than the magnitude of the subsidy as reflected in the rate of subsidization calculated by the U.S. Commerce Department (or comparable administrative agencies in other nations).

Consider, for example, production subsidies (which commonly are at issue in countervailing-duty investigations). A production subsidy may affect the proportion of different factors used in production; it may affect the returns to factors of production; and it may affect the volumes and prices of goods produced. Considerable information must be known to calculate the actual effects of a production subsidy, including the production function of the firms receiving the subsidy and the elasticities of demand for the markets in which those firms sell. Commonly, the production subsidy results both in higher returns to producers and lower prices to consumers, but any calculation of a subsidy rate will include *both* effects and will exceed the proportional change in either producers' gains or consumers' gains. Further, not all of the gains to consumers will be in export markets. The degree to which an increase in the volume of production changes the volume of exports depends on the relative elasticities of demand in the domestic market and export markets, and the change for any given nation depends on the relative demand elasticities of that and other foreign markets. These elasticities are not often known, but it is plain that export supply is much more elastic than production supply, so that a production subsidy's effects will, more than an export subsidy's, be reflected in changes within the home market rather than in changes in export markets. If production subsidies are countervailed because, like export subsidies, they *can* have effects within the export market, the duty rate should reflect the difference in the magnitude of those effects. Although the current U.S. law does not reflect this difference, a smaller export subsidy will produce the same consumer price effect in the export market as a larger production subsidy.[64]

In this section, we examine the arguments respecting the unfairness of practices that lie at the core of antidumping and countervailing-duty laws. The discussion begins with more general issues, proceeds with arguments about dumping, then subsidies, and concludes with analysis of arguments to extend the dumping and subsidy regimes to claims respecting environmental, safety, and labor regulation.

In the United States, even more than with antidumping law, the administrative calculations of subsidy margins and consequent injury seem built on questionable economics and even more questionable statistics. International trading partners have been skeptical of the degree to which application of countervailing-duty law is free of political influence, and have called for modification of the U.S. process in recent negotiations of bilateral, regional, and multilateral accords. The U.S.-Canada Free Trade Agreement and the North American Free Trade Agreement both provide for further attention to the definition and calculation of countervailable subsidies, and the GATT accord from the Uruguay Round restricts the definition of subsidies in several respects.[65] We return below to the predicate for antisubsidy and antidumping laws and the reasons for concern about them.

8.4 Equitable Competition as the Predicate for Antidumping and Countervailing-Duty Law

8.4.1 Unfair Trade Practices, Efficiency, and Competition

The evolution and expansion of antidumping law and countervailing-duty law obscures the analytical basis for those laws. Each began with objections to practices that altered the competition among producers of goods exchanged in international commerce. The objections—to predatory pricing and to export subsidies—focused on both the nature of the practices and their effects. Both practices allow one competitor access to a special advantage that does not depend on skill, hard work, or natural resources. Both allow that competitor to use the advantage to reduce the price of exports to the detriment of producers in the export market.

The expansion of antidumping law to nonpredatory price discrimination and of countervailing-duty law to industry-specific nonexport subsidies moves away from these core cases. These changes might reflect determination that practices cognate to the core cases of predation and export subsidies are similar in nature and effect and thus should be assimilated to the core cases. Or the changes in the law might respond to administrative interests—if the difficulty of separating the additional practices from the core practices is great and the harm from false negatives exceeds the harm from false positives, it would be beneficial to treat the additional practices as if they were the same as the core practices even if they are analytically distinct. Or the changes might flow from political considerations that do not fit any accessible explanation of public interests.

Although it is not our focus in this paper to select among these competing applications, we note that the inquiry we engage in will, necessarily, shed some light on this issue. The choice among these explanations depends on more precise identification of the initial problem perceived with predation and export subsidies. What was the competitive environment that was altered by these practices and what makes the alteration—the introduction of these particular sources of advantage—unfair? Put differently, what is the fair state of play in international commerce, the state of equitable international competition?

At the outset of this inquiry, we must put one argument aside: the cosmopolitan argument for global efficiency. That argument—that the proper goal is maximum efficiency gains worldwide, optimizing global productive resources, and ignoring national boundaries—is an important one. It is offered at times by both economists and noneconomists as a basis for international trade rules. Jagdish Bhagwati, noted trade economist, proposes it as the best normative standard for trade rules.[66] Politicians often assert that trade practices (or, more accurately, particular, selected trade practices) in conflict with that standard should be restrained. Specifically, both predatory pricing and provision of export subsidies have been criticized as efficiency-reducing. The argument also resonates to the same pitch as many arguments built on the notion of equitable competition.

However beneficial its acceptance would be for world welfare and for the welfare of citizens in most nations, the cosmopolitan argument should be put aside as different from the fairness claims we examine here. The desideratum of global efficiency, although invoked in support of fairness claims, does not seem a likely candidate to explain trade laws or to serve even imperfectly as the principle that guides them. As Professor Bhagwati recognizes, the cosmopolitan argument is a useful heuristic, but not what guides policy decisions.[67] It is a commonplace of political science writings that policy makers are motivated by personal interests, not by concern for analytical constructs such as global welfare. But that is not our point. Thoughtful examination of policy decisions gives some scope to analytical arguments about the welfare effects of policy choices, even if only at the margin of political decision making or as a consequence of the benefits of public-interest explanations. However, the arguments that have force in shaping national decisions, so far as analytical arguments can hold sway in a political arena, are predominantly arguments about *national* welfare, not *global* welfare.

The assertion that a given trade practice reduces global efficiency typically mischaracterizes the argument for restriction of the practice. Efficiency implications of trade practices may be a source of useful information, and we will refer to them below, but they are not the direct focus of policy making. The inquiry into the nature of equitable competition, which forms the predicate for constraints on dumping and subsidies, is not simply an inquiry into the sources of global efficiency. It is an inquiry into the basis for asserting that a particular *competitive* practice is or is not fair. We must look to the nature of the competition among producers for the complaint being made.

8.4.2 Dumping and Equitable Competition

In examining the claims that dumping derogates unfairly from conditions of equitable competition, we address two different classes of arguments. First, we consider arguments against predatory pricing to see how far they might support fairness challenges to dumping. Second, we take arguments directed against nonpredatory international price discrimination. Some arguments against price discrimination will be found to turn on the same analytical predicates (for instance, the unfairness of differential access to capital) as arguments against predatory dumping. As we explore these arguments, we endeavor to parse the claims sufficiently to identify the major strands of each complaint.

Predatory Pricing

The Consumers'-Welfare-Loss Argument Predatory pricing, the initial concern of antidumping laws as well as a concern of antitrust laws, can be
examined from the standpoint of consumers or producers. American antitrust literature, led in large measure by the work of Robert Bork, Richard
Posner, and other law professors familiar with economic analysis, has
looked increasingly from the consumers' vantage, a perspective congruent
with allocative efficiency.[68] From this perspective, predatory pricing is
a legitimate, but unlikely, concern. Consumers are injured if a producer
creates a sustainable and exploitable monopoly by pricing goods low
enough to drive other producers out of the market.

Consumers do not object to the low prices charged during the period a
predator is driving rivals from the market. Quite the contrary, that is the
good news to consumers. Their objection is to the subsequent period of
high, monopoly prices. Consumers actually object to two aspects of monopoly. High prices transfer value from consumers to the monopoly producer. And, to support a high price, the profit-seeking monopolist will
limit production and will not produce some goods that consumers value
more than their cost of production. It is the latter objection that is most
troublesome from an efficiency standpoint, as it leads to a loss of social
value, the equivalent of a decline in everyone's standard of living.[69]

Because it is the monopoly and not the price-cutting that is objectionable from the consumer's standpoint, antitrust analysis has devoted
considerable energy to consideration of the circumstances under which
price-cutting can be expected to lead to a monopoly of the sort that will
injure consumers. (The qualifying characteristics of sustainability and ex-
ploitability reflect the fact that not every "monopoly" in fact can be made
to yield monopoly profits, an important observation for antitrust enforcement, but one that need not detain us here.) As Bork and others have
pointed out, predatory price-cutting is an unlikely strategy for securing
monopoly.[70] Price wars may occur in the course of competition among
firms with high fixed investment—witness the recent movements of
U.S. passenger airline fares—but price-cutting is not apt to be a profit-
maximizing method for securing a monopoly. Empirical work by Ken
Elzinga, John McGee, and other scholars who have examined cases in
which predatory price-cutting reputedly occurred confirms that its reputation far exceeds the reality.[71] This should not be taken as the pat
assertion that such price-cutting never occurs (an assertion that may be
likened to the joke about the economist who, when his companion said,

"Look, there's a $20 bill on the street," did not even pause to look, declaring, "There can't be; if there were, someone would have picked it up already!"), but merely that it is sufficiently improbable to be worth relatively little investment in combatting it. That is a basis for skepticism that antidumping law, a major component of trade policy, was erected to protect consumers from this risk.

As discussed earlier, the work skeptical of predation has been challenged by new theoretical writings by economists conversant with game theory and other tools of dynamic analysis.[72] These writings suggest ways other than driving rivals from the market through sustained below-cost pricing to affect rivals though predatory price-cutting, posit reasons that firms might engage in predatory price-cutting in the absence of a prospect for monopoly recoupment, and also explore possible harm to consumers (higher prices, reduced product choice, slower development of innovations) that can occur while the market is occupied by a number of competitors. Like the critiques of predation analysis, the new writings have garnered some empirical support.[73] But there is little evidence of a fit between the conditions necessary for predation under any theory and the conditions that obtain in cases of alleged dumping.[74] And there is especially little evidence of the sort of consumer harms that are hypothesized in the new theoretical writings.[75]

The Capital-Access Argument against Predatory Pricing   From the producer's vantage, however, the matter is different. For producers, predatory price-cutting is not objectionable because it leads to a misallocation of resources. It is objectionable instead because it allows a producer with access to a suspect advantage to injure other producers. For producers, it is the low-cost sales and their immediate consequences, not what happens afterward, that is important.

Low-cost sales, however, do not give rise to a legal or moral claim except when they are made possible by a suspect (unfair) advantage enjoyed by the cost-cutting competitor. The suspect advantage in predation is a sufficient stock of capital to sustain losses from below-cost sales, "sufficient" meaning only that it is very much larger than the stock of similarly priced capital accessible to competitors[76]—this does not mean that the capital is best used, or even sensibly used, for predation. Producers often fear the prospect of competing with better financed rivals, and the existence of rivals who *could* lose large sums of money without dissolving has at times been viewed with alarm. If that fact alone is not troublesome in an era that has seen General Motors post billion-dollar losses and IBM humbled by aggressive price competition from smaller upstarts, it is not coincidence that an antidumping regime was enacted in the United States at the same time as constraints on various practices of domestic "trusts." The large stock of capital that a trust could access was viewed with suspicion wholly apart from the source of the funds that went into the trust's account or the efficiency of the trust form of business.[77]

The producers' argument against predation, however, is an *ipse dixit* unless something else is added. Why is it *unfair* for one competitor to have more money than another or, more accurately, to have access to more money? Certainly, wealthier competitors often have lost to less wealthy competitors. The argument becomes especially problematic when well-functioning capital markets exist. Although the capital markets may be far from perfectly efficient,[78] they provide ample opportunity for many relatively small competitors, with modest personal or institutional stocks of wealth, to access much larger amounts of capital to finance promising commercial ventures. Moreover, antidumping never has been cast as a constraint only against price-cutting from competitors with access to richer, more extensive, or better-functioning capital markets. That is a particularly unlikely direction for U.S. antidumping law to take.

The producers' fairness argument against predatory price-cutting must take one of two possible turns. Either it can invoke the affront that predation gives to efficiency as its support or it can claim an entitlement for producers to a competitive equality that is violated by predatory price-cutting.

The Producers' Efficiency Argument against Predatory Pricing   Despite the inefficiency associated with predation, the efficiency argument will be weak if it depends on the social costs of price-cutting—as Bork observes, these seldom appear to be significant and are likely to be dominated by the gains to consumers from encouraging vigorous price competition generally.[79] If the argument is amended to suggest that the fairness problem lies in asking producers to compete against rivals who can afford to deploy inefficient competitive strategies, it must explain why producers in effect should be granted an entitlement to compete only in a world where rivals are limited to efficient strategies. The efficiency argument here merges with the more direct entitlement argument.

The Entitlement Argument against Predatory Pricing   The entitlement argument might rest on a claim that producers have committed resources to a productive enterprise in the expectation that they would be competing only with rivals whose prices would reflect their costs.[80] The argument also must claim that the producers' commitment of resources merits protection against price-cutting that violates that expectation. In many circumstances, society recognizes property rights and affords protection against their infringement. States can supersede private property rights for certain public purposes, but the United States Constitution guarantees just compensation for such "takings."[81] These protections are supported by claims of efficiency as well as justice.[82] The contours of these protections, however, are seriously debated, and many expectations are better protected by means other than legal entitlements.[83]

If the entitlement claim does rest on producers' expectations, there should be attention to two aspects of producers' behavior that seldom are scrutinized and, while subsumed in some analyses of the effects of dumping, certainly are not specifically highlighted in antidumping law. These are the nature and timing of producers' investments. If producers invest in specialized resources—including workers' investments in specialized human capital—those investments can be devalued by changes in the market for their products. Resources that readily can be turned to other uses, however, would need less protection. In addition, if the entitlement protects the producers' expectations, only those investments made before the unexpected change occurred would merit protection. Inattention to both of these matters suggests that the fairness claim against predatory price-cutting must rest less on the expectations of competing producers than on a more absolute entitlement to conditions for equitable competition.

Desperately Seeking Equity Thus far, inquiry into the argument for constraining predatory dumping reveals no clear description of the conditions of equitable competition. Predatory price-cutting that leads to monopoly is objectionable both because it reduces allocative efficiency and because it injures competing producers. But neither objection provides a suitable explanation for the antidumping law, even in its original form. We turn next to the constraint on price discrimination, which provides the present basis for antidumping law (although, as noted earlier, the analytical case against price discrimination *followed* adoption of the U.S. antidumping law directed against price discrimination, the law being initially justified as a more easily administered restraint of predatory price-cutting).

Price Discrimination
The turn from predation to price discrimination looks at first blush to respond to the same concerns that underlie constraints on predatory price-

cutting. That, indeed, was also the express understanding for adoption of the United States' version of antidumping law based on price discrimination.[84] Cutting prices in export markets was portrayed as a strategy designed to produce a monopoly, and the difference in price between a foreign producer's home market and the producer's exports to the United States was thought to be sufficient evidence of predatory intent to obviate the need for other evidence.[85]

The Capital-Access Argument Redux: Financing Business and Less Competitive Markets   Hence, not surprisingly, the arguments against international price discrimination often track those against predatory dumping. There is, however, a set of arguments about nonpredatory price discrimination that is analytically distinct from claims against predatory dumping. The linchpin of these arguments is the asserted unfairness of an asymmetry in finances between the exporter and domestic producers of closely competing products.[86]

The relation among price discrimination, capital access, and equitable competition usually is presented in the following manner. The exporter by hypothesis (and at times only by hypothesis) enjoys a protected home market and some degree of market power there. That market power, it is assumed, translates into earnings above the competitive norm, providing a source of financing for aggressive price competition to facilitate expansion in the export market. The protected home market most often exists as a consequence of government restrictions on competition, including (but not necessarily limited to) import competition. Because this source of unusual earnings does not flow from production efficiencies, product innovation, or other efficiency-related factors, it is assertedly not a fair source of competitive advantage. The foreign producer does not benefit from mere luck; the foreign producer benefits from something that seems *wrong*—the restriction of competition in the home market. This is the basic capital-access argument against international price discrimination.

There are three problems with this argument. We address these problems in this and the following sections.

First, as with the assertion of unfairness to producers from predatory price-cutting, the assumption that the protected home market yields wealth that can support price-cutting in the export market leaps from the observation of one source of income to an assumption about relative wealth and, even more problematic, relative access to financial support. There is no necessary correlation between a single source of income and wealth; the domestic competitor could be far wealthier than the exporter, notwithstanding the exporter's protected market. This frequently is the case when petitions are filed for relief under U.S. antidumping law.[87] Certainly, there is no necessary correlation between income from a protected market and *access* to capital. It may be more costly for the foreign firm to use retained earnings to finance exports than for the domestic competitor to borrow funds—or it may be less costly or equally costly.

The existence of the foreign protected market does not answer the question. Although retained earnings often are the preferred (least costly) source of financing for firms, that tells us only what the costs of capital tend to be relative to other sources *in that market*.[88] It is true that capital is mobile and that there is a global capital market. But there *are* impediments to capital movement, and the real cost of capital differs for firms in different nations. The existence of the protected foreign market does not automatically create a larger pool of accessible capital for the exporting firm than for its domestic competitor or a pool of capital that is less costly than that available to the domestic competitors.

The Capital-Access Argument Continued: Firm Incentives and Price Discrimination   This brings us to the second, and more important, problem with the capital-access argument against international price discrimination: the fact that a protected foreign market exists does not explain *why* the foreign firm would choose to invest funds in expansion into the more competitive export market, where the return on investment must be lower than in the home market, much less why it would seek at the same time to *depress* prices in the export market through vigorous (nonpredatory) price-cutting.[89] For nonpredatory price discrimination, this behavior would seem particularly odd, as it lowers returns in the export market without the prospect of above-normal returns in subsequent periods.

That puzzle can be solved. The foreign firm faces different demand in the two, separated markets and seeks to maximize returns (over some period) in each market. In most circumstances, the firm would maximize returns by charging a higher price in the market where it faces less elastic demand for its product and a lower price in the market where the firm faces more elastic demand.[90] In common parlance, that is charging "what the market will bear" both at home and abroad. In separated markets, greater total returns are earned by expanding sales at lower—but still above cost—prices in an export market while maintaining returns above the competitive norm by charging prices in the home market that reflect the firm's market power there.[91]

But this solution to the *why* of price discrimination shows that the problem is *not* the existence of wealth that supports price-cutting that otherwise would be unprofitable. Rather, the problem is the existence of separated markets with different demand for a particular product, which leads naturally to differences in the product's price in each market. The differences in price need not be the product of any nefarious act. Such differences may reflect different tastes. The French have a greater affinity for organ meats (animal, not musical) than Americans and pay higher prices for them. Koreans prize Spam ® (for reasons we cannot plumb) and pay higher prices for it than Americans, or anyone else so far as we know.

Perhaps, to exclude cases such as these, the unfairness claim (although not the law) can be recast as a complaint only about demand differences that follow from intentional restrictions of competition in the exporter's home market. That may elide this difficulty with the unfairness complaint against nonpredatory price discrimination. However, it brings us quickly to the third problem with the unfairness argument premised on differences in the competitiveness of the home and export markets.

The Capital-Access Argument Continued Again: The Equity of Less Competitive Markets   The third problem with the capital-access argument against international price discrimination inheres in the argument's assumption that the difference in competitiveness of the home market (from the export market) necessarily is wrong. Certainly, the assumption is correct if two qualifying propositions are accepted: first, that the basis for judgment is global efficiency; second, that the short-term inefficiency of market restrictions always dominates any long-term efficiencies that might result. If these propositions are not accepted, the unfairness of differences in the degree to which markets are open to competition becomes problematic. Why is it unfair *from the perspective of the United States*[92] for, say, Korea or Brazil or Slovakia to have a less open market than the United States?

Clearly, the degree to which a market is open to competition, from internal as well as external sources, will affect the prices, quality, and quantities of goods available in that market. It also will affect the division of returns in an industry between domestic and foreign firms, although only the effect on division of returns in the individual market and not global returns to domestic and foreign firms can be predicted from the degree of domestic restriction, and, except in extreme cases, even this prediction will hold strictly for the short term. Further, the *intra*industry effects of a restriction on competition (such as a trade restriction) largely will be transmitted through labor and capital markets—and at times through the market for goods—into *inter*industry effects that have a different sign. A gain for the restricting economy in one industry will impose costs on that economy in other industries. Think of computer screens or semiconductors as examples of goods with upstream protection for which computer manufacturers downstream bear the costs.

The fairness complaint necessarily casts the different choices that societies have made respecting competition in moral terms. Moreover, there is a peculiar twist to the morality. It is not wrong *per se* to restrict competition in ways that derogate from global efficiency. Instead, it is wrong to restrict competition more than *we* (in the export market) do. That judgment assumes that the decision of the society that is making the judgment on dumping at least has a position on competition that is morally superior to the decision of the exporting nation. But what makes it superior? Is the logical extension of the argument that there should be one standard worldwide, set by the government that is least restrictive of trade in the particular good at issue? (Hong Kong's citizens might, at least at present, embrace that position.) That would be consistent with at least a modified cosmopolitan standard, embracing global efficiency as the goal. Yet it would be quite difficult to square with current antidumping law, which can be applied by nations that are quite restrictive of trade.[93] It also would call into question a great variety of current government actions around the world, indeed in every nation, that inhibit competition. It is doubtful that most of the vigorous advocates of vigilant antidumping regimes would embrace that position.

If the fact of differential openness to competition is not wrongful, as an offense to global efficiency or otherwise, the sale of products at lower prices in export markets cannot be condemned out of hand on efficiency grounds. International price discrimination may lead to greater economic efficiency in the foreign market by permitting foreign industries to achieve scale economies in production—that is, to expand production closer to the volume that corresponds to marginal social cost. Declining-cost industries tend to exploit market power in some manner to fund fixed costs. By funding fixed costs dominantly through higher prices in one's home market, while selling at lower prices that better approximate marginal social costs in export markets, greater economic efficiency is achieved for the firm.[94]

Summary: Price Discrimination, Efficiency, and Harmonization   At bottom, the fairness complaint against dumping qua price discrimination looks either like a pseudo-efficiency argument or a call for all nations to harmonize rules on competition (including trade) at the level set by the nation seeking antidumping protection. The efficiency argument looks too weak and partial to be credited. And the harmonization plea lacks an obvious supporting rationale. It is possible, of course, that some fairness principle is inchoate in international agreements on trade, a principle that, while inarticulate, comports with widely shared intuitions. But that would not support a mandate for harmonization of nations' competition policies. The GATT framework that legitimizes international application of antidumping constraints plainly does not embrace harmonization of restrictions on trade or competition (as opposed to harmonization of *rules*) as a principle. GATT, after all, permits wide variation in the degree of openness to trade in any particular product or in all products by GATT signatories. Tariffs, for instance, can and do differ greatly, both average effective tariff levels for particular nations and tariff levels for individual goods. We hold open for now the question whether some other factor can support the fairness complaint against dumping.

8.4.3 Subsidies and Equitable Competition

The fairness problem in countervailing-duty law is at once simpler and more difficult than in the antidumping context. The call for countervailing duties rests on the notion that a foreign government has acted unfairly in attempting to advantage a set of producers within the foreign nation at the expense of producers in the importing nation. But most strong supporters of countervailing duties in the importing nation would reject the claim that they have a general right to insist that all nations in the world adopt the same economic and social policies as the importing nation. Unfortunately, these two widely shared intuitions—that we are not entitled to choose other nation's policies that affect their employment, industry profits, and trade *but* that it is unfair for another nation to export unemployment, low profits, or other economic or social problems to us— are contradictory.

To examine this contradiction, we begin with a hypothetical situation that illustrates the problem of identifying a subsidy. The following section takes that hypothetical situation as the basis for exploring the *externalization* problem, a necessary step in establishing the claim that bad economic effects have been exported from one nation to another. Next we turn to the fairness claim itself—why externalized effects of a given government policy might be unfair. Finally, we ask what these inquiries suggest about the nature of equitable competition.

Subsidies and Alternative Government Policies: Steeling Ourselves
for the Equity Inquiry

The following example can be used to illustrate the intractability of the fairness claim against subsidies. There is a worldwide decline in demand for, say, steel. The German government determines that the social situation in Germany is too fragile to risk high unemployment among steelworkers, who form a relatively militant (and well-paid) group. The government is choosing among five alternatives. One is a subsidy for German steel exports. A second is providing subsidies to German steel manufacturers to maintain current levels of production. Third, the government considers financing purchases of German steel by German steel-using industries. The fourth alternative is creating a new fund to retrain and give other benefits to workers laid off due to recession in their industry (if certified by a given ministry as an industry that both is important to the national economy and is suffering from a recession). The fifth choice is to press the central bank to accept the risk of increased inflation as a suitable tradeoff for trying to spur the economy generally by reducing key interest rates.

These five alternatives present a continuum of policy actions that at one end clearly would lead to imposition of countervailing duties and at the other end clearly would not. What is the difference among these choices on fairness grounds?

The External-Effect Argument Introduced

One possible distinction is the degree to which effects of the government's decision are felt outside Germany. The first, and plainly countervailable, alternative would lower the price at which German steel makers would be willing to sell steel for export. If the German steel makers are not pure price takers, that will lower the export price of their steel and increase its volume. This, in turn, will lower prices and volumes of competing steel products in the export markets.

The change in the market for other steel products can be expected to result in lower profits and production for other producers, lower employment for those producers, lower wages for their employees, and decreased returns to equity holders in those producers. The more specialized are the resources dedicated to steel production in the export markets, the more likely the consequence will be seen on the price side to a greater degree than on the volume side of the production equation (holding true as well for the tradeoff between wages and employment levels). Specialized resources tend to make supply less elastic, because production factors cannot readily escape low prices by finding alternative (equally remunerative) employment. Less elastic supply in turn implies that any decline in demand will be reflected to a greater extent in low prices rather than in industry contraction.

These effects in the export markets will not be the sole effects of the government's policy, as it will raise the relative cost of steel within Germany and disadvantage German steel-using industries. It also—so far as the labor and capital markets are imperfectly competitive—will maintain relatively high labor and capital costs within Germany as compared to the costs that would be incurred if the steel industry were allowed to contract.

Four Alternative Fairness Claims: Three Equitable Competition Defects
The externalization of costs to steel producers in export markets is the focus of unfairness claims with respect to the export subsidy. But does the *unfairness* stem from the absolute magnitude of those externalized effects, from the relative division of effects between Germany and the export markets, from the fact that Germany benefits while other nations are harmed, or from the concentration of effects in the export markets' steel industries?

Magnitude of External Effects   The *magnitude of the effects* of the decision does not seem to be the key. Of the five alternatives, the last—and the one plainly *non*countervailable choice—probably has the greatest potential impact on the German economy *and* on other economies that trade with Germany (not to mention other members of the European Monetary System). And even a trivial export subsidy to a product sold in highly competitive export markets can be countervailed.

Relative Magnitudes of Internal and External Effects   The *relative division of effects* between Germany and export markets at first looks promising as a source of unfairness. If we do not pretend to have the right to set economic and social policies for other nations, those of us in the export markets should want to adopt a noninterventionist stance to foreign policies that primarily are directed at matters internal to those nations. German decisions that principally affect business and politics within Germany hence would seem not to be sources of unfairness.

But this position is not wholly satisfying. For one thing, the motivation for adopting any one of the alternative policies (so far as we can assign motivation to group actions) is assumed to be strictly internal—external relations may be considered, but they will be secondary in most cases and

opposed to trade-related subsidies in most instances. Germany, our hypothetical subsidizer, does not want to cause any ill effects in export markets,
least of all in a market such as the United States, a nation that has good
relations with Germany, many mutual interests, and considerable economic
and political power. Insofar as external effects are considered, any external
harm is a disadvantage to a policy, and a different policy with equivalent
benefits inside Germany will be preferred.[95]

For another thing, the objection to German policies that work to disadvantage producers in other nations will be voiced whether the disadvantage is large or small relative to the internal effects. That is consistent with
current law. Both the second and third alternatives—which would be apt
to have internal effects considerably greater than their external effects—
would be subject to countervailing duties.[96]

Another problem with the relative division-of-effects argument is its
suggestion that the appropriate time for countervailing duties is the time
they are most difficult to apply. As a matter of international relations, a
rule providing for countervailing duties only if internal effects are smaller
than external effects would seem to get things backward—like a Kaldor-
Hicks compensation rule that only mandated payment where the winners
win less than the losers lose. Where the external effects are a minor
byproduct of internal policies, the effects in export markets can be offset
without great disruption to the relationship between the export nation and
the subsidizing nation and should thus leave each nation better off.[97]

The strength of this last objection depends in part on the remedy being
offered. As we noted earlier, Goetz, Granet, and Schwartz argue that a
sensible and coherent approach to countervailing duties (once it is assumed
that there will be such duties) requires that producers in the export markets
not be granted a right to *deter* other nations from adopting particular
policies but be given only a right to have the ill effects of those policies
offset.[98] This approach would allow the remedy to operate without having
to assess the subsidy's relative effects or risking serious international im-
broglios. The remedy also fits the objection generally voiced in complaints
about subsidies—the typical assertion is that it is wrong for adverse
effects of a given foreign subsidy to be transmitted to the export market,
not that it is wrong for the foreign government to grant the subsidy. As
Goetz, Granet, and Schwartz also point out, however, the effects-oriented
approach they advocate does not describe current U.S. law very well.[99]

Dividing Costs from Benefits: The Externalized-Cost Principle   A different version of the division-of-effects principle—the *externalized-cost* principle—

might object that the policy complained of advantages Germany and disadvantages its trading partners. The problem recognized by this principle is not the relative magnitudes of internal and external effects but the fact that the *sign* of the effect differs, positive for the subsidizing nation and negative for the partner (importing) nation. Very often, however, this is not the pattern of effects we observe. Countervailable subsidies frequently are disadvantageous to the subsidizing nation and advantageous to citizens in the export markets, judged from a welfare-efficiency vantage.[100]

We could examine the issue without accepting the efficiency framework, which improves the odds of supporting the predicate of the *externalized-cost* principle—that a foreign subsidy internalizes benefits to the subsidizing nation and externalizes costs to export markets—but what can we make of this predicate in the absence of any reasonably determinate measure of cost or benefits? And how do we distinguish subsidies, in this framework, from any other government policy? Government policies generally are intended to advantage those who adopt them, even if the advantage is to identifiable political actors rather than in synthetic terms such as national economic welfare judged by efficiency criteria. While not all policies will disadvantage another nation, an extraordinary array of policies will have *some* adverse effect on another nation. All five of the policies set forth above as alternatives for Germany to address the steel industry's woes would have some adverse effects on other nations, albeit affecting different interests and with varying degrees of directness.

This principle does capture some sense of the complaint that always has attached to other nations' economic actions—the common use of the expression "beggar thy neighbor" to describe objectionable practices reflects the sense of wrongly externalized costs. Yet it is difficult to claim that the fact that some costs are externalized is sufficient basis for unfairness.

The real problem here is the ubiquity of actions that create internal benefits and that also generate external costs. If Germany does a better job of training workers, of promoting efficient telephone service, of providing the right infrastructure for industrial development, or of creating incentives for innovation, there will be some adverse effects on other nations as industries competing with German products (and factors of production employed in those industries) will see an erosion in their relative market position and probably an absolute decline as well. Surely, the notion of equitable international competition does not extend to equalizing all economic policies; but then what does the externalized-cost principle require?

Concentration of Effects   The *concentration of effects* on producers in a single industry looks more hopeful as a principle to explain the unfairness of subsidies. In the first place, it bears a family resemblance to the specificity test for the existence of a countervailable subsidy—as a rule, government actions that advantage economic activity generally (or a very large class of business activities) will not be countervailable; only an action that specifically advantages a given industry, singling it out from among the industries in the exporting nation, will be countervailable. This limitation is not, however, linked to the fairness claim of the party affected by it in the importing nation. The specificity test is designed to protect economic sovereignty, to prevent large importing nations from impinging unduly on the liberty of exporting nations to set their own economic policies. Without this limitation, all government actions are potentially countervailable, a fear that was expressed often in the debates during the Tokyo Round. The specificity test, in other words, is a proxy for the division-of-effects principle.

That said, can the concentration of adverse effects in a single industry in the importing nation, which is the likely consequence of a concentration of benefits in a single industry in the exporting nation, provide a distinctive claim of unfairness? Arguably, the answer is "yes" as no principled basis exists for finding the concentration of effects fair. It is, presumably, a matter of serendipity whether the subsidies are provided to products or producers competing with one industry or another. Steel producers, carmakers, shoe manufacturers, or shipbuilders, by hypothesis, are equally vulnerable to harm from foreign subsidies. If it is steel producers who are hurt, the argument goes, it is unfair because they have been singled out *without reason* from a far larger pool of those who could have been injured by foreign subsidies.

This horizontal-fairness argument differs from the preceding arguments. Its focus is not on the terms for equitable international competition. Instead, this argument looks to the different treatment of citizens in the export market as the basis of the unfairness. Germany may choose to subsidize any industry it wants, but if that action injures U.S. steel producers, rather than being spread broadly across the population, then the U.S. producers have a claim to remedy their injury.

This argument presents an empirical issue and a theoretical issue. The empirical issue is whether the injury consequent to a foreign subsidy is, in fact, a matter of pure chance—that steel producers, carmakers, shoe manufacturers, shipbuilders, and others stand equal chances of injury from foreign subsidies. In one sense, the claim surely is correct. The decision respecting subsidies made by a foreign government will be based on a calculus internal to that government. For that reason, it will not be based primarily on factors within the control of the U.S. producers.

Saying that, however, is not enough. It does not separate issues necessary to distinguish different bases for this unfairness claim. One possible source of unfairness is the difficulty of predicting the actions of foreign governments, so that none of us can protect ourselves against them. Another possible source of unfairness is that the foreign government action, predictable or not, cannot be affected by what we do. Although both of those assertions may be largely true, neither is unimpeachable.

Admittedly, governments are a bit like the weather. We talk about them all the time, but they often take us by surprise. Notwithstanding the progress made in positive public choice,[101] prediction of government action over more than the near term is difficult, and foreign government actions tend to be less predictable because we usually have less information about them.

Yet the weather can be predicted within some range of accuracy. And the information necessary to make a better prediction can be obtained with some effort and investment. So, too, with government. Many firms follow carefully the developments around the world that are most likely to affect their business as opposed to business generally. U.S. steel producers are much more apt to know about the potential for German steel subsidies and about the impact that such subsidies would have on their business than they are to know about the prospects for changes in German interest rates. Even if the latter has greater effect, it is part of a set of developments that are more difficult to monitor because more diffuse and its evaluation depends on information that is not specially accessible to people in the steel business. Individual firms, thus, probably are better positioned to anticipate and counter the effects of actions directed specifically at those firms than is anyone else. At the end of the day, it is difficult to say that injury from foreign subsidies is unfair without saying that any adverse business effect from any source is unfair too.[102]

Further, the foreign government's decision may be *principally* affected by considerations outside the control of the injured firms in the export markets, but the decision is not necessarily based *exclusively* on such considerations. Subsidies may be more easily secured by foreign firms in some industries because the competing firms in those industries in the export markets also receive government subsidies. In agriculture, that is a frequent arrow in the quiver of those who seek additional or continued subsidies. Moreover, the injury that ensues will be affected by some factors that are within individual firms' control. The effect of a foreign subsidy of any given magnitude will depend, among other things, on the current demand for the domestic firms' products and the current pricing of those products.[103] These, in turn, are affected by the cost of the firms' inputs, the wage levels of employees, the investments made in research and development, design, marketing, and so on.

If, despite these objections, it is conceded that a particular industry is purely by chance and unpredictably harmed by foreign subsidies, the remedy in current countervailing-duty law seems wrong. The remedy looks back at the subsidy and attempts to eliminate the benefit received by foreign firms (although the benefit is eliminated only in the countervailing export market, not in the home market or in third-world countries).[104] This suggests a premise that it is wrong for the foreign firm to benefit, not that it is wrong for domestic firms in the competing industry to be singled out from other domestic firms for harm. A plausible conclusion is that one of the two is incorrect—either the premise is not what underlies countervailing duties or the duties are not calculated properly.[105]

Equitable Competition: Picking Up the Pieces

The foregoing discussion shows that there is no fairness claim against subsidies that is both a sensible, analytically coherent claim and also a complete match with the shape of countervailing-duty law. But that should not be taken as proof that the fairness claims do not explain countervailing-duty law or that fairness concerns *cannot* explain countervailing-duty law.

We offer two concluding thoughts on this matter. One is that, even if each of the fairness claims fails as an explanation, it may be that some combination of those claims can supply a positive explanation for countervailing-duty law or normative support for it. We are doubtful on both scores, but those prospects have not been examined fully.

The other is that the notion of equitable competition, clearly a central underpinning to countervailing duties, must rest on arbitrary distinctions. Government policies of all kinds affect international competition. The conditions that determine trade flows and the results of interactions between import flows and domestic production are too numerous to allow us to take seriously the proposition that all effects of foreign government actions should be offset or that we can meaningfully segregate effects of most foreign government actions from the effects of other determinants of supply and demand.[106] Equitable international competition hence cannot exclude *all* government actions that affect international competition. Instead, it must exclude a subset of such government actions that are disfavored for other grounds. We continue, however, to have difficulty specifying those grounds.

8.4.4   Equitable Competition in Labor and the Environment

The problem of finding a principled definition of equitable international competition, or of finding a coherent fairness objection to particular practices that affect international competition, is compounded when we shift to the assertion that differences in environmental or safety regulation or in regulation of various labor rules (such as minimum wages, maximum hours, rights to organize unions for collective actions by workers, and so on) should constitute unfair trade practices. The argument is that less strict regulation confers a competitive advantage on a foreign producer by lowering the producer's costs relative to producers in nations with stricter regulation. This argument magnifies the problems with earlier arguments.

Critically, the appropriate baseline against which to compare foreign regulatory practice must be determined. National chauvinism might suggest that to each nation the proper baseline is that nation's regulatory levels—certainly this is the claim put forward in various guises by some American advocates of extending unfair trade rules to cover "environmental dumping," "social dumping," and other differences in regulation of economic and social practices. As vigorously as this position will be pushed, most commentators understand that regulatory standards appropriate for one country are not, in general, appropriate for another.

Environmental Concerns: Back to the Baseline
We begin with environmental regulation. Environmental regulation reflects demand for goods, such as air quality, that, although socially scarce, often are not priced explicitly by the market.[107] The usual source of these externalities resides in the failure to assign property rights in these goods to private parties. As a result, social costs of behavior that harms others—such as pollution—often are not internalized by individual actors (nor are the social benefits of behavior that makes others better off) unless government acts to regulate this behavior. Environmental regulations change the allocation of rights and responsibilities by requiring that specific standards are met, by granting rights to challenge specific types of activities that cause harm, or by proscribing certain types of harm, among other

means.[108] The goal is to bring the social costs and benefits of both the harmful activity and the beneficial activity to which it is attached—manufacturing useful goods, driving automobiles, and so on—into line.

As with other goods, the level of environmental regulation that is ideal for any nation depends on a set of considerations that differs substantially across populations and through time. The demand for specific goods within a country, including environmental quality, depends on factors such as national per capita income (and possibly, the distribution of income), the income elasticity of the good, national tastes, and the scarcity of substitutable and complementary private goods. The supply side depends on the framework within which the good is produced, whether the economy is a command or market economy, what inputs are needed to yield the good (either directly—as by purifying water that has been polluted—or indirectly—as by avoiding the pollution initially), the cost of those inputs, what returns can be generated from producing the good or what penalties will be incurred by failing to do so. Environmental *quality* will be provided in differing degrees in the absence of government regulation depending on the correlation of private and public costs and benefits and on the actual demand for particular types of environmental quality.

The actual level of environmental *regulation* observed in a nation will only in part reflect the national demand for environmental quality. Regulation, after all, is the product of political processes that are not perfectly consonant with national welfare. That may mean that any nation has too little or too much regulation of any type. One well-known study of environmental regulation in the United States demonstrates the way a regulatory initiative can be shaped to confer substantial private gains, even at the expense of turning an effort to increase environmental quality into a net harm to the environment.[109] For our purposes, the question is whether there is a basis on which to judge the propriety of any nation's environmental regulation.

One possibility here is that some nation has decided to limit its environmental regulation in order to allow lower costs of goods that compete in international markets, a decision that looks like a subsidy. Of course, environmental regulation generally must take account of its effect on producers. To do otherwise is to look only at benefits and not costs. In some measure, the approach taken to subsidies under GATT avoids this issue by requiring that subsidies be industry-specific. That simply reformulates the question. If a particular industry is singled out for special exemption from environmental regulation is that tantamount to a subsidy of the sort that would be countervailable? In theory, the answer to this question must be "yes." Deviations from any country's own national standard, as revealed by generally applicable regulation, that permit one industry to meet less stringent environmental quality standards would seem to be evidence of an "input" subsidy, where the input is the ability to (for instance) use the environment as an effluent disposal system. If the government of Mexico, for example, enacted a program that provided government funds for waste disposal for the copper-smelting industry, that would be countervailable under current law. Granting the copper-smelting industry a special exception to otherwise applicable waste disposal regulations is the functional equivalent.

The issue, however, seldom is so simple. Different industries generate different types of environmental problems and face different costs in avoiding them. If we seek parity among industries within each nation, we must define what parity is. Does it mean that each industry (or each firm in each industry) should be allowed to generate the same total amount of pollution, or the same amounts of each, specific pollutant? Does it mean that each industry should be required to spend the same amount in meeting environmental concerns, or that each should be allowed to impose the same dollar-equivalent cost in environmental degradation? A glance at actual environmental standards reveals their extraordinary complexity, born, at least in part, of the array of competing considerations that inform regulation in each particular context. For exactly the same reason, exemptions from generally applicable standards are common. Of course, political considerations not directly related to the social calculus play a role. But it is no mean feat to separate these from the social costs and benefits, as the private costs and benefits that inform investment in efforts to influence political decisions often are congruent with the social calculus.

In practice, the environmental complaint against internationally traded goods seldom is that *intra*national equity has been violated. Instead, the complaint is addressed to *inter*national equity. The U.S. trade restriction related to tuna from Mexico, recently found GATT-illegal by a GATT dispute-resolution panel convened at Mexico's request, is illustrative. The U.S. tuna industry has been required to adopt stringent safeguards to prevent the incidental destruction of dolphins during tuna-fishing operations. Those safeguards reflect special sensitivity of U.S. citizens—at least a politically active group of U.S. citizens—to the fate of dolphins. The U.S. tuna industry unsuccessfully opposed the regulations and, after losing that fight, sought U.S. border protection from Mexican imports which were harvested without the same dolphin-protection standards and expenses. The GATT panel found that it was unreasonable to penalize a foreign producer simply because a more efficient production technology is permitted and employed outside the complaining (high-regulation) nation.[110] Dolphin-protection regulation is solely a national objective within the United States, which cannot abrogate GATT tariff bindings in order to extend extraterritorial regulation to other countries. The failure of Mexico to regulate fishing practices in the same way as the United States does not affect the quality of the product exported, or cause other spillover effects in the United States, apart from its effect on the competing U.S. tuna industry. The panel concluded that, in such circumstances, the differential regulation alone cannot provide a basis for import restriction.[111]

Safety and Labor: From Baseline to Net to Slippery Slope
Safety and labor regulation are generally similar to environmental regulation. They present the same baseline problem. It is difficult to assail other nations' choices of labor policies or safety regulations simply because they differ from one's own. Once that objection is removed, there is no ready baseline against which to measure foreign safety or labor regulation. Having said that, we return below to the question whether there is some level of regulation that can be said to form a moral baseline, perhaps well below the level of the nation seeking to impose constraints on imports.

Coming to Net   In addition to the baseline problem, there is another problem for these forms of regulation as well, what might be called the net problem. Some safety regulation clearly confronts social externalities, such as highway speed regulations, where one's speed endangers others and it is difficult, if not practically impossible, to contract with those others for the speed level that is optimal for all concerned. Much labor and safety regulation, however, is not of this sort. There is, for example, some evidence that workplace safety is adequately addressed by agreement between employer and employee.[112] Even where there is not a set of individual bargains, the parties most affected have ready mechanisms for addressing each others' concerns and reaching an accommodation that satisfies all parties, given what each knows *ex ante*. Greater workplace safety will be provided when an employer believes it will cost less than the alternatives, including the cost of higher wages, increased leave time for injuries or illnesses, and decreased sales due to adverse publicity associated with industrial accidents and injuries. That is not to say that the ideal agreement, viewed *ex post*, will be struck in every case, only that there is seldom a basis to believe that particular social costs or benefits systematically are ignored.[113]

In part because there often is contracting between parties immediately interested in the subject of labor or safety regulation, there is reason to believe that changes in these regulations will be reflected (over time) in changes in other contractual terms. Other things equal, an increase in the costs of employing a worker—higher required payments for health care, for safety, for reduced hours, or whatever—beyond what seemed to be the optimum agreement between worker and employer is likely to be reflected in a decrease in some other form of compensation to the worker— such as lower pay, lower pension benefits, less job security. As a result, the observed level of regulation of labor or safety is not apt to be a good guide to the real cost such regulation imposes on producing goods traded in international markets.

The High Road and the Low Road   Often, however, labor and safety regulations serve as a sort of talisman, indicating general levels of wage costs. Extensive regulation of labor and safety commonly signal high overall wage costs. That is because demand for most goods, including money income, tend to be negatively sloped, reflecting declining marginal utility. At higher income levels, workers are increasingly willing to trade off further money income against greater leisure, increased safety, added control of their work environment, and other goods. As higher levels of regulation impose costs on employers that, *ceteris paribus*, lead to reduced money wages, regulation—like other tradeoffs for money wages—should be observed more at higher wage levels. There is no guarantee of a perfect correlation, especially as too-high levels of regulation can reduce productivity and depress both wages and employment, but there should be a reasonably strong positive relationship between wage levels and levels of labor and safety regulation.

As a result, challenges to foreign imports as unfairly subsidized by low standards of safety regulation or weak workers'-rights laws may in fact be challenges to low-wage levels. The claim being made is that it is unfair to ask workers in high-wage nations to compete against workers in low-wage nations.

This claim should be rejected firmly. One of the principal reasons for trade is to take advantage of differences in the abilities and willingness of people in different places to produce particular goods at given costs. It was Adam Smith's fundamental insight that nations become wealthier when their people have access to a richer variety of goods, each producing and trading the goods it can sell most successfully in international markets.[114] Wage differences, which generally reflect differences in workers' productivity, are an inevitable part of the diversity that leads to gains from trade.

Over time, productivity in some low-wage nation will rise—because of diffusing technology among other reasons—sufficiently that some of its products become competitive in price and quality with those produced elsewhere.[115] As that happens, workers in relatively high-wage nations will be pressed to further increase productivity, reduce wages, or shift into production of other goods. At the same time, the increased productivity of workers in the low-wage nation will produce increased wealth and support increased demand for goods from that nation and other nations. Although open trade will not increase wealth in the low-wage nation under all conditions,[116] it generally will be advantageous to both the high-wage and low-wage nations. The instances in which trade restriction advances the national interest are unrelated to the wage levels in the exporting nation.[117]

Slaving over the Labor Issue: Hitting the Slippery Slopes   Are there, however, exceptional cases, where the foreign practice respecting safety or labor simply cannot be countenanced? For instance, is slave labor to be treated as merely a polar case of low wages?

In our view, slave labor is different. Slavery is a condition of involuntary servitude, unrelated to the cost of maintaining that condition, to the provision of wages or wage equivalents to the slaves. If slaves are well-compensated and well-treated, they nonetheless are held in bondage, unable to change their work or their location, just as they are if they are ill-treated and receive no remuneration. The moral problem of slavery is the same in either instance. The valid objection to slave labor is not that it allows low-cost production of goods—that may or may not be true, as the formal wage payment to any worker, slave or free, is but one aspect of the cost of that worker's labor. Instead the valid objection is that slave labor is immoral. Just as one can make a moral statement by refusing to trade in slaves, a moral statement can be made by refusing to trade in the products of slavery. If it seldom is the true reason for resisting importation of the products of slave labor (a matter as to which we can only speculate), it still must be admitted as a legitimate stance.

The admission of this objection, however, leads quickly to claims that various practices are the moral equivalent of slave labor. Employing children to make carpets in Iran, Iraq, and Turkey; offering pitifully low wages, poor working conditions, and incredibly long hours to seamstresses in Thailand, Indonesia, and India; using prisoners and military conscripts in

China; denying workers the right to organize independent labor unions in Mexico—the list of alleged analogies to slave labor is quite long. But, with the possible exception of China, none of these fit the slave-labor model. Our objection to each of these is not that we truly think it immoral, something that violates basic commands of human behavior. Rather, we think that it is terrible that people can be so desperate that they will work for so little, for so long, in unsafe and unsanitary conditions. Trade is the best hope for changing the lives of misery so many people endure—it is not a certain route to prosperity, but it is the best hope, far better than waiting for charity or wishing that condemnation or other penalties would change the harsh reality of poverty. For those who truly embrace the cosmopolitan standard of world welfare, embargoing trade from nations so impoverished that such pay and working conditions are common would be virtually unthinkable.

The reason for putting China aside is that, where real physical coercion is used, it is not possible to tell whether the situation is truly analogous to slavery. Are people jailed not because they have committed crimes but so the state can have access to their labor on better terms? It seems doubtful, but the possibility must be admitted. Even so, as explained in Section 8.5 below, it probably is preferable to err on the side of understating the risk that this is what is occurring in China rather than overstating it.

8.5   Second-Best Ethics: The Broader Policy Context

8.5.1   The Case for Second-Best Ethics of Unfair Trade Remedies

We have examined the fairness claims on behalf of the antidumping and countervailing-duty laws, finding little in those claims that can sustain the legal regimes now in place. The underlying assumption that we can identify a state of equitable international competition that allows only "natural" and not "unnatural" advantages into play is belied by any effort seriously to define what is wrong in differences between national systems and to connect perceived wrongs to the remedies of international trade laws.

The laws themselves, however, operate in a broader context defined by the objectives and limits of international agreement. Is there a second-best argument for these laws when seen in context?

It is frequently maintained that the GATT Anti-Dumping and Subsidies Codes offer safety valves that have greatly facilitated international consensus about general trade liberalization, which, in turn, has been an engine of postwar economic growth around the world.[118] If so, a law that, when viewed in isolation, appears protectionist may be justified ethically on more encompassing utilitarian grounds.

In a similar vein, the unfair trade laws are defended on a national level in the United States as depoliticizing major portions of trade policy by removing many direct applications by individual industries for trade protection from the doorsteps of Congress. The premise is that Congress would be even more receptive to such pleadings, with less attention to the merits of the claim, than would the quasi-judicial process administered by quasi-judges and reviewed by actual judges.[119] By establishing seemingly objective standards and tests, assuring due process (in form if not always in full substance), and making fact-finding the center of the procedure, it is removed from direct political mediation. Certainly, administrators have denied relief in some instances in which Congress would have granted it.[120] A "lesser-of-two-evils" defense, although not appealing to our sense of Aristotelian perfection, could reflect ethical optimization subject to constraint.

Countervailing-duty laws are also sometimes defended as devices to enlist *national* import-competing interests in the cause of promoting *global* efficiency through tit-for-tat retaliation against trade-distorting (and global welfare diminishing) foreign subsidies.[121] If "retaliation" in the form of countervailing duties typically results in an elimination of the objectionable and trade-distorting foreign practice, this argument would have merit. And, indeed, there are some instances in which countervailing-duty imposition—or even the threat of its imposition—has led a foreign government to abandon a foreign subsidy program that arguably had trade-distorting effects.

8.5.2   The Argument Examined: Opening the Case

Unfortunately, there is much more evidence to the contrary in the extensive history of the unfair trade laws, at least as to the claim that these laws' costs in trade restriction are made up in elimination of trade-distorting practices. Rather than eliminating a trade-distorting practice, both the initiating "unfair" practice and the trade-limiting remedy commonly are in place for years. Further, in many of the cases of greatest potential impact —for example, cases involving large, ongoing government subsidies that support firms otherwise incapable of sustained operation at anything approaching current levels of production—there is agreement to adopt "voluntary export" restraints, a remedy that may be more welfare-reducing and trade-distorting than either the initial practice or the imposition of countervailing duties.[122]

Of course, the countervailing-duty system itself may deter the adoption of some trade-distorting subsidies in the first instance, and the possibility of antidumping sanctions may deter inefficient international price discrimination. This proposition is inherently impossible to prove or disprove, but it is plausible to believe that the existence of trade remedies will deter some of the practices the relevant actors expect to be targets of those remedies.

The crux of the argument, however, is that the trade practices being remedied by antidumping and countervailing-duty regimes should be at least offset and probably deterred. There is considerable difficulty maintaining this predicate. The case for these laws, certainly beyond the central cases of predatory price-cutting and export subsidies, is open to question, and the administration of these laws, as described earlier, is seriously flawed if the goal is to address welfare-reducing trade practices and not simply to protect producers against competition. The appearance of capture by import-competing producer interests is not merely a problem for the United States, as Brian Hindley, Patrick Messerlin, and others have documented.[123] It long has been known that disposition of most trade issues in a representative democracy is skewed toward the interests of import-competing producers, as they commonly represent the most intensely interested group with the lowest costs of exercising political influence.[124] Over time, such producers have exercised increasing influence in the administration of trade-remedy laws and in the amendment of the legislative mandates as well.[125]

8.5.3   The Big Picture: Who Has the Negatives?

Our inquiry is not quite yet at an end. Even if the system of administered antidumping and countervailing duties does not eliminate trade-distorting practices—indeed, even if it is simply a vehicle for relatively inexpensive trade protection—the second-best claim could still hold.

If there is a strong political consensus for protecting import-competing producers against the effects of dumping and subsidization, either because the producers are an effective lobby or because the public generally is persuaded (wrongly, perhaps) that these practices are in some way unfair, these may indeed be the price for trade liberalization. The multilateral GATT agreements are widely credited with the great boom in trade during the post–World War II era. It is not at all clear that these agreements could have gained acceptance, much less the degree of acceptance they have enjoyed, without including a series of escape valves for protection, including through antidumping and countervailing duties. And further accords may depend on providing some scope for additional protections against low-priced imports from nations with less strict protections of the environment, or safety, or workers' rights.

An alternative thesis is that the producers have put one over on the public. If they have sacrificed some protection they might have gotten from the legislature, they have more than made up for it with administrative protection in cases that would not have received legislative attention or acquiescence. And they have succeeded largely by obfuscating the basis for receiving protection. The "level-playing-field" analogy that producers have so freely invoked is inapposite. And equitable international competition is a mirage. We cannot begin to make the conditions of production equivalent across nations, and we should not have that as a goal. The effort to do so is bound to produce mischief and to use up resources unproductively in the process.[126]

The analysis presented here cannot conclusively resolve the conflict between those two theses. We confess to believing that there is something to each, although the second looks to have the better of the argument. It may be that trade protections of the sort we discuss here are necessary costs to secure the benefits of a system of generally open trade. But we do ourselves little good, in that event, making the central principle of administered protection one that, like a mirage, looks from afar to be both attractive and real only to evaporate into mist when approached.

NOTES

Ronald A. Cass is Dean and Melville Madison Bigelow Professor of Law, Boston University School of Law.

Richard D. Boltuck is part of the Trade Resources Company.

The authors are grateful to Jagdish Bhagwati, Robert Bone, Joseph Brodley, Richard Diamond, Robert Hudec, Seth Kaplan, and Kenneth Simons for helpful comments, although these friends deserve to be held harmless for any errors that remain. John Viar provided valuable research assistance, but again merits protection—or perhaps we should say *insulation*—from complaints.

1. Robert E. Hudec, *"Mirror, Mirror, on the Wall": The Concept of Fairness in United States Trade Policy*, in CANADA, JAPAN AND INTERNATIONAL LAW 88, 90 (1990 Proceedings, Canadian Council on Int'l Law) [hereinafter *"Mirror, Mirror"*].

2. This does not mean that trade can never have negative externalities. If trade reflects forces other than those associated with national comparative advantage, arguably it may distort economic activity, and business dislocations consequent to trade (we will put aside

for the moment questions about the causal predicate) can have negative spillover effects just as business dislocations for other reasons (political decisions to close military bases, or to cease procurement of particular goods, for examples). But the general case for trade is positive sum for the immediate participants and for a series of indirect beneficiaries on both sides of the trade.

3. *See* Robert B. Reich, *Who Is Us?*, 68 HARV. BUS. REV. 53 (Jan./Feb. 1990).

4. Equitable competition also is distinct from the notion of global efficiency. *See* discussion in text accompanying notes 66–67 below.

5. *See, e.g.*, Diane P. Wood, *"Unfair" Trade Injury: A Competition-Based Approach*, 41 STANFORD L. REV. 1153, 1172–73 (1989).

6. *See* notes 28–30 below and accompanying text.

7. Professor Stigler suggested in his classroom pedagogy that assigning correction of all market failures to government for remedy is akin to concluding a talent contest between two singers by awarding first place to the second singer after hearing only the first singer perform.

8. *See, e.g.*, *Matsushita Electric Industries Co. v. Zenith Radio Corp.*, 475 U.S. 574 (1986); Phillip Areeda & Donald F. Turner, *Predatory Pricing and Related Practices Under Section 2 of the Sherman Act*, 88 HARVARD L. REV. 697 (1975). Predatory pricing, as presently viewed, also comprehends other adverse effects on rivals, including deterring new product development. *See, e.g.*, Alvin K. Klevorick, *The Current State of the Law and Economics of Predatory Pricing*, 83 AMERICAN ECON. REV., May 1993, at 162. Indeed, it can even be a strategy for maintaining high prices, without driving rivals from the market, if deployed as a punishment for departures from cartel pricing agreements. The concept of predation at the time the original antidumping laws were written, however, was limited to the bankrupting-rivals model, and even today the common assertion in complaints about dumping is the traditional view of predatory pricing. *See, e.g.*, CLYDE V. PRESTOWITZ, JR., TRADING PLACES 325, 396–97 (1988 ed.).

9. *See, e.g.*, Joseph F. Brodley & George Hay, *Predatory Pricing: Competing Economic Theories and the Evolution of Legal Standards*, 66 CORNELL L. REV. 738 (1981); Frank H. Easterbrook, *Predatory Strategies and Counterstrategies*, 48 UNIV. CHICAGO L. REV. 263 (1981). In modern, dynamic models of predation, consumers can bear the costs of higher prices, reduced product choice, and slowed technological development even without predators driving rivals from the market. *See, e.g.*, Janusz Ordover & Garth Saloner, *Predation, Monopolization, and Antitrust, in* 1 HANDBOOK OF INDUSTRIAL ORGANIZATION 537–96 (Richard Schmalensee & Robert D. Willig, eds., 1989).

10. Act of July 2, 1890, §§ 1–2, 26 Stat. 209 (codified as amended at 15 U.S.C. §§ 1–2 (1988)).

11. 15 U.S.C. § 1 [emphasis added].

12. For instance, a foreign producer that exported through an unrelated trading company could engage in predatory pricing providing the trading company itself reported profits on its operations. *But see* Joseph P. Griffin, *Extraterritorial Application of U.S. Antitrust Laws Clarified by United States Supreme Court: An Examination of the Jurisdiction Given Courts Under the Sherman Act*, FEDERAL BAR NEWS & J., Oct. 1993, at 564–69, for a discussion of the present judicial position on the use of the Sherman Act to regulate foreign practices and their impact in the United States. Griffin documents the increasing tolerance of the courts for extraterritorial application of U.S. antitrust laws.

13. Act of Sept. 8, 1916, § 801, 39 Stat. 756, 798 (codified at 15 U.S.C. § 72 (1988)).

14. Although the Trade Agreements Act of 1979, Pub. L. No. 96-39, §§ 101, 106, 93 Stat. 144, 162, 193 (1979) replaced the Antidumping Act of 1921 by adding a new Title VII to the Tariff Act of 1930, Title VII very largely replicates the provisions of the 1921 Act.

15. 15 U.S.C. § 72 (§ 801 of the Act of Sept. 8, 1916).

16. See, e.g., OVERVIEW AND COMPILATION OF U.S. TRADE STATUTES, Committee on Ways and Means, U.S. House of Representatives (1991 ed.), March 25, 1991, at 61, for a brief historical background. The current antidumping law, Title VII, is the direct descendant of the 1921 Act.

17. See, e.g., USX Corporation v. United States, 682 F. Supp. 60 (Ct. Int'l Trade, 1988) (remanding a Title VII dumping investigation to the U.S. International Trade Commission because one Commissioner was found to have required a showing of predation).

18. The 1921 Act represented a sharp departure from antitrust principles. According to BRUCE ARNOLD, CONGRESSIONAL BUDGET OFFICE, A REVIEW OF U.S. ANTIDUMPING AND COUNTERVAILING-DUTY LAW AND POLICY 2 (May 1994):

Over time, antidumping policy and antitrust policy have diverged strikingly. Antidumping law and policy have evolved along a path of ever-increasing protection for U.S. firms from imports and decreasing concern for consumers and the economy as a whole. Antitrust law relating to predatory pricing, at least in recent decades, has taken a path of increasing concern for consumers and the economy as a whole and decreasing concern for firms suffering intense competition.

19. The law also can be read as preferring errors of overinclusion to errors of under-inclusion, although it was not supported in those terms.

20. For example, a thorough examination of a book by the preeminent progenitor of dumping policy, JACOB VINER, DUMPING: A PROBLEM IN INTERNATIONAL TRADE (1923), reveals that he was unaware of the modern price-theoretic explanation of dumping based on differing degrees of market power in separable international markets. Viner was one of the most accomplished price theorists of his day. His book was published just two years after the 1921 Antidumping Act was enacted.

21. See, e.g., Matsushita Electric Industries Co. v. Zenith Radio Corp., 475 U.S. 574 (1986).

22. See Klevorick, note 8 above.

23. Paul Milgrom & John Roberts, Limit Pricing and Entry Under Incomplete Information: An Equilibrium Analysis, 50 ECONOMETRICA 443 (1982); Paul Milgrom & John Roberts, Predation, Reputation, and Entry Deterrence, 27 J. ECON. THEORY 280 (1982).

24. The Milgrom-Roberts model is often presented in the context of limit pricing, but limit pricing is simply forward-looking predation. For a detailed discussion of this model, see JEAN TIROLE, THE THEORY OF INDUSTRIAL ORGANIZATION 367−74 (1988). See also Patrick Bolton & David Scharfstein, A Theory of Predation Based on Agency Problems in Financial Contracting, 80 AMERICAN ECON. REV., Mar. 1990, at 93; Garth Saloner, Predation, Mergers, and Incomplete Information, 18 RAND J. ECON. 165 (1987).

25. James C. Hartigan, Dumping and Signaling, 23 J. ECON. BEHAVIOR & ORG. 69 (1994).

26. See, e.g., Morris E. Morkre & Kenneth Kelly, Perspectives on the Effects of Unfair Imports on Domestic Industries, 61 UNIV. CINCINNATI L. REV. 919 (1993) (describing characteristics of

the dumping, import market shares, and domestic industry at odds with serious effect of price cutting).

27. *See, e.g.*, Brodley & Hay, note 9 above.

28. By consensus, the contemporary understanding of price discrimination was not developed by economists until at least the late 1920s. *See, e.g.*, Edward Chamberlin, THE THEORY OF MONOPOLISTIC COMPETITION (1933). A representative example of the early literature on price discrimination, as applied to dumping, is in Gottfried von Haberler, THE THEORY OF INTERNATIONAL TRADE WITH ITS APPLICATIONS TO COMMERCIAL POLICY (1936), in Chapter 18 generally.

29. For a detailed review of contemporary microeconomic explanations of both price and cost dumping, *see* Richard H. Clarida, *Dumping in Theory, in Policy, and in Practice* (Volume 1, Chapter 9).

30. Protection of the foreign producer's home market is, of course, globally inefficient economically, but the excess social cost falls on consumers or end-users outside of the United States. As is incessantly noted by economists, U.S. national welfare improves when import prices are reduced, whether due to dumping, subsidies, or any other reason. If antidumping policy contributes to correcting the inefficiency, it may generate a global collateral benefit, but obtaining this benefit is not the ostensible domestic purpose of the unfair-trade laws. *See* discussion in text accompanying notes 66–67 below.

31. *See generally* DOWN IN THE DUMPS: ADMINISTRATION OF THE UNFAIR TRADE LAWS (Richard Boltuck & Robert E. Litan, eds., 1991), for a compilation and commentary of methodological biases in the calculation of dumping margins at the Commerce Department.

32. The 1974 Act required the administering authority to omit sales below cost if the sales: "(1) have been made over an extended period of time and in substantial quantities, and (2) are not at prices which permit recovery of all costs within a reasonable period of time in the normal course of trade...." 19 U.S.C. § 1677b(b) (1988). In practice, prices below cost are typically ignored despite part (1) of this provision.

33. Robert E. Baldwin & Michael O. Moore, *Political Aspects of the Administration of the Trade Remedy Laws*, in DOWN IN THE DUMPS 253, 256, note 31 above.

34. Interestingly, the Trade and Tariff Act of 1984 amended Title VII to allow the Commerce Department to use an average-to-average comparison that avoids the problem of zeroing out individual transaction margins:

For the purpose of determining [United States price] or foreign market value under [this and other] section[s] ... [Commerce] may—(1) use averaging or generally recognized sampling techniques whenever a significant volume of sales is involved or a significant number of adjustments to prices is required.

19 U.S.C. § 1677b(f) (1988).
Congress was motivated to amend the law because, as it indicated in the legislative history, zeroing out positive margins causes "a loss of reasonable fairness in the results." H.R. REP. No. 725, 98th Cong., 2nd Sess. (1984).
Nonetheless, Commerce has only rarely applied this provision to base reported margins on average-to-average comparisons. This situation has, in part, changed with the enactment of legislation implementing Uruguay Round agreements. The 1994 Antidumping Code text requires that

the existence of margins of dumping during the investigation phase shall normally be established on the basis of a comparison of a weighted average normal value with a weighted average of prices of all comparable export transactions or by a comparison of normal value and export prices on a transaction-to-transaction basis.

Agreement on Implementation of Article VI of the General Greement on Tariffs and Trade 1994, art. 2.4.2., *in* Final Act Embodying the Results of the Uruguay Round of Multilateral Negotiations, Apr. 15, 1994 (Done at Marrakesh) [hereinafter 1994 Uruguay Round Final Act]. The new GATT text also permits limited exceptions. In a wooden reading of this provision, however, the implementing legislation permits Commerce to continue to use its current method for annual administrative reviews, in which the actual duty payable is calculated. Uruguay Round Agreements Act, Pub. L. 103–465, § 229, 108 Stat. 4889.

35. Richard Boltuck, Joseph F. Francois, & Seth Kaplan, *The Economic Implications of the Administration of the U.S. Unfair Trade Laws*, *in* DOWN IN THE DUMPS 152, 160, note 31 above.

36. Ronald A. Cass & Stephen J. Narkin, *Antidumping and Countervailing Duty Law: The United States and the GATT*, *in* DOWN IN THE DUMPS 200, 213, note 31 above.   '

37. 19 U.S.C. § 1677b(e)(1)(B) (i) & (ii) (1988), *repealed by* Uruguay Round Agreements Act, Pub. L. 103–465, § 224, 108 Stat. 4878.

38. In Article 2.2.2, the Uruguay Round Antidumping Code generally requires that general expenses, profits, and other costs be based on "actual data," rather than arbitrary or historical levels.

39. For an excellent discussion of the various approaches used both currently and histori-cally by ITC commissioners, see Seth Kaplan, *Injury and Causation in U.S. ITC Antidumping Determinations: Five Recent Approaches*, *in* POLICY IMPLICATIONS OF ANTIDUMPING MEASURES (P. K. M. Tharakan, ed., 1991). *See also The Cass/Eckes Debate on the Future of Injury Analysis at the International Trade Commission*, Debate at University Club, Washington, DC (July 17, 1990) (ABA reprint) for a lively exposition of the merits and weaknesses of both method-ological approaches; Richard D. Boltuck, *The Material Injury Determination in Unfair Trade Cases: The U.S. Experience with Competing Analytical Approaches*, Speech at international trade symposium, Institute of Legal Research, National Autonomous University of Mexico, and SECOFI, Mexico City (October 27–29, 1993) (mimeo).

40. *See, e.g.*, Certain Telephone Systems and Subassemblies Thereof from Japan and Taiwan, USITC Pub. 2237, Inv. Nos. 731-TA-426, -428 (Final) (Nov. 1989) (Dissenting Views of Vice Chairman Cass); Antifriction Bearings (Other than Tapered Bearings) and Parts Thereof from the Federal Republic of Germany, France, Italy, Japan, Romania, Singa-pore, Sweden, Thailand and the United Kingdom, USITC Pub. 2185, Inv. Nos. 303-TA-19, -20, & 731-TA-391–399 (Final) (May 1989) (Concurring and Dissenting Views of Vice Chairman Cass); 3.5″ Microdisks and Media Therefor from Japan, USITC Pub. 2076, Inv. No. 731-TA-389 (Preliminary) (April 1988) (Additional Views of Commissioner Cass); Ronald A. Cass, *Economics in the Administration of U.S. International Trade Law*, Ontario Centre for International Business Working Paper No. 16 (July 1989) [hereinafter *Economics*]; Michael Knoll, *Legal and Economic Framework for the Analysis of Injury by the International Trade Commission*, 23 J. WORLD TRADE 95 (June 1989).

41. *See, e.g.*, Certain Telephone Systems and Subassemblies Thereof from Japan and Taiwan, USITC Pub. 2237, Inv. Nos. 731-TA-426 and 428 (Final) (Nov. 1989) (Dissenting Views of Vice Chairman Cass) at 197–220.

42. 19 U.S.C. § 1673 (1988).

43. *Id.*

44. *See* Cass, *Economics*, note 40 above; Ronald A. Cass & Warren F. Schwartz, *Causality, Coherence, and Transparency in the Implementation of International Trade Laws*, in FAIR EX-CHANGE: REFORMING TRADE REMEDY LAWS 24, 35 (Michael J. Trebilcock & Robert C. York, eds., C.D. Howe Inst., 1990) [hereinafter FAIR EXCHANGE].

45. *See, e.g.*, Ronald A. Cass, *Price Discrimination and Predation Analysis in Antitrust and International Trade: A Comment*, 61 UNIV. CINCINNATI L. REV. 877 (1993); Kenneth G. Elzinga, *Antitrust Policy and Trade Policy: An Economist's Perspective*, 56 ANTITRUST L. J. 439 (1987); Kenneth Kelly, *Empirical Analysis for Antitrust and International Trade Law*, 61 UNIV. CINCIN-NATI L. REV. 889 (1993).

46. *Compare* Cass & Schwartz, note 44 above, *with* John J. Barceló III, *A Comment: Judicial Review and Causation in Unfair Trade Remedy Law*, in FAIR EXCHANGE, note 44 above, at 91−102 [hereinafter *Judicial Review*]; J. Michael Finger, H. Keith Hall, & Douglas R. Nelson, *The Political Economy of Administered Protection*, 72 AMERICAN ECON. REV., June 1982, at 453.

47. Act of June 19, 1936, § 1, 49 Stat. 1526 (codified as amended at 15 U.S.C. § 13 (1988)).

48. *See, e.g.*, ROBERT H. BORK, THE ANTITRUST PARADOX: A POLICY AT WAR WITH ITSELF 384−401 (1978); HERBERT HOVENKAMP, ECONOMICS AND FEDERAL ANTITRUST LAW § 6.12 (1985).

49. *See* Aramid Fiber Formed of Poly Para-Phenylene Terephthalamide from the Nether-lands, USITC Pub. 2783, Inv. No. 731-TA-652 (Final) (June 1994).

50. *See, e.g.*, Hudec, "*Mirror, Mirror*," note 1 above.

51. 19 U.S.C. § 1303 (1988).

52. 19 U.S.C. § 1671 (1988).

53. As Professor Hudec has noted, the Supreme Court of the United States has recognized the right of state governments, as "market participants," freely to grant subsidies to indus-tries. Hughes v. Alexandria Scrap Corp., 426 U.S. 794 (1976).

54. The exceptions to this are cases in which states seek to impose a "use tax" on high-priced items (often automobiles) purchased in other states, setting the tax equal to the state sales tax. Formally, all items within the relevant class commonly will be subject to the use tax, but the particular state's sales tax is offset against the use tax, leaving a zero balance for all items purchased within the state. The design of this tax often is to prevent residents from purchasing goods in neighboring states with lower sales tax rates. A lower tax rate in a neighboring state can be seen as a subsidy to the neighboring state's busi-nesses. This is true especially if the low-tax state has a small population relative to the adjacent, higher-tax state (in which case the proportion of the tax that is simply a transfer payment from one group of citizens within the state to another will be low relative to a large state). *See* JEROME R. HELLERSTEIN & WALTER HELLERSTEIN, STATE AND LOCAL TAXATION 638−45 (1978).

55. Hudec, "*Mirror, Mirror*," note 1 above, at 96.

56. *See, e.g.*, Richard D. Boltuck, *Innovations in Support of the Unitary Injury Test in U.S. Unfair Trade Cases*, in ECONOMIC ANALYSIS OF INTERNATIONAL LAW (Jagdeep S. Bhandari & Alan O'Neill Sykes, eds., 1996). *But see* W. M. CORDEN, TRADE POLICY AND ECONOMIC WELFARE 239−45 (1974).

57. GATT 1994 Agreement on Subsidies and Countervailing Measures [hereinafter 1994 Subsidies Code], art. 1.1, *in* 1994 Uruguay Round Final Act, note 34 above.

58. For a review and critique of U.S. decisions on this issue, see Richard Diamond, *Economic Foundations of Countervailing Duty Law*, 29 Virginia J. Int'l L. 767 (1989) [hereinafter, *Economic Foundations*]; Richard Diamond, *A Search for Economic and Financial Principles in the Administration of U.S. Countervailing Duty Law*, 21 Law & Pol'y Int'l Bus. 507 (1990) [hereinafter, *Search*]. *See also* Ronald A. Cass, *Trade Subsidy Law: Can a Foolish Inconsistency Be Good Enough for Government Work?*, 21 Law & Pol'y Int'l Bus. 609 (1990) [hereinafter, *Trade Subsidy*]. The Uruguay Round Agreements and U.S. implementing legislation place some subsidies, such as those to aid "disadvantaged regions," outside the ambit of countervailable subsidies.

59. Charles J. Goetz, Lloyd Granet & Warren F. Schwartz, *The Meaning of "Subsidy" and "Injury" in the Countervailing Duty Law*, 6 Int'l Rev. L. & Econ. 17 (1986).

60. Diamond, *Economic Foundations*, note 58 above; Diamond, *Search*, note 58 above.

61. See Cass, *Trade Subsidy*, note 58 above. *But see* William N. Eskridge, Jr., *Dynamic Interpretation of Economic Regulatory Legislation (Countervailing Duty Law)*, 21 Law & Pol'y Int'l Bus. 663 (1990).

62. 1994 Subsidies Code, note 57 above, art. 19.2.

63. 19 U.S.C. § 1671 (1988).

64. For an explanation of the computation of the export-equivalent subsidy rate—the duty rate needed to offset the trade effects of the associated production subsidy—see Joseph F. Francois, N. David Palmeter & Jeffrey C. Anspacher, *Conceptual and Procedural Biases in the Administration of the Countervailing Duty Law*, *in* Down in the Dumps 95, 95–136, note 31 above (note especially the appendix, at 133–36); Joseph F. Francois, *Countervailing the Effects of Subsidies: An Economic Analysis*, 26 J. World Trade 5–13 (1992).

65. *See, e.g.*, 1994 Subsidies Code, note 57 above, arts. 8, 14. *See also* Canada–United States Free Trade Agreement, Jan. 1, 1988, art. 1908; North American Free Trade Agreement, Aug. 12, 1992, art. 1907.

66. Jagdish Bhagwati, *Is Free Trade Passé After All?*, *in* International Trade and Global Development: Essays in Honour of Jagdish Bhagwati 10, 16–18 (Ad Koekkoek & Loet B. M. Mennes, eds., 1991).

67. Jagdish Bhagwati, *Fair Trade, Reciprocity, and Harmonization: The New Challenge to the Theory and Policy of Free Trade*, *in* Analytical and Negotiating Issues in the Global Trading System 547 (Alan V. Deardorff & Robert M. Stern, eds., 1994).

68. *See, e.g.*, Bork, note 48 above; Richard A. Posner, Antitrust Law: An Economic Perspective (1976).

69. George J. Stigler, The Theory of Price 195–97 (3d ed., 1966).

70. Bork, note 48 above, at 149–55.

71. *See* Kenneth G. Elzinga, *Predatory Pricing: The Case of the Gunpowder Trust*, 13 J. Law & Econ. 223 (1970); Roland H. Koller III, *The Myth of Predatory Pricing: An Empirical Study*, 4 Antitrust L. & Econ. Rev. 105 (1971); John S. McGee, *Predatory Price Cutting: The Standard Oil (N.J.) Case*, 1 J. Law & Econ. 137 (1958). *But see* Ordover & Saloner, note 9 above.

72. *See* discussion in text accompanying notes 22–27 above.

73. *E.g.*, Malcolm R. Burns, *Predatory Pricing and the Acquisition Cost of Competitors*, 94 J. POL. ECON. 266 (1986).

74. *See* Morkre & Kelly, note 26 above.

75. A similar complaint is registered in Edward A. Snyder & Thomas E. Kauper, *Misuse of the Antitrust Laws: The Competitor Plaintiff*, 90 MICHIGAN L. REV. 551 (1991).

76. *See* GEORGE J. STIGLER, THE ORGANIZATION OF INDUSTRY 113 (1968) (noting differential access to capital as a component of predatory price-cutting and similar strategies).

77. HANS B. THORELLI, THE FEDERAL ANTITRUST POLICY: ORIGINATION OF AN AMERICAN TRADITION 564–65, 569–85 (1954).

78. *See, e.g.*, Bolton & Scharfstein, note 24 above.

79. BORK, note 48 above, at 155.

80. An alternative, but bootstrap, claim would be that producers who invested in specialized resources subsequent to the enactment of the trade laws did so in reliance on those laws, even if the laws protect less efficient domestic producers against more efficient foreign firms. A strong argument against recognition of such claims is Louis Kaplow, *An Economic Analysis of Legal Transitions*, 99 HARVARD L. REV. 509 (1986).

81. U.S. CONST., amend. V. Other constitutional provisions protect expectations through guarantees against retroactive legislation, U.S. CONST., art. I, § 9, clause 3 (judicially limited to retroactive imposition of criminal penalties), and against impairment of the obligations of contracts, U.S. CONST., art. I, § 10, clause 1.

82. *E.g.*, RICHARD A. EPSTEIN, TAKINGS: PRIVATE PROPERTY AND THE POWER OF EMINENT DOMAIN (1985).

83. *See* Kaplow, note 80 above.

84. *See, e.g.*, H.R. REP. No. 479, 60th Cong., 2d Sess. (1919).

85. *Id. See also* WILLIAM A. WARES, THE THEORY OF DUMPING AND AMERICAN COMMERCIAL POLICY 19–20 (1977).

86. *See, e.g.*, Terence P. Stewart, *Administration of the Antidumping Law: A Different Perspective, in* DOWN IN THE DUMPS 288, 297–99, note 31 above.

87. For example, AT&T Company, one of the world's giants, petitioned for relief against dumped imports of small business telephone systems from firms such as Biatronic Telecoms Company, Taiwan Nitsuko, and Iwatsu Electric Company. *See* Certain Telephone Systems and Subassemblies Thereof from Japan and Taiwan, USITC Pub. 2237, Inv. Nos. 731-TA-426, 428 (Final) (Nov. 1989).

88. Even if we limit our vision to the role of retained earnings in a single market, there are substantial analytical problems, as the debate over the relationship between dividends, retained earnings, and stock valuation suggests. *See, e.g.*, A. Cosh, *Retention Ratio, in* THE NEW PALGRAVE: FINANCE 243 (John Eatwell, Murray Milgate & Peter Newman, eds., 1989).

89. The same problem is encountered in antitrust analysis. *See* BORK, note 48 above. The explanations for market expansion even at a temporary loss in profits—such as a firm seeking to reap learning-curve effects, establish "first-mover" advantages (such as brand recognition), and exploit large economies of scale—do not engage the question of price discrimination.

90. The same insight explains Ramsey-pricing. *See, e.g.,* BRIDGER M. MITCHELL & INGO VOLGELSANG, TELECOMMUNICATIONS PRICING: THEORY AND PRACTICE 43–61 (1991). The original paper is by Frank P. Ramsey, *A Contribution to the Theory of Taxation,* 37 ECON. J. 47 (1927).

91. *See, e.g.,* GOTTFRIED VON HABERLER, note 28 above, at 296–300.

92. We do not mean to imply that the nation is the unit to which fairness is owed—fairness to a nation is a concept we believe is incoherent. The phrasing in text instead is meant to indicate that the fairness claim premised on differences in national economies is advanced, in this example, *from* the United States; that is, the claim is that trade inflows to the more competitive U.S. economy create unfairness to particular individuals in the United States. But the argument against price discrimination also must be that it is a wrong to persons in the United States for Korea or Brazil or Slovakia to follow policies less supportive of competition than U.S. policies.

93. Indeed, in recent years, nations such as Korea, Turkey, and Mexico, which historically have not been very open to imports (although that is now changing, at an especially rapid rate in Mexico), have established antidumping regimes.

94. Ironically, an alternative means of bringing firm production to the efficient level is a government subsidy to production.

95. This does not, of course, speak to the relative weighting of internal and external interests. *See, e.g.,* ROBERT E. BALDWIN, THE POLITICAL ECONOMY OF U.S. IMPORT POLICY (1985); JAGDISH N. BHAGWATI, PROTECTIONISM (1988); E. E. SCHATTSCHNEIDER, POLITICS, PRESSURES, AND THE TARIFF (1935).

96. *See, e.g., Diamond, Economic Foundations,* note 58 above.

97. "Better off" here does not necessarily mean that the result will be preferred by an "objective" measure such as allocative efficiency or some other metric of social welfare. Certainly, however, the political calculus of social welfare is improved by this action, and it is likely that the social welfare measured by standards such as efficiency will be more congruent with imposition of duties in this situation than in situations where the effects in the importing market are very large compared to those in the exporter's home market. This argument is implicit in Alan O. Sykes, *Second-Best Countervailing Duty Policy: A Critique of the Entitlement Approach,* 21 LAW & POL'Y INT'L BUS. 699 (1990); Alan O. Sykes, *Countervailing Duty Law: An Economic Perspective,* 89 COLUMBIA L. REV. 199 (1989) [hereinafter, *Perspective*].

98. *See* Goetz, Granet & Schwartz, note 59 above.

99. *Id. See also* Cass, *Trade Subsidy,* note 58 above.

100. *See* CORDEN, note 56 above, at 42–57.

101. *See, e.g.,* DENNIS C. MUELLER, PUBLIC CHOICE II (1989).

102. This really is a straightforward extension of the argument made by Louis Kaplow, note 80 above.

103. *See, e.g.,* John J. Barceló III, *Subsidies and Countervailing Duties—Analysis and Proposal,* 9 LAW & POL'Y INT'L BUS. 779 (1977); Boltuck, note 56 above; Sykes, *Perspective,* note 97 above.

104. *See* Boltuck, note 56 above.

105. *See* Goetz, Granet & Schwartz, note 59 above.

106. The same sort of problem affects analysis of causation under § 201 of the Trade Act of 1974, Pub. L. No. 93-618, 88 Stat. 1978 (1975) (codified as amended at 19 U.S.C. § 2251) (1988). *See* Gene M. Grossman, *Imports as a Cause of Injury: The Case of the U.S. Steel Industry*, 20 J. INT'L ECON. 201 (1986); Kenneth Kelly, *The Analysis of Causality in Escape Clause Cases*, 37 J. INDUS. ECON. 187 (1988); Robert S. Pindyck & Julio J. Rotemberg, *Are Imports to Blame? Attribution of Injury Under the 1974 Trade Act*, 30 J. L. & ECON. 101 (1987); Donald J. Rousslang, *Import Injury in U.S. Trade Law: An Economic View*, 8 INT'L REV. L. & ECON. 117 (1988).

107. At times, these goods are capitalized in the value of other goods, such as property located in a relatively smog-free area near Los Angeles or Mexico City.

108. A series of regulatory approaches is set forth, and their application to particular circumstances critiqued, in STEPHEN G. BREYER, REGULATION AND ITS REFORM (1982). Market-based approaches to regulation, such as the creation of tradeable effluent rights, are becoming increasingly common, both in the United States and elsewhere.

109. *See* BRUCE A. ACKERMAN & WILLIAM T. HASSLER, CLEAN COAL/DIRTY AIR (1981).

110. *United States—Restrictions on Imports of Tuna*, GATT Basic Instruments and Selected Documents, 39th Supp. 155 (1993) (Report of the Panel).

111. The tuna case is sensibly grounded in the perception that if any foreign practice not to another country's liking offers a basis for trade restriction, the entire liberal trading system would be at risk. Restrictions against foreign production practices that directly harm U.S. interests could be distinguished and perhaps could be regulated through border measures. For example, a Canadian electrical power plant that causes significant quantities of airborne effluent to enter U.S. territory might be prohibited from selling into the U.S. power grid. Of course, the line between such direct harm and the indirect harm to dolphin lovers from inhabiting a less dolphin-rich world will provide plenty of grist for argument.

112. *See, e.g.*, W. KIP VISCUSI, RISK BY CHOICE: REGULATING HEALTH AND SAFETY IN THE WORKPLACE (1983).

113. If illness or injury does occur, it is seldom easy to reconstruct the values that informed the ill or injured party's initial accord. I may be offered a 20 percent premium for work that involves a higher risk of injury, and may take that work gladly over other work that is less risky and less well compensated. But if I am injured on this job, it is rare that I will deem the compensation already received sufficient. Likewise, losing lottery tickets seldom seem worth their cost after the drawing. This is not to deny that in some cases one party possesses information that, if accessible to the other party, would at the outset have produced a very different deal.

114. ADAM SMITH, THE WEALTH OF NATIONS (Modern Library Edition, 1937) (1776).

115. In addition, declines in the costs of transportation and communication can increase international trade flows even without changes in relative costs of production. *See, e.g.*, Ronald A. Cass & John Haring, INTERNATIONAL TRADE IN TELECOMMUNICATIONS: MONOPOLY, COMPETITION, AND STRATEGY (MIT Press & American Enterprise Institute, forthcoming 1996).

116. Jagdish N. Bhagwati & V. K. Ramaswami, *Domestic Distortions, Tariffs, and the Theory of Optimum Subsidy*, 71 J. POL. ECON. 44 (1963).

117. *See, e.g.*, JAGDISH BHAGWATI & T. N. SRINIVASAN, LECTURES ON INTERNATIONAL TRADE (1983).

118. *See, e.g.*, John H. Jackson, *Perspectives on Countervailing Duties*, 21 LAW & POL'Y INT'L BUS. 739, 745 (1990).

119. *See, e.g.*, John J. Barceló III, *Judicial Review*, note 46 above.

120. *See* Gary N. Horlick, *A Comment, in* FAIR EXCHANGE, note 44 above, at 103–04.

121. For a discussion of the success of the tit-for-tat strategy in repeated games, *see* ROBERT AXELROD, THE EVOLUTION OF COOPERATION (1984); Robert Axelrod, *Effective Choice in the Prisoner's Dilemma*, 24 J. CONFLICT RESOL. 3 (1980).

122. *See* I. M. DESTLER, AMERICAN TRADE POLITICS: SYSTEM UNDER STRESS 118 (1986). *See also* BHAGWATI & SRINIVASAN, note 117 above.

123. *See* Brian Hindley, *Dumping and the Far-East Trade of the European Community*, 11 WORLD ECON. (1988); Patrick Messerlin, *The Antidumping Regulations of the European Community: The "Privatization" of Administered Protection, in* FAIR EXCHANGE, note 44 above, at 107–46.

124. BHAGWATI, PROTECTIONISM, note 95 above; DESTLER, note 122 above; SCHATTSCHNEIDER, note 95 above.

125. *See, e.g.*, J. Michael Finger & Tracy Murray, *Policing Unfair Imports: The United States Example*, 24 J. WORLD TRADE 39 (Aug. 1990).

126. *See* Jagdish N. Bhagwati, *Directly Unproductive, Profit-Seeking (DUP) Activities*, 90 J. POL. ECON. 988 (1982).

9   Defensive Unfairness: The Normative Structure of Section 301

Kenneth W. Abbott

9.1   Introduction

9.1.1   Section 301 and International Trade Policy

Section 301 of the Trade Act of 1974[1] is the only statutory remedy for industries, firms, and workers in the United States—and for the U.S. government itself—that seeks to attack "defensive" trade barriers: acts, practices, and policies of foreign nations that impede U.S. exports of goods, services, or capital.[2] Section 301 appears in the Trade Act under the heading "Relief from Unfair Trade Practices," and practices considered "unfair" have been the focus of activity under the law for the past 20 years. Section 301 can also be used against "offensive" foreign trade practices that displace U.S. exports from third markets, but this activity has been less central to the operation of the remedy.[3]

There have been relatively few proceedings under Section 301 during the early 1990s, as the federal trade bureaucracy and private economic interests alike focused their energies on completing the Uruguay Round trade negotiations. But Section 301 is still a central factor in international trade policy. First, 301 remains the principal means within the U.S. of initiating dispute-resolution procedures within the GATT/WTO system and thus of enforcing the sweeping commitments that America's trading partners have undertaken in the Round. It also remains the principal U.S. tool for attacking foreign trade-distorting practices in areas not subject to GATT discipline. The most controversial aspect of Section 301—the so-called Super 301 procedure, which mandates action against foreign practices identified as especially damaging—expired by its terms in 1990, two years after its enactment. It was reestablished by presidential order in 1994,[4] however, and was reenacted into law in the Uruguay Round Agreements Act, adopted in December 1994.[5]

Second, the success of the Uruguay Round agreements is directly linked to the future role of Section 301. The Understanding on Dispute Settlement adopted at the end of the Round strengthens the GATT dispute-resolution process dramatically; this accomplishment was possible, in large part, because it was seen as a *quid pro quo* for agreement by the U.S. to deal with all of its legal claims within the GATT/WTO system. Such an agreement is explicit in the Understanding.[6] The U.S. government, however, has suggested that it will retain considerable freedom for unilateral action under Section 301.[7] If overly aggressive use of Section 301 were to weaken one of the main political underpinnings of the Understanding, and indeed many of the substantive agreements as well, the results of the Round could be jeopardized.

Third, while they are not dealt with in detail here, other important aspects of U.S. international economic policy reflect the same set of normative ideas and the same sort of unilateral procedures as Section 301. This is particularly true of relations with Japan, notably the Structural Impediments Initiative and the bilateral negotiations currently taking place under the Framework for a New Economic Partnership.

9.1.2   Section 301 as an Analogue to Demands for Domestic Harmonization

In addition to its importance in traditional areas of international economic policy, Section 301 is an important analogue to the recent demands for harmonization of domestic policies in the areas of labor standards, environmental regulation, and competition law, the issues that are the major concerns of this symposium.[8] The most important analogy is that both Section 301 claims and the current demands for harmonization turn on concepts of "fairness." The specific complaints may not be precisely the same, but the underlying demand for fairness in economic relations is at the core of both sets of claims.[9] A second important analogy is the common focus on harmonization of national policies. Section 301 claims have not generally been thought of as efforts to achieve harmonization, but the typical 301 demand for termination or modification of offending foreign practices is in essence a demand that the economic policies of other nations be harmonized with those of the United States. Section 301 claims have for years extended to domestic policies as well as border measures.

A third analogy is that, in both settings, the harmonization procedures are quite similar. In the postwar international economic system, barriers to the movement of goods, services, and capital have generally been reduced through arduous multilateral, regional, and other plurilateral and bilateral negotiations, in which the nations involved barter reciprocal concessions. Section 301 also contemplates negotiations, typically bilateral, to reduce defensive barriers. But three characteristics of the 301 procedure, shared to a considerable degree by current proposals for the harmonization of domestic regulatory policies, set it apart from the prevailing model:

• The agenda for negotiations is set entirely by the United States, as it decides which foreign practices are to be considered "unfair." It is not necessary that such practices be governed by international rules previously negotiated in GATT, the International Labor Organization, or other relevant forums.

• On the assumption that the foreign practices in question are "unfair" in a way that the tariffs dealt with in traditional GATT rounds are not,[10] negotiations are designed to obtain unilateral changes in the respondent nations' policies. Although mutual concessions may sometimes occur in practice, negotiations are not expected to proceed in this way.

• Negotiations proceed under the threat that the United States will retaliate against products or services of the foreign nation should the desired changes not be accepted.[11] Section 301 authorizes executive branch officials to carry out such retaliation, and indeed, since 1988, mandates retaliation in certain circumstances. At least prior to the Uruguay Round agreements, all of this could take place without reference to any international dispute-settlement procedure, and at least in theory even after a dispute-settlement body had ruled against a U.S. claim.[12]

These conceptual similarities have led some to urge that demands for harmonization of labor and environmental policies be incorporated into the established statutory and procedural structure of Section 301. Most notably, Representative Richard Gephardt, as House Majority Leader, regularly spoke in support of a "blue and green 301" that would make actionable the failure of foreign governments to adopt satisfactory labor and environmental standards and to enforce existing domestic laws in those areas.[13] Such a legislative change may still be possible, though the changes in the U.S. political situation since the 1994 elections now appear to militate against it.

9.1.3   Norms of Fairness and Responsibility in Section 301

Section 301 has been extremely controversial over the years, at least among foreign governments and international trade specialists. It has been intensively analyzed by scholars in law, economics, and other disciplines, and the vast majority of them have been critical.[14] As Professor Hudec has observed, however, "Critics have usually focused on the operational aspects of [unfairness claims under 301]—their potentially limitless scope, their unilateral character, their susceptibility to capture and corruption by protectionist forces, and their destructiveness of the multilateral system."[15] In his "Mirror, Mirror" article, Hudec began the task of examining the substance of the fairness claims that underlie a growing portion of U.S. trade law, including the antidumping and countervailing-duty laws and Section 337 of the Tariff Act of 1930 as well as Section 301. He called for scholars to examine these claims on their merits and in their functional setting, without prejudging them.[16]

This approach has substantial merit. Judith Goldstein has shown[17] that ideas, values, norms, and ideologies can have independent influence on the policy processes of American government, separate from the domestic interest group pressures of the public-choice model and from the constraining influences of international structure and relationships emphasized by international relations scholars. The major U.S. trade statutes, for example, were passed in different ideological eras, and are therefore supported by different sets of ideas and norms, each legitimizing different forms of government involvement in private economic activity. The idea of economic liberalism has, of course, dominated U.S. policy throughout the postwar period, but, as Goldstein demonstrates, ideas from the earlier era of mercantilism still survive, institutionalized in laws and legal procedures, while new ideas and variants of old ones rise and fall in influence over time.

This chapter analyzes the ideas embodied in claims of defensive unfairness in international economic relations. What exactly are the normative arguments that support and lend legitimacy to the adoption and implementation of a one-sided statute like Section 301? The best places to locate these ideas and norms are in the text of the statute itself, as enacted in 1974[18] and amended, sometimes radically, in 1979,[19] 1984,[20] 1988,[21] and 1994[22]; and in the legislative history of these enactments, particularly in the demands and arguments of private interests directly affected by foreign trade policies and their colloquies with members of Congress. I cannot claim to have read all of the hearings and debates on the enactment and amendment of Section 301, but I have read a large proportion of them, and have some confidence that the ideas and norms identified here characterize the entire record.[23] Identifying these norms should help us understand not only Section 301 itself, but the analogous claims for harmonization of domestic laws in areas like labor and the environment.

To begin with, it is clear that the general idea that certain trade practices are "unfair," and thus appropriately treated mare harshly than "fair" practices, is deeply embedded in Section 301 and in the nearly 25 years of legislative dialogue on defensive unfairness. This distinction, of course, has been long established with respect to offensive unfair practices like dumping and export subsidies. The search here, however, is for the normative components of the idea of "unfairness." A few specific norms of fairness are reflected in the text of the law itself. For the most part, however, the text is ambiguous on the normative content of such statutory terms as "unfair," "inequitable," and "unreasonable." The statute does include a definition of the term "unreasonable," but this says only that the term means "unfair and inequitable."[24]

This normative ambiguity is not surprising when one realizes that, in the thousands of pages of statements and colloquies on Section 301 and related issues, no witness or member of Congress, so far as I can determine, essays a general definition of either fairness or unfairness, defensive or otherwise. By far the largest number of statements simply refer to "fairness," "equity," or such overworked metaphors as the level playing field. Even under direct questioning,[25] private-sector witnesses complaining of unfair treatment cannot come up with a general definition.[26]

Nonetheless, a relatively small set of normative concepts giving content to the idea of unfairness in international trade, especially in defensive contexts, emerges clearly from the legislative history. Different norms of fairness are emphasized in different periods, but the overall set remains quite consistent over a quarter century. Section 9.2 defines and illustrates these norms of fairness.

It is important to emphasize that the ideas of fairness presented here differ significantly from the free trade norms typically espoused by economists, as set out, for example, in Volume 1 of this symposium. Economic analysis takes place almost exclusively from the perspective of maximizing economic efficiency and welfare at the level of the world or national economy as a whole. Fairness claims under Section 301, in contrast, reflect the world view of the private business engaged in international competition with other firms. This distinction goes far to explain why Section 301 has such strong support among the public and in Congress, even as it is criticized by academics and viewed with caution by the President.

Some norms of fairness reflected in Section 301 are also widely held norms of the international trading system and international law more broadly. Others are less firmly grounded in the established normative systems relevant to international economic activity. Based on this criterion, the concepts of fairness discussed here can be arranged in a rough order of legitimacy, shown in Section 9.2, where the most legitimate norms are presented first. Section 9.3 undertakes a preliminary evaluation of this range of norms in relation to several other criteria.

In addition to the basic norms of unfairness discussed in Sections 9.2 and 9.3, other normative concepts also enter into a determination that taking unilateral action against the practices of a foreign state is appropriate. It is valuable to an understanding of Section 301—and of other developments in the world of unfair trade claims—to examine these ideas separately. Three such "norms of responsibility" seem particularly important in legitimizing an unfairness claim or an act of retaliation against a foreign nation: (1) whether the allegedly unfair practice is properly attributed to the foreign government; (2) whether the practice is within the legitimate scope of international concern, or is insulated from scrutiny by norms of sovereignty, and whether the foreign state has international responsibility to respond to demands for change; and (3) whether the "mental state"—admittedly a fictitious concept, but a useful one—of the foreign government engaging in the practice justifies a response. One can imagine these norms arrayed against the norms of fairness in the form of a matrix; where the practices of a given nation appear on this matrix determines the legitimacy of an unfairness claim. Responsibility norms are discussed in Section 9.4. Section 9.5 is a brief conclusion, emphasizing the similarities and differences between the normative structure of Section 301 and the current demands for harmonization of domestic labor, environment, and competition policies.

9.2 Norms of Fairness

9.2.1 The Norm of Adherence to International Commitments and Law

What we are talking about is the direct violation of a trade agreement with this country. Sen. Lloyd Bentsen.[27]

The least controversial of the defensive unfairness claims made in connection with Section 301 is the charge that particular foreign practices violate an international rule or commitment. Although the 1974 version of Section 301 ("initial 301") did not explicitly mention the violation of international commitments,[28] the 1979 reworking of the section—part of the legislation giving effect to the nontariff-barrier (NTB) agreements of the Tokyo Round—made the enforcement of international commitments an independent normative basis for 301 actions[29] and a principal focus of the law, both substantively and procedurally.[30] As amended in 1988 ("current 301"),[31] moreover, Section 301 makes violations of or denial of rights under a trade agreement, as well as foreign practices "inconsistent" with such an agreement, grounds for mandatory retaliation.[32] Under current 301, in short, observance of international commitments functions as a sort of super-norm.[33]

The allegation that other nations are violating international rules and commitments also appears as a normative argument for action throughout much of the legislative history of Section 301. During the hearings on initial 301, witnesses cited many unlawful practices among the panoply of foreign NTBs complained of, but the normative rationale itself was rarely expressed, much as in the statutory text. In hearings leading up to the 1979 amendment, however, the norm was central to the debate, since Section 301 was then being viewed primarily as a tool to enforce the sweeping agreements the United States was about to enter into. After 1979, claims that foreign states were not carrying out their obligations under GATT, the Tokyo Round codes, or other agreements appear regularly in arguments for strengthening the statute or its implementation by the Executive. Perhaps most notably, in the hearings on current 301, a broad spectrum of witnesses, including influential groups like the Business Roundtable and U.S. Chamber of Commerce, and several members of Congress—including Senator Bentsen—stressed the particular normative quality of violations in support of treating them as a unique basis for mandatory retaliation.

Interestingly, the overall tenor of the normative arguments in the legislative history, and as reflected in statutory text, is not that unlawful conduct, violations of established rules, should be punished. The normative complaint seems to partake more of the idea of reciprocity—the failure of a state to observe its commitments to the United States when we are observing our commitments to it is an illegitimate act—or of the even simpler, unilateral notion that the failure to carry out a commitment is an insult to the United States.[34] It is a normative claim almost purely concerned with the private national interests of the United States, rather than the public interest of the international trading community.[35]

Even so, claims based on violations of international commitments are highly legitimate. Indeed, it is hardly necessary to wrap such claims in the mantle of unfairness. Under general international law, violations of agreements or general legal standards give affected states the right to take responsive actions, under the agreement itself[36] or by way of reprisal, even when those actions would be unlawful in the absence of the violation. GATT article XXIII:1(a) similarly states that the failure to carry out the obligations of the Agreement is justification for initiating dispute-settlement proceedings, and ultimately for restructuring the parties' relationship by a unilateral correction of the violation, compensation, or retaliation. Claims of GATT violations, of course, are tied to institutional procedures which may not be fully observed in Section 301 proceedings.

9.2.2   The Norm of Nullification or Impairment

The world is ... sufficiently complex to make it possible for any government to devise strategems that effectively undo in the marketplace the promises it has made at the bargaining table....

National Association of Manufacturers.[37]

The idea that foreign trade practices can be considered "unfair" if they impair the value of previous trade concessions or agreements is also prominent in Section 301. The text of initial 301, even though it did not specifically mention violations, did provide that import restrictions which impair the value of trade commitments are actionable under the section.[38] As written, initial 301 also required such restrictions to be "unjustifiable or unreasonable," but the presidential message presenting the proposed legislation to Congress, and the administration's section-by-section analysis, essentially equate these broader normative terms to the nullification of commitments. Subsequent versions of the statute also make actions that deny benefits under a trade agreement actionable, while dropping the "unjustifiable or unreasonable" condition. Under current 301, such actions, like violations, are subject to mandatory retaliation.[39]

Arguments that particular foreign practices undercut the value of tariff concessions or other agreements appear regularly in the legislative history. The impairment norm was also used in several legislative proposals to lend legitimacy to extensions of the statute. For example, the principal proposal to bring targeting (which involves a combination of lawful and unlawful practices) within the ambit of Section 301, as was done in 1988, would have made the practice explicitly actionable only when it impaired the benefits of a trade agreement.[40]

The impairment norm derives its legitimacy primarily from its obvious connection with the norm of compliance, as suggested in the quotation at the head of this section. It gains additional legitimacy from GATT Article

XXIII:1(b), which provides that the nullification or impairment of benefits accruing to a state under the General Agreement is a legitimate basis for commencing a dispute-settlement procedure—even if the practices in question do not violate the Agreement—and, if established, to readjust the relationship. This clause, however, has an enormous potential breadth: Any change in economic policy that adversely affects imports could be considered to impair the benefits of prior tariff bindings, for example. If such claims strayed far from traditional commercial policy measures, the principle would likely lose its support. As a result, GATT jurisprudence has interpreted nullification or impairment quite cautiously, principally by requiring that continuation of the original policy be within the foreign state's "reasonable expectations" at the time of the initial negotiation. In this form, nullification or impairment claims stand to benefit fully from the strengthened dispute-settlement rules of the Uruguay Round Understanding.[41]

The measures criticized as impairment in the legislative history of initial 301 were typically standard commercial policy measures: the Northwest Horticultural Council, for example, alleged that many European countries had nullified earlier tariff concessions on fruits and vegetables by means of import licenses, exchange controls, and bilateral quota agreements.[42] Witnesses generally seemed to maintain a narrow interpretation of nullification and impairment, lending their claims the legitimacy of the GATT principle, even if the relevant institutional requirements were not observed.[43] Some of the charges in the legislative history, however, were made with more emotional heat than the narrow nullification or impairment principle of GATT jurisprudence would seem to justify. In these cases, a deeper norm seemed to be at work, the idea that nations should not dodge or evade their commitments. These statements typically included the explicit allegation that the measures in question were intentionally adopted to offset prior trade concessions.[44] In the end, few witnesses seemed willing to base their arguments exclusively on the notion of impairment; most relied as well, or even primarily, on more specific normative claims. But the theme of evasion raised in these early exchanges became ever more prominent over the years.[45]

9.2.3   The Norm of Nondiscrimination

[The bill] will authorize the President to ... respond to the discriminatory service trade practices of foreign governments as they arise. And they certainly are arising.

Coalition of Services Industries, Inc.[46]

The normative claim that foreign acts, policies, or practices are "unfair" when they discriminate against the commerce of the United States is central to Section 301 and its legislative history. Aside from nullification of commitments, discrimination is the only normative concept explicitly identified in every version of the section since its passage in 1974.[47] The nondiscrimination norm was not further explicated in the text of the statute until its 1984 amendment. At that time, "discrimination" was defined (nonexclusively) to include the denial of either national treatment or most-favored-nation treatment to exports of U.S. goods, services, or investment.[48] Some of the practices used to illustrate the standard of unreasonableness also partake of the concept of discrimination.[49]

Discrimination was a particularly prominent normative claim in the legislative history of initial 301. The early 1970s were characterized by the discovery of NTBs as a central problem of international trade policy, one exacerbated by the commercial policies of the European Economic Community. Most of the NTBs reported by private-sector witnesses were inherently discriminatory in the national-treatment sense. These included discriminatory government procurement, import quotas, import prohibitions, the EC variable-levy system, licensing systems for imports and investment, screen-time quotas for U.S. films and TV programs, and similar measures that prevented U.S. firms from selling goods or services or investing capital with the same freedom as local competitors. Many witnesses simply described the NTBs they encountered without explicit normative claims,[50] though their discriminatory nature was clearly part of the problem. Others made the national-treatment argument explicitly. Some also advanced the norm of nondiscrimination in the MFN sense, particularly as to the results of EC enlargement, association agreements, and other external relationships.

Similar claims were advanced frequently, and with increasing ferocity, thereafter, especially in the hearings leading up to the 1984 and 1988 amendments. An amazing range of national barriers to trade, investment, and the provision of services was criticized, explicitly or implicitly, as discriminatory. Preferential procurement, barriers to agricultural imports, and product standards skewed to favor local producers received special attention. As foreign industrial policy and targeting became central concerns in the mid–1980s, the nondiscrimination norm was applied to condemn policies used to incubate sunrise industries and isolate foreign markets so that national firms could grow to competitive size. The intensity and single-mindedness with which private sector witnesses advanced the antidiscrimination norm were captured in the complaint of American broadcasters criticizing Canadian rules restricting advertising on U.S. radio stations broadcasting to Canadian audiences. Confronted with Canada's lofty rationale of protecting its culture and national identity, the broadcasters replied that such concerns could not be allowed to override plainly unfair discrimination.

Norms of nondiscrimination are highly legitimate in international economic law. Both the national treatment principle (Article III) and the MFN principle (Article I) are central to GATT, though both are qualified by a number of exceptions. Additional provisions reflecting these norms are found throughout the Agreement. Indeed, many of the specific substantive rules of GATT, such as the prohibition of most quantitative import restrictions in Article XI, are designed to address particular discriminatory measures. The MFN and national treatment principles also form the core of most other international economic agreements, including FCN treaties, bilateral investment treaties, intellectual property conventions, and the like. While nondiscrimination may not yet be a principle of customary international law, it is a powerful and pervasive norm.

It is important to note, in this connection, that the discrimination claims found in the history of 301, and in its text, cover both discriminatory measures prohibited by GATT or some other international agreement and discriminatory measures not prohibited by any agreement. Thus, a foreign import quota that appeared not to qualify for any GATT exception could be criticized both as a violation of a nation's GATT commitment and as discriminatory. An import quota that did benefit from a GATT exception, like that for certain agricultural quotas in Article XI, or indeed a restrictive measure like a screen-time quota not regulated by GATT or any other agreement, could still be criticized as discriminatory. Such criticism would not support a GATT complaint, except on the ground of nonviolation nullification or impairment, but it would have independent normative power.[51] Claims and proceedings of the latter kind represent a sharp break from those discussed previously: Like many recent demands for harmonization of domestic regulation, they seek the creation of new political or legal norms, rather than merely enforcing existing rules and commitments.

9.2.4   The Norm of Reciprocity

... [L]et others do unto us as we do unto them, or else.

Irving Glass, Tanners Council of America.[52]

Claims based on the idea of reciprocity dominate the legislative history of Section 301. Reciprocity concerns are particularly prominent in the years leading up to the 1984 amendments, when numerous legislative proposals and entire hearings focus on reciprocity issues. Unfortunately, as pointed out by Richard Rivers in a 1982 hearing,[53] "reciprocity" has many different meanings. I have identified two principal uses of the reciprocity norm in the history of Section 301, the second of which includes at least two significant variations. I also discuss a related argument that has become increasingly prominent in U.S. trade policy.

Specific Reciprocity

[E]very time, including the last round, the United States has given more than we have received.

Senator William Roth.[54]

In international trade, the concept of reciprocity has figured most prominently in bilateral and multilaterd negotiations, in which states exchange reciprocal concessions.[55] In GATT, the prevailing concept of reciprocity, especially in the early tariff rounds, involved a balancing of the concessions made by each party in mainly bilateral negotiations, often measured by rough estimates of the increases in trade the concessions might allow. Such concessions were generalized to all parties under the MFN principle, and the overall balance of concessions was roughly assessed at the end.[56] Even this concept of reciprocity, however, is not simple.

Robert Keohane has identified two general approaches to reciprocal negotiations.[57] In *specific* reciprocity, the parties exchange concessions or other items of equal value, at the same time or in a carefully controlled sequence. In *diffuse* reciprocity, the equivalence of exchanges is less precise and their timing less restricted. Diffuse reciprocity requires a sense of obligation to one's partners and a corresponding level of trust. When these conditions exist, parties will not demand precisely equivalent concessions in each exchange, instead counting on their partners to contribute to an acceptable overall balance within a reasonable time. Keohane identifies diffuse reciprocity with the MFN principle of GATT (though in the context of tariff negotiations, specific balancing of concessions has typically taken place both before and after MFN generalization).

In the history of Section 301, the Executive has consistently taken positions at least suggestive of diffuse reciprocity. It has sought authority for new MFN negotiations, defended the results of past negotiations, and opposed more restrictive negotiating approaches.[58] Private-sector witnesses and most of their interlocutors on Congressional committees, however, came to see the diffuse-reciprocity model defended by the Executive as increasingly discredited.

The hearings on Section 301 are replete with assertions that the United States "gave up too much" in past negotiations. Addressing the results of the Kennedy Round, the vegetable growers' association made the general point succinctly: blinded by its free-trade ideals, the U.S. gave more than it got. Rep. Burke (of Burke-Hartke fame) made the point more bluntly, laying responsibility squarely on the Executive: "It is unbelievable what our negotiators did over there." Among many more specific examples, the chemical industry complained that the United States kept in place its Kennedy Round tariff reductions of 50 percent, even though the EC implemented only 20 percent cuts because of the failure of the United States to eliminate its American Selling Price system. The industry criticized this deal as "unfair and not in reciprocal balance." The underlying concern that foreign commercial firms were given greater commercial opportunities than U.S. firms comes through clearly.

Before the Tokyo Round results were announced in 1979, witnesses urged that the Administration be required to obtain equivalent concessions; once the results were known, some agreements were criticized for not having done so. In hearings on the 1984 amendments, many argued that the United States had given up too much in the Tokyo Round, both on tariffs and in the NTB agreements. By the time of the hearings on the 1988 Act, past failures to obtain specific reciprocity had become invested with considerable emotion, exemplified by the comment quoted above.[59]

Congress took action on these concerns over specific reciprocity. The Trade Act of 1974 authorized the President to recommend that future NTB agreements be adopted on a conditional MFN basis, to ensure that states benefiting from such agreements also accept their obligations[60]; this was in fact done for certain Tokyo Round agreements. The 1979 law implementing those agreements also provided that agreements accepted by the United States would not apply to a foreign country unless it had accepted the obligations of the agreement as to the United States, and that the President could not accept any agreement unless all other major industrial countries were also accepting it.[61]

Specific reciprocity in negotiations has considerable normative legitimacy. It is, after all, the basis for most simple contracts and exchanges in all areas of human endeavor, including many aspects of GATT negotiations. The principal weakness of the norm, pointed out by Keohane, is that it limits the prospects for cooperation to situations where exchanges of closely equivalent value can be identified and negotiated. If the necessary conditions can be created, diffuse reciprocity holds out the possibility of greater cooperation.[62]

Equal Access

Don't you think that trade is a two-way street? Why should we allow free trade and have our partners erect all the barriers they do?
Rep. Burke.[63]

More important in the history of Section 301 than the demand for specific reciprocity is the demand for a different notion of reciprocity: equal access. Equal access is a relative norm, like national treatment and MFN, but the comparison here is between the conditions prevailing in the respondent state and in the complainant state. The thrust of the normative claim is that the U.S. and U.S. firms should have access to or commercial opportunities in foreign markets equivalent to those that foreign firms have in the U.S.[64] In the negotiation context, the claim is that negotiations, instead of merely matching equal concessions, should lead to equal levels of access. These claims go well beyond traditional GATT practice, even beyond specific reciprocity. (I will refer to equal-access claims hereafter as reciprocity claims.)

Reciprocity claims appear throughout the history of Section 301, in the context both of negotiations and of unilateral action. Reciprocity is sought within both bilateral and multilateral relationships. Reciprocity is demanded as between national markets as a whole and as between particular economic sectors. Analysis could be organized in any of these ways. The most informative division, however, is between national and sectoral reciprocity, and I will proceed on that basis.

National Reciprocity

Ours is probably the most open market in the world for foreign investors. But look at how other nations treat us in return.
Rep. Shannon.[65]

In the legislative history of Section 301—which often deals simultaneously with authority for trade negotiations[66]—the common theme, repeated over and over again, is that U.S. markets for goods (both manufactured and agricultural), services, and investment are more open than the markets of its trading partners. I will give just a few examples. In the hearings on initial 301, the Cotton Council argued that trade should be a "two-way street"; but other countries want the U.S. to keep its markets open while they close theirs to varying degrees; this situation is inequitable. Rep. Burke fulminated at length on this theme in his inimitable fashion, as suggested by the quotation at the head of the Equal Access section. In a more sober vein, a group of eminent economists, including various Nobel prize winners and veterans of the Council of Economic Advisors, argued during the 1979 hearings that the greater openness of the U.S. was putting its firms at a disadvantage.

One specific complaint, raised throughout the history of the statute, is particularly telling, for it crystallizes the distinction between noncompliance and reciprocity claims. A wide variety of witnesses and members of Congress argue that tariff disparities between the U.S. and foreign nations are unfair (regardless of the relative size of past concessions) because they deny equal access. The complaint begins well before 1974, with Rep. Burke asking, "Shouldn't we have equal tariff rates everywhere? Why do we have to pay seven times the tariff on our exports that others have to pay on imports?"[67] It continues into the hearings on the 1988 amendment, with Rep. Thomas Luken accusing U.S. negotiators of having "sold out" an American industry by agreeing to a seven percent tariff differential, and USTR Clayton Yeutter patiently explaining that tariff rates diverge on many products, and that the tariff rates in question are lawful because they are bound in GATT.[68] To those on the other side, however, lawfulness was not the normative issue; reciprocity was.

By the time of the hearings on the 1984 trade act, the emotional level was high, and reciprocity was the issue of the day. The agenda was filled with legislative proposals designed to achieve reciprocity, and entire hearings were given over to the topic. Sen. Danforth argued that U.S. firms should be able to compete on an equal footing, enjoying the same commercial opportunities the United States provides to others. The U.S. Chamber of Commerce argued that the United States, unlike its trading partners, had an exemplary record of not giving in to interest group demands for import protection and other advantages. The bilateral relationship with Japan was a particular focus of reciprocity claims, summed up by Rep. Gibbons' charge that U.S.–Japan trade was "one-sided free trade."[69] A number of reciprocity bills were aimed solely at Japan.

With foreign industrial policies high on the agenda, a new reciprocity complaint was added: Foreign countries, especially Japan, assisted their industries in ways the U.S. did not, giving them an unfair edge in international competition. As Rep. Dingell put it, "the United States is being had and had good in world trade."[70] Such claims were advanced by a variety of economic interests, from sunset industries to high-technology champions.[71] Rep. Shannon, sponsor of a reciprocity bill, summarized the position: "other countries provide their industries unfair advantages through the use of tax subsidies, preferential treatment, assured markets, and import protection during the early stages of industry development."[72] This line of argument led inevitably to criticism of lax foreign regulation as well as excessive foreign assistance. Indeed, weak government regulation in fields like wage rates, working conditions, and environmental compliance, leading to lower production and operating costs for foreign competitors, were subject to considerable criticism on reciprocity grounds over most of the 25 years of Section 301 legislative history. As compared with the equal-access norm invoked when criticizing trade barriers, these charges might be said to reflect a norm of "equal production conditions."

Throughout the legislative history, the norm of reciprocity, coupled with the assumption (to a significant extent factual) that the U.S. market was more open than others, led naturally to demands for unilateral concessions or changes of policy by other states. Such changes could be achieved in several ways. Unilateral concessions in GATT negotiations were unlikely, of course. Legal action in GATT—focusing on individual barriers or, as in the case of Japan, on the nation's entire economic structure—was perceived by many as too slow, uncertain and, manipulable, and was in any case not available in areas where no GATT rules had been established. Direct bilateral negotiations backed up by threats of retaliation under Section 301, then, emerged as the natural focal point of reciprocity claims.[73]

The demand for equivalent access, let alone for equal production conditions, has little normative support in the established international economic system.[74] Within the United States, however, the claim has strong normative roots. One of those is the belief that the current lack of equal access derives from the absence of specific reciprocity in the past. Another source of the norm is the perception, especially clear during the economic shocks of the 1970s, that the United States is no longer the world's dominant economic power, especially relative to Japan and Europe. In the past, the argument goes, the United States could afford to make nonreciprocal concessions and accept nonreciprocal market opportunities and production conditions; it was justified in doing so, moreover, as the hegemon of the West, responsible for the security of the free world. Now, however, the country can no longer afford to make these sacrifices, and should not be asked to do so. By the mid–1980s, when all the hearings take on a more aggressive and critical tone, the other side of the coin appears: Prosperous countries like Japan and rapidly developing economies like the Asian tigers must "graduate" from the comforts of nonreciprocity, taking on responsibilities commensurate with their development. Even the executive branch agrees.

Some of the energy behind these reciprocity claims stems from the U.S. trade deficit, which was growing, first sporadically, then steadily, throughout the period. The fact that other rich nations, especially Japan, were running large surpluses seemed to confirm that others should take increased responsibility for the international system: "No responsible member of the international trade system can limit access to its market while maintaining large trade surpluses with its major trade partners."[75] The deficit was also treated by members of Congress and many thoughtful witnesses as a serious national problem, contributing to a growing foreign debt and other worrisome effects. No one asserts that unfair trade practices are responsible for more than a small portion of the deficit, but the link between this problem and the lack of reciprocity in commercial activity is inescapable. In addition, the deficit functions for some as rough evidence of a lack of reciprocity, reinforcing more specific examples. Finally, because of the perceived importance of the problem, the deficit was undoubtedly used rhetorically by many private interests to give urgency to their case. In 1985, for example, the Communication Workers refer to the deficit as an "emergency of massive proportions" in order to justify aggressive action.[76] Those utilizing this argument often appear to be as much or more concerned with restricting imports into the United States as with expanding exports; examples include the Steel Workers and UAW.

In the mid–1980s, concern over the trade deficit were crystallized by the Gephardt amendment, an alternative to the strengthening of Section 301. Under this proposal, the government would have identified states with a substantial bilateral trade surplus and a "pattern" of unfair trade practices contributing to the surplus. The U.S. would then have set surplus reduction goals, basically a 10 percent reduction per year for four years. If negotiations on means to achieve these goals were unsuccessful, the President would have been authorized to take a range of retaliatory and non-retaliatory measures. Gephardt steadfastly argued that his bill was not designed simply to achieve surplus reduction by reducing imports, though that is what his critics charged and probably what many of his supporters, like the UAW, hoped to see. Instead, Gephardt argued that the surplus reduction goals of the bill would raise the price of maintaining unfair trade barriers, and predicted that most states would negotiate their barriers away. Much of the debate on this measure concerns these tactical issues. In the end, of course, the concerns over reciprocity and the deficit reflected in the Gephardt amendment led to a significant strengthening of 301, especially the addition of Super 301.

Sectoral Reciprocity

American firms [in our industry] are forced to participate in a "free for all" in their own market while at the same time they are being systematically excluded from foreign markets. The situation ... is both inequitable and intolerable.... The wonder of it all is "Why do we tolerate it"?

Dr. Charles B. Wakeman, Siecor Corporation.[77]

The argument that firms in individual economic sectors in industry, agriculture, and services should have the same access to foreign markets as foreign firms in those sectors have to the American market is at least as common and influential a claim in the history of Section 301 as the demand for reciprocity on a national scale. National reciprocity, which was at first something of a radical demand, becomes by the mid-1980s a conservative alternative to sectoral reciprocity. Interestingly, sectoral reciprocity seems to be the favored claim of individual firms and industry groups throughout the legislative history. Broader-based business groups like the Business Roundtable tend to favor national reciprocity or some compromise such as reciprocity within the industrial, agricultural, and services sectors as a whole. Executive branch officials oppose sectoral reciprocity even more strongly than national reciprocity. Here more than anywhere else in the legislative history, the difference in worldview suggested in the Introduction—the view of the private firm engaged in direct international competition versus a broader view of American business or the national economy as a whole—is starkly apparent.

During the 1974 hearings, which focused on foreign NTBs, virtually every industry group complaining of barriers relied on the norm of sectoral reciprocity, explicitly or implicitly. The Wine Council, for example, observed that foreign wines move freely in the U.S. market, subject only to national taxes and a modest tariff. When U.S. firms try to export wine, however, they face a "nightmare" of restrictions, including outright prohibitions, prohibitive tariffs, and the EC variable levy. "Reciprocity is not a reality" for the wine industry.[78] The Tanners Council similarly noted that U.S. leather is virtually banned in Japan for various "ludicrous," "nonsense" excuses,[79] while Japanese firms are free to ship shoes, gloves, and other leather products here. (The principle the Tanners urged as a way to deal with such problems is quoted at the head of Section 10.5 above.) Sectoral reciprocity did not appear explicitly in initial 301, but it was included as a negotiating objective for the Tokyo Round, along with the instruction that negotiations should be conducted on a sectoral basis to the extent feasible.[80]

Again in 1984, most firms, industry groups, and unions asserted the need for a policy of sectoral reciprocity, and several sectoral reciprocity bills—as well as semisectoral bills like the proposed High Technology Trade Act—were under consideration. In discussions of foreign industrial policy, high-tech industries typified by the Semiconductor Industry Association (SIA) (one of the most active and seemingly influential groups on Section 301) and low-tech sectors like the Raisin Growers joined in arguing that it was also a denial of sectoral reciprocity for foreign competitors to receive more governmental assistance than firms in the U.S. Many of these industries argue for increased assistance from the U.S. government as well as for unilateral changes in foreign practices, an example of what Nicolaides calls the "'me too' syndrome."[81]

The same pattern continues in the hearings on current 301. Industries including auto parts, semiconductors, chemicals, autos, electrical equipment, small aircraft, pharmaceuticals, furniture, and leather hammer away at the fact that foreign competitors in their industry are free to enter the U.S. market, while the home markets of those competitors are closed, at least relatively, sometimes absolutely. These industries demand equal access, and urge the use of 301, including its retaliation provisions, in an aggressive way to force the unilateral concessions needed.[82]

Much of the attention in these hearings focuses on the telecommunications equipment sector, along with related industries like fiber optics. Firms, unions, and associations connected with these industries (like the Siecor Corporation, quoted above) argue the unfairness of operating in a private, open, post–AT&T market when their competitors' markets feature national PTT monopolies with strict buy-domestic policies and discriminatory product standards. Virtually all the relevant members of Congress agree that a lack of reciprocity within these industries is particularly unacceptable, and they express their conclusion in emotional terms, led by the frequently intemperate Rep. Dingell: "Yesterday, the subcommittee heard some truly shocking testimony. Manufacturers of ... fiber optic cable told us how foreign firms exploited technology developed in the United States, ... protected their home markets from U.S. sales, and then flooded our markets with the fruits of their predatory practices."[83] Sectoral reciprocity bills for telecommunications sponsored by Sen. Danforth and other influential members of Congress received much attention, and the 1988 Act gave the sector special treatment.[84]

Sectoral reciprocity has very little normative legitimacy in the established rules and structures of the international economy. An objective reading of the claims set out in the legislative history of 301, however, suggests that there may be good reasons why the idea has such normative force. The norm of sectoral reciprocity stems, after all, from the idea of the competitive market,[85] especially as seen from the "micro" perspective of the individual firm. Even in a low-tech industry, the U.S. firm faces a situation in which its direct competitors can compete with it in the U.S. market, but it cannot compete with them in their home markets. While the foreign firms are able to operate in a large, even unitary, market spanning two or more countries, this market is artificially bifurcated for the U.S. firm by the intervention of foreign governments. The limited scope of the available market restricts the competitive strategies available to the U.S. firm and sets an artificial upper limit to its growth and profitability; it may also give significant competitive advantages to foreign firms.

These competitive advantages are more prominent in the testimony of high-technology firms. The SIA, Electronics Industries Association and other high-tech sectoral groups explain in detail in the Congressional hearings how defensive barriers in a nation like Japan, coupled with relatively open markets in the United States, give foreign firms an opportunity to advance further down the learning curve and achieve greater economies of scale than their U.S. competitors. More active forms of government assistance create other competitive advantages, such as more extensive or less expensive research. This testimony in fact constitutes a relatively early presentation of the theory of strategic trade policy. Many U.S. industries argued that they could not long continue to compete with foreign firms aided by such measures, and made the strategic trade policy argument that national welfare—even national security—would suffer if they were allowed to be victimized.

Representatives of the Executive branch opposed every sectoral reciprocity proposal in the legislative history. They do not, however, seek to rebut the strategic trade policy arguments advanced by industry. Instead, they argue that a policy of sectoral reciprocity would make it more difficult to negotiate liberalizing trade agreements. In negotiations, especially if multilateral, they explain, one must make tradeoffs to get a deal; often these tradeoffs must be between sectors. The alternative, if foreign nations are unwilling to offer concessions in particular sectors, is no deal at all. At the end of the day, the Executive asserts, negotiators can compare the overall concessions in a rough way, and the results are likely to benefit the nation as a whole, even though some individual industries may not benefit, and some may suffer.

Colloquies on this issue between Executive branch officials, on the one hand, and industry representatives and their supporters in Congress, on the other, often read like a dialogue of the deaf. As the foregoing analysis suggests, the two sides are in fact talking past one another. The USTR, responsible for conducting national trade policy in an established international system, cannot assume the perspective of the Raisin Growers; the fiber optics industry finds no solace at all in the USTR's argument about overall national benefit, and indeed advances contrary national-interest arguments of its own. From their own perspectives, both are right.

Equal Outcomes and Measurable Results

I think nations that trade have a responsibility to see that there is reciprocity. I buy what you have, you buy what I have, and we try to come out even. That, to me, is free trade....

Rep. Collier.[86]

In the legislative history of Section 301, someone occasionally takes the position that equal access is not necessarily sufficient; what counts is equal results: equal sales or profits. A particularly colorful, and economically loony, example is the statement of Rep. Collier quoted above, from the hearings on initial 301; few would go this far.

By the time of the hearings on current 301, however, considerable frustration had built up over the perceived failure of negotiations—from the Tokyo Round to the bilateral MOSS talks with Japan—and of a twice-strengthened section 301 to achieve greater reciprocity, especially on a sectoral level. Industries begin to demand specific, if not equal, results. The Telecommunications Group of the Electronics Industries Association, for example, argued that past negotiations, especially those with Japan on procurement by NTT, had focused on "regulatory parity," that is, on equal access; it might now be time, however, to focus on actual increased sales. The SIA, fiber optics industry, and other high-tech sectors, as well as the auto parts and soda ash industries, similarly demanded that Section 301 proceedings and other negotiations focus on obtaining commitments to specific economic results, even if they were not fully comparable to the results of foreign industries in the U.S.

A number of members of Congress supported this position. Even representatives of the USTR asserted that in their current sectoral talks they were seeking concrete, measurable commitments on matters like sales and market share. An important contemporaneous manifestation of this position was the so-called side agreement setting a market share goal or commitment in the U.S.-Japan semiconductor arrangement, an arrangement that led to serious controversy when the U.S. tried to enforce it. The same policy has assumed even greater prominence in U.S. trade policy during the Clinton Administration, particularly in the standoff between the U.S. and Japan over the inclusion of quantitative criteria for measuring results in bilateral, sectoral market-opening agreements negotiated within the Framework for a New Economic Partnership. It has been striking to see the Executive branch—which has opposed sectoral reciprocity arguments for 20 years—buy so completely into this rather extreme position.

A national demand for guarantees of equal results, or even for guarantees of specific, measurable results, has virtually no normative legitimacy of its own within the international economic system.[87] The same demand on the import side—reflected in voluntary export restraint agreements (VERs) and the like—is equally illegitimate, at least in law, and such measures are banned under the Uruguay Round safeguards agreement.[88] These claims could be seen simply as a manifestation of mercantilism, the same sin that critics of foreign defensive barriers perceive in others. In the context of the legislative history of 301 as a whole, however, it appears that these claims (and the Executive's recent reliance on them) are intended less as independent normative positions than as ways of dealing with what are perceived to be duplicitous foreign governments. These issues will be considered further in Section 9.4.

9.2.5   The Norm of the Free Market

In setting trade policies, most nations now follow Clausewitz on war, not Ricardo on comparative advantage.
AFL–CIO.[89]

The claim that foreign government policies and practices are unfair if they distort market forces to the disadvantage of U.S. firms plays several important roles in the history of Section 301.

First, as should already be apparent, the idea of market distortion is inherent in several of the separate normative rationales already considered. In particular, both discrimination and reciprocity, national and sectoral, could be viewed as subdivisions of a fundamental market-distortion norm, although those claims are in fact treated as normatively independent. The relationship is particularly clear in the market-based argument for sectoral reciprocity discussed above.

Second, the norm of market distortion seems to lie behind many other claims, even when it is not made explicit. In the hearings on initial 301, in particular, many industry statements did not advance any specific normative claim at all, but simply described the NTBs they faced in foreign markets. Some of these NTBs could be characterized as unlawful, most as discriminatory, and most as nonreciprocal, at least within the same sectors. The normative claim that one perceives behind these statements, however, is that the foreign barriers interfere with the relatively unimpeded market competition that was supposed to accompany the reduction of tariffs. In the early 1970s most of those concerned with foreign market distortion supported the Nixon Administration's request for broad negotiating authority to deal with NTBs. Later, however, they demanded more aggressive action under Section 301.

Third, especially during the 1980s, as the Tokyo Round negotiations came to be perceived as disappointing, private-sector witnesses began to cast their complaints about foreign practices explicitly in terms of market distortion. Agricultural export interests argued, for example, that foreign import barriers and other government practices artificially constrained the ability of U.S. growers to capitalize on their natural comparative advantage. The Rice Millers complained that Japanese rice growers were completely isolated from the world market, while U.S. growers had begun to move toward market dependence.[90] Many industries charged that foreign governments distorted trade and investment decisions for mercantilist reasons or to achieve social objectives like maintaining employment or national economic goals like conserving foreign exchange. Specific practices criticized in terms of market distortion included investment restrictions, incentives and performance requirements, subsidies of all kinds, and more traditional import restrictions. During this period, most private-sector interests also sought more aggressive action, especially against intentional market distortion. Interestingly, though, the market norm was also used at this time to attack the Gephardt amendment.[91]

Finally, the market norm was the central theme of the attack on foreign targeting and industrial policy that occupied so much of the legislative history of Section 301 during the 1980s. Some concerns with foreign industrial policy were expressed even in the hearings on initial 301. By 1979, the National Association of Manufacturers, arguing in support of the

Tokyo Round Codes, asserted that the heart of the NTB problem was constraining governmental actions that alter and distort trade patterns by fiat; the NAM outlined many of the practices that would figure prominently in the coming debate: a growing public sector that buys and sells on a nationalistic basis; programs to strengthen the competitive strength of local firms through domestic subsidies, R&D support, and infrastructure improvements; discriminatory national technical standards; captive national markets to help firms grow; and encouragement of large investments in productive capacity that can only be justified by substantial exports. From a position closer to the front lines, the steel and semiconductor industries and the AFL-CIO explained the difficulties faced by U.S. firms that must earn a profit in order to remain in business, but are forced to compete with governments, or firms supported by governments, that will be kept alive so long as they continue to provide jobs, profit or no.

By 1984, a growing number of firms, industries, unions and other witnesses assert explicitly or implicitly that the principal problem in international trade is foreign targeting and industrial policy, particularly in high-tech industries. Advancing a strategic trade policy analysis, witnesses repeatedly argue that foreign governments are taking advantage of market conditions like declining costs and learning curves to incubate domestic firms that can later be "unleashed" on world markets. The strongest advocate of this position is the SIA, which argues that Japan and other countries use targeting and other beggar-thy-neighbor, market-distorting measures for traditional mercantilist reasons: to build strong, prosperous states.

Other witnesses, including broad business associations like the U.S. branch of the International Chamber of Commerce, the U.S. Chamber of Commerce, and the Business Roundtable, as well as advocacy groups like the Labor-Industry Coalition for International Trade (LICIT), take up the argument that foreign governments implement industrial policies to achieve social, regional, industrial, and financial goals, both long and short term, instead of deferring to the market. As a result, public and private enterprises alike are able to operate in disregard of basic market principles, such as the need to compete for capital, please shareholders, and make a profit. Individual firms argue, often poignantly, that they cannot compete with such enterprises. It is suggested at least once that some foreign government intervention might well be justified to correct domestic market failures; in the cases at hand, however, that justification is alleged not to apply: Japan, in particular, is seen not to be offsetting disadvantages faced by its firms, but as grooming them to dominate world markets.

Many of the same points are repeated in hearings on the 1988 Act. Unions, including the AFL-CIO, firms and industry groups, and associations like the Chamber of Commerce all criticize foreign industrial policies and targeting as distortive of the market. By this time, however, the claim has been thoroughly ventilated and accepted by the relevant members of Congress. Most of the 1988 hearings are devoted to demands for more aggressive action. While the 1984 Act added the elimination of harmful targeting practices to the statute as a negotiating objective,[92] the 1988 Act designated any combination of acts, policies, and practices found to constitute "export targeting" as an "unreasonable," and thus actionable, practice.

The fact that the 1988 amendment applied to "export targeting," rather than "targeting" or "industrial policy" more broadly, raises an important point. In discussions based on the market-distortion norm, and indeed on some other norms as well, the distinction between defensive and offensive unfairness rather quickly begins to break down. Even purely defensive barriers are often viewed as having offensive implications, or as being part of a package designed for offense as much as defense. This is certainly the case in the targeting debate, where foreign industrial policies are viewed as primarily designed to grow successful export industries. Industry groups like the SIA are as much concerned with dumped or subsidized exports from foreign targeted industries to the United States and third markets as they are in obtaining access to foreign markets for their own products. Firms like Houdaille, the machine tool manufacturer that brought the first legal action based on foreign targeting, and industries like steel are primarily concerned with foreign exports. These are not simply protectionist responses, however: They comport perfectly with the economic analysis of targeting as strategic trade policy.

Even outside the area of targeting, those complaining about defensive barriers are often concerned with import competition. Unfortunately, many of these complaints seem to be transparent attempts to turn norms of defensive unfairness to protectionist advantage. From the early 1970s until 1988, many of the "usual suspects" in the field of import relief—industries like steel, leather, autos, fruits and vegetables, and footwear—complain regularly about closed foreign markets. In 1974, the AFL-CIO complains vigorously about foreign trade barriers, but comes down in support of the Burke-Hartke bill, which would have established quotas on imports and restrictions on outgoing foreign investment, without attacking defensive barriers in any significant way. Others complain about foreign barriers and argue for retaliation, sometimes mandatory retaliation, as a way to obtain some protection from imports. Even if transparent, this kind of testimony has had political effects: It has led many to support a strengthened Section 301 to deal with defensive barriers in order to head off more direct protectionist demands.

The market-distortion rationale—at least when used properly—has some legitimacy. After all, many rules of GATT, from broad principles like MFN and national treatment to more specific rules like the prohibition of quantitative restraints, are designed precisely to restrict governmental practices that distort market behavior to an unacceptable degree. The same is true of other international agreements, like BITs. None of these agreements, however, gives the principle of market disruption much authority outside these specific, negotiated, often qualified rules.

9.2.6   Structural Unfairness

The Japanese, by sleight-of-hand, magic, tradition, or downright subterfuge, have been able to see to it that . . . , in spite of the U.S. comparative advantage, nothing can happen.

Tanners Council of America.[93]

Under the heading of structural unfairness, I combine two rather different arguments sometimes found in the history of Section 301. The two are united by the fact that neither deals with specific governmental measures.

First, private-sector witnesses frustrated by efforts to enter foreign markets, especially Japan, occasionally make a sweeping argument to the following effect: Even though we are unable to identify the particular governmental measures that protect the foreign market, *something* improper must be at work in those markets, or else we would be able to sell there. The argument is often supported by assertions about product quality and statistics demonstrating success in other markets. In 1981, for example, the Tanners Council described their earlier 301 case against Japan, as a result of which the USTR had negotiated a special quota for U.S. leather. Once the quota was established, the Tanners asserted, they began an export push in Japan—but with no results. After three years, they had only been able to fill 14 percent of their quota. While they cited certain specific NTBs, the Tanners were largely reduced to advancing the kind of argument quoted above. Comments to the effect that those seeking to sell in Japan face an "impenetrable maze" or a "wall of fog" fall in the same general category. Experiences like those of the Tanners, if true, certainly carry some intuitive persuasive power, but these are not truly normative arguments. The Japanese government and other experts have also argued that such statistical comparisons can be misleading.[94]

Second, and more important, is the argument that such fundamental characteristics of foreign nations as their political systems, economic systems, and culture may be at least partly responsible for difficulties in entering or operating in their markets, and that these situations are in some sense unfair. This claim too is typically aimed at Japan. In the legislative history of 301, for example, private interests like the Machinists Union as well as legislators such as Rep. Gibbons claim that a relatively closed Japanese culture is part of the explanation for the difficulty of selling and investing there; Gibbons argues that this structural difference places a responsibility on Japan to show outsiders how to penetrate it. The Association of Exporters and Importers argues that Japanese business structures and practices are the heart of the market-access problem. Kent Caldor argues that capture of the Japanese bureaucracy by industry and the pattern of cooperation between them is the principal problem. Sen. Heinz, after a visit to Japan, asserts that there are deep problems with the Japanese political system, from the bureaucracy to the Diet. Fred Bergsten complains of Japanese "group think." Others simply lay the blame on the Japanese system across the board.

There seems to be no question that structural differences like these can make economic intercourse difficult. Neutral observers might well say, moreover, that it could benefit both sides to work on harmonizing such national structures, although few would expect this approach to be easy, and some might hold out for preserving important elements of distinct national cultures. The normative claim, however, that structural differences like these are unfair by themselves would seem to have virtually no legitimacy.[95] This assessment is basically reflected in U.S. trade policy: cultural and other structural differences are not dealt with under Section 301, but efforts at harmonization have been made in such settings as the U.S.–Japan Structural Impediments talks.

9.2.7   Mercantilist Claims

Where other nations bar U.S. products ..., U.S. laws to gain access should be [enforced] to even out the burdens in the world.

AFL-CIO.[96]

With a wealth of normative claims available to them, few in either Congress or the private sector find it necessary to adopt straightforward mercantilist positions in comments on Section 301, though foreign governments are regularly portrayed as pursuing traditional and neomercantilist policies. The AFL-CIO, other unions, and import-competing industries, however, certainly base their positions on the assumptions that imports are economically damaging to local competitors and indeed that the costs they create for local workers, producers, and communities outweigh their benefits to consumers. The AFL-CIO philosophy is summed up in the memorable phrase, often repeated, that is quoted above: "trade" means imports, and imports are an unalloyed burden. By the same token, most of the witnesses supporting a strengthened Section 301 treat exports as an unalloyed benefit, the main goal of international trade policy, though few argue that the coercive power of 301 should be deployed simply as an effective way to increase exports.

From time to time, however, comments suggestive of a mercantilist approach do appear, independently or in discussions of structural problems, measurable commitments to market access, and other issues. These comments are nonnormative by nature, and are virtually without normative legitimacy. The related argument that the United States must in some way protect itself from mercantilist policies (like targeting) that other countries follow, putting their national interests as they see them ahead of free-trade principles, is complex, interesting, and powerful. It is basically a tactical point, however, not a normative one.

9.3   Assessment

This section sets forth a preliminary assessment of the validity and power of the fairness norms described in Section 9.2. Several introductory points should be noted. First, I focus here on the normative arguments themselves. I am not concerned, except incidentally, with the "operational" aspects of these arguments, such as their unilateral administration and their tendency to bypass established institutional structures like the GATT dispute-resolution procedure. Those are valid grounds for criticism, but not the subject of this paper. Second, it is also necessary to separate the normative claims from the facts to which they are applied. Experts will undoubtedly differ on the accuracy of the factual claims made in the legislative history of Section 301, but for the present I am not disputing them. The same holds true for matters of theory, such as the economic analysis of the effects of foreign industrial policies. If the facts or theories are false, the conclusions drawn are also false; but I wish to examine the normative part of the syllogism. Finally, recall that the task of assessment was begun in Section 9.2, which presented the norms of fairness roughly in order of their legitimacy within the international economic system.

9.3.1   Internal Consistency and Coherence

These two related standards are important logical tests of any set of normative propositions. Applying these standards to the norms of fairness underlying Section 301 produces mixed results: In general, the norms of fairness are closely interrelated and well integrated, yet they also pose significant problems of coherence.

(1)   The norm of compliance with commitments and rules is by itself unexceptionable; the nullification or impairment norm is in a real sense a logical corollary of the compliance norm.

(2)   The nondiscrimination norm, especially in the national treatment sense, is highly coherent. Few if any problems of consistency with the compliance and nullification norms arise, either, because discrimination is the underlying rationale for most of the rules and commitments in international economic law.

(3)   The norm of reciprocity has some problems of coherence because of the several senses in which the term is used. Specific reciprocity in the negotiated exchange of concessions, equivalent levels of trade restriction at the national level, and equivalent levels of restriction at the sectoral level are all sensible concepts, though they may be difficult to apply to complex regulatory programs. In the legislative history of Section 301, however, they have proven not to be fully consistent with each other. Thus, it is possible to complain of a lack of equal access even if specific reciprocity in previous negotiations has been achieved; it is also possible to complain of a lack of equal access at the sectoral level even if on average national levels of access are equivalent. The reciprocity norm is only truly coherent, then, when only one of its variations is invoked.

While the reciprocity norm is logically different from the norm of nondiscrimination, many reciprocity claims are also discrimination claims: If a complainant firm could benefit from the protections or benefits foreign governments are said to offer, it would have no reason to criticize them.[97] Thus, few inconsistencies between these norms arise. A significant problem of consistency may, however, arise with the compliance norm. The problem is best illustrated by the continuing complaint, based on the equal-access version of the reciprocity norm, that it is unfair for foreign nations to maintain significantly higher tariff rates on particular products than the United States does. Tariffs are subject to a complex system of rules and institutions, under which tariff rates are capped and periodically negotiated downward. The tariffs that result from that system are essentially declared lawful under GATT Article II. Thus, while the existence of legal rules and the norm of compliance support many reciprocity complaints and are irrelevant to others (those dealing with as yet unregulated areas), in this case the norm of compliance cuts against the norm of reciprocity. The same conflict can be observed in the application of the market distortion and other norms.

The force of the reciprocity norm is significantly reduced when this kind of conflict exists, especially when the norm is invoked as a rationale for unilateral concessions. But the norm of reciprocity is extremely powerful, especially within the worldview of the private firm engaged in international competition. In the legislative history of Section 301, private-sector witnesses have typically dealt with conflicts between legal rules and norms like reciprocity by impugning the validity of the relevant legal system. In the tariff case, for example, they have criticized not only the procedures of GATT negotiations but also the United States negotiating positions, reflective of diffuse reciprocity, and the skill of the U.S. negotiators. To some extent, the claim could be analogized to an argument that the outcome of a legal proceeding was invalid because one party lacked adequate counsel. Congress and the Executive have generally been unwilling to act on claims that fly in the face of legal authority. The normative conflict has, however, fed a deep sense of disrespect for traditional negotiating postures and procedures.

(4)   Market distortion is the theoretical underpinning for most claims of discrimination and nonreciprocity, as well as for most international rules. In addition, almost all of the measures criticized in the history of Section 301 as market-distorting involve elements of discrimination and nonreciprocity, and many involve violations of commitments as well. The market-distortion norm, then, has little problem of consistency.

There are, however, significant problems of internal coherence. First, market distortion is a remarkably flexible principle. All governments, including that of the United States, intervene in markets in myriad ways, most of which have both economic and political rationales. All of these interventions cannot be considered "unfair," yet how does one decide where to stop? Which forms of intervention are acceptable, which not? Is there some "natural" set of governmental measures outside of which the market-distortion norm becomes applicable? Countervailing-duty (CVD) law has struggled with these questions for years, though with only limited success. The most important line drawn in CVD jurisprudence is between "specific" and "general" governmental measures; this line has economic justification, since only distortion of the relative costs between industries can change comparative advantage. The specificity test is not explicitly advanced in the legislative history of Section 301, but it seems to be generally accepted: Virtually all the governmental measures complained of would be considered "specific."

Second, while the neoclassical market model does offer a theoretical basis for distinguishing between optimal interventions to correct specific market failures and measures that are inappropriately distortive, it is virtually impossible to apply these theoretical insights empirically. To assess a particular government intervention, one must first drastically expand the frame of reference to include all aspects of the market in question, including the many other governmental interventions, since the measure in question may simply offset some other market failure or distortion.[98] Even then the interrelationships are likely to be too complex and dynamic to unravel.

Third, states have very different conceptions of the proper role of government in the market. In the absence of consensus, however, there must inevitably be a tendency to regard forms of market intervention practiced by one's own government as "natural" and acceptable, while regarding the practices of others as distortive and unacceptable. The problem is accentuated in the administration of a unilateral statute like Section 301. If American standards of market intervention were to become the operative principles of Section 301, claims advanced under the statute would become much less legitimate.

In the end, one must conclude that market distortion has limited normative legitimacy as an independent principle.

(5)   "Wall-of-fog"-type structural claims are intended to suggest discrimination, nonreciprocity and market distortion in conditions where concrete evidence is hard to find. Such claims are consistent with prior norms, though they share the weaknesses of those norms as well as their strengths. Most structural claims are, however, normatively weak, if not incoherent, because of their lack of specificity. Claims that the culture, politics, or economic system of Japan or some other country are unfair to U.S. firms are also essentially discrimination and reciprocity claims, reflecting the

assumptions that it is easier for Japanese to operate in their own society and that U.S. society is more open. The principal normative weaknesses of these claims are their lack of specificity and the fact that they seem to attack the nature of things. If it could be shown that particular cultural or economic institutions were actually artifacts of intentional government action, especially action designed to disadvantage foreign firms, the normative criticism would be much stronger, in terms both of norms of fairness and norms of responsibility.

The most significant problem of consistency and coherence arising in connection with the entire set of fairness norms has to do not so much with the norms themselves as with the procedures used to implement them. The threat of retaliation is virtually the only method anyone has suggested by which the U.S. can marshall enough power to obtain the unilateral correction of allegedly unfair foreign trade practices under Section 301. If retaliation is actually carried out, however, the U.S. becomes guilty of discrimination, nonreciprocity, and market distortion. In addition, while retaliation under the aegis of the GATT dispute-settlement process will be justified by international agreement, unilateral retaliation will often violate international commitments. The very structure of Section 301, then, places the U.S. government in the position of committing most of the wrongs with which it charges others.

A related procedural issue is that noted above as a criticism of the Gephardt amendment. Even if a Section 301 action successfully elicits a commitment to correct an allegedly unfair trade practice, the foreign government must often intervene in its economy to ensure compliance. Such intervention will be especially likely if specific quantitative results are required. In these circumstances, what is seen as a remedy for, let us say, some form of discrimination could well lead to increased market distortion, in both the short and long terms.

9.3.2   Mirror-Image Issues

Criticisms of other nations' policies lose normative force to the extent that the United States follows similar policies. This is a particular problem for reciprocity claims, of course, but the point applies to any normative claim made in connection with Section 301. The United States has been adjudged to have breached GATT and to have instituted discriminatory trade policies. There are products on which U.S. tariffs are higher than those of other countries, and nations with which the United States runs a large trade surplus. U.S. agricultural quotas and price supports, as well as various VERs, have created situations of nonreciprocal market access for foreign suppliers. United States policies from trade preferences for Caribbean products to tax and budget measures affect ("distort") various product, service, and capital markets.

Professor Hudec has observed that Congress regularly acts as if the United States were wholly blameless in matters of trade policy.[99] Perhaps surprisingly, though, the mirror-image problem was not simply glossed over during the legislative history of Section 301. Representatives of the Executive branch pointed out the problem repeatedly, explicitly noting that other nations would be justified not only in criticizing the United States on similar grounds, but in initiating 301-type procedures, and even in retaliating, against it. The latter threat is minimized by the relative economic strength of the United States, of course, but the Executive, at least, seemed to take it seriously. Mirror-image problems were also pointed out by private-sector groups such as retailers, the Association of Exporters and Importers, and others vulnerable to retaliation and counter-retaliation. Most surprising of all, the problem was on more than one occasion pointed out by members of Congress to witnesses urging aggressive action under Section 301. Although the statute has been strengthened several times, it has always left the Executive with considerable discretion, even under Super 301 and the mandatory retaliation provisions. It would be a reasonable hypothesis that recognition of the mirror-image problem is at least in part responsible for this (relative) restraint.

Most supporters of a strong Section 301 respond to the existence of restrictive U.S. measures in one of three ways. First, many assert differences in scope and intensity: True, the United States may have import restrictions, but they are neither so numerous nor so restrictive as in the EC or Japan. This is basically a factual distinction, but one that introduces troublesome gradations of reciprocity into the basic norm. Second, many witnesses seek to distinguish U.S. restrictions in terms of their legal nature. The most significant U.S. import restrictions—VERs, antidumping and countervailing duties, for example—are cast as either temporary safeguard measures or lawful responses to unfair practices, while the foreign measures complained of are simply protectionist devices.[100]

Third, numerous supporters of Section 301 address the mirror-image problem from the slippery ground of intent. The argument that U.S. restrictions are designed to respond to unfair practices while foreign barriers are simply protectionist is not just a matter of legal form; it is a normative argument asserting the greater legitimacy of the mental state behind the U.S. restrictions. Supporters also argue that U.S. policies which might be criticized as targeting are actually innocent (and commercially inefficient) byproducts of military or NASA operations, which were, after all, undertaken on behalf of the free world while others took free rides. Foreign practices, in contrast, are typically characterized as intentional efforts to implement strategic trade policy by protecting sunrise industries, growing dominant firms, and the like.

None of these arguments responds completely to the mirror-image problem. In addition, the underlying facts and the characterizations applied to them by the proponents are often complex and controvertible. To the extent that they apply, they have some plausible normative force. Rarely, however, is this force great enough to overcome the effects of mirror-image restrictions and recapture the original power of reciprocity and other norms.

Witnesses who advance sectoral reciprocity claims typically adopt a position on mirror-image issues similar to that taken on GATT negotiations: Whether another sector benefits from some protective measure or price support or receives some spinoff benefit from a NASA program is of little relevance to us; our only concern is the artificial advantages of the firms that compete with us in the narrow market where we do business.[101] From the private firm's micro perspective, this position, like sectoral reciprocity in general, makes perfect sense. From a national perspective, however, the existence of equivalent practices in any sector weakens a normative claim advanced by the U.S. government, especially one based on reciprocity. The result is another dialogue of the deaf: Industry representatives see mirror-image problems raised by the Executive as irrelevant, while the Executive feels itself constrained by those problems from taking up the industry's complaint. Efforts to resolve this conflict—which engenders considerable tension—have hardly begun.

9.3.3 Workability

A third basis of assessment is whether the norms of fairness advanced in connection with Section 301 would be workable as a basis for national trade policy in dealing with the acts, policies, and practices of foreign governments. Operational issues, legitimacy, factual determination, and mirror-image problems are of course all relevant to this issue.

(1) The norm of compliance with rules and commitments and the norm of nondiscrimination both seem quite workable in practice. Both

are implicated in the operation of virtually all international economic agreements, not only GATT—with its dispute-resolution procedure and requirement of involvement by the Contracting Parties—but numerous bilateral treaties where unilateral demands for corrective action, negotiations, and the possibility of retorsions,[102] reprisals,[103] and withdrawal are routine. Unilateral determinations of noncompliance are the stuff of traditional international law. Charges of discrimination can typically be made on a relatively objective basis, and are a staple of relations under most economic agreements. Most actual Section 301 proceedings, moreover, are based on one of these norms.

(2)   Reciprocity, on the other hand, is a rather slippery norm, particularly because it can mean different things to different people: There is a vast distance between specific reciprocity in trade negotiations and equal or measurable economic outcomes. There are other ambiguities as well. Is strict bilateral reciprocity required, or will overall multilateral reciprocity suffice? Should reciprocity be achieved bilaterally at the expense of the MFN principle? Must reciprocity be national or sectoral? If sectoral, how should the relevant sector be defined? How are mirror-image issues to be handled? Should one take account of similar practices in other sectors of the complainant state's economy? Other kinds of benefits that the complaining sector may receive? Whichever kind of reciprocity is at issue, how close must the equivalence be? How is it to be measured? How is reciprocity to be achieved? What of the possible conflict between reciprocity and prevailing legal standards? On these and other issues, the reciprocity principle seems difficult to administer, and even more difficult to administer even-handedly. Even specific reciprocity in trade negotiations, as witnesses from the Executive have argued throughout the legislative history of Section 301, is not easily achieved, whether on tariff rates or on the rule-based issues of the Tokyo and Uruguay Rounds.

(3)   Market distortion seems the most unworkable norm of all, for the reasons already given. If states disagree on the proper role of government and thus on the very meaning of market distortion, if every government (including those favoring relatively free markets) intervenes frequently in its economy, and if the principal theoretical understandings are virtually impossible to apply, the market-distortion principle hardly offers a workable basis for trade policy. It also seems likely that foreign governments will resist market-distortion claims more strongly than, say, charges of discrimination, since such claims go to the heart of the foreign state's

economic system. Finally, because of the universality of market intervention, mirror-image issues will plague market-distortion claims.

(4) "Wall-of-fog" structural claims are clearly unworkable because of
their lack of specificity. Structural claims of the "different-culture" variety
can at least be grappled with, but may require such deep or sweeping
change—much of which may be beyond governmental control[104]—as to
be unmanageable even in long-term negotiating contexts like the Structural Impediments Initiative, let alone in demands for unilateral change
constrained by statutory time limits.

(5) Discrimination, reciprocity, market distortion, and structural/
cultural claims share a final problem of workability that does not arise with
claims of noncompliance with rules or commitments. In the latter context,
the universe of potential claims is rather clearly delimited. Rules may
require interpretation at the margin, but there are only so many rules to
be broken. The other normative claims, however, pose serious "slippery-
slope" problems. The problem is perhaps greatest with the reciprocity
norm. It is one thing to say that state A should not be allowed to target
export industries in a way that state B does not. Experience with Section
301 suggests, however, that there is no way to limit reciprocity claims to
such discrete economic policy measures. Reciprocity claims can expand
along at least two dimensions. First, demands can grow in intensity, from
the removal of an offending foreign measure, to the addition of equivalent
domestic measures, to quantitative economic results, to equal outcomes
(demands that are increasingly at odds with free-market norms). Second,
reciprocity claims can grow in breadth, from border measures, to domestic
measures aimed at exporting or import-competing industries, to more
general domestic economic policy measures, to noneconomic measures like
environmental protection, to structural and cultural issues. Norms as un-
controllable as this are not workable bases for national trade policy.

9.4 Norms of Responsibility

As noted in the Introduction, whatever norm of fairness is applied to
particular foreign measures or practices, several other issues are also relevant in determining whether it is appropriate to demand that a foreign
state change its policies. These go to the question whether, and to what
extent, a foreign government can be properly held responsible for particular measures or conditions in an international forum. A number of re-

sponses to these issues have been suggested in the text of Section 301 and in its legislative history. I call these norms of responsibility.

Three issues of responsibility are discussed here:

(1) whether the measure or condition at issue in a particular proceeding can be attributed to the government of the respondent state. The text of Section 301 itself requires that the issue of attribution be considered: At least since 1979, only "acts, policies and practices of a foreign state or instrumentality" are actionable. In addition, to the extent that a measure or condition cannot be considered a governmental act, demands for a governmental response become less legitimate and less likely to succeed.

(2) whether the measure at issue is, even if attributable to the foreign government, within the appropriate scope of international concern, and within the ambit of state responsibility, such that the foreign government has an obligation to respond to foreign demands for change.

(3) what motive or "mental state" can be ascribed to the foreign government. To illustrate, the normative force of a demand for revision of a domestic product standard adopted long before formal barriers to imports were eliminated or reduced, even if that standard now functions in a discriminatory fashion, would seem weaker than that of a demand for removal of a recently adopted measure aimed explicitly at limiting imports. More generally, certain heightened mental states might justify more aggressive responses and more extreme remedies, much as criminal penalties are increased for premeditation and other aggravating factors.

All of these issues are raised in the legislative history of Section 301, but they are not typically dealt with in as much depth as, say, the elements of the market-distortion rationale. What is more, these issues have not received much focused attention in public and academic discussion of Section 301 and other U.S. demands for unilateral changes in foreign economic policies. With these points in mind, the main goals of this section are to present the basic issues of responsibility as they have appeared in the Section 301 context and to add some preliminary analysis, so that the issues can be considered more thoroughly in the future.

9.4.1   Attribution

Tariff elimination must be accompanied by a public pledge by the Japanese Government to ... overcom[e] the pervasive attitude of Japanese businessmen that it is disloyal to purchase competitive foreign goods.

Semiconductor Industry Assoc.[105]

For the most part, the question of attribution to government has been easily dealt with in the legislative history of Section 301. The vast majority of the "acts, policies and practices" complained of are official, positive acts of government: quotas, tariffs, variable levies, discriminatory procurement by the government itself or its instrumentalities, subsidies, concerted targeting programs or industrial policies, investment barriers, performance requirements, and the like. Proponents of action under Section 301 have, however, argued that a considerably broader range of measures and conditions should be attributed to foreign governments.

(1)   Some witnesses take the position, at least implicitly, that private practices which function as trade barriers should be attributed to government, even in the absence of any official act, if the government informally plays a role in creating or sustaining them. The most common issue raised here is the existence of private cartels in Japan and other countries. The ubiquitous SIA and other industries assert, for example, that the Japanese and other governments "encourage" the formation of private cartels and other restrictive business practices. The soda ash industry describes a complex trade-restricting scheme carried out by a cartel, and argues that this is an appropriate issue for action under 301 because the government had "blessed" the arrangement. The SIA also alleges that the Japanese government had "encouraged" buy-Japanese attitudes.

If a government actively participates in the creation of a trade barrier, even by informal means—assuming, of course, that the facts can be determined—attribution is rather easily established, at least for normative purposes.[106] There is, of course, a vast range of ways in which a government can informally lend support to some private course of action; near the lower end of the range—say where a single midlevel official privately expresses a positive opinion—the link might not be sufficient, either normatively or legally, to attribute the action to government. Questions of mental state may also be relevant. There appears to be a clear normative difference, for example, between covert official encouragement of a cartel designed to substitute for a recently repealed import quota and a public statement by a government official urging people to buy domestic products during a recession. Unfortunately, such careful distinctions have rarely been made in the 301 context.

(2)   Other witnesses argue that the mere "toleration" of cartels and restrictive business practices, intellectual property piracy, and similar private acts should be attributable to government. Interestingly, Section 252

of the Trade Expansion Act of 1962—the predecessor of Section 301, primarily applicable to measures affecting agriculture—explicitly made "toleration of cartels" an actionable practice. Numerous private-sector witnesses in the legislative history of Section 301 seek restoration of this phrase.

"Toleration" is a less active form of involvement than "encouraging."[107] If the government is aware of the private activity and its effects on others, however, the difference may be insubstantial. This sort of consideration probably explains USTR Yeutter's statement to Congress that his office already considered toleration of cartels actionable under 301, "if the facts are strong enough." Toleration of systematic anticompetitive private activities was in fact added to Section 301 as an actionable practice in 1988. This attribution rule will have substantial normative validity so long as the restraining conditions just discussed are observed in its administration; the modifier "systematic" sets the right tone by limiting coverage to practices whose existence and external effects are likely to be known to government.

(3) Finally, some witnesses argue, especially as to Japan, that "trade barriers" such as buy-local attitudes, private business practices difficult for foreign firms to penetrate, economic structures like the "keiretsu" system, and various cultural matters should be seen as the responsibility of the Japanese government. Even before it asserted that the Japanese government encourages buy-Japan attitudes, for example, the SIA argued simply that the government had a positive duty to overcome them, as in the statement quoted above. In terms of governmental awareness, these assertions are similar to the toleration cases discussed above. They raise troubling problems, however, in the area of state responsibility.

9.4.2 State Responsibility

Each nation-state has a sovereign right to establish whatever social and economic policies ... it believes are necessary for the internal workings of its nation. However, when they deal in international commerce, they take on an additional responsibility; one that ... diminishes their sovereign right to act....

Coalition for International Trade Equity.[108]

As the examples in Section 9.4.1 indicate, supporters of Section 301 criticize numerous aspects of domestic policy in foreign states, typically on grounds of discrimination or reciprocity, sometimes as market distortion.

Essentially, the demand is that the states in question harmonize their policies with those of the United States or of market-oriented states in general. In terms of official policies, three areas stand out as subjects of criticism: industrial policy, competition policy, and labor policy. (Environmental policy, though occasionally mentioned, is not a significant factor in the history of 301, at least until the 1990s.) Private conduct said to be attributable to foreign states is also subject to criticism.

Industrial Policy

As far back as the early 1970s, private firms argue to Congress that foreign government measures dealing with the domestic structure of industry can have significant external effects, distorting markets and creating barriers to trade and investment, and that they should be dealt with under Section 301. In the absence of any positive legal rules restricting such measures, their adverse external effects seem to be the principal normative justification for international concern and state responsibility, as suggested in the quotation appearing above.

The Executive branch typically seeks to rebut this sort of argument because of the danger that it could be turned against the United States. The Executive's basic position is that differences in industrial structure, even when supported by official government action, create essentially neutral interface problems. It may well be appropriate to deal with such problems by attempting to harmonize domestic policies through negotiation, but the sovereign choices of other governments on the structure of their economies should not be considered unfair or attacked by other states.[109]

Several industries attempt to compromise these stark differences by suggesting tests to determine whether particular domestic policies are appropriate for international criticism. One group argues that measures adopted for valid domestic public purposes are beyond foreign criticism, while those that encourage unfair trade are within the scope of 301. This appears to be a circular proposition, unless it means only that issues of motive are relevant. Another group suggests that only measures that are "excessive" in "purpose or administration" should be considered proper subjects for foreign concern. This test too is less than helpful.

Eventually, issues of industrial structure come to be addressed largely in terms of the concept of targeting, a form of industrial policy that bundles together a variety of lawful and unlawful, domestic and international measures. As defined in the 1988 amendment to Section 301, however, such measures must be "bestowed on a specific enterprise, industry or group." This definition creates a new compromise, putting broad industrial policy decisions out of bounds and focusing Section 301 on programs similar to those dealt with under the countervailing-duty law.

Competition Policy
Domestic competition policy, including particularly matters related to the operation of cartels, other forms of collaborative activity, vertical relationships (as in the Japanese distribution system), and restrictive business practices generally, is a frequent issue in the legislative history of Section 301. It is clear from the years of testimony that many U.S. firms find private anticompetitive practices among the most serious foreign impediments they face, often more significant, in fact, than official measures. These practices are treated as unfair under the norms of discrimination, reciprocity, and market distortion. Frequently, it is the private conduct itself that is criticized, raising all the attribution questions discussed above. Assuming attribution to government, it again appears, to the extent that any rationale is suggested, that the existence of adverse external effects is the normative basis for criticizing another nation's internal competition policy and the private actions of its firms.

Labor Policy
Criticism of the domestic labor policy of foreign states is surprisingly significant in the history of Section 301. This is primarily the result of the significant political role played in the debate by organized labor, which has maintained a consistent policy on the subject since the early 1970s, and probably long before.

   The labor issue is complicated by the existence of a large number of widely adopted international labor standards, most of them embodied in treaties sponsored by the International Labor Organization (ILO). On the one hand, the existence of such standards increases the legitimacy of a charge that a lax or repressive foreign labor policy is unfair. Instead of merely asserting that the policy is discriminatory, or nonreciprocal, or perhaps market-distorting, it can be criticized as, or assimilated to, a violation of international law. The existence of international standards also helps to bring the labor rights issue into the international arena, weakening claims of domestic jurisdiction. Organized labor testifies repeatedly that it has long looked to the ILO process as the best way to raise labor standards worldwide.

At the same time, however, many nations have not adopted all of the ILO conventions (the United States is among the laggards, though numerous witnesses observe that equivalent rights are granted workers under U.S. domestic law). One way of justifying demands for change in these countries is to argue that ILO standards have become customary international law, binding on all states. United States statutes conditioning trade preferences and foreign assistance on observance of "internationally recognized worker rights" incorporate an argument of this sort, though without reference to any source.[110] If applicable international legal norms cannot be established, however, one must resort to other norms of fairness.[111]

In addition, if accepted international rules are not applicable, labor advocates must assert alternative grounds for state responsibility. In large part, the arguments for foreign concern, state responsibility, and unilateral action turn again on the adverse external economic effects of foreign labor policies, typically reflecting the "equal-production-conditions" (or "level-playing-field") version of the reciprocity norm. But the argument also includes the additional "altruistic" theme that lax or repressive foreign labor policies are a proper subject of international concern because of their destructive effects on workers in the foreign country. (A similar argument is made in connection with lax environmental laws.)[112] In this context, the AFL-CIO argues that the limited achievements of the consensual ILO process strengthen the case for unilateral action by the U.S.

This combination of arguments, combined with the political power of organized labor, has proven nearly irresistible to Congress, at least in recent years. Section 301 now makes persistent denial of a variety of labor rights actionable as an "unreasonable" practice.[113] Yet in the absence of agreed international rules it remains unclear on what basis the effects of foreign government policies on their own people are appropriate subjects for foreign criticism, much less foreign demands for unilateral change under threat of economic retaliation.

Generalizing from the discussion of these three areas of policy, it seems clear that the case for foreign state responsibility, and hence for unilateral action under Section 301, is strongest when the foreign activity being criticized contravenes international rules accepted by the foreign state, or at least widely enough accepted to constitute customary law.[114] Not only do such rules bind the foreign government; they are typically designed, at least in part, to protect other nations from the effects of the conduct, making them legitimate complainants.

A less obvious situation is that in which the conduct in question—normally private conduct—is condemned under the foreign state's own rules. Such situations arise under Section 301 primarily in connection with competition policy. Within the broader harmonization debate, however, they also arise in connection with the lax enforcement of labor, environment, and other policies. Here the foreign government has undoubted responsibility for implementation of the policies in question. It may, however, also be entitled to considerable sovereign discretion in terms of the resources it employs in enforcing the many regulatory statutes for which it is responsible. In addition, it is not at all clear that the U.S. is an appropriate complainant in such a situation, although a negotiated approach would be more legitimate than a unilateral, coercive one.[115]

The most important situations in the history of Section 301, however, fall into two very different and more troublesome categories. The first includes cases in which the conduct attributed to a foreign government violates norms applicable only within the complaining state. Some complaints by U.S. firms about the toleration of private anticompetitive conduct abroad, for example, fall into this category, since the foreign governments criticized do not have antitrust laws equivalent to those of the United States. When foreign governments have not adhered to international labor conventions and the case for customary law is weak, complaints about foreign labor practices may also fall into this category. There seems little question here that the United States is simply using its economic power to spread its own norms, however valid and important it holds those norms to be.

The second troublesome category includes cases where no legal norm is violated, even in the complaining country; instead, the complaint is based solely on the external effects of the foreign practice. Certain kinds of assistance to industry, for example, are not forbidden by any international norm or any rule of foreign or U.S. domestic law. Yet private interests in the U.S. and members of Congress are willing to assert that such assistance should be actionable under Section 301 merely because of its competitive impact on U.S. firms (and, of course, because it is "unfair"). Complaints about social and cultural practices in foreign nations also fall into this category: It is probably the absence of any convincing argument for state responsibility that makes the more extreme of those claims so laughable. More broadly, the argument that states should be responsible for modifying any economic or social policy or practice that has negative external effects would amount to a substantial expansion of the normal rules of state responsibility under international law, one that the U.S. would almost certainly oppose in the abstract.

9.4.3   Governmental State of Mind

This is not only an unfair trade practice, this is a con game. This is a fraud perpetrated by Japan, by its government and by its business to fleece my constituents.... [The remedy] should be just as sure as if somebody is caught robbing you on the street.... If an American trying to do business in another country isn't confident that where they are fleeced and conned and cheated ..., they can get relief ... under Section 301 ..., they will have no confidence in the trade laws.

Sen. John Danforth.[116]

Much as with the issue of attribution, the question whether the "mental state" or motive of the foreign government normatively justifies a foreign response rarely arises in the legislative history of Section 301. Almost all the measures complained of (other than certain structural barriers) can be seen as intentional, either because they are positive acts, formal or informal, or because they are knowingly tolerated. In addition, most of those measures are plausibly alleged to be intentionally aimed at disadvantaging foreign interests. This is even true of many of the industrial policy measures that figure in the debate. This combination is certainly sufficient to justify foreign criticism and action, assuming all other conditions are satisfied.

A few witnesses suggest that a weaker "mental state" could also be sufficient for action. At least one group, for example, observes that the restrictive effects of a domestic product standard could be either intentional or "inadvertent"—as in the case of a standard adopted before there was significant international trade in the products concerned—but that in either case the standard should be equally actionable. Other witnesses take the same position, arguing, for example, that all foreign standards that burden U.S. commerce, whether "by design or by effect," should be treated alike. These issues are not raised with enough frequency, however, to be able to assess them.

The more prominent issue of governmental motivation in the history of Section 301 is the alleged existence of aggravated mental states, thought to justify harsher responses, in certain foreign governments. Even in the early 1970s, various private groups, as well as Rep. Burke, assert that Japan and the EC have established many of the NTBs under discussion, not only with the intention of discriminating against foreign commerce, but with the additional intention of evading their tariff commitments. This suggests a deceitful mental state, associated with evasion provisions in criminal and regulatory law. Even the panel of eminent economists mentioned earlier suggests a similar deceitful mental state, observing that foreign governments are disguising protection with obscure regulations.

By 1984, when the tone of the legislative process is generally more critical and aggressive, allegations of venal motive are commonplace. The governments of Japan, the EC, and other nations are said to be adopting beggar-thy-neighbor policies, attempting to "steal" technology, using domestic measures as a "subterfuge," and seeking world dominance for their firms. At least one concrete and highly visible fact situation, described repeatedly by the SIA, lent support to these characterizations, especially those suggesting deceitfulness: After Japan agreed to remove certain formal barriers to semiconductor imports, the SIA alleged, it promptly instituted "countermeasures" (the term said to have been used in Japanese memoranda) to blunt the effects of the action.

The hearings on current 301 include more of the same, though even more extreme. Japan, as characterized by Rep. Dingell, is a "willing participant" in a "ruthless trade war," an "economic aggressor." States that tolerate intellectual property counterfeiting are "economic pirates." Japan negotiates "in bad faith," using a variety of deceitful methods to evade its commitments. To the auto parts industry, Japan is a "carnivore," anxious to take over additional markets.

Some of these statements amount to national insults. Most are purely subjective, extreme interpretations of disputed facts. Many are surely made for rhetorical purposes, not as serious analysis. Nowhere in the legislative history, in fact, is there any serious analysis of what should constitute an aggravated mental state or what consequences should flow from the existence of one. Whatever the explanation, though, allegations like these have been a prominent part of the background of Section 301, especially in its 1988 version. To this author, it appears that a belief in the venal motives of at least some foreign governments was more responsible for the adoption of mandatory retaliation and the other harsh procedures incorporated in current 301 than any other issue discussed in this chapter.

9.5   Conclusion

What light does the normative analysis of Section 301 shed on the recent demands for harmonization of domestic national policies in areas like environmental regulation, labor, and competition law? There are both similarities and differences between the two areas of discourse, and each helps to illuminate the current claims.

9.5.1 Similarities

(1)   First, it is important to recall the extent to which both Section 301 claims and demands for domestic harmonization are unilateral in nature. Some of these similarities have been pointed out in the Introduction, and it is not necessary to elaborate on them here.

(2)   The history of Section 301, juxtaposed against current harmonization claims, suggests how completely the idea of fairness permeates debate within the United States on issues of international economic policy, and how long it has done so. Claims relating the adverse economic effects of differences in domestic regulation have been prominent in the history of Section 301 for nearly 25 years, dating back to the discovery of foreign NTBs in the early 1970s. Labor policy has been the most fertile source of complaints, followed by competition policy and the varied aspects of industrial policy. Claims relating to differing environmental policies have been much less prominent, presumably because environmental regulation in the United States has only recently become sufficiently pervasive and costly to raise the issue. The altruistic claims now prominent in demands for harmonization of environmental and labor policy can also be found in the history of Section 301, mainly in connection with worker rights, but debate over 301 has been principally concerned with economic effects.

(3)   In general, both areas of discourse draw from the same palette of fairness norms and are confronted with the same issues of state responsibility. Unfortunately, however, both are also characterized by similar failings: failure to specify clearly the meaning, ambit, and implications of the concepts of fairness relied upon; to grapple with the nagging mirror-image issue and questions of internal coherence and workability; and to devote any serious attention to resolving the challenging problems of state responsibility.

(4)   The history of Section 301 demonstrates how easily norms of fairness, and similar rhetorical devices, can be captured and manipulated by self-interested groups; this is also a significant problem with current demands for domestic harmonization. Advocates of worker rights, for example, press for action under Section 301 both for the "altruistic" benefits to foreign workers and for the "level-playing-field" advantage to U.S. workers in their own unions and electoral districts; it is impossible to separate the two motives. Even worse, the rhetorical tools of fairness in the 301

setting—where the primary issues are defensive barriers to U.S. exports—are regularly advanced by interests whose principal concern is the reduction of imports into the United States. Potent rhetorical concepts like environmental protection are ripe for misuse in similar ways.

9.5.2   Contrasts

(1)   Perhaps the most striking contrast between these two areas of discourse is the relative poverty of the fairness norms advanced in the domestic harmonization debate. Altruistic claims are a more important aspect of the current harmonization debate, but many of the competition-oriented norms of fairness discussed in Section 9.2 are notably absent.

Domestic harmonization claims involve relatively few claims of violation of international commitments, and thus relatively few nullification claims. Such compliance problems as do arise tend to be dealt with in the ILO or the appropriate environmental regime, rather than as a demand for domestic harmonization or for coercive trade measures. This distinction, however, may simply be the result of differences in the extent of applicable international law.

Discrimination, too, is rarely an issue in the harmonization debate. Indeed, the fact that U.S. firms can relocate business operations to foreign nations and obtain the benefits of lax regulation without discrimination is one of the greatest concerns of those who advocate regulatory harmonization.

Several aspects of the reciprocity norm prominent in the history of Section 301 are also notably absent in the current debate. These include the controversy over specific reciprocity in trade negotiations and the pervasive "equal-access" issue, both national and sectoral. Again, however, these distinctions appear to stem primarily from differences in the issue areas involved in the two areas of discourse.

Since these other norms are not regularly available, claims for domestic regulatory harmonization tend to be based primarily on the variant of the equal-access reciprocity norm that I have called "equal-production-conditions" reciprocity, and to some extent on suggestions of market distortion. In his analysis of demands for unilateral action in pursuit of environmental harmonization,[117] Professor Hudec refers to competition-oriented claims for environmental harmonization as "level-playing-field" claims. This is an accurate characterization, since the level-playing-field or equal-production-conditions norm dominates and largely defines the claims at issue.

(2)　A second striking point is that the norms of fairness prominent in domestic harmonization discourse are among the least persuasive of the range of norms described here. For one thing, both equal-production-conditions reciprocity and market distortion are near the bottom of the list in terms of legitimacy under the standards of the existing international economic system. The foregoing analysis has suggested, moreover, that the market-distortion norm becomes very nearly incoherent when examined in detail, and that it provides an unworkable basis for national policy.

The equal-production-conditions norm is also less persuasive than the more traditional versions of equal-access reciprocity employed in the history of Section 301. There, the normal complaint is that *my* government gives *you* a benefit that *your* government does not give *me*; it is not fair for us to compete under those circumstances. In demands for domestic harmonization, however, the complaint is that *your* government gives *you* something that *my* government does not give *me*. This is not surprising at all, given the nation-state system, and does not intuitively seem unfair. What is more, even compared to the complaints advanced in connection with Section 301, there appears to be no easy way to contain demands for equal production conditions. All differences in conditions would seem to become fair game for criticism, and even for unilateral action, posing a serious "slippery-slope" problem.

(3)　Finally, most traditional Section 301 complaints are addressed to affirmative governmental actions: trade barriers, subsidies, performance requirements, and the like. Demands for domestic harmonization, in contrast, generally focus on instances of governmental inaction: failure to adopt or enforce stricter regulatory standards. This difference has several implications. First, claims based on inaction typically face more difficult problems of attribution and state responsibility. Second, in most areas of international interaction—human rights is a particularly important example—international standards that would require affirmative government action have proven significantly more controversial, especially in the United States.

Third, the general thrust of the norms of the international economic system is to restrain government intervention in markets. Most domestic harmonization claims, however, call for increased intervention. This poses a number of risks: an increased possibility of regulatory capture, inappropriate or inefficient responses to urgent foreign demands, and other forms of "government failure." Finally, as a tactical matter, theory and experience both suggest that it is more difficult to force governments to take specific actions ("compellence") than to refrain from acting ("deterrence").

In sum, the fairness arguments made in the current debate over harmonization of domestic national regulation are not new, but they do involve some of the most complex problems that have arisen in more traditional commercial contexts—where they are still poorly understood—in particularly perplexing forms.

NOTES

Kenneth W. Abbott is Elizabeth Froehling Horner Professor of Law and Commerce, Northwestern University School of Law.

1. Trade Act of 1974, Pub. L. No. 93-618, §§ 301–310, 88 Stat. 1978 (1975) (codified as amended at 19 U.S.C. §§ 2411–20 (1988)).

2. The distinction between defensive and offensive trade measures—those that spur exports to the U.S. or to third markets in which U.S. firms compete—begins to break down under close analysis. Dumping, for example—clearly an offensive measure—is often possible only because of defensive measures that insulate home markets. Many of the measures that have been criticized in connection with Section 301 have effects on exports as well as on imports. And the "remedy" against foreign defensive measures under Section 301 is the imposition of new import barriers by the U.S. On a macro level, however, the distinction can be a useful one.

3. Although U.S. trade law contains a number of remedies against unfair offensive practices, all come into play as goods enter the territory of the United States. They are thus virtually useless in the third-market situation.

4. Executive Order No. 12,981 (Mar. 3, 1994).

5. Uruguay Round Agreements Act, Pub. L. No. 103-465, § 314(f), 108 Stat. 4809 (1994).

6. Article 23:1 of the Understanding on Rules and Procedures Governing the Settlement of Disputes in Final Act embodying the Results of the Uruguay Round of Multilateral Trade Negotiations, Apr. 15, 1994 (Done at Marrakesh) provides: "When members seek the redress of a violation of obligations [or of related legal claims], they shall have recourse to, and abide by, the rules and procedures of this Understanding."

7. In addition, the Uruguay Round Agreements Act, in Section 102, provides both that no provision of any Uruguay Round agreement will prevail over any inconsistent U.S. law and that nothing in the Act itself (including approval of the Uruguay Round agreements) is to be construed as modifying any other law—specifically including Section 301—except to the extent explicitly amended.

8. The seeds of the present controversy, especially in competition policy, industrial policy, and labor policy, can also be found in the history of Section 301.

9. Because of its economic focus, the history of Section 301 has involved primarily "level-playing-field" issues rather than independent values such as protecting the environment. In the area of labor policy, however, claims based on the independent value of protecting workers have also appeared. This issue is discussed further in section 9.5.

10. As will appear later, however, it has been alleged in connection with Section 301 that high foreign tariffs are in fact unfair, in spite of the long-standing tariff negotiation system.

11. In the context of harmonization demands, the equivalents of 301 retaliation are the suggestions that countervailing duties be imposed on products from countries with lower domestic standards, that preferential trade treatment be made conditional on acceptable domestic standards, that trade not be liberalized with countries (such as Mexico before NAFTA) having lower standards, and that other economic responses be taken to promote harmonization.

12. Under Section 301(a)(2), part of the section of the law prescribing mandatory retaliation for violations of trade agreements and similar situations, the U.S. Trade Representative "is not required to take action" in cases in which a formal dispute resolution proceeding under GATT or some other trade agreement rules against the U.S. claim. Presumably, however, the USTR could take action if it chooses to do so. Even though the Uruguay Round Understanding on Rules and Procedures Governing the Settlement of Disputes attempts to channel all legal disputes into the GATT/WTO dispute-settlement system, this language was not amended by the Uruguay Round Agreements Act.

13. *See, e.g., Gephardt Reveals Plans for 'Green and Blue 301,'* 10 Int'l Trade Rep. (BNA) 776 (1993); *Trade Legislation Could Target Japan, China, Uruguay Round, Gephardt Says,* 11 Int'l Trade Rep. (BNA) 212 (1994); *Gephardt Bill to Allow Sanctions for Not Enforcing Environmental Laws,* 11 Int'l Trade Rep. (BNA) 500 (1994).

14. *See, e.g.,* AGGRESSIVE UNILATERALISM: AMERICA'S 301 TRADE POLICY AND THE WORLD TRADING SYSTEM (Jagdish Bhagwati & Hugh T. Patrick, eds., 1990), especially Professor Bhagwati's introductory chapter.

15. Robert E. Hudec, *"Mirror, Mirror on the Wall": The Concept of Fairness in United States Foreign Trade Policy, in* CANADA, JAPAN AND INTERNATIONAL LAW 88 (1990 Proceedings, Canadian Council of Int'l Law).

16. Another call for an examination of the arguments underlying fair trade demands is Phedon Nicolaides, *How Fair Is Fair Trade?,* 21 J. WORLD TRADE L. # 4 at 147 (1987).

17. *See, e.g.,* Judith Goldstein, *Ideas, Institutions, and American Trade Policy,* 42 INT'L ORG. 179 (1988).

18. Trade Act of 1974, Pub. L. No. 93-618, §§ 301–302, 88 Stat. 1978 (1975).

19. Trade Agreements Act of 1979, Pub. L. No. 96-39, title IX, 93 Stat. 144, 295 (1979).

20. Trade and Tariff Act of 1984, Pub. L. No. 98-573, § 304, 98 Stat. 2948, 3002 (1984).

21. Omnibus Trade and Competitiveness Act of 1988, Pub. L. No. 100-418, §§ 1301–1302, 102 Stat. 1107, 1164–79 (1988). *See also id.* § 1303, 102 Stat. at 1179.

22. After this chapter had been completed, Congress passed the Uruguay Round Agreements Act, note 5 above. The Act does not appear to work any significant change in the matters discussed herein. The Act: (1) expands the range of retaliatory actions that the USTR is authorized to take (Sec. 314(a)–(b)); (2) strengthens the extent to which inadequate intellectual property protection in foreign nations is to be considered "unreasonable" under Section 301 (Sec. 314(c)); (3) revises the time limits for Section 301 proceedings in relation to certain trade agreements (Sec. 314(d)); (4) revises the procedure for enforcing agreements to conform with the Uruguay Round Understanding on dispute resolution (Sec. 314(e)); and (5) extends the Super 301 procedure (Sec. 314(f)). I have attempted to refer to the 1994 amendments where necessary.

23. The following hearings are drawn on in this chapter:

Trade Act of 1974. (a) Trade Reform: Hearings Before the House Ways and Means Comm. (Parts 1–15), 93d Cong., 1st Sess. (1973). (b) The Trade Reform Act of 1973: Hearings Before the Senate Finance Comm. (Parts 5–6), 93d Cong., 2d Sess. (1974).

Trade Agreements Act of 1979. (a) Implementation of the Multilateral Trade Negotiations: Hearings Before the Subcomm. on International Trade of the Senate Finance Comm., 96th Cong., 1st Sess. (1979). (b) Trade Agreements Act of 1979: Hearings Before the Subcomm. on International Trade of the Senate Finance Comm. (Parts 1 and 2), 96th Cong., 1st Sess. (1979).

Trade and Tariff Act of 1984. (a) U.S. Trade Policy, Phase II: Private Sector: Hearings Before the Subcomm. on Trade of the House Ways and Means Comm. (Parts A and B), 97th Cong., 1st Sess. (1981–82). (b) Reciprocal Trade and Market Access Legislation: Hearing Before the Subcomm. on Trade of the House Ways and Means Comm., 97th Cong., 2d Sess. (1982). (c) Trade Reciprocity: Hearing Before the Subcomm. on International Trade of the Senate Finance Comm., 97th Cong., 2d Sess. (1982). (d) Options to Improve the Trade Remedy Laws: Hearings Before the Subcomm. on Trade of the House Ways and Means Comm. (Parts 1–2), 98th Cong., 1st Sess. (1983). (e) General Trade Policy: Hearings Before the Subcomm. on Commerce, Transportation, and Tourism of the House Comm. on Energy and Commerce, 98th Cong., 1st Sess. (1983).

Omnibus Trade and Competitiveness Act of 1988. (a) United States Trade and Competitiveness: Hearings Before the Subcomm. on Economic Stabilization of the House Comm. on Banking, Finance and Urban Affairs, 99th Cong., 1st Sess. (1985). (b) Unfair Foreign Trade Practices: Hearings before the Subcomm. on Oversight and Investigations of the House Energy and Commerce Comm. (Parts 1–2), 99th Cong., 1st Sess (1985). (c) United States-Japan Trade: Hearing Before the Subcomm. on International Trade of the Sen. Finance Comm., 99th Cong., 1st Sess. (1985). (d) Trade Policy: Hearing Before the Subcomm. on Commerce, Transportation, and Tourism of the House Comm. on Energy and Commerce, 99th Cong., 2d Sess. (1986). (e) Trade Reform Legislation: Hearings Before the Subcomm. on Trade of the House Ways and Means Comm. (Part 1), 99th Cong., 2d Sess. (1986). (f) Presidential Authority to Respond to Unfair Trade Practices: Hearing Before the Senate Finance Comm., 99th Cong., 2d Sess (1986). (g) Improving Enforcement of Trade Agreements: Hearing Before the Sen. Finance Comm., 100th Cong., 1st Sess. (1987).

24. Trade Act of 1974, note 1 above, at § 301(d)(3)(A) & (B).

25. *See, e.g.,* Oversight Hearings on U.S. Trade Policy: Hearing Before the Senate Finance Comm., 99th Cong., 1st Sess. (1985): "My question is, can you kind of give some guiding principle as to what should be unfair that all countries should stop? (Sen. Baucus); "What are the things that are fair and unfair ...? (Sen. Packwood).

26. This fact was regularly used to argue against the adoption and strengthening of Section 301; with no definitions, the statute was derided as an "unguided missile."

27. Improving Enforcement of Trade Agreements, note 23 above, at 13 (statement of Sen. Bentsen).

28. Initial 301 did mention practices that impair the value of trade commitments, however. Trade Act of 1974, note 1 above, § 301(a)(1).

29. Section 301(a), as amended in 1979, authorized the President to enforce the rights of the U.S. under any trade agreement, and to act against any act, policy, or practice of a foreign state that was inconsistent with such an agreement.

30. The 1979 amendment, for example, required USTR to initiate dispute-settlement proceedings under the relevant agreement when violations were alleged and consultation with the respondent country had failed to resolve the issue.

31. As noted earlier, in December 1994, after this chapter had been prepared, Section 301 was amended by the Uruguay Round Agreements Act. It is thus not strictly correct to refer to the statute as amended in 1988 as "current 301." However, the 1988 amendments significantly changed the structure of Section 301, while the 1994 amendments, as outlined in note 22 above, are quite narrow. Substantively, then, the designation remains reasonably accurate.

32. Section 301(a)(1).

33. Judging from a preliminary examination of a large number of private petitions requesting initiation of Section 301 proceedings, claims of rule violation dominate the Section 301 complaint procedure. Although a broad range of nonviolative conduct can be the subject of Section 301 complaints, the great majority of private petitions appear to focus almost exclusively on alleged violations of some trade agreement, frequently GATT itself, raising other normative claims, if at all, seemingly as an afterthought or a way to cover all the bases. This was true, moreover, even before the statute required mandatory retaliation for violations.

34. It might be noted in this connection that the "trade agreements" covered by Section 301 would include agreed, but essentially unilateral, market-access commitments, even those negotiated under a previous 301 action.

35. *See* Kenneth W. Abbott, *GATT as a Public Institution: The Uruguay Round and Beyond*, 18 Brooklyn J. Int'l L. 31 (1992).

36. *See* Vienna Convention on the Law of Treaties, art. 60 ("material breach" authorizes affected state to terminate agreement or suspend its operation in whole or part).

37. Trade Policy, note 23 above, at 130 (comments of the National Association of Manufacturers).

38. Trade Act of 1974, note 1 above, § 301(a)(1).

39. Sec. 301(a)(1)(B)(i).

40. This limitation did not, however, survive in the final enactment. Current 301 defines "export targeting" as an "unreasonable" act, policy, or practice. Sec. 301(d)(3)(B)(ii); as such, it is subject to discretionary action by the USTR. Sec. 301(b)(1).

41. Dispute Settlement Understanding, note 12 above, art. 26.

42. Trade Reform, note 23 above, at 4316.

43. Impairment claims can retain considerable legitimacy even if all institutional requirements are observed. In the recent Oilseeds case against the EC, for example, the U.S. came close to implementing trade sanctions even though the GATT Council had not approved retaliation under Article XXIII. Because of the EC's conduct in the case, including its blocking of Council decisions, many believed the U.S. position was justified.

44. *See, e.g.,* Unfair Foreign Trade Practices, note 23 above, Part I at 46, 48 (statement of Communication Workers of America: Japan refused to put NTT under Procurement Code, but promised that it would act consistently with Code; then used discriminatory product standards to evade commitment).

45. The idea of intentional evasion is dealt with further in Section 9.4.

46. General Trade Policy, note 23 above, at 86, 87 (statement of Harry H. Freeman on behalf of Coalition of Services Industries, Inc.).

47. *See, e.g.,* Trade Act of 1974, note 1 above, § 301(a)(1)–(2); Omnibus Trade and Competitiveness Act of 1988, note 21 above, § 301(b).

48. Trade and Tariff Act of 1984, note 20 above, § 301(e)(5). The definition of "unjustifiable" in paragraph (e)(4), covering violations of legal rights, also mentioned denial of MFN or national treatment.

49. Sec. 301(d)(3)(B)(i)(I), (III).

50. One reason for this seems to have been that the hearings leading up to the Trade Act of 1974 were more focused on supporting multilateral negotiations to deal with the newly identified problems than on normative criticism.

51. For further discussion of the interplay between these claims, see Section 9.3.

52. Trade Reform, note 23 above, at 4774 (statement of Irving Glass, President, Tanners Council of America).

53. Reciprocal Trade and Market Access Legislation, note 23 above, at 198 (statement of Richard Rivers).

54. Trade Reciprocity, note 23 above, at 11 (remarks of Sen. William V. Roth, Jr.).

55. *See, e.g.,* Reciprocal Trade Agreements Act of 1934, Act of June 12, 1934, c. 474, 48 Stat. 943; GATT art. XXVIII bis (negotiations on a reciprocal and mutually advantageous basis).

56. *See* Statement of Richard Rivers, note 53 above.

57. Robert O. Keohane, *Reciprocity in International Relations,* 40 INT'L ORG. 1 (1986).

58. *See, e.g.,* Reciprocal Trade and Market Access Legislation, note 23 above, at 6 (statement of Deputy USTR David Macdonald), Reciprocal Trade and Market Access Legislation; Trade Reciprocity, note 23 above, at 27 (statement of USTR William Brock); General Trade Policy, note 23 above, at 677 (statement of USTR General Counsel Claud Gingrich).

59. It is interesting to note that, under the Uruguay Round Final Act, states adhering to the Agreement Establishing the World Trade Organization thereby readopt GATT as GATT 1994, along with all previous legal instruments relating to tariff concessions and many other prior instruments and decisions, as well as adopting the Uruguay Round tariff concessions and agreements. Any legal argument that previous concessions were improper will thereby be extinguished by ratification.

60. Trade Act of 1974, note 1 above, § 102(f).

61. Trade Agreements Act of 1979, note 19 above, § 2(b).

62. *See* Keohane, note 57 above.

63. Trade Reform, note 23 above, at 1185 (remarks of Rep. Burke).

64. At first, the idea of equal access refers only to the absence of nonreciprocal barriers, primarily governmentally imposed barriers. Later, a stronger version of equal access becomes prominent. See Section 9.2.4.

65. Options to Improve the Trade Remedy Laws, note 23 above, Part 1 at 65 (remarks of Rep. Shannon).

66. The discussions of equal-access reciprocity also found their way into the negotiation provisions of trade legislation. For example, one of the stated legislative purposes of the 1974 Trade Act was to harmonize, reduce, or eliminate trade barriers in such a way as to assure "substantially equivalent commercial opportunities" for U.S. commerce. Trade Act of 1974, note 1 above, § 2(2); *see also id.* § 126. The 1979 statute implementing the Tokyo Round provided that no Tokyo Round NTB agreement should apply to a foreign country unless the President determined that the country has accorded adequate benefits, including substantially equal commercial opportunities, to the United States. Trade Agreements Act of 1979, note 19 above, § 2(b)(2). Similar provisions appear in 1984 and 1988. Trade and Tariff Act of 1984, note 20 above, § 302(1); Omnibus Trade and Competitiveness Act of 1988, note 21 above, § 1105(b).

67. Remarks of Rep. Burke, note 63 above.

68. Unfair Foreign Trade Practices, note 23 above, Part 2 at 488 (remarks of USTR Clayton Yeutter).

69. Reciprocal Trade and Market Access Legislation, note 23 above, at 2 (statement of Rep. Sam M. Gibbons).

70. Unfair Foreign Trade Practices, note 23 above, Part 2 at 129 (statement of Rep. John Dingell).

71. While these claims involved reciprocity, both sectoral and national, I discuss them below in terms of the market-distortion rationale, which was the more prominent normative feature of the claims.

72. Statement of Rep. Shannon, note 65 above, Part 1 at 64.

73. The 1988 amendment added a provision to Section 301 under which reciprocal market-access opportunities in the United States are to be considered, where appropriate, in determining whether a foreign practice is to be designated "unreasonable." Omnibus Trade and Competitiveness Act of 1988, note 21 above, § 1301, amending Section 301(d)(3)(D).

74. To some extent, however, both claims seem to be reflected in the increasing popularity of regional free-trade areas.

75. Reciprocal Trade and Market Access Legislation, note 23 above, at 30 (statement of (former USTR) William Eberle, on behalf of U.S. Chamber of Commerce).

76. Statement of Communications Workers of America, note 44 above, Part 1 at 46.

77. Unfair Foreign Trade Practices, note 23 above, Part 2 at 39, 67 (statement of Dr. Charles B. Wakeman, President, Siecor Corporation).

78. Trade Reform, note 23 above, at 3044 (statement of U.S. Wine Council).

79. To many observers, the excuses were hardly ludicrous, turning as they did on Japan's desire to protect the livelihood of a uniquely disadvantaged group of workers. Later, a GATT panel ruled that this excuse was insufficient, since less restrictive measures could have been used.

80. Trade Act of 1974, note 1 above, § 104.

81. Nicolaides, note 16 above, at 149.

82. Ultimately, sectoral reciprocity received little textual recognition in the 1988 Act. *See, e.g.,* Omnibus Trade and Competitiveness Act of 1988, note 21 above, § 1301, amending Section 301(c)(4), (d)(3)(D).

83. Statement of Rep. John D. Dingell, note 70 above, Part 2 at 129.

84. *See* Omnibus Trade and Competitiveness Act of 1988, note 21 above, §§ 1371–1382, codified at 19 U.S.C. §§ 3101–3111.

85. For further discussion of the market as norm, see Section 9.2.5.

86. Trade Reform, note 23 above, at 1064 (statement of Rep. Collier).

87. GATT itself, however, has negotiated commitments for specified levels of imports as part of agreements for the accession of nations to the General Agreement.

88. Agreement on Safeguards § VI.

89. Unfair Foreign Trade Practices, note 23 above, Part 1 at 9, 10 (statement of Howard D. Samuel, Industrial Union Dept., AFL-CIO).

90. Lionel Olmer of the Commerce Department argued even more broadly that the U.S. and Japan have deeply different economic philosophies, with the former strongly committed to the free market and the latter inclined to leave little scope for the market to operate. United States–Japan Trade, note 23 above, at 28 (statement of Lionel Olmer).

91. The criticism was that the amendment might force foreign governments to assume a larger role in their economies in order to meet deficit-reduction targets, endangering free markets there over the longer run.

92. *See* Trade and Tariff Act of 1984, note 20 above, § 305, adding new Section 104A to the Trade Act of 1974; *see especially* the new Section 104A(c) in *id.*

93. U.S. Trade Policy, Phase II: Private Sector, note 23 above, Part B at 899 (remarks of Elinor D. Talmadge, Tanners Council of America).

94. *See* Problems Arising from Comparing Shares of Foreign Products and Foreign Investments in Japan with Those in Third Countries, prepared by Japanese Ministry of International Trade and Industry, on file with the author.

95. I have previously addressed both the relevance of cultural differences and the folly of treating them as unfair trade practices. *See* Kenneth W. Abbott, *"Black Ships" and Balance Sheets*, 3 NORTHWESTERN J. INT'L L. & BUS. 103 (1981).

96. U.S. Trade Policy, Phase II: Private Sector, note 23 above, Part A at 59 (statement of Rudy Oswald, AFL-CIO).

97. Of course, it may not be the discriminatory nature of the foreign programs that prevents the complaining U.S. firm from taking advantage of them, but simply the fact that the U.S. firm does not operate in the relevant foreign nations.

98. Nicolaides, note 16 above, at 157.

99. *See* Hudec, *"Mirror, Mirror"*, note 15 above.

100. Much of the recent academic criticism of U.S. antidumping law attempts to demonstrate that this distinction is one of form alone, not of substance. *See, e.g.,* the article by Ronald A. Cass and Richard D. Boltuck, at Chapter 9 in this volume.

101. Occasionally in the legislative history an industry is itself shown to receive benefits like those of which it is complaining. *See, e.g.,* Trade Reform, note 23 above, at 1437 (colloquy between Rep. Waggoner and American Farm Bureau Federation).

102. Retorsions are relatively minor, lawful responses to unfriendly acts of foreign governments.

103. Reprisals are more serious, otherwise unlawful responses to agreement violations.

104. *See* John McMillan's chapter 14 in volume I.

105. U.S. Trade Policy, Phase II: Private Sector, note 23 above, Part A at 579 (statement of Dr. Alexander Lidow for the Semiconductor Industry Assn.).

106. A stricter standard is adhered to in some legal contexts, such as the U.S. doctrine of foreign sovereign compulsion for antitrust purposes. The narrow view of attribution incorporated in this doctrine serves to allow the U.S. to apply its own antitrust standards to private activities abroad. It is an unfortunate inconsistency for a more expansive view to be adopted in the context of Section 301, where it again permits action against a broader range of foreign practices.

107. *See* Kenneth W. Abbott, *Economic Sanctions and International Terrorism,* 20 Vanderbilt J. Transnat'l L. 289 (1987).

108. Trade Reform Legislation, note 23 above, Part I at 449 (statement of Coalition for International Trade Equity).

109. *See, e.g.,* Reciprocal Trade and Market Access Legislation, note 23 above, at 21, 23 (statement of Lionel Olmer, Dept. of Commerce).

110. Labor advocates argue that internationally recognized workers' rights stem from human rights instruments, such as the International Covenants on Civil and Political and on Economic, Social and Cultural Rights, as well as the ILO conventions. *See* Virginia A. Leary's article at Chapter 5 in this volume.

111. In addition to the norms of fairness outlined above, labor advocates have offered specific arguments in criticism of foreign labor policies. For example, groups such as the UAW argue that most of the issues dealt with under Section 301 involve the rights of capital; for U.S. policy to be equitable, the rights of labor should be given equal treatment. Somewhat similarly, the AFL-CIO, Rep. Pease, and other labor advocates call on the theory of comparative advantage. Under economic theory, they argue, international trade is intended to increase the welfare of all parties. But the "parties" in question should not be just the states involved; the component interests within each state should be considered. Thus, while trade based on lax labor rules will benefit consumers and producers, it will do so at the expense of workers. To right the balance, at least some minimal labor protections should be incorporated into U.S. and international trade policy.

112. The United States has sought to make a similar point by arguing that Japanese industrial and competition policies harm Japanese consumers as well as foreign competitors. The environmental analogue, of course, is more clear: Lax foreign environmental policies harm the global environment as well as creating adverse competitive effects.

113. Omnibus Trade and Competitiveness Act of 1988, note 21 above, § 301(d)(3)(B)(iii).

114. Of course, the normative case for "unfairness" is strongest in those circumstances as well. *See* Section 9.2.

115. The NAFTA side agreements on labor and environmental policy, which require Mexico to enforce its own laws in those areas, were negotiated agreements, but the U.S. had enormous bargaining leverage because of the expectation that NAFTA would not be approved by the U.S. Congress if the agreements were not completed. This episode stands somewhere between a true negotiation on the basis of reciprocity and a unilateral, coercive approach under Section 301.

116. Presidential Authority to Respond to Unfair Trade Practices, note 23 above, at 61–62 (remarks of Sen. John Danforth).

117. *See* Robert E. Hudec's article at Chapter 3 in this volume.

Index

Abbott, Kenneth, 12–13, 16
Adherence to commitments, norm of, 420–22
Ad hoc review procedures, GATT rules concerning, 141–42, 171n.158
"Adjustment for losers" position, 249–50
African Elephant Conservation Act, 163n.53
"Aggressive unilateralism," workers' rights policy, 212–13, 220–21
Agreement Establishing the World Trade Organization (WTO), 46–47
Agreement on Agriculture (GATT), 21, 41
Agreement on Technical Barriers to Trade (GATT), 21
Agreement on the Application of Competition Law (US-EU), 344, 346, 348n.12
Agreement on the Application of Sanitary and Phytosanitary Measures (SPS), 21
environmentalist concerns over, 62
facially neutral measures in, 78–80, 90n.80
legal restraints on domestic regulations and, 60
Agreement on Trade-Related Aspects of Intellectual Property Rights (GATT), 21, 42–44, 52
Airbus venture, 330n.140
Alchain, Armen R., 243–45, 252
Alleged anticompetitive practices (AACPs)
conditions for action, 341–42, 348n.10
private practices, 337–39, 348n.8
role of governments in, 333–34
Allen, William R., 243–45, 252
Alston, Philip, 181, 212, 216–17
American Bar Association, competition harmonization initiatives, 274–75, 299–300

American Federation of Labor-Congress of Industrial Organizations (AFL-CIO), 187, 440–42
Animal protection legislation
environmental harm concept and transborder activities, 112–13
foreign countries' measures concerning, 104–105, 165nn.78–79
unilateral trade restrictions, 146
U.S. laws and regulations, 100
Antarctic Marine Living Resources Convention Act, 163n.53
Antidumping Act of 1921, 16–18, 20, 124, 329nn.121, 361–65, 406nn.14
Antidumping Code, 368, 408n.38
Antidumping Law of 1916, 361–62
Antidumping laws
administrative expansion of, 365–68
asymmetry in domestic and international price regulation, 371–72
common agreement among nations concerning, 278
concepts and implementation, 360–76
efficiency as norm in reforms of, 11
equitable competition and, 376–401
equity of less competitive markets and, 385–86, 412n.92
evolution and expansion of, in U.S., 361–72
fairness norms and, 12–13, 355–60
financing business and less competitive markets, 383–84, 411n.87
firm incentives and price discrimination, 384–85, 411nn.88–91
harmonization of antitrust and trade policy through, 124–126, 297–301, 329nn.121
historical roots of, 361